T0145260

Lecture Notes in Artificial Intelligence   11531

Subseries of Lecture Notes in Computer Science

More information about this series at http://www.springer.com/series/1244

Stephan Chalup · Tim Niemueller ·
Jackrit Suthakorn · Mary-Anne Williams (Eds.)

RoboCup 2019:
Robot World Cup XXIII

Springer

Editors
Stephan Chalup ⓘ
University of Newcastle
Callaghan, NSW, Australia

Jackrit Suthakorn ⓘ
Mahidol University
Nakhon Pathom, Thailand

Tim Niemueller
Google
X, The Moonshot Factory
Munich, Germany

Mary-Anne Williams ⓘ
University of Technology
Sydney, NSW, Australia

ISSN 0302-9743　　　　　　　　ISSN 1611-3349　(electronic)
Lecture Notes in Artificial Intelligence
ISBN 978-3-030-35698-9　　　　ISBN 978-3-030-35699-6　(eBook)
https://doi.org/10.1007/978-3-030-35699-6

LNCS Sublibrary: SL7 – Artificial Intelligence

This Springer imprint is published by the registered company Springer Nature Switzerland AG
The registered company address is: Gewerbestrasse 11, 6330 Cham, Switzerland

Preface

This volume contains the proceedings of the 23rd Annual RoboCup International Symposium, held on July 8, 2019, at the International Convention Centre Sydney.

RoboCup was first held in 1997 and counts now as one of the most significant international annual events in autonomous robotics and artificial intelligence (AI). RoboCup has a competition, that ran July 2–7, 2019, with participants from about 40 countries, and a research conference, the International RoboCup Symposium, held on the final day.

The Competition comprised 11 major leagues, with about 1,200 participants, and 3 junior leagues, with about 900 participants. The individual leagues addressed specific challenges including Soccer, Rescue, Industrial, @Home, and On Stage (see robocup. org). The winners of each league were invited to submit papers describing their approach. 15 Champion Papers were submitted and reviewed by at least two Trustees or Executive Members of the RoboCup Federation. 14 of the submitted Champion Papers were accepted and are included in the Champion Papers Track of this volume.

There were 59 research paper submissions for presentation at the 2019 RoboCup International Symposium. All of them were peer reviewed by at least three reviewers of the international Program Committee. The accepted papers included 27 papers in the Regular Track reporting innovative, original research with relevance to areas of robotics and AI, and 11 papers in the Development Track describing innovative hardware developments, software frameworks, and open-source software developments. All 38 accepted research papers were presented at the symposium either as interactive posters or as oral talks. No distinction in paper quality was associated with the two presentation modes. The review mode for all papers was single-blind.

The symposium program comprised 3 outstanding keynote presentations, the 38 research paper presentations, and an additional poster track reporting on 8 RoboCup Federation sponsored projects.

Keynote 1 was presented by Manuela Veloso on "A Brief History of RoboCup and a Discussion of the Future." Keynote 2 by Peter Corke had the title "Creating Robots That See," and Keynote 3 by Gamini Dissanayake was on "Robots in the Wild."

The 23rd Annual RoboCup International Symposium was a joint effort of a large group of people who contributed in various roles to make this event and these proceedings possible:

- Claude Sammut and the Local Organizing Committee of RoboCup 2019
- President Daniel Polani and the Trustees and Executive Board Members of the RoboCup Federation
- Keynote speakers
- Authors of submitted papers and their supporting institutions
- Authors of eight RoboCup Federation supported project posters
- International Program Committee and associated reviewers
- Local organizing team of ICMS Australasia Pty Ltd

- Staff of the International Convention Centre Sydney
- Local volunteers and helpers
- EasyChair support
- Springer Verlag Heidelberg LNCS team

We hope these proceedings will be a useful contribution not only to RoboCup, but generally to the rapidly developing fields of AI and Robotics.

October 2019

Stephan Chalup
Tim Niemueller
Jackrit Suthakorn
Mary-Anne Williams

Organization

Program Co-chairs

Stephan Chalup   The University of Newcastle, Australia
Tim Niemueller   X, The Moonshot Factory, Google Munich, Germany
Jackrit Suthakorn   Mahidol University, Thailand
Mary-Anne Williams   University of Technology Sydney, Australia

Local Chair

Stephan Chalup   The University of Newcastle, Australia

Program Committee

H. Levent Akin   Bogazici University, Turkey
Hidehisa Akiyama   Fukuoka University, Japan
Minoru Asada   Osaka University, Japan
Sven Behnke   University of Bonn, Germany
Reinaldo A. C. Bianchi   Centro Universitário da FEI, Brazil
Joydeep Biswas   University of Massachusetts Amherst, USA
Esther Colombini   Unicamp, Brazil
Klaus Dorer   Hochschule Offenburg, Germany
Amy Eguchi   University of California San Diego, USA
Vlad Estivill-Castro   Griffith University, Australia
Thomas Gabel   Frankfurt University of Applied Sciences, Germany
Katie Genter   The University of Texas at Austin, USA
Justin Hart   The University of Texas at Austin, USA
Dirk Holz   X, The Moonshot Factory - formerly Google [x], USA
Trent Houliston   4Tel Pty Ltd, Australia
Benjamin Johnston   University of Technology, Sydney, Australia
Piyush Khandelwal   The University of Texas at Austin, USA
Robert King   The University of Newcastle, Australia
Gerhard Kraetzschmar   Bonn-Rhein-Sieg University, Germany
Nuno Lau   University of Aveiro, Portugal
Olivier Ly   LaBRI - Bordeaux 1 University, France
Patrick MacAlpine   The University of Texas at Austin, USA
Frederic Maire   Queensland University of Technology, Australia
Eric Matson   Purdue University, USA
Alexandre Mendes   The University of Newcastle, Australia
Çetin Meriçli   Carnegie Mellon University, USA
Tekin Meriçli   Carnegie Mellon University, USA
Daniele Nardi   Sapienza University of Rome, Italy

Oliver Obst	Western Sydney University, Australia
Paul G. Plöger	Bonn-Rhein-Sieg University of Applied Science, Germany
Daniel Polani	University of Hertfordshire, UK
Mikhail Prokopenko	The University of Sydney, Australia
Luis Paulo Reis	University of Porto - FEUP/LIACC, Portugal
Thomas Röfer	Deutsches Forschungszentrum für Künstliche Intelligenz GmbH, Germany
Raul Rojas	Freie Universität Berlin, Germany
Javier Ruiz-Del-Solar	Universidad de Chile, Chile
Maarouf Saad	École de Technologie Supérieure, Canada
Raymond Sheh	Curtin University, Australia
Saeed Shiry	Amirkabir University of Technology, Iran
Jivko Sinapov	The University of Texas at Austin, USA
Frieder Stolzenburg	Harz University of Applied Sciences, Germany
Peter Stone	University of Texas at Austin, USA
Komei Sugiura	NICT, Japan
Yasutake Takahashi	University of Fukui, Japan
Flavio Tonidandel	Centro Universitário da FEI, Brazil
Meg Tonkin	University of Technology Sydney, Australia
Arnoud Visser	University of Amsterdam, The Netherlands
Ubbo Visser	University of Miami, USA
Jonathan Vitale	University of Technology Sydney, Australia
Oskar von Stryk	TU Darmstadt, Germany
Josiah Walker	Rome2rio Pty Ltd, Australia
Alfredo Weitzenfeld	University of South Florida, USA
Timothy Wiley	The University of New South Wales, Australia
Aaron Wong	4Tel Pty Ltd, Australia

Additional Reviewers

Pedro Amaro	Masahide Ito
Seyed Ehsan Marjani Bajestani	Yuqian Jiang
Alexander Biddulph	Haresh Karnan
Xiaoping Chen	Ulrich Karras
Farshid Faraji	Irene Kipnis
Brígida Mónica Faria	Daniel Lee
Mohamadreza Faridghasemnia	Pedro Lima
Grzegorz Ficht	Guilherme Cano Lopes
Reinhard Gerndt	Aly Magassouba
Daniel Ginn	Mauricio Matamoros
Jarrett Holtz	Julia Maurer
Mojtaba Hosseini	Kazuhito Murakami
Wouter Houtman	Tomoharu Nakashima
Luca Iocchi	Angelica Nakayama

Luis Gustavo Nardin
Itsuki Noda
Asadollah Norouzi
Maike Paetzel
Pedro Peña
Arul Selvam Periyasamy
Daniel Polani
Elena Prieto
Sadegh Rabiee
Caleb Rascon
Secret Reviewer
Francesco Riccio
Alana Santana
Rico Schillings
Falk Schmidsberger

Sören Schwertfeger
Rishi Shah
Masaru Shimizu
Sophie Siebert
Marco Simões
Kai Steckhan
Gerald Steinbauer
Peter Turner
Rudi Villing
Sven Wachsmuth
Hugh Mee Wong
Junhao Xiao
Rong Xiong
Sebastian Zug

Contents

Regular Research Papers

Learning to Run Faster in a Humanoid Robot Soccer Environment Through Reinforcement Learning

Miguel Abreu[1]([⊠])[iD], Luis Paulo Reis[1][iD], and Nuno Lau[2][iD]

[1] University of Porto, LIACC/FEUP, Artificial Intelligence and Computer Science Lab, Faculty of Engineering of the University of Porto, Porto, Portugal
{m.abreu,lpreis}@fe.up.pt
[2] University of Aveiro, DETI/IEETA, Institute of Electronics and Informatics Engineering of Aveiro, Aveiro, Portugal
nunolau@ua.pt

Abstract. Reinforcement learning techniques bring a new perspective to enduring problems. Developing skills from scratch is not only appealing due to the artificial creation of knowledge. It can also replace years of work and refinement in a matter of hours. From all the developed skills in the RoboCup 3D Soccer Simulation League, running is still considerably relevant to determine the winner of any match. However, current approaches do not make full use of the robotic soccer agents' potential. To narrow this gap, we propose a way of leveraging the Proximal Policy Optimization using the information provided by the simulator for official RoboCup matches. To do this, our algorithm uses a mix of raw, computed and internally generated data. The final result is a sprinting and a stopping behavior that work in tandem to bring the agent from point a to point b in a very short time. The sprinting speed stabilizes at around 2.5 m/s, which is a great improvement over current solutions. Both the sprinting and stopping behaviors are remarkably stable.

Keywords: Reinforcement learning · Machine learning · Humanoid · Robot · Soccer · Running

1 Introduction

Reinforcement learning is constantly expanding its reach to replace outdated solutions. Its ability to overcome problems with large state and action spaces is becoming more relevant as the computational power increases and new optimization algorithms are developed. Competitive environments are particularly prone to adopt this trend given the intense demand for new and improved solutions. This is particularly noticeable in the RoboCup competition. Every year, new robotic skills are designed, making the competition more exciting. Ultimately, developing and optimizing high performance behaviors can be useful for real life situations in the future.

© Springer Nature Switzerland AG 2019
S. Chalup et al. (Eds.): RoboCup 2019, LNAI 11531, pp. 3–15, 2019.
https://doi.org/10.1007/978-3-030-35699-6_1

One of the most important skills in a 3D soccer simulation match is running. The first player to reach the ball has an advantage over the opposing team, which may prove to be decisive if done consistently. To improve the odds, researchers should focus on developing fast and stable running mechanisms. With this in mind, every competing team has perfected their algorithms along the years. However, none is making use of the full potential of the robotic soccer agents. This is clear in the main event as well as secondary challenges of the RoboCup competition. Recent work has introduced new perspectives on this long-established problem [1]. Nonetheless, the proposed solution is not mature enough to be integrated in existing teams.

To bring the robotic soccer agents closer to their full potential, this paper introduces a way of leveraging the Proximal Policy Optimization using the information provided by the simulator for official RoboCup matches. To do this, our algorithm uses a mix of raw, computed and internally generated data. To complement the sprinting stage, we also optimize a stopping algorithm which brings the robot back to a stationary pose. We expect to improve the running performance and bring a new pace for future RoboCup competitions.

In Sect. 2 we present some work related with the RoboCup competition. Then, we introduce the methods used to train and test our approach (Sect. 3), including a description of the simulator and agent, the employed state and action spaces and the optimization method. In Sect. 4 we describe the results concerning the learned sprinting and stopping behaviors. Then we discuss those results (Sect. 5) and present some conclusions and future work (Sect. 6).

2   Related Work

RoboCup is an annual international robotics competition which gathers teams from multiple countries annually since 1997 [2]. Since the adoption of the 3D Soccer Simulation League (3DSSL) in 2004, low level behaviors have evolved considerably. Every year, each participating team releases their binary to a public repository [3], which contains every team until the 2018 champion [4]. This repository is important to analyze competing teams and develop improved solutions. One of the most important research fields in the competition is bipedal locomotion. Contributions in this area extend over different areas, including omnidirectional walk [8,9], contextual-based walking [10,11], and fast walking [12]. Currently, there is a lot of room for improvement concerning running speed.

There is a RoboCup competition called Gazebo running challenge [5], which tests the agents' speed and stability using the Gazebo simulator. The last RoboCup event that included this challenge was in 2017. Every participating team would run for 20 s at the highest possible speed. Only two of the four participants were able to complete the challenge [6]. UTAustinVilla averaged 1.19 m/s on the best three of four runs, while magmaOffenburg averaged 0.38 m/s on the same conditions. Previously, in 2014, the RoboCup's running challenge was conducted in SimSpark. In this version UTAustinVilla also had the best results, achieving a speed of 1.343 m/s [7].

Recent work on this subject has brought improvements to the running performance [1]. The Proximal Policy Optimization algorithm was used to develop running behaviors from scratch using data provided by the robot's sensors, as well as the real orientation and coordinates provided by the server. This last type of data is not allowed in official RoboCup matches, and thus the resulting behavior is not ready to be integrated in a team. Furthermore, some components can be improved, including speed, stability and integration convenience.

3   Methods

Two complementary behaviors are being developed – sprinting and stopping. The former is concerned with making the transition from a stationary position to a running gait, while the latter is responsible for reversing that transition. Most of the features introduced below while describing the used methods are common for both behaviors.

3.1   Simulator and Agent

SimSpark [13] – the official simulator for the RoboCup 3D Soccer Simulation League – was the chosen simulator to conduct the learning process. This option ensures that the optimization results can run seamlessly in official RoboCup matches. Also, SimSpark uses a realistic and stable physics engine – the Open Dynamics Engine (ODE). The learning agent is a version of the NAO humanoid robot [14], created by SoftBank Robotics.

Since the objective of this work is to integrate the learned behaviors in a competing team, the simulator was configured with current official RoboCup rules. However, during the learning stage, to accelerate the optimization, the real-time mode was disabled to allow synchronous communication with the agent. Comparing with previous work [1], in our approach, the noise was not disabled and the visual perception was not extended (i.e., the position and orientation were not obtained from the server, since this kind of features is not available during the competition).

3.2   State Space

The state space is composed of 80 continuous variables represented by the single-precision (32b) floating-point data type. These variables are grouped in Table 1, according to their meaning. The gyroscope, accelerometer and joints data is obtained directly from the simulator. There are a total of 22 joints in the NAO robot version without toes, as seen in Fig. 1, from which only 20 are being optimized. The head pitch and yaw are excluded from the state space. The feet force data is acquired directly when the feet are touching the ground, and it includes 3D contact coordinates and 3D force vectors for each foot. When the agent's feet are not touching the ground, SimSpark will not provide information in the

Table 1. State parameters

Parameter	Data size ($\times$32b)	Acquisition method
counter	1	generated
z-coordinate	1	computed
orientation*	1	computed
gyroscope*	3	raw
accelerometer*	3	raw
feet force*	12	raw
joint's position*	20	raw
*differentiation	39	computed

*differentiation is performed on parameters followed by an asterisk

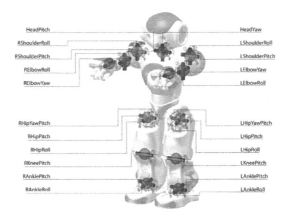

Fig. 1. NAO robot – joints and actuators (adapted from [22])

respective cycle and our agent assumes that the corresponding variables are all set to zero.

The counter is generated by the agent. It starts from zero, when the robot is stopped, and it is incremented at every 3 time steps (which is related to the control cycles explained in the next section). This counter works like a timer for the optimization algorithm, and, during our preliminary tests, its inclusion in the state space yielded about 20% of speed improvement after the optimization was concluded. In this phase, we also attested the importance of the robot torso's z-coordinate and orientation. The former provides useful information when the feet data is unavailable and the orientation is essential to keep the robot aligned with the objective.

The orientation is easily determined from the visual references provided by the simulator. However, these references are not good enough to provide accurate z-coordinate estimates. Therefore, this variable is computed with a linear predictor function that was modeled using linear regression on some of the other state space variables. The best single features and features crosses were initially filtered based on their correlation with the ground-truth, which was obtained directly from SimSpark. Then, an algorithm based on the Akaike information criterion was used to refine the feature selection [15, 16]. Currently, this predictor uses 368 features (including raw observations and feature crosses). In a new data set, corresponding to a reinforcement learning optimization with 20M time steps, it yielded an average absolute error of 0.011 m. This is accurate, considering that all the data provided to the agent by SimSpark (under the configuration for official matches) has an associated error of 0.005 units, due to rounding precision.

Finally, the variables in Table 1 followed by an asterisk are differentiated with respect to time, considering the length of one time step (20 ms). The majority of them constitute first-order derivatives of linear or angular positions. The exceptions are the rate of force change (df/dt); the torso's angular acceleration; and the torso's jerk (time derivative of acceleration).

3.3 Action Space

All joints of the simulated NAO robot (Fig. 1) have an associated actuator. Analogously to the state space, 20 actuators were used. The head pitch and yaw actuators were excluded since their optimization was not part of the objective. To control each actuator, the simulator requires angular speeds between $-7°/s$ and $+7°/s$, provided through continuous variables. Our agent produces these values through an indirect control approach [1], where the optimization algorithm produces target angles for each joint instead of speed values for each actuator. The scaled target angle for joint i (θ_i^{target}) and the output angular speed for actuator i at time step t (ω_i^t) are obtained by the following equations:

$$\theta_i^{target} = (x_i + 1) * \frac{b_i - a_i}{2} + a_i,$$
$$\omega_i^t = (\theta_i^{target} - \theta_i^{t-1})/k, \tag{1}$$

where x_i is the optimization algorithm output value for joint i, clipped to the range $[-1, 1]$; a_i and b_i are the lower and upper bounds, respectively, of the joint's angular range; θ_i^{t-1} is the angular position of joint i in the previous time step; and k is a constant that adjusts the speed at which the target angle is reached. Finally, ω_i^t is clipped to the range $[-7, 7]$ before being sent to the simulator. After a random search, k was set to 7.

In official RoboCup matches, the NAO robot's vision perception is limited to an interval of 3 time steps, and all observations are delayed 1 time step. The latter limitation allows the simulator to process the current action at the same time the agents compute the next action using the last available observations. This improves computational time but hinders the performance of reinforcement learning algorithms, since the current action must take into account the last action without knowing its result. To manage these issues, the agent control cycle was synchronized with the arrival of visual information. The observations fed to the optimization algorithm carry information about the last action, and the following yielded action is repeated for the next 3 time steps. This solves the disruption of time continuity and reduces computational requirements from the agent's side.

3.4 Optimization Method

We chose the Proximal Policy Optimization (PPO), introduced by Schulman et al. [17], as the preferred optimization method. This decision was based on its simplicity and good performance on producing high quality behaviors [17].

The chosen implementation was obtained from OpenAI baselines [18], which uses the clipped surrogate objective:

$$L(\theta) = \hat{\mathbb{E}}_t[min(r_t(\theta)\hat{A}_t, clip(r_t(\theta), 1 - \epsilon, 1 + \epsilon)\hat{A}_t],$$

$$where \quad r_t(\theta) = \frac{\pi_\theta(a_t|s_t)}{\pi_{\theta_{old}}(a_t|s_t)}, \tag{2}$$

where $\hat{A}_t$ is an estimator of the advantage function at timestep t. The clip function clips the probability ratio $r_t(\theta)$ in the interval given by $[1-\epsilon, 1+\epsilon]$. This implementation alternates between sampling data from multiple parallel sources, and performing several epochs of stochastic gradient ascent on the sampled data, to optimize the objective function.

Hyperparameter optimization requires a large number of iterations to cover a significant part of the hyperparameter space. Therefore, due to the similarity between case studies, we opted to base our hyperparameter tuning on the best solution found by OpenAI, when training the mujoco 3D humanoid [18]. They proposed the optimization of a multilayer perceptron with two hidden layers with 64 neurons. On top of that solution, we changed to 4096 time steps per actor batch and increased the maximum number of time steps to 200M (to learn the sprinting behavior) and 40M (to learn the stopping behavior).

3.5 Experimental Setup and Testing

The simulator was configured identically for the experimental and test setups. The real-time mode was switched on during testing to allow for visual inspection of the resulting behavior. Otherwise, it remained off to reduce computational time. For the sprinting behavior, the experimental and test setups were the same. The agent is initially placed near the field's left goal at $(-14\,m, 0\,m)$, facing the field's right goal. The initial pose is shown in Fig. 2a. To achieve this pose all joints must be set to $0°$, with the exception of: knees pitch $(-60°)$, hips pitch $(30°)$, ankles pitch $(30°)$, shoulders pitch $(-90°)$, elbows yaw (L: $-90°$, R: $90°$), elbows roll (L: $-90°$, R: $90°$). The agent is encouraged to run as fast as possible in a straight line since the reward is only given by the robot torso's x-coordinate difference from the last time step. As the traveled distance in the x-axis increases, so does the reward. The episode ends if the robot falls (torso's

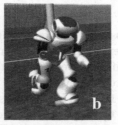

Fig. 2. Initial poses for the sprinting (**a**) and stopping (**b**) behaviors

z-coordinate is below $0.27\,$m) or reaches the finish line (torso's x-coordinate is above $14\,$m).

The stopping behavior is trained after the optimization of the sprinting behavior. It does not have a fixed initial position or pose. The robot starts from a stopped position and runs for a random period of time. Then, the control of the robot is assumed by the stopping optimization algorithm, which must ensure that it goes back to a stationary position without falling. One possible initial position and pose is shown in Fig. 2b. The reward is given by the difference between the distance of the current joint's position to the desired pose, and the distance of the previous joint's position to the desired pose. In other words, the agent is compensated for getting closer to the desired pose, and penalized for getting farther. Furthermore, it also receives a fixed unitary bonus for surviving another control cycle without falling.

The target pose is the same as shown in Fig. 2a but with both arms lowered to bring the center of mass down and increase stability. To ensure that the final pose is completely achieved, after the episode reaches 50 time steps ($1\,$s), an algorithm gradually takes over (using a weighted average) to force the joints to the desired angles. This also means that if the robot is not stable in under a second, it will probably fall and the episode will end. If successful, the episode ends when the robot achieves the final pose and remains stable for 100 time steps ($2\,$s), receiving a fixed unitary bonus per control cycle.

During testing, the only difference is the extent of the running stage, before the stopping algorithm takes control. Instead of randomly assigning a value to the extent, it was gradually increased from $0.42\,$s to $1.80\,$s, allowing 100 episodes to run before incrementing $0.06\,$s (3 time steps). This test was implemented to compare the stopping behavior performance under different initial conditions.

4 Results

This section presents the results obtained while testing the sprinting and testing behaviors, according to the conditions established in Sect. 3.5. A video demonstration is available online at https://youtu.be/lkSVad_tjOY.

4.1 Sprinting

The learning process took 73 h on a single Intel Xeon E5-2620 v3 at 2.40 GHz. The results for this experiment were averaged over 1000 episodes executed under the conditions specified in Sect. 3.5. After the optimization was concluded, the trained agent deviated, on average, $-3°$ from the x-axis, with a standard deviation (SD) of $\pm 5.9 \times 10^{-2\circ}$. This bias was compensated by adjusting the orientation observation on the opposite direction. The following results were obtained after this fix was implemented.

Figure 3 shows the robot's average speed along the x-axis (x-speed) from a given starting line (perpendicular to the x-axis) until the end of the episode. When the starting line is defined at 0 m, the average x-speed covers the entire episode, including the initial stopped position. If the line is defined at 1 m, only the trajectory performed after the robot torso's center crosses it is considered for the average x-speed computation.

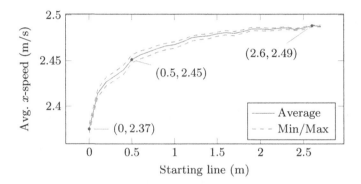

Fig. 3. Average robot speed along the x-axis from a given starting line (perpendicular to the x-axis) until the end of the episode (blue line). The dashed red lines represent the minimum and maximum values. These results were averaged over 1000 episodes. (Color figure online)

In this experiment, the robot has not fallen once in 1000 episodes. Considering the entire trajectory, from a stopped position until the robot travels 28 m, the average x-speed ranged between 2.37 m/s and 2.38 m/s, with a SD of ± 2.8 mm/s. Using the technique employed by the magmaChallenge benchmark tool [19], which starts measuring the robot's x-speed after it crosses the 0.5 m line, our approach averaged 2.45 m/s on SimSpark, with a SD of ± 2.1 mm/s. After 2.5 m the agent stabilizes at around 2.49 m/s.

Figure 4 allows the analysis of a single episode. Figure 4a shows the instantaneous x-speed, represented by a continuous blue line. The average speed is defined by a dotted red line. It is computed by considering the current time instant t until the episode's end T, where the travelled distance is given, analogously, from x_t until x_T, as denoted by $(x_T - x_t)/(T - t)$. Note that this expression is dependent on time instants instead of x-coordinates.

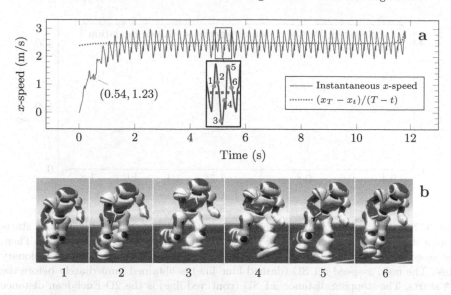

Fig. 4. Robot's speed along the x-axis in a single episode, on top (**a**). The continuous blue line indicates the instantaneous speed while the dotted red line represents the average speed from the current time value t until the end of the episode T. A sequence of frames from that episode is shown on the bottom (**b**). Each frame corresponds to one of the numbered time steps in (**a**). (Color figure online)

Initially, the robot was standing still. Then it accelerated and crossed the 0.5 m imaginary line. At that moment, 0.54 s had passed, and the robot's instantaneous x-speed (for which we consider the last 3 steps = 60 ms) was 1.23 m/s. This point in the graph is near a local minimum, which is explained by the current running gait cycle. By observing Fig. 4b, it is possible to study the movement dynamics which leads to the speed oscillations while running.

As Adelaar and Novacheck defined [20,21], running, in comparison with walking, is characterized by longer double floating periods, where there is no support from any limb. This characteristic is seen during 27% of the time for the episode shown in Fig. 4. The sequential frames displayed on the figure's bottom correspond to the numbered time steps on top. Each pose is associated with a specific cycle of the running gait. The lowest speed is registered when the robot is still floating (frame no. 3).

4.2   Stopping

The stopping behavior is coordinated with the sprinting behavior to bring the robot, once again, to a stationary pose. The results for this experiment were averaged over 2400 episodes executed under the conditions specified in Sect. 3.5. Figure 5 shows the stopping behavior results for different initial conditions. The robot has not fallen once during this evaluation. In the first batch of 100 episodes, the robot ran for 0.42 s, achieving an average maximum speed of 1.24 m/s. After

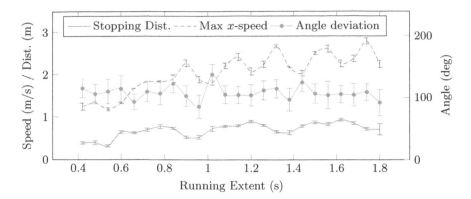

Fig. 5. Stopping results as a function of the initial running extent. The robot starts from a stopped position and runs for a certain extent, between 0.42 s and 1.80 s. Then, the stopping algorithm (SA) tries to bring the robot back to a predefined stationary pose. The max. x-speed ±1 SD (dashed blue line) is obtained immediately before the SA starts. The stopping distance ±1 SD (cont. red line) is the 2D Euclidean distance traveled by the robot while the SA is operating. Analogously, the angle deviation ±1 SD (green dots) is the absolute rotation angle measured while the SA is running. In total, 24 running extents were tested, with 100 episodes each, totalling 2400 episodes. (Color figure online)

that moment, the stopping algorithm took control and stopped the robot, on average, in 0.39 m with an angle deviation of 115°. In the following batches, the initial speed increases, although not monotonically, for the reasons already stated in Sect. 4.1. The fastest initial speed was obtained for a running extent of 1.74 s, for which the average max. speed was 2.79 m/s. With these initial conditions, the robot stopped, on average, in 0.72 m with an angle deviation of 109°.

5   Discussion

Regarding the sprinting behavior, the obtained results were a considerable improvement over current RoboCup standards. Our agent is 82% faster than the 2014 RoboCup's running challenge champion [7]. It is also considerably faster than the 2017's champion [6], although the comparison is not entirely fair due to differences between SimSpark and Gazebo. To the best of our knowledge, there is currently no team in the RoboCup 3D Soccer Simulation League that can run at a similar speed. Also, in comparison with previous work [1], several metrics were improved. The average speed after the robot crosses the 0.5 m line increased from 1.46 m/s to 2.45 m/s and the standard deviation reduced from 0.13 m/s to 0.002 m/s. This can be translated as greater speed, determinism and reliability, which is supported by the fact that the robot did not fall in 1000 consecutive episodes. The conditions tested in this work were harder, since the agent had no access to the original robot torso's x, y and z coordinates. However, this also made the solution more robust, since it is easier to run towards a different direction without having to align the Cartesian plane with the agent's initial orientation. Two factors that largely contributed to the optimization quality were the new initial pose introduced in Sect. 3.5 and the longer optimization session with 200M time steps.

The stopping behavior is directly linked with the running style, and it is harder to compare with existing solutions. From the obtained results, it is possible to conclude that the agent learned to rotate its body approximately 100°, while trying to stop, to avoid falling. From a physics standpoint, this trick seems logical. The NAO robot is more prone to tip forward than sideways, because its base is wider than it is long. Nonetheless, this is not ideal, since most times the agent is expected to end the sprint with the same orientation that it had on the beginning. We tried penalizing the orientation deviation but the quality of the solution decreased, as the robot would sometimes fall after the optimization was concluded. Despite this limitation, the proposed solution always kept control of the robot, which did not fall in 2400 consecutive episodes.

6 Conclusion and Future Work

We have successively trained a sprinting and stopping behavior that is now integrated into our team and can be used in official RoboCup matches. This solution was obtained from scratch using the Proximal Policy Optimization algorithm. The sprinting performance is highly stable. It is largely superior to previous running challenge champions and, to the best of our knowledge, it is also considerably better than current running algorithms used by RoboCup 3D Soccer Simulation League teams.

Regarding the stopping behavior, there is still room for improvement on multiple fronts. Despite its impeccable ability to stop the agent without falling, its ending orientation is, on average, very different from when the stopping algorithm takes control. Moreover, the stopping distance can also be improved.

On the future, the focus will be set on improving the stopping algorithm and expanding both behaviors to other versions of the NAO robot, with special emphasis on the version with controllable toes. We expect that the larger solution space may produce even better results.

Acknowledgment. The first author is supported by FCT under grant SFRH/BD/139926/2018. The work was also partially funded by COMPETE 2020 and FCT Portuguese Foundation for Science and Technology under project UID/CEC/00027/2019 (LIACC) and UID/CEC/00127/2019 (IEETA).

References

1. Abreu, M., Lau, N., Sousa, A., Reis, L.P.: Learning low level skills from scratch for humanoid robot soccer using deep reinforcement learning. In: 19th IEEE International Conference on Autonomous Robot Systems and Competitions (IEEE ICARSC 2019), Gondomar, Porto, Portugal, 24–26 April 2019

2. Noda, I., Suzuki, S.J., Matsubara, H., Asada, M., Kitano, H.: RoboCup-97: the first robot world cup soccer games and conferences. AI Mag. **19**(3), 49 (1998)
3. Glaser, S.: RoboCup Soccer - 3D Simulation League. https://archive.robocup.info/Soccer/Simulation/2D/binaries/RoboCup/2018/. Accessed 19 Apr 2019
4. MacAlpine, P., Torabi, F., Pavse, B., Sigmon, J., Stone, P.: UT Austin Villa: RoboCup 2018 3D simulation league champions. In: Holz, D., Genter, K., Saad, M., von Stryk, O. (eds.) RoboCup 2018. LNCS (LNAI), vol. 11374, pp. 462–475. Springer, Cham (2019). https://doi.org/10.1007/978-3-030-27544-0_38
5. Gazebo support for the RoboCup 3D simulator league. https://bitbucket.org/osrf/robocup3ds. Accessed 19 Apr 2019
6. MacAlpine, P., Stone, P.: UT Austin Villa: RoboCup 2017 3D simulation league competition and technical challenges champions. In: Akiyama, H., Obst, O., Sammut, C., Tonidandel, F. (eds.) RoboCup 2017. LNCS (LNAI), vol. 11175, pp. 473–485. Springer, Cham (2018). https://doi.org/10.1007/978-3-030-00308-1_39
7. MacAlpine, P., Depinet, M., Liang, J., Stone, P.: UT Austin Villa: RoboCup 2014 3D simulation league competition and technical challenge champions. In: Bianchi, R.A.C., Akin, H.L., Ramamoorthy, S., Sugiura, K. (eds.) RoboCup 2014. LNCS (LNAI), vol. 8992, pp. 33–46. Springer, Cham (2015). https://doi.org/10.1007/978-3-319-18615-3_3
8. Snafii, N., Abdolmaleki, A., Lau, N., Reis, L.P.: Development of an omnidirectional walk engine for soccer humanoid robots. Int. J. Adv. Rob. Syst. **12**(12), 193 (2015)
9. Moradi, K., Fathian, M., Ghidary, S.S.: Omnidirectional walking using central pattern generator. Int. J. Mach. Learn. Cybernet. **7**(6), 1023–1033 (2016)
10. Abdolmaleki, A., Lau, N., Reis, L.P., Peters, J., Neumann, G.: Contextual policy search for linear and nonlinear generalization of a humanoid walking controller. J. Intell. Rob. Syst. **83**(3), 393–408 (2016)
11. Abdolmaleki, A., Lau, N., Reis, L.P., Peters, J., Neumann, G.: Contextual policy search for generalizing a parameterized biped walking controller. In: 2015 IEEE International Conference on Autonomous Robot Systems and Competitions, pp. 17–22. IEEE (2015)
12. Shafii, N., Lau, N., Reis, L.P.: Learning to walk fast: optimized hip height movement for simulated and real humanoid robots. J. Intell. Rob. Syst. **80**(3), 555–571 (2015)
13. Xu, Y., Vatankhah, H.: SimSpark: an open source robot simulator developed by the RoboCup community. In: Behnke, S., Veloso, M., Visser, A., Xiong, R. (eds.) RoboCup 2013. LNCS (LNAI), vol. 8371, pp. 632–639. Springer, Heidelberg (2014). https://doi.org/10.1007/978-3-662-44468-9_59
14. SoftBank Robotics: Nao the humanoid robot. https://www.softbankrobotics.com/emea/en/nao. Accessed 19 Apr 2019
15. Akaike, H.: A new look at the statistical model identification. IEEE Trans. Autom. Control **19**(6), 716–723 (1974)
16. Sugiura, N.: Further analysis of the data by Akaike's information criterion and the finite corrections. Commun. Stat. Theory Methods **7**(1), 13–26 (1978)
17. Schulman, J., Wolski, F., Dhariwal, P., Radford, A., Klimov, O.: Proximal policy optimization algorithms. CoRR, vol. abs/1707.06347 (2017)
18. Dhariwal, P., et al.: Openai baselines. https://github.com/openai/baselines. Accessed 20 Apr 2019
19. The MagmaOffenburg RoboCup 3D Simulation Team: magmaChallenge: Benchmark tool for RoboCup 3D soccer simulation. https://github.com/magmaOffenburg/magmaChallenge. Accessed 19 Apr 2019

20. Adelaar, R.S.: The practical biomechanics of running. Am. J. Sports Med. **14**(6), 497–500 (1986)
21. Novacheck, T.F.: The biomechanics of running. Gait Posture **7**(1), 77–95 (1998)
22. SoftBank Robotics: Aldebaran documentation: Nao - actuator & sensor list. http://doc.aldebaran.com/2-1/family/nao dcm/actuator sensor names.html

High-Frequency Multi Bus Servo and Sensor Communication Using the Dynamixel Protocol

Marc Bestmann[1](✉), Jasper Güldenstein[2], and Jianwei Zhang[3]

[1] Hamburg Bit-Bots, Technical Aspects of Multimodal Systems (TAMS), Department of Informatics, University of Hamburg, Vogt-Kölln-Straße 30, 22527 Hamburg, Germany
bestmann@informatik.uni-hamburg.de
[2] Hamburg Bit-Bots, Department of Informatics, University of Hamburg, Vogt-Kölln-Straße 30, 22527 Hamburg, Germany
5guelden@informatik.uni-hamburg.de
[3] Technical Aspects of Multimodal Systems (TAMS), Department of Informatics, University of Hamburg, Vogt-Kölln-Straße 30, 22527 Hamburg, Germany
zhang@informatik.uni-hamburg.de
http://robocup.informatik.uni-hamburg.de

Abstract. High-frequency control loops are necessary to improve agility and reactiveness of robots. One of the common limiting bottlenecks is the communication with the hardware, i.e., reading of sensors values and writing of actuator commands. In this paper, we investigate the performance of devices using the widespread Robotis Dynamixel protocol via an RS-485 bus. Due to the limitations of current approaches, we present a new multibus solution which enables typical humanoid robots used in RoboCup to have a control loop frequency of more than 1 kHz. Additionally, we present solutions to integrate sensors into this bus with high update rates.

Keywords: Robotics · Humanoid · Servo · Sensor · Control · Bus · Open source

1 Introduction

Daisy chained servo motors with bus communication are an essential component of many robots. They reduce the complexity of the mechanical system by minimizing the number of cables required for controlling the actuators. Especially in robots with many degrees of freedom, i.e., humanoids, it is impractical to control motors in parallel. Daisy chaining sensors into the bus can further reduce the number of needed cables.

A widely used standard for peripheral communication is RS-485 (also known as TIA-485 or EIA-485) [9]. Robust communication in electrically noisy environments is achieved with a differential signal. One widely used servo motor series using RS-485 for communication are Dynamixel servos by Robotis[1]. They are

---

[1] Some subseries (e.g., the MX or X series) are also available with a buffered TTL interface as a physical communication layer. Servos with a TTL interface can be connected to the same hardware as ones with an RS-485 interface as explained in Sect. 2.

© Springer Nature Switzerland AG 2019
S. Chalup et al. (Eds.): RoboCup 2019, LNAI 11531, pp. 16–29, 2019.
https://doi.org/10.1007/978-3-030-35699-6_2

used in a wide range of scenarios from robot arms and end effectors to small to full-size humanoids. Some of these applications are described in Sect. 3.

Fast and reliable communication with the actuators is essential for most use cases. Since lower latency is synonymous with a faster response to sensory inputs, motions can be more dynamic and reactive. This is especially important in scenarios such as collision detection and for motions that maintain or restore balance of the robot.

In this paper, we survey the existing controller boards to communicate with servos that utilize RS-485 (or TTL) for serial communication. Furthermore, we propose new approaches to improve the control loop rate using multi-bus approaches.

This paper is structured as follows: Sect. 2 introduces the communication with Dynamixel servo motors. In Sect. 3 we present existing controller boards. Section 4 explains two approaches. First, we show our improved firmware for an existing controller board. Second, we present our newly developed controller board. We evaluate the performance of controlling Dynamixel servo motors in Sect. 5. Afterward, the integration of sensors into the bus is discussed and evaluated in Sect. 6. The ROS [7] based software which interfaces with the controller boards is described in Sect. 7. A collection of lessons learned which might be helpful to anyone using the Dynamixel bus is provided in Sect. 8. Finally, the paper concludes with Sect. 9.

2 Dynamixel Communication

The Dynamixel bus uses a specified master/slave half-duplex protocol with 8 bit, 1 stop bit, and no parity [1]. All Dynamixel MX, X and Pro servos use either RS-485 or TTL as a physical communication layer. TTL communication can be emulated using RS-485 transceivers by tying the inverting data line to 2.5 V using a simple voltage divider. Since the minimum differential voltage on the RS-485 bus is 1.5 V, the 5 V TTL logic level is interpreted correctly. Each servo is assigned a unique ID number which is used to address the servo from the master.

There are two types of packages: instruction packages, sent by the master, and status packages, sent by the slaves. The master can send *write* instructions to set values to the slave's registers and *read* instructions to get current register values returned through a status package. The instruction packages can be either *single, sync,* or *bulk.* Single instructions are only processed by one slave. Sync packages specify a set of slaves and a range of registers with consecutive addresses which are read or written. All specified slave devices answer this instruction sequentially. Bulk packages are similar to sync packages, but it is possible to specify the registers for each slave individually. All packages start with a header, the corresponding ID, and the length of the package. The package ends with a checksum to verify its correctness.

Several features were introduced in the second version of the protocol, i.e. higher maximum package size, improve checksum and byte stuffing to prevent occurents of headers inside a package. Furthermore, version 2.0 specifies sync

Table 1. Number of bytes needed for different package types.

read	sync read	bulk read
$i = n * 14$	$i = 14 + n$	$i = 10 + n * 5$
$s = n * (11 + r)$	$s = n * (11 + r)$	$s = n * (11 + r)$
write	sync write	bulk write
$i = n * (12 + r)$	$i = 14 + n * (r + 1)$	$i = 10 + n * (5 + r)$

i: Instruction length [B]
s: Status length [B]
n: Slaves to address
r: Registers to read/write

Table 2. Comparison of multiple devices available for controlling RS485 or TTL servo Motors. The maximum bus speed describes the theoretically achievable maximum with the hardware. Some boards are limited in baud rate by firmware.

Name	Microchip	Max. bus speed [MBaud]	No. bus	Prot. 2	Cost
CM730[a]	FT232R+STM32F103	4.5	1	No	
OpenCM9.04	STM32F103	2.5[b]	1	Yes	50$
OpenCR	STM32F746	10	1	Yes	180$
Arbotix Pro	FT232R+STM32F103	4.5	1	No	150$
Rhoban DXL	STM32F103	4.5 (2.25)[c]	3	Yes[d]	~20$
USB2DXL	FT232R	3	1	Yes	50$
U2D2	FT232H	6	1	Yes	50$
QUADDXL	FT4232H	12	4	Yes	~40$

[a] Discontinued;
[b] Limited by transceiver on extension board;
[c] Bus 1 can operate at 4.5 Mbps, bus 2 and 3 only at 2.25 Mbps;
[d] Not supported by original firmware

read and bulk write instruction packages which were not officially included previously. Since it is not compatible but superior to version 1, we are only considering the newer version of the protocol in the following.

While the protocol can be used for any device, it is most commonly used for the Dynamixel servos. They are a combination of a DC motor, a gearbox and a microprocessor which acts as a PID controller. The servo can be controlled by current, velocity, position or a combination of position and maximal current. In a typical closed-loop application the sensor values of the servos are read, and new commands are given to the servos in a fixed rate. The performance of the system depends thereby on how long a read and write cycle takes. Multiple factors influence the cycle time. These are the baud rate, the number of servos on the bus, and the number of bytes read and written. Table 1 gives the calculations for the required lengths of the packages required for *single*, *sync* and *bulk read* and *write* instructions. It is visible that the use of sync or bulk packages can decrease the number of needed bytes and therefore increase the performance.

3   Related Work

The Dynamixel bus system is widespread in different areas of robotics, mainly legged robots and robotic arms. Multiple robot platforms that use this bus

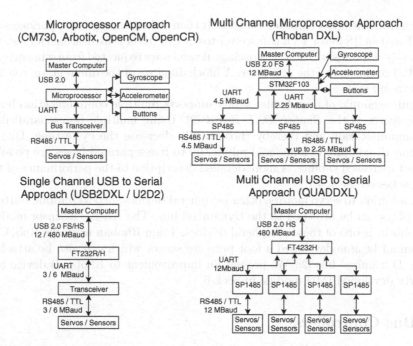

Fig. 1. Block diagram of different approaches to communicate with servo motors, sensors and other peripheral devices using the Dynamixel bus. They can be differentiated by the number of buses (**horizontal**) and the used chip type (**vertical**). Our newly proposed solution is the QUADDXL (**bottom right**).

system are produced by the manufacturer of the Dynamixel motors. These include the mobile robot TurtleBot3 [4], the small size humanoid robot DarwinOP [5], the full-size humanoid robot THORMANG, and the robotic arm OpenManipulator-X. Many research groups have also developed robot platforms that use this bus. They are especially widespread in the Humanoid League of the RoboCup where 32 of 34 teams use the Robotis servos and therefore the Dynamixel bus system[2]. They are also used in multiple other leagues of the RoboCup, e.g., the Rescue League.

Since the actuators are used in many robot platforms, multiple controller solutions are available. Some of them are commercially available from Robotis or other distributors, e.g., the *Arbotix* controllers from Interbotix. Furthermore, there are multiple boards designed by research groups for their robotic platform, especially in the RoboCup domain. An overview of these boards is shown in Table 2.

All of these boards connect to a host computer via USB. They can be grouped into two different approaches. One approach uses a USB to serial converter to directly translate the USB signal to UART and afterward, by using a transceiver, to RS-485 or TTL. Two widespread representatives of this approach are the *USB2DXL* and *U2D2* boards from Robotis, which provide no direct sensor interface. The other approach uses a microprocessor which parses the packages

---

[2] Data from team description papers available at https://www.robocuphumanoid.org/hl-2019/teams/.

coming from the host computer via USB. It then either transmits the packages via UART and an RS485 or TTL transceiver to the bus (if they are destined for a slave) or directly responds with a status package if values are requested from sensors (e.g., an IMU) connected to the processor. A block diagram of the different approaches is shown in Fig. 1.

The only example of a controller which supports multiple communication buses to the servos is the *Rhoban DXL Board* [2]. Using multiple buses parallelizes the communication and thereby theoretically decrease the cycle time. Due to the limbed structure of humanoid robots, up to five separated buses are possible without increased cabling. A more detailed description of the performance of the approaches see Sect. 4.1.

In addition to servo motors, other peripheral devices such as sensors, buttons or displays can be attached to the Dynamixel bus. The AX-S1, a sensor module by Robotis, is one of these peripheral devices. Team Rhoban from the RoboCup Humanoid League developed a foot pressure sensor which can also be attached to the Dynamixel bus [2]. We present an improvement to Rhoban's device and a newly developed IMU module in Sect. 6.

4 Bus Controllers

Two different approaches were taken to improve the performance of the bus. First, we improved the well-performing Rhoban DXL Board by changing its firmware to adapt to protocol 2.0, enabling the use of sync commands. Second, a USB to four-channel serial chip was used to further increase the performance. The two approaches are presented in the following and evaluated in Sect. 5.

4.1 DXL Board

Since the DXL Board was the only available multi-bus controller, this board was chosen as the current baseline. It supports up to three buses. The original version had a firmware supporting only protocol 1.0 with a custom implementation of a sync read. The host computer can send a special sync read command to the board which translates it into regular read packages for the individual slave devices. Those instructions are then transmitted on the corresponding bus where the slave is connected. All status package are then aggregated and returned as a special response package. Thereby, the board can increase the throughput in comparison to a single bus, but it violates the protocol specifications.

Since protocol 2.0 specifies a sync read, there is no need for a custom sync read and it can be replaced by sending a standard sync package from host computer to the DXL board. This package is split up on the microprocessor of the board into three sync read packages for the three buses. The resulting status packages are transmitted to the host computer in correct order to stay in the protocol specifications. This way the number of required bytes on the servo bus can be further decreased and no extension of the protocol is necessary. The required bytes on the USB bus increase since single status packages are transmitted, but its influence is low since the USB bus has a higher throughput than the servo bus.

As a comparison, we implemented a second firmware version which only uses one bus system. Here, all instructions from the main computer are parsed and transmitted to the bus if it is not a reading of the directly connected sensors, i.e., the IMU or connected buttons. The resulting status packages do not have to be parsed and can be transmitted directly to the main computer. This reduces the workload on the microprocessor and the latency resulting from parsing packages. Furthermore, only one of the UART ports of the microprocessor is capable of 4.5 MBaud. The other two can only achieve a maximum speed of 2.25 MBaud. Therefore, this is the only way to utilize the highest possible baud rate of the Dynamixel servos.

4.2   QUADDXL

We developed a simple, high speed, low latency alternative to the DXL Board using the FT4232H chip from FTDI. It is a single USB 2.0 High Speed to 4 serial channel converter. Its schematic is presented in Fig. 2. The virtual com port drivers required for using the device have been included in the Linux kernel since version 3.0.0, and the buses are directly accessible as serial device files. The interface is comparable to the USB2DXL and U2D2, but it offers four bus systems with up to 12 MBaud each while requiring only one USB connection. No firmware is required since the chip directly transmits the bytes without parsing packages. It is therefore also usable for both Dynamixel protocol versions and any future versions. Furthermore, the latency is lower since no parsing is involved.

5   Evaluation of Servo Communication

The typical control strategy of servo motors in a humanoid robot is a continuous cycle of reading their sensors' information and writing new goals. In contrast to other robot types (e.g., robotic arms or wheeled robots), continuous control is necessary to keep the robot from falling. A higher frequency of this cycle results in faster reaction time to disturbances, for example by correcting the torso pose after an applied force to keep the robot standing. Since using sync reads/writes is the most efficient way to achieve this (see Sect. 2), we focused our evaluation on these instructions.

In our experimental setup, we used 20 Dynamixel MX-64 servos using RS-485. 10 bytes are necessary to read the current position, velocity and used current from a single servo motor. The current is used to identify the torque applied by the servo. Additionally, it is necessary to write 4 bytes to each servo to set a goal position. If all servos are on the same bus, this results in 568 bytes of data per update cycle, including header and checksum bytes (see Table 1). In the case of splitting it up on four buses, the necessary data is 163 byte per bus, due to additional header bytes. We chose this 20 motor setup since it is similar to many humanoid robots, such as Darwin-OP [5] and most of the robots in the Humanoid

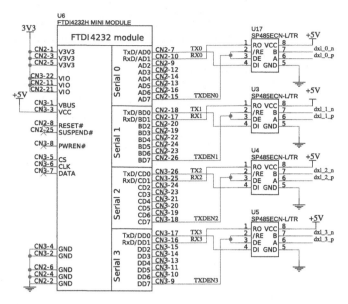

Fig. 2. Schematic of the QUADDXL. An FT4232H Mini Module (**left**) is connected to the host computer via USB. The four RS485 transceivers (**right**) are connected via the UART interface. The transceivers provide the required physical communication layer to a Dynamixel bus each.

League which were profoundly influenced by it. We measured the mean update cycle rate of our approaches together with the USB2DXL as a baseline and additionally provided the theoretical maximum that could be achieved if the bus would be transmitting these bytes without downtime between packages. The results are displayed in Table 3 and a comparison between the QUADDXL and the theoretical maximum is displayed in Fig. 3. We were not able to communicate with the servos on 4.5 MBaud with any controller. Therefore the highest tested baud rate is 4 MBaud. The reasons for this remain unknown.

For a single bus, the best performance was reached in 1 and 2 MBaud by the USB2DXL, closely followed by the QUADDXL. The Rhoban DXL performed worse in single and multi-bus approach. 4 MBaud is not possible with the USB2DXL but would have been with the U2D2. We expect it to perform slightly better than the QUADDXL in the single bus case (as the USB2DXL did on lower baud rates), but it was not available to us for testing.

Considering multiple buses, the Rhoban DXL performed worse than the QUADDXL. Furthermore, the performance of the Rhoban DXL board does not scale linearly with increasing bus number and baud rate. This indicates that the processing on the microprocessor is a bottleneck.

Overall, the QUADDXL manages to increase the cycle rate with increasing bus number and baud rate. It reaches a maximum of 1373 Hz which is three times higher than its speed on a single bus, and two times higher than the maximum possible speed on a single bus. The disparity between the real update rates and the theoretically possible rate is very high (see Fig. 3).

Table 3. Mean update rates for different numbers of buses and baud rates with sync commands in protocol 2.0. The Rhoban DXL board (R-DXL) was tested with our newly programmed firmware in single- and multi-bus version. The QUADDXL approach provides the best results. We believe that the low rate for the R-DXL on 4 MBaud is due to the microcontroller being to slow, resulting in massive package loss.

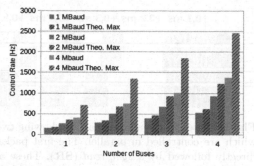

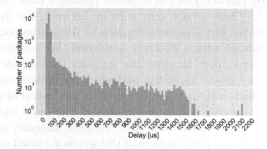

Fig. 3. Comparison of theoretically possible control rates with results from QUADDXL. The disparity between both is getting higher with increasing bus speed due to the constant response delay time.

Fig. 4. Histogram of delays between status packages in a sync read response from Dynamixel MX-64 servos. The y-axis is scaled logarithmically. A total of 61,913 packages was analyzed. The bucket size for each bar is 20 us.

No. buses	MBaud	Board	Rate [Hz]
		Theoretical Max	176
		R-DXL Single	132
	1	R-DXL Multi	125
		USB2DXL	153
		QUADDXL	149
1		Theoretical Max.	352
		R-DXL Single	215
	2	R-DXL Multi	179
		USB2DXL	272
		QUADDXL	261
		Theoretical Max.	704
	4	R-DXL Single	40
		QUADDXL	398
		Theoretical Max.	336
	1	R-DXL Multi	185
		QUADDXL	285
2		Theoretical Max.	671
	2	R-DXL Multi	219
		QUADDXL	497
		Theoretical Max.	1342
	4	QUADDXL	744
		Theoretical Max.	461
	1	R-DXL Multi	224
		QUADDXL	390
3		Theoretical Max.	922
	2	R-DXL Multi	250
		QUADDXL	670
		Theoretical Max.	1843
	4	QUADDXL	1003
		Theoretical Max.	613
	1	QUADDXL	524
4		Theoretical Max.	1227
	2	QUADDXL	923
		Theoretical Max.	2545
	4	QUADDXL	**1373**

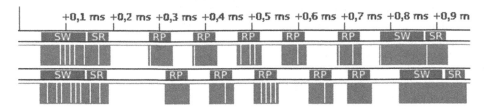

Fig. 5. Screenshot of a logic analyzer showing two buses with 5 servos each at 4 MBaud, which are controlled in parallel. The first package on the left is a *sync write* (**SW**), directly followed by a *sync read* (**SR**). These are followed by the response packages (**RP**) of the servos and then again followed by the *sync read* of the next cycle. The delay before response packages caused by the parsing of the packages is clearly visible.

To further investigate this significant difference, a logic analyzer was used. The results show that a significant portion of the available bus time is used up by the delay of the response packages from the servos (see Fig. 5).

There is not only a delay between the sync read instruction and the first status but also between each of the status packages. This delay length does not change with a different baud rate. We assume that this delay derives from the servo's need to parse the previous package on the bus. In a sync read, the servo only sends its status package after it has read the status package of the servo which was specified before it in the instruction. This ensures that there are not two servos writing on the bus at the same time. This time varies as an analysis of the data recorded with the logic analyzer shows (Fig. 4).

Since the firmware of the servos is closed source, there is no direct possibility to solve this problem. When comparing the performance influence of a higher baud rate and more buses on a system with long response delays, more buses scale better than a higher baud rate (see also Fig. 3). A higher baud rate can only decrease the bus time needed for transferring data but does not shorten the delays. More buses, on the other hand, can parallelize this delay.

The theoretically possible update rate for one bus can be computed using Eq. 1, where *data* is the number of bytes that have to be sent on the bus in each cycle (see Table 1). Since 10 bit are required to transmit 1 byte of data (1 start and 1 stop bit), this factor has to be added.

The optimal real rate, i.e., without possible delays introduced by the bus controller or main computer, can be approximated with Eq. 2 by introducing an additional factor that takes the response delay of the servo into account. In this equation, n is the number of servos on the bus and the $50\,\mu s$ are an approximation for the mean delay time.

While the experiments were conducted on MX-64 servos, we expect other motors from the MX and X series to behave identically since the same microprocessor (STM32F103) is used in all of them.

$$rate[Hz] = \frac{1}{\frac{data[B]*10[bit/B]}{baud[bit/s]}} \quad (1) \quad rate[Hz] = \frac{1}{\frac{data[B]*10[bit/B]}{baud[bit/s]} + n*50[\mu s]} \quad (2)$$

6   Sensors

Besides the sensor data from the servos themselves, additional modalities are often needed in the control cycle. In the RoboCup Humanoid League, those are mostly IMUs and foot pressure sensors. If we want to benefit from the higher control rate of the servos we also need a similarly high reading rate of the sensors.

Different possibilities to connect sensors to the main computer exist. The most practical way is to include them on the Dynamixel bus since this reduces the number of required cables. Furthermore, it allows for interfacing the sensors with the same software as the servos.

We present and evaluate two different sensor boards that use the Dynamixel bus for communication to the main computer. Firstly, an IMU sensor module is introduced in Sect. 6.1. Secondly, a foot pressure sensor based on Rhoban's ForceFoot [2] is presented in Sect. 6.2.

While only these two boards are presented and evaluated, practically any sensor using common physical communication interfaces can be attached to the Dynamixel bus using a microprocessor. Furthermore, other peripheral electronics such as buttons and displays can be added to the bus system. The general approach is presented in the schematic shown in Fig. 6.

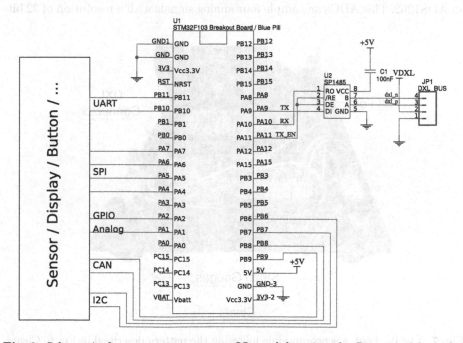

Fig. 6. Schematic for a generic sensor or IO module using the Dynamixel bus. An STM32F103 breakout board (**center**), e.g., a Blue Pill, connects via UART to an RS485 transceiver (**right**) which is connected to the Dynamixel bus. A multitude of peripheral devices (**left**) may be attached to the various communication interfaces provided by the microcontroller.

6.1   IMU

We used an MPU6050 IMU connected to a Maple Mini using I2C at 400 KHz. The Maple Mini is connected to the Dynamixel Bus using an RS-485 transceiver. The IMU provides the raw linear accelerations and angular velocities in a resolution of two bytes each. Therefore it was necessary to read 12 bytes in each cycle on one device. Since this only requires a single read and status package, 37 Bytes needed to be transmitted (see Table 1). Due to the low number of bytes needed for this process, it was possible to reach an update cycle of 1 kHz. The rate is limited by the fact, that the microprocessor has a single core can not read the IMU and communicate on the Dynamixel bus at the same time. Using a multi core microprocessor could solve this, if higher update rates are required.

6.2   Foot Pressure Sensor

The most widespread foot pressure sensor in the Humanoid League was developed by Rhoban [8] and consists of four strain gauges with an HX711 ADC and an ATMega328PB chip to connect it with the Dynamixel bus. While this approach proved successful, the employed ADC limits the update rate to 80 Hz. Therefore, we developed an improved version, called *Bit Foot* (see Fig. 7), using an ADS1262. This ADC can sample four analog signals with a resolution of 32 bit

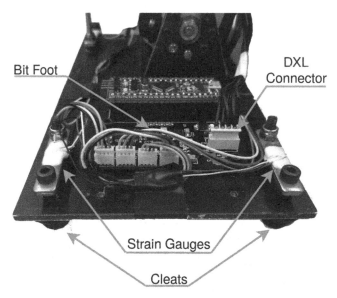

Fig. 7. The Bit Foot, a sensor module following the pattern described in Fig. 6. Cleats are attached to strain gauges at four corners of the foot to measure the contact forces of the robot's foot. The analog signals of these strain gauges are fed into an ADC. SPI is used to interface this microchip from the STM32F103. The board is connected to the Dynamixel bus via an RS485 transceiver.

at a rate of up to 38400 Hz. It provides integrated filtering and multiple analog channels. It is connected via SPI to a STM32F103 breakout board called *Blue Pill*. This board is connected to the Dynamixel bus via an RS-485 transceiver. We use the raw data for all four strain gauges (32 bytes), but it would also be feasible to directly provide the center of pressure.

We evaluated the sensor similar to the IMU using regular read packages but only reached a cycle rate of 697 Hz. The readout of the ADC limits this rate. It can not read the four sensors at the same time but is only multiplexing between the different inputs. When changing the input channel, a delay time is needed before reading new values. This problem could be solved by using a different or multiple ADCs. Our result is still a significant improvement to the current baseline.

7   Interface Software

In order provide sensor and servo data to other software components, interfacing software is required. We chose the ros_control framework [3], which abstracts hardware and provides different controllers. Furthermore, it directly integrates the hardware into ROS [7] and provides the same interface when using the Gazebo simulator [6], simplifying the transfer from simulation to the real robot.

We implemented a hardware interface which can connect the servos and the previously mentioned sensors. The protocol implementation is based on the Robotis Dynamixel SDK[3] and Workbench[4] with the addition of a multi-register *sync read* which is necessary to read all values of the servos in a single *sync read*. The devices and values which should be read can be specified in a configuration file. Multiple buses can be used in parallel by initiating multiple instances of this interface, which is essential for the QUADDXL approach.

Different controllers provided by ros_control, e.g., position or effort, can be directly used with this hardware interface. Since the Dynamixel servos provide the possibility to use *Current-based Position Control*, where the servo is position controlled but with a maximum current, an additional controller was implemented to make this possible.

8   Lessons Learned

This section provides some important practical information which was learned during the work.

Sync Reads. The use of *sync reads* and *writes* is essential to increase performance since they reduce the number of bytes needed for each control loop cycle. If registers are used which have no sequential addresses, the indirect addressing feature should be used to reduce the number of needed sync packages.

---

[3] http://emanual.robotis.com/docs/en/software/dynamixel/dynamixel_sdk/ overview/.

[4] http://emanual.robotis.com/docs/en/software/dynamixel/dynamixel_workbench/.

Return Delay Time. The Dynamixel servos have a *return delay time* value which adds an additional delay to the response time. The default value is 250 us, which can make fast communication impossible, even when this delay is set in just a single servo. At each startup of the robot, this register value should be written to 0, in case that a servo was replaced or reset, since difficult to debug bus timeouts and performance drops can happen.

Linux Kernel Latency. The default value of the Linux USB-serial device latency timer is 16 ms. This is done to reduce the number of needed headers for the USB packages and the load on the CPU. We set it to 0 to reach the best performance. Due to the high baud rate of USB 2.0 HS (480 MBaud) the additional header bytes do not slow down the sensor and servo communication.

Use Highest Baud Rate Possible. Even if a fixed cycle time is used which would be achievable with a lower baud rate, the transfer time of a package is lowered, thus making the reaction of the servos faster. We did not encounter any problems with noise or corrupted packages on higher baud rates.

FTDI Bus Controller. The latency of the USB to serial devices is lower than the microprocessor-based approaches since those have to parse the packages which introduces an additional delay. Furthermore, with the USB to serial approaches, no additional firmware is necessary, thus simplifying deployment and debugging.

Open Source Firmware. It was not possible for us to improve the long reply delays of the Dynamixel servos. This problem could possibly be solved if the firmware would have been open sourced.

9   Conclusion

In this paper, we evaluated methods to improve the interfacing of servos and sensors using the widespread Dynamixel protocol. Our approach of using multiple buses showed to be the most effective due to the long reply times of the Dynamixel servos and their limitations in baud rate. Using this, we achieved a cycle rate of more than 1 KHz on the servos of our robot. Furthermore, we showed an approach to integrate other sensors with high update rates into the same bus, thus reducing the number of cables in the robot. The presented solutions are very low-cost and easy to reproduce.

Further improvements on cycle rates could be reached by reducing the response time of the servos or by extending the Dynamixel protocol to reduce the number of bytes per cycle. One approach would be a *cyclic read* and *cyclic write*, where the master specifies which values are written and read each cycle before starting. Afterward, only shortened request and response packages can be sent since all slaves know which data they need to transmit.

We invite other teams to use our controller board[5], control software[6], foot pressure sensors[7] and sensor connection board[8].

---

[5] https://github.com/bit-bots/bitbots_quaddxl.

[6] https://github.com/bit-bots/bitbots_lowlevel/tree/master/bitbots_ros_control.

[7] https://github.com/bit-bots/bit_foot.

[8] https://github.com/bit-bots/dxl_sensor.

Acknowledgments. Thanks to the Hamburg Bit-Bots for support. Thanks to team Rhoban for making their hardware and software open source. This research was partially funded by the German Research Foundation (DFG) and the National Science Foundation of China (NSFC) in project Crossmodal Learning, TRR-169.

References

1. Robotis e-manual. http://emanual.robotis.com/. Accessed 21 Apr 2019
2. Allali, J., et al.: Rhoban football club: RoboCup humanoid kid-size 2016 champion team paper. In: Behnke, S., Sheh, R., Sarıel, S., Lee, D.D. (eds.) RoboCup 2016. LNCS (LNAI), vol. 9776, pp. 491–502. Springer, Cham (2017). https://doi.org/10.1007/978-3-319-68792-6_41
3. Chitta, S., et al.: ros_control: A generic and simple control framework for ROS. J. Open Source Softw. **2**, 456 (2017). https://doi.org/10.21105/joss.00456
4. Guizzo, E., Ackerman, E.: The TurtleBot3 teacher [resources_hands on]. IEEE Spectr. **54**(8), 19–20 (2017)
5. Ha, I., Tamura, Y., Asama, H., Han, J., Hong, D.W.: Development of open humanoid platform DARwIn-OP. In: SICE Annual Conference 2011, pp. 2178–2181. IEEE (2011)
6. Koenig, N., Howard, A.: Design and use paradigms for Gazebo, an open-source multi-robot simulator. In: 2004 IEEE/RSJ International Conference on Intelligent Robots and Systems (IROS), vol. 3, pp. 2149–2154. IEEE (2004)
7. Quigley, M., et al.: ROS: an open-source robot operating system. In: ICRA Workshop on Open Source Software, Kobe, Japan, vol. 3, p. 5 (2009)
8. Rouxel, Q., Passault, G., Hofer, L., N'Guyen, S., Ly, O.: Rhoban hardware and software open source contributions for robocup humanoids. In: Proceedings of 10th Workshop on Humanoid Soccer Robots, IEEE-RAS International Conference on Humanoid Robots, Seoul, Korea (2015)
9. Soltero, M., Zhang, J., Cockril, C.: RS-422 and RS-485 Standards Overview and System Configurations. Technical report, Texas Instruments (2002)

Positioning of Active Wheels for Optimal Ball Handling

A Guide for Designing a New Ball Handle Mechanism for Middle-Size-League at RoboCup

Maximilian Beuermann, Marie Ossenkopf$^{(\boxtimes)}$, and Kurt Geihs

EECS Department — Distributed Systems, University of Kassel,
Wilhelmshöher Allee 73, 34121 Kassel, Germany
{maximilian.beuermann,geihs}@uni-kassel.de, ossenkopf@vs.uni-kassel.de

Abstract. The RoboCup is an international competition in robot science. In the Middle Size League (MSL), which is one of the robotic soccer leagues, dribbling a ball is an essential capability. This task needs both hardware and software consideration. The position of the active dribbling wheels determines the movement possibilities of the dribbling robot and software control can only limitedly make up for poor hardware design decisions. We present a guide that leads through the decision-making process for positioning the wheels of the ball handle mechanism. We show a variety of considerations that need to be taken into account when designing a ball handle mechanism. We weight the requirements and conclude an optimal positioning for the ball handle mechanism of the Carpe Noctem Cassel team. We also present the kinematic solution of the ball actuation for the essential movement directions.

Keywords: Active dribbling · Robot soccer · Ball handle mechanism · RoboCup · MSL · Carpe Noctem Cassel

1   Introduction

The Carpe Noctem Cassel team of the University of Kassel has been participating in the Middle Size League (MSL) of the RoboCup since 2006. Our latest hardware and construction update is the CN2010 robot, which we still use today. In recent years it has become essential to focus on hardware elaboration in order to keep up with the competition. Not only do the competing teams advance, but the rules also get updated to move the challenge closer to human soccer.

In robot soccer, as in human soccer, it is essential to control the ball and dribble it alongside the player according to the applicable rules. The robot dribbles around opponents, runs free for a pass to a fellow player or turns on the spot to find a free fellow player. The movements of the robot with the ball are limited by the rules to shift the gameplay to fast passes instead of long distance forward driving. Due to the fast and highly dynamic movements, the reliable

© Springer Nature Switzerland AG 2019
S. Chalup et al. (Eds.): RoboCup 2019, LNAI 11531, pp. 30–43, 2019.
https://doi.org/10.1007/978-3-030-35699-6_3

guiding of the ball on the robot becomes particularly important. This movement is carried out by the ball handle mechanism as an actuator of the robot.

One of the latest updates in the MSL rules [12] was "natural dribbling", meaning, that the ball has to rotate in the direction of its movement during dribbling. That imposes high demands on the ball handling mechanism. A passive mechanism, like most teams used in the first years, would either lose the ball quickly or prevent the ball from rolling naturally. Another significant advantage of the active versus the passive ball handle mechanism is the duel strength. Hence, an active mechanism, which actuates the ball according to the movement of the robot, is inevitable. This paper portraits the kinematic and dynamic challenges of actuating the ball, especially the role of the robot design and the active wheel positioning.

There is a set of rules that define the hardware and construction criteria for soccer robots in the MSL, but leave the design itself to each team for the promotion of innovation. In the MSL, the de facto standard uses two actively driven wheels attached to movable arms for the ball handle mechanism [1–3,7]. As this approach turned out the most promising so far, we stay with this concept for the redesign of the Carpe Noctem robots. We collect the aspects that need to be taken into account when designing an effective ball handling. We analyze requirements like the rules of the MSL and the conditions for a stable run, as well as the strategic consideration of robot movements in certain game situations. We figured out that the first most crucial decision for reasonable ball control is the choice of contact points between the wheels and the ball. As our examination of the topic might be useful to other teams redesigning their robots in the future, we want to deliver a guide for this decision process. Therefore, this paper shows how to quantify the optimal position of the wheels on the ball to have a safe grip and move as if the ball was rolling freely at the same time.

The remainder of this paper is organized as follows: Sect. 2 presents related work. We gather the requirements that are imposed on the system by rules and desirable behavior in Sect. 3. In Sect. 4, we analyze how two active wheels can induce the required ball movements. We present their kinematic solution depending on the wheel positioning. We analyze the aspects that need to be taken into account regarding the stability of the ball guidance in Sect. 5 and discuss the optimal position in Sect. 6. There we also discuss changes that would occur with other hardware choices. Eventually, we conclude with Sect. 7.

2 Related Work

Junkai et al. [2] present the history of various approaches to ball dribbling in the MSL from the beginnings with passive ball handling to the present use of active ball handling. As a best practice, the concept of ball handling with two actively driven wheels on movable lever arms [1] has established and is now the de facto standard in the MSL. Each team has adapted this basic concept for its robots.

The stabilization of the ball to solve the handling problem is currently solved via a closed-loop-control [1,2,4,6,7] by most teams. They treat the motion model as Lagrange equations after a linearization in the control algorithm. From the measured position of the lever arms, the position of the ball in the ball handle is estimated and, in case of deviation from the ideal position, compensated by adjusting the wheel speeds. In order to obtain stable dribbling, at least one iteration of the closed-loop-control must have been performed, because a stable condition can only be achieved by constantly adjusting the wheel speeds based on measured values.

Another approach is the application of the nonlinear equations of motion of rigid bodies from classical mechanics. The kinematics of ball motion can be described by the velocity state, as shown by Chikushi et al. [3] and Kimura et al. [5]. The spectrum of modeling motion problems reaches from mathematical models and continuous systems over multi-body-systems to finite element systems. There is a vast number of formalisms to describe multi-body-systems, but all of them are based either on Lagrange equations or Newton-Euler equations. Saha et al. give an overview of the evolution of these formalisms in the last decades [14]. The way via Newton-Euler equations is more error-prone than Euler-Lagrange equations because they consider nonlinear effects between bodies. For solving the motion problem with Newton-Euler equations, it is crucial to know the joints between and the types of bodies in the multibody system. We use the work of Kimura et al. [5] and extend their model by properties of the actuation with two active wheels. Chikushi et al. [9] also pursued this extension with an experimental approach. We use a more theoretic approach instead.

The rolling behavior of the ball imposed by two active wheels is similar to the driving behavior of cars, which has been researched in the automotive sector for decades [8]. The results from this extensively researched field are suitable for optimizing the driving behavior of a car through the design of the wheel suspension. We apply them to choose the optimal position of the contact point between wheel and ball concerning a stable dribbling behavior. Proper positioning can create a solid basis for subsequent control. We will elaborate on the similarities to car driving behavior in detail in the following sections.

3   Requirement Analysis

3.1   Artificial Requirements by Rules of the MSL [12]

A The diameter of the ball is 22.28 cm according to the current FIFA rules [11].

B There is maximum coverage of the ball by the robot at 1/3 of the top projection convex hull.

C The ball has to rotate continuously in the direction of its movement. We call this requirement further on natural rolling.

D Movement with the ball is only allowed within a radius of 3 m around the place where the ball was picked up.

E Reverse travel with the ball is limited to a maximum of 2 m and can only be repeated after the ball has been picked up again.

3.2 Gameplay Situation (User Story)

If opponents occupy the robot that holds the ball, it is essential for this robot to react quickly to gaps in the opponent's formation. The reaction can be dribbling around the opponent or aligning to play a pass to a fellow player. Both options require an agile behavior of the robot, which guides the ball safely. An agile behavior means to execute many different movement possibilities in a quick fashion. Due to the rigid position of the wheels on the ball, some movements are possible with safer ball guidance than others.

Regarding these situations, we set the focus on fast cornering, hence combining movement in x- and y-direction as well as rotating with fast direction changes. However, the ball should still be guided reliably in a longitudinal direction. The forward motion is more important than the backward motion because the backward motion is only allowed in a smaller range than the forward motion though it is necessary after gaining the ball in a duel. Turning on the spot and the transversal movement to the side is also useful, but less critical since the robot usually acts from a forward movement when it is not stopped. Braking and acceleration must also be observed so that the ball is not lost due to the nonholonomic constraint.

4 Movement Analysis

The main focus of our analysis lies in the question, how two active wheels can generate a natural rolling movement and how the positioning affects the movement possibilities of the robot-ball combination. The movement of the robot guiding the ball determines the desired movements of the ball. This section contains a holistic analysis of the guided ball movement. We follow the explanations of Lynch and Park on nonholonomic constraints [13]. The aspects of friction, the characteristic of the rigid steering axle, and the resulting movements are covered. We extend the motion analysis from Kimura et al. [5].

The basis of this study is the natural rolling movement of a ball on the ground. This movement is described by Eq. (1) and means a simultaneous translation V_{trans} and rotation ω_{ball} of the ball, where the point of the ball touching the ground has an instantaneous speed of zero (Eq. 2) and thereby forms the instantaneous pole at this moment. The rotational axis of the ball runs through the instantaneous pole.

$$V_{rolling} = \begin{bmatrix} V_{trans} \\ \omega_{ball} \end{bmatrix} \quad with \quad V_{trans} = \omega_{ball} r_{ball} \tag{1}$$

$$V_{IU} = 0 \tag{2}$$

To achieve this configuration, the rolling friction between the ball and floor $F_{friction}$ (Fig. 1a) has to be higher than the summed up force in x-direction F_x introduced onto the instantaneous pole by the ball handling mechanism. During braking and acceleration, the position of the instantaneous pole on the Z-axis of the ball is shifted in proportion to the velocity gradient. The resulting

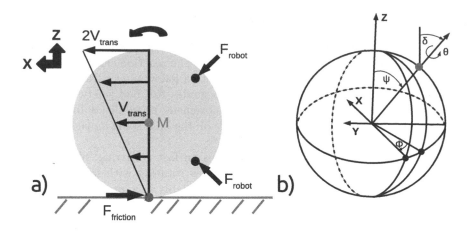

Fig. 1. (a) Forces on the ball for movement in the positive x-direction. The upper pushing force is transmitted by the active wheels, the lower one by the passive balls. The rolling condition holds when the instantaneous pole of the ball lies at the contact point between the ball and the ground (blue point). The momentary velocity at this point is zero and defines the position of the ball's rotational axis. (b) Four angles describe the positions of the wheels on the ball. The angles ϕ and ψ describe the point of contact between the ball and the wheel. The other angles δ and θ describe the pose of the wheel at this point. (Color figure online)

behavior: When braking too hard, the ball is pressed so firmly against the ground that it jams. In the opposite case, the acceleration force is so strong that the instantaneous pole of the ball is at the center of the ball, causing the ball to rotate on the spot.

4.1 How to Generate the Desired Ball Movement

The position of the contact point and the corresponding pose of the wheel is described by the four angles ϕ, ψ, θ, and δ in Fig. 1b.

An active wheel can transmit a velocity onto the surface of the ball. The virtual path that it would take on the surface of the ball is called centrode and forms a circle. It is determined by the intersection of the ball surface and a plane, that is formed by the wheel's velocity vector and the ball center (see $V_{wheel,left}$ in Fig. 2a). Two active wheels can actuate a ball supported without friction in various rotations. The virtual velocity results from Jourdain's principle of virtual power [8]. To determine the resulting movement of the ball, the virtual velocity vector of each wheel can be mentally shifted along the centrode of the wheel. At the point of contact of the two centrodes, the two vectors of the virtual velocities add up. The resulting vector forms the real centrode of the two active wheels. As the wheels have one DOF each, they cannot fully access all three rotational DOFs of the ball. That means the actuation cannot generate a rotation around the axis that is formed by the intersection of the centrodes and the center of the ball. When the ball is rolling on a floor with friction, the instantaneous pole at the contact point between the ball and floor forms a third centrode on the ball. Its alignment depends on the movement direction of the ball. This third centrode can add another DOF to the ball actuation, making its rotation fully controllable. However, for an arbitrary wheel positioning, the intersection of the three centrodes only coincides in one single movement direction. This makes the calculation of the resulting ball movement difficult and complex because the transmitted velocities can only be compared in pairs. The resulting velocity of one combination forms a new centrode that intersects with the third centrode. The final resulting velocity can be determined at this new intersection, but the location of this intersection changes for every variation in velocities. When all three centrodes intersect at the same point, the calculation is less complicated, but the third rotational DOF is lost again. In reality, the transverse forces created through transverse slip between the wheel and ball change this theoretic movement. Hence some ball movements might be actuatable which are not in theory and the other way around.

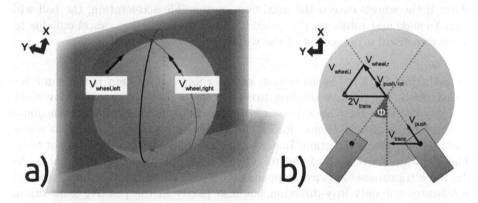

Fig. 2. (a) The centrode (red circles) is formed by the intersection of the ball surface and the plane (brown) defined by the wheel velocity vector and the ball center. At the point of contact of the two centrodes (blue point), the two vectors of the virtual velocities add up. The resulting vector forms the real centrode (black circle) of the two active wheels. (b) The sideways translation of the robot leads to a momentary velocity V_{push} of the ball orthogonal to the contact area. To produce a sideways movement, the wheel actuation $V_{wheel,left}$ and $V_{wheel,right}$ have to sum up with the rotational part of the momentary velocity $V_{push,rot}$ to $2\,V_{trans}$ in the y-direction. (Color figure online)

For the following thoughts on actuatable robot ball movements, we assume a symmetrical arrangement of the active wheels, so the intersection of the centrodes lies somewhere on the x-z-plane.

Translation in X. The simultaneous movement of the robot and ball in positive x-direction can be fully controlled. The translation part of the rolling motion V_{trans} from Eq. (1) is actuated through the push by the robot's translation. The rotation part ω_{ball} is generated by the two driving wheels of the ball handle mechanism. The linear combination of the wheel velocities has to be twice the translation velocity to follow the rolling condition, as shown in Fig. 1a. It is almost indifferent where the active wheels are located, as long as they are positioned symmetrically around the x-z-plane and do not share the same moving centrode. When the centrodes intersect at the z-axis, the following velocities for the wheels can be deduced from the kinematic relationship (with ϕ and ψ as defined in Fig. 1b).

$$V_{wheel,l} = V_{wheel,r} = \frac{V_{trans}}{cos\phi} \tag{3}$$

The opposite movement in negative x-direction can only be influenced by the rotation of the wheels. It follows the same rules of the ratio between translation and rotation, but the friction between the ball and the ground limits the maximum acceleration. The translational part of the rolling motion is generated solely by the friction $F_{friction}$ in Fig. 1a that hinders the ball from sliding over the ground, because the pushing force $F_{robot,x}$ of the robot can not become negative. If the wheels exceed the maximum permissible acceleration, the ball will start to slide and rotate on the ground. Forces in y-direction cancel out due to the symmetrical arrangement of the wheels.

Translation in Y. The movement of the robot-ball system is the same for translation in the positive and negative y-direction. In contrast to the movement in the x-direction, the wheels are not symmetrical to the plane that is orthogonal to the rotational axis. Hence, forces and velocities do not cancel out as easily when moving into y-direction. Imagine the case where both wheels do not turn. The sideways movement of the robot will push the ball with one wheel. As the force transmission always happens orthogonal to the contact area, the ball accelerates not only in y-direction but also partly in the positive x-direction. The x-fraction of the contact force will lead the ball to leave the ball handle mechanism. The actuation of the wheels can partially compensate this effect, by adding the actuation velocities as shown in Fig. 2(b). With the right amount, the actuation can add up to a rotation around the x-axis, which would be natural rolling in the y-direction.

$$V_{push} = sin\phi V_{trans}; \qquad V_{push,rot} = V_{push}\frac{2}{1 + cos\psi} \tag{4}$$

$$V_{wheel,l} = -\frac{V_{trans}}{sin\phi} \tag{5}$$

$$V_{wheel,r} = V_{trans}\left(\frac{1}{sin\phi} - \frac{2\,sin\phi}{1 + cos\psi}\right) \tag{6}$$

Rotation. A pure rotation around the z-axis of the robot resembles the translation in the y-direction because the desired momentary velocity of the ball center is purely directed in the y-direction (we assume the ball handling mechanism is symmetrical in front of the robot). The difference arises from the varying momentary velocities of the two wheels. One wheel has a slightly positive x-velocity, while the other one has a negative one. This means the wheel actuation has to give the ball the same velocity as the backward moving wheel to prevent it from losing contact with it. This is equivalent to the desired acceleration towards the rotational center, which ensures a circular orbit.

$$V_{push} = sin\phi \, d\omega; \qquad V_{push,rot} = V_{push} \frac{2}{1 + cos\psi} \tag{7}$$

$$V_{wheel,l} = -\frac{d\omega}{sin\phi} - sin\psi \, r\omega \left(\frac{sin\phi}{cos\phi} - \frac{cos\phi}{sin\phi} \right) \tag{8}$$

$$V_{wheel,r} = \frac{d\omega}{sin\phi} - \frac{sin\psi \, r\omega}{sin\phi cos\phi} + 2d\omega \frac{sin\phi}{1 + cos\psi} \tag{9}$$

Combinations. The omnidirectional drive of the robot allows any combination of the three above mentioned behaviors. With the intersection of the centrodes located at the z-axis, every x-y-combination is a simple linear combination of the wheel velocities as seen in Fig. 2, following the ration between translation and rotation.

Combining translational and rotational movement of the robot leads to a curve and hence cornering. This is important in order to avoid obstacles while using the properties of movement in positive x-direction as often as possible. In most cases, the right actuation can be approximated by the linear combination of the solution for translation and rotation. There are some cases, like the combination of rotation in the positive z and translation in the negative y-direction in which a natural ball movement cannot be actuated. In this case, the ball should lay still while the robot rotates around it.

5   Effects of the Wheel Positioning on Stability

The arrangement of the wheels is of particular importance under the condition of the fixed steering axle because it cannot be changed during the game. We will, therefore, analyze the alignment of the wheels from a strategic and mechanical point of view in this section. We will transfer results from the automotive sector on driving stability with wheels to the problem of ball guidance. This section elaborates the effect positioning in a purely qualitative fashion. The quantitative aspects follow in the next section.

The geometric arrangement of the wheels in the multi-body system influences the motion behavior of the ball. Positioning is, therefore, of decisive importance for the ball's stable motion behavior. The position of the contact point and the corresponding pose of the wheel is described by the four angles ϕ, ψ, θ, and δ in Fig. 1b. Thus four degrees of freedom are available for the positioning of the respective wheel. The four angles influence each other under the constraints of the rules and cannot be chosen independently. This situation will be discussed in detail in the next section. In this section, the conditions for a stable running behavior are mentioned and set in context to the four DOFs of the wheel position.

A rest position is a stable system state. The arrangement of the wheels on the ball can achieve a rest position of the ball movement in positive x-direction. Small deviations from the ideal x-direction will then be compensated by automatically returning the ball to the track in the positive x-direction. All other directions of movement need to be transferred into a stable condition in another way.

The models for driving stability from the automotive sector [10] take many parameters into account. We limit ourselves to the parameters that are most relevant for us and which directly influence the stability of the running behavior through the position and pose of the tire, namely caster, toe, and camber angle.

5.1 Caster

The caster is the distance from the momentary pole of a wheel to the intersection between the steering axis and the ground. The higher this distance, the more stable is the running behavior of the wheel, which also leads to an increased cornering angle. The ball handle mechanism does not have a real steering axis, but we can approximate it as the line between the middle of the active wheel contacts and the ball center (Fig. 3a). For the caster to produce a stable running behavior of the ball, the wheel contacts must lie behind the ball and above its equator. Then this line intersects with the ground in the direction of the ball movement and small disturbances do not threaten the stability of the running behavior. The highest caster can be achieved with $\phi = 0$ and $\psi = \frac{\pi}{2}$. However, the caster behavior can only be assumed to be valid, as long as the ball stays in the holonomic state with the ball handling mechanism.

5.2 Toe

The preset deviation of the running direction of a wheel from the moving direction in the x-direction is called toe. It influences the cornering behavior by creating an artificial slip angle. This increases grip by tensing the tread particles in the tire and creating a slip. The orientation of the tires inwards, i.e., towards each other, is called toe-in. This decreases the cornering radius because the outer wheel already points in curve direction and the wheel inside the curve brakes the ball and thus reduces the radius of the curvature. The opposite is the toe-out, in which the cornering radius is increased because the outer wheel tends to break while the inner wheel pushes in curve direction. The angle θ influences the toe.

5.3 Camber Angle

The camber angle describes the degree of lateral tilting of the wheel, whereby the running surface is pressed more firmly against the ball on either the inside or the outside of the tire. This increases the slip effect and hence the amount of transversal force, that can be transmitted from the wheel to the ball in the

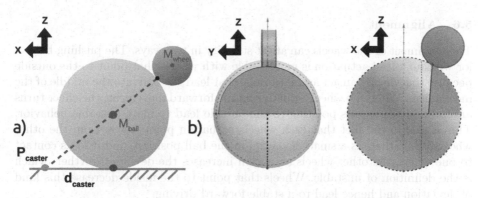

Fig. 3. (a) Transfer of the caster idea from a steered wheel to the actuated ball. The distance d_{caster} between the intersection of the steering axis with the ground and the instantaneous pole (blue point) defines the stability of the forward movement. (b) The red line shows the 1/3 limit to the wheels given by the rules. The blue line shows the progression of the contact point between wheel and ball by positioning the wheels far as possible to the limit as possible when the running direction of the wheels shows to the z-axis. The blue area shows the possible contact positions with regards to the rules and a positive caster. (Color figure online)

defined direction. It can be used to allow smaller cornering angles and higher backward grip by tilting the wheel in positive x-direction or faster forward acceleration by tilting the wheel in the negative x-direction. It is presented by the angle δ in our model.

5.4 Symmetrical Arrangement of the Wheels

The uniform arrangement of the wheels around the x-z-plane causes a stable behavior by uniform force and torque transmission via the contact surfaces onto the ball. This results in a defined movement without disturbing secondary movement. The angles ϕ and ψ from Fig. 1b are primarily affected by this condition.

5.5 Arrangement in y-direction

An important measure of stability is the possible deviation from the stable position that does not lead to unstable behavior. For the ball handle mechanism, the switching point between stable and unstable behavior is when an active wheel changes the hemisphere of the ball, e.g., the ball moves so much to one side, that it is considered as besides the ball handling mechanism. The wider the two wheels spread in the y-direction, the bigger is the distance the ball has to travel to leave the handler to the side and the more stable is the forward driving behavior. This also affects ϕ and ψ.

5.6   Alignment

The alignment of the wheels can affect stability in two ways. The pushing behavior without wheel actuation is more stable with wheels that point to the outside because the wheels can act as guard rails, that lead the ball into the middle of the mechanism. When the wheels spin during the forward movement, the effect turns around and the wheels pointing to the outside lead to more unstable behavior. This is due to the fact that each wheels actuation points away from the other wheel. When there is a small deviation in the ball position, and it loses contact to one wheel, the other wheels actuation increases the deviation further, which is the definition of unstable. Wheels that point to the inside decrease this kind of deviation and hence lead to a stable forward driving.

5.7   Intersecting the Z Axis

Aligning the wheels in a way that their centrodes intersect at the z-axis enables a more straightforward calculation of the resulting ball movement, as shown in Sect. 4. This does not mechanically affect stability, but it leads to an easier calculation of control, which makes the design of a stable control loop much more manageable. The angles ϕ and θ of the respective wheel must coincide so that the effect occurs.

6   Discussion

We will discuss the weighting of the different design decisions for stability against each other to find an optimal positioning of the wheel contact and find quantitative values.

6.1   Finding the Optimal Contact Point

First, we construct the possible range for the angles ϕ and ψ on the ball surface. The caster from Sect. 5.1 must be confident of having a positive effect on the stability. Therefore the wheels must be placed above the ball equator. The permissible range for the placement, as given by the MSL rules in Sect. 3.1, is inside the 1/3 of the ball surface facing the robot. Hence, every part of the wheel must be within the maximum 1/3 boundary line. We model the real expansions of the wheels as ideal cylinders with the real dimensions of the wheels. In our case, the wheels are 3 cm wide with a diameter of 8 cm. Together with the condition of intersecting the wheel centrodes at the z-axis, we get that the possible course of the positions results in the blue half circle in Fig. 3(b). The slightly tilted track of the possible positions results from the changing angle θ and the resulting different expanse of the wheel in the x-direction.

   Although we could choose any position in the blue area, only positions on the blue line are desirable, considering the requirements and conditions. The intuition would tell us, to grab a ball around the center instead of balancing it one finger for higher control and the stability conditions and actuation requirements support this intuition. The wider the distance in the y-direction is, the more stable is the guided forward movement. The closer the wheels are to the y-z-plane, the higher is the force that they can transmit into negative x-direction, which affects the duel strength and the possible backward acceleration. We therefore only consider positions on the blue line, which makes ϕ, ψ, and θ dependent.

The volume of the wheels gives the maximum z-position, so they do not touch each other. The highest located position follows as $\phi = 20.57°$ and $\psi = 20.80°$. The minimal z-position is given by the ball equator, which lies at $\psi = 90°$ with $\phi = 63,96°$. This gives us a dependent range for ϕ, ψ, and θ, which we analyzed regarding their stable movement possibilities.

6.2 Possible Stable Movements

The possible movements with the fixed steering axles of the wheels are limited. When the running directions of the wheels point in another direction than the movement of the ball, this creates slippage on the contact surface between the wheel and the ball. If the slippage is in the low ideal range (deviation angle up to 50°), the grip increases. Otherwise (deviation angle higher than 50°), the slippage is too high and the wheel starts sliding. This sliding effect has non-linear behavior, which causes instability. Therefore, directions in which sliding occurs should be avoided.

We analyzed four different wheel positions in the before defined range on the amount of critical area in x-y-direction. The result is shown in Fig. 4.

For $\phi = 30°$ this would completely exclude sideways travel and hence rotation. The strategic analysis of the dribbling movements from Sect. 3.1 gave us a prioritization of short, agile movements. Therefore, the ball handling mechanism should be able to cope with fast sideways direction changes.

The requirement for the natural rolling behavior is a sufficiently high friction force at the momentary pole between ball and ground. This friction force depends on the weight of the ball and the contact force introduced by the wheel. The contact force is always orthogonal to the ball surface, which defines the lowest position of the wheels. $\phi = 60°$ has only a few critical directions and therefore many movement possibilities, but the proportion of contact force in the z-direction is too small to support the friction between ball and ground. We chose a minimal proportion of 50% force in the z-direction. This decision might differ for heavier or lighter balls and a floor with higher or lower friction.

We determined that the position with the angle $\phi = 54°$ is the optimal position for stable dribbling. At this position, the contact force has $\sim$50% in the z-direction (Table 1). The critical area is smaller than the non-critical area, i.e., more than 50% of the directions can be approached. In the X direction, a deviation of 15.55° from the longitudinal drive is possible without restriction due to friction effects on the tire. The corresponding gap in the Y direction is larger (67.1°) and allows the ball to roll sideways. The critical direction at 36° between the orientation of the robot and that of the ball should not be approached.

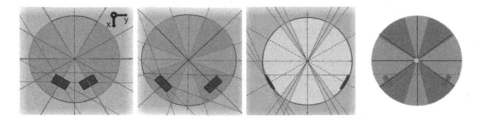

Fig. 4. Critical areas (orange) with $\phi = 30°, \phi = 45°, \phi = 60°$ and $\phi = 54°$ from left to right. (Color figure online)

Table 1. Comparison of contact force in the negative z-direction and the amount of critical area in x-y-direction, depending on the position for different angles of ϕ/θ

$\phi = \theta$	30°	45°	54°	60°
z-proportion [%]	76.5	65.5	50.78	15.43
critical area [°]	59.38	53	40.9	12.78
y-distance [cm]	9.18	13.02	20.05	70.73

The inclination of the wheels by the toe-in causes a slip angle when the robot moves straight ahead. In combination with a negative camber angle δ the grip increases, allowing higher forward dribbling speeds. The heavy wear as a disadvantage of this arrangement can be ignored because the support possibilities at the tournament are given to change a wheel between games and the wheels are low cost. A combination with a positive camber angle would instead lead to a smaller cornering radius. We chose a camber angle of zero to make a compromise between both options.

The position of the wheels that we found as optimal for our requirements is hence is given by $\boldsymbol{P}_{wheel} = (\phi\ \psi\ \theta\ \delta)^T = (54°\ 60.95°\ 54°\ 0°)^T$.

7 Conclusion

We presented an all-embracing analysis of the mechanical ball handling problem with two active wheels. We indicated the general open-loop control inputs for movement with the ball. The difficulties in calculating the complete systems lie in the displacement of the wheel contact points when the ball moves out of the handler. The centrodes would no longer intersect at one point, which leads to highly nonlinear behavior of the system. The analysis would, however, benefit from a complete simulation. We hope that this analysis is of use to other teams designing or redesigning a ball handle mechanism. We offer help to anyone interested in deriving the full kinematic equations. Our findings can be used for a ball handling mechanism that actively changes the contact point with the ball, by reweighting the requirements for different game situations, which would lead to different optimal contact positions.

References

1. de Best, J., van de Molengraft, R.: An active ball handling mechanism for RoboCup. In: 10th International Conference on Control, Automation, Robotics and Vision (2008)
2. Junkai, R., Chenggang, X., Junhao, X., Kaihong, H., Huimin, L.: A control system for active ball handling in the RoboCup middle size league. In: 2016 Chinese Control and Decision Conference (CCDC), Yinchuan, pp. 4396–4402 (2016)
3. Chikushi, S., Weerakoon, T., Ishii, K., Sonoda, T.: Motion analysis and control of the ball operation for dribbling action in RoboCup soccer robot. In: 2016 Joint 8th International Conference on Soft Computing and Intelligent Systems and 2016 17th International Symposium on Advanced Intelligent Systems, pp. 532–536 (2016)
4. Bigelow, F.F., Kalhor, A.: Robust adaptive controller based on evolving linear model applied to a Ball-Handling mechanism. Control Eng. Pract. **69**, 85–98 (2017). https://doi.org/10.1016/j.conengprac.2017.09.008
5. Kimura, K., Ishii, K., Takemura, Y., Yamamoto, M.: Mathematical modeling and motion analysis of the wheel based ball retaining mechanism. In: 2016 Joint 8th International Conference on Soft Computing and Intelligent Systems (SCIS) and 17th International Symposium on Advanced Intelligent Systems (ISIS), Sapporo, pp. 518–523 (2016)
6. Mas' udi, M.I., et al.: Implementation of PID control in active ball handling system of middle size robot soccer. In: 2018 10th International Conference on Information Technology and Electrical Engineering (ICITEE), pp. 242–247. IEEE (2018)
7. Cunha, B.; Neves, A. J.R.; Dias, P.; Azevedo, J. L.; Lau, N.; Dias, R. et al.: CAMBADA'2015. Team Description Paper (2015)
8. Popp, K., Schiehlen, W.: Ground vehicle dynamics (2010)
9. Chikushi, S., Weerakoon, T., Sonoda, T., Ishii, K.: Kinematics of two-roller-driven ball for RoboCup soccer robot. JRNAL 4(3), 248 (2017). https://doi.org/10.2991/jrnal.2017.4.3.15
10. Genta, G., Morello, L.: The Automotive Chassis. Springer, Dordrecht (2009). pp. 59, 91, 137, 217
11. FIFA: Laws of the game 2015/2016. Fédération Internationale de Football Association (2015). p. 15
12. RoboCup (2018). RoboCup Official site. www.robocup.org
13. Lynch, K.M., Park, F.C.: Modern Robotics. Cambridge University Press, Cambridge (2017)
14. Saha, S.K., Shah, S.V., Nandihal, P.V.: Evolution of the DeNOC-based dynamic modelling for multibody systems. Mech. Sci. 4, 1–20. https://doi.org/10.5194/ms-4-1-2013

Cooperative Multi-agent Deep Reinforcement Learning in a 2 Versus 2 Free-Kick Task

Jim Martin Catacora Ocana$^{(\boxtimes)}$, Francesco Riccio, Roberto Capobianco, and Daniele Nardi

Department of Computer, Control and Management Engineering,
Sapienza University of Rome, Via Ariosto 25, 00185 Rome, Italy
{catacora,riccio,capobianco,nardi}@diag.uniroma1.it

Abstract. In multi-robot reinforcement learning the goal is to enable a team of robots to learn a coordinated behavior from direct interaction with the environment. Here, we provide a comparison of the two main approaches to tackle this challenge, namely independent learners (IL) and joint-action learners (JAL). IL is suitable for highly scalable domains, but it faces non-stationarity issues. Whereas, JAL overcomes non-stationarity and can generate highly coordinated behaviors, but it presents scalability issues due to the increased size of the search space. We implement and evaluate these methods in a new multi-robot cooperative and adversarial soccer scenario, called 2 versus 2 free-kick task, where scalability issues affecting JAL are less relevant given the small number of learners. In this work, we implement and deploy these methodologies on a team of simulated NAO humanoid robots. We describe the implementation details of our scenario and show that both approaches are able to achieve satisfying solutions. Notably, we observe joint-action learners to have a better performance than independent learners in terms of success rate and quality of the learned policies. Finally, we discuss the results and provide conclusions based on our findings.

1 Introduction

Multi-agent reinforcement learning is concerned with the application of reinforcement learning (RL) techniques to situations having multiple agents learning at the same time in the same environment. Multi-agent reinforcement learning is important because it could provide solutions for challenging domains involving robot teams or robot swarms, see [2,6,9,11].

Two main MARL approaches have been proposed for handling multi-agent domains. In independent learners (IL), every agent performs standard RL, but in the presence of other agents. IL has the drawback that each individual sees the environment as non-stationary; and hence, guarantees of single-agent RL do not longer hold. Meanwhile, in joint-action learners (JAL), the state and action spaces of all agents are merged together, and a single policy is learned

© Springer Nature Switzerland AG 2019
S. Chalup et al. (Eds.): RoboCup 2019, LNAI 11531, pp. 44–57, 2019.
https://doi.org/10.1007/978-3-030-35699-6_4

that maps joint-observations to joint-actions. Any single-agent RL algorithm can readily be used to learn such joint-policy. JAL overcomes the non-stationarity problem, but it presents scalability issues as the joint state and action spaces can grow exponentially larger with the number of agents. Additionally, from a practical perspective, communication range/bandwidth and memory capacity could also limit JAL's scalability.

In this work, we implement IL and JAL and compare them on a robotic task. We consider a simplified version of soccer, referred to as 2 versus 2 offensive free-kick task. In soccer domains, the number of agents is normally small (up to eleven agents per team in a full soccer scenario); hence, it is conceivable for JAL to converge within a reasonable amount of time, contrary to domains with hundreds or more agents where JAL is impractical. JAL may still be slower than IL in such soccer scenarios, but it is also more likely to find better policies. Therefore, these special domains provide a motivating opportunity for investigating the tradeoff between optimality and convergence rate across MARL approaches.

A previous work, Hausknecht [3], compares parameter/memory sharing IL and JAL within a partially observable Robocup 2D domain, called 2-vs-1 half-field offense. This study reports that neither approach succeeds in the multi-agent sense. With IL, agents learn to unreliably score single-handedly; meanwhile, JAL finds no competent policies. By contrast, we manage to generate successful solutions grounded on cooperation for both approaches and within a similar domain. Furthermore, our results reveal that on average IL converges slightly faster than JAL; on the other hand, JAL discovers more synchronized strategies than IL, which may allow the attacking team to score goals within a shorter period of time. On top of that, JAL shows a higher success rate than IL, 60% versus 20% respectively, where the success rate indicates the percentage of runs in which a perfect scoring solution was found by the learning algorithm.

Summarizing, our contributions are: (1) we provide satisfactory results from IL and JAL in a new domain; namely, in the 2-vs-2 offensive free-kick task, (2) we compare the performances of IL and JAL, confirming that JAL should not be overlooked when facing analogous domains, and (3) we carry out experiments on a physically realistic 3D simulator, whereas, as far as we know, all previous studies concerning MARL in soccer domains involved 2D environments.

1.1   Markov Decisions Processes (MDPs)

MDPs [4] are a formalism for modeling sequential decision problems that concisely encode the interactions between agents and their environments. An MDP is a tuple $\langle S, A, T, R, \gamma \rangle$, comprising:

- The set S of all states in the world,
- The set A containing every action a learning agent can execute,
- A probability distribution over transitions $T : S \times A \times S \rightarrow [0,1]$ from a current state to a next state given the action performed by the agent in the starting state,
- A reward function $R : S \times A \rightarrow \mathbb{R}$ that quantifies the immediate goodness of the action performed in the current state,

– And a discount factor γ that weights down the value of future rewards.

An MDP must satisfy the Markov property [16], such that the next state and expected next reward depend, in general, probabilistically only on the state and action representations at the current time step, which means that the following equality holds true for all r and s':

$$\Pr\{R_{t+1}=r, S_{t+1}=s'|S_t, A_t\} = \Pr\{R_{t+1}=r, S_{t+1}=s'|S_0, A_0, R_0, ..., S_t, A_t\} \quad (1)$$

Given an MDP, the goal is to find a policy π, i.e. a generally stochastic mapping from states to actions that fully encodes the decision-making behavior of an agent.

1.2 Markov Games

Markov Games [14], also called Stochastic Games, are the straightforward extension of MDPs to situations where there are multiple agents capable of making decisions in the same environment. In a Markov Game, all agents perceive the complete state of the world, i.e. they have full observability. In addition, in the general case, each agent has a distinct reward function, but for strictly cooperative tasks the entire team can be granted a single reward. The general formulation of a Markov Game is a tuple $\langle S, \mathcal{A}, T, R, \gamma \rangle$, comprising:

– The set S of all states in the world,
– The collection $\mathcal{A}$ of action sets pertaining to each agent $A^1, ..., A^k$,
– A probability distribution over transitions $T : S \times \mathcal{A} \times S \rightarrow [0,1]$ from a current state to a next state given the joint-action performed simultaneously by all agents in the starting state,
– A reward function, possibly different for each agent i, $R^i : S \times A^1 \times ... \times A^k \rightarrow \mathbb{R}$ that quantifies the immediate goodness of the joint-action performed by the agents in the current state,
– And a discount factor γ that weights down the value of future rewards.

1.3 Reinforcement Learning (RL)

Reinforcement Learning is concerned with learning in MDPs without having an a priori model of the domain (transition and reward functions). The main characteristics of RL is that learning is accomplished through raw experience by executing actions and receiving rewards; and that learning is synonymous with the maximization of the sum of rewards collected over time [16]. The core objective of RL is to find the optimal policy π^* that yields the highest sum of rewards, which is usually defined in terms of the cumulative discounted reward. Formally, if an agent with policy π is at state S_t after t timesteps, and thereafter it receives a sequence of future rewards of $\{R_{t+1}, R_{t+2}, ...\}$, then the expected cumulative discounted reward G_t is expressed as:

$$E_\pi[G_t|S_t = s] = E_\pi\left[\sum_{k=0} \gamma^k R_{t+k+1}|S_t = s\right] \quad (2)$$

The term $E_\pi[G_t|S_t = s]$ is also called the value of s under π. A function $v_\pi(s)$ that encodes this information for every state in S is known as a value function. This definition can be extended to every state-action pair in $S \times A$, yielding an action-value function, also called a q-function, which is formalized as:

$$q_\pi(s,a) = E_\pi\left[\sum_{k=0}\gamma^k R_{t+k+1}|S_t = s, A_t = a\right] \qquad (3)$$

1.4 Deep Reinforcement Learning

Deep RL relies on deep neural networks for representing the value functions or policies that are learned. These networks are trained through some efficient variant of stochastic gradient descent (SGD), which minimizes a loss function that measures the difference between the current predictions of the network and the target values it must approximate to. For example, for a network with parameters θ, prediction vector $\mathbf{y}_\theta$ and target vector $\mathbf{d}$, the L2-loss function is defined as:

$$\mathcal{L}(\mathbf{d}, \mathbf{y}_\theta) = (\mathbf{d} - \mathbf{y}_\theta)^T \cdot (\mathbf{d} - \mathbf{y}_\theta) \qquad (4)$$

The update rule of SGD given a learning rate α and a uniformly random perturbation $\mathbf{e}_t$ is then computed as:

$$\theta_{t+1} = \theta_t - \alpha\nabla_\theta\mathcal{L}(\mathbf{d}, \mathbf{y}_\theta)|_{\theta_t} + \mathbf{e}_t \qquad (5)$$

Deep Deterministic Policy Gradient (DDPG) was developed by Lillicrap et al. [8]. It employs two separate deep neural networks, denoted as critic and actor. The critic learns a parametrized q-function (Q_θ). Meanwhile, the actor learns and executes a parametrized policy (π_θ). During training, at each time step t the learning agent collects $[S_t, A_t, R_{t+1}, S_{t+1}]$. Naïve updates for the critic and actor can be computed as follows. In the case of the critic, we feed the network with the most recent state-action pair (S_t, A_t) to obtain a prediction $Q_\theta(S_t, A_t)$, then we set the corresponding target (see Eq. (6)), by computing an approximation through temporal differences [15] and relying on the current actor network in order to estimate the next action $A_{t+1} = \pi_\theta(S_{t+1})$.

$$R_{t+1} + \gamma Q_\theta(S_{t+1}, \pi_\theta(S_{t+1})) \qquad (6)$$

When training the actor, we take advantage of the gradients of the critic with respect to its action inputs [1] to set the following direction of improvement, which is then used to update the actor's parameters as in Eq. (5):

$$\nabla_a Q_\theta(S_t, a = \pi_\theta(S_t))\nabla_\theta\pi_\theta(S_t) \qquad (7)$$

Stable DDPG. Naïve updates will lead to instabilities during training. Two extra mechanisms proposed by Mnih et al. [10] need to be enforced to overcome this problem.

First of all, SGD requires that samples are independent and identically distributed. To break the ordering of the collected samples, an experience replay buffer is introduced that gathers samples $[S_t, A_t, R_{t+1}, S_{t+1}]$ from several episodes. Afterwards, off-policy updates are performed by drawing a batch of random experiences from this buffer.

Second, in Eq. (6) targets depend on the current critic and actor networks. This could lead to learning oscillations and divergence, since the targets themselves will also change after each update. To deal with this issue, two target networks Q'_θ and π'_θ are introduced. Their architectures are identical to the critic and actor networks but their parameters are updated less frequently. Given these target networks, the critic's targets are computed as:

$$R_{t+1} + \gamma Q'_\theta(S_{t+1}, \pi'_\theta(S_{t+1})) \tag{8}$$

1.5   Independent Learners Approach

In independent learners, each agent applies RL on its own. There is no direct communication among agents. Furthermore, agents are not explicitly aware of the actions executed by other learners. Because of this, from the perspective of each individual the world appears non-stationary, i.e. the reward signal each agent receives depends on hidden, random and time-varying variables, which are the unknown policies of other agents. As a result, directly applying single-agent RL techniques is no longer guaranteed to produce good results.

One approach to diminish the negative effects of non-stationarity is homogeneous learners, applicable only when all agents have identical state and action spaces. In this scenario, it is possible to reduce the problem to one in which we learn a single shared q-function or policy from the combined experiences of all agents. Previous works, such as [5] and [7], report satisfactory results from such approach.

1.6   Joint-Action Learners Approach

The key idea of JAL is to reformulate the learning problem such that instead of having as many independent MDPs as the number of agents, only a single Markov Game is defined over the joint-action space corresponding to the group of agents. Moreover, when a single reward is handed to the team of agents in cooperative tasks, the Markov Game formulation can effectively be treated as a single-agent problem; completely avoiding non-stationarity.

On the downside, JAL presents scalability issues, as the joint-state and joint-action spaces as well as the size of any parametrized structure must increase. Notoriously, this growth is only linear for approximate methods that explicitly learn a policy, such as DDPG. However, even a linear growth can be quite restrictive compared to the constant complexity of IL for domains involving hundreds of agents or more.

2   Evaluation

2.1   Implementation

Task Specification. Experiments were carried out on the 2 vs. 2 offensive free-kick task. It involves an offensive team (2 attackers) and a defending team (defender and goalkeeper). The game takes place in the half-field belonging to the latter team. An episode starts with the offensive team being granted a free kick. From the beginning of a match and until an attacker makes contact with the ball, the players of the defending team are forbidden to remain less than 0.75 m away from the ball. The attackers' goal is to score a goal within a time limit and without losing control of the ball.

In this work, we made use of a RoboCup Standard Platform League [12] simulator, called the B-Human framework [13]. This framework allows teams of NAO humanoid robots to compete against each other in a physically grounded and fairly realistic virtual environment. Therefore, the offensive free-kick task is played by four NAO robots with identical sensing and actuation capabilities.

World Settings. Figure 1 shows a random initialization of the task. At the beginning of each episode, the ball is placed at position [1.0, 2.0] m. The defender is positioned 0.75 m away from the ball and in between the ball and the center of the goal line; hence, it blocks a direct kick to goal. The goalkeeper is placed at the center of the goal line.

Moreover, one attacker is initially placed 0.3 m from the ball and according to the angular variable β with range $[0, \pi/4]$ rad. The other attacker is fixed to -2.5 m on the y-axis, whereas its position on the x-axis varies uniformly at random within [1.0, 2.0] m at each initialization.

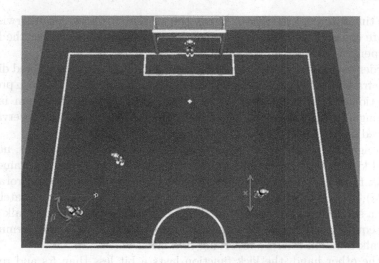

Fig. 1. Random initial world state.

The defensive players follow handcrafted policies. The defender's policy considers two conditions: (1) before the ball is touched, it stands in-place, and (2) after the ball is touched, it approaches it as fast as it can. The goalkeeper is only allowed to move from post to post along the goal line. It moves towards the intersection of the goal line and the ball's velocity vector or until it reaches a post, as long as the ball moves forward.

An episode terminates if:

- The offensive team has scored a goal;
- a sufficient time limit of 20 s has expired;
- one player of the defending team has made contact with the ball;
- the ball has left the field.

MDP Formulation for IL. Since both attackers are identical, an homogeneous learners strategy is enforced for IL; hence, effectively only one MDP is formulated. From the point of view of each agent, its associated MDP comprises an 18-dimensional state vector, consisting of the following high-level information:

- The agent's absolute pose, $[x^A, y^A, \theta^A] \in \mathbb{R}^3$, which encodes the current Cartesian position $\mathbf{p}^A = [x^A, y^A]$ and 2D orientation of the agent;
- the absolute pose of its teammate, $[x^T, y^T, \theta^T] \in \mathbb{R}^3$, which likewise encodes position $\mathbf{p}^T = [x^T, y^T]$;
- the ball's absolute position, $\mathbf{p}^B = [x^B, y^B] \in \mathbb{R}^2$;
- the ball's absolute velocity, $[v_x^B, v_x^B] \in \mathbb{R}^2$;
- the defender's absolute position, $[x^D, y^D] \in \mathbb{R}^2$;
- the goalkeeper's spot over the goal line, $y^G \in \mathbb{R}$, which indicates a location on the y-axis of the world's frame;
- a 5-bit timestamp, $[t^4, t^3, t^2, t^1, t^0] \in \{0,1\}^5$, representing the current time step of the episode. The timer increases by one step every 1 s of game play.

This timestamp is essential to satisfy the Markov Property, as otherwise, the next state could either be a new configuration of players and ball or the failure state depending on the time remaining.

In order to perform fast simulations, location information is gathered directly from the framework's oracle. Nevertheless, the B-human framework also provides the functionality to preprocess the same high-level information from images, considering a simulated camera located over the field, such that full observability is achieved as well.

Each agent is permitted to execute only one of two macro actions, namely: walk and kick, which come as pre-built functions with the B-Human framework. The walk function requires three arguments (relative Cartesian and rotational velocities), it loops indefinitely step after step, taking a robot approximately 0.5 s to make a single step. Wrapped around this function, we declare the walk action to be a sequence of a couple of steps and we implement it by forcing termination of the walk function after 1 s according to a clock.

On the other hand, the kick function lasts a bit less than 5 s and requires no extra arguments (an agent always kicks with the same leg). We define the kick action given the kick function plus some idle time such that it lasts exactly 5 s. The action space of the MDP is represented by a 5-dimensional real-valued vector, composed of:

- Two selectors in the range $[0.0, 1.0]$. The agent executes the action whose associated selector is the highest.
- Three walking arguments taking values in $[-1.0, 1.0]$.

It is worth mentioning that each agent receives observations and makes decisions only during the first time step of an episode and time steps immediately after a robot terminates an action (time instances when the walk and kick functions release control back to the main execution), all other intermediate time steps are ignored by the agent. Thus, when the kick action is called, the agent then waits 5 s (time steps) before making its next decision.

As the free-kick task is fairly complex, being unlikely that the attacking team scores as a result of random actions, and since we choose to use algorithms that are not optimized for handling sparse rewards, in order for learning to happen it was necessary to design a shaped reward function that reinforces the agents in a continuous manner for getting closer to scoring a goal.

Therefore, at each time step t, both agents are independently given shaped rewards based on the same function, which is shown below. Said function is similar to the one used in [3], except that we add the term D_B^T. In the following equations, $\mathbf{p}$ corresponds to a 2D position with components x and y; furthermore, scripts A, T, B, L, R and P refer to the agent, its teammate, the ball, the left goal post, the right goal post and either post, respectively.

$$R = D_A^B + max(D_B^T, D_B^G) + G \tag{9}$$

Where:

$$D_A^B = d(\mathbf{p}_t^B, \mathbf{p}_{t-1}^A) - d(\mathbf{p}_t^B, \mathbf{p}_t^A) \tag{10}$$

$$D_B^T = \begin{cases} \text{if the agent pushed the ball, } d(\mathbf{p}_{t-1}^B, \mathbf{p}_t^T) - d(\mathbf{p}_t^B, \mathbf{p}_t^T) \\ \text{else,} \qquad\qquad\qquad\qquad\qquad 0 \end{cases} \tag{11}$$

$$D_B^G = \begin{cases} \text{if the agent pushed the ball, } d_{goal}(\mathbf{p}_{t-1}^B) - d_{goal}(\mathbf{p}_t^B) \\ \text{else,} \qquad\qquad\qquad\qquad\qquad 0 \end{cases} \tag{12}$$

$$G = \begin{cases} \text{if goal, } +20 \\ \text{else,} \quad 0 \end{cases} \tag{13}$$

$$d(\mathbf{p}, \mathbf{q}) = \sqrt{(x_p - x_q)^2 + (y_p - y_q)^2} \tag{14}$$

$$d_{goal}(\mathbf{p}^B) = \begin{cases} \text{if } y^B \geq y^L, \, d(\mathbf{p}^B, \mathbf{p}^L) \\ \text{if } y^B \leq y^R, \, d(\mathbf{p}^B, \mathbf{p}^R) \\ \text{else,} \qquad |x^B - x^P| \end{cases} \tag{15}$$

This reward function integrates the following terms:

- D_A^B: Rewards an agent for approaching the ball.

- D_B^T: Promotes cooperation, since it incentivizes an agent for passing the ball to a teammate.
- D_B^G: Rewards an agent for hitting the ball to goal.
- G: Assigns a large positive reward to all agents of the attacking team when a goal is scored, and assigns zero otherwise.

Markov Game Formulation for JAL. Since full observability is assumed in both formulations, the state space of the Markov Game associated with the free-kick task is also 18-dimensional, embedding the same components as the previous MDP. Because a parametrized policy will be learned, the joint-action space (10D) is constructed simply by concatenating each agent's 5-dimensional action vector, as presented in the precedent sub-section. Likewise, the team makes decisions only during the first time step and time steps following the culmination of an action executed by anyone of the attackers.

For instance, if during time step 0 the team decides one attacker to walk and the other to kick, then, the next team decision will be made during time step 1, but it will only have a meaningful effect over the next action performed by the first attacker as the second one still has to complete the kick action. Assuming that the next action of the first attacker is to kick, then the next team decision will occur during time step 5 (skipping time steps from 2 to 4), when the next action to be executed by the second attacker will have to be selected.

A shaped reward is also considered for JAL, for the same reasons as previously stated. In this case, the offensive team as a whole is rewarded given the following function that employs the notation found in the previous sub-section, but introduces subscript A_i denoting the i-th agent in the attacking team.

$$R = \sum_i D_{A_i}^B + max(\{D_B^{A_i}, \forall i\}, D_B^G) + G \tag{16}$$

Where:

$$D_{A_i}^B = d(\mathbf{p}_t^B, \mathbf{p}_{t-1}^{A_i}) - d(\mathbf{p}_t^B, \mathbf{p}_t^{A_i}) \tag{17}$$

$$D_B^{A_i} = d(\mathbf{p}_{t-1}^B, \mathbf{p}_t^{A_i}) - d(\mathbf{p}_t^B, \mathbf{p}_t^{A_i}) \tag{18}$$

$$D_B^G = d_{goal}(\mathbf{p}_{t-1}^B) - d_{goal}(\mathbf{p}_t^B) \tag{19}$$

The G term and functions $d(\mathbf{p}, \mathbf{q})$, $d_{goal}(\mathbf{p}^B)$ are computed according to Eqs. (13), (14) and (15), respectively. The terms of this function convey the following information:

- $\sum_i D_{A_i}^B$: Rewards the team for every attacker that approaches the ball.
- $\{D_B^{A_i}, \forall i\}$: Rewards the team whenever the ball is passed to any member.
- D_B^G: Rewards the team if any agent shoots to goal.
- G: Assigns a large positive reward to the attacking team when a goal is scored, and assigns zero otherwise.

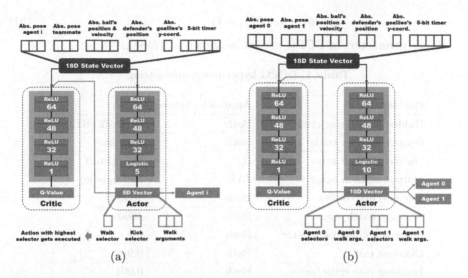

(a)   (b)

Fig. 2. Neural architectures. On the left, the architecture for independent learners; while on the right, the architecture for joint-action learners.

Deep RL Settings. The DDPG algorithm is used in IL as well as in JAL. Accordingly, four separate deep neural networks are maintained during training: critic, actor, target critic and target actor.

All four networks are represented by dense networks with 3 hidden layers (Fig. 2). This choice was taken because the offensive free-kick task has a low dimensional state and it does not require a memory of past states to be solved; thus, convolutional or recurrent networks are not necessary. Critics receive as input the concatenation of state and action vectors of the corresponding MDP (18D + 5D) or Markov Game (18D + 10D) and predict a single Q-value. Actors are fed only state vectors (18D) and produce an output of size equal to the cardinality of the action (5D) or joint-action (10D) vector corresponding to IL or JAL.

An ϵ-greedy strategy is followed during training. By setting $\epsilon = 0.5$ and fixing this value for the entire run, the action that will be executed by the agent or the team will agree exactly with the output of the corresponding actor half the time; and the other half, macro actions will be selected uniformly at random, while a small uniform noise of ± 0.05 will be added to the walking velocities initially determined by said actor.

After each iteration (single match/episode), all networks are updated once given a mini-batch of experiences, randomly selected from the replay buffer. Training of the critic and actor relies on the L2-loss and Adam optimizer. In turn, target networks are updated smoothly based on the recently-updated parameters of their references (represented as vectors θ^Q and θ^π) and on the scalar hyperparameter τ, as follows:

$$\theta'^Q_{t+1} = \tau\theta^Q_{t+1} + (1-\tau)\theta'^Q_t \qquad (20)$$

$$\boldsymbol{\theta}'^{\pi}_{t+1} = \tau\boldsymbol{\theta}^{\pi}_{t+1} + (1-\tau)\boldsymbol{\theta}'^{\pi}_t \tag{21}$$

Hyper-parameters of DDPG are set as shown in Table 1:

Table 1. DDPG hyper-parameter setting

Parameter	Approach	Symbol	Value
Hidden units/layer critic/actor	Both	-	64,48,32 (RELU)
Output units in critic	Both	–	1 (linear)
Output units in actor	IL	–	5 (logistic)
Output units in actor	JAL	–	10 (logistic)
Size of replay buffer	Both	–	100000
Training batch size	Both	–	4000
ϵ-greedy control parameter	Both	ϵ	0.5
Discount rate	Both	γ	0.9
Learning rate critic/actor	Both	α	0.001
Update rate target networks	Both	τ	0.01

2.2 Results

IL and JAL were executed 10 runs each, over the offensive free-kick task. Each run continued for 400K iterations, i.e. 20-s matches. Policies were validated on 50 randomly initialized episodes after every 200 iterations, where the ϵ hyper-parameter is set to zero.

Independent Learners. IL achieved successful team strategies in two out of ten runs. In the remaining runs, IL scored zero goals at every validation step. Figure 3(a) shows that initially IL gets stuck in a bad local minimum, but it eventually manages to converge to a satisfactory policy after 200K iterations on average. In this local minimum, the attacker further away from the ball, only approaches the ball but never kicks it; likely because it is seldom close enough to the ball to perform a kick with positive effects.

Figure 3(b) reveals the typical behavior of a successful strategy attained by IL. In particular, it shows the trajectories followed by attackers, defenders and ball at different time steps, where the chevrons' apices point to the direction of motion, triangles denote a kick action and circles indicate ball at rest. We can notice that the attacker that receives the ball displays a reactive behavior, i.e. it does not know where to go until its teammate makes a pass; as a result, it spends extra time readjusting and searching for the ball.

Joint-Action Learners. JAL accomplished a perfect goal percentage in validation in six out of ten runs. Another two ended with percentages of 0.52 and 0.78, and the last two stayed at zero the entire time. Figure 4(a) reveals that in

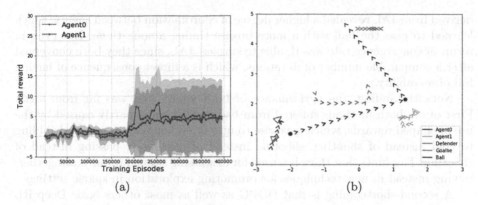

Fig. 3. Independent Learners. On the left, the average total reward per episode; while on the right, an execution of the learned policy.

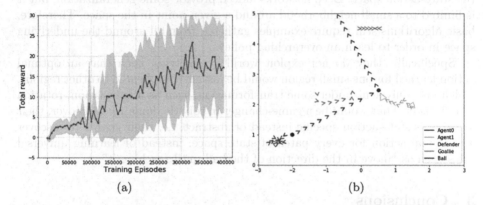

Fig. 4. Joint-Action Learners. On the left, the average total reward per episode; while on the right, an execution of the learned policy.

some cases JAL suffers from the same local minimum encountered by IL. However, in other cases, JAL can discover effective policies quickly, but it does not truly converge until several steps later (after 300K iterations on average).

Figure 4(b) shows the response of a successful policy usually derived by JAL. It can be observed that when executing a pass, there is a beforehand understanding between the agents about where the ball will be directed, such that the receiver moves straight to intersect the ball without wasting much time. Needless to say, this strategy shows more coordination than the one learned by IL.

2.3   Discussion

By comparing the results obtained from IL and JAL, it is evident that the latter approach outperforms the former. JAL learned well-performing strategies much more consistently (60% of runs) than IL (20% of runs). In addition, final policies derived from JAL revealed a higher degree of coordination between agents, which learned to pass the ball with a more precise timing among them. Not even in terms of convergence rate was IL able to surpass JAL, since they both converged after a comparable number of iterations, which is a direct consequence of having full observability.

Notwithstanding, the performance of both approaches was far from ideal. First of all, both methods suffered from bad local minima partly caused by the use of shaped rewards, which gave rise to unwanted behaviors such as: dribbling to goal instead of shooting, shooting instead of passing or passing instead of shooting. This hints that there is a need for dismissing shaped rewards altogether, relying instead in new techniques for promoting exploration in sparse settings.

A second shortcoming is that DDPG as well as most others basic Deep RL algorithms are extremely sample-inefficient. Certainly, there are several sources of inefficiency; yet, the most fundamental is the lack of generalization throughout the state-action space. Deep networks indeed provide some generalization, but it is limited to a small neighborhood around a given point in the space. Therefore, basic algorithms still require examples gathered from all around the underlying space in order to learn an overarching policy.

Specifically, they do not exploit world symmetries, such that an optimal action learned for one small region would be instantly replicated to other regions, which are equivalent under some transformation, such as a translation, rotation or reflection. That would be a game-changer in robotic domains. Moreover, their learning is state-action specific instead of abstract, i.e. their goal is to discover an optimal action for every patch of state space, instead of learning universal rules such as "move in the direction of the ball until reaching it".

3   Conclusions

This work achieved successful implementations of both independent learners and joint-action learners in the 2-vs-2 offensive free-kick task and within a complex 3D simulator.

Joint-action learners were clearly superior to independent learners. They both converged after a comparable number of iterations. However, JAL discovered good strategies more consistently than IL; furthermore, policies found by JAL reveal a greater inter-agent coordination than those found by IL. Hence, we conclude that for similar robotic domains JAL constitutes a MARL alternative that should not be ignored.

Despite its effectiveness in discovering a solution, the learning procedure was quite inefficient. It suffered from bad local minima; in addition, there were no mechanisms for exploiting symmetries or abstractions found in the world in order to make use of fewer training examples. These issues will be addressed in future work.

References

1. Hafner, R., Riedmiller, M.: Reinforcement learning in feedback control. Mach. Learn. **84**(1–2), 137–169 (2011)
2. Haksar, R.N., Schwager, M.: Distributed deep reinforcement learning for fighting forest fires with a network of aerial robots. In: IEEE/RSJ International Conference on Intelligent Robots and Systems, IROS, pp. 1067–1074 (2018)
3. Hausknecht, M.J.: Cooperation and communication in multiagent deep reinforcement learning. Ph.D. thesis, University of Texas at Austin, USA (2016)
4. Howard, R.A.: Dynamic Programming and Markov Processes. MIT Press, Cambridge (1960)
5. Kalyanakrishnan, S., Stone, P.: Learning complementary multiagent behaviors: a case study. In: Baltes, J., Lagoudakis, M.G., Naruse, T., Ghidary, S.S. (eds.) RoboCup 2009. LNCS (LNAI), vol. 5949, pp. 153–165. Springer, Heidelberg (2010). https://doi.org/10.1007/978-3-642-11876-0_14
6. Knopp, M., Aykın, C., Feldmaier, J., Shen, H.: Formation control using GQ(λ) reinforcement learning. In: 26th IEEE International Symposium on Robot and Human Interactive Communication (RO-MAN), pp. 1043–1048, August 2017
7. Kurek, M.: Deep reinforcement learning in keepaway soccer. Master's thesis, Poznan University of Technology, Poland (2015)
8. Lillicrap, T.P., et al.: Continuous control with deep reinforcement learning. CoRR abs/1509.02971 (2015). http://arxiv.org/abs/1509.02971
9. Liu, Y., Nejat, G.: Multirobot cooperative learning for semiautonomous control in urban search and rescue applications. J. Field Rob. **33**(4), 512–536 (2016)
10. Mnih, V., et al.: Human-level control through deep reinforcement learning. Nature **518**(7540), 529–533 (2015)
11. Pham, H.X., La, H.M., Feil-Seifer, D., Nguyen, L.V.: Cooperative and distributed reinforcement learning of drones for field coverage. CoRR abs/1803.07250 (2018). http://arxiv.org/abs/1803.07250
12. RoboCup Technical Committee: Robocup standard platform league (nao) rule book. Rules2018.pdf, August 2018. https://spl.robocup.org/downloads/
13. Röfer, T., et al.: B-human: team report and code release 2017. Technical report, Deutsches Forschungszentrum für Künstliche Intelligenz, Universität Bremen (2017)
14. Shapley, L.S.: Stochastic games. Proc. Natl. Acad. Sci. **39**(10), 1095–1100 (1953)
15. Sutton, R.S.: Learning to predict by the methods of temporal differences. Mach. Learn. **3**, 9–44 (1988)
16. Sutton, R.S., Barto, A.G.: Introduction to Reinforcement Learning, 1st edn. MIT Press, Cambridge (1998)

Similarity Analysis of Action Trajectories Based on Kick Distributions

Takuya Fukushima[1]([✉])[ID], Tomoharu Nakashima[1][ID], and Hidehisa Akiyama[2][ID]

[1] Osaka Prefecture University, Osaka, Japan
{takuya.fukushima,tomoharu.nakashima}@kis.osakafu-u.ac.jp
[2] Fukuoka University, Fukuoka, Japan
akym@fukuoka-u.ac.jp

Abstract. This paper discusses the validity of similarity measures for action trajectories based on kick distributions. We focus on action trajectories for analyzing team strategies. Kick distribution is then obtained from the action trajectories, which allows us to quantitatively calculate the dissimilarity (or distance) between two team strategies. In this paper, three distance metrics are investigated as the similarity measure: Earth mover's distance, L^2 distance, and Jensen-Shannon divergence. A series of numerical experiments are conducted to compare the evaluation of the similarity obtained by the distances with human subjective evaluations. The effectiveness of the distance metrics is also discussed in terms of the computational cost for calculating the distance.

Keywords: Strategy analysis · Data mining · Similarity measure · RoboCup Soccer Simulation 2D

1 Introduction

Now that sensor devices and the global positioning system are popular and image processing technologies have made a great progress, the data analysis of movement trajectories have been actively studied. For example, Lin et al. [1] presented a model of person's movement trajectory with a graph and formulated the elderly's disorientation detection problem as abnormality detection in the trajectories. In the domain of weather analysis, Dodge et al. [2] investigated the validity of the similarity in analyzing the trajectory of tropical cyclones. Especially with regard to sports, the similarity analysis of player's actions and movement trajectories has been performed for various kinds of sports [3–6]. For the RoboCup soccer simulation, Michael et al. [7] proposed a method that represents the trajectories of the ball and players in a game with a recurrent neural network.

Nakashima et al. [8] performed a tactical analysis based on kick distributions obtained by kicks of a soccer team in RoboCup soccer 2D simulation. In their analysis method, soccer teams were grouped in an unsupervised way such as hierarchical clustering using the kick distributions. The distance between two

© Springer Nature Switzerland AG 2019
S. Chalup et al. (Eds.): RoboCup 2019, LNAI 11531, pp. 58–70, 2019.
https://doi.org/10.1007/978-3-030-35699-6_5

kick distributions was calculated to measure the similarity between them during the clustering process. In their paper, Earth Mover's Distance (EMD) was used as the distance metric between two kick distributions. However, EMD has some problems. For example, the computational cost becomes intractably high as the number of kicks in the kick distributions increases. It is for this reason that EMD is not suitable for online tactical analysis. Furthermore, it is not clear whether the distance calculated by EMD agrees with the subjective similarity by human.

The purpose of this research is to show the validity of a computational way to understand team strategies in a similar manner to human's subjectivity. This paper tackles the above problems in the kick distribution. That is, we try to reduce the computational cost for calculating the distance between kick distributions, and also we investigate the validity of various distance metrics for kick distributions. There are two key aspects in this research. One is to convert a discrete kick distribution into a continuous probability distribution called a kick probability distribution by using kernel density estimation for reducing the computational complexity. The other is to see whether the distance metrics conform to human subjectivity on the similarity between any two kick distributions.

The dissimilarity (or the distance) between two kick distributions is measured by calculating EMD, L^2 distance and Jensen-Shannon (JS) divergence. In order to check whether these dissimilarity metrics agree with the human subjectivity, we use a paired comparison method in questionnaires and analyze them quantitatively. This paper examines the relationship between dissimilarity evaluation of human-subjective and dissimilarity analysis using kick distribution by calculating rank correlation. This allows us to show the effectiveness of using kick distributions as a method to calculate the dissimilarity in the team behavior in the same way as the human evaluate it.

2   Similarity in Team Strategies

Team strategy can be represented by the combinations of taken actions (e.g., passes and dribbles) and positional roles (e.g., forward and defender). This paper focuses on the actions taken by the players during games. The positional role is not discussed and left for future research.

In the RoboCup soccer 2D simulation, various strategies are developed by various teams. It is generally accepted that there is no perfect strategy which works well against any others. Thus, teams should adapt themselves by switching their strategies according to their opponent. In order to achieve this strategy switching, it is necessary to distinguish the strategies by similarity analysis. The similarity analysis can be also used to predict the game result (i.e. win or lose) with an assumption that both teams keep using their current strategies for the rest of the game. Based on the prediction result, we can switch the team strategy to more appropriate one which leads the team to win the game against the opponent team with a higher probability. Thus, the similarity analysis of team strategies is useful and necessary to increase the winning rate of the team.

The similarity between two team strategies is based on the similarity metrics between the corresponding kick distributions that are generated by the teams [8].

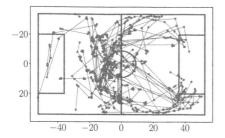

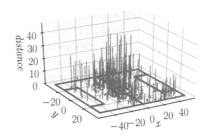

Fig. 1. An example of action trajectories

Fig. 2. Converted kick distribution from Fig. 1

A kick distribution of a team is generated by collecting all kicks made by the team during the course of the game. An action trajectory (or an episode) is defined as a set of sequential actions by the team starting from the time when the team firstly intercepts the ball and ending with the time when the ball is intercepted or is delivered into the opponent penalty area. Figure 1 shows an example of such action trajectories. In this figure, dots represent the points where the ball was kicked during a game. The points are connected with a line if they were sequentially executed in an episode.

2.1   Kick Distribution

A kick distribution is a set of kicks that are executed during a game. Each kick includes the following information: (i) The position in the soccer field where the action was taken, and (ii) the movement length of the ball that was brought by the kick. Thus, each kick is represented by a three-dimensional vector (i.e., xy-coordinate of the kick point in the soccer field and the distance made by the kick). Figure 2 shows the kick distribution that is converted from the action trajectories shown in Fig. 1. In Fig. 2, the height of the poles represents the distance made by the kicks, and the position of the poles shows the place where the ball was kicked.

The high computational time and a large amount of data become necessary to assume distributions as the dimensionality increase. In this paper, we assume that the kick distributions will be utilized for tactical analysis in an online manner, thus we only employ the absolute value of the kick point and the movement length of the ball to avoid the problem. In addition, another reason is that the kick distributions in the previous research [8] were expressed in the same say.

2.2   Kick Probability Distribution

As the kick distribution is a collection of individual kicks, it is time-consuming to calculate the distance (or dissimilarity) between two kick distributions. This is because the calculation involves individual consideration of the kicks in the

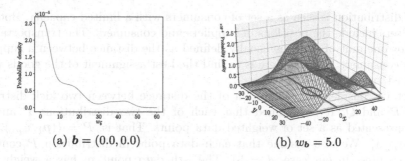

(a) $b = (0.0, 0.0)$ (b) $w_b = 5.0$

Fig. 3. Kick probability distribution

kick distribution. In order to calculate the distance efficiently, we propose to convert a kick distribution to a continuous probability distribution represented. Kernel Density Estimation (KDE) is employed for this purpose. KDE is a non-parametric method to estimate the probability density function of a population from a sample. In the KDE process of this paper, three-dimensional Gaussian kernels are used as each kick is represented by a three-dimensional vector.

Let us define $p(b, w_b)$ as the probability that the kick is executed at the position b with the distance w_b. This probability is estimated by KDE using a set of Gaussian functions. We show the kick probability distribution in Fig. 3(a) and (b). These figures were generated by converting from the kick distribution shown in Fig. 2. Since it is not possible to graphically show the three-dimensional probability density function, Fig. 3(a) shows the kick probability distribution on the condition that the ball was kicked at the position $b = (0.0, 0.0)$, and the kick probability distribution in Fig. 3(b) shows the probability density at the distance $w_b = 5.0$.

3   Distance Metrics for Kick Distributions

In order to measure the dissimilarity between two kick distributions, we use three distance metrics to compare. The problem here is how to calculate such distance metrics. The following subsections present the three distance metrics considered in this paper.

3.1   Earth Mover's Distance

The number of data points in kick distribution is not constant because the number of kicks in a game is variable. Thus, it is not possible to use a straight-forward approach for calculating the distance between two kick distributions. Earth Mover's Distance (EMD) [9] is such a metric to measure the dissimilarity between two sets that may have different number of data points. This distance metric is defined as a solution of a transportation problem where one kick distri-bution is seen as a set of suppliers with the amount of available goods while the other distribution is seen as a set of consumers with a limited capacity. Both of these sets include the positions of suppliers and consumers. The transportation cost for one unit of goods is usually defined as the distance between a supplier and a consumer. The task here is to find the best assignment of the goods with the least transportation cost.

Let us consider the calculation of the distance between two kick distributions P and Q. It is assumed that each of the two distributions P and Q are represented as a set of weighted data points. That is, $P = \{(\boldsymbol{p}_1, w_{\boldsymbol{p}_1}), \ldots, (\boldsymbol{p}_m, w_{\boldsymbol{p}_m})\}$. We also assume that each data point in distribution P consists of d features (in our case, $d = 3$). The i-th data point $\boldsymbol{p}_i$ has a weight w_i. Likewise, the other distribution Q is assumed to be a set of n data points (i.e., $Q = \{(\boldsymbol{q}_1, w_{\boldsymbol{q}_1}), \cdots, (\boldsymbol{q}_n, w_{\boldsymbol{q}_n})\}$). EMD between P and Q can be calculated even though the number of data points is different from each other.

Let us denote the ground distance between two data points $\boldsymbol{p}_i$ and $\boldsymbol{q}_j$ as d_{ij}. In this paper, Euclidean distance is used as the distance between two data points. By calculating the distances for all combinations, we can obtain a ground distance matrix $\mathbf{D} = [d_{ij}]$. Let us define the transportation amount of goods from $\boldsymbol{p}_i$ to $\boldsymbol{q}_j$ as f_{ij}. Then, we have a transportation matrix $\mathbf{F} = [f_{ij}]$. EMD is calculated as the transportation amount $\mathbf{F}^*$ that minimizes the cost function in Eq. (1). The formulation of the optimization with a cost function W is defined in Eq. (2).

$$\mathbf{F}^* = \arg\min_{f_{ij}} \mathrm{W}, \tag{1}$$

$$\mathrm{W} = \sum_{i=1}^{m}\sum_{j=1}^{n} d_{ij} f_{ij}. \tag{2}$$

The restrictions in the minimization of the cost function W are as follows; $f_{ij} \geq 0 (1 \leq i \leq m, 1 \leq j \leq n)$; $\sum_{j=1}^{n} f_{ij} \leq w_{\boldsymbol{p}_i} (1 \leq i \leq m)$; $\sum_{i=1}^{m} f_{ij} \leq w_{\boldsymbol{q}_j} (1 \leq j \leq n)$; $\sum_{i=1}^{m}\sum_{j=1}^{n} f_{ij} = \min(\sum_{i=1}^{m} w_{\boldsymbol{p}_i}, \sum_{j=1}^{n} w_{\boldsymbol{q}_j})$.

EMD between the distributions P and Q is determined with the optimal transportation matrix $\mathbf{F}^* = [f_{ij}^*]$ as follows:

$$\mathrm{EMD}(P, Q) = \frac{\sum_{i=1}^{m}\sum_{j=1}^{n} d_{ij} f_{ij}^*}{\sum_{i=1}^{m}\sum_{j=1}^{n} f_{ij}^*}. \tag{3}$$

A metric $d(\cdot, \cdot)$ is defined as a distance when the following conditions are satisfied for any x, y, and z; (a) non-negative $d(x, y) \geq 0$; (b) non-degenerate $d(x, y) = 0 \Leftrightarrow x = y$; (c) symmetry $d(x, y) = d(y, x)$; (d) triangle inequality $d(x, z) \leq d(x, y) + d(y, z)$.

There are some problems in applying EMD to RoboCup environment. By definition, the value of EMD always satisfies the properties (or axioms) of distance (a) and (c). On the other hand, (b) and (d) hold only when the total weights in the supplier group and those in the consumer group are exactly the same. In the case of the RoboCup soccer, these conditions are not usually satisfied. More concretely, the non-degenerate and the triangle inequality of EMD for kick distribution does not holds in almost all the time. Another problem in EMD is that the computational cost becomes intractably high with the number of data points. Therefore, EMD cannot work in an online manner.

3.2 L^2 Distance

Another distance metrics for distributions is known as L^2 distance. This subsection consider the L^2 distance a distance measure between two kick distributions. This distance measure uses probability density functions $p(x)$ and $q(x)$ and is defined as follows.

$$L^2(p,q) = \int (p(x) - q(x))^2 dx, \tag{4}$$

where the probability density functions $p(x)$ and $q(x)$ are the kick probability distributions obtained from kick distributions by KDE (in Sect. 2). The L^2 distance satisfies the properties of distance, that is, (a), (b), (c) and (d) that are discussed in the last subsection.

3.3 Jensen-Shannon Divergence

Jensen-Shannon (JS) divergence is known as another metric between probability distributions. The distance between the probability density functions $p(x)$ and $q(x)$, using the JS divergence is obtained as follows:

$$D_{JS}(p||q) = \frac{1}{2}D_{KL}(p||\frac{p+q}{2}) + \frac{1}{2}D_{KL}(q||\frac{p+q}{2}), \tag{5}$$

where D_{KL} is Kullback-Leibler (KL) divergence obtained by Eq. (6)

$$D_{KL}(p||q) = \int p(x)\log\frac{p(x)}{q(x)} dx. \tag{6}$$

By putting $M = \frac{p+q}{2}$, we have

$$D_{JS}(p||q) = \frac{1}{2}D_{KL}(p||M) + \frac{1}{2}D_{KL}(q||M)$$

$$= \frac{1}{2}\int p(x)\log\frac{p(x)}{M(x)} dx + \frac{1}{2}\int q(x)\log\frac{q(x)}{M(x)} dx.$$

Note that the probability density functions $p(x)$ and $q(x)$ are the kick probability distributions described in Subsect. 2.2. JS divergence has properties of distance (a), (b) and (c), but does not satisfy (d).

4   Experiment

We would like to know whether the distance metrics for kick distributions are suited to human subjectivity. Through numerical experiments, the similarity of action trajectories is calculated by using the distance measures described in Sect. 3. In addition, we conduct a questionnaire to verify how much these dissimilarity measures in Sect. 3 agree with the human subjectivity. We also compare the calculation time of the three different distance measures.

Note that it might be faster to calculate the distance using the kick distributions than using the kick probability distributions when the number of data points in the kick distribution (i.e., the number of kicks) is extremely small. In this paper, we assume that the kick distribution has so a large amount of data points that the calculation on the kick distribution is computationally unfeasible.

4.1   Experimental Settings

In the numerical experiments in this section, the dissimilarity between two action trajectories is calculated by using the distance between the corresponding kick (or kick probability) distributions. Action trajectories are extracted from logs of those games where the following seven teams played against a well-known base team agent2D [10].

A. CYRUS2018 [11]   B. FRA-UNIted [12]
C. Gliders2016 [13]   D. HELIOS2018 [14]
E. MT2018 [15]   F. Oxsy [16]
G. WrightEagle [17]

The above teams are top teams in the world competitions of RoboCup Soccer Simulation 2D League. The action trajectories of HELIOS2018 playing against agent2D are set as target action sequences. The task of the experiment participants is to evaluate how close the strategies of the seven teams are to those of the target team (in our experiments, the target team is HELIOS2018). Note that Team D is actually the target team, which means that the experiment participants are expected to identify Team D as the target team. Note also that the action trajectories of Team D are different from those of the target teams because different game logs are used to extract the action trajectories.

The action trajectories for each team are extracted from logs of five games against agent2D. The distance between the action trajectories of Teams A~G and the target trajectories is calculated by using the kick distributions in the case of EMD. For the other distance measures (i.e., L^2 distance and JS divergence), the probability density functions generated by the KDE method are used. The value of the distance is expected to be small when the corresponding two action trajectories (i.e., the corresponding team strategies) are close to each other. In the numerical experiments of this section, a paired-comparison method is used in order to verify whether the similarity matches with the human subjectivity. In our numerical experiments, the paired comparison is performed where

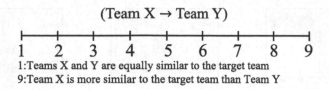

1:Teams X and Y are equally similar to the target team
9:Team X is more similar to the target team than Team Y

Fig. 4. Nine scale rating for evaluating the similarity between two action trajectories

"similarity to the target team" is evaluated by the experiment participants. In a questionnaire, each experiment participant answers the degree of similarity between two teams in one of the nine scale ratings as shown in Fig. 4.

In the paired comparison method, the experiment participants should pick up one scale out of them for each combination of the action trajectories. That is, the experiment participant subjectively selects one scale regarding how close Team i is to the target team in comparison to how close Team j is to the target team (for $i \neq j$ in A~G). For each scale, the point is assigned and used for summarizing later.

For example, if the selected scale corresponding to "Team A is *more similar to the target team* than Team B", nine points are added to A→B and 1/9 points are added to B→A. By continuing this procedure for all combinations, we can obtain a 7×7 pairwise comparison matrix $\boldsymbol{A}$. Then, the principal eigenvector $\boldsymbol{w}$ for the principal eigenvalue λ_{max} of the paired comparison matrix $\boldsymbol{A}$ is obtained. The principal eigenvector normalized by $\sum_{i=1}^{n} w_i = 1$ is treated as the similarity. In this way, similarity evaluations of the human subjectivity between the target trajectories and each team's ones are calculated quantitatively.

We rank the "similarity to the target trajectory" according to the dissimilarity between the target and each team's trajectories. The rank correlation are calculated by the four types of distance metrics, EMD, L^2 distance, JS divergence and human subjectivity. By using the calculated correlations, we show the effectiveness of kick distributions in calculating the similarity of action trajectories.

The rank correlation is calculated using Spearman's rank correlation coefficient. Spearman's rank correlation coefficient r_{xy} is obtained by the following equation:

$$r_{xy} = 1 - \frac{6}{n(n^2 - 1)} \sum_{i=1}^{n} (x_i - y_i)^2, \tag{7}$$

where each of x and y represents one of the four distance metrics, i means each team from which action trajectories are extracted, and n is the number of the experiment participants. That is, $x, y \in \{\text{EMD}, L^2 \text{ distance}, \text{JS divergence}, \text{human subjectivity}\}$, $i \in \{\text{A, B, C, D, E, F, G}\}$ and $n = 7$.

4.2   Experimental Results

The action trajectories that are used in the questionnaire are shown in Fig. 5(a)–(g). These are only a subset of the action trajectories that were presented during

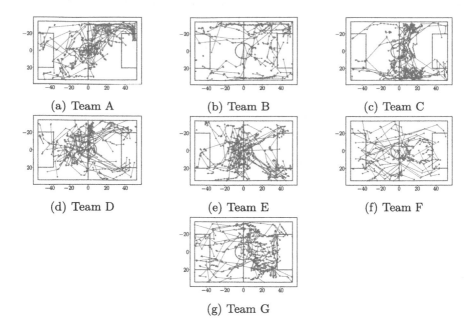

(a) Team A   (b) Team B   (c) Team C

(d) Team D   (e) Team E   (f) Team F

(g) Team G

Fig. 5. Kick sequences extracted from the teams (excerpt)

the questionnaire. In the experiments with the experiment participants, five figures (which correspond to five games) are presented for each team.

One of the action trajectories by the target team is already shown in Fig. 1. The calculated distances between the kick distributions using the three types of distance metrics and their rank of similarity are presented in Table 1(a)–(c). From these results, we can see that the distances between the kick (probability) distributions of the target and ones of the Team D (same as the experimental setting of the target) is the smallest for any distance metrics. This demonstrates the validity of using kick distributions for similarity analysis. We can also see from Fig. 1 that kick distributions consider strategic positioning of the players without the ball possession. For example, Team A (i.e. Fig. 5(a)) have asymmetrical strategy by assigning offensive players to the upper side in the soccer field.

Table 2 shows the calculated similarity between each of the seven teams and the target team for all the experiment participants. Note that this table shows the similarity, not dissimilarity. In addition, Fig. 6 depicts the box plot of the similarities between the target and each team's action trajectories using human subjectivity. We can see that most of the experiment participants have evaluated the action trajectories of Team D (or Team C, E) as close to the target team. On the other hand, we can also see that there is a large variances in the evaluations among the experiment participants. The Consistency Index (C.I.) tended to be high when the similarity of the action trajectories was measured by the paired comparison method as shown in Table 2. Generally, the

Table 1. Calculated similarities of action trajectories

(a) EMD

Team	Distance	Rank
A	10.46	7
B	5.876	4
C	7.316	6
D	2.035	1
E	3.419	2
F	4.786	3
G	6.602	5

(b) L^2 distance

Team	Distance	Rank
A	5.922×10^{-6}	5
B	5.348×10^{-6}	4
C	6.923×10^{-6}	7
D	2.495×10^{-7}	1
E	1.313×10^{-6}	2
F	6.273×10^{-6}	6
G	4.757×10^{-6}	3

(c) JS divergence

Team	Distance	Rank
A	3.142×10^{-1}	3
B	3.840×10^{-1}	7
C	3.387×10^{-1}	6
D	1.131×10^{-1}	1
E	1.986×10^{-1}	2
F	3.334×10^{-1}	5
G	3.267×10^{-1}	4

(d) Human subjectivity

Team	Similarity	Rank
A	9.968×10^{-2}	4
B	6.212×10^{-2}	6
C	1.747×10^{-1}	3
D	3.228×10^{-1}	1
E	2.337×10^{-1}	2
F	5.164×10^{-2}	7
G	7.241×10^{-2}	5

consistency is very low when C.I. is very high (≥ 0.15). Therefore, we found that it was difficult for humans to measure the similarity of action trajectories. Table 1(d) shows the average value of the similarities obtained by the eigenvectors in the paired comparison metrics of all experiment participants. We can find that the results with a high similarity when using the same team (HELIOS2018) as the target is obtained for the setting regardless the distance metrics. Even consistent evaluation is difficult with human subjectivity.

We can see that EMD and JS divergence have a positive correlation with the human subjectivity. We also find that L^2 distance has a weak correlation as compared to the other distance metrics. Therefore, it is shown that there is no significant difference between similarity analysis of action trajectories by kick distributions and human subjectivity for the evaluation of the similarity. That is, the presented way of calculating the dissimilarity between action strategies using kick distribution agrees with human subjectivity.

We now discuss the relationship between the rank correlation and the computational time to calculate the distances. These are shown in Table 3. We can see that the calculation time and the computational cost can be significantly reduced in the distance metric by using the continuous kick probability distributions as compared to the discrete kick distributions. Thus, it is possible to analyze the dissimilarity more quickly by converting the discrete kick distributions to the continuous ones when calculating the distance between kick distributions during a game in an online manner.

Table 2. Calculated similarity with the human subjectivity

Experiment participant	Team							
	A	B	C	D	E	F	G	C.I.
1	0.0612	0.0446	0.3119	0.2892	0.2064	0.0495	0.0371	0.0748
2	0.0321	0.0280	0.1235	0.4620	0.2374	0.0681	0.0488	0.1401
3	0.2127	0.0740	0.2399	0.2562	0.1763	0.0271	0.0137	0.3457
4	0.1078	0.0278	0.0524	0.4387	0.2396	0.0780	0.0559	0.1593
5	0.0460	0.0721	0.1345	0.3436	0.3471	0.0374	0.0194	0.2263
6	0.0983	0.0564	0.0975	0.3658	0.2939	0.036	0.0521	0.1508
7	0.0477	0.0417	0.0517	0.3564	0.1533	0.0924	0.2569	0.2168
8	0.1207	0.2640	0.1589	0.2341	0.2925	0.0231	0.1443	0.5327
9	0.2465	0.0521	0.3815	0.1468	0.1193	0.0286	0.0251	0.1349
10	0.0630	0.0268	0.0477	0.2445	0.3367	0.1112	0.1702	0.1895
11	0.0624	0.0627	0.1168	0.3308	0.3100	0.0292	0.0881	0.5340
12	0.0594	0.0412	0.2285	0.4664	0.1594	0.0260	0.0191	0.2282
13	0.1554	0.0472	0.3275	0.2922	0.1024	0.0435	0.0318	0.1372
14	0.0823	0.0311	0.1732	0.2918	0.2976	0.0728	0.0513	0.2685
Average	0.0997	0.0621	0.1747	0.3228	0.2337	0.0516	0.0724	0.2385
Variance	0.0041	0.0036	0.0117	0.0084	0.0067	0.0008	0.0050	0.0201

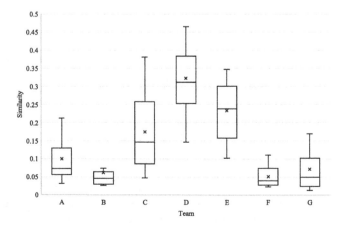

Fig. 6. The similarity in action trajectories using human subjectivity.

Table 3. Spearman's rank correlation and calculation time

Distance metric	Rank correlation	Time (sec.)
EMD	6.429×10^{-1}	7650
L^2 distance	3.929×10^{-1}	130
JS divergence	7.143×10^{-1}	0.404

5   Conclusions

In this paper, we calculated the distance between kick distributions for dissimilarity analysis of action trajectories. We used EMD, L^2 distance, and JS divergence as metrics for the distance between kick distributions. In order to show the validity of kick distributions for the similarity analysis, we compared the proposed similarity analysis methods with the human subjective evaluations.

The human subjective evaluations for the similarity of the action trajectories were calculated by using a paired comparison method. We showed that our similarity analysis methods have a positive correlation with the human subjectivity. Thus, we also showed that our method has the validity for the similarity analysis. Another contribution of the paper is that the calculation time can be reduced by using the continuous kick probability distributions.

For future work, we will consider a new similarity analysis method that can distinguish kick directions. Moreover, we will apply the proposed method to other experimental environment.

References

1. Lin, Q., Zhang, D., Connelly, K., Ni, H., Zhiwen, Y., Zhou, X.: Disorientation detection by mining GPS trajectories for cognitively-impaired elders. Pervasive Mob. Comput. **19**, 71–85 (2015)
2. Dodge, S., Weibel, R., Laube, P.: Trajectory similarity analysis in movement parameter space. In: Proceedings of the 19th GIS Research UK Annual Conference 2011, pp. 270–279 (2011)
3. Zhu, G., et al.: Trajectory based event tactics analysis in broadcast sports video. In: Proceedings of the 15th ACM International Conference on Multimedia, pp. 58–67 (2007)
4. Mutschler, C., Kókai, G., Edelhäußer, T.: Online data stream mining on interactive trajectories in soccer games. In: Proceedings of the 2nd International Conference on Positioning and Context-Awareness, pp. 15–22 (2011)
5. Stein, M., Janetzko, H., Schreck, T., Keim, D.A.: Tackling similarity search for soccer match analysis: multimodal distance measure and interactive query definition. In: Proceedings of the 4th Symposium on Visualization in Data Science, 10 pages (2018)
6. Mehrasa, N., Zhong, Y., Tung, F., Bornn, L., Mori, G.: Deep learning of player trajectory representation for team activity analysis. In: Proceedings of the 11th MIT Sloan Sports Analytics Conference, 8 pages (2018)

7. Michael, O., Obst, O., Schmidsberger, F., Stolzenburg, F.: Analysing soccer games with clustering and conceptors. In: Akiyama, H., Obst, O., Sammut, C., Tonidandel, F. (eds.) RoboCup 2017. LNCS (LNAI), vol. 11175, pp. 120–131. Springer, Cham (2018). https://doi.org/10.1007/978-3-030-00308-1_10
8. Nakashima, T., Mifune, S., Henrio, J., Obst, O., Wang, P., Prokopenko, M.: Kick extraction for reducing uncertainty in RoboCup logs. In: Yamamoto, S. (ed.) HCI 2015. LNCS, vol. 9173, pp. 622–633. Springer, Cham (2015). https://doi.org/10.1007/978-3-319-20618-9_61
9. Rubner, Y., Tomasi, C., Guibas, L.J.: The earth mover's distance as a metric for image retrieval. Int. J. Comput. Vision **40**(2), 99–121 (2000)
10. Akiyama, H., Nakashima, T.: HELIOS base: an open source package for the RoboCup soccer 2D simulation. In: Behnke, S., Veloso, M., Visser, A., Xiong, R. (eds.) RoboCup 2013. LNCS (LNAI), vol. 8371, pp. 528–535. Springer, Heidelberg (2014). https://doi.org/10.1007/978-3-662-44468-9_46
11. Zare, N., et al.: Cyrus 2D simulation team description paper 2018. In: RoboCup2018 Montreal, 6 pages (2018)
12. Gabel, T., Klöppner, P., Godehardt, E.: FRA-UNIted – team description 2018. In: RoboCup2018 Montreal, 6 pages (2018)
13. Prokopenko, M., Wang, P., Obst, O., Jauregui, V.: Gliders 2016: integrating multi-agent approaches to tactical diversity. In: RoboCup2016 Leipzig, 6 pages (2016)
14. Akiyama, H., Nakashima, T., Suzuki, Y., Ohori, A., Fukushima, T.: HELIOS2018: team description paper. In: RoboCup2018 Montreal, 6 pages (2018)
15. Yang, Z., et al.: MT2018: team description paper. In: RoboCup2018 Montreal, 6 pages (2018)
16. Marian, S., Luca, D., Sarac, B., Cotarlea, O.: OXSY 2018 team description. In: RoboCup2018 Montreal, 6 pages (2018)
17. Li, X., Chen, R., Chen, X.: WrightEagle 2D soccer simulation team description 2015. In: RoboCup2015 Hefei, 5 pages (2015)

Modelling and Optimisation
of a RoboCup MSL Coilgun

Valentin Gies[1][(✉)] (iD), Thierry Soriano[2], Christopher Albert[3],
and Nicolas Prouteau[3]

[1] Université de Toulon, CNRS, IM2NP - UMR 7334, 83130 La Garde, France
`gies@univ-tln.fr`
[2] Université de Toulon, CNRS, COSMER - EA 7398, 83130 La Garde, France
`thierry.soriano@univ-tln.fr`
[3] Université de Toulon, SeaTech, Robot Club Toulon, Toulon, France
`rct@univ-tln.fr`
`http://rct.univ-tln.fr`

Abstract. This paper focuses on the modelling and optimization of a
RoboCup Middle Size League (MSL) coil-gun. A mechatronic model coupling electrical, mechanical and electromagnetic models is proposed. This
model is used for optimizing an indirect coil-gun used on limited size
robots at the RoboCup for kicking real soccer balls. Applied to a well
defined existing coil gun [6], we show that optimizing the initial position
of the plunger and the length of a plunger extension leads to increase
the ball speed by 30% compared to the results presented in a previous
study.

Keywords: Coil gun · Electro magnetic launcher · Mechatronics ·
Modelling · RoboCup

1 Introduction

An electromagnetic launcher (EML) is a system using electricity for propelling
a projectile [5]. A coil gun is a type of EML, having only the ability to launch
magnetic objects (such as iron rods) by converting electrical energy into kinetic
energy using a coil [1].

Launching non-magnetic objects cannot be done directly using coil guns
because they are not affected by magnetic field but can be done using an *"indirect
coil gun"*, having a magnetic plunger accelerated by a coil, propelling an non-
magnetic object by continuous contact or elastic shock. Both these propelling
techniques can be combined in a multi-phase EML. Optimization of this type of
launcher is the purpose of this work.

Optimizing limited size indirect coil guns is the scope of this paper. For
illustrating our purpose, we have chosen to optimize a kicking system used at
the RoboCup in Middle Size League, which is a competition of robot playing
soccer and having a limited size and weight for embedding soccer balls launching
systems. This article is divided into three parts:

© Springer Nature Switzerland AG 2019
S. Chalup et al. (Eds.): RoboCup 2019, LNAI 11531, pp. 71–85, 2019.
https://doi.org/10.1007/978-3-030-35699-6_6

- In Sect. 2, principles of coil guns are presented with limitations concerning their modelling.
- In Sect. 3, a mechanic and electromagnetic model is proposed and implemented using finite elements simulation tools for the electromagnetic part of the coil gun, and using Matlab Simulink for the mechanical and electrical aspects.
- In Sect. 4, simulation results are discussed in order to optimize the parameters of an existing indirect coil gun.

RoboCup is an international competition of robot teams playing soccer with a goal: winning against a soccer professional team by 2050. In Middle Size League (MSL), teams are composed of 5 robots playing autonomously on a 22 m by 14 m soccer field with a real soccer ball (diameter 22 cm) weighting 450 g. Each robot have a maximum length of 52 cm, a maximum width of 52 cm and a maximum height of 80 cm. Current kicking systems used in MSL have the ability of propelling balls with a speed of $12\,\mathrm{m.s^{-1}}$. This speed is interesting and allows to kick balls at a distance of 15 m but is limited compared with real soccer players. In order to make a comparison, a shoot from a professional soccer player can reach $130\,\mathrm{km.h^{-1}}$, compared with $43\,\mathrm{km.h^{-1}}$ for current MSL robots. In terms of kinetic energy, $E_K = \frac{1}{2}\mathrm{mv}^2 = 32\,\mathrm{J}$ is transmitted to the ball at the RoboCup, compared to $E_K = 300\,\mathrm{J}$ transmitted by a real professional player. The ratio is about 10 times, showing that an important step has to be done in order to compete with humans.

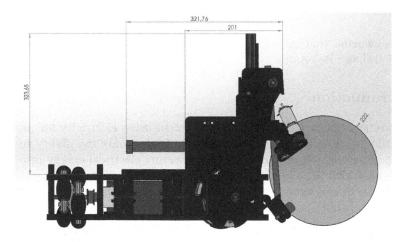

Fig. 1. Kicking system in a RoboCup robot

RoboCup MSL case study has been chosen due to the relevancy of trade-off consisting in an optimization of the speed of a ball kicked by an indirect coil gun, while having strong size constraints due to competition rules. RoboCup robots need compact but powerful coil guns. Existing systems able to strike a ball at

$12\,\mathrm{m.s^{-}1}$ have an acceleration of about $100\,\mathrm{G}$ and a strike time of about $20\,\mathrm{ms}$. As shown in Fig. 1, the size of the whole kicking system, including the indirect coil gun, is about $30\,\mathrm{cm}$ including the coil and the iron rod, with a coil size of about $10\,\mathrm{cm}$ to $12\,\mathrm{cm}$ in length, a rod size of about $13\,\mathrm{cm}$ in length, and a rod stroke of about $12\,\mathrm{cm}$.

2   Principles of Coil Guns

2.1   Physical Concept

Coil guns are made using a variable reluctance magnetic circuit composed of a fixed magnetic circuit looped by an magnetic iron projectile. A coil is placed around the stroke of the iron rod in order to magnetize the magnetic circuit and to create a magnetic force on the rod.

Considering that the magnetic field in a magnetic circuit tends to be maximized if possible, the air gap in a magnetic circuit tends to be reduced, resulting in a force on the rod propelling it when the magnetic circuit is excited with a coil crossed by a current pulse as shown in Fig. 2. This is the principle of a variable reluctance actuator.

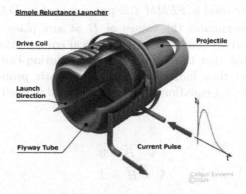

Fig. 2. Coil gun principle

In our case study, a large capacitor $(4700\,\mu\mathrm{F})$ is discharged in the coil in order to produce a high current generating the magnetic field and force. A mobile plunger (iron rod) is able to move in this field, sliding in a stainless steel tube. Iron rod is attracted to the centre of the stainless steel tube and thus accelerated until it reaches this point. It can be slowed down if the plunger goes over this point while the current in the coil is still present, but this doesn't happens in real conditions as shown later.

Current discharge on the coil can be described by a second order RLC differential equation, but having non-constant coefficients because of the changing value of the inductor over the time. In this paper, we propose an electrical model taking into account the variation of the inductance when the iron rod slides forward in the coil.

2.2   Electromagnetic Theory and Simulation Software

Hopkinson law is the base a variable reluctance actuators: $\mathscr{F} = NI = R\Phi$, with:

- $\mathscr{F}$: magnetomotive force (MMF and the unit is ampere-turn: At)
- N: number of turns of the coil
- I: intensity in the coil (A)
- R: reluctance (H^{-1})
- Φ: flux (Wb)

Consequently, magnetic flux is equal to: $\Phi = \dfrac{NI}{R}$ and coil force is equal to: $\overrightarrow{F} = \overrightarrow{grad}(\overrightarrow{M} \cdot \overrightarrow{B})$ with $\overrightarrow{M} = IS\overrightarrow{n}$.

Going deeper into a theoretical electrical model is interesting if the reluctance is constant, in order to find an analytical solution. However, there are 2 main factors making it non-constant: the first one is the position of the plunger, and the second one is the saturation of the magnetic circuit as shown in Fig. 3, which can be very important if the coil current is high. In order to take these non-linearities into account, a finite-element model based simulator is used for calculating the force and the inductance values under different conditions [4]. Open source software used is *FEMM 4.2*, programmed by D.C. Meeker.

FEMM 4.2 approximates the values of $\overrightarrow{B}$ at any place of the system for each plunger and current combination. Numerical computation is performed in a static way, meaning that the kicking system evolution can be considered as a succession of short time independent magneto-static problems. For each of these problems, following equations link magnetic field intensity B and magnetic excitation H:

$$\nabla \cdot \overrightarrow{B} = 0 \tag{1}$$
$$\nabla \times \overrightarrow{H} = J \tag{2}$$

$\overrightarrow{B}$ and $\overrightarrow{H}$ can be linked together in a linear approach:

$$\overrightarrow{B} = \mu \overrightarrow{H} \tag{3}$$

or in a more realistic non-linear approach:

$$\overrightarrow{B} = \mu(\overrightarrow{H})\overrightarrow{H} \tag{4}$$

FEMM software tries to find a field that satisfies the linear approach and the flux density equation with the magnetic vector potential $\overrightarrow{A}$ defined as:

$$\overrightarrow{B} = \nabla \times \overrightarrow{A} \tag{5}$$

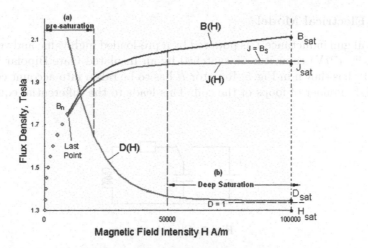

Fig. 3. Magnetic field saturation in iron

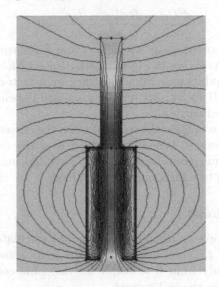

Fig. 4. FEMM 4.2 simulation with the plunger outside the coil

$\vec{A}$ can be found by the software using Eq. 4 with a conjugate gradient method, so we can rewrite Eq. 2 as:

$$\nabla \times \left(\frac{1}{\mu(\vec{H})} \nabla \times \vec{A}) \right) = J \tag{6}$$

Using this equation, the software calculates $\vec{A}\,\vec{B}$ in every place of the EML as shown on Fig. 4. It also evaluates integral values on a specific part of the system such as the inductance of the coil or the force applied on the iron plunger.

2.3   Electrical Model

The coil gun inductance L is powered by a pre-loaded high value and voltage (*i.e.* 4700 μF, 450 V) capacitor C, switched by an Insulated Gate Bipolar Transistor (IGBT) has shown in Fig. 5. Resistor R has to be taken into account considering the high number of loops of the coil. This leads to the differential equation 7.

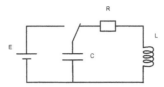

Fig. 5. Electric circuit

$$\frac{d^2 U_C}{dt^2} + \frac{R}{L}\frac{dU_C}{dt} + \frac{U_C}{LC} = 0 \tag{7}$$

This equation can be solved easily when L, C and R are constants, but L is not constant in our case. As shown in Fig. 6, simulations on *FEMM 4.2* using a LUA script shows that L inductance value can vary by a factor 18 in our studying case, going from 19 mH to 342 mH for the same coil depending on the plunger position and on the coil current.

When the plunger is outside the coil and when the current is high, the inductance has the lowest values. When the plunger is at the centre of the coil and when current is low, magnetic field is well guided and magnetic materials are not saturated, leading to a high inductance value.

2.4   Mechanical Model

As explained before, force on the plunger cannot be calculated analytically. Simulations using *FEMM 4.2* combined with a LUA script shows (Fig. 7) that force varies in our case study from 0 to 850 N for the same coil depending on the plunger position and on the coil current.

When the plunger is outside the coil, the force is very small due to the size of the air gap which is too important. When the plunger is exactly at the centre of the coil, force is null for any value of the current because air gap is minimal. The maximal force strength is obtained for high currents and plunger positions between 40 mm and 80 mm from the centre of the coil.

3   Mixed Electrical and Mechanical Model of the Indirect Coil Gun

Inductance and magnetic force values are necessary to build a model of the coil gun for simulating it precisely. Calculated using *FEMM 4.2*, they are imple-

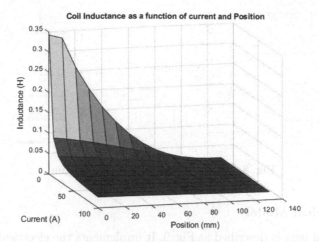

Fig. 6. Variation of the inductance value depending on the plunger position and the coil current

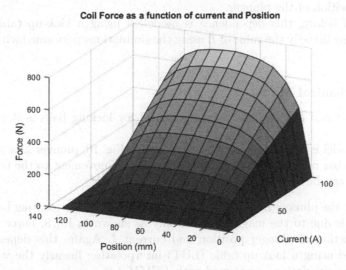

Fig. 7. Variation of the force on the plunger depending on its position and the coil current

mented using look-up tables taking into account plunger position and coil current in order to approximate inductance and force for every configurations of the system.

For this mechatronic model combining mechanic, electric and magnetic modelling, Matlab Simulink tool has been used as shown in Fig. 8.

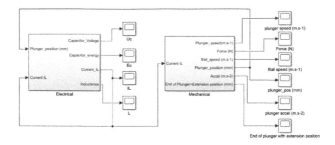

Fig. 8. Mechatronic model of the coil gun

3.1   Electrical Model

The electrical part is described at Fig. 9. It implements the electrical differential equation 7 using discrete blocks. This is necessary because coefficients of the equation are not constant due to the dependence of inductance L to the current and the position of the plunger.

As said before, this dependence is modelled using a look-up table (LUT) interpolating linearly the value of L using the simulations performed with *FEMM 4.2*.

3.2   Mechanical Model

The indirect coil gun mechanical system used for kicking balls is described at Fig. 10.

This model is not simple because as shown in Fig. 10, plunger hits a rotating aluminium bar near its centre, in order to transmit movement to the ball. Thus, movement can be split in 3 phases as shown in Fig. 11:

- Phase 1: the plunger is accelerated without contact on the rotating bar. Acceleration is due to the magnetic force only as shown in Eq. 8. Force $F_{magneto}$ is a function of plunger position and current I. Again, this dependence is modelled using a look-up table (LUT) interpolating linearly the value of F using the simulations performed with *FEMM 4.2*.

$$m_p \ddot{x} = F_{Magneto}(x, I) \tag{8}$$

- Phase 2: an elastic shock happens when plunger hits the rotating bar. We assume that kinetic energy is conserved as described in Eq. 9, even if for a few milliseconds a part of this one is absorbed by the ball and then given back before the ball is kicked. In theory, speeds of ball, bar and plunger are not similar after the shock, but in reality they are all moving together thanks to the deformation of the ball which ensure that the contact is permanent after the shock as shown in the slow motion picture in Fig. 12.

$$\frac{1}{2} m_p \dot{x_{Init}}^2 = \frac{1}{2} m_p \dot{x_{Final}}^2 + \frac{1}{2} m_B \frac{R_2^2}{R_1^2} \dot{x_{Final}}^2 + \frac{1}{2} J \frac{\dot{x_{Final}}^2}{R_1^2} \tag{9}$$

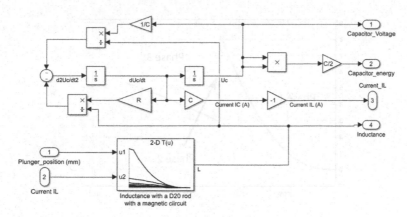

Fig. 9. Electrical part of the coil gun model, including a look-up table obtained with *FEMM 4.2*

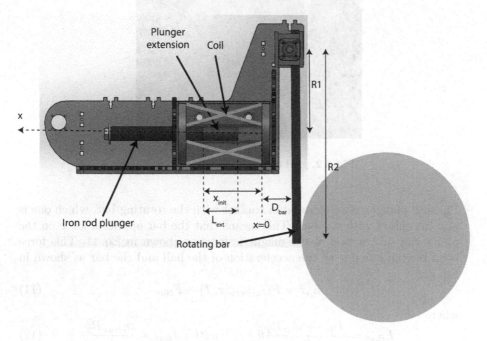

Fig. 10. Simulated kicking system

This leads to a plunger speed just after the shock equal to the $\dot{x}_{final}$ given in Eq. 10.

$$\dot{x}_{Final} = \sqrt{\frac{m_p}{m_p + m_B\frac{R_2^2}{R_1^2} + \frac{J}{R_1^2}}}\,\dot{x}_{Init} \qquad (10)$$

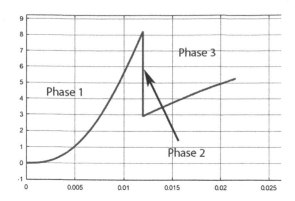

Fig. 11. Plunger speed in $m.s^{-1}$ over the time in s

Fig. 12. Ball deformation after phase 2

– Phase 3: plunger is accelerated in contact with the rotating bar, which one is also in contact with the ball. This means that the bar applies a force on the plunger in subtraction of the magnetic force as shown in Eq. 11. This force is an inertial one due to the acceleration of the ball and the bar as shown in Eq. 12.

$$m_p\ddot{x} = F_{Magneto}(x, I) - F_{Bar} \tag{11}$$

where

$$F_{Bar} = \frac{J_{Bar} + m_B R_2^2}{R_1}\ddot{\theta} \qquad with : J_{Bar} = \frac{m_{Bar} R_2^2}{3} \tag{12}$$

For small θ angles, $\ddot{\theta} \simeq \dfrac{\ddot{x}}{R_1}$, this leads to:

$$\frac{m_p R_1^2 + J + m_B R_2^2}{R_1^2}\ddot{x} = F_{Magneto}(x, I) \tag{13}$$

This mechanical model is implemented with Matlab Simulink using discrete blocks and switches for simulating the different phases of the movement (Fig. 13).

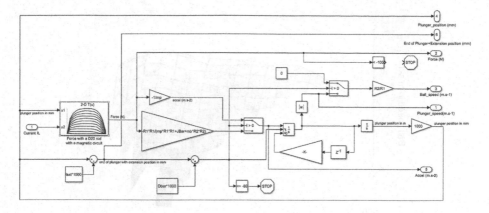

Fig. 13. Mechanical part of the coil gun model

4 Indirect Coil Gun Simulation Results

The indirect coil gun system presented before and used in robots at the RoboCup has been simulated using Matlab Simulink. Even if the mechanical structure and the electromagnetic properties of the kicking system have been completely defined as in Fig. 10, there are 2 remaining degrees of freedom in order to optimize its power: the initial position x_{init} of the plunger, and the length L_{ext} of the non-magnetic extension of the plunger.

In order to compare results with other previous studies, the kicking system simulated is Tech United Team one described in [6]. Parameters of the model are the following ones:

- Distance from rotating bar axis to plunger touch point: $R_1 = 13$ cm
- Distance from rotating bar axis to ball touch point: $R_2 = 24$ cm
- Coil length: $L_{Coil} = 11.5$ cm
- Coil number of turns: $N_{Coil} = 1050$ turns
- Plunger iron rod diameter: $D_{Plunger} = 25$ mm
- Plunger iron rod length: $L_{Plunger} = 11.5$ cm
- Plunger iron rod mass: $m_{Plunger} = 690$ g
- Plunger extension diameter: $D_{Ext} = 18$ mm
- Plunger extension length: L_{Ext} cm
- Plunger extension mass: $m_{Ext} = 0.68 * L_{Ext}$ (in m)
- Distance from coil to rotating bar: $D_{Bar} = 4$ cm
- Vertical bar mass: $m_{Bar} = 80$ g
- Ball mass: $m_{Ball} = 450$ g
- Capacitor value: 4700 uF
- Capacitor charge voltage: 450 V
- Coil resistance: 2.5 Ω

Considering these parameters, we can notice that if $L_{ext} < x_{init} + D_{Bar}$, the plunger with its extension is not in contact with the vertical bar at the beginning

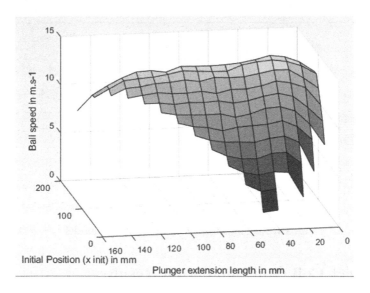

Fig. 14. Impact of initial plunger position and plunger extension length on the ball kicking speed

of the move, and consequently this one will be divided in 3 phases. In the limit case where $L_{ext} = x_{init} + D_{Bar}$, the move will have only on phase: the third one with the plunger in contact with the vertical bar from the start.

In order to find the best set-up corresponding to the highest ball speed, the kicking system has been simulated for different values of x_{init} and L_{ext} chosen as: $x_{init} \in [0; 12\,\text{cm}]$ and $L_{ext} \in [0; x_{init} + D_{Bar}]$.

Results are presented on Fig. 14. The best configuration is to have a plunger initial position $x_{init} = 120\,\text{mm}$, and a plunger extension length $L_{ext} = 30\,\text{mm}$, leading to a ball speed of $v_{Ball} = 14.46\,\text{m.s}^{-1}$. This means that the plunger must be nearly outside the coil at the start and have a short extension of 30 mm only. In this optimal configuration, the movement is a three phase one, with an elastic shock.

4.1 Comparison with Previous Experimental Results

In [6], Tech United Team use the same indirect coil gun in another configuration, using a plunger non magnetic extension always connected to the rotating bar. Their case corresponds to $x_{init} = 110\,\text{mm}$ with a plunger extension length $L_{ext} = 150\,\text{mm}$. Measured ball speed at full switch duty cycle is 11.2 m ([6] in page 1664), compared with $11.1\,\text{m.s}^{-1}$ obtained by our simulation.

Even if the comparison with external samples is too limited, this shows that our model fits very well a real behaviour. It is interesting to note that without changing the mechanical and electromagnetic structure of the coil gun, our optimization leads to a ball speed of $14.46\,\text{m.s}^{-1}$. This speed is 30% higher than the

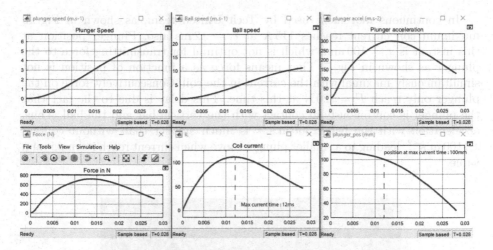

Fig. 15. Simulation using Tech United [6] one phase configuration

obtained speed, corresponding to 70% more energy transmitted using a 3 phases move.

This can be explained comparing the simulation results. In the optimal case, as shown in Fig. 16 maximum coil current reaches 115 A at $t = 12$ ms. Plunger position at this instant is $x = 75$ mm optimal for transmitting force to the plunger as shown in Fig. 7. That means force as a function of position is maximal simultaneously with the current in the coil, leading to an optimal force on the plunger, reaching $F = 850$ N.

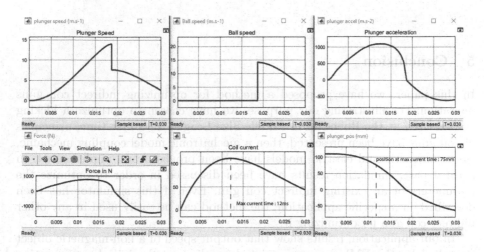

Fig. 16. Simulation using the optimal three phases configuration

In continuous movement used by Tech United team, as shown in Fig. 15 maximum coil current reaches 115 A at $t = 12$ ms also. Plunger position at this instant is $x = 100$ mm, which is not optimal for transmitting force to the plunger as shown in Fig. 7. That means force as a function of position is not simultaneously maximal with the current in the coil. Consequently, force on the plunger only reach $F = 720$ N at this time. This delay is due to the fact that the plunger is continuously in contact with the vertical bar and the ball. Thus, acceleration with the ball $\simeq 300$ m.s^{-2} is much smaller than without contact $\simeq 1100$ m.s^{-2}, leading to a smaller plunger move when current reach its maximum value.

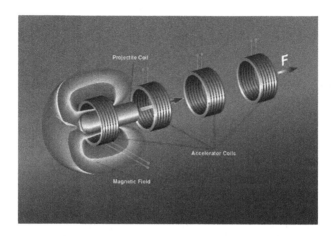

Fig. 17. 3D diagram of a system with multiple coils [3]

5   Conclusion

In this paper, we have proposed a method for optimizing indirect coil guns operation. For illustrating our purpose, we have chosen to optimize a kicking system used at the RoboCup in Middle Size League. In a first time, principles of coil guns have been presented, then a mechatronic model coupling mechanic, electromagnetic and electric models have been proposed and implemented. In a third part, simulation results have been discussed in order to optimize the parameters of an existing indirect coil gun. Even if this simulator has been described on a specific application, the method can be easily used in any other indirect coil gun for optimizing it.

In our application, results show that output speed of a non-magnetic object propelled by the EML can vary a lot depending on the initial configuration of the iron plunger, and depending on the size of its non-magnetic extension. Optimal results are obtained with a three phase propulsion, including an elastic shock. However, this result rely on the assumption that deformation of the non-magnetic object ensures a permanent contact after the shock. This is a strong hypothesis, but easily true when the projectile is deformable. Moreover, in case of a non-deformable contact, the non-magnetic object would have to be very resistant to the very important instantaneous acceleration during the shock.

In a further work, the structure of our coil gun will be optimized dividing the coil in several smaller coils activated sequentially. For example, scenarios using 2, 3 or 4 coils (each one having a half, a third or a quarter of the total turns of the initial coil), triggered sequentially by software or using a position sensor instead of a single coil as shown in Fig. 17 will be evaluated as in [2,7]. This will lead to have successively a maximum current on each coil when the rod is optimally placed in the coil, leading to a increased projectile speed.

References

1. Abdo, T.M., Elrefai, A.L., Adly, A.A., Mahgoub, O.A.: Performance analysis of coil-gun electromagnetic launcher using a finite element coupled model. In: 2016 Eighteenth International Middle East Power Systems Conference (MEPCON), pp. 506–511, December 2016. https://doi.org/10.1109/MEPCON.2016.7836938
2. Bencheikh, Y., Ouazir, Y., Ibtiouen, R.: Analysis of capacitively driven electromagnetic coil guns. In: The XIX International Conference on Electrical Machines - ICEM 2010, pp. 1–5, September 2010. https://doi.org/10.1109/ICELMACH.2010.5608023
3. Kang, Y.: Conceptual diagram of coilgun system, July 2008
4. Lequesne, B.P.: Finite-element analysis of a constant-force solenoid for fluid flow control. IEEE Trans. Ind. Appl. **24**(4), 574–581 (1988). https://doi.org/10.1109/28.6107
5. Meessen, K.J., Paulides, J.J.H., Lomonova, E.A.: Analysis and design of a slotless tubular permanent magnet actuator for high acceleration applications. J. Appl. Phys. **105**(7), 07F110 (2009). https://doi.org/10.1063/1.3072773
6. Meessen, K.J., Paulides, J.J.H., Lomonova, E.A.: A football kicking high speed actuator for a mobile robotic application. In: IECON 2010 - 36th Annual Conference on IEEE Industrial Electronics Society, pp. 1659–1664, November 2010. https://doi.org/10.1109/IECON.2010.5675433
7. Williamson, S., Horne, C.D., Haugh, D.C.: Design of pulsed coil-guns. IEEE Trans. Magn. **31**(1), 516–521 (1995). https://doi.org/10.1109/20.364639

A Review of Robot Rescue Simulation Platforms for Robotics Education

Josie Hughes[1](✉) ⓘ, Masaru Shimizu[2] ⓘ, and Arnoud Visser[3] ⓘ

[1] Downing College, Cambridge University, Cambridge, UK
jaeh2@cam.ac.uk
[2] School of Engineering, Chukyo University, Nagoya, Japan
[3] Intelligent Robotics Lab, Universiteit van Amsterdam,
Amsterdam, The Netherlands
https://github.com/IntelligentRoboticsLab/Joint-Rescue-Forces/wiki/
RoboCup-2019

Abstract. This review explores a natural learning curve which gives an appropriate RoboCup Rescue challenge at the right age. Children who got involved in the age group 14+ should continue their learning experience until they reach graduate level. To reduce the cost of such a learning experience, simulation is an attractive option in a large part of the world. The realism of the simulations and challenges should increase step-by-step, which are supported by more powerful but also more complex interfaces at each level/age-group. The result is a natural learning curve which allows for life-long learning. In this paper, we detail the requirements for such a platform and review a number of different simulation platforms and accompanying interfaces focusing on suitability for use for education rescue robotics. Resulting from this review of simulation platforms, a case-study of an example 'game field' rescue simulation platform suitable for students at different points along the learning curve.

Keywords: Educational kit · Search and rescue · Simulation

1 Introduction

Robot rescue is seen as a grand challenge for intelligent systems [13]. The mission of the urban search and rescue (USAR) robot competitions is to increase awareness of the challenges involved in search and rescue applications and to provide an objective evaluation of robotic implementations [23]. Rescue competitions have been a key part of the RoboCup Competition, and Rescue Simulation Leagues have been introduced from 2000 [2]. Simulation of rescue scenarios enables a more concerted focus on multi-agent collaboration, sensing, and mapping.

Although primarily viewed as a research activity, rescue robot simulation has also got the potential to make a significant impact to robotics education, and rolling such activity out could significantly benefit both the research community and education [7,22]. Rescue simulation provides a means of teaching

© Springer Nature Switzerland AG 2019
S. Chalup et al. (Eds.): RoboCup 2019, LNAI 11531, pp. 86–98, 2019.
https://doi.org/10.1007/978-3-030-35699-6_7

key robotics and computer science principles in an engaging and meaningful way, while requiring minimal hardware development [8,11]. There has been the development of previous rescues robot platforms, most notably CoSpace Rescue Simulation, which has formed part of the RoboCup Junior Competition. In this robot rescue platform, robots autonomously navigate a small indoor environment with infrared sensors [11]. This replicates the RoboCup Rescue Virtual Robot competition, users can simulate multiple agents, whose capabilities closely mirror those of real robots [2]. The simulated environment models both indoor (building, factory) and outdoor environment (street) that have partially collapsed due to an earthquake [28]. The indoor map includes a maze of walls, doors, different floors, overturned furniture, and problematic rubble which provide various tests for robot navigation, communication, and mapping capabilities [25](See Fig. 1). The victims are distributed throughout the environment and the mission for the robots and its operators is to find victims, determine their location in its global map while each robot stays near a victim for further assistance [29].

Fig. 1. Example of indoor environments with different types of smoke (Courtesy RoboCup Rescue Simulation Technical Committee [28]).

There is a need for a rescue simulation platform which bridges education to research, specifically targeted at older secondary students (14+) to undergraduate university students [4]. This requires a platform which has a low barrier to entry to allow wide-scale uptake from schools while also providing the scope to explore the more interesting and challenging concepts which Rescue Simulation such as navigation and sensing.

In this paper, we summarize the requirements for a rescue based education simulation platform, review a number of different simulation platforms and associated interfaces, and provide some initial proof-of-concept platforms and approaches.

2   Current Challenge

Robotics has been demonstrated to be an excellent tool for teaching computer science and engineering and also exciting and engaging students [27]. However, obtaining suitably robust robots or robot kits can require significant financial

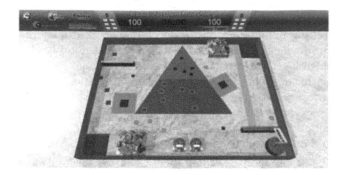

Fig. 2. A simple CoSpace world in the RoboCup Junior Rescue Simulation competition (Courtesy RoboCup Junior Technical Committee).

outlay by a school, and can also demand a substantial time commitment from already busy teachers who need to become confident using the robot systems.

Yet, the current challenge is based on simple robots with a limited sensor suite (see Fig. 2), which makes it difficult to continue the learning experience with more advanced topics as computer vision, path-planning and simultaneous localization and mapping problem (SLAM). These are topics one would expect at the undergraduate level [19].

3   Requirements and Methods

To evaluate the suitability and potential of different simulation environments and interface, it is first necessary to define the requirements from both an education standpoint and a research perspective. From these requirements, metrics by which the different simulation platforms can be evaluated and can be determined.

3.1   Requirements

- Free access to the software such that it is fully accessible to students to use, and, not a high requirement for high-performance computation facilities.
- Ease of install such that installation does not become a barrier to entry.
- Interface that is intuitive to use.
- Scope in the platform such that it can be used to underpin robotics teaching from fundamentals to higher complexity to provide scope for students to explore and test.
- A pathway that allows an easy transition to research-based platforms after use of the focused educational platform.

Following the defined requirements, we compared a number of free open source 3D robot simulators. In particular, the simulators Gazebo and Webots are considered, which both have different advantages and disadvantages.

4   Analysis of Simulation Platforms

In this section, we present an analysis of two different simulation environments and three associated interfaces. We provide a quantitative and qualitative assessment of the simulation environments which tie into the metrics and requirements provided in the previous section.

4.1   Gazebo and Associated Interfaces

Gazebo is the simulation environment integrated in Robot Operating System (ROS), although it was originally developed for the Player-Stage environment [14]. Gazebo development boosted when it was selected as the simulation environment for the DARPA Robotics Virtual Challenge (VRC) [1]. Although the aim of the VRC is also to rescue people, the fundamental difference between RoboCup Rescue and the DRC/VRC is the breadth of capabilities required of the robots [2].

In 2016 Gazebo was selected as the simulation environment for the RoboCup Rescue Virtual Robot competition [24]. Previously, the RoboCup Rescue Virtual Robot competition was based on a simulation environment which was based on Gamebots on top of the Unreal Engine [12]. This simulation environment was called USARSim [3], which at the end also provided a ROS-interface [16]. Because also a USARSim interface in Gazebo was created [24], both backward and forward compatibility was guaranteed.

The main advantage of Gazebo is that it actively maintained by the Open Source Robotics Foundation[1], which allows a variety of robots and environments to be simulated. To give an example of the diversity of possible environment; Gazebo was recently used as the simulation platform for the DARPA Subterrain Challenge[2], the RoboNation maritime Virtual RobotX competition[3] and NASA's Space Robotics Challenge [10]. The tight coupling with Robot Operating System (ROS) allows the usage of state-of-the-art ROS modules directly to the robots, simulated or real [15]. Yet, those state-of-the-art modules requires a deep understanding of robotics; an experience that has to build up at the undergraduate and graduate level [6]. An interface has been developed to allow Scratch, a GUI based programming language typically used in schools, to be used to control and interface with ROS topics[4]. This has the potential to provide a far easier and more intuitive interface to ROS and Gazebo.

4.2   Webots and Associated Interfaces

Webots is a simulation environment with a long history [18]. From the beginning, the environment was meant for both education and research. Webots was

---

[1] https://www.openrobotics.org/.
[2] https://www.subtchallenge.world/.
[3] https://robotx.org/index.php/about/about-virtual-robotx.
[4] http://wiki.ros.org/scratch.

Table 1. A comparison of the different interfaces to Webots.

	Blockly	Matlab Interface	Python Interface
Ease of Install	Easy	Easy but many toolboxes	Several 'easy' ways
Free/Cost/Open source	Free	Complimentary for RoboCup (Junior) teams	Open source
GUI/Interface			
Suitability for Age <14	Yes	-	-
Suitability for Age 14–18	-	Yes	-
Suitability for Age 18+	-	-	Yes
CV/ML Possible	No	Integrated CV and ML Toolboxes	Interface with OpenCV and ML Libraries
SLAM/Localisation	None	Integrated Robotics System Toolbox	Possible [21]
Sensory Data	None	Integrated Sensor Fusion and Tracking Toolbox	Possible but not standardized
Existing Support/ Online Resources	Forum	Extensive	Community
Level of Support Provided	Minimal	Dedicated	Fragmented

designed as a sensor-based simulator for mobile robotics [17], which allows transferring the behavior developed in simulation to be transferred to a real robot, due to the realistic responses of the IR proximity-sensors and a particular vision sensor, the EDI artificial retina.

Recently, Webots has become free open source software, released under the terms of the Apache 2.0 license, which makes it fulfill one of the requirements to be used at high-schools world-wide. In addition, the professional support of the Cyberbotics Ltd. has made installation easy and reliable on Windows, Linux and MacOS platforms. In addition, Olivier Michel, the founder of Cyberbotics, has initiated a WikiBook, which was further developed by Fabien Rohrer and Nicolas Heiniger. The WikiBook *Cyberbotics' Robot Curriculum*[5] contains beginner, novice, intermediate and advanced levels (Table 2).

The interface of Webots is intuitive to use [9]. At the beginner level, BotStudio is used as an interface, which teaches the students the concept of an automaton. At the novice level, this is used to create simple behaviors as line following. On the intermediate level, several behavioral modules are combined,

---

[5] https://en.wikibooks.org/wiki/Cyberbotics'_Robot_Curriculum.

to the level of a full subsumption architecture [5]. At this level, also, the concept of image processing is introduced. On an advanced level, one can think of pattern recognition and simultaneous localization and mapping problem (SLAM) [26]. At the advanced level, one no longer works in the BotStudio, but directly programs the robot in a programming language as C (or C++, Python, Java, Matlab).

A number of third parties have created graphical interfaces to the simulator. For the younger age groups, Blockly[6] appears to be the most suitable as it provides a Scratch[7] like environment while also allowing the potential for reasonable levels of complexity.

4.3   Comparison Between Webots and Gazebo

A comparison can be made between the simulation environments provided by Webots and Gazebo. This is provided in Table 2. This demonstrates how the scope and support of Gazebo are extensive in comparison to Webots. However, the windows compatibility and previously use in educational platforms makes Webots more suited for younger students.

Table 2. Comparison between different simulation environments: Webots and Gazebo

Simulation Platform	Gazebo	Webots
Physics Engine	ODE, Bullet, Simbody, and DART	ODE: Open Dynamics Engine
Realism	Advanced 3D Graphics	3D Graphics
Sensory Modelling	Sensors and Noise	Some Sensors, lower controllability
Windows/Linux	Linux	Windows/Linux
Gamification	Can be implemented	Can be implemented
Open-Source	Open Source	Free, Open Source
Existing Education Applications	Limited	Extensive, many platforms
Long Term Support	Well-established Online Support	Some Support & many examples

5   Case Studies: Prototype Platforms

5.1   Gamification in Gazebo

One of the smart tricks to enhance the involvement of students in the current design of the CoSpace challenge [8] is that the scoreboard is integrated into the

---

[6] https://developers.google.com/blockly/.
[7] https://scratch.mit.edu/.

environment, which increases the suspense and directly gives feedback on the progress. In principle, this sort of integration is also possible in Gazebo, yet it had to be demonstrated, which is done in this case study. A Gazebo environment has been developed, which recreates many of the elements which can be found in a CoSpace arena (see Fig. 3).

Gazebo supports a variety of research robots, such as the PR2 and the Atlas robot [1], but has no model for the small direct-drive robots typically used in education. Because the size of the robot directly has an influence on the design of the challenges (both objects and obstacles), a new model of a small direct-drive robot was created for this challenge. This robot not only has the size, but also the sensor suite typically used in education (see Fig. 4).

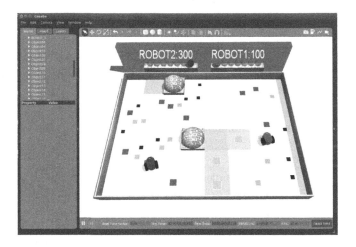

Fig. 3. The creation of a simple CoSpace world in the Gazebo environment.

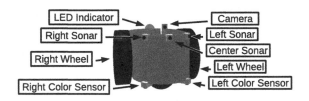

Fig. 4. The Robot functionality.

So, to recreate the important elements which define the interaction with the world in a CoSpace-like challenge the following functionality had to be added to Gazebo:

1. Two small direct-drive robots, each with an own color.
2. The sensor suite which can be expected on such small robot: a webcam (Fig. 5), three distance sensors and two color sensors.

3. Controllable LEDs to indicate the status of the robot.
4. 2D objects which indicate the location of victims (and disappear when driven over).
5. A scoreboard which indicates how many victims are picked up by team Red and Blue.
6. A game manager who implements the rule of the game, such as creating victims on new (random) locations once they're picked up.

A sensor which is not part of the current CoSpace-like challenge, but which could facilitate an interesting challenge for the age 14–18, is the webcam mounted on the simulated robot (see Fig. 5).

Fig. 5. A view image from the webcam on the robot.

The camera feed allows introducing Computer Vision and Pattern Recognition to those students. An example of such an assignment would be the recognition of a few landmarks on the walls by combining a simple artificial neural network with a backpropagation algorithm.

The result is a world which resembles one of the CoSpace worlds, which can now be controlled with standard ROS-commands as cmd_vel(See Fig. 6).

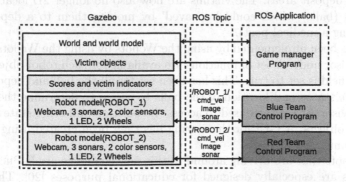

Fig. 6. A connection diagram between the robot models and the team control programs.

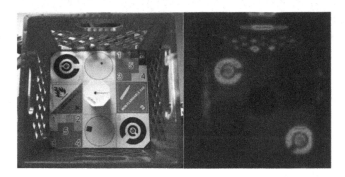

Fig. 7. The detection of thermal activity in a standard test crate (Courtesy RoboCup Rescue Technical Committee).

This challenge can be easily extended to more advanced challenges in the future. One of the challenges which seems to be on an appropriate level for undergraduates (and in the spirit of the RoboCup Rescue Virtual Robot competition) is the virtual equivalent of the perception tasks as defined in the RoboCup Rapid Manufacturing Challenge, such as visual/thermal activity, motion, color, and Hazmat tests (see Fig. 7).

5.2   An Advanced Challenge in Webots

A prototype environment has been created based upon the Webots simulation platform. An environment has been created using Python to create a rescue scenario which includes gamification. Within this environment, two E-Puck robots are active (one for each team), as illustrated in Fig. 8. The environment is more complicated than the current CoSpace challenge because there are now also crate based obstacles (which could be pushed out of the way, but also intentionally or accidentally pushed to a location where it blocks the route (of the other team) to the ball deposit area). The victims are now also no longer 2D locations, but 3D objects (balls) which could be 'saved' by moving them to a deposit area (representing a medical post).

This has been implemented by using the Webots by using the Webots concept of a supervisor node. A set of functions are available for each robot object whose supervisor field is set to true. This has been set for all the ball and deposit areas to allow the status and location of the balls to access to determine the scoring. The Supervisor API is then used to access the position and other state variables of the ball objects. A GUI for the scoring has then been created using Tkinter. This is summarized in Fig. 9.

The robots that are driving around in this new challenge are E-Puck robots. The robots are especially designed for educational purposes [20]. The robots can be controlled with code inside the Webots environment, or controlled by an external program. The same E-Puck Monitor program which can control a real E-Puck via its wifi-interface can also be used to control the simulated robot (see

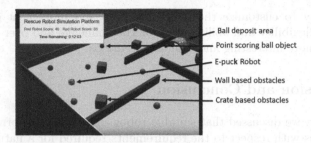

Fig. 8. Webots simulation environment created.

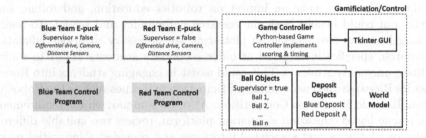

Fig. 9. Summary of the different components to implement the simulation.

Fig. 10). The task for the students is to make autonomous decisions based on the sensor information which is available.

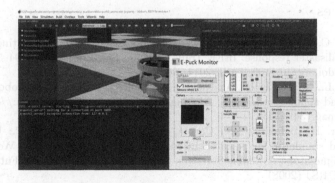

Fig. 10. Connection of the official E-Puck Monitor with Webots.

Going forwards, this platform will be tested with student groups to explore and test how best this meets the requirements. In particular, this process will investigate the level of complexity, to explore if it has a sufficiently low entry barrier, yet lets students explore high-level concepts.

The ability to customize the rescue scenario and implement gamification provides the flexibility and ability to tailor the challenge and over time, create increasingly more interesting and complex scenarios.

6 Discussion and Conclusion

In this review, we discussed that suitable robot simulation platforms for different age groups with respect to the requirements required for a natural learning curve. In particular, we focused on the appropriate platforms for a RoboCup Rescue Challenge for various age groups. The rescue robot simulation has also got the potential to make an impact on robotics education, and rolling such activity out could benefit both the research community and school. To realize the long learning, new simulation platforms are necessary to bridge education to research, specifically targeted at older secondary students (14+) to undergraduate university students. This could assist in engaging students into Rescue Robotics Research and encouraging participation in leagues such as the RoboCup Virtual Robotic Simulation Competition. Also, we summarized the requirements for a rescue based education simulation platform, review two suitable different simulation platforms and associated interfaces and provided some initial proof-of-concept platforms and approaches.

Acknowledgement. This work is funded by RoboCup Federation Support 2019. We like to thank Fatemeh Pahlevan Aghababa, Amirreza Kabiri and Francesco Amigoni for their suggestions.

References

1. Agüero, C.E., et al.: Inside the virtual robotics challenge: simulating real-time robotic disaster response. IEEE Trans. Autom. Sci. Eng. **12**(2), 494–506 (2015). https://doi.org/10.1109/TASE.2014.2368997
2. Akin, H.L., Ito, N., Jacoff, A., Kleiner, A., Pellenz, J., Visser, A.: Robocup rescue robot and simulation leagues. AI Mag. **34**(1), 78–78 (2013). https://doi.org/10.1609/aimag.v34i1.2458
3. Balaguer, B., Balakirsky, S., Carpin, S., Lewis, M., Scrapper, C.: Usarsim: a validated simulator for research in robotics and automation. In: Workshop on Robot Simulators: Available Software, Scientific Applications, and Future Trends at IEEE/RSJ (2008)
4. Blank, D., Meeden, L., Kumar, D.: Python robotics: an environment for exploring robotics beyond legos. In: Proceedings of the 34th SIGCSE technical symposium on Computer Science education (2003). https://doi.org/10.1145/792548.611996
5. Brooks, R.: A robust layered control system for a mobile robot. IEEE J. Rob. Autom. **2**(1), 14–23 (1986). https://doi.org/10.1109/JRA.1986.1087032
6. Crick, C., Jay, G., Osentoski, S., Pitzer, B., Jenkins, O.C.: Rosbridge: ROS for Non-ROS users. In: Christensen, H.I., Khatib, O. (eds.) Robotics Research. STAR, vol. 100, pp. 493–504. Springer, Cham (2017). https://doi.org/10.1007/978-3-319-29363-9_28

7. Eguchi, A.: RoboCupJunior for promoting STEM education, 21st century skills, and technological advancement through robotics competition. Rob. Auton. Syst. **75**, 692–699 (2016). https://doi.org/10.1016/j.robot.2015.05.013

8. Eguchi, A., Shen, J.: Student learning experience through cospace educational robotics: 3d simulation educational robotics tool. In: Cases on 3D Technology Application and Integration in Education, pp. 93–127. IGI Global (2013). https://doi.org/10.4018/978-1-4666-2815-1.ch005

9. Guyot, L., Heiniger, N., Michel, O., Rohrer, F.: Teaching robotics with an open curriculum based on the e-puck robot, simulations and competitions. In: Proceedings of the 2nd International Conference on Robotics in Education, Vienna, Austria (2011). https://www.cyberbotics.com/publications/RiE2011.pdf

10. Hambuchen, K.A., et al.: Nasa's space robotics challenge: advancing robotics for future exploration missions. In: AIAA SPACE and Astronautics Forum and Exposition (2017). https://doi.org/10.2514/6.2017-5120

11. Hughes, J.: Robotic rescue simulation for computing teaching in the UK: a case study. In: 2016 IEEE Global Engineering Education Conference (EDUCON), pp. 1051–1055. IEEE (2016). https://doi.org/10.1109/EDUCON.2016.7474683

12. Kaminka, G.A., Veloso, M.M., Schaffer, S., Sollitto, C., Adobbati, R., Marshall, A.N., Scholer, A., Tejada, S.: Gamebots: a flexible test bed for multiagent team research. Commun. ACM **45**(1), 43–45 (2002). https://doi.org/10.1145/502269.502293

13. Kitano, H., Tadokoro, S.: Robocup rescue: a grand challenge for multiagent and intelligent systems. AI Mag. **22**(1), 39–39 (2001). https://doi.org/10.1609/aimag.v22i1.1542

14. Koenig, N., Howard, A.: Design and use paradigms for gazebo, an open-source multi-robot simulator. In: Proceedings of 2004 IEEE/RSJ International Conference on Intelligent Robots and Systems, 2004 (IROS 2004), vol. 3, pp. 2149–2154. IEEE (2004). https://doi.org/10.1109/IROS.2004.1389727

15. Kohlbrecher, S., Meyer, J., Graber, T., Petersen, K., Klingauf, U., von Stryk, O.: Hector open source modules for autonomous mapping and navigation with rescue robots. In: Behnke, S., Veloso, M., Visser, A., Xiong, R. (eds.) RoboCup 2013. LNCS (LNAI), vol. 8371, pp. 624–631. Springer, Heidelberg (2014). https://doi.org/10.1007/978-3-662-44468-9_58

16. Kootbally, Z., Balakirsky, S., Visser, A.: Enabling codesharing in rescue simulation with USARSim/ROS. In: Behnke, S., Veloso, M., Visser, A., Xiong, R. (eds.) RoboCup 2013. LNCS (LNAI), vol. 8371, pp. 592–599. Springer, Heidelberg (2014). https://doi.org/10.1007/978-3-662-44468-9_54

17. de Meneses, Y.L., Michel, O.: Vision sensors on the webots simulator. In: Heudin, J.-C. (ed.) VW 1998. LNCS (LNAI), vol. 1434, pp. 264–273. Springer, Heidelberg (1998). https://doi.org/10.1007/3-540-68686-X_25

18. Michel, O.: Webots: symbiosis between virtual and real mobile robots. In: Heudin, J.-C. (ed.) VW 1998. LNCS (LNAI), vol. 1434, pp. 254–263. Springer, Heidelberg (1998). https://doi.org/10.1007/3-540-68686-X_24

19. Michieletto, S., Ghidoni, S., Pagello, E., Moro, M., Menegatti, E.: Why teachrobotics using ros? J. Autom. Mob. Rob. Intell. Syst. **8** (2014). https://doi.org/10.14313/JAMRIS_1-2014/8

20. Mondada, F., et al.: The e-puck, a robot designed for education in engineering. In: Proceedings of the 9th Conference on Autonomous Robot Systems and Competitions, vol. 1, pp. 59–65. IPCB: Instituto Politécnico de Castelo Branco (2009). https://repositorio.ipcb.pt/handle/10400.11/2863

21. Sakai, A., Ingram, D., Dinius, J., Chawla, K., Raffin, A., Paques, A.: Python-robotics: a python code collection of robotics algorithms. arXiv:1808.10703 (2018)
22. Sammut, C., Sheh, R., Haber, A., Wicaksono, H.: The robot engineer. In: ILP (Late Breaking Papers), pp. 101–106 (2015). http://ceur-ws.org/Vol-1636/
23. Sheh, R., Schwertfeger, S., Visser, A.: 16 years of robocup rescue. KI - Künstliche Intell. **30**(3), 267–277 (2016). https://doi.org/10.1007/s13218-016-0444-x
24. Shimizu, M., Koenig, N., Visser, A., Takahashi, T.: A realistic robocup rescue simulation based on gazebo. In: Almeida, L., Ji, J., Steinbauer, G., Luke, S. (eds.) RoboCup 2015. LNCS (LNAI), vol. 9513, pp. 331–338. Springer, Cham (2015). https://doi.org/10.1007/978-3-319-29339-4_27
25. Takaya, K., Asai, T., Kroumov, V., Smarandache, F.: Simulation environment for mobile robots testing using ros and gazebo. In: 2016 20th International Conference on System Theory, Control and Computing (ICSTCC), pp. 96–101 (Oct 2016)
26. Thrun, S., Leonard, J.J.: Simultaneous localization and mapping. In: Siciliano, B., Khatib, O. (eds.) Springer handbook of robotics, pp. 871–889. Springer, Heidelberg (2008). https://doi.org/10.1007/978-3-540-30301-5_38
27. Toh, L.P.E., Causo, A., Tzuo, P.W., Chen, I., Yeo, S.H., et al.: A review on the use of robots in education and young children. Educ. Technol. Soc. **19**(2), 148–163 (2016). https://doi.org/10.1111/j.1467-8535.2009.00944.x
28. Visser, A.: A guide to the RoboCup Virtual Rescue worlds. Technical report, IRL-UVA-16-01 - University of Amsterdam (2016). https://staff.fnwi.uva.nl/a.visser/publications/GuideToUSARSimWorlds.pdf
29. Williams, A., Sebastian, B., Ben-Tzvi, P.: Review and analysis of search,extraction, evacuation, and medical field treatment robots. J. Intell. Rob. Syst., 1–18 (2019). https://doi.org/10.1007/s10846-019-00991-6

A Fast and Stable Omnidirectional Walking Engine for the Nao Humanoid Robot

Mohammadreza Kasaei[✉], Nuno Lau, and Artur Pereira

IEETA / DETI, University of Aveiro, 3810-193 Aveiro, Portugal
{mohammadreza,nunolau,artur}@ua.pt

Abstract. This paper proposes a framework designed to generate a closed-loop walking engine for a humanoid robot. In particular, the core of this framework is an abstract dynamics model which is composed of two masses that represent the lower and the upper body of a humanoid robot. Moreover, according to the proposed dynamics model, the low-level controller is formulated as a Linear-Quadratic-Gaussian (LQG) controller that is able to robustly track the desired trajectories. Besides, this framework is fully parametric which allows using an optimization algorithm to find the optimum parameters. To examine the performance of the proposed framework, a set of simulation using a simulated Nao robot in the RoboCup 3D simulation environment has been carried out. Simulation results show that the proposed framework is capable of providing fast and reliable omnidirectional walking. After optimizing the parameters using genetic algorithm (GA), the maximum forward walking velocity that we have achieved was 80.5 cm/s.

Keywords: Humanoid robots · Walking engine ·
Linear-Quadratic-Gaussian (LQG) · Genetic algorithm · Linear
Inverted Pendulum Model (LIPM)

1   Introduction

Developing a fast and reliable walking for a humanoid robot is a complicated subject due to dealing with a naturally unstable system. In particular, humanoid robots are known as hyper Degree of Freedom (DOF) systems which generally have more than 20 DOFs. Humanoid robots can easily adapt to our dynamic environment because of their kinematic similarity with a human. However, developing reliable locomotion is a complex subject that absorbs the attention of researchers. Unlike wheeled robots, humanoid robots can handle real environment limitations like gaps, stairs, uneven terrain, etc. Thus, they can be used in a wide range of applications from helping elderly people to performing dangerous tasks like fire fighting.

Over the past decades, several stable walking engines have been presented and tested on real and simulated robots. Although the performance of robots in

© Springer Nature Switzerland AG 2019
S. Chalup et al. (Eds.): RoboCup 2019, LNAI 11531, pp. 99–111, 2019.
https://doi.org/10.1007/978-3-030-35699-6_8

simulators are not perfectly equal with their performance in the real world, the significant advantage of using realistic simulators instead of real robot experiments is that researchers can perform much experimentation without worrying about mechanical damages on the devices of the robot (e.g., wear and tear).

Recently, the number of researches in this field shows an increasing interest in investigating humanoid locomotion. Studies in this field can be divided into two main groups: *(i) model-based approaches*: these approaches consider a physical template model of the robot, and a walking engine will be designed based on this model and some stability criteria; *(ii) model-free approaches*: researches in this group are biologically inspired and typically focus on generating some rhythmic patterns for the limbs of robot without considering any physical model of the robot.

In this paper, we propose a fully parametric closed-loop walking framework for a simulated soccer humanoid agent. The core of this framework is an extended version of Linear Inverted Pendulum (LIPM) which is one of the well-known walking dynamics models. LIPM considers a restricted dynamics of the COM and represents the dynamics of the robot by a first-order stable dynamics. This framework is developed and successfully tested within the RoboCup 3D simulation environment.

The main contributions of this paper are the following: *(i)* an integrated framework for humanoid walking that incorporates capabilities for walking, optimization and learning; *(ii)* investigating the effect of releasing the height constraint of the COM in LIPM and examining how it can increase the walking speed and also improve the stability; *(iii)* investigating how the torso motion can be used to keep the Zero Momentum Point (ZMP) inside support polygon to provide more stable walking; *(iv)* A Genetic algorithm (GA) is used to find the optimum value for the walking parameters and the optimized walking engine is tested within the RoboCup 3D simulation environment.

The remainder of this paper is organized as follows: Sect. 2 gives an overview of related work. In Sect. 3, firstly, the gait stability criterion is explained, then, an overview of the LIPM is presented, afterward, the effects of releasing the height constraint of the COM and considering the mass of torso are discussed. Section 4 explains the structure of our robust low-level controller. Then, the overall architecture of our framework is presented and explained in Sect. 5. Simulation scenarios, optimization method and the results are presented in Sect. 7. Finally, conclusions and future research are presented in Sect. 8.

2   Related Work

Successful approaches exist in both model-based and model-free biped locomotion groups and each group has its advantages and disadvantages. For instance, although model-free approaches avoid dealing with dynamics model of the system, their structure is composed of several oscillators which have many parameters that should be tuned. Besides, adopting sensory feedback to all the oscillators is a complicated subject. Indeed, tuning the parameters for performing a particular motion is typically based on optimization algorithms which are iterative procedures and need to a large number of tests. In the remainder of this section, we briefly review some approaches of both groups and focus on those which are more related to this paper.

One of the popular ways to develop a model-based walking is using a dynamics model of the robot and the concept of ZMP. ZMP is a point on the ground plane where the ground reaction force acts to compensate gravity and inertia [17]. The fundamental idea of using ZMP as a criterion is that keeping the ZMP within the support polygon guarantee the stability of the robot. Based on this idea, generally, a predefined ZMP trajectory is used to generate a feed-forward walking. Given that the feed-forward approaches are not stable enough due to their sensitivity to the accuracy of the dynamics model, a feedback controller should be used to keep the ZMP inside the supporting polygon. Kajita et al. [5] proposed a walking pattern generator based on LIPM and preview control of ZMP. They conducted a simulation to show the performance of their approach. In this simulation, a simulated robot (HRP-2P) should walk on spiral stairs. They specified the foot placement in advance and based on that the trajectories of the COM were generated. Simulation results showed that the robot could successfully walk on the spiral stairs. Nowadays, their approach is widely used and has been successfully implemented on different humanoid platforms. Although their method has several benefits such as simplicity in implementation, it also has some drawbacks like needing to specify future steps in advance and also requiring more computational power in comparison with simple methods because its use of an optimization method. Another variant of this method has been proposed which used the analytical solution of the ZMP equation to generate the COM trajectories [4,10,16]. This method is sufficient for robots with constrained computation resources.

LIPM assumes motion of the upper body parts are negligible and do not have effects in the overall dynamics of the robot. Although considering this assumption simplifies the walking control problem, it is not an appropriate assumption because the upper body of a humanoid robot has several DOFs that their motions generate momentum around COM. Moreover, controlling this momentum not only causes significant improvements in stability of the robot but also can be used as a push recovery strategy. Therefore, several extended versions of LIPM have been proposed to improve the accuracy of the dynamics model of the robot. Napoleon et al. [11] used two masses inverted pendulum to represent the lower and the upper body of a humanoid robot in their dynamics model and proposed a ZMP feedback controller based on this model. Later, Komura et al. [8] and also Pratt et al. [14] considered angular momentum around COM in their dynamics model and proposed an extended version of LIPM. They conducted several simulations and showed that using their model, the robot was not only able to generate walking but also could regain its stability after applying pushes. Recently, Kasaei et al. [6] extended this model by considering the mass of stance leg to improve the accuracy of the controller. Using this model, they proposed an optimal closed-loop walking engine and showed the performance of their system using walking and push recovery simulation scenarios.

Several model free approaches as possible alternative to generate humanoid locomotion have been proposed. The approaches based on the concept of Central Pattern Generators (CPG) are one of the important categories in this group. Picado et al. [13] used some Partial Fourier Series (PFS) oscillators to generate a forward walk for a simulated humanoid robot and used GA to optimize the parameters of the oscillators. They showed the optimized version of their approach was able to achieve a fast forward walking (51 cm/s). Later, Shahriar et al. [1] extended their approach and developed a walking engine which not only was able to generate faster forward walking but also able to generate stable sidewalk. It should be noted that several hybrid approaches have been proposed [7,9,12] which used the ZMP concept to modify the outputs of the oscillators, consequently providing more stable walking. Some of these approaches, try to find an appropriate way to adapt sensory feedback based on classical control approaches. In some others approaches, using learning algorithms, robots learn how to modify the output of each oscillator to track the reference trajectories and compensate the errors. For instance, in [2], a framework based on neural network has been developed to learn a model-free feedback controller to balance control of a quadruped robot walking on rough terrain.

In most of the proposed walking engines described above, the height of COM was considered to be fixed, moreover, the effects of the motion of the torso were not considered. In the rest of this paper, we propose a closed-loop model based walking framework and show how the motion of torso and changing the height of COM can improve the walking performance.

3   Gait Stability and Dynamics Model

Our proposed framework stays on the model-based group and the core of this framework is an abstract dynamics model of the robot. In this section, firstly, we briefly describe the ZMP as our main criterion for gait stability and then present an overview of LIPM and investigate the effects of changing the height of COM as well as moving the torso.

3.1   ZMP and Gait Stability

Several criteria for analyzing the stability of the robot have been proposed [3,17]. According to the nature of normal human gait which is composed of 80% of single support and 20% of double support [18], most of the proposed criteria focus on the single support phase of walking. In this phase, one foot is in contact with the ground and the other one swings forward. In this work, the concept of ZMP is used as our main criterion to analyze the stability of the robot and is defined using the following equation:

$$p_x = \frac{\sum_{k=1}^{n} m_k x_k (\ddot{z}_k + g) - \sum_{k=1}^{n} m_k z_k \ddot{x}_k}{\sum_{k=1}^{n} m_k (\ddot{z}_k + g)}, \tag{1}$$

where n is the number of masses that are considered in the dynamics model, m_k is the mass of each part, $(x_k, \ddot{x}_k)$, $(\ddot{z}_k, \ddot{z}_k)$ represent the horizontal and vertical position and acceleration of each mass, respectively.

3.2 Dynamics Model

LIPM is one of the well-known dynamics model which is used to generate and analyze the locomotion of robots. This model abstracts the dynamics of the robot using a single mass that is connected to the ground via a massless rod. This model considers an assumption that the mass is restricted to move along a defined horizontal plane. In this model, the motion equation in sagittal and frontal planes are equivalent and independent. Therefore, we derive the equation in the sagittal plane. According to the Eq. 1 and based on LIPM assumptions, the overall dynamics of the robot can be represented using a first-order stable dynamics as follows:

$$\ddot{x}_c = \omega^2 (x_c - p_x), \tag{2}$$

where $\omega = \sqrt{\frac{g+\ddot{z}}{z}}$ represents the natural frequency of the pendulum, x_c and p_x are the positions of COM and ZMP, respectively. According to the assumptions of LIPM, knee joints have to be crouched to keep the COM at a constant height which consumes more energy during walking. In order to generate more energy efficient and also more human-like locomotion, a sinusoidal trajectory is assigned to the vertical motion of COM. The vertical trajectory of COM in this model is as follows:

$$z_c = z_0 + A_z \cos \left(\frac{2\pi}{StepTime} t + \phi \right), \tag{3}$$

where Z_0 is the initial height of COM, A_z, ϕ represent the amplitude and the phase shift of vertical sinusoidal motion of the COM, respectively. It should be mentioned that these parameters can be adjusted using sensory feedback to deal with environmental perturbations. However, the current version of dynamics model is good enough to generate a fast walking but it is not suitable for generating a very fast walking. During a very fast walking, COM accelerates forward and ZMP moves behind the center of gravity (COG), based on this dynamics model, COM should be decelerated to keep the ZMP inside the support polygon. This deceleration causes the ZMP to move to the boundary of the support foot and consequently, the robot starts to roll over. One of the possible approaches to regain ZMP inside the support foot is using the torso movement for compensating the ZMP error and prevent falling. Although it is possible to modify the dynamics model by adding another mass as a torso, this modification changes our linear dynamics into a nonlinear dynamics model which does not have an analytical solution generally and should be solved numerically. According to the biomechanical analysis of human walking and running, torso moves in a sinusoidal form and the amplitude of its movement depends on some parameters like walking speed, the amplitude of changing the height of COM, etc. To consider the effect of torso motion based on biomechanical analysis, a mass with

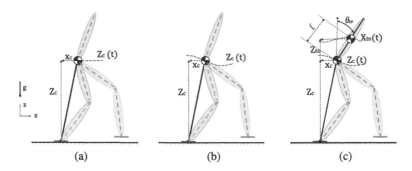

Fig. 1. Schematics of the dynamics models: (a) LIPM; (b) LIPM with vertical motion of COM; (c) LIPM with vertical motion of COM and torso motion.

a sinusoidal movement is added to our dynamics model. Therefore, the motion equation of this model can be obtained using Eq. (1) as follows:

$$\ddot{x}_c = \mu(x_c + \frac{\alpha l}{1 + \alpha}\theta_{to} - p_x) - \frac{\alpha \beta l}{1 + \alpha \beta}\ddot{\theta}_{to}$$

$$\alpha = \frac{m_{to}}{m_c}, \quad \beta = \frac{z_{to}}{z_c}, \quad \mu = \frac{1 + \alpha}{1 + \alpha \beta}\omega^2, \quad x_{to} = x_c + l\theta_{to} \tag{4}$$

where x_{to} is the position of torso, l, θ_{to} represent the torso length and torso angle, m_{to}, m_c, z_{to}, z_c are the masses and heights of torso and lower body, respectively. Equation 4 can be represented as a linear state space system as follows:

$$\dot{x} = Ax + Bu$$

$$\begin{bmatrix} \dot{x}_c \\ \ddot{x}_c \\ \dot{\theta}_{to} \\ \ddot{\theta}_{to} \end{bmatrix} = \begin{bmatrix} 0 & 1 & 0 & 0 \\ \mu & 0 & \frac{\mu \alpha l}{1 + \alpha} & 0 \\ 0 & 0 & 0 & 1 \\ 0 & 0 & 0 & 0 \end{bmatrix} \begin{bmatrix} x_c \\ \dot{x}_c \\ \theta_{to} \\ \dot{\theta}_{to} \end{bmatrix} + \begin{bmatrix} 0 & 0 \\ -\mu & \frac{-\alpha \beta l}{1 + \alpha \beta} \\ 0 & 0 \\ 0 & 1 \end{bmatrix} \begin{bmatrix} p_x \\ \ddot{\theta}_{to} \end{bmatrix}. \tag{5}$$

In the next section of this paper, we will explain how this state space system can be used to design an optimal low-level controller to generate a very fast and stable walking.

4   Low Level Controller

In this section, an optimal state-feedback controller will be designed based on the obtained state space system in the previous section. This controller is a Linear-Quadratic-Gaussian (LQG) controller which is robust against process disturbances and also measurement noise.

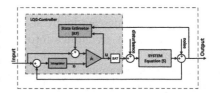

Fig. 2. Block diagram of the proposed low-level controller.

The overall architecture of this controller is depicted in Fig. 2. As is shown in this figure, the controller is composed of an integrator for eliminating steady-state error and also two other fundamental modules which are the state estimator and the optimal controller gain that will be described in the following of this section.

4.1 State Estimator

Typically measurements are affected by noise that occur because of modeling errors and sensors noise. In particular, to design a controller which could be able to robustly track the reference trajectories in presence of uncertainties, firstly, the states of the system should be estimated based on the control inputs and the observations. In this paper, we assume that the states of the system are observable but the observations are noisy. According to this assumption and also linearity of the dynamics system (Eq. 5), a Kalman Filter (KF) was used to estimate the states of the system. Indeed, KF is a recursive filter that can estimate the

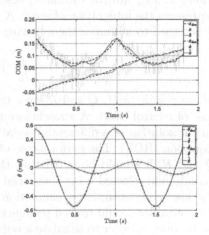

Fig. 3. Simulation results of the examining the state estimator performance.

states of a linear dynamics system in the presence of noise. To examine the performance of the KF, we carried out a simulation by modeling the observations as a stochastic process by applying two independent Gaussian noises to the measured states. The simulation results are depicted in Fig. 3. As is shown, KF was be able to estimate the states of the system.

4.2 Optimal Controller Gain

Based on the estimation of the states and also the integration of error which are available in each control cycle, we formulate the control problem as optimal control. Indeed, this controller finds a control law for our system based on a cost

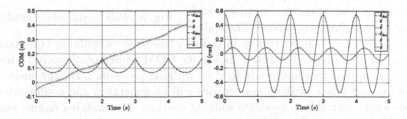

Fig. 4. Simulation results of examining the controller performance in presence of noises.

function which is a function of state and control variables. The optimal control law for the tracking is designed as follows:

$$u = -K \begin{bmatrix} \tilde{x} - x_{des} \\ x_i \end{bmatrix}, \tag{6}$$

where $\tilde{x}$, x_{des} are the estimated states and the desired states, respectively. x_i represents the integration of error, K is the optimal gain of the controller which is designed to minimize the following cost function:

$$J(u) = \int_0^\infty \{z^\mathsf{T} Q z + u^\mathsf{T} R u\} dt, \tag{7}$$

where $z = [\tilde{x} \quad x_i]^\mathsf{T}$, Q and R are a trade-off between tracking performance and cost of control effort. A straightforward solution exists for finding the K based on the solution of a differential equation which is called the Riccati Differential Equation (RDE). The performance of the controller is sensitive to the choice of Q and R. It should be noted that they are positive-semidefinite and positive-definite and selected using some trial and error. To examine the performance of the low-level controller, a simulation has been carried out. In this simulation, the controller should track a reference trajectory in the presence of noise. In this simulation, in order to simulate a noisy situation, independent zero-mean Gaussian noises are added to the measurements. The simulation results are depicted in Fig. 4. The results show that the controller is able to robustly track the reference even in a noisy situation. In the next section, we will explain how this low-level controller can be used to generate stable walking.

5   Walk Engine

In this section, based on the presented dynamics model and the low-level controller in previous sections, a walking engine will be designed. Walking is a periodic motion which is composed of four phases: Idle, Initialize, Single Support, Double Support. In the Idle phase, the robot is loading the initial parameters from its database and standing in place and waiting for a walking command. The walk-

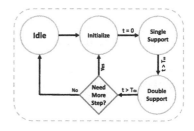

Fig. 5. Walk engine state machine.

ing phase will be changed to the initialize phase once a walking command is received. In this phase, the robot moves its COM from initial position to the first single support foot and ready to start walking procedure. During single and double support phase walking trajectories will be generated and commanded to the low-level controller to generate walking motion. This walking engine can be modeled by a state machine which has four distinct states. In this state machine, each state has a specific duration and a timer is used to trigger state transitions. The architecture of this state machine is depicted in Fig. 5.

6 Reference Trajectories Planner

Generally, a walking reference trajectories planner is composed of five sub planners which are connected together in a hierarchical manner. The first level of this hierarchy is foot step planner which generates a set of foot positions based on given step information, terrain information and some predefined constraints (e.g., maximum and minimum of the step length, step width, the distance between feet, etc.). The second planner is the ZMP planner that uses the planned foot step information to generate the ZMP reference trajectories. In our target framework, our ZMP reference planner is formulated as follows:

$$r_{zmp} = \begin{cases} \begin{cases} f_{i,x} \\ f_{i,y} \end{cases} & 0 \le t < T_{ss} \\ \begin{cases} f_{i,x} + \frac{L_{sx} \times (t - T_{ss})}{T_{ds}} \\ f_{i,y} + \frac{L_{sy} \times (t - T_{ss})}{T_{ds}} \end{cases} & T_{ss} \le t < T_{ds} \end{cases}, \quad (8)$$

where $f_i = [f_{i,x} \quad f_{i,y}]$ are the planned footsteps on a 2D surface ($i \in \mathbb{N}$), L_{sx} and L_{sy} represent step length and step width, T_{ss}, T_{ds} are the single support duration and double support duration, respectively. t is the time which will be reset at the end of each step ($t \ge T_{ss} + T_{ds}$). The third planner is the swing leg planner which generates the swing leg trajectory using a cubic spline function. This planner uses three control points that are the position of swing leg at the beginning of the step, the next footstep position and a point between them with a predefined height (Z_{swing}). The fourth planner is the global sinusoidal planner which generates three sinusoidal trajectories for the height of COM, the torso angles and the arm positions. The fifth planner is the COM planner which uses the planned ZMP trajectories and the analytical solution of the LIPM to plan the COM trajectories. This planner is formulated as follows:

$$x(t) = r_{zmp_x} + \frac{(r_{zmp_x} - x_f)\sinh(\omega(t - t_0)) + (x_0 - r_{zmp_x})\sinh(\omega(t - t_f))}{\sinh(\omega(t_0 - t_f))}, \quad (9)$$

where r_{zmp_x} represents the current ZMP position, t_0, t_f, x_0, x_f are the times and corresponding positions of the COM at the beginning and at the end of a step, respectively. In this work, T_{ds} is considered to be zero, it means ZMP transits to the next step at the end of each step instantaneously [6]. Moreover, x_f is assumed to be in the middle of current support foot and next support foot ($\frac{f_i + f_{i+1}}{2}$).

7 Result

To validate the performance of our proposed walking engine, a simulation scenario is designed which focused on omnidirectional walking. This simulation scenario has been set up using the RoboCup 3D simulation league simulator

108   M. Kasaei et al.

which is based on SimSpark[1] multi-agent simulator. This simulator simulates rigid body dynamics using the Open Dynamics Engine (ODE) and provides a realistic simulation. In this simulator, the physics simulation is updated every 0.02 s. The overall architecture of this simulation setup is depicted in Fig. 6.

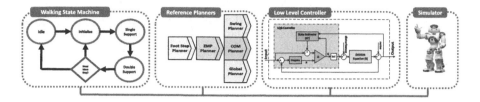

Fig. 6. Overall architecture of the proposed walking engine.

The omnidirectional walking scenario is focused on examining the ability of the proposed walking engine to provide a robust omnidirectional walking. In this simulation, a simulated robot should turn right while walking diagonally (forward and sideward simultaneously) without falling. Indeed, the robot starts from the stop state and should smoothly increase the walking speed to reach its target velocity. It should be noted that in this simulation, the walking parameters have been tuned using some trial and error. Four snapshots of this experiment are shown in Fig. 7. A video of this simulation is available online at: www.dropbox.com/s/z99xpncxscje97z/OmniWalk.mkv?dl=0.

Fig. 7. Four snapshots of the omnidirectional walking simulation scenario.

Fig. 8. Four snapshots of the maximum walking speed simulation scenario.

---

[1]   http://simspark.sourceforge.net/.

7.1 Maximum Walking Speed

One of the major metrics of a walking engine is the maximum velocity of the forward walking. To evaluate this metric, another simulation scenario has been set up. In this simulation, the robot starts from a specific point that is 10 m far from the midline of the field. The robot should walk toward this line as fast as possible without deviating to the sides or being unstable. After several simulations, the best hand-tuned velocity that was achieved was 53 cm/s. As described in previous sections, the proposed framework is fully parametric which allows using optimization algorithms to find the optimum parameter. Therefore, in order to find the maximum forward walking speed, an optimization based on the GA algorithm has been set up to find the optimum values of the parameters. In this optimization, 8 parameters of the framework have been selected to be optimized that were expected step movement (x, y, θ) , the maximum height of swing leg (Z_{swing}), the step duration (T_{ss}), the constant torso inclination TI_{to}, amplitudes of the center of mass movement (A_z) and also torso movement (A_{to}). In this scenario, the simulated robot is allowed to walk forward during 10 s, and a simple but efficient fitness function f with parameters ϕ is defined as:

$$f(\phi) = -|\varDelta X| + |\varDelta Y| + \epsilon \tag{10}$$

where $\varDelta X$ is the total distance covered in X-axis, $\varDelta Y$ represents the deviated distance in the Y-axis, ϵ is zero if the simulated robot did not fall and 100 otherwise. Based on this fitness function, the robot is rewarded for moving forward toward the midline of the filed and it is penalized for deviating or falling. Each iteration has been repeated three times and the average of the fitness has been used.

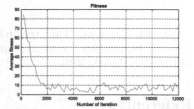

Fig. 9. Evolution of the fitness.

After around 12000 iterations of optimization, GA improved the robot walking speed and reached a maximum stable velocity of 80.5 cm/s which is 54% faster than the best hand-tuned solution. Our optimized walking is faster than the agents in [1,7,13,15]. The average fitness value of different parameters setting is depicted in Fig. 8. Four snapshots of this simulation are shown in Fig. 9. A video of this simulation is available online at: https://www.dropbox.com/sh/0kk0i0ucoxy7dav/AAAMkDxLlObsmwc2PgL-dl-ha?dl=0.

8 Conclusion

In this paper, we presented an architecture to generate a model-based walking engine. In particular, we used the ZMP concept as our main stability criterion and extended the LIPM to investigate the effects of vertical motion of COM and also torso inclination while walking. Using the obtained dynamics model, we formulated the problem of the low-level controller of humanoid walking as an optimal controller. We performed some simulations to show how this controller can optimally track the desired trajectories even in the presence of noise. After that, according to the periodic nature of human walking and using the proposed dynamics model and also low-level controller, we modeled the walking engine using a state machine which was composed of four distinct states: Idle, Initialize, Single Support and Double Support. We formulated all the procedures of generating the reference trajectories and validated them using designing an omnidirectional waking simulation scenario. The simulation result shows that our framework is able to generate stable omnidirectional walking. We carried out several simulations and tuned the parameters manually to find the maximum forward walking speed that the simulated robot can walk using our framework. The best hand-tuned speed that we achieved was 53 cm/s. In order to find the optimum value of the parameters and improve the walking speed, we selected 8 major parameters of our framework and optimized them using GA. After 12000 iterations, the walking speed reached a maximum stable velocity of 80.5 cm/s which was 52% faster than our best hand-tuned version and also was faster than [1,7,13,15].

In future work, we would like to investigate the effects of considering the mass and inertia of the swing leg in the dynamics model. Additionally, we intend to port the proposed framework to the real hardware to show the performance of this framework.

Acknowledgement. This research is supported by Portuguese National Funds through Foundation for Science and Technology (FCT) through FCT scholarship SFRH/BD/118438/2016.

References

1. Asta, S., Sariel-Talay, S.: Nature-inspired optimization for biped robot locomotion and gait planning. In: Di Chio, C., et al. (eds.) EvoApplications 2011. LNCS, vol. 6625, pp. 434–443. Springer, Heidelberg (2011). https://doi.org/10.1007/978-3-642-20520-0_44
2. Gay, S., Santos-Victor, J., Ijspeert, A.: Learning robot gait stability using neural networks as sensory feedback function for central pattern generators. In: 2013 IEEE/RSJ International Conference on Intelligent Robots and Systems, pp. 194–201. IEEE (2013)
3. Goswami, A.: Postural stability of biped robots and the foot-rotation indicator (FRI) point. Int. J. Rob. Res. 18(6), 523–533 (1999)
4. Harada, K., Kajita, S., Kaneko, K., Hirukawa, H.: An analytical method for real-time gait planning for humanoid robots. Int. J. Humanoid Rob. 3(01), 1–19 (2006)
5. Kajita, S., et al.: Biped walking pattern generation by using preview control of zero-moment point. In: Proceedings of the IEEE International Conference on Robotics and Automation, 2003, ICRA 2003, vol. 2, pp. 1620–1626. IEEE (2003)
6. Kasaei, M., Lau, N., Pereira, A.: An optimal closed-loop framework to develop stable walking for humanoid robot. In: 2018 IEEE International Conference on Autonomous Robot Systems and Competitions (ICARSC), pp. 30–35. IEEE (2018)

7. Kasaei, S.M., Simões, D., Lau, N., Pereira, A.: A hybrid ZMP-CPG based walk engine for biped robots. In: Ollero, A., Sanfeliu, A., Montano, L., Lau, N., Cardeira, C. (eds.) ROBOT 2017. AISC, vol. 694, pp. 743–755. Springer, Cham (2018). https://doi.org/10.1007/978-3-319-70836-2_61

8. Komura, T., Leung, H., Kudoh, S., Kuffner, J.: A feedback controller for biped humanoids that can counteract large perturbations during gait. In: Proceedings of the 2005 IEEE International Conference on Robotics and Automation, 2005, ICRA 2005, pp. 1989–1995. IEEE (2005)

9. Massah, A., Zamani, A., Salehinia, Y., Sh, M.A., Teshnehlab, M.: A hybrid controller based on CPG and ZMP for biped locomotion. J. Mech. Sci. Technol. **27**(11), 3473–3486 (2013). https://doi.org/10.1007/s12206-013-0871-7

10. Morisawa, M., et al.: Experimentation of humanoid walking allowing immediate modification of foot place based on analytical solution. In: Proceedings 2007 IEEE International Conference on Robotics and Automation, pp. 3989–3994. IEEE (2007)

11. Nakaura, S., Sampei, M., et al.: Balance control analysis of humanoid robot based on ZMP feedback control. In: IEEE/RSJ International Conference on Intelligent Robots and Systems, vol. 3, pp. 2437–2442. IEEE (2002)

12. Or, J.: A hybrid CPG-ZMP control system for stable walking of a simulated flexible spine humanoid robot. Neural Netw. **23**(3), 452–460 (2010)

13. Picado, H., Gestal, M., Lau, N., Reis, L.P., Tomé, A.M.: Automatic generation of biped walk behavior using genetic algorithms. In: Cabestany, J., Sandoval, F., Prieto, A., Corchado, J.M. (eds.) IWANN 2009. LNCS, vol. 5517, pp. 805–812. Springer, Heidelberg (2009). https://doi.org/10.1007/978-3-642-02478-8_101

14. Pratt, J., Carff, J., Drakunov, S., Goswami, A.: Capture point: A step toward humanoid push recovery. In: 2006 6th IEEE-RAS International Conference on Humanoid Robots, pp. 200–207. IEEE (2006)

15. Shafii, N., Reis, L.P., Lau, N.: Biped walking using coronal and sagittal movements based on truncated fourier series. In: Ruiz-del-Solar, J., Chown, E., Plöger, P.G. (eds.) RoboCup 2010. LNCS (LNAI), vol. 6556, pp. 324–335. Springer, Heidelberg (2011). https://doi.org/10.1007/978-3-642-20217-9_28

16. Sugihara, T., Nakamura, Y.: A fast online gait planning with boundary condition relaxation for humanoid robots. In: Proceedings of the 2005 IEEE International Conference on Robotics and Automation, pp. 305–310. IEEE (2005)

17. Vukobratovic, M., Frank, A., Juricic, D.: On the stability of biped locomotion. IEEE Trans. Biomed. Eng. **1**, 25–36 (1970)

18. Winter, D.A., Ruder, G.K., MacKinnon, C.D.: Control of balance of upper body during gait. In: Winters, J.M., Woo, S.L.Y. (eds.) Multiple muscle systems, pp. 534–541. Springer, New York (1990). https://doi.org/10.1007/978-1-4613-9030-5_33

Utilizing Temporal Information in Deep Convolutional Network for Efficient Soccer Ball Detection and Tracking

Anna Kukleva$^{(\boxtimes)}$, Mohammad Asif Khan$^{(\boxtimes)}$, Hafez Farazi$^{(\boxtimes)}$, and Sven Behnke$^{(\boxtimes)}$

Computer Science Institute VI, Autonomous Intelligent Systems, Universität Bonn, Endenicher Allee 19a, 53115 Bonn, Germany
{s6ankukl,s6mokhan}@uni-bonn.de, {farazi,behnke}@ais.uni-bonn.de

Abstract. Soccer ball detection is identified as one of the critical challenges in the RoboCup competition. It requires an efficient vision system capable of handling the task of detection with high precision and recall and providing robust and low inference time. In this work, we present a novel convolutional neural network (CNN) approach to detect the soccer ball in an image sequence. In contrast to the existing methods where only the current frame or an image is used for the detection, we make use of the history of frames. Using history allows to efficiently track the ball in situations where the ball disappears or gets partially occluded in some of the frames. Our approach exploits spatio-temporal correlation and detects the ball based on the trajectory of its movements. We present our results with three convolutional methods, namely temporal convolutional networks (TCN), ConvLSTM, and ConvGRU. We first solve the detection task for an image using fully convolutional encoder-decoder architecture, and later, we use it as an input to our temporal models and jointly learn the detection task in sequences of images. We evaluate all our experiments on a novel dataset prepared as a part of this work. Furthermore, we present empirical results to support the effectiveness of using the history of the ball in challenging scenarios.

Keywords: Robocup · Deep learning · Ball detection · Fully convolutional neural network · Spatio-temporal neural network

1 Introduction

The RoboCup introduced by Kitano et al. [15] serves as the central problem in understanding and development of Artificial Intelligence. The challenge aims at developing a team of autonomous robots capable of playing soccer in a dynamic environment. It requires the development of collective intelligence and an ability to interact with surroundings for effective control and decision making. Over the years several humanoid robots [8,9,21] have participated in the challenge.

A. Kukleva and M. A. Khan—Equal Contribution.

© Springer Nature Switzerland AG 2019
S. Chalup et al. (Eds.): RoboCup 2019, LNAI 11531, pp. 112–125, 2019.
https://doi.org/10.1007/978-3-030-35699-6_9

One of the main hurdle identified within the tournament is perceiving the soccer ball. The efficient detection of soccer ball relies on how good the vision system performs in tracking the ball. For instance, consider cases where the ball disappears or gets occluded from robots point of view for a few frames. In such situations using the current frame is not useful. However, a dependence on the history of frames can help in making a proper move. In this work, we propose an approach which can effectively utilize the history of ball movement and improve the task of ball detection. We first utilize the encoder-decoder architecture of SweatyNet model and train it for detection of the ball in single images. Later we use it as a part of our proposed layers and learn from temporal sequences of images, thereby developing a more robust detection system. In our approach we make use of three spatio-temporal models: TCN [2], ConvLSTM [26] and ConvGRU [3].

For this work, we recorded a new dataset for the soccer ball detection task. We make our data as well as our implementation available on GitHub so that the results can be easily reproduced. research[1]. We used Pytorch [19] for our implementation.

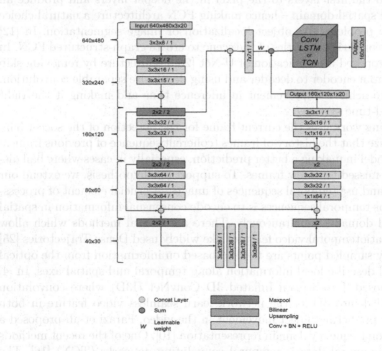

Fig. 1. The proposed architecture with feed-forward and temporal parts.

[1] https://github.com/AIS-Bonn/TemporalBallDetection.

2   Related Work

Numerous works have been done in the area of soccer ball detection. Before RoboCup 2015 the ball was orange, and many teams used color information [22]. Since RoboCup2015, the ball is not color coded anymore, which forced teams to use more sophisticated learning based approaches like HOG cascade classifier [7]. In recent years, the convolutional approaches with their innate ability to capture equivariance and hierarchical features in images have emerged as a favorite choice for the task. In [23] authors use CNN to perform localization of soccer ball by predicting the x and y coordinates. In a recent work [17] use proposal generators to estimate regions of soccer ball and further use CNN for the classification of regions. In [13] authors compared various CNN architectures namely LeNet, SqueezeNet, and GoogleLeNet for the task of a ball detection by humanoid robots. In [21] authors inspired by work of [20] proposed a Fully Convolutional Networks (FCN) that offers a robust and low inference time, which is an essential requirement for the soccer challenge. As the name suggests, the FCN is composed entirely of convolution layers which allows them to learn a path from pixels in the first layers to the pixel in the deeper layers and produce an output in the spatial domain – hence making FCN architecture a natural choice for pixel-wise problems like object localization or image segmentation. In [12] authors use geometric properties of the scene to create graph-structured FCN. In [6] authors proposed a modification of U-Net [20] architecture by removing skip connections from encoder to decoder and using depthwise separable convolution. This allows to achieve improvement in inference time and making it the right choice for real-time systems.

The existing work uses the current frame for the detection of the soccer ball. We hypothesize that the history of frames (coherent sequence of previous frames) could help model in making a better prediction, especially in cases where ball disappears or is missed for a few frames. To support our hypothesis, we extend our experiments and use temporal sequences of images. A crucial element of processing continuous temporal sequences is to encode consensual information in spatial and temporal domains simultaneously. There are several methods which allow extracting spatiotemporal video features like widely used Dense Trajectories [25] where densely sampled points are tracked based on information from the optical flow field and describe local information along temporal and spatial axes. In [4] authors proposed Two-Stream Inflated 3D ConvNet (I3D) where convolution filters expanded into 3D let the network learn seamless video feature in both domains. For predicting object movement in the video, Farazi et al. proposed a model based on frequency domain representation [10]. One of the recent methods in modeling temporal data is temporal convolution networks (TCN) [16]. The critical advantage of TCN is the representation gained by applying the hierarchy of dilated causal convolution layers on the temporal domain, which successfully capture long-range dependencies. Also, it provides a faster inference time compared to recurrent networks, which make it suitable for real-time applications.

Additionally, there are successful end-to-end recurrent networks which can leverage correlations within sequential data [5,11,26]. ConvLSTM [26] and ConvGRU [3] are recurrent architectures which compound convolutions to determine the future state of the cell based on its local neighbors instead of the entire input.

In this work, we propose a CNN architecture which utilizes sequences of ball movements in order to improve the task of soccer ball detection in challenging scenarios.

3   Detection Models

3.1   Single Image Detection

In this paper, the task of soccer ball detection is formulated as a binary pixel-wise classification problem, where for a given image, the feed-forward model predicts the heatmap corresponding to the soccer ball. In this part we utilize three feed-forward models namely SweatyNet-1, SweatyNet-2 and SweatyNet-3 as proposed in [21].

All three networks are based on an encoder-decoder design. The SweatyNet-1 consists of five blocks in the encoder part and two blocks in the decoder part. In the encoder part, the first block includes one layer, and the number of filters is doubled after every block. In the decoder part, both blocks contain three layers. Each layer comprises of a convolutional operator followed with batch normalization and ReLU as the non-linearity. In addition, bilinear upsampling is used twice: after the last block of the encoder and after the first block of the decoder. Skip connections are added between layers of encoder and decoder to provide high-resolution details of the input to the decoder. Similar approaches have been successfully used in Seg-Net [1], V-Net [18] and U-Net [20].

All convolutional filters across the layers are of the fixed size of 3×3. The encoder part includes four max-pooling layers where each one is situated after the first four blocks. The number of filters in the first layer is eight, and it is doubled after every max-pooling layer. In the decoder, the number of filters is reduced by a factor of two before every upsampling layer.

The other two variants of SweatyNet, are designed to reduce the number of parameters and speed up the inference time. In SweatyNet-2, the number of parameters is reduced by removing the first layer in each of the last five blocks of the encoder. In SweatyNet-3, the number of channels is decreased by changing the size of convolutions to 1×1 in every first layer of last five encoder blocks and both of the decoder blocks.

3.2   Detection in a Sequence

Temporal extensions capture spatio-temporal interdependence in the sequence and allow to predict the movement of the ball capturing its size, direction, and speed correctly. In our experiments, we utilize the temporal series of images to improve the task of soccer ball detection further.

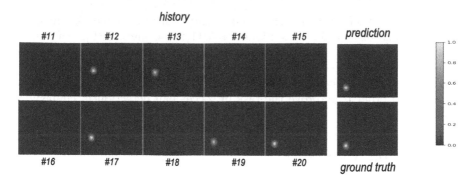

Fig. 2. The prediction results, on the synthetically generated sequences. The network correctly predicts the future position and successfully keeps the size of *slow* moving ball with $\sigma = 4$ even when the history is sparse. Note that sparse history resembles an occluded ball.

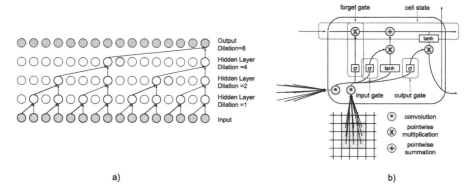

Fig. 3. Visualization of (a) a stack of causal convolutional layers which compose TCN architecture. (b) a convolutional LSTM cell.

Our approach illustrated in Fig. 1 propose a temporal layer and learnable weight w which makes use of the history of sequences of fixed length to predict the probability map of the soccer ball. We use a feed-forward layer TCN and compare it with recurrent layers ConvLSTM and ConvGRU. The three approaches differ in the type of connections formed in the network.

We train our model to learn heatmaps of a ball based on the sequence of frames representing the history of its movement. More precisely, if the timestamp of the current frame is t, given the heatmaps from $(t - h)$ to $(t - 1)$ the output of the network is the sequence of heatmaps from timestamp t to $(t + p)$, where h is the history length and p is the length of predicted sequence.

The ConvLSTM and ConvGRU layers are stacks of several convolutional LSTM and GRU cells, respectively, which allows for capturing spatial as well as temporal correlations. Each ConvLSTM cell acts based on the *input, forget* and *output* gates, while the core information is stored in the *memory* cell controlled by the aforementioned gates. Each ConvGRU cell adaptively captures time dependencies with various time ranges based on *content* and *reset* gates. Convolutional structure avoids the use of redundant, non-local spatial data and results in lower computations. Figure 3 depicts the structure of convolutional LSTM cell where the input is a set of flattened 1D array image features obtained with the convolutions layers. Convolutional GRU cell also differs from standard GRU cell only in the way how input is passed to it.

Unlike the two recurrent models, where gated units control hidden states, TCN hidden states are intrinsically temporal. This is attributed to the dilated causal convolutions used in TCN, which generates temporally structured states without explicitly modeling connection between them. Thus, TCN captures long term temporal dependencies in a simple feed-forward network architecture. This feature further provides an advantage of the faster inference time. Figure 3 shows dilated causal convolutions for dilations 1, 2, 4, and 8. For our work, we replicated the original TCN-ED structure with repeated blocks of dilated convolution layers and normalized ReLU as activation functions.

For sequential data, it is challenging to train a network from scratch because of the limited size of the dataset and the difficulties in collecting the real data. Besides, the training process requires more memory to store a batch of sequences, resulting in a choice of smaller batch size. To address this problem, we use transfer learning and finetune the weights of our model on the sequences of synthetic data. We use SweatyNet-1 as the feature extractor and finetune it with the temporal layers.

For the input to temporal layers; TCN, ConvLSTM, and ConvGRU, we also take advantage of high-resolution spatial information by concatenating the output of 2nd and 6th block of SweatyNet-1. To speed up the training process and propagate spatial information, we apply a convolution of size 7×7 on the combined features. Moreover, we take an element-wise product of the output of convolution with a learnable weight of w and add it to the output of SweatyNet. This combination serves as an input to the temporal layers. The weight w serves as a gate which learns to control how much of high-resolution information is transferred from the early layers of Sweaty-Net and helps the network in detecting soccer ball with subpixel level accuracy.

4   Experiments

In this section, we describe the details of the training process for our two sets of experiments. In the first experiment, we consider a problem of localization of the object in an image. In the second experimet, we evaluated our temporal approach. The evaluation of our experiments is discussed in Sect. 4.3.

4.1   Training

Detection in an Image: For our work, we created a dataset of 4562 images, of which 4152 images contain a soccer ball. We refer to it as *SoccerData*.

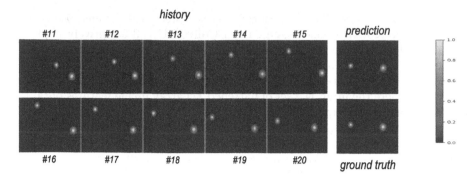

Fig. 4. The result of the temporal part, trained on a dataset with one ball per frame. Note that the network can generalize to detect two moving objects.

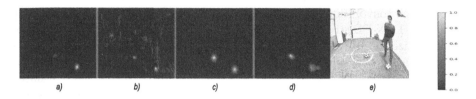

Fig. 5. Qualitative results of the trained network in detecting two balls. (a) SweatyNet prediction (b) residual information (c) ground truth (d) temporal prediction (e) real image

The images are extracted from a video recorded from the robot's point of view and are manually annotated using the imagetagger[2] library. The images are from three different fields with different light sources. Note that since the data is recorded on walking robot, in many images we have blurry data.

Each image is represented by a bounding box with coordinates: $x_{min}, y_{min}, x_{max}, y_{max}$. For teaching signal we generated a binormal probability distribution centered at $c = 0.5(x_{max} + x_{min}, y_{max} + y_{min})$ and with the variance of $r = 0.5min(x_{max} - x_{min}, y_{max} - y_{min})$. In contrast to the work of [21] where authors consider ball of fixed radius, we take into account the variable radius of a ball by computing the radius based on the size of the bounding box.

We apply three variants of SweatyNet model as described in Sect. 3 on the *SoccerData*. For the fair evaluation of the model, we randomly split our data into 70% training and 30% testing. In the training phase, mean squared error (MSE) is optimized between a predicted and a target probability map. We use Adam [14] as the optimizer. We trained all of our models for a maximum of 100 epochs on the Nvidia GeForce GTX TITAN GK110. Similar to [21] the hyperparameters used in our experiments are learning rate of 0.001 and a batch size of 4. In addition, we experiment with dropout probability of 0.0, 0.3 and 0.5.

---

[2] https://imagetagger.bit-bots.de/.

Detection in a Sequence: We train the temporal part in two ways: (i) we pre-train the temporal model on artificially generated sequences and finetune it on top of the pre-trained SweatyNet-1 for the real sequences,
(ii) finetune the joint model on the real sequences where the pre-trained weights are used only for the SweatyNet-1 model.

Algorithm 2 details the procedure for synthetic data generation. To get heatmaps of a particular sequence L_i at each time step j we generate a multi-normal probability distribution centered at (x_j, y_j) with a variance equal to the radius R_i.

To finetune the model on the real sequential data, we extracted a set of real soccer ball frames from bags recorded during RoboCup2018 Adult-Size games. Since video frames do not always contain a ball in the field of view, we preprocess videos to make sure that we do not use a sequence of frames without any ball present. With such restrictions, we got 20 sets of consecutive balls with an average length of 60. For all of our experiments, we fixed the history size h to 20 and prediction length p to 1.

For training on real data, we use learning rates of $1e-5$ for the detection task and $1e-4$ for the temporal part after pretraining. In the temporal network on the artificial sequences, the learning rate is set to $1e-5$. We train on synthetic data for 20 epochs and 30 epochs for the real data.

TCN: Encoder and decoder of TCN are two convolutional networks with two layers of 64 and 96 channels, respectively. We set up all parameters following the work of [16] except that we use Adam as an optimizer with MSE loss.

ConvLSTM and ConvGRU: We use four layers of ConvLSTM/ConvGRU cells with the respective size of 32, 64, 32, 1, and fixed kernel of size five across all layers.

Multiple Balls in a Sequence: To verify that our model can generalize, we test it on a more complex scenario with two present balls. Note that the network was only trained on a dataset containing a single ball. The qualitative results can found in Figs. 4 and 5. These figures depict that the model is powerful enough to handle cases not covered by training data. The temporal part leverages the previous frames and residual information and can detect the ball which is absent in SweatyNet output (Fig. 4 (a) vs. (d)).

4.2   Postprocessing

The output of a network is a probability map of size 160×120. We use the contour detection technique explained in Algorithm 1 to find the center coordinates of a ball. The output of the network is of lower resolution and has less spatial information than the input image. To account for this effect, we calculate sub-pixel level coordinates and return the center of contour mass, as the center of the detected soccer ball.

Algorithm 1. Postprocessing to find coordinates of a ball.

$M \leftarrow$ A matrix of size 120×160 representing predicted output of a network.
$A_{min} \leftarrow$ Area of a smallest ball in the training set.
$B_M \leftarrow M > 0.1$, binary map.
List $L \leftarrow$ detect contours in B_M.
$C \leftarrow$ contour in L with maximum area.
if area of $C \le A_{min}$. **then**
    $(c_x, c_y) \leftarrow (-1, -1)$
else
    $W_C \leftarrow$ mask M with C.
    $(c_x, c_y) \leftarrow$ center of mass of W_C.
end if
return (c_x, c_y)

Algorithm 2. Artificial sequences creation.

$N \leftarrow$ Number of sequences.
$L_N \leftarrow []$ A list to store a list of coordinates of a moving ball for all sequences.
$R_N \leftarrow []$ A list to store radius of a ball for all sequences.
for i = 1 **to** N **do**
    $R_i \sim \mathcal{U}(\{3, 4, 5\})$, $x_1 \sim \mathcal{U}(\{0, ..., frame_x\})$, $y_1 \sim \mathcal{U}(\{0, ..., frame_y\})$
    $steps_i \sim \mathcal{U}(\{30, ..., 60\})$ and $dist_i \sim \mathcal{U}(\{50, ..., 500\})$
    $dx_i \leftarrow x_1/steps_i, dy_i \leftarrow y_1/steps_i$
    $R_N \leftarrow R_i, L_i \leftarrow [(x_1, y_1)]$
    for j = 1 **to** $steps_i$ **do**
        $direction\_x_j, direction\_y_j \sim \mathcal{U}(\{-1, 1\})$
        $x_j \leftarrow x_j + direction\_x_j.dx_i, y_j \leftarrow y_j + direction\_y_j.dy_i$
        $L_i \leftarrow (x_j, y_j)$
    end for $L_N \leftarrow L_i$
end for
return L_N, R_N

4.3 Evaluation

To analyze the performance of different networks we use several metrics: false
discovery rate (FDR), precision (PR), recall (RC), F1-score (F1) and accuracy
(Acc) as defined in Eq. 1, where TP is true positives, FP is false positives, FN
is false negatives, and TN is true negatives.

$$FDR = \frac{FP}{FP + TP}, PR = \frac{TP}{TP + FP}, RC = \frac{TP}{TP + FN},$$
$$F1 = 2 \times \frac{PR \times RC}{PR + RC}, Acc = \frac{TP + TN}{TP + FP + TN + FN}$$
$$(1)$$

An instance is classified as a TP if the predicted center and actual center of
the soccer ball is within a fixed distance of $\gamma = 5$ (Fig. 6).

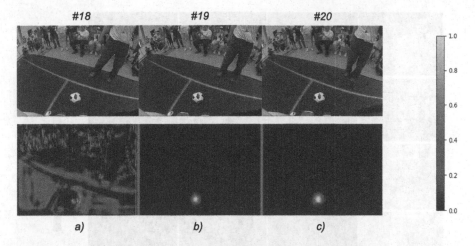

Fig. 6. Top row is the part of the input history (frame {18,19,20}). The bottom row consists of heatmaps where (a) visualization of the residual information from Sweaty Net to temporal, (b) ground truth ball position and (c) predicted output by the temporal part.

Fig. 7. Example of correctly detected ball after finetuning with the temporal model while the confidence of just the SweatyNet is very low, resulting in false negative detection. The left image is the real image; the middle is SweatyNet output without finetuning; the right one is SweatyNet output after finetuning.

5 Results

The results of our experiments are summarized in Table 1. The performance of all three models are comparable. To improve generalization and prevent overfitting, we further experiment with different dropout [24] probability values. We train all our models on a PC with Intel Core i7-4790K CPU with 32 GB of memory and a graphics card Nvidia GeForce GTX TITAN with 6 GB of memory. For real-time detection, one major requirement is of a faster inference time. We report the inference time of the model on the NimbRo-OP2X robot in Table 2(a). The NimbRo-OP2X robot is equipped with Intel Core i7-8700T CPU with 8 GB of memory and a graphics card Nvidia GeForce GTX 1050 Ti with 4 GB of memory. Since all three models don't use the full capacity of GPU during inference, which allows bigger models to perform extra computations in parallel; as a result, all three SweatyNet networks are comparable in real time inference.

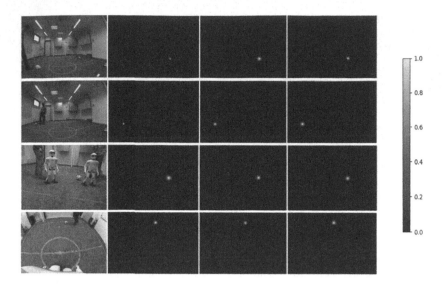

Fig. 8. From left to right: input image, the ground truth, prediction of the neural network, and the final output after post-processing.

Figure 8 demonstrates the effectiveness of the model for the task of soccer ball detection. For this study, we only consider SweatyNet-1.

The results of sequential part are further summarized in Table 2(b). The sequential network successfully captures temporal dependencies and gives an improvement over the SweatyNet. Usage of artificial data for pre-training the temporal network is beneficial due to the shortage of real training data and boosts performance. Figure 2 illustrates artificially generated ball sequences with the temporal prediction. We observed that when the temporal model is

Table 1. Evaluation of SweatyNets on the task of soccer ball detection. The highlighted numbers are the best performance for a particular dropout probability.

Performance metric											
Model	Dropout	FDR		PR		RC		F1		Accuracy	
		Train	Test	Train	Test	Train	Test	Train	Test	Train	Test
SweatyNet-1	0.0	**0.001**	**0.017**	**0.999**	**0.981**	0.987	**0.949**	0.993	**0.964**	0.989	**0.945**
SweatyNet-2	0.0	0.003	0.020	0.997	0.980	0.986	0.912	0.992	0.948	0.988	0.916
SweatyNet-3	0.0	0.002	0.019	0.998	**0.981**	**0.990**	0.935	0.994	0.959	**0.991**	0.933
SweatyNet-1	0.3	0.017	**0.019**	0.984	0.979	**0.988**	0.950	0.986	**0.966**	0.978	**0.945**
SweatyNet-2	0.3	**0.014**	0.022	**0.986**	**0.980**	0.986	0.949	0.986	0.964	**0.979**	0.941
SweatyNet-3	0.3	**0.014**	0.024	**0.986**	0.978	0.987	**0.956**	**0.987**	**0.966**	**0.979**	**0.945**
SweatyNet-1	0.5	0.039	0.024	0.960	0.975	**0.989**	**0.972**	**0.974**	**0.973**	**0.961**	**0.955**
SweatyNet-2	0.5	**0.029**	**0.015**	**0.970**	**0.983**	0.870	0.812	0.917	0.899	0.882	0.844
SweatyNet-3	0.5	0.048	0.022	0.952	0.981	0.982	0.940	0.967	0.959	0.949	0.932

pre-trained on the artificial data, the learnable weight for the residual information takes a value of 0.57 on average, though without pre-training, the value
is 0.49. The performance of TCN is comparable to ConvLSTM and ConvGRU,
but it considerably outperforms ConvLSTM and ConvGRU in terms of inference
time, which is a critical requirement for a real-time decision-making process.
Table 2(a) presents a comparison between temporal models on inference time.

To support our proposal of using sequential data, in Fig. 7 we present an
example image where the SweatyNet alone is uncertain of the prediction, though
the network gives an strong detection when further processed with the temporal
model.

Table 2. (a) Inference time comparison. For sequential models, we report time on top
of the base model, (b) Evaluation of different tested models. Note *real* denotes that
training of the sequential part is performed only on real data and *ft* means that a
pre-training phase on the artificially generated ball sequences is done before finetuning
on real data.

Method	Time in ms measured on the robot
SweatyNet-1	4.2
SweatyNet-2	3.5
SweatyNet-3	4.7
LSTM	219.6
GRU	178.5
TCN	**1.1**

(a)

Performance Metric on Test set				
Method —	FDR —	PR —	RC —	F1 — Acc
SweatyNet-1 (0.5)	**0.024**	0.975	0.972	0.973 0.955
Net+LSTM(*real*)	0.025	**0.976**	0.979	0.977 0.962
Net+LSTM(*ft*)	0.026	0.975	**0.987**	**0.981 0.967**
Net+GRU(*real*)	**0.024**	0.975	0.980	0.978 0.963
Net+GRU(*ft*)	0.026	0.972	**0.987**	**0.980 0.966**
Net+TCN(*real*)	**0.024**	**0.976**	0.982	0.979 0.964
Net+TCN(*ft*)	0.026	0.974	**0.985**	**0.980 0.966**

b

6 Conclusion

In this paper, we address the problem of soccer ball detection using sequences
of data. We proposed a model which utilizes the history of ball movements for
efficient detection and tracking. Our approach makes use of temporal models

which effectively leverage the spatio-temporal correlation of sequences of data and keeps track of the trajectory of the ball. We present three temporal models: TCN, ConvLSTM, and ConvGRU. The feed-forward nature of TCN allows faster inference time and makes it an ideal choice for real-time application of RoboCup soccer. Furthermore, we show that with transfer learning, sequential models can further leverage knowledge learned from synthetic counterparts. Based on our results, we conclude that our proposed deep convolutional networks are effective in terms of performance as well as inference time and are a suitable choice for soccer ball detection. Note that the presented models can be used for detecting other soccer objects like goalposts and robots.

References

1. Badrinarayanan, V., Kendall, A., Cipolla, R.: Segnet: a deep convolutional encoder-decoder architecture for image segmentation. IEEE Trans. Pattern Anal. Mach. Intell. **39**(12), 2481–2495 (2017)
2. Bai, S., Kolter, J.Z., Koltun, V.: An empirical evaluation of generic convolutional and recurrent networks for sequence modeling. arXiv preprint arXiv:1803.01271 (2018)
3. Ballas, N., Yao, L., Pal, C., Courville, A.: Delving deeper into convolutional networks for learning video representations. In: ICLR (2016)
4. Carreira, J., Zisserman, A.: Quo vadis, action recognition? a new model and the kinetics dataset. In: Proceedings of the IEEE Conference on Computer Vision and Pattern Recognition, pp. 6299–6308 (2017)
5. Chung, J., Gulcehre, C., Cho, K., Bengio, Y.: Empirical evaluation of gated recurrent neural networks on sequence modeling. arXiv preprint arXiv:1412.3555 (2014)
6. van Dijk, S.G., Scheunemann, M.M.: Deep learning for semantic segmentation on minimal hardware. arXiv preprint arXiv:1807.05597 (2018)
7. Farazi, H., Allgeuer, P., Behnke, S.: A monocular vision system for playing soccer in low color information environments. In: Proceedings of 10th Workshop on Humanoid Soccer Robots, IEEE-RAS International Conference on Humanoid Robots, Seoul, Korea (2015)
8. Farazi, H., et al.: Autman kid-size team description 2013. Amirkabir University of Technology, Technical report (2013)
9. Ficht, G., et al.: Nimbro-op2x: Adult-sized open-source 3d printed humanoid robot. In: 2018 IEEE-RAS 18th International Conference on Humanoid Robots (Humanoids), pp. 1–9. IEEE (2018)
10. Farazi, H., Behnke, S.: Frequency domain transformer networks for video prediction. In: European Symposium on Artificial Neural Networks, Computational Intelligence and Machine Learning (ESANN), Bruges, Belgium (2019)
11. Hochreiter, S., Schmidhuber, J.: Long short-term memory. Neural Comput. **9**(8), 1735–1780 (1997)
12. Houliston, T., Chalup, S.K.: Visual mesh: real-time object detection using constant sample density. arXiv preprint arXiv:1807.08405 (2018)
13. Javadi, M., Azar, S.M., Azami, S., Ghidary, S.S., Sadeghnejad, S., Baltes, J.: Humanoid robot detection using deep learning: a speed-accuracy tradeoff. In: Akiyama, H., Obst, O., Sammut, C., Tonidandel, F. (eds.) RoboCup 2017. LNCS (LNAI), vol. 11175, pp. 338–349. Springer, Cham (2018). https://doi.org/10.1007/978-3-030-00308-1_28

14. Kingma, D.P., Ba, J.: Adam: a method for stochastic optimization. arXiv preprint arXiv:1412.6980 (2014)
15. Kitano, H., Asada, M., Kuniyoshi, Y., Noda, I., Osawa, E.: Robocup: the robot world cup initiative. In: Proceedings of the First International Conference on Autonomous Agents, pp. 340–347. ACM (1997)
16. Lea, C., Flynn, M.D., Vidal, R., Reiter, A., Hager, G.D.: Temporal convolutional networks for action segmentation and detection. In: proceedings of the IEEE Conference on Computer Vision and Pattern Recognition, pp. 156–165 (2017)
17. Leiva, F., Cruz, N., Bugueño, I., Ruiz-del Solar, J.: Playing soccer without colors in the spl: a convolutional neural network approach. arXiv preprint arXiv:1811.12493 (2018)
18. Milletari, F., Navab, N., Ahmadi, S.A.: V-net: fully convolutional neural networks for volumetric medical image segmentation. In: 2016 Fourth International Conference on 3D Vision (3DV), pp. 565–571. IEEE (2016)
19. Paszke, A., et al.: Automatic differentiation in pytorch (2017)
20. Ronneberger, O., Fischer, P., Brox, T.: U-Net: convolutional networks for biomedical image segmentation. In: Navab, N., Hornegger, J., Wells, W.M., Frangi, A.F. (eds.) MICCAI 2015. LNCS, vol. 9351, pp. 234–241. Springer, Cham (2015). https://doi.org/10.1007/978-3-319-24574-4_28
21. Schnekenburger, F., Scharffenberg, M., Wülker, M., Hochberg, U., Dorer, K.: Detection and localization of features on a soccer field with feedforward fully convolutional neural networks (fcnn) for the adultsize humanoid robot sweaty. In: Proceedings of the 12th Workshop on Humanoid Soccer Robots, IEEE-RAS International Conference on Humanoid Robots, Birmingham (2017)
22. Schulz, H., Strasdat, H., Behnke, S.: A ball is not just orange: using color and luminance to classify regions of interest. In: Proceedings of Second Workshop on Humanoid Soccer Robots, Pittsburgh (2007)
23. Speck, D., Barros, P., Weber, C., Wermter, S.: Ball localization for robocup soccer using convolutional neural networks. In: Behnke, S., Sheh, R., Sarıel, S., Lee, D.D. (eds.) RoboCup 2016. LNCS (LNAI), vol. 9776, pp. 19–30. Springer, Cham (2017). https://doi.org/10.1007/978-3-319-68792-6_2
24. Srivastava, N., Hinton, G., Krizhevsky, A., Sutskever, I., Salakhutdinov, R.: Dropout: a simple way to prevent neural networks from overfitting. J. Mach. Learn. Res. 15(1), 1929–1958 (2014)
25. Wang, H., Kläser, A., Schmid, C., Liu, C.L.: Dense trajectories and motion boundary descriptors for action recognition. Int. J. Comput. Vis. 103(1), 60–79 (2013)
26. Xingjian, S., Chen, Z., Wang, H., Yeung, D.Y., Wong, W.K., Woo, W.C.: Convolutional LSTM network: a machine learning approach for precipitation nowcasting. In: Advances in Neural Information Processing Systems, pp. 802–810 (2015)

Analysis of the PSO Parameters for a Robots Positioning System in SSL

Marcos Aurelio Pchek Laureano[1,2](✉) (iD) and Flavio Tonidandel[2](✉) (iD)

[1] Federal Institute of Parana, Curitiba, PR, Brazil
marcos.laureano@ifpr.edu.br
[2] University Center of FEI, São Bernardo do Campo, SP, Brazil
flaviot@fei.edu.br
http://curitiba.ifpr.edu.br/, https://portal.fei.edu.br/

Abstract. The changes in the Small Size League rules have brought greater possibilities of playing. With the increased complexity of soccer matches, the positioning of the robots has become important as a defense and attack mechanism. The learning of opposing team game playing has been shown to be effective, but an SSL soccer match indicates the need for solutions that analyze the strategy of the opposing team during the game and make any necessary adaptations. This paper proposes the use of the Particle Swarm Optimization (PSO) algorithm as an option to determine the positioning during the match. A prototype has been developed to validate the configuration parameters. Experiments in a simulator, analysis of game logs and results in a real matches have demonstrated the feasibility of applying the PSO algorithm to find the robots positions.

Keywords: Robot soccer · Particle Swarm Optimization (PSO) · Small Size League (SSL)

1 Introduction

RoboCup is a robotics competition designed to encourage research into artificial intelligence techniques through friendly matches. RoboCup Small Size League (SSL) competition focuses on the problem of cooperation and multi-agent control in a dynamic environment. SSL-related surveys focus on analyzing the historical records with learning algorithms to identify and classify sets of opponent's moves. The learning has proved to be effective [8,12], but the complexity of a soccer match indicates the need for solutions that can analyze the strategy of the opposing team during the game and make any necessary adaptations. In this context, it's necessary to use techniques that result in low computational time.

This study was financed in part by Instituto Federal do Paraná – Brasil and the Coordenação de Aperfeiçoamento de Pessoal de Nível Superior – Brasil (CAPES) – Finance Code 001.

SSL has already implemented certain changes and others are being addressed for the near future [17]. The main changes in the SSL category in 2018 were the division into two leagues (A and B), a new field design and an increased number of robots in the field. Since these changes enable various combinations of defense and attack moves, a dynamic system for positioning the defense is important for the success of a soccer team [4].

Many papers involving swarm intelligence and robotic algorithms can be found in the literature [1,11,13,16]). Studies on the social behavior of organisms have inspired the development of efficient optimization algorithms. The Particle Swarm Optimization (PSO) proposed by Kennedy and Eberhart [6] is an optimization algorithm based on a population of particles. It has been acknowledged for solving several problems with simplicity and a few computational resources.

The first objective of this paper is to test, verify, and determine the configuration parameters (inertia, confidence, number of iterations and population size) of the PSO algorithm in order to optimize robot positioning in the field. The second is to demonstrate the effective positioning of robots based on the defense fitness function developed for this study.

The remainder of the paper is organized as follows: Sect. 2 describes the PSO algorithm; Sect. 3 refers to papers on soccer robots applications; Sect. 4 explains the defense fitness function applied to the PSO; Sect. 5 explains the PSO parameter choices for this proposal; Sect. 6 addresses the simulations; Sect. 7 analyzes the simulations, and Sect. 8 presents the conclusions of this paper.

2   Particle Swarm Optimization

Particle swarm optimization (PSO) is a computational method that optimizes a problem by iteratively trying to improve a candidate solution with regard to a given measure of quality. It solves a problem by having a population of candidate solutions, here called particles, and moving these particles around in the search space according to the mathematical formula over the particles position and velocity [6]. To find the ideal solution, each particle moves toward its best position (*pbest*) and the best overall position (*gbest*) in the swarm. These equations can be observed in (1)[19]:

$$
\begin{aligned}
pbest(i,t) &= min[f(P_i(k))], i \in 1, ..., N_p, k = 1, ..., t \\
gbest(t) &= min[f(P_i(k))], i = 1, ..., N_p, k = 1, ..., t
\end{aligned}
\tag{1}
$$

Where i is the index of the particle; N_p indicates the total number of particles; t informs the current iteration; f is the function fitness, and, P_i indicates the position of the particle. Each particle has a randomly associated velocity, thus allowing it to move through the search space of potential solutions to the problem being optimized. In the implementation of the PSO algorithm, the particle velocity is updated based on inertia, cognition and social components. The velocity V and the position P of the particles are updated from Eqs. (2) and (3), respectively:

$$V_i(t+1) = \underbrace{\underbrace{\omega V_i(t)}_{\text{inertia}}}_{\text{diversification}} + \underbrace{\underbrace{c_1 r_1(pbest(i,t) - P_i(t))}_{\text{cognitive}} + \underbrace{c_2 r_2(gbest(t) - P_i(t))}_{\text{social}}}_{\text{intensification}} \quad (2)$$

$$P_i(t+1) = P_i(t) + V_i(t+1) \quad (3)$$

Where V denotes velocity, ω is the inertia factor used to balance global and local exploration, r_1 and r_2 are randomly distributed in the range $[0, 1]$, and c_1 and c_2 are constant parameters called acceleration coefficients. The variable c_1 represents how much the particles tend to follow their past behaviors in case of success, and c_2 represents their tendency to follow the success of other particles.

The PSO algorithm can work with several neighborhood topologies, the most frequent of which are best global (*gbest*) and local best (*lbest*) topologies [7,19]. The neighborhood topology determines the set of particles that contribute to the calculation of the best result of a particle. The *gbest* topology is represented by a fully connected graph. Each particle is influenced by its best position and also by the best position of a swarm particle. In the *lbest* topology, each particle is bound to k particle. Each particle is influenced by its personal best position and the best neighborhood position.

A PSO algorithm with global best topology converges rapidly because all particles are strongly attracted by the best particle in the swarm, thus producing sub-optimal results when the best particle is trapped in a local minimum. On the other hand, a PSO algorithm with local best topology converges slowly, but with greater chances of finding the global optimum, because each particle is influenced only by its adjacent neighbors and, therefore, groups of neighbors can explore different regions or great places in the search space [7].

The PSO was chosen as the base algorithm due to some of its characteristics: it is versatile, applied in several areas of knowledge, converges rapidly to a set of satisfactory answers, has low computational cost in comparison with other optimization algorithms, is less complex and requires a small number of parameters to be optimized, and allows a greater flexibility between local and global exploration in the desired search space when compared to other algorithms. The authors Wahab et al. [15] demonstrated that the PSO is considered one of the best optimization algorithms.

3   Related Studies

Many techniques have been applied to the decision-making of a robot soccer game, including: Case-based Reasoning, Learning from Observation, Reinforcement Learning, Pattern Recognition, Fuzzy Theory, Neural Network, Evolutionary Algorithm and Decision Tree.

Wang et al. [16] proposed to use the PSO to calculate route planning and detour. Their proposal was applied and simulated in a soccer game of robots with five members on each side. According to the authors, the use of PSO has proved to be possible, simple and easy to implement. However, the speed of the ball and the robots were considered constant, which does not reflect a real game situation. Saska et al.'s proposal [13] uses the PSO algorithm combined with Fergunson splines for the calculation of trajectories of robots on a soccer field. According to the authors, the use of splines is an implementation of movement that is natural for robots and easy to implement. Such calculation of trajectories reduces the computational cost of processing since one does not need to explore all possible paths as in traditional path-planning algorithms.

In Okada et al. [11], PSO is used to find soccer team positions in the 2D Simulator League field. In the simulations, the ball had 15 fixed positions and the PSO was used to find possible configurations of the position of the players in the field. According to the authors, the formations found showed no tendency for offensive or defensive positions, so the players can remain close to midfield.

There are other studies related to SSL. Mendoza et al. [9] suggested a Selectively Re-active Coordination (SRC) algorithm, which contains two layers: a coordinated opponent-agnostic layer enables the team to create its plans, setting the space for an offensive game, and an individual opponent-reactive action selection layer enables the robots to maintain re-activity to different opponents. This approach allows a tradeoff between team's ability to create team plans independently of the opponents, and its ability to react appropriately to different opponent behaviors. Quintero et al. [12] applied machine learning techniques to the problem of predicting soccer plays. The authors demonstrated experimentally that it is possible to predict the play that certain team will perform in a SSL game. Schawb et al. [14] applied deep reinforcement learning (DRL) to train skills. They have demonstrated learning of two different skills: navigating to a ball and aiming and shooting. Although they are not perfect, these learned skills allow a performance close to that of hand-coded baseline skills.

Albad et al. [1] applied the swarm algorithm to robot soccer to try to solve strategy, learning or positioning problems. For RoboCup community, solutions about strategy, learning or positioning applied in robot soccer is an open problem, even of exists many researches about this.

This proposal differs from other approaches because it uses an optimization algorithm for defensive positions that can respond during a SSL match and based on the movements of the opponent team's robots. A fitness function for a PSO algorithm was created to meet certain behavioral conditions respecting some criteria based on human soccer games.

4   Proposal of This Paper

In this paper, the PSO algorithm is used to find a positioning that meets some characteristics of human soccer. According to Costa et al. [4], a soccer match is divided into two concepts: defense and attack. The defense of a team must (a) hinder offensive passes (that might result in a goal) and kicks on goal, (b) recover ball possession, (c) prevent opponent's progression, (d) protect the goal and (e) reduce opponent's playing space. The attack must: (a) maintain ball

Table 1. Types of punishments

Type	Value	Meaning
PLOW	100	Low Punishment (only to differentiate minor cases)
PMLOW	500	Mid Punishment (low impact)
PMID	1000	Mid Punishment
PMHIGH	2000	Mid Punishment (high impact)
PHIGH	5000	High Punishment, violation of SSL rules

possession, (b) build up offensive actions, (c) progress through the opponent's half, (d) create situations of shooting and (e) shoot on opponent's goal.

To meet the defense requirements similar to those in human soccer, a fitness evaluation function is used in simulations applied to the defense position. It evaluates four desirable situations for a defense formation:

- A minimum distance among the robots in order to make opponent's movements more difficult and decrease the opponent's chances to receive the ball, make passes or kick to goal;
- The view of the opponent's robots in relation to a certain point of interest is blocked;
- The view of the goal of all the opponent's robots is blocked by least one robot of team, especially opponent robot with ball possession;
- Respect for the SSL rules on collisions between robots and invasion of the goal area.

In equations, field size is considered in centimeters and the *Goal* term can be any point of interest in the search space. For example: the left or right corner of the goalkeeper or a set of points from the opponent's field attack.

4.1   Robot Movements

The new robots positioning in the field is calculated by the motion of the particle $p(i, t)$ in search space. The velocity and the position of the robots are based in Eqs. (2) and (3). The new calculated position (new particle $p(i, t+1)$) is checked in (4) to determine if the new fitness value of particle has become smaller than the current value of *pbest*. If so, then new particle is the new *pbest* ($pbest(i, t) = p(i, t+1)$). Subsequently, the PSO checks whether the new *pbest* is lower than the current *gbest* value. If so, then the new particle is also the new *gbest* ($gbest(t) = pbest(i, t)$) of the swarm.

4.2   Punishments and Notations

Table 1 shows the punishments applied in the equations. These values represent centimeters in the SSL field. The punishments are used to differentiate situations that may occur during a SSL match.

4.3   General Equation

Equation (4) represents the four desirable situations for a defense formation. It comprises of another five functions (detailed in the following subsections).

$$
\begin{aligned}
\text{fitness}(A, p(i,t), goal) = & \; f_{\text{MinDistance}}(A, p(i,t)) + \\
& \; f_{\text{CheckStraight}}(A, p(i,t), goal) + \\
& \; f_{\text{ProtectGoal}}(A, p(i,t)) + \\
& \; f_{\text{Colission}}(A, p(i,t)) + \\
& \; f_{\text{InvasionGoalArea}}(p(i,t))
\end{aligned}
\tag{4}
$$

Where A represents the set of opponent's robots, $p(i,t)$ represents the set of robots that make up the defense (it is the particle of the swarm), i is a particle in iteration t, and $goal$ represent the goal or another point of interest. The set A considered in the other equations follows the rule described in (5).

$$
RA = \downarrow_1^9(\angle)A
$$

$$
A = \begin{cases}
RA_{1...l} \in RA, & \text{if } l = k \\
RA_b + RA_{1...(l-k+1)} \subset RA, & \text{if } l > k \; . \\
RA_{1...l} \in RA, & \text{if } l < k
\end{cases}
\tag{5}
$$

Where RA is the set A ordered according to the angular view of the goal, RA_b represents the opponent robot with ball possession, l is the number of opposing robots, and k is the number of robots that make up the defense. Robots with lower angles of vision of the goal will have more difficulties to kick the ball in its direction.

4.4   Minimum Distance

The $f_{\text{MinDistance}}$ (6) function sums the distances between the opponent's robots and the robots that make up the defense. A minimum distance is desirable to obstruct kicks and passes.

$$
f_{\text{MinDistance}}(A, P) = \{
$$

$$
\text{distance}(p, a) = \sqrt{(p_x - a_x)^2 + (p_y - a_y)^2}
$$

$$
d = \text{distance}(p, a)
$$

$$
I_{c_d}(p, a) = \begin{cases}
(1 - \frac{40}{d}), & \text{if } (1 - \frac{40}{d}) > 0 \\
\text{PMID}, & \text{otherwise}
\end{cases}
\tag{6}
$$

$$
\sum_{a \in A} \sum_{p \in P} I_{c_d}(p, a)
$$

$$
\}
$$

P represents the set of robots that make up the defense, A represents the set of opponent's robots, a is a robot from set A, and p is a robot from set P. The I_{c_d} operator is used to ensure the minimum distance between a team robot and an opponent robot. Value 40 indicates a dimension of two robots in SSL (≈ 40 cm). One value >0 indicates that the robot is behind the opponent's robot.

4.5   Blocking the View of Points of Interest

The $f_{CheckStraight}$ (7) function verifies if the opponent robots' view of the goal or another point of interest is blocked, which is desirable to make passes and kicks difficult. A high sum indicates that several of the opponent's robots have vision of the goal.

$$
f_{CheckStraight}(A, P, goal) = \{
$$
$$
straight(a, p, g) = \{((g_y - p_y) \times a_x +
$$
$$
(p_x - g_x) \times a_y + (g_x \times p_y - p_x \times g_y))\}
$$
$$
s = \begin{cases} 0, & \text{if } a \text{ has the ball} \\ PLOW, & \text{otherwise} \end{cases}
$$
$$
I_{c_s}(p, a, goal) = straight(a, p, goal) + s
$$
$$
\sum_{a \in A} \sum_{p \in P} I_{c_s}(p, a, goal)
$$
$$
\}
$$
(7)

The straight operators returns the distance between robot p and the line formed between a and $goal$. If a does not have the ball, $PLOW$ punishment is applied, so the formations that protect the goal of the player with the ball tend to be privileged.

4.6   Blocking the View of the Goal

The $f_{ProtectGoal}$ is a function to penalize whenever robot p does not protect its team's goal from the opponent's robot with the ball. A high sum indicates that the opponent's robot A_b has a view of the goal and is free to kick or pass the ball. In that case, if there are more robots in the defense than opponent's robots, the opponent's robot with ball possession may be blocked by more robots.

$$
f_{ProtectGoal}(A, P) = PMID \times (\sum_{p \in P} \forall \, p \notin A_{ball})
$$
(8)

4.7   Respect SSL Rules

The function $f_{Colission}$ (9) prevents a collision among a team's own robots or the opponent's robots.

$$f_{\text{Colission}}(A, P) = \text{PHIGH} \times ((\sum_{a \in A} \sum_{p \in P} \text{pos}(a) = \text{pos}(p) +$$
$$(\sum_{p \in P} \sum_{q \in P} \text{pos}(p) = \text{pos}(q) \wedge p_{id} \neq q_{id})) \tag{9}$$

In (9) the comparison between robots uses the field coordinates. Example: $\text{pos}(a) = \text{pos}(p)$ indicates that $a_x = p_x$ and $a_y = p_y$, and $p_{id} \neq q_{id}$ comparing team robots id.

Function $f_{\text{InvasionGoalArea}}$ (10) prevents the invasion of the goalkeeper's area.

$$f_{\text{InvasionGoalArea}}(P) = \text{PHIGH} \times (\sum_{p \in P} \forall\, p \in \text{Goal area}) \tag{10}$$

5   Simulation Parameters

To perform the experiments, the opponent's robots were positioned in the classic 2–2–3 formation applied 8 × 8 soccer. In this formation, the players have a well defined field of attack and defense (Fig. 1a). Figure 1b shows an example of the position of the opponents used in the simulations, chosen randomly according to the distribution in Fig. 1a and respecting the SSL rules. One robot was randomly chosen to possess the ball.

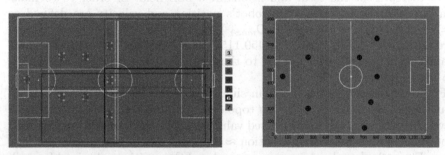

(a) 2–2–3 formation – colors indicate area of action for each robot   (b) Example of distribution in simulations

Fig. 1. 2–2–3 Formation in 8 versus 8 Soccer.

Inertia weight (ω) plays a key role in providing balance in the local and global exploitation process. It determines the contribution rate of the particle's previous velocity to its velocity in the next step. Bansal et al. [2] compared several proposals of inertia weights and concluded that the constant value 0.7298 (proposed by Clerc and Kennedy [3]), the random value $0.5 + \frac{rand(0,1)}{2}$ (proposed by Eberhart and Shi [5]), and the linear value $(\omega_{start} - \omega_{end}) \times \frac{it_{Max} - it}{it_{Max}} + \omega_{end}$ proposed by Xin et al. [18] (where $\omega_{start} = 0.9$ and $\omega_{end} = 0.4$, it_{Max} is the maximum of iterations, and it the current iteration) have a smaller number of iterations or less error.

The acceleration coefficients (c_1 and c_2) were chosen based on literature, according to which the most used values are: $c_1 = c_2 = 2$ and $c_1 = c_2 = 1.496$, in the simulations the values $c_1 = c_2 = 1$, $c_1 = 2, c_2 = 1$ and $c_1 = 1, c_2 = 2$ were adopted. Coefficient c_1 controls the diversity of each particle and c_2 controls their the global diversity. When $c_1 > c_2$, the particle tends to move to the *pbest* position and when $c_1 < c_2$, the particle tends to move to the *gbest* position in the swarm. Neighborhood topologies for global best (*gbest*) and local best (*lbest*) were used in the simulations.

Fifteen simulation scenarios were chosen to find the best parameters for inertia (ω) and the cognitive (c_1) and social coefficients (c_2). Each scenario comprised 5 instants (15 s of movement) to simulate a real game situation. The population size (from 50 to 200) and the number of iterations (from 50 to 500) varied in each scenario.

The configurations that provided best results were with 100 particles in the swarm population and 300 iterations, above this there was no improvement in results. Each particle consists of five robots positioned in the defense (with the coordinates x, y and velocities vx, vy – a robot is only one point in the search space), goalkeeper was not considered. The current position of the robots in the field is always part of the swarm population, since the movement may have been minimal and the current position can continue to have the best fitness. The search space dimensions are defined by 900 (D_{maxY}) × 1200 (D_{maxX}) points to represent the total dimensions of a SSL field. In order to to make up a particle in the swarm, each robot's position and velocity are defined as ($x = rand(0, D_{maxX})$, $y = rand(0, D_{maxY})$) ($vx = 1, vy = 1$), and fixed position representing the goal is defined at 450,1150. The *lbest* topology with the same parameters obtained results similar to those for the *gbest* topology but with a 30% higher average execution time.

Figure 2 presents the results from simulation scenarios with 300 iterations, population of 100 particles, and *gbest* topology after 10.000 simulations. As Fig. 2 shows, the minimum value (the desired value, since it is a minimization function) is the same in all simulations (variation ≈ 0.1). Other field positions get similar values. Figure 3a, b and c show some examples of the positions obtained for each inertia factor.

All scenarios with $c_1 = c_2 = 2$ have the best results, followed by the scenario with $c_1 = c_2 = 1.496$. In the tests performed, the inertia adopted showed little influence on the final result of the algorithm. A fixed inertia ($\omega = 0.7298$) was chosen (proposed by Clerc and Kennedy [3]). These values are the most used in several studies about PSO.

6   Experiments

Three types of experiment were performed using (2) and (3) with parameters $\omega = 0.7298, c_1 = c_2 = 2$ to calculate the velocity and position of each robot that

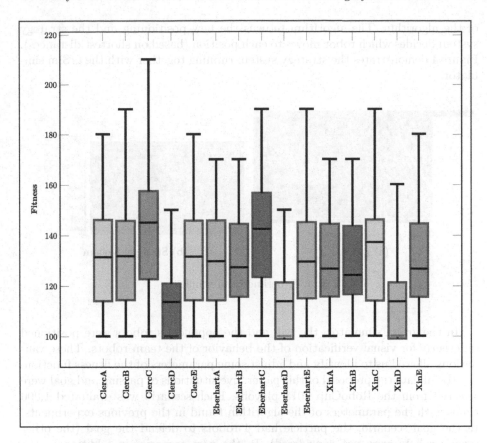

Fig. 2. Scenario settings: (a) $c_1 = 1$ and $c_2 = 2$; (b) $c_1 = 2$ and $c_2 = 1$; (c) $c_l = c_2 = 1$; (d) $c_1 = c_2 = 2$ and (e) $c_1 = c_2 = 1.496$.

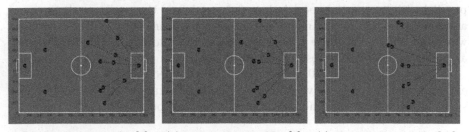

(a) Inertia proposed by [3].   (b) Inertia proposed by [5].   (c) Inertia proposed by [18].

Fig. 3. Some results for each inertia.

make up the particle, a grSim simulator [10], log analysis of RoboCup 2018 and the *Latin American Robotics Symposium* 2018 (LARS 2018) in five real matches.

In the simulator and in real matches the algorithm runs every 100ms. The current positioning is a particle that makes up the swarm of the next execution of the algorithm. The algorithm returns the new positioning and the strategy system decides which robot moves to each position (based on shortest distances). Figure 4 demonstrates the strategy system running together with the grSim simulator.

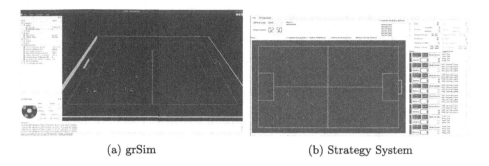

(a) grSim   (b) Strategy System

Fig. 4. Experiments in simulator.

In the grSim simulator, the ball and the opponent's robots were positioned differently for visual verification of the behavior of the team robots. These validations allowed us to identify and adjust some parameters of the fitness function.

To validate the proposal of this paper, five situations of passing and goal were selected from the RoboCup 2018 playoffs. Each scenario was evaluated 1,000 times with the parameters of the algorithm found in the previous experiments. In the goal scenario, the particle had 4 robots to defend the goal (the other team's robots were not considered). In the pass scenario, in addition to the defense particle (previously with 4 robots), another particle was made up with the remaining 3 robots in order to block the pass. The algorithm was run in parallel with two particle populations (one to defend the goalkeeper's area and another to block passes). In the ball interception scenario, the fitness function was adjusted to receive the opponent's robots that did not have ball possession as points to defend. The results can be seen in Fig. 5.

Finally, during LARS 2018 the proposal was applied in five real games. These experiments allowed us to verify the positioning limitations caused by the time spent in processing and sending commands to the robots.

7   Analysis

The various simulations and matches have show that using parameters for $c_1 = c_2 = 2$ leads to the positions that are closest to the ideal. Even the worst positioning found, based on the worst minimized value that was calculated (Fig. 6a) provides a satisfactory positioning for the goal defense.

Figure 6b shows the worst positioning situation ($c_1 = c_2 = 1$). In this case, the solution found is far below the ideal for a defense positioning system. For

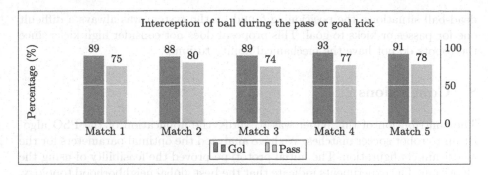

Fig. 5. Percentage of interception success in five RoboCup 2018 matches.

this scenario and search space, higher values for c_1 and c_2 are more effective because they result in the gradual decrease of the amplitude of the trajectory of the particles, thus ensuring the convergence of the algorithm [19].

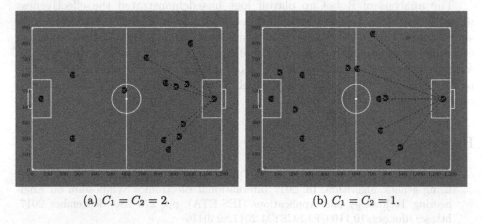

(a) $C_1 = C_2 = 2$.   (b) $C_1 = C_2 = 1$.

Fig. 6. Worsts cases – Inertia proposed by Clerc and Kennedy [3].

Experiments with logs have demonstrated the effectiveness of the proposal of this paper, but the opponent's strategy system would probably make other moves to succeed in goal-kicking or pass-through. In the scenario to block passes, as there were more opponent's robots in the attack area that could receive a pass than defenders to block them, the percentage of success was lower than in the scenario to defend the goalkeeper's area.

Experiments conducted during LARS 2018 have shown that it is necessary to anticipate position of the opponent's robot and ball. For the time between the processing of the new positions is no longer desired due to the movement of the opposing team (about 3 s for calculating the positioning, the system sending the commands to robots and robots performing the movement). In games with dead-ball situations, the positioning found by the system was always a difficult one for passes or kicks to goal. This proposal does not consider high kicks since the robots do not have the mechanical ability to jump.

8   Conclusions

The contribution of this paper was to verify the application of the PSO algorithm to robot soccer matches. We have analyzed the optimal parameters for the algorithm configuration. The initial prototype proved the feasibility of using the algorithm. The experiments indicate that the best global neighborhood topology, the number of iterations (300), acceleration coefficients ($c_1 = c_2 = 2$), and the size of the population (100) meet the project requirements in terms of computational costs to be run during a real soccer match. For inertia, all the evaluated strategies were effective, and we adopted the value $\omega = 0.7298$.

The main advantage of this approach is the possibility of optimizing, in real time and without previous knowledge, combinations of positioning with a low computational cost, which would not be possible with other techniques [12,14].

The analysis of RoboCup playoff logs has demonstrated the effectiveness of the proposal for this paper. Experiments conducted during LARS 2018 have shown that it can be used to find field positioning during an real SSL soccer game, especially in games with dead-ball situations (e.g. indirect kicks). However, for a dynamic game, the movements of the opponent's must be considered in order to calculate the future positioning, which is the main challenge to be improved on future studies.

References

1. Albab, R.T.U., Wibowo, I.K., Basuki, D.K.: Path planning for mobile robot soccer using genetic algorithm. In: 2017 International Electronics Symposium on Engineering Technology and Applications (IES-ETA), pp. 276–280, September 2017. https://doi.org/10.1109/ELECSYM.2017.8240416
2. Bansal, J.C., Singh, P.K., Saraswat, M., Verma, A., Jadon, S.S., Abraham, A.: Inertia weight strategies in particle swarm optimization. In: 2011 Third World Congress on Nature and Biologically Inspired Computing, pp. 633–640, October 2011. https://doi.org/10.1109/NaBIC.2011.6089659
3. Clerc, M., Kennedy, J.: The particle swarm - explosion, stability, and convergence in a multidimensional complex space. IEEE Trans. Evol. Comput. **6**(1), 58–73 (2002). https://doi.org/10.1109/4235.985692
4. da Costa, I.T., da Silva, J.M.G., Greco, P.J., Mesquita, I.: Princípios táticos do jogo de futebol: conceitos e aplicação. Motriz. Revista de Educação Física **15**(3), 657–668 (2009)
5. Eberhart, R.C., Shi, Y.: Tracking and optimizing dynamic systems with particle swarms. In: Proceedings of the 2001 Congress on Evolutionary Computation (IEEE Cat. No.01TH8546), vol. 1, pp. 94–100 (2001). https://doi.org/10.1109/CEC.2001.934376

6. Kennedy, J., Eberhart, R.: Particle swarm optimization. In: 1995 Proceedings of the IEEE International Conference on Neural Networks, vol. 4, pp. 1942–1948, November 1995. https://doi.org/10.1109/ICNN.1995.488968
7. Kennedy, J., Mendes, R.: Population structure and particle swarm performance. In: Proceedings of the 2002 Congress on Evolutionary Computation, 2002, CEC 2002, vol. 2, pp. 1671–1676 (2002). https://doi.org/10.1109/CEC.2002.1004493
8. Larik, A.S., Haider, S.: A survey of nature inspired optimization algorithms applied to cooperative strategies in robot soccer. In: 2018 International Conference on Advancements in Computational Sciences (ICACS). IEEE, February 2018. https://doi.org/10.1109/icacs.2018.8333485
9. Mendoza, J.P., Veloso, M., Simmons, R.: Selectively reactive coordination for a team of robot soccer champions. In: Proceedings of the Association for the Advancement of Artificial Intelligence Conference (AAAI) (2016)
10. Monajjemi, V., Koochakzadeh, A., Ghidary, S.S.: grSim – RoboCup small size robot soccer simulator. In: Röfer, T., Mayer, N.M., Savage, J., Saranlı, U. (eds.) RoboCup 2011. LNCS (LNAI), vol. 7416, pp. 450–460. Springer, Heidelberg (2012). https://doi.org/10.1007/978-3-642-32060-6_38
11. Okada, H., Wada, T., Yamashita, A.: Evolving RoboCup Soccer player formations by particle swarm optimization. In: SICE Annual Conference 2011, pp. 1950–1953 (2011)
12. Quintero, C., Rodríguez, S., Pérez, K., López, J., Rojas, E., Calderón, J.: Learning soccer drills for the small size league of RoboCup. In: Bianchi, R.A.C., Akin, H.L., Ramamoorthy, S., Sugiura, K. (eds.) RoboCup 2014. LNCS (LNAI), vol. 8992, pp. 395–406. Springer, Cham (2015). https://doi.org/10.1007/978-3-319-18615-3_32
13. Saska, M., Macas, M., Preucil, L., Lhotska, L.: Robot path planning using particle swarm optimization of ferguson splines. In: 2006 IEEE Conference on Emerging Technologies and Factory Automation, pp. 833–839, September 2006. https://doi.org/10.1109/ETFA.2006.355416
14. Schwab, D., Zhu, Y., Veloso, M.: Learning skills for small size league RoboCup. In: Holz, D., Genter, K., Saad, M., von Stryk, O. (eds.) RoboCup 2018. LNCS (LNAI), vol. 11374, pp. 83–95. Springer, Cham (2019). https://doi.org/10.1007/978-3-030-27544-0_7
15. Wahab, M.N.A., Nefti-Meziani, S., Atyabi, A.: A comprehensive review of swarm optimization algorithms. PLoS ONE **10**, e0122827 (2015). https://doi.org/10.1371/journal.pone.0122827
16. Wang, L., Liu, Y., Deng, H., Xu, Y.: Obstacle-avoidance path planning for soccer robots using particle swarm optimization. In: 2006 IEEE International Conference on Robotics and Biomimetics, pp. 1233–1238, December 2006. https://doi.org/10.1109/ROBIO.2006.340104
17. Weitzenfeld, A., Biswas, J., Akar, M., Sukvichai, K.: RoboCup small-size league: past, present and future. In: Bianchi, R.A.C., Akin, H.L., Ramamoorthy, S., Sugiura, K. (eds.) RoboCup 2014. LNCS (LNAI), vol. 8992, pp. 611–623. Springer, Cham (2015). https://doi.org/10.1007/978-3-319-18615-3_50
18. Xin, J., Chen, G., Hai, Y.: A particle swarm optimizer with multi-stage linearly-decreasing inertia weight. In: 2009 International Joint Conference on Computational Sciences and Optimization, vol. 1, pp. 505–508, April 2009. https://doi.org/10.1109/CSO.2009.420
19. Zhang, Y., Wang, S., Ji, G.: A comprehensive survey on particle swarm optimization algorithm and its applications. Math. Probl. Eng. **2015**, 38 (2015). https://doi.org/10.1155/2015/931256

Collision Avoidance for Indoor Service Robots Through Multimodal Deep Reinforcement Learning

Francisco Leiva[1](✉), Kenzo Lobos-Tsunekawa[1], and Javier Ruiz-del-Solar[1,2]

[1] Department of Electrical Engineering, Universidad de Chile, Santiago, Chile
{francisco.leiva,kenzo.lobos,jruizd}@ing.uchile.cl
[2] Advanced Mining Technology Center (AMTC),
Universidad de Chile, Santiago, Chile

Abstract. In this paper, we propose an end-to-end approach to endow indoor service robots with the ability to avoid collisions using Deep Reinforcement Learning (DRL). The proposed method allows a controller to derive continuous velocity commands for an omnidirectional mobile robot using depth images, laser measurements, and odometry based speed estimations. The controller is parameterized by a deep neural network, and trained using DDPG. To improve the limited perceptual range of most indoor robots, a method to exploit range measurements through sensor integration and feature extraction is developed. Additionally, to alleviate the reality gap problem due to training in simulations, a simple processing pipeline for depth images is proposed. As a case study we consider indoor collision avoidance using the Pepper robot. Through simulated testing we show that our approach is able to learn a proficient collision avoidance policy from scratch. Furthermore, we show empirically the generalization capabilities of the trained policy by testing it in challenging real-world environments. Videos showing the behavior of agents trained using the proposed method can be found at https://youtu.be/ypC39m4BlSk.

1 Introduction

Collision avoidance is an indispensable ability in mobile robotics. Avoiding a wide range of both static and dynamic obstacles is a key requirement for safe autonomous navigation, autonomous exploration, and multi-agent coordination. Classical formulations to address the collision avoidance problem often consist of several subsystems interacting in a modular fashion. These subsystems extract and process information from the environment, and then use it to plan and execute collision-free trajectories. The main problem that arises when utilizing these classical, modularized systems is that they generally have many adjustable parameters, whose tuning is time consuming and strongly environment-specific.

In this work, we present an end-to-end approach to endow a mobile robot with the ability to avoid collisions using Deep Reinforcement Learning (DRL). The proposed method allows a controller to derive continuous velocity commands for an omnidirectional mobile robot using depth images, odometry based speed

© Springer Nature Switzerland AG 2019
S. Chalup et al. (Eds.): RoboCup 2019, LNAI 11531, pp. 140–153, 2019.
https://doi.org/10.1007/978-3-030-35699-6_11

estimations, and laser measurements as inputs. The latter are incorporated despite the use of depth cameras in order to increase the robot's field of view, thus, improving the observability of the problem. The controller is parameterized by a multimodal neural network and trained using the Deep Deterministic Policy Gradient (DDPG) algorithm [8].

We consider perceptual restrictions commonly found in robots equipped with depth and laser sensors. Consequently, we address the limited observability caused by these restrictions by adding Long Short-Term Memory (LSTM) [4] layers to the controller's network architecture [10]. To further enhance observability, instead of directly using laser measurements as inputs, these readings are aggregated in time as a point-cloud during the policy execution, and handled in a way similar to that proposed in PointNet [14].

As large amounts of data are required to learn a proficient collision avoidance policy, we use the Gazebo simulator [7] for the training process, and then directly transfer the trained controller to a real-world platform by leveraging on ROS [15] interfaces. Because of the aforementioned procedure, we also address the reality gap problem that arises due to the mismatch between simulated and real sensor measurements. In this regard, we use a simple processing pipeline to reduce the differences between simulated and real depth images.

As a case study, we consider indoor collision avoidance using the Pepper robot [12], currently the official Social Standard Platform of the RoboCup@Home competition. The Pepper robot has a 3D sensor on its head, and three fixed laser range finders near its omnidirectional base, which provide sparse range measurements. These sensors provide noisy, short-ranged perception, and are used as inputs to the trained collision avoidance controller.

Through simulated and real-world testing, we show that our approach is capable of learning an effective collision avoidance policy from scratch through DRL. Furthermore, we show that the obtained controller is robust to noisy sensors, and is able to behave adequately when deployed in unseen environments.

The main contributions of this work are the following: (i) An efficient approach to train a robust collision avoidance policy in an end-to-end manner. (ii) A novel method to exploit range measurements through sensor integration and feature extraction (akin to PointNet) for a DRL application. (iii) The utilization of a depth image preprocessing pipeline and its validation as a means to improve the performance of the deployed policy in the robot, by reducing the reality gap.

2   Related Work

Obstacle avoidance and similar tasks have been solved by a variety of methods for a long time, with machine learning based methods taking the lead in performance and popularity [5,10,17,18,23]. Methods that rely on labeled data, such as imitation learning, usually require huge amounts of supervised data that is cumbersome to obtain [17,23]. Furthermore, such methods usually limit the system's performance to the ability of the supervisor. On the other hand, DRL-based methods do not require labeled data and are unbounded by the performance of a supervisor; however, they require large quantities of interactions with the environment to produce good results. Although there are several works on DRL for obstacle avoidance, they either use laser measurements or depth images (thus limiting both performance and applicability) [5,18,20,21], use simplistic environments (halls and fixed environments) [5,20,21], or even fail to converge using just sparse laser measurements [20]. In contrast, we use a multimodal DRL approach [9,13], using both depth images and sparse laser measurements, and consider complex training and validation scenarios.

In some case studies, such as trivial environments, hallways, and some mazes, visual clues and patterns are enough to infer information about regions outside the agent's perceptual range. However, generally, the limitations of such constrained perception must be addressed. A simple approach to overcome the partial observability produced by a limited perceptual range is simply adding more sensors and integrating them using multimodal strategies. However, this method is not always feasible due to physic or monetary contraints. Another common strategy is using recurrent neural networks to alleviate the partial observability [10]. In this work we complement this strategy by integrating sensor readings at different time steps, which allows us to keep a representation of areas outside the perceptual range, while also increasing the density of the measurements.

Finally, we also address the issue of transferring policies trained in simulations to the real world (reality gap) from the perspective of the mismatch between simulated and real observations. Increasingly popular methods to produce real-like observations rely on generative strategies [22], which require labeled data that in the case of depth sensors is difficult or impossible to obtain. Another standard method to produce realistic observations consists of the study of noise and artifact models of 3D sensors [11,21]. In this work, we use a simple pipeline to reduce the mismatch between simulated and real depth images, based on some of the ideas introduced in [6].

3   Preliminaries

We consider the standard RL framework, in which an agent interacts with an environment E in discrete time steps. At each discrete time step t the agent observes o_t, picks an action a_t, and receives a scalar reward r_t. In most real world settings the environment E is partially observed, so the entire history of observation-action tuples may be required to describe the current state s_t, that is, $s_t = (o_1, a_1, ..., o_t, a_t)$.

The environment E is modeled as a Markov Decision Process (MDP) with a state space $\mathcal{S}$, an action space $\mathcal{A}$, transition dynamics $p(s_{t+1}|s_t, a_t)$, and a reward function $r(s_t, a_t)$. The agent's behavior is determined by a policy which may be either stochastic $\pi(a_t|s_t) = \mathbb{P}(a|s)$ or deterministic $a = \pi(s)$.

The return $R_t = \sum_{i=t}^{T} \gamma^{i-t} r(s_i, a_i)$ is defined as the total discounted future reward at time step t, being $\gamma \in [0, 1]$ the discount factor, and T a finite time horizon. The goal in RL is to learn a policy that maximizes the expected return starting from an initial state: $\mathbb{E}_{(r_i, s_i) \sim E, a_i \sim \pi}[R_1]$.

4 Collision Avoidance for the Pepper Robot

Collision avoidance can be treated as a sequential decision making problem, where an agent has to navigate through a given environment while avoiding static and dynamic obstacles. In this case we consider indoor environments, and the Pepper robot as the physical agent. To solve this problem using the RL framework we formulate it as an MDP. Namely, the state space $\mathcal{S}$, action space $\mathcal{A}$, and reward function $r(s_t, a_t)$ are designed in an ad-hoc fashion.

For the state space we consider processed sensor readings (depth images and laser measurements) and normalized odometry based speed estimations. While depth images are processed primarily to bridge the reality gap due to training in simulations (see Sect. 4.1), laser measurements are processed to address the limited perception range of the robot (see Sect. 4.2).

Like several other works on collision avoidance through DRL [5,17,21], velocity commands are used to control the agent. Since Pepper has an omnidirectional mobile base, an action at time t is defined by the tuple $a_t = (v_x^t, v_y^t, v_\theta^t)$, where v_x^t and v_y^t correspond to the robot's instantaneous linear speeds in the x and y-axis, whereas v_θ^t to its angular speed around the z-axis.

The reward function is designed based on several agent's desirable behaviors when interacting with the environment. To encourage navigation through safe, collision-free regions, the reward defined in Eq. 1 is utilized.

$$r_t = \begin{cases} \dfrac{v_x^t}{v_x^{\max}} \cos\left(\dfrac{\pi}{2} \dfrac{K_{v_\theta}^t}{v_\theta^{\max}}\right) & v_x^t \geq 0 \\[2ex] \dfrac{v_x^t}{v_x^{\max}} & v_x^t < 0 \end{cases} \tag{1}$$

The variables $v_x^{\max}$ and $v_\theta^{\max}$ correspond to the maximum values for v_x and v_θ, whilst $K_{v_\theta}^t$ is defined in Eq. 2.

$$K_{v_\theta}^t = \min\left\{\max\left\{\left|v_\theta^t\right|, \left|v_\theta^t - v_\theta^{t-1}\right|\right\}, v_\theta^{\max}\right\} \tag{2}$$

To prevent the agent from getting dangerously close to obstacles, a punishment signal is provided according to Eq. 3, where $l_{\min}^t$ denotes the distance to the nearest obstacle according to the processed laser measurements at time t, and K is a constant set to 1.5. A stronger punishment $r_t = -10$ is given to the agent whenever it fails to avoid an obstacle.

$$r_t = K(l_{\min}^t - 1), \quad l_{\min}^t < 0.6 \tag{3}$$

In this work, the collision avoidance problem is modeled as an episodic task, where an episode ends when the robot collides, or when a fixed number of time steps is reached. To encourage generalization, each episode has randomized initial poses for the robot and most of the obstacles of the environment.

4.1   Depth Images Processing

There is a big difference between simulated depth images and those obtained from the Pepper's 3D sensor. Simulated depth images obtained from Gazebo are ideal, completely noise-free and undistorted. Pepper's 3D sensor readings, on the contrary, usually have many patches of lost, mixed and noisy pixels, and present a clear distortion in the predicted relative distance to some objects. Due to this mismatch, directly transferring the trained policy in simulations to the real world would be unfeasible.

To solve the aforementioned issue, both simulated and real depth images are subjected to a preprocessing stage. Because of the information loss inherent to the 3D sensor embedded in Pepper, it is almost impossible to reconstruct accurate depth maps, specially when the scenes include several shiny or dark objects. Given this limitation, we focus on improving the real sensor readings, but also on corrupting the simulated depth images so they resemble their real-world counterpart.

Mixed and lost pixels are usually found near the border of different objects in a depth map. Therefore a Canny edge detector [2] is applied over the simu-lated depth images to find regions where pixel corruption would exist. The edge detector is also applied over the depth map's corresponding RGB image, as some edges cannot be directly extracted from the simulated depth map. The extracted edges are aggregated and filtered since some of them arise because of textures, which are usually not associated to places where corruption in real depth images is present. To filter these edges, a Hough transform [3] is applied over the aggre-gated edge map to detect lines, and the value of pixels parallel to each of the detected lines is compared. If the difference between the average value of the compared pixels is below a threshold, the edge associated to the detected line is likely to be produced because of textures, and consequently is discarded. Finally, the filtered edge map is dilated, and pixel patches are marked over random-sized regions whose position matches the filtered edges. The resulting mask resembles the distribution of corrupted pixels of real depth images, and is applied over the original simulated depth image.

For the real depth images, we only tackle the problem introduced by lost pixels, which we found to be the main cause of image distortion of the real 3D sensor used. A mask is constructed to mark all the lost pixels in the real depth images, and then their value is predicted using Telea's inpainting technique [19]. The same procedure is applied over the corrupted simulated depth maps. Finally, both real and simulated images are decimated (and subjected to an anti-aliasing filter) to reduce their dimensionality to 60×80 pixels. Figure 1 shows a diagram of the described pipeline.

4.2   Laser Integration

Laser range information is usually used in DRL applications as fixed dimensional representations. Some examples are a fixed-number of sparse laser readings [18], a fixed number of candidates from a dense laser sensor [16], and image-like

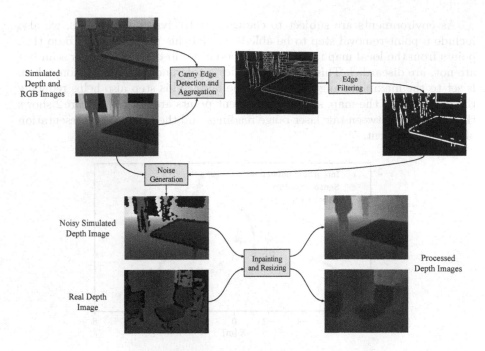

Fig. 1. Diagram of the preprocessing pipeline for simulated and real depth images.

representations [13] (e.g 3D LiDAR). For sparse lasers and fixed candidates, their distribution and resolution become critical in the observability of the MDP, but a high dimensionality may produce slow learning since in most cases these elements are fed to fully connected layers, which do not necessarily exploit the nature of the representation. While image-like representations do exploit the nature of the readings through convolutional layers, all these representations fail to identify openings (areas without obstacles in the sensor range) since in those cases the readings must be saturated to their maximum value to maintain a consistent representation. Furthermore, in all cases, the representations only consider obstacles in a direct line of sight, failing to model complex environments.

In this work we construct and unordered, size-independent representation of the environment, which we will refer to as "local map". This local map is made by simply integrating laser scans across time in a fixed-frame, and storing them as a point-cloud. In in this case, the fixed-frame utilized to perform such integration is set by the robot's odometry. As odometry also integrates the error of the encoders, navigating through large environments using this methodology produces clearly distorted local maps. To address this issue, the laser scan integration is limited to a fixed distance D from the robot's local frame, as points within this range are less likely to be distorted by the odometry error. In the case of the Pepper robot, D is set to 6.5 m.

As environments are subject to change due to dynamic obstacles, we also include a point-removal step to be able to model this phenomenon. To do this, points from the local map that should be perceived in the current laser scan but are not, are discarded. This process includes a tolerance in the criterion, which is set to the maximum angular error of the laser. This step also helps reducing the distortion of the map, since non-coherent points are deleted. Figure 2 shows the difference between raw laser range readings and the proposed representation of the environment.

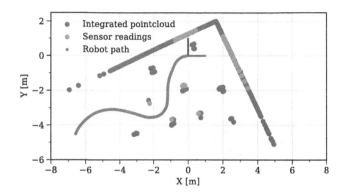

Fig. 2. Difference between raw laser measurements and the proposed odometry based local map. The green dots represent the trajectory followed by the robot, whilst orange points correspond to its raw laser range measurements. The blue points represent the obtained local map, constructed by integrating and filtering laser readings. (Color figure available online)

The advantages of this representation are clear. It encapsulates information to distinguish between opening areas from objects at the saturation distance. It also allows to model the environment with increasingly precision as the robot navigates through it, while modeling out-of sight objects. Finally, it allows the use of cheaper sensors, as it can artificially augment the sensor's resolution.

4.3   Algorithm and Networks' Architecture

To train the collision avoidance policy we use DDPG [8], a continuous control DRL algorithm. Since DDPG is an actor-critic method, two independent neural networks are designed to parameterize the policy (actor) and the state-action value function (the critic). In this work, both of these networks share almost the same structure, differing only in their inputs and outputs.

As we combine different sensor measurements to conform the state space, a multimodal strategy is followed to perform sensor fusion. In this regard, every sensor is processed independently by different feature extractors (which are part of the same neural network), and the resulting embeddings are concatenated. However, given that the laser measurements representation (the local map) has a non-fixed dimensionality, neither fully-connected nor convolutional layers can directly take it as input. Instead, we follow the approach presented in [14], using shared weights and symmetric activation functions to go from a variable input size to a fixed dimensionality embedding.

The approach followed consists of two steps. First, every point from the map is processed by a series of fully connected layers independently (the same fully connected layers are applied to every point). Then, the outputs from this operation are aggregated using max pooling to obtain a global feature vector, which encapsulates the input's information in a fixed-dimensional representation. Even though the number of points conforming the local map may vary at every time step during the policy execution, we select a fixed number of points from this representation during training to allow batch processing. If the number of points from the local map exceeds the fixed selected number of points, uniform sampling is performed. On the contrary, if the points from the local map are not enough, we randomly repeat points until the requirement is satisfied. At test time, the complete local map is utilized.

The architectures of the designed actor and critic are summarized in Fig. 3, where hyper parameter and design choices were primarily taken from [10]. The depth image feature extractor is conformed by three convolutional layers: Conv1 with 16 8×8 filters (stride 4), Conv2 with 32 4×4 filters (stride 2), and Conv3 with 32 2×2 filters (stride 2). The feature extractor for the local map consists of three fully connected layers of 64, 64 and 1024 hidden units respectively. Finally, the feature extractor for the odometry speed estimations (and actions, for the critic) consists of two fully connected layers of 32 and 64 hidden units each.

The embeddings obtained from these modules are concatenated and used as input for a fully connected layer (FcFus), which has 200 hidden units. The output from this layer goes to an LSTM layer, and then to another fully connected layer (FcPre), both having 200 cells/hidden units. The final layer (FcOut) outputs the action for the actor and the state-action value for the critic, respectively.

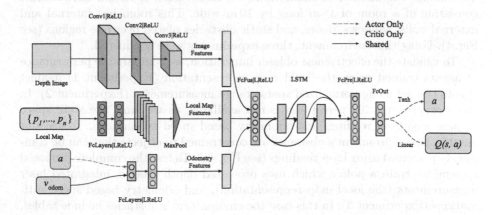

Fig. 3. Representation of the proposed multimodal network architecture.

We use LSTM layers to address the partial observability due to the robot's sensors limitations, that is, to rely on several observations to approximate the actual environment state at each time step. These layers process the concatenated embeddings obtained from the inputs, thus, being able to integrate sensory information through time. To effectively train the neural network with these layers, uniform sampling from the replay buffer cannot be performed. Instead, the method proposed in [10] is utilized to sample sequential experience traces.

5   Evaluation Results

5.1   Experimental Setup

The training environments are constructed using the Gazebo simulator [7], whilst TensorFlow [1] is used to implement DDPG and the associated neural network models. To bridge the simulations with the training algorithm, we rely on ROS [15] interfaces.

Episodes are limited to 500 time steps, but may end prematurely whenever a collision between the agent and any obstacle is detected. At every time step, a velocity command is executed for 400 ms. The maximum instantaneous speeds for the Pepper robot are set to 0.5 and 0.3 m/s for the x and y-axis, and 0.5 rad/s for the angular speed around the z-axis.

We utilize a batch size of 64 for training, whereas learning rates, weight initializations and exploration strategy remain the same as in the original DDPG paper [8]. All processing is conducted in a laptop equipped with an Intel i7-7700HQ processor, and a Nvidia GeForce GTX 1060 GPU. With the available hardware, 7,500 training steps take approximately one hour.

5.2   Simulation Results

To validate our method in simulations, we constructed a virtual environment consisting of a room of 18 m long by 10 m wide. This room has internal and external walls, windows, doors, and static obstacles placed over free regions (see Fig. 4). Using this environment, three experiments were conducted.

To validate the effectiveness of laser integration, we compare the performance of agents trained using the local map representation (Experiment 1) against agents trained using normalized sparse range measurements (Experiment 2). In these experiments 3D perception is not available, as we limit the state space to processed laser readings and odometry based speed estimations. To account for this, the environment's obstacles are constrained to objects that can be completely perceived using laser readings (see Fig. 4a). To test the complete proposed system, we train a policy which uses processed depth images, integrated laser measurements (the local map representation), and odometry based speed estimations (Experiment 3). In this case the environment's obstacles include tables, as 2D range measurements are not enough to model their collision geometry (see Fig. 4b).

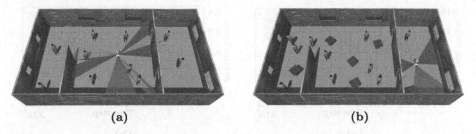

Fig. 4. Virtual environments constructed for training and validation in simulations. (a) Environment used for Experiments 1 and 2. Contains 10 simple obstacles (persons). (b) Environment used for Experiment 3. Contains 10 simple obstacles (persons) and 6 complex obstacles (tables).

To evaluate the performance of the trained agents, two metrics are utilized: the total reward obtained in an episode $R = \sum_{t=1}^{T} r(s_t, a_t)$, and the average instantaneous forward speeds of an episode (penalizing high angular speeds) $V_{\Sigma} = \frac{1}{T} \sum_{t=1}^{T} v_x^t \cos(v_\theta^t)$.

Figure 5 shows the obtained results for the conducted experiments. The training process was limited to 7.2×10^4 time steps (approximately 10 hours per trial) for Experiments 1 and 2 (Fig. 5a and b). For Experiment 3 (Fig. 5c and d), training was conducted for 11×10^4 time steps (that is, for approximately 15 hours per trial). Every 8×10^3 and 10×10^3 time steps, respectively, 50 validation episodes are performed (the policy is executed directly, i.e., the exploration is turned off). The graphs show the average and standard deviations from 10 independent trials.

The obtained results show that policies trained using the proposed method (using both high and low dimensional state spaces) are able to efficiently avoid obstacles in the constructed virtual environment. From Fig. 5a and b it is clear that agents trained using raw sparse laser measurements fail to get a good performance, as the environment's observability is heavily limited by the robot's perception range. In contrast, including the local map in the state space allows the trained agents to learn proficient obstacle avoidance policies, thus, validating the benefits of such representation.

Figure 5c and d show that agents trained with the proposed method consistently get good performance, regardless of the high variance across training and validation episodes due to robot and obstacles initial pose randomization. This also shows the ability of the proposed method of combining multisensory inputs, as the trained policies successfully learn to avoid tables in spite of contradictory information between lasers and depth images (the constructed local map detects tables as point obstacles or collision free regions, and their 3D geometry is only captured by the depth images).

There is a slight reduction in the overall performance and its variance (both in terms of the reward and average speeds) compared to the results obtained using only the local map (Fig. 5a and b); however, this is due to the difference

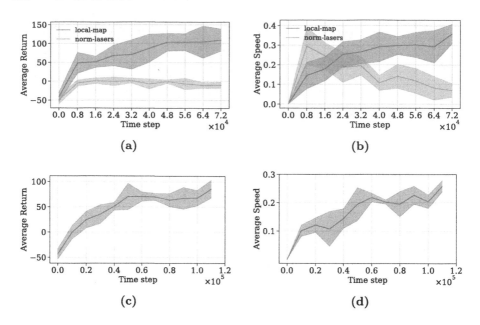

Fig. 5. Performance evaluations for the experiments carried out. (a) and (b) show the comparison between agents trained using the proposed local-map representation, and agents trained using normalized sparse range measurements (Experiments 1 and 2). (c) and (d) show the performance of agents trained using the complete proposed method (Experiment 3).

between the number of obstacles utilized for Experiment 1 and Experiment 3 (refer to Fig. 4). As we randomize the initial pose of the robot and the obstacles for each episode, a small number of obstacles allows the existence of easy episodes (which results in occasionally higher rewards). On the other hand, the difficulty is higher, but remains similar across episodes, when the environment is highly cluttered (which results in lower rewards).

5.3 Validation on the Physical Robot

The collision avoidance policy trained using the full proposed method in simulations (Experiment 3) was directly transferred to a real Pepper robot by using external processing and ROS interfaces. Depth images and laser measurements were manipulated according to the methodology described in Sects. 4.1 and 4.2, respectively. To evaluate the performance of the policy, we considered three different indoor environments (see Fig. 6): A study room (static obstacles), a hall (static and dynamic obstacles) and a cluttered laboratory (dynamic obstacles, maze-like environment).

The agent was able to navigate successfully through collision free regions in all these environments, regardless of the variety of unseen obstacles it encountered with respect to simulations. Furthermore, it behaved adequately even when undergoing maze-like environments. Examples of the trained policy deployed in real world environments can be found at https://youtu.be/ypC39m4BlSk.

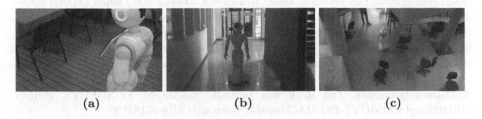

(a)   (b)   (c)

Fig. 6. Real work environments utilized to validate the trained collision avoidance policy. (a) Study room, (b) hall, and (c) laboratory.

The generalization capabilities of the trained policy may be explained considering that (i) simulated and real local maps are similar, and (ii) the avoidance of 3D obstacles in the real world only requires coarse information regarding their shapes, which can be obtained using the processed depth images. These conditions allowed the policy to perform well in the testing environments even though it was trained with limited information in simulations.

On the other hand, it was observed that the policy's performance was severely undermined when the robot was deployed in environments where outdoor lighting was present, as Pepper's depth sensor produced highly corrupted images under such conditions. The same performance detriment was observed when unprocessed depth images were used as observations. This behavior can be explained considering the domain mismatch between simulated depth images used for training the policy, and the heavily corrupted depth maps that were being fed to the policy in the aforementioned scenarios.

6   Conclusions and Future Work

In this work we presented a successful approach to solve the obstacle avoidance problem using the Pepper robot, with experimental validations in real-world environments. We also presented a novel approach to use point-clouds, and more generally, unordered and non-fixed dimensional inputs for RL applications. Finally, a simple preprocessing stage to bridge the reality gap between simulated and real depth images was presented and validated.

Although in this work we only tackled the obstacle avoidance problem, similar tasks, such as visual navigation, could be solved relying on the proposed modelling. Furthermore, during our experiments, the real world performance of the policy was strongly dependent of the input preprocessing applied during training and deployment. Consequently, realistic input simulation and domain adaptation arise as interesting areas of study for future work.

Finally, in this implementation we integrate laser scans using encoder-based odometry to construct the unordered representation of laser measurements. This greatly limits the quality of the integration. We propose the use of proper point cloud registration (for instance, using Iterative Closest Point) when LiDAR information allows the use of such methods, and also the use of point-clouds produced by methods such as visual SLAM as inputs of our policy. Furthermore, these methods could also be applied to register point-clouds from the depth sensor, as the local map feature extraction extends to 3D points.

Acknowledgements. This work was partially funded by FONDECYT Project 1161500 and CONICYT-PFCHA/Magíster Nacional/2018-22182130.

References

1. Abadi, M., et al.: TensorFlow: large-scale machine learning on heterogeneous systems (2015). Software available from tensorflow.org. https://www.tensorflow.org/
2. Canny, J.: A computational approach to edge detection. IEEE Trans. Pattern Anal. Mach. Intell. PAMI **8**(6), 679–698 (1986). https://doi.org/10.1109/TPAMI.1986.4767851
3. Duda, R.O., Hart, P.E.: Use of the hough transformation to detect lines and curves in pictures. Commun. ACM **15**(1), 11–15 (1972). https://doi.org/10.1145/361237.361242
4. Hochreiter, S., Schmidhuber, J.: Long short-term memory. Neural Comput. **9**(8), 1735–1780 (1997). https://doi.org/10.1162/neco.1997.9.8.1735
5. Kahn, G., Villaflor, A., Ding, B., Abbeel, P., Levine, S.: Self-supervised deep reinforcement learning with generalized computation graphs for robot navigation. In: 2018 IEEE International Conference on Robotics and Automation (ICRA), pp. 1–8, May 2018. https://doi.org/10.1109/ICRA.2018.8460655
6. Kim, S., Kim, M., Ho, Y.: Depth image filter for mixed and noisy pixel removal in rgb-d camera systems. IEEE Trans. Consum. Electron. **59**(3), 681–689 (2013). https://doi.org/10.1109/TCE.2013.6626256
7. Koenig, N., Howard, A.: Design and use paradigms for gazebo, an open-source multi-robot simulator. In: 2004 IEEE/RSJ International Conference on Intelligent Robots and Systems (IROS) (IEEE Cat. No.04CH37566), vol. 3, pp. 2149–2154, September 2004. https://doi.org/10.1109/IROS.2004.1389727
8. Lillicrap, T.P., et al.: Continuous control with deep reinforcement learning. In: ICLR (2016)
9. Liu, G.H., Siravuru, A., Prabhakar, S., Veloso, M., Kantor, G.: Learning end-to-end multimodal sensor policies for autonomous navigation. In: Proceedings of the 1st Annual Conference on Robot Learning. Proceedings of Machine Learning Research, 13–15 November 2017, vol. 78, pp. 249–261. PMLR (2017)
10. Lobos-Tsunekawa, K., Leiva, F., Ruiz-del-Solar, J.: Visual navigation for biped humanoid robots using deep reinforcement learning. IEEE Rob. Autom. Lett. **3**(4), 3247–3254 (2018). https://doi.org/10.1109/LRA.2018.2851148
11. Nguyen, C.V., Izadi, S., Lovell, D.: Modeling kinect sensor noise for improved 3d reconstruction and tracking. In: 2012 Second International Conference on 3D Imaging, Modeling, Processing, Visualization Transmission, pp. 524–530, October 2012. https://doi.org/10.1109/3DIMPVT.2012.84

12. Pandey, A.K., Gelin, R.: A mass-produced sociable humanoid robot: pepper: the first machine of its kind. IEEE Rob. Autom. Mag. **25**(3), 40–48 (2018). https://doi.org/10.1109/MRA.2018.2833157

13. Patel, N., Choromanska, A., Krishnamurthy, P., Khorrami, F.: A deep learning gated architecture for UGV navigation robust to sensor failures. Rob. Auton. Syst. **116**, 80–97 (2019). https://doi.org/10.1016/j.robot.2019.03.001

14. Qi, C.R., Su, H., Mo, K., Guibas, L.J.: Pointnet: deep learning on point sets for 3d classification and segmentation. CoRR abs/1612.00593 (2016). http://arxiv.org/abs/1612.00593

15. Quigley, M., et al.: ROS: an open-source robot operating system. In: Proceedings of the IEEE International Conference on Robotics and Automation (ICRA) Workshop on Open Source Robotics, Kobe, Japan, May 2009

16. Sampedro, C., Bavle, H., Rodriguez-Ramos, A., de la Puente, P., Campoy, P.: Laser-based reactive navigation for multirotor aerial robots using deep reinforcement learning. In: 2018 IEEE/RSJ International Conference on Intelligent Robots and Systems (IROS), pp. 1024–1031, October 2018. https://doi.org/10.1109/IROS.2018.8593706

17. Tai, L., Li, S., Liu, M.: A deep-network solution towards model-less obstacle avoidance. In: 2016 IEEE/RSJ International Conference on Intelligent Robots and Systems (IROS), pp. 2759–2764, October 2016. https://doi.org/10.1109/IROS.2016.7759428

18. Tai, L., Paolo, G., Liu, M.: Virtual-to-real deep reinforcement learning: continuous control of mobile robots for mapless navigation. In: 2017 IEEE/RSJ International Conference on Intelligent Robots and Systems (IROS), pp. 31–36, September 2017. https://doi.org/10.1109/IROS.2017.8202134

19. Telea, A.: An image inpainting technique based on the fast marching method. J. Graph. Tools **9**(1), 23–34 (2004)

20. Xie, L., Wang, S., Rosa, S., Markham, A., Trigoni, N.: Learning with training wheels: Speeding up training with a simple controller for deep reinforcement learning. In: 2018 IEEE International Conference on Robotics and Automation (ICRA), pp. 6276–6283, May 2018. https://doi.org/10.1109/ICRA.2018.8461203

21. Xie, L., Wang, S., Markham, A., Trigoni, N.: Towards monocular vision based obstacle avoidance through deep reinforcement learning. CoRR abs/1706.09829 (2017). http://arxiv.org/abs/1706.09829

22. Yang, L., Liang, X., Xing, E.P.: Unsupervised real-to-virtual domain unification for end-to-end highway driving. CoRR abs/1801.03458 (2018). http://arxiv.org/abs/1801.03458

23. Yang, S., Konam, S., Ma, C., Rosenthal, S., Veloso, M.M., Scherer, S.: Obstacle avoidance through deep networks based intermediate perception. CoRR abs/1704.08759 (2017). http://arxiv.org/abs/1704.08759

YoloSPoC: Recognition of Multiple Object Instances by Using Yolo-Based Proposals and Deep SPoC-Based Descriptors

Patricio Loncomilla$^{(\boxtimes)}$ and Javier Ruiz-del-Solar

Advanced Mining Technology Center, Universidad de Chile, Santiago, Chile
{ploncomi,jruizd}@ing.uchile.cl

Abstract. The recognition of particular objects instances (e.g. my coffee cup or my wallet) is an important research topic in robotics, as it enables tasks like object manipulation in domestic environments in real-time. However, in recent years most efforts have been aimed to solve generic object detection and object class recognition problems. In this work, a method for performing recognition of particular objects instances, named YoloSPoC, is proposed. It is based on generation of high-quality object proposals by using YOLOv3, computing descriptors of these proposals using a MAC (Maximal Activation of Convolutions) based approach, recognizing the object instances using an open-set nearest neighbor classifier, and filtering of overlapping recognitions. The proposed method is compared to state-of the-art methods based on local features (SIFT and ORB based methods) using two datasets of home-like objects. The obtained results show that the proposed method outperforms existing methods in the reported experiments, being robust against conditions like (i) occlusions, (ii) illumination changes, (iii) cluttered backgrounds, (iv) presence of multiple objects in the scene, (v) presence of textured and non-textured objects, and (vi) object classes not available when training the proposal generator.

Keywords: Object recognition · Object instance recognition · Robocup@Home

1 Introduction

In recent years, advances in computer vision have been impressive, as convolutional neural networks (CNN), and in general deep learning, has enabled the use of large datasets for training models with millions of parameters. Then, hand-engineered systems have fallen in favor of flexible network architectures trained with large datasets, where each specific task to be solved is specified by means of an optimization loss.

One of the hottest research topics is generic object recognition, in which objects are classified into a set of possible categories, each having thousands of labeled examples. The accuracy of these systems is constantly rising, having outperformed humans in this task. The same applies to the task of object detection in images, where impressive results have been obtained using deep-based approaches such as YOLO [7].

© Springer Nature Switzerland AG 2019
S. Chalup et al. (Eds.): RoboCup 2019, LNAI 11531, pp. 154–165, 2019.
https://doi.org/10.1007/978-3-030-35699-6_12

However, in some applications like manipulation of objects in domestic environments (see Fig. 1), the recognition of particular objects instances (e.g. my coffee cup, my wallet, my key chain), using just one or very few stored views (the number depends on the objects symmetry) of the object, is required. In this case it is difficult to apply the standard deep learning pipeline, because it is not always possible to obtain hundreds or thousands of images of the object instances to be recognized. Also, the number of particular objects to recognize can be much higher than those in standard datasets like COCO [14], which consider only 80 possible object categories. This topic has not been fully addressed by the computer vision or the deep learning communities.

Fig. 1. Pepper robot detecting instances of domestic objects.

In this work, we analyze this problem and propose a method for solving the particular object instance recognition task. The method is based on the use of YOLOv3 [8] for generating high-quality proposals, and computing descriptors for each proposal using a MAC (Maximal Activation of Convolutions) based procedure [4, 5]. Then, the descriptors in the current test image are compared to reference descriptors using an open-set nearest-neighbor classification procedure, followed by a post-processing step, which filters multiple, overlapping recognitions of the object instance.

This paper is organized as follows: Sect. 2 presents the related work, and in Sect. 3 the proposed method is described. Then, in Sect. 4 results are presented and analyzed, and in Sect. 5 conclusions are drawn.

2 Related Work

While general object recognition has been successfully addressed by the computer vision community by using CNNs, recognition of particular object instances has not been at the aim of current research. However, some works address this problem by following different approaches.

In [9, 10], the SIFT L&R object recognizer, which uses matches between local descriptors followed by geometric verification, is used for comparing several local descriptor implementations. This object recognizer can detect successfully textured objects and can deal with cluttered backgrounds. However, it is not able to recognize objects which are untextured, or far from the camera.

In [12], a system which can recognize object instances from RGBD data is presented. For classifying images in which the object is cropped, local descriptors (spin images, SIFT) are extracted for representing shape, while SIFT is extracted from images. An EMK feature is generated for pooling information from the descriptors, and a classifier (SVM or random forest) is applied to predict the label from the object. For detecting objects, a sliding window approach using a HoG-based detector is tested. Also, in this work two benchmarks named *Washington RGB-D object dataset* and *Washington RGB-D scene dataset* are introduced.

It must be also noted that, in previous RoboCup conferences, there are not papers related to particular object instance recognition using deep learning techniques.

3   Proposed Method

In this work, we aim to solve a particular object instance recognition by using methods based on CNNs and nearest-neighbor classification. By changing the paradigm from local descriptors to global descriptors based on CNNs, we aim to recognize objects that are very hard to recognize by using just local descriptors.

Thus, the proposed method is based on four main blocks: (i) computation of region proposals, (ii) computation of global descriptors, and (iii) recognition of object instances using an open-set nearest-neighbor classification scheme, which can reject detections generated by objects outside the training dataset, and (iv) suppression of redundant detections. The blocks that define the method are shown in Fig. 2.

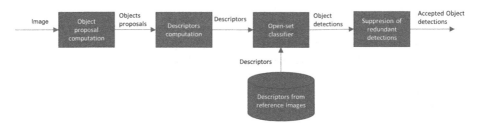

Fig. 2. Block diagram of the system

3.1   Object Proposal Detection

The generation of object proposals is based on the YOLOv3 object detector [8]. It is a CNN, which takes an image as input and generates a list of bounding boxes as output, each considering a confidence and probabilities of belonging to each class. The system works by considering an initial set of bounding boxes spread over the image, and then, by using regression, each bounding box is fitted to an object present in the image. Also, both probabilities of belonging to each object class, and an objectness score are computed for each proposal. Finally, non-maximal suppression is applied over the resulting bounding boxes. YOLOv3 is improved respect to previous YOLOs, by considering multiple scales and modifying the loss function for improving accuracy on small objects. The network is trained on large datasets like COCO [14], which includes about 200,000 labeled images, divided into 80 classes. As YOLOv3 is trained to detect a predefined set of classes, it is not feasible to use it as a general proposal generator, which must be class-agnostic. However, this problem can be handled by lowering the confidence threshold from 0.5 to 0.01, which enables detection of most of the objects to recognize, at the cost of generating misdetections that need to be handled by an open-set classifier. As YOLOv3 assigns labels to the detections, and this work is aimed at detecting objects that can be manipulated by a robot, detections with labels related to non-manipulable objects (like furniture) are discarded.

3.2   Descriptors Computation

Global descriptors are computed for describing the proposals. The used methodology [4, 5] is aimed to another application, image retrieval, in which it achieves state-of-the-art performance. However, it can be used successfully for generating global descriptors. The method consists on computing features using CNNs over the object proposals and then pooling them channel-wise into a descriptor [4, 5]. The used architecture consists of the convolutional layers of a ResNet-101 network [16], which is a high performant CNN that includes residual blocks containing shortcut connections, as shown in Fig. 3. The network is pretrained on ImageNet [15], but it can be fine-tuned by using a Siamese network approach, which consists on modeling the network as an embedding function, which maps inputs into a metric space.

The use of channel-wise pooling operations enables the system to be robust against small translations and small changes in the scale of the objects. Also, for improving robustness against scale change and translation, these descriptors can be computed for several sub regions of the image, and then summed up.

These descriptors are very robust, and able to outperform all previous methods on image retrieval. For computing the global descriptors, different variants of pooling described in [5] are used, including MAC (maximum activations of convolutions), SPoC (sum-pooled convolutional features) and gem (generalized mean). The CNN Image retrieval toolbox [11], which implements the computation of global descriptors, is used for computing a descriptor for each proposal. Also, this toolbox is able to train the network by using a Siamese network approach, by using Structure from Motion on outdoor scenes.

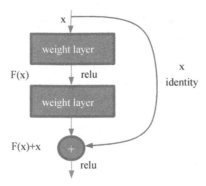

Fig. 3. Residual block used in ResNet networks, which can include more than 100 layers.

3.3 Open-Set Nearest Neighbor Classifier

A nearest neighbor classifier is used for assigning labels to each proposal from the test image, by using its global descriptor. As the environment could contain objects different that those stored in the training database, the system must be able to reject unknown objects.

Open-set classifiers can deal with data different from that available during training, labeling them as unknown. An open-set classifier is used for classifying the proposals, and for rejecting those related to objects outside the training dataset. A nearest neighbor classifier considering a second-to-first nearest neighbor distance ratio test [3] is used for rejecting detections that does not correspond to any of the known objects.

$$\frac{d_2}{d_1} < threshold \rightarrow reject$$

where d_1 is the Euclidean distance between the test descriptor and the nearest descriptor in the database, and d_2 is the Euclidean distance between the test descriptor and the nearest descriptor from a different object in the database. Then, in case the two distances are similar, the classifier cannot be confident about the class of the object, and the detection is discarded.

3.4 Suppression of Redundant Detections

The invariance of the descriptor against different translations and scales is useful for managing occlusions and different object poses. However, it can generate multiple detections from a same object, because several small proposals intersecting the true object can be labeled as positives. Then, a post-processing step is required. Detections related to a same object are sorted by its size. Then, when the bounding box from a given detection is completely contained inside another bounding box related to the same object, it is eliminated. A tolerance threshold of 30 pixels is used for deciding when a given object detection is contained inside another object.

Table 2. F1-scores on DSLL, per subset

Subset	Method				
	YoloSPoC	YoloSPoC-triplet	YoloSPoC-gem	SIFT L&R	ORB L&R
S1	0.861	0.836	0.836	0.679	0.632
S2	0.840	0.841	0.864	0.329	0.244
S3	0.902	0.910	0.944	0.312	0.208
S4	0.923	0.877	0.857	0.247	0.169
S5	0.695	0.620	0.631	0.465	0.337
M1	0.863	0.841	0.861	0.143	0.090
M2	0.814	0.829	0.817	0.076	0.045
Mean	0.843	0.822	0.830	0.322	0.246

YOLOv3 is trained on the COCO dataset, which considers 80 object classes. Then, degradation of proposal's quality can be expected when detecting objects not contained in COCO. Then, the second set of experiments analyses which would be the performance of the proposed method in case of having ideal proposals. In order to test this, the real ground truth boxes are used instead of the YOLO-based proposals. Results are shown in Table 3. The proposed systems achieve impressive F1-scores over 0.92, except in the dataset S5 which includes occlusions. The best variant is again YoloSPoC, and the use of triplet learning is not useful again because of the domain shift.

Table 3. F1-Scores on DSLL, considering truth bounding boxes, per subset

Subset	Method				
	YoloSPoC	YoloSPoC-triplet	YoloSPoC-gem	SIFT L&R	ORB L&R
S1	1.0	1.0	1.0	0.679	0.632
S2	1.0	0.981	0.997	0.329	0.244
S3	0.987	0.978	1.0	0.312	0.208
S4	0.961	0.939	0.975	0.247	0.169
S5	0.865	0.836	0.823	0.465	0.337
M1	0.965	0.936	0.955	0.143	0.090
M2	0.928	0.916	0.919	0.076	0.045
Mean	0.941	0.931	0.934	0.322	0.246

The following conclusions can be drawn of the results presented in Tables 2 and 3:

(i)   Multiple objects: The performance of YoloSPoC does not degrade when multiple objects are present in the images. In Table 2 a F1-score of 0.839 is obtained in multiple objects cases (M1, M2) v/s 0.847 in single object cases.
(ii) Occlusions: YoloSPoC is able to detect occluded objects, but its performance is slightly decreased with occlusions. In Table 2, a F1-score of 0.695 is obtained in occluded cases (S5) v/s 0.867 when no occlusions occur.
(iii) Illumination changes: The performance of YoloSPoC is almost not affected by changes in illumination. In Table 2, the F1-score is 0.840 in cases of variable illumination (S2), v/s 0.843 in cases of no illumination changes.
(iv) Cluttered backgrounds: The performance of YoloSPoC is almost not affected by cluttered backgrounds. In Table 2, a F1-score of 0.869 is obtained when cluttered backgrounds are considered (S4, M2) v/s 0.832 when uniform backgrounds are used.
(v)   Non-textured objects: YoloSPoC is able to detect non-textured objects. In Table 3, YoloSPoC can get a perfect F1-score on cases S1 and S2, in which non-textured objects are present. Then, the SPoC descriptor is useful for detecting both textured and non-textured objects.

Examples of different conditions (i), (ii), (iii), (iv), (v) are shown in Fig. 4.

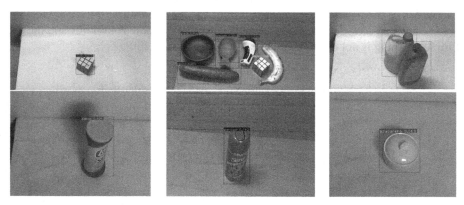

Fig. 4. Objects to recognize under different conditions: single object, multiple objects, occlusions, illumination changes, cluttered background and non-textured objects.

Finally, the third set of experiments consists on analyzing the dependence between the F1-score and the nearest neighbor ratio. Results are shown in Table 4. It can be noted that the best nearest neighbor ratio threshold for detections considering YOLO proposals is 0.95. However, when ground truth bounding boxes are used instead of YOLO, the best nearest ratio threshold is 1.0, which is equivalent to not using the nearest neighbor ratio at all. In consequence, the use of the nearest neighbor ratio is not useful in this case. Then, it can be concluded that the nearest neighbor ratio is useful for discarding proposals not containing objects from the dataset, because they are only present when YOLO-based proposals are used.

Table 4. F1-scores over all subsets using different methods, using different nearest neighbor ratios, both for YOLO proposals and for ground truth bounding boxes

Variant	Method				
	YoloSPoC	Yologem triplet	Yologem	SIFT L&R	ORB L&R
YOLO proposals @ 0.90	0.770	0.769	0.763	0.322	0.246
YOLO proposals @ 0.95	0.834	0.820	0.837	0.322	0.246
YOLO proposals @ 0.98	0.824	0.816	0.820	0.322	0.246
YOLO proposals @ 1.00	0.803	0.774	0.795	0.322	0.246
GT proposals @ 0.90	0.875	0.871	0.860	0.322	0.246
GT proposals @ 0.95	0.947	0.928	0.938	0.322	0.246
GT proposals @ 0.98	0.966	0.940	0.952	0.322	0.246
GT proposals @ 1.00	0.967	0.940	0.952	0.322	0.246

4.3   Washington RGB-D Scenes Dataset Experiments

The Washington RGB-D Scenes dataset [12] includes eight sequences, each generated by a moving camera. A total set of 300 object instances can be included in the sequences. Each object is represented by around 830 views.

In this work, we compare YoloSPoC against the instance object detector proposed in [12], which uses a variant of HoG descriptors applied over sliding windows and a linear SVM classifier for detecting and classifying the objects. Only 12 views per training object are used when testing our system, while for [12] around 830 views of each training object are used, as the last system is unable to work when few views are available. The precision-recall curves are shown in Fig. 5. Results indicate that our system, using only 12 views per object, improves largely on the original work, which uses around 830 views per object. Also, the original system [12] requires the use of background images from the same scenes for training a classifier, while our system is able to work without any kind of extra training, and it is shown to be robust against different backgrounds.

Note that, in YoloSPoC, predictions do not have a meaningful score, because nearest neighbors are used for labeling the object proposals. Then, the precision-recall curve is generated by modifying the nearest neighbor ratio threshold.

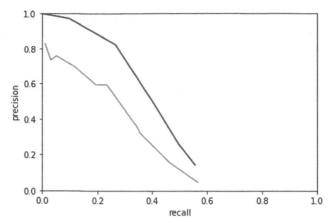

Fig. 5. Precision-recall curves over all WRGBD Scenes dataset. The original system [12] using RGB data is shown in red, and the proposed system YoloSPoC is shown in blue. (Color figure online)

5   Conclusion

In this work, a novel method named YoloSPoC for solving the particular object recognition task is proposed. It is composed by an object proposal generator based on YOLOv3, a SPoC CNN used for generating global descriptors, a nearest neighbor classifier, a nearest neighbor ratio test for rejecting misdetections, and a final post-processing step for eliminating multiple detections from a same object. The method is compared against several state-of-the-art methods based on local descriptors and geometric verifications. Extensive experiments are performed, by using the DSLL dataset, which contains images of objects which can be manipulated by a robot, captured under different conditions, and also by using the Washington RGB-D Scenes dataset. In the reported experiments, the proposed system is shown to consistently outperforms previous methods on all of the tests performed by a large margin. YoloSPoC is robust against conditions like (i) multiple objects, (ii) occlusions, (iii) illumination changes, (iv) cluttered backgrounds, (v) non-textured objects, and (vi) object classes not available when training the proposal generator.

The use of triplet learning is not useful in our case because of domain shift, as the Siamese network used for computing global descriptors was trained on outdoor images, while our application is related to manipulable objects. Also, the nearest neighbor ratio test is shown to be useful for discarding proposals not associated to objects from the dataset. Future work includes evaluating the system in other datasets and fine-tuning the networks that compute global descriptors by using triplet learning, on a new dataset of domestic objects to be built.

Acknowledgement. This work is partially funded by Fondecyt 1161500 and CONICYT PIA grant AFB18004.

References

1. Koch, G., Zemel, R., Salakhutdinov, R.: Siamese neural networks for one-shot image recognition. In: ICML Deep Learning Workshop, vol. 2 (2015)
2. Hoffer, E., Ailon, N.: Deep metric learning using triplet network. In: Feragen, A., Pelillo, M., Loog, M. (eds.) SIMBAD 2015. LNCS, vol. 9370, pp. 84–92. Springer, Cham (2015). https://doi.org/10.1007/978-3-319-24261-3_7
3. Lowe, D.G.: Distinctive image features from scale-invariant keypoints. Int. J. Comput. Vis. 60(2), 91–110 (2004). https://doi.org/10.1023/B:VISI.0000029664.99615.94
4. Tolias, G., Sicre, R., Jégou, H.: Particular object retrieval with integral max-pooling of CNN activations. https://arxiv.org/abs/1511.05879 (2016)
5. Radenović, F., Tolias, G., Chum, O.: Fine-tuning CNN image retrieval with no human annotation. IEEE Trans. Pattern Anal. Mach. Intell. 41(7), 1655–1668 (2019)
6. Ren, S., He, K., Girshick, R., Sun, J.: Faster R-CNN: towards real-time object detection with region proposal networks. In: Advances in Neural Information Processing Systems (NIPS), pp. 91–99 (2015)
7. Redmon, J., Farhadi, A.: YOLO9000: better, faster, stronger. In: Computer Vision and Pattern Recognition (CVPR) (2017)
8. Redmon, J., Farhadi, A.: YOLOv3: an incremental improvement. https://arxiv.org/abs/1804.02767 (2018)
9. Martínez, L., Loncomilla, P., Ruiz-del-Solar, J.: Object recognition for manipulation tasks in real domestic settings: a comparative study. In: Bianchi, R., Akin, H., Ramamoorthy, S., Sugiura, K. (eds.) RoboCup 2014. LNCS (LNAI), vol. 8992, pp. 207–219. Springer, Cham (2015). https://doi.org/10.1007/978-3-319-18615-3_17
10. Loncomilla, P., Ruiz-del-Solar, J., Martínez, L.: Object recognition using local invariant features for robotic applications: a survey. Pattern Recogn. 60, 499–514 (2016)
11. CNN Image Retrieval in PyTorch: Training and evaluating CNNs for Image Retrieval in PyTorch. https://github.com/filipradenovic/cnnimageretrieval-pytorch
12. Lai, K., Bo, L., Ren, X., Fox, D.: A large-scale hierarchical multi-view RGB-D object dataset. In: 2011 IEEE International Conference on Robotics and Automation, pp. 1817–1824 (2011)
13. Georgakis, G., Reza, M.A., Mousavian, A., Le, P.-H., Kosecka, J.: Multiview RGB-D dataset for object instance detection. In: International Conference on 3DVision (3DV) (2016)
14. COCO Dataset. http://cocodataset.org
15. ImageNet. http://www.image-net.org
16. He, K., Zhang, X., Ren, S., Sun, J.: Deep residual learning for image recognition. In: 29th IEEE Conference on Computer Vision and Pattern Recognition (CVPR 2016) (2016)

A Model-Free Algorithm of Moving Ball Interception by Holonomic Robot Using Geometric Approach

Pavel A. Makarov$^{(\boxtimes)}$ [ID], Tolga Yirtici, Nurullah Akkaya, Ersin Aytac, Gorkem Say, Gokhan Burge, Berk Yilmaz, and Rahib H. Abiyev [ID]

Near East University, TRNC, 99138 Nicosia, Cyprus
pavel.makarov@neu.edu.tr

Abstract. In this paper, one common problem for the teams competing in the RoboCup Small Size League (SSL) is addressed, namely the interception of a moving ball at an arbitrary aspect angle relative to the direction of the shot. We present a simple, robust and efficient algorithm for the interception of a moving ball by an omnidirectional SSL robot. The algorithm, designed on the basis of a heuristic approach, requires minimal knowledge of robot dynamics and relies on two key ideas. The first idea is the consideration of ball motion via transition to a reference frame where the ball is static, and the second one is planning the motion of the robot in such a reference frame from the geometric viewpoint. Experiments conducted in a real SSL environment confirmed the beneficial properties of the algorithm: it provides successful interception in a variety of scenarios, characterized by different directions of ball motion and the positional relationships between the ball, robot and goal.

Keywords: Interception skill · Pass and shoot · Mobile robot · Holonomic motion · Model-free methods

1 Introduction

Efficient control in a dynamic environment without precise data characterizing the environment and the agent is strongly required for a mobile robot to accomplish various missions concerned with a certain motion scenario. With a sufficiently accurate model of robot motion, the objective is attainable using the methods of optimal control theory, once the mathematical formulation for the "most desirable" motion is given in terms of cost function. In the absence of such a model, the machine learning approach, which is rather trendy nowadays, appears to be a reliable and flexible solution. However, machine learning usually needs a huge amount of training data, and significant computational resources. Another potential hurdle is the fine tuning of the resulting controller, as the approach features almost no transparency. Alternatively, heuristic methods can be applied to obtain a fast and practical solution for the problem. The main drawback of the heuristic approach is its weak universality, *i.e.* the necessity to design a separate algorithm for each particular objective. Nevertheless, a well-designed heuristic algorithm

© Springer Nature Switzerland AG 2019
S. Chalup et al. (Eds.): RoboCup 2019, LNAI 11531, pp. 166–175, 2019.
https://doi.org/10.1007/978-3-030-35699-6_13

can provide near-optimal performance of the robot within the scope of the objective, with minimal development and computational costs.

In this paper we address a common problem experienced by the teams competing in the RoboCup Small Size League (SSL), namely the interception of a moving ball at an arbitrary aspect angle relative to the direction of the shot. Recently, the "NEUIslanders" SSL team, whom the authors are with, has significantly improved in this area, using the aforementioned heuristic approach to create the relevant control algorithm without the knowledge of a robot motion model.

SSL teams use omnidirectional four-wheel (rarely – three-wheel) cylinder-shaped robots, equipped with a single kicker. Computer renderings of the "NEUIslanders" soccer robot are depicted in Fig. 1. As a rule, the translational motion of the robots is controlled via set velocity (two components). Both robot and ball tracking is provided by common vision system relying on several ceiling-mounted cameras. Commands for all robots of a team are generated on a single off-board computer and transmitted to the agents. Therefore, measurement errors together with the delays in the delivery of vision data and commands are typical factors that should be taken into account in the design of any control algorithm.

Fig. 1. Soccer robot of the "NEUIslanders" SSL team and its omnidirectional chassis.

The problem of ball interception is reduced to the alignment of the intercepting robot's kicker with the ball at a certain moment of time in such a way that robot orientation at this moment corresponds to the aimed direction of the shot. For particularity only, we will assume that the robot aims at the adversary's goal. A natural requirement for efficient interception is to minimize the time elapsed until the shoot.

Unfortunately, few works on the problem have been reported in literature. Three different techniques – precise computation of the interception point, reinforcement learning and the method of qualitative velocity – are considered in [1], but all within the framework of the RoboCup soccer simulator (Soccer Server), where the major part of real-world adverse factors is ignored. The same limitation concerns [2]: the authors suggest a combination of reinforcement learning with the off-line computation of an optimal trajectory for the agent, and validate their approach through computer simulations only. As for the teams of the RoboCup soccer community, the prediction of future ball location and the relevant planning of interceptor trajectory are primarily used, according to the available

168 P. A. Makarov et al.

releases [3–5]. It should be noted that the prediction-based approach is not free of some inherent shortcomings, emanating, on the one hand, from the limited prediction accuracy owing to measurement errors for the instantaneous ball speed, combined with the uncertainty of friction deceleration [6], and, on the other hand, from the necessity to estimate the required time for the robot to attain a certain position.

The algorithm presented in this work has been developed with the aim of providing a robust, reliable and easy-tunable interception skill, avoiding the drawbacks of prediction-based methods, to our robots. Optimal performance in terms of rapidity was not demanded, but the ability to align the kicker with the ball (static or rolling) regardless of the direction of ball motion and the positional relationship between the ball, robot and goal was a strict requisite. Examples of nontrivial interception scenarios are schematically depicted in Fig. 2: we will refer to these cases as head-on, cross and overtake interception.

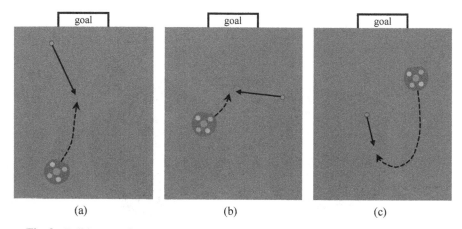

Fig. 2. Ball interception scenarios: (a) head-on, (b) cross and (c) overtake interception.

2 Interception Algorithm

2.1 Overview

The inputs for the proposed algorithm are the current position vectors $\mathbf{r}^r$ and $\mathbf{r}^b$ of the intercepting robot and the ball accordingly, ball velocity $\mathbf{V}^b$, and polar angle φ specifying the desired shooting direction. Vectors $\mathbf{r}^r$, $\mathbf{r}^b$, $\mathbf{V}^b$ are obtained from the tracking system (a Kalman filter is conventionally used for this purpose). The algorithm produces set velocity $\mathbf{V}^{set}$ for the intercepting robot as the output, and runs at each iteration of the control loop independently, avoiding the necessity to store any specific data in memory.

The first key idea of the algorithm is to consider robot motion in the reference frame, where the ball is static. Formally, we determine the *relative* set velocity $\mathbf{W}^{set}$ for the robot with respect to the moving ball first, and then convert it into the absolute set velocity $\mathbf{V}^{set} = \mathbf{W}^{set} + \mathbf{V}^b$. This concept, on the one hand, ensures robot alignment with the moving ball under condition that $\mathbf{W}^{set}$ is produced by a reliable algorithm of static ball interception, and, on the other hand, serves as a good alternative to prediction-based techniques.

The second key idea, related to static ball interception, is prompted by the lack of knowledge about robot dynamics. Assuming that only a few reference characteristics of robot motion are known, such as maximal speed and admitted acceleration, we have chosen a geometric approach as the most suitable for the synthesis of the algorithm. Namely, a family of desired paths of approach to the ball, where each path depends on the initial position of the interceptor, is introduced, and the field of set velocities $\mathbf{W}^{set}(\mathbf{r}^b)$ is set in order to guide the robot along the desired path, avoiding significant deviations from it. By "significant deviations" we mean discrepancies that can lead to the failure of interception.

2.2 Detailed Description

Relative set velocity $\mathbf{W}^{set}$ is representable by its magnitude and direction. Unit vector $\mathbf{n}^W$, specifying the direction of $\mathbf{W}^{set}$, is determined as follows. First, we compute the target robot position (robot coordinates are defined as the coordinates of its center) with respect to the current ball location as $\mathbf{r}^{trg} = \mathbf{r}^b - d \cdot \mathbf{n}^{shoot}$, where $\mathbf{n}^{shoot}$ is the unit vector pointing in the direction of the shot, and d denotes the distance from the center of the robot to the ball when the latter is aligned with the kicker. It is assumed that robot orientation corresponds to $\mathbf{n}^{shoot}$. Then, two virtual circles of radius ρ are introduced around the ball, as depicted in Fig. 3a: these circles are located symmetrically about the line joining $\mathbf{r}^{trg}$ and $\mathbf{r}^b$ (shoot line), and intersect at $\mathbf{r}^{trg}$ with the angle 2α between their tangent lines. The circles should serve as some boundaries to be rounded by robot trajectory.

The following simple logic underlies the computation of $\mathbf{n}^W$:

- if the robot is behind the ball (relative to shooting direction) within the 2α-segment, it can move directly to the target position;
- if the robot position does not fall into the 2α-segment, and the robot is outside the virtual circles, it is directed along the tangent line to one the circles, dropped through the current position of the robot, so that the circle will be bent round. The choice of the circle depends on which side from the shoot line the robot is located;
- if the robot occurs inside one of the circles (which is quite possible when it bends a circle round), the direction is set as tangent to the closest point of the circle and turned slightly to push the robot outside. The "deeper" is the robot, the stronger is the turn of the vector $\mathbf{n}^W$.

Omitting the formulas describing such logic, we illustrate it by Fig. 3b, where the field of relative set velocity is plotted on a rectangular grid of robot positions.

The found vector $\mathbf{n}^W$ is multiplied by certain set speed W: $\mathbf{W}^{set} = \mathbf{n}^{set} \cdot W$. The latter is equated to maximal robot speed V_{max} when the robot is far enough from the ball, and is decreased as it comes closer. The idea of decreasing the relative set speed is twofold: on the one hand, it allows the robot to bend the circles round more accurately, reducing its acceleration; on the other hand, it ensures better kicker alignment under the adverse conditions (measurement errors and delays) typical in real-world operation. In our implementation we use the formulas

$$W = \min\{W_0, V_{max}\}, \quad W_0 = W_{close} + \frac{|\mathbf{r}^r - \mathbf{r}^{trg}|}{D_{close}}(V_{max} - W_{close}),$$

where W_{close} stands for the relative speed when the robot is close to the ball, and D_{close} is the distance at which we start to decrease speed.

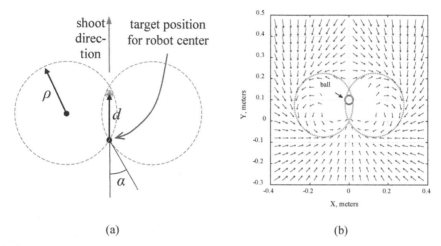

(a)   (b)

Fig. 3. (a) The geometry used to determine the direction of relative set velocity, and (b) relative set velocity calculated for different robot positions by the proposed algorithm.

Radius ρ is specified with respect to some admitted robot acceleration a_{adm}. According to the centripetal acceleration formula, one should assign this radius as $\rho = W^2/a_{adm}$, where the reasonable choice for W, under the presumption that the virtual circles are rather small, is W_{close}. However, we should take into account that the intercepted ball is not stationary, hence *absolute* robot speed might significantly differ from W_{close}. Owing to a greater load on the electric motors, the behavior of the robots at the disposal of "NEUIslanders" (and presumably the same problem is faced by all omnidirectional robots with limited motor power) is less stable at high speeds, which confines robot maneuverability in case of rapid motion. Concerning the algorithm, it means that the radius of turn should be increased in order to suppress unpredictable deviations from the nominal trajectory. We have come to the following *ad-hoc* formulas assigning the radius of turn:

$$\rho = \min\{\rho_{max}, \max\{\rho_{min}, \rho_0\}\}, \quad \rho_0 = \frac{(\kappa|\mathbf{V}^b| + W_{close})^2}{a_{adm}},$$

with ρ_{min} and ρ_{max} confining the range of ρ, and coefficient κ introduced to consider the increase of robot speed due to ball motion.

Once $\mathbf{W}^{\text{set}}$ is computed, we determine the output set speed $\mathbf{V}^{\text{set}}$ as

$$\mathbf{V}^{\text{set}} = \mathbf{W}^{\text{set}} + \mathbf{V}_0^b, \ \mathbf{V}_0^b = \mathbf{V}^b \cdot \min\left\{1, \frac{|\mathbf{V}^b|}{V_{\max}}\right\}$$

In these formulas, $\mathbf{V}_0^b$ is ball velocity, clipped by the maximal robot speed – this operation was introduced to avoid unnecessary back motion of the robot when the ball is rapidly rolling towards it.

Table 1 summarizes all parameters present in the interception algorithm and their assigned values in its current implementation by the "NEUIslanders". The majority of the listed values were selected empirically – due to the lack of time we had no opportunity to create a tool, which could automate the search of the optimal ones.

Table 1. Parameters of ball interception algorithm.

Notation	Description	Value
d	Distance from robot center to the ball aligned with the kicker	10 cm
$\rho_{\min}$	Minimal radius of virtual circle	15 cm
$\rho_{\max}$	Maximal radius of virtual circle	40 cm
α	Half-angle between the tangents to virtual circles	30°
a_{adm}	Nominal admitted acceleration of robot	2.25 m/sec^2
$V_{\max}$	Maximal robot speed	2.8 m/sec
W_{close}	Assigned relative speed in the vicinity of the ball	0.35 m/sec
D_{close}	Distance to the target point, when the approach speed is reduced	1.5 m
κ	Coefficient for ball speed consideration	0.7

3 Experimental Results

The experiments conducted in the real SSL environment (soccer field, vision system, *etc.*) confirmed the robustness and efficiency of the presented algorithm with parameters according to Table 1. Visually, the behavior of the intercepting robot resembles the motion to a predicted point, and the performed trajectories do not look redundant for any of the interception scenarios, with the possible exception of the final stage, when the robot has to be aligned (in velocity) with the moving ball.

The figures below present the observed interceptor behavior in dynamics, with the time step of 0.15 s. The coordinates used for presentation were obtained from raw vision data, and interpolated to the appropriate time grid. Small vectors laid from the center of the robot indicate the set velocity generated by the algorithm at each moment of time. Figure 4 depicts the head-on scenario; Figs. 5, 6 and 7 – different cases of cross interception, and Fig. 8 – overtake interception. One can clearly see that in all cases the robot is able to shoot towards the goal at the time of the final snapshot.

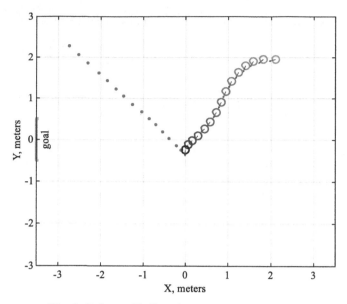

Fig. 4. Robot and ball motion: head-on interception.

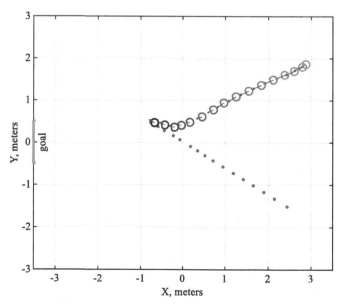

Fig. 5. Robot and ball motion: semi-cross interception.

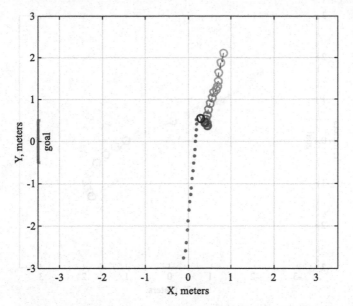

Fig. 6. Robot and ball motion: cross interception towards the ball.

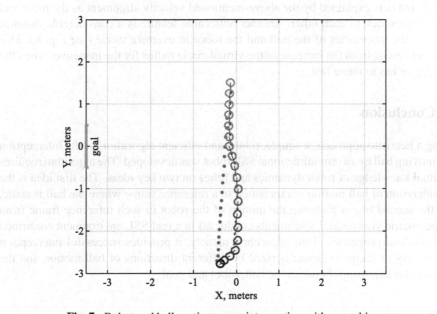

Fig. 7. Robot and ball motion: cross interception with overtaking.

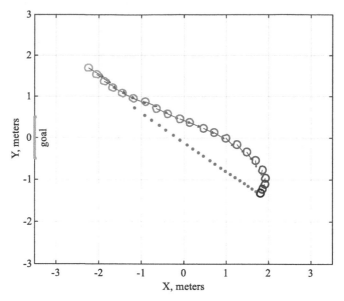

Fig. 8. Robot and ball motion: overtake interception.

It should be noted that the change of the direction of robot motion, observed in Figs. 5 and 6, is explained by the above-mentioned velocity alignment as the robot and the ball approach to each other. Another noticeable feature is a considerable distance between the trajectories of the ball and the robot in overtake mode (see Fig. 8). This behavior results from the increase of the virtual circle radius for the maneuver when the interceptor has to move fast.

4 Conclusion

Using a heuristic approach, a simple, robust and efficient algorithm for the interception of a moving ball by an omnidirectional SSL robot was developed. The algorithm requires minimal knowledge of robot dynamics and relies on two key ideas. The first idea is the consideration of ball motion via transition to a reference frame where the ball is static, and the second one is planning the motion of the robot in such reference frame from the geometric viewpoint. Experiments conducted in a real SSL environment confirmed the beneficial properties of the algorithm: namely, it provides successful interception in a variety of scenarios, characterized by different directions of ball motion and the positional relationships between the ball, robot and goal.

References

1. Stolzenburg, F., Obst, O., Murray, J.: Qualitative velocity and ball interception. In: Jarke, M., Lakemeyer, G., Koehler, J. (eds.) KI 2002. LNCS (LNAI), vol. 2479, pp. 283–298. Springer, Heidelberg (2002). https://doi.org/10.1007/3-540-45751-8_19

2. Maire, F., Taylor, D.: A quadratic programming formulation of a moving ball interception and shooting behaviour, and its application to neural network control. In: Stone, P., Balch, T., Kraetzschmar, G. (eds.) RoboCup 2000. LNCS (LNAI), vol. 2019, pp. 327–332. Springer, Heidelberg (2001). https://doi.org/10.1007/3-540-45324-5_34
3. Maeda, K., Kohketsu, A., Takahashi, T.: Ball-receiving skill dependent on centering in soccer simulation games. In: Asada, M., Kitano, H. (eds.) RoboCup 1998. LNCS (LNAI), vol. 1604, pp. 152–161. Springer, Heidelberg (1999). https://doi.org/10.1007/3-540-48422-1_12
4. Bowling, M., Veloso, M.: Motion control in dynamic multi-robot environments. In: Veloso, M., Pagello, E., Kitano, H. (eds.) RoboCup 1999. LNCS (LNAI), vol. 1856, pp. 222–230. Springer, Heidelberg (2000). https://doi.org/10.1007/3-540-45327-X_17
5. Rahimi, M.M., et al.: Parsian extended team description for RoboCup. Robocup SSL, Nagoya, Japan (2017)
6. Abiyev, R.H., et al.: NEUIslanders Team Description Paper RoboCup 2019. Robocup SSL, Sydney, Australia (2019)

Toward Data Driven Development
in RoboCup

Heinrich Mellmann[(✉)], Benjamin Schlotter, and Philipp Strobel

Adaptive Systems Group, Humboldt-Universität zu Berlin,
Unter den Linden 6, 10099 Berlin, Germany
`mellmann@informatik.hu-berlin.de`

Abstract. Conducting games in RoboCup incurs high cost in terms of
effort, time, and money. The scientific outcome, however, is quite limited
and often not very conclusive. Especially, analyzing and drawing conclusions about the performance of complex processes like decision making
of an individual robot or the behavior on the team level poses a considerable challenge. Collecting more data during the competition games
will help to analyze the performance of algorithms, identify errors and
areas for improvement, and make more significant statements regarding
the performance of the robots. In this work we investigate the possibilities for collection of the large scale RoboCup data and its analysis.
We present a system for automatic recording of synchronized videos of
RoboCup games and an application for exploration and annotation of
large sets of RoboCup-related data. We also present data sets collected
during the competitions in 2018 and an algorithm for visual detection
and tracking of robots in the RoboCup videos. A first empirical evaluation shows promising results and demonstrates how such data can be
integrated and used to validate robot's behavior.

Keywords: Data driven development · Robot detection · Visual robot
tracking · Camera localization

1 Introduction

An empirical scientific discipline requires a set of methods and practices for
evaluation and comparison of proposed models and solutions. RoboCup provides
a unique *common test scenario* for robotics, but its potential is, by far, not
realized. Conducting games incurs high cost in terms of effort, time, and money.
The scientific outcome, however, is quite limited and often not very conclusive.
In most cases only the final score of the games provides feedback about the
performance of a team.

Our aim is to shift the focus of the games more towards scientific experiments.
This requires a comprehensive data collection infrastructure in order to enable
empirical analysis and to generate quantifiable results. This might provide a basis
for analysis of complex high level algorithms like team strategy. This might in

© Springer Nature Switzerland AG 2019
S. Chalup et al. (Eds.): RoboCup 2019, LNAI 11531, pp. 176–188, 2019.
https://doi.org/10.1007/978-3-030-35699-6_14

turn enable for a quantifiable analysis of the overall progress of the league over the years.

Collecting more data during the competition games will help to analyze the performance of algorithms, and identify errors and areas for improvement. In particular, analysis of the team behavior, like role change, require global synchronized data. This kind of data can be more easily collected in a controlled experiment in a lab environment. However, the algorithms running on a robot tend to behave differently in the isolated environment of the lab compared to real conditions during a competition. From this perspective each RoboCup competition can be seen as a large scale collective experiment evaluating the abilities of the robots. In order to build understanding based on this large scale experiment, we need to capture data more effectively and to make this rich data comparable across the community and over time. For human soccer extensive data collected from games is available which allows researchers to learn behavior models of teams from tracking data. For example in [5] the authors use such models to answer *what if* type of questions.

Teams in the Standard Platform League already collect data during the games. Common team communication and data sent by the game control computer during the game is recorded and made publicly available. [1]Individual teams are collecting the data they need to analyze their team's performance and to solve bugs, e.g., images for ball detection. Many teams record videos of their games. All this data is however unorganized and there are no shared tools and common practices to effectively analyze and evaluate large amounts of data specific to RoboCup. At the same time many teams do not have access to extensive logging infrastructure, this includes in particular new teams joining RoboCup.

So far there have been only few attempts to analyze the game data on a large scale within the Standard Platform League (SPL). A noteworthy example is the technical report [3] by the team Nao Devils from 2016, where the authors analyze the final outdoor game. And in [8] the team B-Human analyses their robot positions in final game against Team HTWK at the RoboCup 2017. Their analysis shows that the both teams do not utilize the corners of the field which might be used for future tactic improvements. In [7] we extracted and annotated events where the robots kicked the ball to draw conclusions about the performance of the proposed decision making mechanism. In the continuation of the work [6], more complex decisions were introduced and evaluated in simulated experiment. A rigorous empirical analysis in this case would require more extensive data collection and more sophisticated analysis methods. These publications outline the motivation and the direction of our work.

The work presented in this paper is the result of an ongoing effort to push forward the development of an ecosystem of tools and practices to support collection, organization and analysis of large amounts of RoboCup-specific data enabling detailed analysis and promoting data driven research and development in RoboCup. Although our current work focuses on the SPL, the developed tools and methods are applicable to other leagues.

---

[1] https://spl.robocup.org/downloads/.

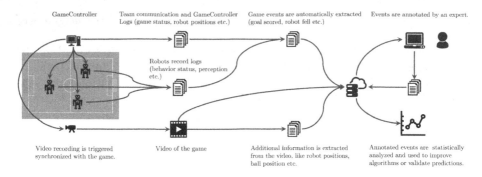

GameController   Team communication and GameController   Game events are automatically extracted   Events are annotated by an expert.
                 Logs (game status, robot positions etc.)   (goal scored, robot fell etc.)

Robots record logs
(behavior status, perception
etc.)

Video recording is triggered   Video of the game   Additional information is extracted   Annotated events are statistically
synchronized with the game.   from the video, like robot positions,   analyzed and used to improve
                                                     ball position etc.   algorithms or validate predictions.

Fig. 1. Overview over the data flow of the implemented data processing ecosystem.

The remainder of the paper is structured as follows. The Sect. 2 gives an overview over the different components of the data collection system and the flow of the data. The Sect. 3 describes the automatic recording system for automatic collection of synchronized RoboCup videos. In the Sect. 4 we discuss the data collected during German Open and RoboCup in 2018. Section 5 describes the *RoboCup Explorer*, a server based application for inspection and annotation of RoboCup data. In the Sect. 6 we present a method for the detection of robots in the game videos based on deep learning. The position of the camera which recorded the video can be determined through alignment of the field lines in the video. This allows to track the detected robots in the global field coordinates resulting in a low cost visual tracking system. The details of the tracking are discussed in Sect. 7 alongside first empirical results.

Technical information about the system as well as links to the open source repository and the collected data can be found on the project page [2].

2   System Overview and Data Flow

At the current point we distinguish between three types of sources from which data can be gathered during a RoboCup soccer game: The *video* of the game, recorded by cameras on the side of the field; The *network communication* between the robots and data sent by the *game control computer* to the robots; and *log data* recorded by each individual robot.

Figure 1 depicts the used components and the data flow of the implemented system. For the collection of the data we utilize existing infrastructure within the SPL. In particular we make use of the *GameController*[1], a specialized software, which is used to control the games within SPL. The network communication of the GameController and all the robots is recorded and made publicly available. The data communicated by the robots contains such information like the estimated position on the field, perceived ball, but also information about the robot's role. We extend the data collection with the automatic recording system of synchronized game videos, which will be discussed in more details in the Sect. 6.

After a game is completed, the video as well as the log files of the Game-Controller and the log files of each individual robot are collected and stored on a server. The collected data is organized by a defined scheme and named by the date, time and participating teams. On the server, a pipeline of different processing task are executed. In particular, spatial and temporal information is extracted from communication data and individual log files. Spatial information may contain robot's estimated position on the field, perceptions of the ball etc. Temporal information may contain game events like changes of the game state (*READY, PLAY*, etc.) or penalties, but also other events like cases where a robot fell or a particular decision was made or a particular action executed, e.g., a kick (cf. Sect. 5). Further information can be extracted from the recorded video. At the current moment we focus on detecting and tracking robots in the video, as discussed in Sect. 5 in more detail. In the future, the detected robot trajectories could be integrated with the data from the log files to reconstruct a full and reliable view of the robot's behavior.

The collected and processed data can be inspected and further enriched with annotations with the *RoboCup Explorer*, which will be discussed in Sect. 5 in more details. The annotations can be used for empirical evaluation of the behavior patterns and decisions similarly to [9], and perhaps as input for machine learning approaches in the future.

3   Collection of Videos and Data

A central piece of the collected data are videos of the games taken from a global perspective. In order to generate and retrieve the ground truth for the whole game, those videos need to capture the whole field with all robots visible. It is also crucial for the videos to be synchronized with other data collected from the network and from the individual robots, to easily compare them with the generated ground truth. A low cost system, that is quickly deployable and largely automatic, can be best adopted and used by other teams throughout the league. In this section we give a brief overview over a low cost system for automatic synchronized recording of RoboCup videos.

In the Standard Platform League (SPL) the games are controlled by a dedicated computer with a specialized software called *GameController*. The Game-Controller is operated by a human and acts effectively as a translator of the commands given by the human main referee to the robots. The changes in the state of the game, like *READY, PLAY* or *FINISH*, and other relevant information are broadcast to the robots through WiFi. Our system is utilizing these messages to synchronize the data from different sources. They are recorded by each individual robot, they are part of the recorded network communication, and are used to start and stop the recording of the video of the game.

For the recording of the videos we currently use GoPro cameras (tested with GoPro Session and GoPro Hero 5 Black). They have a wide angle and are capable of capturing the whole field when placed on the side of the field. These cameras are widely available and provide high video quality. The recording can be triggered over a WiFi interface of the camera.

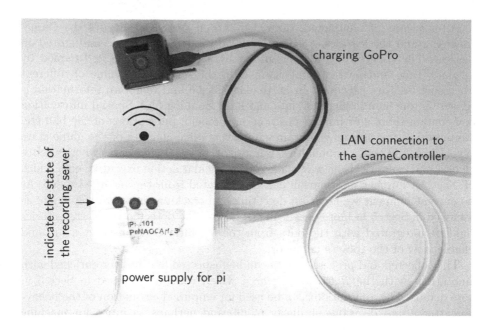

Fig. 2. System for automatic recording of synchronized RoboCup videos. The recording server is based on raspberry pi with the colored indicator LEDs. The GoPro is charged via USB from the raspberry. A LAN cable connects the pi to the GameController network. The Recording server sends commands to the GoPro via WiFi.

The central piece of the video recording system is a *recording server*. The code for the recording server software has been made open source and can be found through the project page [2]. The task of the recording server is to control the recording process of the video, in particular, to start and stop recording of the video based on the messages received from the GameController. The current version of the recording server is running on a *Raspberry Pi 3 Model B*. It is very compact and is equipped with a LAN, WiFi, USB and GPIO pins where additional components can be attached. The recording server is connected to the GameController network through LAN interface and simultaneously to the GoPro camera through the WiFi. It has been equipped with indicator LED-lights in order to enable a fast and robust monitoring of the system's health during a competition. The lights indicate whether the connection to the camera could established successfully, whether a GameController is currently online or if a recording is running. The overview over the recording system can be seen in the Fig. 2.

The system requires to be set up only once at the beginning of the competition and ensures that each game is recorded and *synchronized* with the corresponding network data. At the current stage, the videos are recorded on the memory card (microSD) of the GoPro camera and can be retrieved in the breaks between the games or at the end of the day. Depending on the available Internet

Fig. 3. Left: An example image from a recording at the German Open 2018. Right: An example image from a recording at the RoboCup 2018

connection, collected data can be immediately uploaded to a server or directly copied by the teams to be used *during* the competition.

The system was tested and used to collect synchronized communication data and video at several events during 2018 and 2019. Most notable, the data gathered during the German Open 2018 and the RoboCup 2018 will be discussed in more details the Sect. 4.

4   Data Sets from GO18 and RC18

The recording system described in the Sect. 3 was successfully deployed during the German Open 2018 and at the RoboCup 2018 in Montreal. The videos and data from both competitions were made publicly available and can be found on our project website [2]. In the following we give a brief overview over the collected data sets.

German Open was played on a single field. For the game recording one camera, GoPro Session, was installed on the side of the field in about 4 m height. With that, the entire playing field could be recorded with only small occasional occlusions by the referees or other persons on the field. An example can be seen in Fig. 3. All of 23 played competition games were completely and correctly recorded. The system was running completely autonomously without errors. All recorded video were made available to interested teams on site and can be found on our project website [2].

RoboCup 2018 in Montreal was played on 5 fields in parallel (numbered A–E), which posed a significant infrastructural challenge. For each of the fields a separate video recording system was deployed. In this case, two different versions of the GoPro cameras were used: *GoPro Session* on the fields A, B and E, and *GoPro Hero 5 Black* on the fields C and D. All Cameras were installed on the side of the field in 2.5 m height.

During the RoboCup 2018 we collected approximately 500 GB of data. The GoPro Videos constitute about 450 GB. The rest is mostly the log data collected by the individual robot of our team, Berlin United. The GameController logs have a negligible size with only 20 MB per halftime. During the competition a number of noteworthy issues have occurred which led to some videos being

Table 1. Evaluation of the video recording during the RoboCup 2018 in Montreal

Field	Camera	Missing	Partially	Complete	Sum
A	GoPro Hero 4 Session	3		19	**22**
B	GoPro Hero 4 Session	4		12	**16**
C	GoPro Hero 5 Black	2	5	9	**16**
D	GoPro Hero 5 Black	2	4	8	**14**
E	GoPro Hero 4 Session	2		6	**8**
Sum		**13**	**9**	**54**	**76**

incomplete, corrupted or missing. In the following we briefly outline those. The evaluation of the recorded games reveals, that of the totally 76 games played

- 54 games were completely recorded
- 9 games were only partially recorded, with only few seconds missing in some cases, but also a complete half
- 13 games were not recorded at all.

The Table 1 shows the statistics of the collected videos in more detail.

The main reason for missing recordings turned out to be the teams unplugging the power supply of the recording system or the LAN connection to the GameController, and re-purposing the ports for their needs, because of the limited number of ports. Two of the incomplete videos were fractured in a large number of segments. Which was most likely caused, by a second instance of a GameController on the same network, probably accidentally started for testing by one of the teams. The two competing instances would start and stop recording in repeated succession. This behavior was verified in an isolated experiment. To prevent this issue we plan to add a configuration option to the raspberry pi server, in order to set the IP address of the gamecontroller and ignore messages of unofficial instances. In another approach, once a recording has started, messages of other instances of the gamecontroller are discarded and therefore prevent fractured video files.

Another minor issue was the stability of the WiFi connection between the raspberry pi and the GoPro Hero 5. The reason for the disconnections could not be fully explained. Probably the interference of other WiFi networks or on a similar frequency sending devices was a factor. Another issue observed with the GoPro Hero 5 was, that the camera draws more power during the video capturing than could be provided by the Raspberry Pi. In some cases, this resulted in incomplete or missing videos after the battery was depleted and the camera shut down. After some research we found that the GoPro Hero 5 can be charged via USB-PD 3.0. With an USB-C charger we were able to provide sufficient power to charge both, the raspberry pi and the GoPro Hero 5.

Fig. 4. Left: overview over the data collected during different RoboCup events. Right image: example session for inspection and event annotation for the first half of the game with the team *Nao Team HTWK* at the RoboCup 2018. Main components are timelines with events represented by colored buttons (bottom); visualization of the robots state, position on the field and perceived ball (right) and possible labels for the events (left).

The recorded matches were made available to the interested teams during and after the competition. After the preparation and evaluation the videos were uploaded to YouTube. The links can be found on the project website [2].

5   RoboCup Data Explorer

The *RoboCup Data Explorer* is a web based server application which has been developed for organization, inspection and annotation of large amounts of RoboCup data (videos, network communication and individual logs).

The data can be stored on the same server or provided by another, e.g., the game video are stored on YouTube. The RoboCup Data Explorer provides two different views on the data. The data set view shows a list of *data units* sorted by the event and the game half as illustrated in Fig. 4 (left). Each of these data units contains the data collect during a contiguous game sequence, which is usually a half of an SPL game. Such a data unit can be inspected in a inspection and annotation view as illustrated in Fig. 4 (right).

As can be seen in the Fig. 4 (right), the inspection and annotation view has four main components: video of the game (center), global field view (right), game events (bottom) and annotations panel (left). The communication data as well as data collected by the individual robots can be presented in spatial manner in the global field view, e.g., positions of the robots and the ball, and in form of events in the event view, e.g., game states, penalties, fall downs. In order to be displayed the events and spatial information is automatically extracted from the log files and saved in a unified event log format. The events and spatial information can also be extracted from the videos as discussed in Sect. 6.

The human operator can navigate the game data by selecting the events of interest and jumping to the corresponding position in the video. Selected event can also be annotated to gather human feedback for quantitative analysis or as

Fig. 5. Example of detected robots in a video recorded with a GoPro camera at the RoboCup 2018 in Montreal/Canada.

training data for machine learning. The annotation tool was used to annotate different kick actions executed by the robots in the videos recorded during the games at the RoboCup in 2015. The kick events were automatically extracted from the log files recorded by the individual robots and synchronized with the video. The results were used to evaluate the performance of the kick decision algorithm and were published in [7].

6   Robot Detection in Videos

Additional information can be automatically extracted from the video using machine vision techniques. Detected robots and ball can be used to verify the perception of the robots or as input for automatic referee system in a future project [10]. On standard datasets like *COCO* or *PASCAL VOC* the state of the art object detection algorithms already achieve impressive results. Since there is no publicly available detector trained to detect Nao robots from that view we used transfer learning to retrain a state of the art detector to detect the Nao robots.

For our experiments we used DC-SPP-YOLO [4] which is based on the YOLO object detection algorithm. To speed up the training performance pretrained weights for the convolutional layers provided by the authors of the YOLO papers were used[2]. Figure 5 illustrates an example for an SPL game scene with detected robots. The training was performed on the video recording of the quarterfinals game[3] between the teams *Nao Team HTWK* and *Berlin United* from the RoboCup 2018 as described in Sect. 4. In total 3300 labeled images from the first half of a game were used. Additional 200 images were used for validation during training and further 2500 images were used for testing.

---

[2] https://pjreddie.com/media/files/darknet53.conv.74.
[3] https://youtu.be/KKtQmRtP06A.

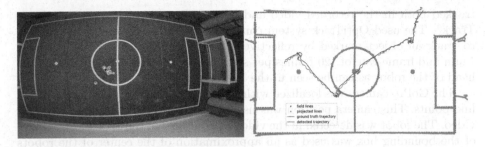

Fig. 6. Tracking of the robot in the laboratory conditions. Left: a frame from the recorded video. Right: trajectory of the robot determined based on the video in comparison to the ground truth recorded by the OptiTrack system. Projected line points are also shown in comparison to the model of the field. Note the goal posts being treated as lines.

On the 2500 test images the mean average precision is 0.999786. The precision and recall values are both 1.0 which means that the correct number of robots were detected in each images and the average IOU for the robot detection is 87.41%. So far the robot detection was tested only on a very limited dataset taken from one game. In recordings of other games the performance of the detection might be impacted by different lighting, different jersey colors and different height and angle of the camera. The results show however that accurate robot detection is possible given enough labeled data. The next section shows that based on the presented robot detection a fairly accurate localization of the robots is possible as well.

7   Visual Robot Tracking

In this section we explore the feasibility of visual tracking of the positions of the robots during the game in RoboCup videos as recorded in Sect. 4. For this we localize the robots detected in the Sect. 6 in relation to the global coordinates of the field. In order to do so, we need to estimate the position and rotation of the camera as well as distortion parameter of the lens.

The distortion of the lens can be determined with standard methods. Here it is important to note, that the GoPro-Videos are recorded in a so called *Super-View* format, which distorts the image additionally in the post-processing and needs to be corrected separately.

In order to localize the camera we use the field lines. The field lines are detected by a simple thresholding. The line points in the image are projected on the field and matched with the expected field lines in a nearest neighbor fashion. The location and rotation of the camera are determined by a classical minimization routine, such that the matching distance error is minimized.

We conducted an isolated experiment in order to evaluate the accuracy of the visual tracking. The robot NAO is dribbling the ball into a goal while being tracked both in the recorded video and by a dedicated tracking system Opti-Track[4]. The used OptiTrack system consists of 10 infrared cameras being able to track an object marked by reflective markers with a precision of less than 1 mm and frame rate of 120 frames per second. The markers were placed on the head of the robot as can be seen in the Fig. 6 (left).

The GoPro camera was localized with a mean error of 66 mm on the projected line points. This camera position was used to project the detected robot in the video. The robot was detected in the video as described in the Sect. 6. The center of the bounding box was used as an approximation of the center of the robots body and projected with the assumed height of 260 mm.

The resulting projected trajectory of the robot is shown alongside the ground truth recorded by the OptiTrack system in Fig. 6 (right). The error between the both trajectories is 14.93 mm, while maximal deviation is 98 mm. Considering the comparably simple and rudimentary setup of the system and calibration of the camera, the precision is surprisingly high.

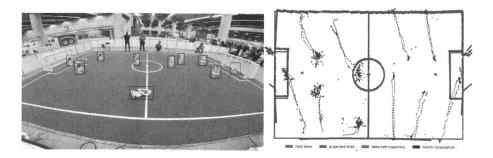

Fig. 7. Tracking of the robots on field conditions during the *Ready* phase. Left: final positions of the robots in the *READY* phase. Right: trajectories of the robots determined based on the video [green] in comparison to the communicated positions of the robots [red]. Projected line points are also shown in comparison to the model of the field. Note the goal posts being treated as lines (Color figure online).

For the second experiment we used a game recording of the quarterfinals between the teams *Nao Team HTWK* and *Berlin United* from the RoboCup 2018 as described in Sect. 6. For this video the camera was localized with an estimated precision of 66 mm on the projected line points. Figure 7 (right) illustrates the trajectories of the robots in the READY-phase, i.e., the first 45 s of the game, where robots assume their kickoff positions. The detected positions (green) are shown alongside the positions determined by the robots (red), which have been extracted from the network communication. Estimated deviation between both positions for the localization of the HTWK robots is mean 87 mm with standard deviation of 82 mm. For the Berlin United robots the mean deviation is 55 mm and standard deviation 44 mm.

---

[4] https://optitrack.com/.

The results of both experiments constitute a basic proof of concept for the feasibility of visual robot tracking in the videos recorded with a wide angle camera. Merged with the communicated localization of the robots a reliable motion trajectory for all robots can be reconstructed. Possible future applications include verification of the robot localization, live tracking, and analysis of the behavior patterns.

At the current stage the algorithm contains a number of heuristics and simplifying assumptions, which may introduce errors. Most notably, the assumed fixed height of the robots center used for projection, might vary depending on the walking height of the robot and doesn't hold for fallen robots. Replacing those heuristics with more accurate estimates might significantly improve the accuracy of the final position estimation.

Note that the identification of a robot's player number and its belonging to the team is currently not implemented. To solve this the player numbers could be assigned manually at the beginning and tracked through the game. Positions estimated by the robots' own self localization and communicated through WiFi can be used to estimate their numbers as well. The classification of a robot's team could be done based on the color of the jerseys.

8   Conclusions

We presented the current progress of our ongoing work towards a data driven development and analysis in RoboCup. The key components of the ecosystem presented in the paper are the automatic recording system for recording synchronized videos of RoboCup games and the RoboCup Explorer - an application for organization and annotation of the RoboCup data. We discussed the data collected during the German Open and RoboCup in 2018. Based on this data we developed a method for detection of the robots in the videos and their tracking on the field.

The results discussed in the paper show a clear path for the future development. On one hand we will continue to improve the tools and the process for collection and organization of the data, e.g., in order to reduce the risk of game video not being recorded. A more extensive analysis of the robot detection is needed in order to evaluate the generalization of the presented work. Furthermore visual tracking methods can be used to increase the robustness of the detection. On the other hand the ecosystem reached enough maturity allowing us to push forward to work on methods for analysis of complex behavior patterns of the robots and bring machine learning techniques to the level of decision making and planing. For example the effect of behavior decisions such as *how many robots stay near the own goal when the ball is in the opponent half* on the game score or other metrics can be analyzed over multiple teams and competitions.

Acknowledgements. This work was supported by the RCF grants in 2017 and 2018.

References

1. B-Human: GameController 2018 - RoboCup Edition (2018). https://spl.robocup.org/downloads/. Accessed 22 Apr 2019
2. Berlin United: Tools for Data Driven Research and Development in RoboCup (2019). http://www.robocup.tools. Accessed 22 Apr 2019
3. Hofmann, M., Moos, A., Rensen, F., Schwarz, I., Urbann, O.: Playing robot soccer outdoor. In: The 11th Workshop on Humanoid Soccer Robots at 16th IEEE-RAS International Conference on Humanoid Robots (2016). http://d-fence.sytes.net/research/files/Playing%20Soccer%20Outdoors%20with%20Humanoid%20Robots.pdf
4. Huang, Z., Wang, J.: DC-SPP-YOLO: dense connection and spatial pyramid pooling based YOLO for object detection. CoRR (2019). arXiv:1903.08589
5. Le, H.M., Carr, P., Yue, Y., Lucey, P.: Data-driven ghosting using deep imitation learning (2017)
6. Mellmann, H., Schlotter, B.: Advances on simulation based selection of actions for a humanoid soccer-robot. In: Proceedings of the 12th Workshop on Humanoid Soccer Robots, 17th IEEE-RAS International Conference on Humanoid Robots (Humanoids), Madrid, Spain (2017)
7. Mellmann, H., Schlotter, B., Blum, C.: Simulation based selection of actions for a humanoid soccer-robot. In: Behnke, S., Sheh, R., Sarıel, S., Lee, D.D. (eds.) RoboCup 2016. LNCS (LNAI), vol. 9776, pp. 193–205. Springer, Cham (2017). https://doi.org/10.1007/978-3-319-68792-6_16
8. Röfer, T., Laue, T., Hasselbring, A., Richter-Klug, J., Röhrig, E.: B-Human 2017 – team tactics and robot skills in the standard platform league. In: Akiyama, H., Obst, O., Sammut, C., Tonidandel, F. (eds.) RoboCup 2017. LNCS (LNAI), vol. 11175, pp. 461–472. Springer, Cham (2018). https://doi.org/10.1007/978-3-030-00308-1_38
9. Zhu, D., Veloso, M.: Virtually adapted reality and algorithm visualization for autonomous robots. In: Behnke, S., Sheh, R., Sarıel, S., Lee, D.D. (eds.) RoboCup 2016. LNCS (LNAI), vol. 9776, pp. 452–464. Springer, Cham (2017). https://doi.org/10.1007/978-3-319-68792-6_38
10. Zhu, D., Veloso, M.: Event-based automated refereeing for robot soccer. Auton. Robots 41(7), 1463–1485 (2017). https://doi.org/10.1007/s10514-016-9607-8

"Lucy, Take the Noodle Box!": Domestic Object Manipulation Using Movement Primitives and Whole Body Motion

Alex Mitrevski[✉], Abhishek Padalkar, Minh Nguyen, and Paul G. Plöger

Hochschule Bonn-Rhein-Sieg, Sankt Augustin, Germany
{aleksandar.mitrevski,abhishek.padalkar,minh.nguyen,
paul.ploeger}@h-brs.de

Abstract. For robots acting - and failing - in everyday environments, a predictable behaviour representation is important so that it can be utilised for failure analysis, recovery, and subsequent improvement. Learning from demonstration combined with dynamic motion primitives is one commonly used technique for creating models that are easy to analyse and interpret; however, mobile manipulators complicate such models since they need the ability to synchronise arm and base motions for performing purposeful tasks. In this paper, we analyse dynamic motion primitives in the context of a mobile manipulator - a Toyota Human Support Robot (HSR) - and introduce a small extension of dynamic motion primitives that makes it possible to perform whole body motion with a mobile manipulator. We then present an extensive set of experiments in which our robot was grasping various everyday objects in a domestic environment, where a sequence of object detection, pose estimation, and manipulation was required for successfully completing the task. Our experiments demonstrate the feasibility of the proposed whole body motion framework for everyday object manipulation, but also illustrate the necessity for highly adaptive manipulation strategies that make better use of a robot's perceptual capabilities.

Keywords: Learning from demonstration · Dynamic motion primitives · Whole body motion · Everyday object manipulation · Toyota HSR

1 Introduction

When acting in complex everyday environments, robots are prone to experiencing failures. For instance, Fig. 1 illustrates two failure examples with our Toyota Human Support Robot (HSR)[1,2], namely failures in grasping an object from a table and placing it on a confined shelf.

---

[1] https://www.toyota-global.com/innovation/partner_robot/robot/.
[2] We call our HSR Lucy, hence the title.

© Springer Nature Switzerland AG 2019
S. Chalup et al. (Eds.): RoboCup 2019, LNAI 11531, pp. 189–200, 2019.
https://doi.org/10.1007/978-3-030-35699-6_15

(a) A toy about to slip out of the gripper   (b) The robot knocks down a yogurt cup

Fig. 1. Unsuccessful attempts at grasping and placing an object

Failures such as these can be caused by various factors [18], for instance incomplete knowledge about the environment or sensory limitations. Regardless of the causes, robots should have the ability to not only recover from such failures, but also use those as learning opportunities in order to improve. In practice, this is usually difficult to achieve, often due to limitations of the paradigm with which robot programs are created. For instance, the problem of planning manipulation trajectories for performing a specific manipulator motion is generally complex and can be solved by randomly searching for feasible solutions[3], which however makes it difficult to predict and analyse the behaviour of a robot. Particularly in the context of manipulation, learning from demonstration [2] is a popular alternative to randomised planners and complex manipulation models that aims to replace explicitly programmed motion models by a process in which feasible and predictable motions are demonstrated to a robot by a human demonstrator.

In this paper, we study the problem of learning from demonstration in the context of domestic robots by considering the dynamic motion primitive (DMP) framework [6] for representing manipulator trajectories. Dynamic motion primitives encode demonstrated motion trajectories by a dynamic model, often in Cartesian space with respect to a manipulator's end effector. Such an explicit representation is beneficial when considering failures and failure analysis since a motion primitive in this format can be used as a predictive model of a robot's behaviour. Domestic robots are however mobile manipulators in principle, so a representation of pure manipulator trajectories is generally insufficient for executing purposeful tasks; instead, such robots need to synchronise arm and base motions. We thus present a minor extension to motion primitives that allows whole body motion of a robot, such that arm motions are favoured whenever possible, but base motions are introduced when a manipulator is unable to move anymore without reaching a singular configuration.

To validate the feasibility of our whole body motion framework, we present an extensive set of experiments in which a Toyota HSR was grasping various

---

[3] One popular example is the MoveIt! library https://moveit.ros.org, which provides a seamless interface to the Open Motion Planning Library (OMPL) http://ompl.kavrakilab.org/core/.

everyday objects in a common domestic environment. The experiments evaluate the whole body motion framework in a scenario in which the robot had to grasp objects from tables with two different heights, such that, due to the variation of object poses, arm motion was sufficient for success in some of the trials, while whole body motion was required in others.

2   Related Work

Learning from demonstration [2,10] is a popular technique for robot knowledge acquisition where the aim is to let a robot learn an execution policy by generalising over one or more demonstrations by an expert operator. In the context of manipulation, such policies are often based on a representation of motion primitives. Motion primitives can be represented in different manners, such as combinations of basis functions extracted by performing principal component analysis on a set of demonstrations [11], distributions over trajectories [16], dynamic equations [6], as well as neural networks [4]. In this work, we use the dynamic motion primitive representation due to its easy interpretability and predictive nature, but also because of the potential to improve such learned models using reinforcement learning [9] and create sequences of complex motions by combining individual motion primitives together [12]. In this paper, we analyse motion primitives in the context of grasping everyday objects in a common domestic environment, such as the objects used in the RoboCup@Home competition [14], such that we synthesise grasps based on 3D object representations using point cloud data [3].

3   Methodology

3.1   DMP Preliminaries

In the dynamic motion primitives framework [6], a motion trajectory is represented by a second-order differential equation of the form

$$\tau \ddot{\mathbf{y}} = \alpha \left(\beta (\mathbf{g} - \mathbf{y}) - \dot{\mathbf{y}} \right) + \mathbf{f} \tag{1}$$

where τ is a time constant that can be used for controlling the motion duration, α and β are positive constants, $\mathbf{g}$ is a motion goal, $\mathbf{y}$ is the current state of the system, and $\mathbf{f}$ is a forcing term. This equation converges to $\mathbf{g}$ if the forcing term vanishes, such that by varying the forcing term, arbitrary trajectories can be represented with the above model. Dynamic motion primitives can be learned, where learning reduces to finding a model of the forcing term that describes the desired motion; the model should ensure that the forcing term eventually tends to zero so that the system can converge to the desired goal. Motion primitives are usually learned from demonstrations, which is what we also do here.

In their general form, DMPs are robot-independent, as they represent trajectories in Cartesian space; the conversion to joint motion commands is done by an inverse kinematics solver. In other words, given a Cartesian velocity vector $\dot{\mathbf{y}} = J\dot{\mathbf{q}}$, where J is the manipulator Jacobian and $\dot{\mathbf{q}}$ is a vector of joint velocities, we can find the joint velocity vector as

$$\dot{\mathbf{q}} = J^{-1}\dot{\mathbf{y}} \tag{2}$$

Particularly for non-redundant manipulator, singular solutions of the above equation are likely in practice. To handle the singularities of such manipulators, we use the weighted damped least squares method [15, 21] to determine the joint velocities.

DMPs themselves do not provide a direct way of dealing with kinematic and dynamic constraints on the robot joints, which have to be dealt with at the control level. In practice, this is not as significant an issue as it might seem due to two main reasons: (i) a primitive generated from a demonstrated trajectory generally represents feasible reproducible motions (though this is largely determined by the manner in which trajectories are demonstrated [2]); (ii) a primitive-based policy is often not used directly, but is improved in a reinforcement learning scenario [9]. What is a practical issue however, particularly in the context of domains such as domestic robotics, is the fact that $\mathbf{g}$ is likely to lie outside the dexterous workspace of a robot's manipulator (for instance, a robot may need to grasp a table object that is not reachable from the robot's current position); in such cases, a motion primitive on its own is clearly insufficient for performing a task.

3.2   Combining DMPs and Whole Body Motion

Considering that we work with mobile robots, we overcome this problem by using a whole body motion framework that performs only arm motions when the manipulator Jacobian is well-conditioned, but introduces motion of the robot's base when the Jacobian is nearing a singularity. Near-singularities of a manipulator can be detected by monitoring the smallest singular value σ_{min} of the Jacobian J defined above, which tends to zero in such configurations [8]; this follows directly from the fact that the condition number of a matrix is given by the ratio $\frac{\sigma_{max}}{\sigma_{min}}$, such that singular or near-singular matrices have a large condition number.

The distribution of linear velocities amongst the mobile base platform and the end effector is governed by the following relations:

$$m_{cap} = \frac{\sigma_{min} - \sigma_l}{\sigma_h - \sigma_l} \tag{3}$$

$$\mathbf{v}_{ee} = m_{cap}\mathbf{v} \tag{4}$$

$$\mathbf{v}_b = (1 - m_{cap})\mathbf{v} \tag{5}$$

where m_{cap} is what we call a capability coefficient of the manipulator, σ_{min} is the smallest singular value of J, σ_l is a lower threshold on σ_{min}[4], σ_h is an

---

[4] This value is experimentally tuned in such a way that the manipulator remains away from singular configurations.

upper threshold on σ_{min}[5], $\mathbf{v}$ is the desired linear velocity of the end effector in the global frame of reference, $\mathbf{v}_{ee}$ is a velocity command for the end effector, and $\mathbf{v}_b$ is a velocity command for the mobile base. Here, it should be noted that the motion of the base is introduced only when σ_{min} drops below σ_h. In a similar fashion, it is possible to incorporate limitations of the base motion, such as obstacles sensed by a distance sensor, in a modified version of the above policy to ensure safe base motion.

As mentioned above, the desired end effector velocities are converted to joint velocities using an inverse kinematics solver[6]. The obtained joint velocities are then interpreted by a low-level joint velocity controller, which performs the actual joint motions. Base velocity commands are similarly interpreted by the robot's base velocity controller.

3.3   Demonstrating and Learning Motion Primitives

Learning from demonstration can be done in various different ways, all of which impose different constraints on the robot and demonstrator [2]. In the context of this work, we use external observations for recording motion primitives, namely we record the motion of a demonstrator using a camera placed on the robot, which tracks the position of an ArUco marker board [5]. The demonstration process is illustrated in Fig. 2.

By recording the board poses at a predefined frequency, we obtain a set of n points $D = \{d_i \mid d_i \in \mathbb{R}^6, 1 \leq i \leq n\}$. D is thus a representation of the demonstrated trajectory in Cartesian space, which is then used for learning the forcing term of a motion primitive. As done in [6], we represent the forcing term as a sum of weighted basis functions

$$f(x) = \frac{\sum_{i=1}^{k} \Psi_i(x) w_i}{\sum_{i=1}^{k} \Psi_i(x)} x(\mathbf{g} - \mathbf{y_0}) \tag{6}$$

where y_0 is the initial position, g is the goal, w_i are weights that need to be learned, and each $\Psi_i(x)$ has the form

$$\Psi_i(x) = \exp\left(-\frac{1}{2\sigma_i^2}(x - c_i)^2\right) \tag{7}$$

such that the weighting terms are learned using weighted linear regression.

It should be noted that we learn a separate primitive for each Cartesian dimension, which means that a complete motion primitive is a combination of six dimension-specific primitive motions that need to be followed together when the motion has to be reproduced. Here, it is important to mention that we actually only control the position of the end effector, which means that the orientation

---

[5] The value of σ_h is also experimentally tuned and prevents the introduction of base motions prematurely.

[6] https://github.com/b-it-bots/mas_common_robotics/tree/kinetic/mcr_manipulation/mcr_arm_cartesian_control.

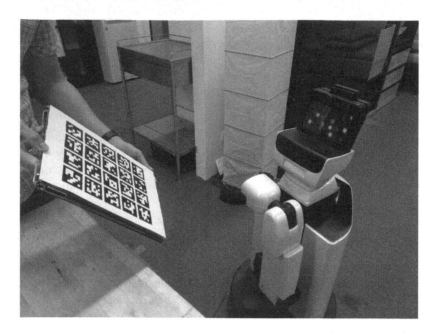

Fig. 2. DMP demonstration by observing an ArUco marker board

primitives are not taken into account at runtime, but this is only because the external observation method makes it difficult to represent the orientation reasonably; using a different demonstration method, such as kinesthetic teaching [2], would make it possible to use those in practice as well[7].

3.4 Purposeful Manipulation in Domestic Environments

We represent manipulation trajectories using motion primitives that can be demonstrated and learned in order to have a predictable and generalisable model that allows a robot to perform tasks in a domestic environment. In particular, assuming that we have m motion primitives $M_i, 1 \leq i \leq m$ and s skills $S_j, 1 \leq j \leq s$, we associate each M_i with a skill S_j, where this mapping need not be a bijective one; in particular, each M_i can be associated with multiple skills (for instance, a single primitive can be used for grasping and placing), but also each S_j can utilise multiple primitives (for instance, we could have multiple grasping primitives that change depending on the context)[8].

As can be noticed above, the representation of motion primitives we apply does not directly use any dynamic information about the environment, such as

---

[7] An implementation of the complete DMP learning and execution workflow can be found at https://github.com/b-it-bots/ros_dmp.

[8] Our implementation that currently only makes use of a single dynamic primitive per skill is embedded into our domestic robotics architecture: https://github.com/b-it-bots/mas_domestic_robotics.

obstacles that are in the way of a robot. We do not deal with such factors in this paper, but note that information about obstacles can be incorporated in the form of repulsive fields [17]. We consider this to be an essential future extension for the practicality of our framework in complex everyday scenarios.

4 Evaluation

To evaluate motion primitives for performing purposeful tasks in the context of domestic robots, we recorded a grasping primitive for a Toyota Human Support Robot (HSR) and performed a set of grasping experiments in which the robot had to grasp objects from two different surfaces - an ordinary dining table and a living room table[9]. To detect objects, we used the SSD object detector [13] trained on the COCO dataset; our experimental evaluation is not concerned with recognising objects, so the pretrained model suffices for our purpose and we did not retrain it on a new dataset. For calculating the object poses, we used a grasp synthesis method that assumes a fixed grasping orientation (resulting in a sideways grasp) and determines the position of the object to be grasped from the object's point cloud by averaging the positions of the points:

$$\begin{pmatrix} x \\ y \\ z \end{pmatrix} = \begin{pmatrix} \frac{1}{N} \sum_{i=1}^{o} O_{x_i} \\ \frac{1}{N} \sum_{i=1}^{o} O_{y_i} \\ \frac{1}{N} \sum_{i=1}^{o} O_{z_i} \end{pmatrix} \qquad (8)$$

where O is the object's point cloud and o is the number of points[10].

The experimental setup was the same for both surfaces, namely a single object was placed on the surface, such that the robot had to (i) detect the object, (ii) determine its pose, (iii) choose a grasping pose, and (iv) execute a grasping motion using the previously recorded motion primitive. The pose of the object was varied in each experimental trial; in some of the trials, the robot could reach the object with pure arm motion, while the object was out of reach and thus whole body motion was required in all other trials. Runs in which the object could not be detected were repeated until the object was found. Due to the design of the HSR, the robot has to align with the object before performing a grasping motion; in addition, the arm goes to a pregrasp position before executing a motion primitive, such that two different pregrasp positions were used depending on the surface. The sequence of steps for grasping an object on the dining table is depicted in Fig. 3.

The overall experimental setup is illustrated in Fig. 4, such that we used the objects in Fig. 5 for evaluation. We performed 10 experimental trials per object; this resulted in 150 trials per surface or 300 trials in total. Trials in which the object was grasped and remained in the gripper until manual removal

---

[9] A video of an earlier trial run of our experiment can be found at https://www.youtube.com/watch?v=OC7vttt4-Jo.

[10] Further details about our perception pipeline can be found at https://github.com/mas-group/mas_tutorials.

(a) The pose of the object is detected first

(b) The robot then aligns with the object

(c) The arm goes to a pre-grasp configuration

(d) The object is grasped by applying whole body motion

(e) The arm retrieves back to a safe configuration

Fig. 3. Object grasping sequence

(a) Dining table

(b) Coffee table

Fig. 4. Setup and objects used in the grasping experiments. In the case of the coffee table, the white board was placed in order to block out some reflections due to bad lighting conditions. In both cases, only one object at a time was placed at different positions on the table, such that the robot had to detect the object, estimate its pose, and then grasp it (10 times for each object and surface combination), resulting in 300 grasping experimental trials in total.

were considered successful provided that the manipulator did not have a strong collision with the table; trials in which there was a collision or the object was not grasped successfully were counted as failures.

Plots of representative planned and executed trajectories when grasping the noodle box are shown in Fig. 6. As can be seen there, the executed trajectories do not exactly match the predicted trajectories, although this can be tolerated in most practical scenarios.

The results of the baseline grasping experiment are shown in Table 1.

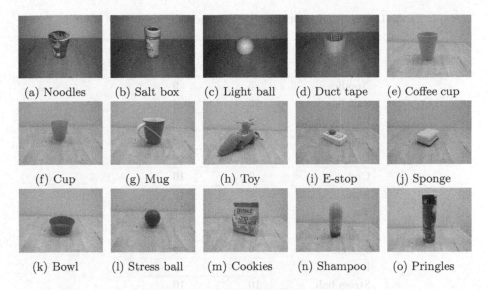

(a) Noodles   (b) Salt box   (c) Light ball   (d) Duct tape   (e) Coffee cup

(f) Cup   (g) Mug   (h) Toy   (i) E-stop   (j) Sponge

(k) Bowl   (l) Stress ball   (m) Cookies   (n) Shampoo   (o) Pringles

Fig. 5. Objects used in the grasping experiments

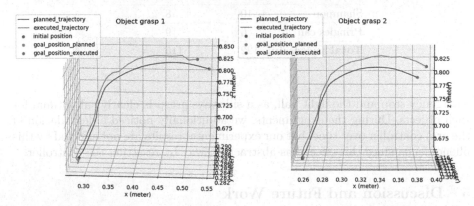

Fig. 6. Planned and executed DMP-based trajectories by the Toyota HSR in the noodle box grasping experiment

A large number of failed attempts in the experiments were caused by a slip of the object due to an incorrectly detected object pose; for instance, this was the case for the bowl when turned upside down, the mug and noodle box on the dining table, as well as the shampoo on the coffee table. Occasional failures were due to collisions with the table that triggered a safety stop. While grasping the e-stop, most failures were due to the fact that the object is too low for a sideways grasp; on the coffee table, neither the e-stop nor the light ball could be grasped due to this issue. Failures such as these clearly indicate the necessity for a more general grasp planner that is able to adapt based on the context and task; for instance, a top-down grasp is more suitable for objects such as the

Table 1. Successful grasps in the grasping experiment (out of 10)

Object	Surface	
	Dining table	Coffee table
Noodles	5	9
Salt box	10	4
Light ball	10	0
Duct tape	9	10
Coffee cup	9	10
Cup	9	10
Mug	7	10
Toy	8	7
E-stop	4	0
Sponge	10	9
Bowl	7	9
Stress ball	10	10
Cookies	8	10
Shampoo	10	8
Pringles can	6	9
Total successful	122	115

emergency stop and the light ball, as a sideways grasp is clearly suboptimal for such objects. During the experiments, we additionally noticed a degradation of the arm controller over time, but our experimental results are not affected by this phenomenon since this effect was abstracted away by resetting the controller.

5   Discussion and Future Work

The evaluation of dynamic motion primitives extended with a whole body motion policy has shown the feasibility of the approach for everyday object manipulation with a mobile manipulator, but has also illustrated various limitations of the framework as presented here that need to be addressed for increasing the method's practical applicability. As would be expected, the quality of the demonstrated motion primitive significantly affects the motion executed by the manipulator. We have found that the method based on recording trajectories using external observations is not ideal since it requires a trial-and-error procedure for finding a suitable primitive; we are thus investigating ways to use admittance control for demonstrating trajectories using kinesthetic teaching.

As illustrated by the experimental analysis, motion primitives can be reasonably generalised, but there are natural limits to the generalisation capabilities. In our experiments, the motion primitive was originally recorded for manipulation on the dining table, where a concave trajectory is executed, while a convex trajectory is needed for manipulation on the coffee table. In order to generalise the primitive, we manually specified two different pregrasp positions of the manipulator for the two tables, but an adaptive strategy that automatically selects pregrasp positions and motion primitives is needed for fully autonomous operation; various ideas in this direction are presented in [20]. As discussed before, it is also necessary to consider dynamic information about the environment, such as obstacles and external forces acting on the robot during the execution of trajectories, in order to increase the practical usefulness of primitive-based execution. Improving faulty motion primitives based on corrective demonstrations [7] and teacher feedback [1] is another possible extension. Finally, our primary motivation for using motion primitives is having a model that can be used for detecting and diagnosing robot execution failures; a consistency-based method as discussed in [19] provides some ideas for that, although its direct applicability needs to be investigated in a separate study.

6   Conclusions

In this paper, we analysed learning from demonstration in general as well as the use of dynamic motion primitives for representing motion trajectories of a mobile manipulator in particular and investigated the framework in the context of a specific mobile manipulator - a Toyota Human Support Robot. To allow executing trajectories that require synchronised arm and base motion, we discussed a small extension of manipulation-only motion primitives to whole body motion using which motions of a mobile base are introduced if the manipulator is approaching a singular configuration. We additionally presented an extensive set of experiments in which the robot was grasping different everyday objects in a common domestic environment. Future work will address the manner in which trajectories are demonstrated to the robot, but the adaptation of primitives to different contexts and tasks as well as the use of primitives for predicting execution failures need to be studied as well.

Acknowledgements. We gratefully acknowledge the support by the b-it International Center for Information Technology. We would like to thank Sven Schneider for all useful discussions and insights.

References

1. Argall, B.D., Browning, B., Veloso, M.: Teacher feedback to scaffold and refine demonstrated motion primitives on a mobile robot. Robot. Auton. Syst. **59**(3–4), 243–255 (2011)
2. Argall, B.D., Chernova, S., Veloso, M., Browning, B.: A survey of robot learning from demonstration. Robot. Auton. Syst. **57**(5), 469–483 (2009)
3. Bohg, J., Morales, A., Asfour, T., Kragic, D.: Data-driven grasp synthesis: a survey. IEEE Trans. Robot. **30**(2), 289–309 (2014)
4. Chen, N., Bayer, J., Urban, S., van der Smagt, P.: Efficient movement representation by embedding dynamic movement primitives in deep autoencoders. In: IEEE-RAS 15th International Conference on Humanoid Robots (Humanoids), pp. 434–440 (November 2015)

5. Garrido-Jurado, S., Muñoz-Salinas, R., Madrid-Cuevas, F.J., Marín-Jiménez, M.J.: Automatic generation and detection of highly reliable fiducial markers under occlusion. Pattern Recogn. **47**(6), 2280–2292 (2014)
6. Ijspeert, A.J., Nakanishi, J., Hoffmann, H., Pastor, P., Schaal, S.: Dynamical movement primitives: learning attractor models for motor behaviors. Neural Comput. **25**(2), 328–373 (2013)
7. Karlsson, M., Robertsson, A., Johansson, R.: Autonomous interpretation of demonstrations for modification of dynamical movement primitives. In: Proceedings of 2017 IEEE International Conference on Robotics and Automation (ICRA), pp. 316–321 (2017)
8. Kirćanski, M.V., Boric, M.D.: Symbolic singular value decomposition for a PUMA robot and its application to a robot operation near singularities. Int. J. Robot. Res. 12(5), 460–472 (1993)
9. Kober, J., Peters, J.: reinforcement learning in robotics: a survey, pp. 579–610 (2012)
10. Lee, J.: A survey of robot learning from demonstrations for human-robot collaboration. https://arxiv.org/abs/1710.08789 (2017)
11. Lim, B., Ra, S., Park, F.C.: Movement Primitives, Principal Component Analysis, and the Efficient Generation of Natural Motions. In: Proceedings of the 2005 IEEE international conference on Robotics and Automation, pp. 4630–4635 (April 2005)
12. Lioutikov, R., Kroemer, O., Maeda, G., Peters, J.: Learning manipulation by sequencing motor primitives with a two-armed robot. In: Menegatti, E., Michael, N., Berns, K., Yamaguchi, H. (eds.) Intelligent Autonomous Systems 13. AISC, vol. 302, pp. 1601–1611. Springer, Cham (2016). https://doi.org/10.1007/978-3-319-08338-4_115
13. Liu, W., et al.: SSD: single shot multibox detector. CoRR. arXiv:1512.02325 (2015)
14. Matamoros, M., Rascon, C., Hart, J., Holz, D., Beek, L.: RoboCup@Home 2018: Rules and Regulations (2018). http://www.robocupathome.org/rules/2018_rulebook.pdf
15. Nakamura, Y., Hanafusa, H.: Inverse kinematic solutions with singularity robustness for robot manipulator control. J. Dyn. Syst. Meas. Control **108**(3), 163–171 (1986)
16. Paraschos, A., Daniel, C., Peters, J., Neumann, G.: Probabilistic movement primitives. In: Proceedings of 26th International Conference on Neural Information Processing Systems, vol. 2, pp. 2616–2624 (2013)
17. Park, D.H., Hoffmann, H., Pastor, P., Schaal, S.: Movement reproduction and obstacle avoidance with dynamic movement primitives and potential fields. In: Humanoids 2008–8th IEEE-RAS International Conference on Humanoid Robots, pp. 91–98 (December 2008)
18. Pettersson, O.: Execution monitoring in robotics: a survey. Robot. Auton. Syst. **53**(2), 73–88 (2005)
19. Provan, G.: Diagnosing hybrid systems using consistency-based methods. In: 29th International Workshop Principles of Diagnosis DX 2018 (2018)
20. Ude, A., Gams, A., Asfour, T., Morimoto, J.: Task-specific generalization of discrete and periodic dynamic movement primitives. IEEE Trans. Robot. **26**(5), 800–815 (2010)
21. Wampler, C.W.: Manipulator inverse kinematic solutions based on vector formulations and damped least-squares methods. IEEE Trans. Syst. Man Cybern. **16**(1), 93–101 (1986)

Estimation of Subjective Evaluation of HRI Performance Based on Objective Behaviors of Human and Robots

Yoshiaki Mizuchi[1]([✉]) [iD] and Tetsunari Inamura[1,2] [iD]

[1] National Institute of Informatics,
2-1-2 Hitotsubashi, Chiyoda-ku, Tokyo 101-8430, Japan
{mizuchi,inamura}@nii.ac.jp
[2] The Graduate University for Advanced Studies, SOKENDAI,
2-1-2 Hitotsubashi, Chiyoda-ku, Tokyo 101-8430, Japan

Abstract. The conventional approach to the evaluation of the performance of human-robot interaction (HRI) is subjective evaluation, such as the application of questionnaires. As such subjective evaluation is time-consuming, an alternative automatic evaluation method based on only objectively observable factors (i.e., human reaction behavior) is required for autonomous learning by robots and for scoring in robot competitions. To this end, we aim to investigate the extent to which subjective evaluation results can be approximated using objective factors. As a case study, we designed and carried out a VR-based robot-competition task in which the robot was required to generate comprehensible and unambiguous natural language expressions and gestures to guide inexpert users in everyday environments. In the competition, both event data and human behavioral data (i.e., interaction histories) were observed and stored. Additionally, to acquire subjective evaluation results, we asked third-parties to evaluate the HRI performance by reviewing the stored interaction histories. From the analysis of the relationship between objective factors and subjective evaluation results, we demonstrate that the subjective evaluation of HRI can indeed be reasonably approximated on the basis of objective factors.

Keywords: Human-robot interaction · Natural language generation · RoboCup@Home · Virtual reality

1 Introduction

The evaluation of human-robot interaction (HRI) is important to improve the social skills of interactive robots. Moreover, there is a particular need for automated evaluation; for example, for autonomous learning of human-interaction

This paper is based on results obtained from a project commissioned by the New Energy and Industrial Technology Development Organization (NEDO). This work was also supported by JST CREST Grant Number JPMJCR15E3, Japan.

© Springer Nature Switzerland AG 2019
S. Chalup et al. (Eds.): RoboCup 2019, LNAI 11531, pp. 201–212, 2019.
https://doi.org/10.1007/978-3-030-35699-6_16

skills, robots need to be able to evaluate their interactions, responding appropriately to both positive and negative results to improve their HRI policies without specific interventions by developers. Due to the fact that the requirement exists in the context of robot competitions such as RoboCup@Home, these provide an appropriate and effective context for investigating techniques and approaches for the improvement of HRI.

The evaluation of HRI performance is generally subjective, with the standard method being the use of questionnaires for the evaluation of social and cognitive factors. However, subjective evaluation suffers from two drawbacks: first, the acquisition of answers from test subjects is time-consuming, and second, the number of samples is limited to the number of available human respondents. Accordingly, the conventional questionnaire-based approach to subjective evaluation is impractical for fair and efficient evaluation of HRI performance in contexts such as robot competitions.

One of the solutions to these problems is an alternative method that approximates the subjective evaluation results from only observable objective factors, namely, human reaction behaviors. In order to achieve this, we need to analyze the relationship between the subjective evaluation results and the objective factors. Therefore, it is necessary to observe and store data on all the events and human behaviors in question, in addition to acquiring subjective evaluation results. As experiments of this nature are time-consuming and costly, we chose to utilize immersive virtual reality (VR) techniques as a more time- and cost-effective solution to carry out HRI experiments, and thereby to acquire the requisite data. We have already proposed a VR-based software platform, SIGVerse [7], which enables human users to log in and make use of an avatar to interact with virtual robots and environments through immersive VR interfaces. A basic concept has been also proposed for the evaluation of the performance of the HRI in a VR-based robot competition task [3]; however, no evaluation method that approximates subjective evaluation results has been proposed or discussed to date.

The aim of this study is to investigate how to approximate subjective evaluation results of HRI performance on the basis of objective factors. In this paper, we present a case study of a robot competition in which the virtual robot had to guide non-expert human users to complete a certain task by means of verbal/nonverbal communication. Data on human reaction behaviors occurring in response to the instructions given by different robots were recorded and stored. Additionally, to acquire subjective evaluation results, we asked third-parties to evaluate the HRI performance by reviewing the stored interaction histories. From the analysis of the relationship between objective factors and subjective evaluation results, we demonstrate that the subjective evaluation of HRI could be reasonably approximated using objective factors.

2   Related Works

With respect to the evaluation of the social and cognitive effects of robots, various measurement scales have been developed. In research fields relating to human-agent interaction and social robotics, developing psychological scales is a common focus area (e.g., [4,8]). Although Bartneck et al. [1] developed the 'godspeed questionnaire' as a standardized measurement tool for the measurement of the psychological effects of HRI, their study and similar works in the field have focused on psychological effects, using only questionnaire-based subjective evaluations.

In cases of targeting objectively measurable factors such as comfortable distances [9], the effects of HRI can be evaluated directly. However, the effects of most of HRI functions, particularly natural language instructions and gestures generated by robots, are not measurable directly. With respect to measurable factors to verify the effectiveness of HRI functions, the focus has been on metrics such as required time and success rates in a specific task (e.g., [6]). Although using those metrics is a reasonable approach to compare the performance of HRI, it is not clarified what metrics are appropriate for the evaluation and how to choose appropriate metrics.

With respect to experiments to evaluate the effects of HRI, a few research groups have carried out field studies in real-world environments (e.g., [2]). Although such field studies are important for the development of social robots, in terms of the efficient evaluation, especially for robot competitions, they offer somewhat infeasible solutions for evaluating parallel sessions, easily controlling experimental conditions, or reproducing interaction histories. The utilization of VR techniques offers a feasible solution to these problems. The Generating Instructions in Virtual Environments (GIVE) challenge [10] was proposed to evaluate natural language generation (NLG) systems which guide human users to perform a task in a virtual environment, but HRI is not a focus area in this challenge. In the absence of any similar challenges focusing on HRI, no forum exists in which the embodiment of both robots and human instruction-followers (i.e., gestures by a virtual robot and physical actions of an avatar to interact with objects) are not targeted.

Kanda et al. [5] focused on the analysis of the relationship between objective results (the body movements of subjects) and subjective impressions. To determine an evaluation method for HRI performance, they attempted to estimate the subjective evaluation results from the body movements with multiple linear regression analysis. Ideally, the scoring methods and rules for robot competitions should be developed through this sort of analysis. However, there is no such work on direct evaluation of HRI performance involving generated natural language sentences/utterances and gestures generated by robots, nor is there an appropriate platform available. Accordingly, as the primary step towards this ultimate goal, we focus on a case study of a robot competition to demonstrate the contribution our platform can make, and propose and validate an approach to determine the most effective evaluation method for HRI performance.

3   Case Study

We designed a robot competition task in which the virtual robot has to guide non-expert human users to achieve a certain task by verbal communication.

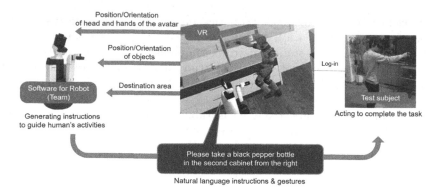

Fig. 1. Flow of the proposed competition task.

Figure 1 shows the flow of the proposed competition task. At the start of the task, only the robot receives the pre-defined label name and position/orientation of the target object, the position/orientation/size of the destination area, and the position/orientation of other objects (i.e., all existing furniture objects and graspable objects except the target object). The position/orientation of the head and both hands of the avatar can be determined by the robot at any time. The role of the robot is to generate natural language instructions and gestures to properly control the navigation actions of a human instruction-follower (i.e., a test subject); in other words, the robot needs to convert positional information to natural language instructions and gestures. The generated natural language instructions are given to the avatar visually and audibly. The role of the test subject is to find/take a target object and then carry it to a destination by following the instructions from the robot. The test subjects is not told about room layouts, the target object, or the destination area. Accordingly, while the conventional robot competition tasks have focused on the understanding of requests from human operators by a robot, the roles of robot and human are reversed in this task.

We developed the competition system on the SIGVerse ver.3 platform [7]. Each team could develop controller software for the virtual robot by utilizing existing ROS-based software packages and libraries for real robots. The test subject logs in to a virtual avatar through the VR interface (e.g., Oculus Rift and Touch) and can interact with the virtual robot and objects in the virtual environment. With visual feedback and the tracking of head/hand poses, the test subject can manipulate virtual objects and the drawers/doors of furniture in a manner similar to that in which they would interact with the real physical environment. The test subject can move around the virtual environment by using the joystick of a hand-held controller. Additionally, they can request instructions at any time by using a button on the hand-held controller.

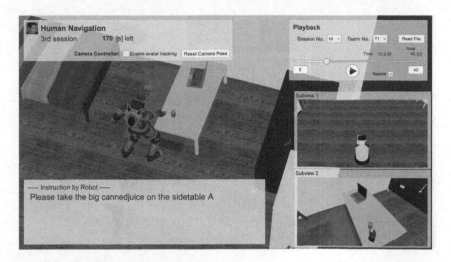

Fig. 2. Screenshot of the playback system for subjective evaluation by third-parties.

We organized a VR-based HRI competition at the World Robot Summit, Service Category, Partner Robot Challenge[1], held in October 2018 in Tokyo. This provided the context for the case study used in the research. The proposed competition task falls into the 'Human Navigation' in the rulebook[2]. We shared the competition software on GitHub[3] in advance, and only required participants to develop controller software (i.e., instruction generators) for the virtual robot. In the competition, the test subjects learned in advance, and practiced enough operational procedures to move, grasp objects, open/close doors and drawers, and request additional instructions from the robot in a test environment.

In addition to the robot competition, to analyze the relationship between objective factors and the result of subjective evaluation by humans, we asked third-parties to watch the recorded interaction histories from the competition and to subjectively evaluate these. Figure 2 shows the playback system for use in facilitating evaluation by third-parties. The evaluators are able to control the pose of a camera in the VR environment and observe all the events from an arbitrary point of view, and can watch a scene as many times as necessary. The behavior of the robot and the first-person user perspective are provided in sub-windows. The scores in the competition were hidden during the playback of the interaction histories, to prevent evaluator-bias. The evaluators rated the efficiency of the interaction between the robot and the test subject using a 5-point Likert scale questionnaire.

---

[1] http://worldrobotsummit.org/en/wrc2018/service/.

[2] http://worldrobotsummit.org/download/rulebook-en/rulebook-simulation_league_partner_robot_challnege.pdf.

[3] https://github.com/PartnerRobotChallengeVirtual/.

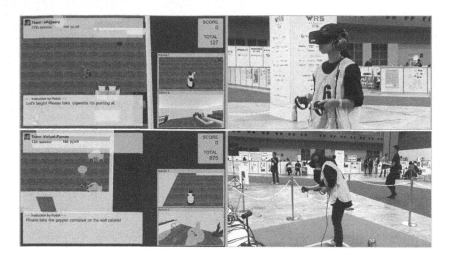

Fig. 3. Screen-shots of the Human Navigation task.

4   Results

Figure 3 shows screen-shots of the competition system and the behavior of a test subject. The recordings of all the competition sessions are available on a YouTube channel[4]. In the competition, we evaluated 7 robot-software controller submissions developed by 7 participating team. Each team competed in 28 sessions in parallel, making a total of 196 sessions. Each session lasted up to 180 s. Different room layouts were used in each session. We invited 16 test subjects to take part in the evaluation; each subject acted in the testing role up to twice for each team (either 7 or 14 sessions per tester). Consequently, 7.9 h of human-robot interaction history data were collected. The history data include not only the sentences generated by the robots, but also all the test subject's embodied reactions, such as wandering motions due to a vague instructions from the robot, mistakes due to misunderstandings, and so on.

We evaluated interaction behaviors according to the competition rulebook (See footnote 2) As no criteria existed to directly evaluate the generated utterance, we formulated the scoring method empirically based on the following objectively measurable factors:

- Required time to complete the task.
- Required time to grasp the target object.
- Frequency of incorrect object-grasps.
- Number of instructions given by the robot.

The score distribution for each team is shown in Fig. 4. Each dot denotes the average score and the error bar denotes 95% confidence intervals. The average

---

[4] https://bit.ly/2QOjJAZ.

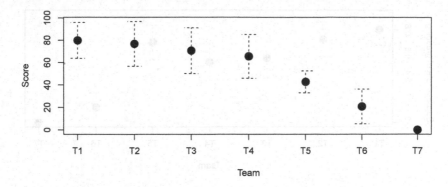

Fig. 4. Score distribution of the teams.

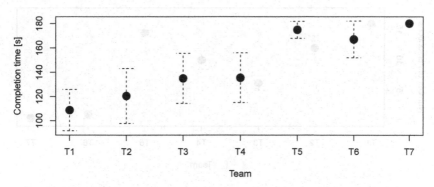

Fig. 5. Required time to complete the task for each session.

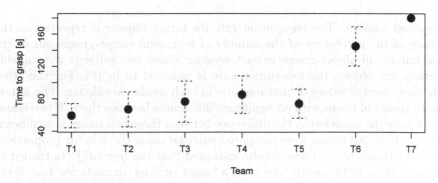

Fig. 6. Required time to grasp the target object for each session.

values and 95% confidence intervals of the objective measures are also shown in
Figs. 5, 6, 7 and 8. Table 1 compares the scores and the results of the objective
measures. The time taken is assumed to be 180 s if a task remains incomplete
then 180 s have elapsed. The completion rate is the percentage of successfully

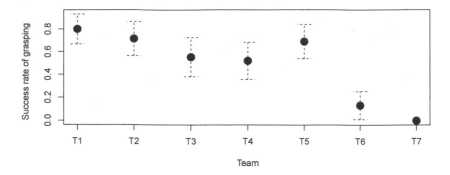

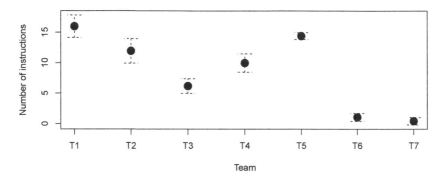

Fig. 7. Recognition rate of target object for each session.

Fig. 8. Number of instructions given by robots in each session.

completed sessions. The recognition rate for target objects is reported as the average of the percentage of the number of successful target-grasps out of the total number of object-grasps in each session; where test subjects were unable to grasp any object, the recognition rate is assumed to be 0%. For the other measures, average values of that measure in each session are shown. The letters denote groups of teams with no significant differences between them. If two teams do not have the same letter, the difference between those two teams is significant with $p < 0.05$. All teams were compared pairwise using the test for proportions and Steel-Dwass tests. These results indicated that the test subjects tended to fail the task more frequently and need a longer time to complete the task if the robot instructions were incomprehensible.

For a subjective evaluation, we invited 10 third-party evaluators. Each evaluator was asked to evaluate 168 sessions (7 teams × 24 sessions); we excluded 4 sessions which were affected by a log-file that was accidentally corrupted. Figure 9 shows the result of the subjective evaluation using a 5-point Likert scale questionnaire. The comparison of the subjective scores given in Table 2. The scores were compared pairwise using a post-hoc Steel-Dwass test. Some differences exist between the evaluated and competition scores, with a significant

Table 1. Comparison for objective measures.

Team	T1	T2	T3	T4	T5	T6	T7
Score	79.7	76.6	70.6	65.5	42.7	20.7	0.0
	A	A	A	A			
		B	B	B	B		
						C	C
Completion rate [%]	82.1	60.7	50.0	50.0	14.3	10.7	0.0
	A	A					
		B	B	B			
					C	C	C
Required time to complete the task [s]	108.8	120.4	134.9	135.4	174.8	167.0	180.0
	A	A	A	A			
			B	B	B		
					C	C	C
Recognition rate of target object [%]	80.0	71.5	55.4	52.2	69.0	13.2	0.0
	A	A	A	A	A		
						B	
							C
Required time to grasp the target [s]	59.2	67.1	70.2	85.1	73.9	145.0	180.0
	A	A	A	A	A		
						B	B
Number of instructions	16.0	11.9	6.2	10.0	14.4	1.1	0.4
			A			A	A
			B				
		C		C			
	D				D		

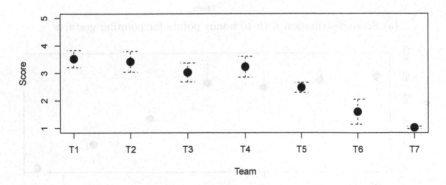

Fig. 9. Score of efficiency of interaction between each robot and test subjects subjectively evaluated by third-parties

difference between T2 and T5 and in the order of T3 and T4; these can be attributed to the fact that we decided the scoring method subjectively.

Table 2. Comparison result of subjective scores.

Team	T1	T2	T3	T4	T5	T6	T7
Efficiency of HRI (subjective result)	3.5	3.4	3.0	3.2	2.5	1.6	1.0
	A	A	A	A			
			B		B		
						C	C

To improve the validity of the scoring method, we analyzed the relationship with the subjective evaluation results and modified the scoring method used in the robot competition. Evaluator comments indicated that the key factor in the higher T4 score was the inclusion of robot pointing gestures. Accordingly, we awarded bonus points for pointing gestures; if the robot had been able to correctly point out a target object and destination, bonus points were added once for each of these achievements. Figures 10(a) and (b) show the modified scores

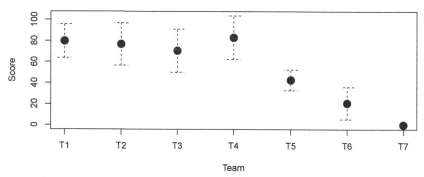

(a) Score distribution with 10 bonus points for pointing gestures

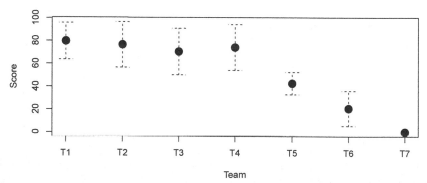

(b) Score distribution with 5 bonus points for pointing gestures

Fig. 10. Modified score distributions that were added bonus points for pointing gestures.

when 5 or 10 points were added for each pointing gestures. From the results shown in Fig. 10(a), if 10 points were added, the score distribution would be distorted because T4's score would exceed those of T1 and T2. The order of score distribution in Fig. 10(b) corresponds to the subjective evaluation results. We were, thus, able to modify the evaluation method appropriately while continuing to utilize our system and the recorded interaction histories. The importance of such a revision process in the development of valid evaluation methods for HRI performance was, thereby, demonstrated effectively.

5   Discussions

With respect to system efficiency, the third-party evaluators required 15 h on average (with a maximum of 30 h) to review all the interaction histories and respond to the questionnaire. The time-consuming nature of the subjective evaluation of HRI performance is a weakness of this approach. Additionally, evaluation based on objective measures of human behavior, such as the time required to complete tasks, did not correspond to the subjective evaluation results. This supports our supposition that using only such objective measures is inadequate for the evaluation of HRI performance, and underscores the importance of creating an evaluation method that approximates the subjective evaluation result from objective factors.

In the robot competitions, we often face the similar problem in the process of defining scoring methods. Although organizers define the scoring method by discussion, often heated, the validity thereof has never been assessed to date. In other words, conventional evaluation criteria for the evaluation of HRI performance have only been subject to manual and empirical modification. Our proposed improvement process, modelled in this work, demonstrates its potential for improving evaluation methods without human intervention.

Another contribution of our study was the development of a VR system and the demonstration, through a case study in a robot competition, of its applicability in facilitating the observation of interaction histories. Playback of recorded events and human behaviors recorded by the system facilitates subjective evaluation by enabling the evaluator to observe the HRI they are evaluating form arbitrary points of view.

6   Conclusions

In this study, we aimed to devise a method for evaluating the performance of HRI that uses objective factors to approximate subjective evaluation. As a case study, we organized a VR-based HRI competition during the World Robot Summit held in October 2018. Analysis of the relationship between objective/observable factors and the results of subjective evaluation by third-parties was described.

One of the main contributions of this work was to demonstrate the necessity for a method of objective evaluation that can approximate subjective evaluation results from only objective factors. Another important contribution was the proposal and trial of an improvement process for the evaluation method that can function effectively without manual intervention.

In this study, we subjectively revised the evaluation method as a first step. However, numerical analysis methods such as multiple regression analysis should be used to more approximate the human subjectivity. Additionally, although our system can obtain embodied human behavior, such as changes to the head directions of avatars which can be assumed to present the frequency with which a test subject loses their way, such factors are not currently used for evaluation. In future work, we would like to focus on embodied behavior so as to determine a more effective evaluation method.

References

1. Bartneck, C., Kulić, D., Croft, E., Zoghbi, S.: Measurement instruments for the anthropomorphism, animacy, likeability, perceived intelligence, and perceived safety of robots. Int. J. Soc. Robot. 1(1), 71–81 (2009)
2. Brščić, D., Kidokoro, H., Suehiro, Y., Kanda, T.: Escaping from children's abuse of social robots. In: Proceedings of ACM/IEEE International Conference on Human-Robot Interaction, pp. 59–66 (2015)
3. Inamura, T., Mizuchi, Y.: Competition design to evaluate cognitive functions in human-robot interaction based on immersive VR. In: Akiyama, H., Obst, O., Sammut, C., Tonidandel, F. (eds.) RoboCup 2017. LNCS (LNAI), vol. 11175, pp. 84–94. Springer, Cham (2018). https://doi.org/10.1007/978-3-030-00308-1_7
4. Kamide, H., Kawabe, K., Shigemi, S., Arai, T.: Anshin as a concept of subjective well-being between humans and robots in Japan. Adv. Robot. 29(24), 1624–1636 (2015)
5. Kanda, T., Ishiguro, H., Imai, M., Ono, T.: Development and evaluation of interactive humanoid robots. Proc. IEEE 92(11), 1839–1850 (2004)
6. Knepper, R.A., Tellex, S., Li, A., Roy, N., Rus, D.: Recovering from failure by asking for help. Auton. Robots 39(3), 347–362 (2015)
7. Mizuchi, Y., Inamura, T.: Cloud-based multimodal human-robot interaction simulator utilizing ROS and unity frameworks. In: IEEE/SICE International Symposium on System Integration, pp. 948–955 (2017)
8. Nomura, T., Kanda, T.: Rapport-expectation with a robot scale. Int. J. Soc. Robot. 8(1), 21–30 (2016)
9. Rossi, S., Staffa, M., Bove, L., Capasso, R., Ercolano, G.: User's personality and activity influence on HRI comfortable distances. In: Lecture Notes in Computer Science, vol. 10652, pp. 167–177 (2017). https://doi.org/10.1007/978-3-319-70022-9_17
10. Striegnitz, K., Denis, A., Gargett, A., Garouf, K., Koller, A., Theune, M.: Report on the second second challenge on generating instructions in virtual environments (GIVE-2.5). In: Proceedings of European Workshop on Natural Language Generation, pp. 270–279 (2011)

Adaptive Walk-Kick on a Bipedal Robot

Pedro Peña(✉) and Ubbo Visser(✉)

University of Miami, Coral Gables, FL 33146, USA
{pedro,visser}@cs.miami.edu

Abstract. Using the NAO robot as a testbed, we propose a walk-kick framework that can generate a kick trajectory with an arbitrary direction without prior input or knowledge of the parameters of the kick in the midst of walking while still guaranteeing reaching a reference trajectory. The walk-kick uses kick interpolators from a dynamic kick engine and the walk trajectories generated from adaptive walking engine to generate motions in any direction that allow a robot to reach its destination while also allowing it to move the ball in further distances without transitioning in different states to accommodate both tasks. The system has been extensively tested on the physical robot, taking into account ten different target angles. The stability and reliability of each kick has been evaluated 30 times for each kick motion trajectory while performing demanding motions. Results show that our proposed walk-kick framework and its integration is reliable in terms of the kick directions and stability of the robot overall (<1% falling rate), and our experiments verify that the walk-kick trajectories were consistent with an average absolute bearing of <6° within any given direction.

Keywords: Dynamic kick · Dynamic walking · Humanoid robots

1   Background and Motivation

Generating dynamic kick motions on a robot while the robot is walking allows the robot to quickly kick the ball towards the goal. This is difficult because the robot can become unstable and might fall as a result. Kick engines such as [2,3,10,12,17,18] have been developed for the NAO robot and although they are dynamic, the kick engines need the robot to be in a stable position where momentum is minimal before they can begin generating kick motions. Although walk-kick controllers such as [19] that use an analytic Zero Moment Point (*ZMP*) have been developed, there are no walk-kick controllers that can generate kick motions in arbitrary directions while the robot is walking. The difficulty of the task lies in generating kick motions that allow the robot to walk while also being in a stable equilibrium.

Wenk et al. [17] developed a kick engine that generates online kick motions using trajectories generated by Bézier curves, but in order to create such motions, the humanoid robot has to dynamically balance on one foot so it can handle any force generated by the kick. In order to find these forces, Wenk et al. use

© Springer Nature Switzerland AG 2019
S. Chalup et al. (Eds.): RoboCup 2019, LNAI 11531, pp. 213–226, 2019.
https://doi.org/10.1007/978-3-030-35699-6_17

inverse dynamics to calculate the ZMP. Böckmann et al. [3] provided a mass spring damper model to model motor behavior, and modified the ZMP equation to account for this behavior to get the actual motor position rather than a believed state. The authors also adapted Dynamic Motion Primitives (*DMP*) to generate kick trajectories, and used a PD controller with a forcing term in the transformation system to control the shape of the trajectory.

Sung et al. [15] use full body motion planning and via-point representation to generate joint angle trajectories. In order to create efficient full body motion trajectories, the authors use optimization techniques such as Semi-Infinite Programming (*SIP*) to specify constraints such as minimal energy and torque, and also deal with joint redundancy. Yi et al. [20] use THOR-OP (*Tactical Hazardous Operations Robot - Open Platform*), a full sized humanoid robot to generate kick and walk motions for the AdultSize League in RoboCup. The robot has a hybrid walking system that uses two types of controllers: a ZMP preview controller and a ZMP based reactive controller. The kick motions generated are handled by the hybrid walking controller to create smooth transitions between the dynamic walk and strong kick.

The kick engine of Xu et al. [18] is separated into four phases: preparation, retraction, execution, and wrap-up phase. The authors use a grid space to find the kick that maximizes the distance in the retraction point and minimizes the angle between the direction of the foot and the direction of the ball. The stabilization of the robot is done with a Body Inclination Control that controls the torso angle to maintain the center of mass (*CoM*) in the support polygon. Becht et al. [2] use a proportional controller to minimize the distance of the CoM with regards to the support polygon of the supporting foot, and the kick trajectory is determined by the retraction point and the contact point. Kim et al. [7] use Whole-Body Operational Space Control to generate stable dynamic motions and use a virtual model as an interface for a real robot using an extended Kalman-filter; the controller was tested on a NAO robot generating dynamic kick motions. Lengagneua, Fraisse, and Ramdani [8] use Interval Analysis to find viable motion parameter sets that allow the robot to replan motions based on an offline optimization. A motion optimization for a 30° of freedom humanoid robot, HRP-2, was also done for kick motions where the minimization of energy and joint friction is considered in [9]. Choi et al. [4] developed an impact-based trajectory planner for a kicking robot where the initial velocity and launch angle of the ball are determined by modeling external and aerodynamic forces. Learning kick motions for the NAO robot in simulation has also been investigated [1, 5, 16].

All of these controllers except the controller from Yi et al. [19] assumes that the robot has no momentum before the kick motion is executed, and there are none that consider dynamic kick motions in any direction while walking. Therefore, we propose a walk-kick controller which integrates a kick controller that generates kick trajectories derived from Peña et al. [12,13] and the walking engine from Seekircher and Visser [14] which makes no assumption of the walk model and allows the robot to use the model as a black box to plan steps while also utilizing a torso angle controller to keep the robot from falling.

In Sect. 2, we will discuss the framework for the walk-kick controller. In Sect. 3, we will describe the experiment design for the walk-kick controller, and the results of the walk-kick trajectories and stabilization will be discussed in Sects. 3.1 and 3.2, respectively. Future directions based on the results of the experiments will be discussed in Sect. 4 and conclusion of the paper will be stated in Sect. 5.

2   Approach

Seekircher and Visser [14] developed a dynamic walking engine that uses a 3D linear inverted pendulum model (*LIPM*) to generate a gait. Since there is an analytical solution for the LIPM, it is used to compute the change of the CoM trajectory with respect to the state of the robot which in this case is the foot positions of the robot.

The authors optimize the parameters of the step value that satisfies the stable CoM trajectory on the given surface. This relieves the engineer from having to calibrate the robot on different surfaces. The reason for this manual calibration is due to the simplicity of LIPM which does not capture the complete dynamics of the robot such as Coriolis effects from the ground friction forces and nonlinear

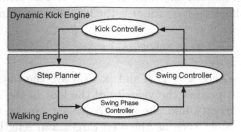

Fig. 1. Walk-kick framework

forces applied to the robot. There are other techniques to find stable motions such as linear and angular momentum control [6] but requires more computation. To generate a kick motion, the robot is required to execute a stable stop motion where the robot has to decrease linear momentum and both foot positions need to be in an initial configuration. Henceforth, it is inefficient and expensive to generate a kick motion unless a kick can be executed while the robot is walking because it will allow the robot to use its linear momentum and generate a kick motion without disrupting the original reference trajectory.

2.1   Integration of Walking and Kick Engine

The kick controller resides in the dynamic kick engine [11,12] developed by Peña et al. When the agent sends a request for a walk-kick, the motion request, e.g., kick direction and kicking foot, is received by the step planner. The step planner chooses the next steps of the gait cycle that minimizes the amount of time it takes to reach the reference trajectory dictated by the model which in this case is LIPM. Therefore if the agent requests a kick while the robot is walking, the step planner has to plan for the kick motion while guaranteeing a stable walk. In order to do this, the step planner waits until the current foot for the kick motion is in the swinging phase. When this is the case, the step planner sends a kick direction request to the swing control for a kick motion trajectory. The step planner sends this information to the swing phase controller which keeps track of the current swing foot, and when the swing foot phase of the kick starts, the walking engine communicates with the omnidirectional kick controller from Peña et al. [11,12] to generate a kick trajectory. The walk-kick framework is shown in Fig. 1.

2.2   Walk Trajectory

LIPM is derived from the approximation of a floating-base robot where the robot is approximated by a centroid, i.e., the CoM. The movement of the CoM causes the CoM to tip over because the rest of the body of the robot is approximated by a spoke that is in contact with the ground. Therefore the objective of the floating-base robot is to move its feet such that the inverted pendulum is always balanced and does not tip over. The other assumption made for the LIPM of a floating-base robot is the height is constant. The equation of LIPM is defined as:

$$\mathbf{x}_t = \mathbf{x}_0 cosh(kt) + \dot{\mathbf{x}}_0 \frac{1}{k} sinh(kt) \qquad \dot{\mathbf{x}}_t = k\mathbf{x}_0 sinh(kt) + \dot{\mathbf{x}}_0 cosh(kt)$$

Where $k = \sqrt{\frac{g}{h}}$ and $[\mathbf{x}_0, \dot{\mathbf{x}}_0]$ are the initial conditions of the system. In order to predict the velocity of the foot in the support exchange, the requested walk velocity and the step frequency can be used to derive the initial seed of the model such as the step target and length. After, Newton's method is used to find a velocity in the first support exchange such that it equals the velocity of the third exchange so the base can walk with constant velocity. In order to maintain the robot balanced, a torso angle controller is used to maintain the robot upright. When the step planner finds a viable foot placement, the walking engine interpolates the feet position to this position.

2.3   Walk-Kick Trajectory

The foot positions provided by the step planner are used to generate motions that allow the robot to hit a ball while still following the reference trajectory. In pursuance of a kick motion, the kick controller has to have a notion of the step planning of the robot. The kick motion trajectory is then generated using a trajectory generated from one of the interpolators [13]: sextic, cubic, or Hermite cubic splines. Hence the walk-kick trajectory controller is as follows:

$$\mathbf{x}_{t+1} = \psi(\mathbf{x}_s, \mathbf{x}_f, \mathbf{x}_{via}, t_f, t_{curr}), \qquad \dot{\mathbf{x}}_{t+1} = \dot{\psi}(\mathbf{x}_s, \mathbf{x}_f, \mathbf{x}_{via}, t_f, t_{curr})$$

where $\mathbf{x}_t = [x_t, y_t, z_t]$ and $\dot{\mathbf{x}}_t = [\dot{x}_t \dot{y}_t, \dot{z}_t]$. ψ is one of the interpolators from [13], and in every time step the swing controller uses ψ and $\dot{\psi}$ to calculate the position and velocity of the swinging foot. For the kick motion, two cubic polynomials are generated when the cubic spline interpolator is used. The point where the two polynomials meet is called the via-point. The cubic polynomial is as follows,

$$\alpha_1(t) = a_{13}t^3 + a_{12}t^2 + a_{11}t + a_{10}, \quad \alpha_2(t) = a_{23}t^3 + a_{22}t^2 + a_{21}t + a_{20}.$$

In order to generate an arbitrary motion, specific constraints need to be put upon the polynomials. Since there are two cubic polynomials (i.e., eight coefficients/DOF), there are eight constraints. Every piece of the cubic Hermite spline is a polynomial of three degrees. The cubic Hermite spline is specified by it's end points and the tangents of those points (i.e., derivatives at the end points). The cubic Hermite spline is a smooth continuous function and to interpolate the Hermite polynomial, the following definition is used:

$$\boldsymbol{p}(t) = (2t^3 - 3t^2 + 1)\boldsymbol{p}_0 + (t^3 - 2t^2 + t)\boldsymbol{m}_0 + (-2t^3 + 3t^2)\boldsymbol{p}_1 + (t^3 - t^2)\boldsymbol{m}_1.$$

This equation can be used to interpolate the foot of the robot through the kick trajectory. The above interpolator is for unit intervals. Therefore, $0 \leq t \leq 1$ and $\boldsymbol{p}(t)$ is the position of the foot at time t. $\boldsymbol{p}_0$ and $\boldsymbol{p}_1$ are the end points of the kick trajectory, and $\boldsymbol{m}_0$ and $\boldsymbol{m}_1$ are the derivatives of the end points. The velocity of the foot at time t can be defined as the derivative of $\boldsymbol{p}(t)$:

$$\dot{\boldsymbol{p}}(t) = (6t^2 - 6t)\boldsymbol{p}_0 + (3t^2 - 4t + 1)\boldsymbol{m}_0 + (-6t^2 + 6t)\boldsymbol{p}_1 + (3t^2 - 2t)\boldsymbol{m}_1.$$

Using sextic polynomials as a kick interpolator lets us define seven constraints due to the seven coefficients in the polynomial. The sextic polynomial is defined as:

$$\alpha(t) = a_6 t^6 + a_5 t^5 + a_4 t^4 + a_3 t^3 + a_2 t^2 + a_1 t + a_0.$$

The seven constraints of the kick trajectory are used to control the position, velocity, and acceleration of the kick. It is also used to control the height of the foot from the ground at the via point. There is still a notion of the via point in the sextic polynomial but a knot where two polynomials meet does not exist. The via point is only used to control the swing shape of the kick trajectory. With these seven constraints, the linear system can now be solved to obtain a polynomial that is able to generate the kick trajectory desired.

The starting position (retraction point), $\mathbf{x}_s$, of the kick trajectory is the same starting position of the step planner. In fact, the only difference between a regular walk trajectory and a walk-kick trajectory will be the via point, $\mathbf{x}_{via}$, in which the via point is the actual contact point of the foot and the ball, and it is what makes the trajectory a kick motion.

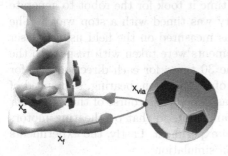

Fig. 2. Walk-kick motion where the via point is the point of contact with the ball.

Lastly, the final position of the swinging leg, $\mathbf{x}_f$, is the same as the step planner, and when the swing phase ends, the swing control sends a finish signal to the kick controller. The time constraint, t_f, for the trajectory is decided by the step planner, and it is not altered so that the step trajectory of the gait cycle is not tampered with allowing the walking engine to seamlessly reach its reference trajectory while also executing kick trajectories to move the ball at further distances.

In order to interpolate the kick trajectory during the swinging phase, the swing controller sends the kick controller, shown in Fig. 1, the current time, t_{curr}, to interpolate the spline. While the walk-kick trajectory is executed in the swing phase, the swing controller is communicating with the kick controller for the position $\mathbf{x}_t$ and velocity $\dot{\mathbf{x}}_t$ of the foot in the next state. When the swinging foot reaches $\mathbf{x}_f$ at time t_f, the kick controller ends. The kick controller now waits for another request and the cycle starts again. An example of how the walk-kick trajectory is generated is shown in Fig. 2. The start position, $\mathbf{x}_s$, is the first point in the curve from the left. The second point is the via point, $\mathbf{x}_{via}$, i.e., the contact point to the ball, and the end position, $\mathbf{x}_f$, is the next step position for the support phase. Note that the first and second position are the same positions from the step planner.

3   Experimental Design and Results

To test the validity of the integration of both the kick and walk controllers, we designed two experiments that tested the reliability of the kick trajectories and the ball trajectory while also testing the stability of the system while it generates these motions in the course of walking. The first experiment conducted was to test the performance of the kick controller while the robot walks as explained in Sect. 3.1, and in the second experiment, the stability of the robot was tested by observing the CoM trajectory which will be discussed in Sect. 3.2. The experiments were done on a soccer SPL field for ten kick directions: front, back, front-diagonal (45°), back-diagonal (45°), and side for the right and left foot. The experiments were done with Softbank's NAOv4 robot. The robot was placed on the field such that the kick direction of the robot was perpendicular to the goal line. For example, for the front kick, the robot was placed facing the goal, while for the side kick, the robot was placed parallel to the goal line. For all kicks, the robot was placed by the half line. On the other hand, the ball was placed near the kicking foot of the robot and the robot walked roughly in place for several steps and kicked. The reason for this was to mitigate the variability of the kick direction as the robot walked up to the ball. When the robot walk-kicks, the controller timed the amount of time it took for the robot to generate the kick trajectory, and the ball trajectory was timed with a stop watch. The x and y distance of the ball trajectory was measured on the field using a laser instrument, Bosch GLM50c. The measurements were taken with respect to the kick direction of the robot. This was done 30 times for each direction and for each foot for a total for 300 kicks; results of the position, bearing, and speed of these kicks are visualized in Fig. 3. This was done in the course of three days for about $\sim$40 − $\sim$75 min for each direction and foot, so that overheating motors do not become an influencing factor in the experiment. Lastly, the experiments were done on the physical robot and not in simulation.

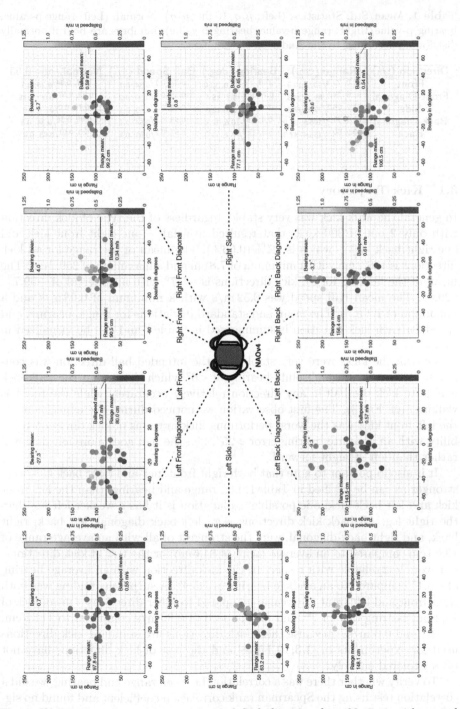

Fig. 3. Walk-kick range and bearing for each kick direction done 30 times with a total of 300 kicks

220   P. Peña and U. Visser

Table 1. Mean/Std. Statistics: (Left: μ, σ/Right: μ, σ). Normal: (Left: range p-value, bearing p-value/Right: range p-value, bearing p-value), numbers are bold if normally distributed according to the Anderson-Darling test.

Direction (L/R)	Range (cm.)	Bearing (deg.)	Ball Speed (m/s)	Normal, $\alpha = 0.05$
Front	80.0, 22.3/90.5, 19.3	-27.3, 19.1/4.0, 12.0	0.37, 0.1/0.34, 0.1	**0.47, 0.04**/0.35, 0.1
Front-Diagonal	97.8, 24.8/99.2, 24.3	0.7, 19.5/-5.7, 15.4	0.55, 0.1/0.59, 0.2	**0.32, 0.67**/0.02, **0.15**
Side	63.2, 25.1/77.1, 17.6	-5.0, 17.9/0.8, 12.6	0.48, 0.2/0.45, 0.1	**0.79, 0.0**/0.73, 0.0
Back-Diagonal	148.1, 21.5/106.5, 22.9	-0.9, 8.8/-10.6, 17.8	0.65, 0.1/0.54, 0.1	**0.48, 0.36**/0.34, **0.5**
Back	143.5, 50.0/156.4, 47.3	-9.3, 15.0/-3.7, 11.7	0.57, 0.2/0.61, 0.1	0.0, 0.01/0.05, 0.0

3.1 Kick Trajectory

In general the walk-kick was very stable, regardless of the type of kick direction with only 2 out of 300 kicks that resulted in a fall – one right front kick and one right back kick – which is <1% (0.66%). The mean of the range for all kick directions is 106.2 cm with a minimum of 7.8 cm and a maximum of 259.2 cm. The mean of the bearing for all kick directions is −5.7° with an interval of −59.7°– 129.8°. The mean ball speed was 0.52 m/s with a minimum of 0.08 m/s and a maximum of 1.1 m/s. The mean and standard deviations for range, bearing, and speed for each kick direction is summarized in Table 1 and can be visualized in Fig. 3.

Overall the kicks were very stable and the intended ball direction was consistent with an average absolute bearing of <6° which shows that the walk-kick is able to kick the ball in any direction relatively accurately while the robot is walking. (cf. Fig. 3). The first observation we noticed during the experiments is the left front kick was the worst performing kick in terms of kick direction reliability with an absolute bearing error >25°, i.e., the ball goes more left diagonal rather than left straight forward.

It is also important to note that both right front kick and right back kick were stronger as can be verified in Table 1, i.e., range and bearing, than the left front kick and left back kick; one possible explanation is it has a weaker left leg than the right leg. All back kick directions, e.g., left back diagonal, left back, right back, and right back-diagonal, were the strongest of all with an average range of 138.6 cm compared to an average mean of 84.6 cm for the rest of kick directions, but were less reliable with respect to the kick direction with an average bearing of −6.1° compared to an average bearing of −5.4°. A surprising finding was both right front and left front are weaker compared to other directions – mean kick of 85.3 cm, bearing of −11.7°, and mean speed of 0.36 m/s compared to 111.5 cm, −4.2°, and 0.6 m/s – because these kick directions are standard kick directions used for experiments in [2,3,10,17,18] and the rest of kick directions have not been explored entirely.

To verify whether there was a correlation between range and bearing, we did a correlation test using the Spearman rank correlation coefficient and found no significant result for range and bearing but found a significant correlation between range and speed with a p-value of 0.0 (the result can be seen in Fig. 4(a); the

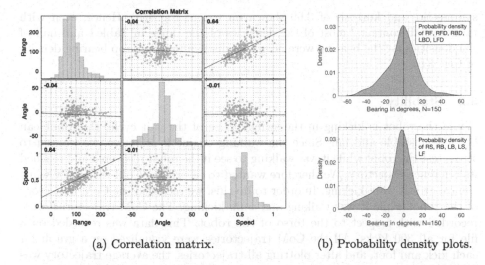

(a) Correlation matrix.   (b) Probability density plots.

Fig. 4. (a) Correlation matrix between range, bearing and ball speed using the Spearman rank correlation coefficient. Only the correlation between range and speed is significant (r = 0.64; p = 0.0). (b) Probability density plots for various kicks Top: Right front (RF), Right Front Diagonal (RDF), Right Back Diagonal (RBD), Left Back Diagonal (LBD), Left Front Diagonal (LFD). Bottom: Right Side (RS), Right Back (RB), Left Side (LS), Left Back (LB).

histograms of the correlation matrix in Fig. 4(a) are also approximately normal. Because of the walk-kick variability when the robot walked up to the ball and kicked, it was possible for the ball to take curved trajectories. Although this might have been possible, all measurements were taken as if the ball traveled in a straight trajectory. For this reason, there was variability in the relation between ball speed and range for all kicks, but overall, the statistics in Fig. 4(a) show that range and speed were correlated. The normality of the densities were tested with the Anderson-Darling test with an α of 0.05. Table 1 shows the results of each kick direction density for range and bearing. As can be observed, most of the densities for range with the exception of left back and right front-diagonal are normally distributed. Because the experiment was done from a position where the robot had to walk up to the ball and walk-kick, contact with the ball was inconsistent and most of the kick direction densities for bearing were approximately negatively skewed as can be verified in Table 1. The bottom density of Fig. 4(b) shows the density of the bearing for all kick directions that were below the α value in the Anderson-Darling test, e.g., right side, right back, left back, left side, and left front, where the density is approximately normal with a skewness value of −0.62 which means it is moderately negatively skewed and it is leptokurtic, with a kurtosis of 3.7, compared to the density of the bearing for all the kick directions that were above the α value in the Anderson-Darling test, e.g., right front, right front-diagonal, right back-diagonal, left back-diagonal, and left front-diagonal, with a skewness value of −0.28, i.e., approximately symmetric, and kurtosis of 3.69 shown on top of Fig. 4(b). Hence, even with random ball contacts, most of the densities of the range in Table 1 and half of the densities for the bearing were normally distributed, e.g., top bearing density of Fig. 4(b).

3.2   Stability

While the robot is kicking in the swing phase of the gait cycle, the robot can become unstable and fall. Since the walking engine is adaptive, we wanted to stress test the robot while it was walking to see if the robot recovered and reached its reference trajectory. We therefore wanted to record the CoM trajectory while the robot was walk-kicking. In order to do this, we recorded the CoM trajectory of the robot while it was walking and walk-kicking. The CoM trajectories were recorded with respect to the torso of the robot. This data was recorded on a file for all 300 kicks. All the CoM trajectories were visualized on a graph for each kick and foot, and after plotting all trajectories, the average trajectory was plotted.

As shown in Fig. 5a–f, the CoM trajectories follow a similar pattern, and as expected they follow a trajectory that is predictable and expected when the stability of the system is guaranteed. Figure 5a–f show all the CoM trajectories exhibited by all 300 kicks and show very interesting results. The first observation is that each graph shows the CoM behaving uniquely where the walk-kick region, which is shaded in Fig. 5a–f, shows three different behaviors: positive slope, negative slope, and constant.

Each of these behaviors explains a different phenomenon and every combination of the x-axis and y-axis describes a unique kick direction where even the kicking foot can be derived. Figure 5a is the CoM trajectories for all kick trajectories that moved on the positive y-axis, positive slope, of the robot, e.g., left front-diagonal, left side, and left back-diagonal. As can be seen in the graph, all the y-axis kick trajectories moved as expected: as the robot kicks the CoM shifts on the positive y-axis because of the swinging foot leaves the center of the robot while also showing that CoM stays in the center of the support polygon shown in Fig. 6a. When the robot kicks in the negative y-axis, negative slope, such as the right side, right front-diagonal, and right back-diagonal, the CoM shifts toward the negative y-axis. When the robot kicks on the x-axis and has a constant y-value, e.g., right and left front kicks and right and left back kicks, the CoM stays relatively close to zero on the y-axis such as can be seen in Fig. 5e.

The same effects can be seen for kicks that move in the positive x-axis, Fig. 5b, the negative x-axis, Fig. 5f, or relatively close to zero such as in the case when the robot does a side kick with either foot as shown in Fig. 5d. Since all these kick trajectories can be classified with these CoM trajectories, the combination of two CoM trajectories can explain a unique kick direction. For instance, if the robot will execute a left front-diagonal kick, we expect the CoM to shift towards the positive x-axis, positive slope, and y-axis in which Fig. 5a and b explain this phenomenon. The same can be said for any kick direction – e.g., Fig. 5a and f for right back-diagonal kick and Fig. 5a and f for left back-diagonal kick – and this concept was supported in the experiments conducted.

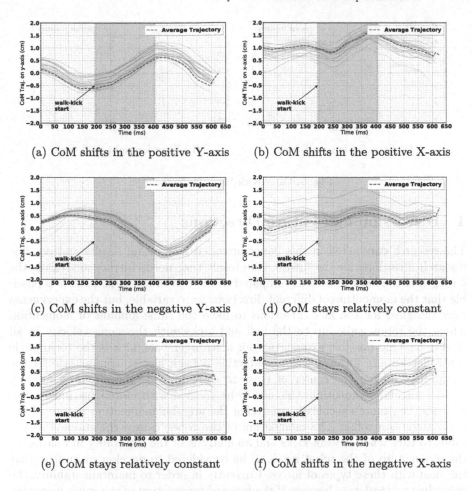

(a) CoM shifts in the positive Y-axis   (b) CoM shifts in the positive X-axis

(c) CoM shifts in the negative Y-axis   (d) CoM stays relatively constant

(e) CoM stays relatively constant   (f) CoM shifts in the negative X-axis

Fig. 5. Walk-kick CoM trajectories

An important question that is raised is whether the robot becomes unstable when all these shifts of CoM occur. As can be verified in these graphs, the CoM for the 300 kicks were bounded between -2.0–2.0 cm, Fig. 5a–f, in which the supporting foot trajectories were bounded by -6.0–6.0 cm, Fig. 6a and b, which shows that the CoM was always in the support polygon of the robot; this verifies why the likelihood of the robot falling when walk-kicking is $<1\%$. Figure 6a and b also shows that while the walk-kick is executed, the robot still follows the support foot trajectory planned by the step planner, which in consequence, the walk trajectories are neither disrupted when the robot is walk-kicking nor does it become unstable. The area that is shaded in Fig. 6a and b is when the robot is walk-kicking. Figure 6a shows when the robot is doing a left kick and Fig. 6b is the step trajectory when the robot is doing a right kick.

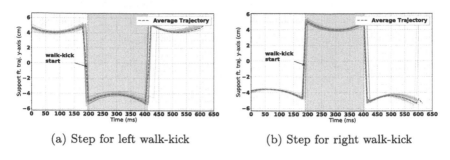

(a) Step for left walk-kick   (b) Step for right walk-kick

Fig. 6. Walk-Kick Step Trajectories

4 Discussion and Future Directions

The research conducted in this paper provided interesting results and possible research directions for the future. One result that needs further analysis is the strength of the back directions compared to the rest of the directions. It is possible that the momentum of different directions were variable, but the experiments were designed for the kick directions to have the same amount of momentum where the robot walks up to the ball and kicks with the same velocity in all directions. One possible explanation for a stronger back kick is the torso angle controller leaning forward when conducting a back kick to compensate for the instability causing the center of mass to shift towards the center generating greater angular momentum; this has to be verified with more experiments and analysis, i.e., more specifically analyzing the angular momentum output of the torso angle controller. The momentum of the robot causes the stability of the robot to vary when it walk-kicks and an analysis of the instability in relation to the momentum of the robot needs to be considered to develop controllers that can deal with these types of forces. Currently in order to maintain stability, the robot has to decelerate because if the forward momentum of the robot increases, the robot may fall. Therefore, making the step position a parameter of the walk-kick controller while the robot kicks will definitely help with the stability. This entails optimizing the step planner to minimize instability while maintaining the reference trajectory. The current controller for the walk-kick is open loop allowing the robot to passively use its momentum to generate kicks while walking, but the momentum of the robot and the kick trajectory acceleration can be actively controlled to generate a desired momentum allowing a closed-feedback loop system, i.e., this controller will also enable passing capabilities by controlling the force of the foot when it is in contact with the ball. Lastly, testing the dynamics of the walk-kick on different platforms will be important to determine the causes found in this paper and verify the system.

5 Conclusion

Although a variety of kick engines have been implemented over the years, there are none that demonstrate an omni-directional kick motion while walking. We therefore propose a walk-kick controller that enables a robot to kick in any direction while walking. The kick trajectories are generated by kick interpolators: cubic polynomials, sextic polynomials, and cubic Hermite splines. The kick trajectories are generated when the swinging foot is the kicking foot requested. The step planner handles the synchronization of both kick and step planners, while the swing controller communicates with the kick controller for the interpolation of the swinging foot. The balance controller used for the walking engine uses the walking model as a black box, essentially enabling modularity in the controller to add features such as the kick controller, which grants the kicking trajectories to integrate with the walking engine without causing the robot to destabilize. The walk-kick controller was tested on a NAOv4 robot by kicking in ten directions (front, front-diagonal, side, back-diagonal, and back) for each foot. Our experiments verified that the walk-kick trajectories were consistent with an average absolute bearing of $<6°$ which shows that the walk-kick is able to kick the ball in any direction while the robot is walking, and the CoM trajectories were also very stable within the bounds of the step trajectories. The step trajectories also followed the reference trajectories while executing the kick motions with a consistent average trajectory.

References

1. Abdolmaleki, A., Simões, D., Lau, N., Reis, L.P., Neumann, G.: Learning a Humanoid kick with controlled distance. In: Behnke, S., Sheh, R., Sarıel, S., Lee, D.D. (eds.) RoboCup 2016. LNCS (LNAI), vol. 9776, pp. 45–57. Springer, Cham (2017). https://doi.org/10.1007/978-3-319-68792-6_4
2. Becht, I., de Jonge, M., Pronk, R.: A dynamic kick for the NAO robot. University of Amsterdam, Intelligent Robotics Lab, Tech. rep. (2013)
3. Böckmann, A., Laue, T.: Kick motions for the NAO robot using dynamic movement primitives. arXiv preprint. arXiv:1606.00600 (2016)
4. Choi, J.Y., So, B.R., Yi, B.J., Kim, W., Suh, I.H.: Impact based trajectory planning of a soccer ball in a kicking robot. In: Proceedings of the 2005 IEEE International Conference on Robotics and Automation, pp. 2834–2840 (April 2005). https://doi.org/10.1109/ROBOT.2005.1570543
5. Ferreira, R., Reis, L.P., Moreira, A.P., Lau, N.: Development of an omnidirectional kick for a NAO humanoid robot. In: Pavón, J., Duque-Méndez, N.D., Fuentes-Fernández, R. (eds.) IBERAMIA 2012. LNCS (LNAI), vol. 7637, pp. 571–580. Springer, Heidelberg (2012). https://doi.org/10.1007/978-3-642-34654-5_58
6. Kajita, S., et al.: Resolved momentum control: humanoid motion planning based on the linear and angular momentum. In: Proceedings 2003 IEEE/RSJ International Conference on Intelligent Robots and Systems (IROS 2003) (Cat. No. 03CH37453), vol. 2, pp. 1644–1650 (October 2003). https://doi.org/10.1109/IROS.2003.1248880
7. Kim, D., Jorgensen, S.J., Stone, P., Sentis, L.: Dynamic behaviors on the NAO robot with closed-loop whole body operational space control. In: 2016 IEEE-RAS 16th International Conference on Humanoid Robots (Humanoids), pp. 1121–1128 (November 2016). https://doi.org/10.1109/HUMANOIDS.2016.7803411

8. Lengagneua, S., Fraisse, P., Ramdani, N.: Planning and fast re-planning of safe motions for humanoid robots: application to a kicking motion. In: 2009 IEEE/RSJ International Conference on Intelligent Robots and Systems, pp. 441–446 (October 2009). https://doi.org/10.1109/IROS.2009.5354002

9. Miossec, S., Yokoi, K., Kheddar, A.: Development of a software for motion optimization of robots - Application to the kick motion of the HRP-2 robot. In: 2006 IEEE International Conference on Robotics and Biomimetics, pp. 299–304 (December 2006). https://doi.org/10.1109/ROBIO.2006.340170

10. Müller, J., Laue, T., Röfer, T.: Kicking a ball – modeling complex dynamic motions for humanoid robots. In: Ruiz-del-Solar, J., Chown, E., Plöger, P.G. (eds.) RoboCup 2010. LNCS (LNAI), vol. 6556, pp. 109–120. Springer, Heidelberg (2011). https://doi.org/10.1007/978-3-642-20217-9_10

11. Peña, P.: An omni-directional kick engine for NAO humanoid robots. Master's thesis, University of Miami, 1365 Memorial Drive Coral Gables, FL. 33146 (January 2019)

12. Pena, P., Masterjohn, J., Visser, U.: An omni-directional kick engine for humanoid robots with parameter optimization. In: Akiyama, H., Obst, O., Sammut, C., Tonidandel, F. (eds.) RoboCup 2017. LNCS (LNAI), vol. 11175, pp. 385–397. Springer, Cham (2018). https://doi.org/10.1007/978-3-030-00308-1_32

13. Peña, P., Masterjohn, J., Visser, U.: optimizing kick trajectory: a comparative study. In: Müller, C., Lisetti, C., Theobald, M. (eds.) 3rd Global Conference on Artificial Intelligence, GCAI 2017. EPiC Series in Computing, vol. 50, pp. 239–245. EasyChair (2017). https://doi.org/10.29007/3f7v, https://easychair.org/publications/paper/Xw6m

14. Seekircher, A., Visser, U.: An adaptive LIPM-based dynamic walk using model parameter optimization on humanoid robots. KI **30**(3), 233–244 (2016)

15. Sung, C.H., Kagawa, T., Uno, Y.: Planning of kicking motion with via-point representation for humanoid robots. In: 2011 8th International Conference on Ubiquitous Robots and Ambient Intelligence (URAI), pp. 337–342 (November 2011). https://doi.org/10.1109/URAI.2011.6145987

16. Wang, J., Liang, Z., Zhou, Z., Zhang, Y.: Kicking motion design of humanoid robots using gradual accumulation learning method based on Q-learning. In: 2016 Chinese Control and Decision Conference (CCDC), pp. 5274–5279 (May 2016). https://doi.org/10.1109/CCDC.2016.7531941

17. Wenk, F., Röfer, T.: Online generated kick motions for the NAO balanced using inverse dynamics. In: Behnke, S., Veloso, M., Visser, A., Xiong, R. (eds.) RoboCup 2013. LNCS (LNAI), vol. 8371, pp. 25–36. Springer, Heidelberg (2014). https://doi.org/10.1007/978-3-662-44468-9_3

18. Xu, Y., Mellmann, H.: Adaptive motion control: dynamic kick for a humanoid robot. In: Dillmann, R., Beyerer, J., Hanebeck, U.D., Schultz, T. (eds.) KI 2010. LNCS (LNAI), vol. 6359, pp. 392–399. Springer, Heidelberg (2010). https://doi.org/10.1007/978-3-642-16111-7_45

19. Yi, S.J., McGill, S., Lee, D.D.: Online kick generation method for humanoid soccer robots. In: The 8th Workshop on Humanoid Soccer Robots (2013). http://www.ais.uni-bonn.de/humanoidsoccer/ws13/papers/HSR13_Yi.pdf

20. Yi, S.J., McGill, S., He, Q., Hong, D., Lee, D.: Walk and kick motion generation for a general purpose full sized humanoid robot. In: Workshop on Humanoid Soccer Robots, IEEE-RAS International Conference on Humanoid Robots (Humanoids). IEEE (2014)

JET-Net: Real-Time Object Detection for Mobile Robots

Bernd Poppinga[1,2] and Tim Laue[1(✉)]

[1] Universität Bremen, Bremen, Germany
{poppinga,tlaue}@uni-bremen.de
[2] JUST ADD AI GmbH, Bremen, Germany

Abstract. In most applications for autonomous robots, the detection of objects in their environment is of significant importance. As many robots are equipped with cameras, this task is often solved by image processing techniques. However, due to limited computational resources on mobile systems, it is common to use specialized algorithms that are highly adapted to the respective scenario. Sophisticated approaches such as Deep Neural Networks, which recently demonstrated a high performance in many object detection tasks, are often difficult to apply. In this paper, we present JET-Net (**J**ust **E**nough **T**ime), a model frame for efficient object detection based on Convolutional Neural Networks. JET-Net is able to perform real-time robot detection on a NAO V5 robot in a robot football environment. Experiments show that this system is able to reliably detect other robots in various situations. Moreover, we present a technique that reuses the learned features to obtain more information about the detected objects. Since the additional information can entirely be learned from simulation data, it is called *Simulation Transfer Learning*.

1 Introduction

Depending on the application domain, a mobile robot needs to detect different objects with a certain reliability and precision. In the RoboCup Standard Platform League, to which our work has been applied, two important categories of moving objects are the ball and the other robots. For the ball, multiple sophisticated detection techniques, mostly based on machine learning, already exist [15,19,25]. However, the reliable detection of other robots is a much more complex problem fur multiple reasons: a robot is not fully symmetric and thus looks different depending on the angle of view, it can have different postures (e.g. standing, lying, or getting up), and, especially when it is close, often only parts of a robot are in the current field of view. Futhermore, changing lighting conditions might make it difficult to use the robot's colored jersey as a reliable cue. Nevertheless, some highly spezialized robot detection approaches have already been implemented and are currently in use, as described in Sect. 2.2.

© Springer Nature Switzerland AG 2019
S. Chalup et al. (Eds.): RoboCup 2019, LNAI 11531, pp. 227–240, 2019.
https://doi.org/10.1007/978-3-030-35699-6_18

In recent years, detecting objects by using Deep Neural Networks has been very successful in many domains, some examples are given in Sect. 2.1. These approaches are able to robustly generalize over deviations in perspective, shape, and lighting conditions. However, to achieve a certain level of robustness and precision, many network layers are required, resulting in a high demand of computing power, which is not available on many mobile platforms such as the NAO V5, which was the target platform for our development and which also needs to carry out many other tasks that require computing time.

The main contribution of this paper is an adaptable network architecture that is able to perform object detection on computationally limited robot platforms. Although the architecture itself is kept general, its performance is demonstrated for the task of robot detection, which it is able to carry out with a precision and robustness that is suitable for robot football. In comparison to most related works, the network carries out the full detection process and does not only classify preselected candidate regions. An additional contribution is an extension to the main network that makes it possible to not only perform object detection but also to learn additional properties of the objects entirely from the simulation. This is demonstrated by learning the distances to detected robots.

The remainder of this paper is organized as follows: First, Sect. 2 discusses related approaches for object detection by Deep Neural Networks in general as well as for object detection in the RoboCup Standard Platform League domain in particular. Afterwards, a description of our approach is given in Sect. 3. An evaluation of the accuracy and the performance of our approach is presented in Sect. 4. Finally, the paper concludes in Sect. 5.

2   Related Work

2.1   Object Detection by Deep Neural Networks

There are many recently published works regarding object detection, most of them aim for two major objectives: a high mean average precision (MAP) and a low inference time. Published in 2015, Faster R-CNN [24] was the state of the art in terms of MAP for a long time. This is due to its two-staged architecture, which comes at the costs of increased runtime. Furthermore, Faster R-CNN has introduced anchor boxes, which are used until today. The Single Shot MultiBox Detector (SSD) [14] approach takes many aspects of Faster R-CNN and puts them into a one-staged detector by removing the preselection step. This means that the classifier has eventually to deal with many simple negatives that take away the focus form the hard examples. To compensate these disadvantages, the hard negative mining was presented, which allows the detector to concentrate on the difficult examples. In contrast to SSD, the YOLO approach [21,22] is optimized to reach extraordinary inference time. This approach has been iteratively improved so that the latest version YOLOv3 [23] offers a good trade-off between MAP and inference time. In 2017, the Retina Net [13] one-staged detector made it finally possible to outperform two-staged detectors by applying a technique called Focal Loss. Additionally, it uses a feature pyramid architecture which presents the current state of the art [12].

2.2 Object Detection in RoboCup Soccer

In recent years, Deep Learning has already been successfully used for the detection of the Standard Platform League's new ball [15,19,25]. A similar approach is also used by [1] for detecting robots. However, all these approaches have in common that they use neural networks for classifying previously computed candidate regions and thus depend on other software components. In the RoboCup Humanoid League, a full detection approach, which would not have real-time inference on a NAO robot, has been presented by [26].

In addition to these machine learning approaches, many other solutions exist that heavily rely on the particular design of the robot football environment and a robust color classification. By knowing that everything takes place on an even green floor, objects can be detected by just finding gaps in green [6,11]. In the SPL, the colors of the robots as well as their jersey colors are known, this makes a direct detection based on a previously conducted color classification possible, as described, for instance, by [16] and [3]. This approach is also applied in some other leagues, for instance in the Small-Size Robot League's SSL-Vision [28].

However, due to changes in the RoboCup rules that require more natural lighting conditions, these approaches become less maintainable und applicable by the time. One recently published approach by [10] therefore combines basic robot vision techniques on grayscale images with candidate classification through a Convolutional Neural Network to detect all objects on an SPL field. Furthermore, approaches that rely on a neural-network-based semantic segmentation also become applied, for instance by [2].

3   JET-Net: The Just Enough Time Approach

In this section, we explain JET-Net's model design, followed by the applied training. Then we show how we use JET-Net for robot detection in the SPL. In the end, we explain how to use *Simulation Transfer Learning* to predict more characteristics while only using data from simulation.

3.1   General Model Design

Even though we want to apply the object detection to the specific task of robot detection in the SPL, JET-Net provides a general framework that can be adapted to different tasks. Therefore, we do not use any special features of the NAO as in [18] and restrict ourself to the size and ratio of the object. However, within these restrictions, we want to make everything as task-specific as possible. That means that we adapt our resolution to the camera and computational power of the robotic system. Furthermore, we do not predict thousands of classes but one or two. Whenever there is a design question, we always take just enough to fulfill the task. This results in an efficient architecture that needs just enough time to do its task, without any significant overhead. Our model design frame is used to define a basic architecture, which is optimized afterwards.

Model Frame. For the model design, we define a frame that leads the design process. This frame consists of three units. We start by using alternating *Feature Modules* and *Scale Modules* to get features of different hierarchy levels. In the end, we add a layer for the bounding box prediction, which uses anchor boxes as introduced in [24].

- **Feature Module:** This module uses stacked 3×3 convolutions to extract the important features. The number of layers per module and the number of filters are hyperparameters. Each *Feature Module* starts with a Batch Normalization.
- **Scale Module:** This module follows directly after every *Feature Module*. It reduces the image size by a factor of two. We tried different approaches for the scaling. As we have a natural lack of parameters in small neural networks, we choose 3×3 convolutions with a stride of 2 over 2×2 convolutions and Max Pooling. However, the number of filters will remain a hyperparameter.
- **Box Prediction:** This very last network layer predicts the bounding boxes. Here, 1×1 convolutions are used to determine the five box parameters for every cell in the remaining image. The number of anchor boxes per cell is a hyperparameter here.

Speed Up. Even though one should choose a minimal input size and a lightweight model design to achieve a fast inference, we are not satisfied by the efficiency of normal convolutions. For this purpose, we chose the MobileNet [7] approach over other techniques such as SqueezeNet [8]. Admittedly, SqueezeNet reduces the number of parameters, but there is hardly a faster inference. Therefore, its usage would be rather counterproductive, as our small network has a natural lack of parameters. This is why we go with the MobileNet approach and replace some convolutions with *Separable Convolutions*.

For 3×3 convolutions, one can save for example 15.3% of the calculations when using 24 filters like we did for our robot detector. However, it is not always advisable to use Separable Convolution. When working with grayscale images, we only have one channel at the input layer and the use of Separable Convolution would lead to an increase in calculations. The same goes for the box prediction layer, where 1×1 convolutions are applied. Furthermore, since layers deeper in the network operate on smaller images, the acceleration has not such a big influence. Therefore, it is sometimes worth to choose normal convolution in those layers to get more parameters while retaining a good inference time.

3.2 Training

As usual for this kind of object detector, we used two different loss functions for training. Additionally, we present our augmentation steps and show, how we can achieve even more speed up the inference time by applying pruning.

Loss Functions. The task of finding bounding boxes for objects in the image consists of two subtasks: Determining if a certain area shows a wanted object and finding the exact box. For the corresponding training, we propose the following loss functions:

MACE Loss. Each anchor box needs to be classified whether it contains an object whose bounding box needs to be found or not. This is not a trivial task. As we have so many potential anchor boxes, many of them are quite easy to classify as negatives. This causes the problem that the optimization does not concentrate on the hard examples. But we actually care more about those that are hard to classify. This is also the big advantage of two-staged detectors, as they filter the easy examples in the first step, so that they only need to classify the hard examples in the second stage. Other one-staged detectors already tried to deal with this problem: SSD proposed hard negative mining, where only a fixed number of the hardest examples are used to calculate the loss. The *Focal Loss* approach introduces a weighting which weights bigger errors higher. For a vector of errors between label and prediction y_{err}, (Eq. 1) shows how the Focal Loss is calculated. We took that approach but replaced the negative logarithmic error by the mean squared error. This allows to sum up the equation into $i^{2+\gamma}$. Furthermore, we discovered that $\gamma = 1$ works quite well for our tasks. Therefore, we will refer to the used loss function (Eq. 2) as mean absolute cubed error (MACE).

$$\text{FocalLoss}(y_{err}) = \frac{1}{|y_{err}|} \cdot \sum_{i \in y_{err}} -log(1-i) \cdot i^\gamma \tag{1}$$

$$\text{MACE}(y_{err}) = \frac{1}{|y_{err}|} \cdot \sum_{i \in y_{err}} i^2 \cdot i^1 = \frac{1}{|y_{err}|} \cdot \sum_{i \in y_{err}} i^3 \tag{2}$$

IoU Loss. The loss, which rates the position and size of the bounding box, is responsible for the other four parameters of the bounding box: x-position, y-position, width, and height. Other approaches use a variant of the absolute distance between the wanted values and the predictions (Faster R-CNN) or the relative distance (SSD). We propose a more abstract measurement of the loss by using the mean IoU (Intersection over Union) value as the loss function. We argue that those four values do not contribute equally to a good matching bounding box. However, the IoU value does take all aspects into account and returns one value.

$$\text{IoU-Loss}(true, pred) = 1 - \text{MEAN}(\text{IoU}(true_{box}, pred_{box})) \tag{3}$$

Augmentation. To achieve a better generalization, we use data augmentation. While some publications propose an exhausting approach for augmentation, we concentrate on creating only images that could actually appear in reality. This ensures that we don't use capacities for images that will never appear. This leaves us with the following procedures:

- **Zoom:** For the zoom operation, the image size is increased by a factor between 1.0 and 1.5. Since the input size remains untouched, we can now pick a cutout from the zoomed image.
- **Flip:** Since the playing field and the robots are symmetrical, we can flip the image at the vertical axis. A flip at the horizontal axis is not performed, as it would produce impossible images.
- **Ground Truth Box Noise:** To apply more noise, the borders of the ground truth boxes are varied. This makes it way harder to memorize certain boxes. To vary the boxes, each border line is moved in a certain area ($\pm 5\%$).

Table 1. Final model design for robot detection on a NAO V5. The table shows our JET-Net instantiation for robot detection. Filter b.p. means before pruning and a.p. after pruning, respectively. The inference time has been measured on a NAO V5 robot.

Layertype	Filter b.p	Filter a.p	Filter Size	Strides	Padding	Output
BNorm	–	–	–	–	–	80×60
Conv	24	16	3×3	1	Same	80×60
SConv	24	24	3×3	2	Same	40×30
BNorm	–	–	–	–	–	40×30
SConv	24	16	3×3	1	Same	40×30
SConv	24	20	3×3	1	Same	40×30
SConv	24	20	3×3	2	Same	20×15
BNorm	–	–	–	–	–	20×15
SConv	24	20	3×3	1	Same	20×15
SConv	24	20	3×3	1	Same	20×15
SConv	24	24	3×3	1	Same	20×15
SConv	24	24	3×3	2	Same	10×8
BNorm	–	–	–	–	–	10×8
Conv	24	24	3×3	1	Same	10×8
Conv	24	24	3×3	1	Same	10×8
Conv	24	24	3×3	1	Same	10×8
Conv	24	24	3×3	1	Same	10×8
Conv	20	20	3×3	1	Same	10×8
Inference time	*12.0 ms*	*9.0 ms*				

Fig. 1. Sampling Levels. For the robot detection application, we tried different sampling levels from 640×480 (outer left) to 40×30 (outer right). Each images shows a quarter of the pixels used in the image before. We chose 80×60 (second from right) for input, as it is the lowest resolution that still shows every robot.

Pruning. Another way of speeding up calculations is to not execute them in the first way. For that reason, we use pruning to remove those filters that contribute the least. In [17], many pruning methods are compared. Although the normed activation was not the best pruning method, it was still a very good one and is comparatively easy to implement and calculate. A crucial part of the pruning is the fine tuning between the different pruning runs to compensate the damage. This leaves us with an iterative algorithm that looks for the filter with the least activation, removes it, and treats the dealt damage with fine tuning. This can be repeated until a certain size is reached or the loss drops under a certain threshold. As the number of filters in the box prediction unit is fixed, we excluded this from the pruning process. The resulting filter counts can be seen in Table 1. The pruning allowed us to reduce the inference time from 12.0 ms to 9.0 ms.

3.3 Application: Just Enough Robot Detection

For the scenario of the SPL, we created an instantiation of our model frame. As we use the current B-Human software stack [25], the inference on the robot is performed by B-Human's JIT compiler [27], which is able to process four convolutional filters at a time and which can process up to 24 filters fast. Our proposed network takes this into account. Furthermore, we take advantage of the fact that convolutions are cheaper on smaller images, as they don't need to be applied so often. The final model is described in Table 1. For the training, we used images from both sources, reality as well as simulation. As the B-Human framework provides images with a resolution of 640×480 pixels in YUV422 color space, some preprocessing is needed before we can pass the data to the network:

- **Color space conversion:** As multiple ball detectors for this domain have already shown, the use of only one channel, the Y channel, is enough to achieve good results and contributes to more robustness.
- **Normalization:** Because mobile robots might deal with changing and challenging lighting conditions, a 2% min-max normalization is applied.
- **Subsampling:** Object classifiers such as the ball detectors often classify 32×32 pixels or less. However, in this scenario, we deal with the whole image instead of small patches. Therefore, we scale the image to an input size of 80×60 pixels (see Fig. 1).

GAN-Training	Discriminator Accuracy	
	Both sources	Sim only
before	75,7%	58,4%
after	64,2%	58,2%

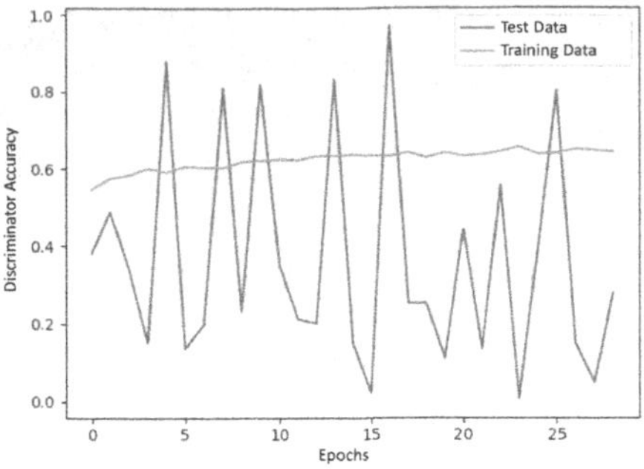

Fig. 2. GAN-Training. The table shows the training results before and after the GAN training. You can see that only the use of images from both sources provides us with us a high level of anonymization. While the discriminator is able to find some rule for the real images of the training data to tell them apart, it is more or less randomly guessing for the simulation data in the training data. And finally, the discriminator has no clue for the test data.

3.4 Simulation Transfer Learning

When we look from a more global point of view, a further possibility for optimization appears: Instead of just improving the inference time, we can reuse the features created for the detection task and use them to estimate further characteristics of the detected object, such as the distance. However, labeling those features is an annoying and exhausting task. Therefore, we want our network to use features for the robot detection that exist in the reality as well as in the simulation. To achieve this, we train our network not only with real images but also with images generated by a simulation. This forces the network to learn features for both sources. Those features could end up in two separated sets: one for real images and one for artificial images. However, as our network is so small, it already learns some features that appear in both sources. We finalize those features by applying a form of training that is similar to Generative Adversarial Network (GAN) training [5]. For this, we define the whole network, except for the box prediction layer, as the generator and create a discriminator which is almost as powerful as the box prediction layer (see Fig. 3). Afterwards, we alternatinatly train the discriminator and the box prediction layer with the generator. This results in a state, where the network cannot tell apart the simulated images and the real ones. When we reach this state, we can learn additional feature, like the distance, by using simulated images only. To do this, we freeze the generator and ignore the loss of the real images for the additional features, as we don't have valid labels for them. In this way, the real images are only used for the bounding boxes while we can obtain other characteristics from the simulation. In Fig. 2, you can see that even before the GAN training the learned features deliver almost no information from which we can derive the source. Only through overfitting on the training data, the discriminator is somehow able to label some of the images right. These are promising results, which imply that it could be possible to use these features to learn more characteristics only from simulation images as almost every information about the image source is vanished. We refer to this technique as *Simulation Transfer Learning*.

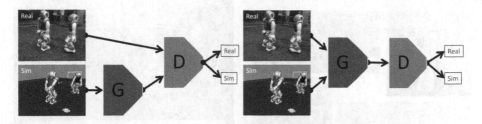

Fig. 3. GAN Architectures. The left image shows a typical GAN architecture. The image from the simulation is processed by the generator (G) to look like a real image. Afterwards, both images are passed to the discriminator (D) which tries to distinguish both real images and simulation images. On the right side, our adapted architecture is shown: We send images from both sources through the generator (G), as we just want them to look alike.

4   Evaluation

For the evaluation of our approach, we measure the performance of the robot detector. Therefore, we trained the proposed model (Table 1) with 27.000 publicly available images from ImageTagger [4] and 28.000 images generated in simulation by SimRobot [9][1]. Additionally, we used the simulated images to gather the distances of the robots, which were used for Simulation Transfer Learning. We do this by executing two experiments: a static setup and a dynamic one.

4.1   Different Distances and Poses

For evaluating the static setup, we placed one of our robots at the end of the field. Then we defined five distances (1.5 m, 3 m, 4.5 m, 6 m, 9 m) and three different angles for each distance (left, center, right). For each distance, we tested nine different poses, most of them used for the center position: robot stands frontal (1), robots stands sidewards (2), like 1 but at left position (3), like 1 but at right position (4), gorilla position (5), robot lies on the floor (6), like 1 but with ball in front of the robot (7), two robots standing behind each other (8), after goalkeeper jump (9). Some poses are shown in Fig. 4, Fig. 5 provides an overview of the setup. Furthermore, we evaluate pose 1 and 2 also for 0.3 m to evaluate close-ups. For each distance and pose, we checked, if the robot is detected as well as the error of the estimated distance. For more meaningful results, we compare our robot detector to the B-Human's current implementation [25].

---

[1] The generated images as well as a script for downloading the datasets that we used from ImageTagger are available online at https://sibylle.informatik.uni-bremen.de/public/JET-Net/.

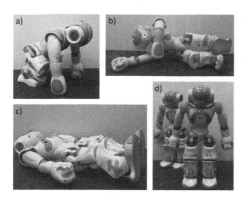

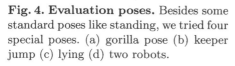

Fig. 4. Evaluation poses. Besides some standard poses like standing, we tried four special poses. (a) gorilla pose (b) keeper jump (c) lying (d) two robots.

Fig. 5. Overview of the evaluation setup. We placed the robot that has to be detected on one the positions marked by balls after the other. The robot in the red jersey has to detect it.

The results show that our proposed network detects the robot in every pose in the area until 4.5 m. Only the lying robot is problematic from 1.5 m on, which is probably because its representation in the box prediction layer is too small. Until the distance of 1.5 m it is also possible to tell the two robots from pose 8 apart. Starting from the distance of 6 m almost no robot is recognized. The B-Human detector in comparison is able to detect robots in a distances between 1.5 m and 3 m independently from the pose. However, lying robots are often detected as two robots. The B-Human detector calculates the distance to a robot by detecting a

Table 2. Results of the static evaluation. The column *Detected Robots* shows how many of the nine poses have been recognized. *Distance Mean* and *Standard Deviation* show the results of the distance prediction through all poses.

Distance	Detected Robots		Distance Mean		Distance Std Deviation	
	JET-Net	B-Human	JET-Net	B-Human	JET-Net	B-Human
0.3 m	**2/2**	0/2	–	–	–	–
1.5 m	**9/9**	8/9	**1.4 m**	1.2 m	0.2 m	**0.1 m**
3.0 m	8/9	8/9	**3.0 m**	2.7 m	0.5 m	0.5 m
4.5 m	**7/9**	1/9	**5.1 m**	3.7 m	0.6 m	0.6 m
6.0 m	**1/9**	0/9	–	–	–	–
9.0 m	0/9	0/9	–	–	–	–

Table 3. Results of the dynamic evaluation. Comparing JET-Net to B-Human. As B-Human does not provide probabilities, there is no MAP to be calculated.

Approach	Recall			Precision	IoU			MAP
	total	until 6 m	until 3 m	total	total	until 6 m	until 3 m	total
B-Human	0.204	0.285	0.583	**0.972**	0.657	0.657	0.662	–
JET-Net	**0.662**	**0.781**	**0.929**	0.856	**0.683**	**0.705**	**0.793**	0.591

robot's feet and then incorporating the knowledge about its camera's perspective. Within an area of 3 m the mean of the estimated distance over all poses of our approach is more accurate than the B-Human solution. Which has, on the other hand, a smaller variance. An overview of the results is given in Table 2.

4.2 Robot Detection During a Game

We also evaluated the performance for a test game of B-Human. During the game, we measured the precision, recall, IoU, and MAP for both approaches. As the B-Human approach does not rank the detections, there is no MAP value for this approach. While the precision of B-Human is still a bit better than our approach, we outperform the B-Human approach in every other category. Especially, we are able to achieve a much higher recall (see Table 3). The B-Human detector is tuned to strongly prefer precision over recall.

4.3 Performance

The software on the NAO robot alternatingly processes the image of the upper and the lower camera. As each camera runs at 30 fps, this results in an overall 60 fps. When processing the upper image, which we use in a higher resolution than the lower one, the B-Human detector only needs 0.5 ms per frame on average but relies on a previously executed color segmentation that takes more than 3 ms. While the main task of the upper camera is the raw robot detection, the lower camera is mainly used for calculating the robot distances. As shown before in Table 1, JET-Net takes 9.0 ms for the inference of one image on a NAO V5 robot. However, as our network is able to predict the distances only from one image, the lower camera is not needed anymore, which can be considered as a reduction of the average runtime to 4.5 ms. This makes it still possible to run each camera at 30 fps. Furthermore, recent measurements on a new NAO V6 robot revealed a runtime of only 2.5 ms.

5   Conclusion and Future Work

In this paper, we presented a framework for designing and training object detectors for mobile robots that are real-time capable, which is called JET-Net. By defining a coarse structure that only depends on few hyperparameters, we provide an easily adaptable network with advice for finding those few hyper-parameters. We used that framework for instantiating a robot detector for the RoboCup SPL that runs on a NAO V5 in real-time. Furthermore, in comparison to the current robot detector of B-Human, we are able to recognize three times more objects by only losing a few percents in precision. As our system delivers probabilities, this ratio can be shifted to the one or the other direction. When comparing the maximum distance to which a robot can be detected, we are able to detect robots for further 1.5 m compared to B-Human's approach.

Additionally, we presented Simulation Transfer Learning, a technique that makes further use of the features that are already created for the robot detection. In doing so, it is able to receive more information about a detected object with almost no further calculations. The reuse of the already learned features makes it possible to learn these additional features from simulation only. This provides a simple method for crossing the simulation reality gap. In our experiments, we used this approach for estimating the distance to detected robots. The results show that in general, we can provide a better measure than current approaches that calculate the distance regarding to the current pose of the robot. However, this depends strongly on the pose of the detected robot. Thus, we have a bigger standard deviation than the geometric approach.

Further works can investigate the detection of other objects like a ball or goal posts in the SPL or entirely new scenarios on other robot platforms. As we did not use any special characteristics of the NAO V5, our approach should be easily transferable to these scenarios. Moreover, the computation of other characteristics than the distance, like the orientation, could be obtained from the simulation and applied to real world scenarios. Although the inference time of JET-Net is already satisfying, it could probably be improved by using approximations techniques like XNOR-Net [20].

Acknowledgements. We would like to thank the members of the team B-Human for providing the software framework for this work as well as everybody who contributed labeled data to the ImageTagger platform, especially the Nao Devils team.

References

1. Cruz, N., Lobos-Tsunekawa, K., Ruiz-del-Solar, J.: Using convolutional neural networks in robots with limited computational resources: detecting NAO robots while playing soccer. In: Akiyama, H., Obst, O., Sammut, C., Tonidandel, F. (eds.) RoboCup 2017. LNCS (LNAI), vol. 11175, pp. 19–30. Springer, Cham (2018). https://doi.org/10.1007/978-3-030-00308-1_2
2. van Dijk, S.G., Scheunemann, M.M.: Deep learning for semantic segmentation on minimal hardware. In: Holz, D., Genter, K., Saad, M., von Stryk, O. (eds.) RoboCup 2018. LNCS (LNAI), vol. 11374, pp. 349–361. Springer, Cham (2019). https://doi.org/10.1007/978-3-030-27544-0_29
3. Fabisch, A., Laue, T., Röfer, T.: Robot recognition and modeling in the robocup standard platform league. In: Proceedings of the Fifth Workshop on Humanoid Soccer Robots in conjunction with the 2010 IEEE-RAS International Conference on Humanoid Robots, Nashville, TN, USA (2010)

4. Fiedler, N., Bestmann, M., Hendrich, N.: ImageTagger: an open source online platform for collaborative image labeling. In: Holz, D., Genter, K., Saad, M., von Stryk, O. (eds.) RoboCup 2018. LNCS (LNAI), vol. 11374, pp. 162–169. Springer, Cham (2019). https://doi.org/10.1007/978-3-030-27544-0_13
5. Goodfellow, I.J., et al.: Generative Adversarial Networks, pp. 1–9, June 2014. http://arxiv.org/abs/1406.2661
6. Hoffmann, J., Jüngel, M., Lötzsch, M.: A vision based system for goal-directed obstacle avoidance. In: Nardi, D., Riedmiller, M., Sammut, C., Santos-Victor, J. (eds.) RoboCup 2004. LNCS (LNAI), vol. 3276, pp. 418–425. Springer, Heidelberg (2005). https://doi.org/10.1007/978-3-540-32256-6_35
7. Howard, A.G., Wang, W.: MobileNets: Efficient Convolutional Neural Networks for Mobile Vision Applications. arXiv preprint arXiv:1704.04861 (2017)
8. Iandola, F.N., Han, S., Moskewicz, M.W., Ashraf, K., Dally, W.J., Keutzer, K.: SqueezeNet: AlexNet-level accuracy with 50x fewer parameters and <0.5MB model size, pp. 1–5 (2016). http://arxiv.org/abs/1602.07360
9. Laue, T., Spiess, K., Röfer, T.: SimRobot – a general physical robot simulator and its application in robocup. In: Bredenfeld, A., Jacoff, A., Noda, I., Takahashi, Y. (eds.) RoboCup 2005. LNCS (LNAI), vol. 4020, pp. 173–183. Springer, Heidelberg (2006). https://doi.org/10.1007/11780519_16
10. Leiva, F., Cruz, N., Bugueño, I., Ruiz-del Solar, J.: Playing soccer without colors in the SPL: a convolutional neural network approach. arXiv preprint arXiv:1811.12493 (2018)
11. Lenser, S., Veloso, M.: Visual sonar: fast obstacle avoidance using monocular vision. In: Proceedings of the 2003 IEEE/RSJ International Conference on Intelligent Robots and Systems (IROS 2003), Las Vegas, USA, vol. 1, pp. 886–891 (2003)
12. Lin, T.Y., Dollár, P., Girshick, R., He, K., Hariharan, B., Belongie, S.: Feature pyramid networks for object detection. In: Proceedings - 30th IEEE Conference on Computer Vision and Pattern Recognition, CVPR 2017 2017-Janua, pp. 936–944 (2017)
13. Lin, T.Y., Goyal, P., Girshick, R., He, K., Dollár, P.: Focal Loss for Dense Object Detection, August 2017. http://arxiv.org/abs/1708.02002
14. Liu, W., et al.: SSD: single shot multibox detector. In: Leibe, B., Matas, J., Sebe, N., Welling, M. (eds.) ECCV 2016. LNCS, vol. 9905, pp. 21–37. Springer, Cham (2016). https://doi.org/10.1007/978-3-319-46448-0_2
15. Menashe, J., et al.: Fast and precise black and white ball detection for robocup soccer. In: Akiyama, H., Obst, O., Sammut, C., Tonidandel, F. (eds.) RoboCup 2017. LNCS (LNAI), vol. 11175, pp. 45–58. Springer, Cham (2018). https://doi.org/10.1007/978-3-030-00308-1_4
16. Metzler, S., Nieuwenhuisen, M., Behnke, S.: Learning visual obstacle detection using color histogram features. In: Röfer, T., Mayer, N.M., Savage, J., Saranlı, U. (eds.) RoboCup 2011. LNCS (LNAI), vol. 7416, pp. 149–161. Springer, Heidelberg (2012). https://doi.org/10.1007/978-3-642-32060-6_13
17. Molchanov, P., Tyree, S., Karras, T., Aila, T., Kautz, J.: Pruning Convolutional Neural Networks for Resource Efficient Inference (2015), pp. 1–17 (2016). http://arxiv.org/abs/1611.06440
18. Mühlenbrock, A., Laue, T.: Vision-based orientation detection of humanoid soccer robots. In: Akiyama, H., Obst, O., Sammut, C., Tonidandel, F. (eds.) RoboCup 2017. LNCS (LNAI), vol. 11175, pp. 204–215. Springer, Cham (2018). https://doi.org/10.1007/978-3-030-00308-1_17
19. Nao-Team HTWK: Team research report 2018 (2019). https://htwk-robots.de/documents/TRR_2018.pdf

20. Rastegari, M., Ordonez, V., Redmon, J., Farhadi, A.: XNOR-Net: ImageNet Classification Using Binary Convolutional Neural Networks, pp. 1–17, March 2016. http://arxiv.org/abs/1603.05279
21. Redmon, J., Divvala, S., Girshick, R., Farhadi, A.: You Only Look Once: Unified, Real-Time Object Detection (2015). http://arxiv.org/abs/1506.02640
22. Redmon, J., Farhadi, A.: YOLO9000: Better, faster, stronger. In: Proceedings - 30th IEEE Conference on Computer Vision and Pattern Recognition, CVPR 2017 2017-Janua, pp. 6517–6525 (2017)
23. Redmon, J., Farhadi, A.: YOLOv3: An Incremental Improvement, April 2018. http://arxiv.org/abs/1804.02767
24. Ren, S., He, K., Girshick, R., Sun, J.: Faster R-CNN: towards real-time object detection with region proposal networks. IEEE Trans. Pattern Anal. Mach. Intell. **39**(6), 1137–1149 (2015)
25. Röfer, T., et al.: B-Human team report and code release 2018 (2018). http://www.b-human.de/downloads/publications/2018/coderelease2018.pdf
26. Speck, D., Barros, P., Weber, C., Wermter, S.: Ball localization for robocup soccer using convolutional neural networks. In: Behnke, S., Sheh, R., Sariel, S., Lee, D.D. (eds.) RoboCup 2016. LNCS (LNAI), vol. 9776, pp. 19–30. Springer, Cham (2017). https://doi.org/10.1007/978-3-319-68792-6_2
27. Thielke, F., Hasselbring, A.: A JIT compiler for neural network inference. In: Chalup, S., Niemueller, T., Suthakorn, J., Williams, M.-A. (eds.) RoboCup 2019: Robot World Cup XXIII. LNCS(LNAI), vol. 11531, pp. 448–456. Springer, Cham (2019)
28. Zickler, S., Laue, T., Birbach, O., Wongphati, M., Veloso, M.: SSL-vision: the shared vision system for the robocup small size league. In: Baltes, J., Lagoudakis, M.G., Naruse, T., Ghidary, S.S. (eds.) RoboCup 2009. LNCS (LNAI), vol. 5949, pp. 425–436. Springer, Heidelberg (2010). https://doi.org/10.1007/978-3-642-11876-0_37

Towards S-NAMO: Socially-Aware Navigation Among Movable Obstacles

Benoit Renault[1,2]([✉]), Jacques Saraydaryan[1,3], and Olivier Simonin[1,2]

[1] CITI Lab., Inria Chroma, Université de Lyon, Villeurbanne, France
benoit.renault@insa-lyon.fr
[2] INSA Lyon, Université de Lyon, Villeurbanne, France
[3] CPE Lyon, Université de Lyon, Villeurbanne, France

Abstract. In this paper, we present an in-depth analysis of Navigation Among Movable Obstacles (NAMO) literature, notably highlighting that social acceptability remains an unadressed problem in this robotics navigation domain. The objectives of a Socially-Aware NAMO are defined and a first set of algorithmic propositions is built upon existing work. We developed a simulator allowing to test our propositions of social movability evaluation for obstacle selection, and social placement of objects with a semantic map layer. Preliminary pushing tests are done with a Pepper robot, the standard platform for the Robocup@home SSPL (SSPL: Social Standard Platform League), in the context of our participation (LyonTech Team).

Keywords: Navigation Among Movable Obstacles (NAMO) ·
Socially-Aware Navigation (SAN) · Path planning · Simulation

1 Introduction

In 2005, Stilman et al. [6] formulated the field of Navigation Among Movable Obstacles (NAMO). The NAMO problem consists in planning a path from a start to a goal position, while moving obstacles if necessary. It extends the well known Piano Mover's Problem by differentiating static and movable obstacles, and allowing the manipulation of the later if it minimizes the chosen cost function (eg. travel distance, time, energy). Contexts like service robotics or search and rescue, in particular, would definitely benefit from algorithms capable of dealing with manipulable clutter, doors or objects.

In the last two decades, the growing interest in service robotics, implying robot navigation in human-populated environments, has sparked interest in Social Robotics, and more specifically Socially-Aware Navigation (SAN) [20,24,30]. Basically, it also extended the basic navigation problem: now not only must the robot find a plan that ensures physical safety (no collisions), minimizes the travel distance, time or energy, but also the disturbance to humans[1].

Until now, to the best of our knowledge, has never been considered in NAMO problems the necessity of minimizing disturbance to humans (or any other type

---

[1] In Socially-Aware Navigation, disturbance is used as synonym for 'discomfort', the feeling of being unsafe [24].

© Springer Nature Switzerland AG 2019
S. Chalup et al. (Eds.): RoboCup 2019, LNAI 11531, pp. 241–254, 2019.
https://doi.org/10.1007/978-3-030-35699-6_19

of autonomous agents). Thus, we want to create Social NAMO algorithms: ones that allow an autonomous agent to go from an initial pose to a goal pose, forbidding collision with obstacles but not their displacement, minimizing both robot's displacement cost (distance, time or energy) and disturbance to humans.

To achieve this, we make the following contributions: in Sect. 2, we provide an analysis of existing NAMO-related works. Then, in Sect. 3, we define the expectations for Social NAMO and propose two extensions applied to Wu & Levihn's approach [14, 16, 23]. We introduce social movability evaluation in obstacle selection, and a semantic map layer to deal with social placement of objects. Finally, in Sect. 4, we propose experiments based on our open simulator and the Pepper robot, in the view of our RoboCup@Home participation (LyonTech Team). We provide closing remarks and discuss future work in Sect. 5.

2 NAMO: Analysis of Existing Works

The following paragraphs give an overview of NAMO through the discussion of the used world representations, notion of cost & optimality, manipulation characteristics and finally, the actual planning algorithms that rely on them. Also, we will point out how they relate to socially-aware navigation and its constraints. A synthesis of the main comparison criteria is given in Table 1.

World Representation. NAMO relies on an object-based representation of the world [2,5,6,8,10–14,16–19,22,23,26–29,31,33] (in opposition to an occupation-space-based one): in order to chose the best obstacle placement, it is necessary to reason about them as separate entities. Final placement selection is what actually tells NAMO apart from the well-known field of Rearrangement Planning [4]. Inspired by the works of Kim et al. on traversability affordance [7], Clingerman et al. [21,25] represent movable obstacles as high values in a costmap, but they recon that it can't be called a NAMO algorithm, since it does not allow to control obstacle placement (the robot simply tries to "go through the obstacle").

Semantic information about Movable Obstacles is key to these algorithms. The most basic need is the 'movability' attribute, in addition to the obstacles position and shape. In the literature, individual obstacles are simply assumed to have a boolean attribute of being movable or not. This attribute has until now been given as input [2,5,6,8,10–12,17,18,26–28] (mainly for simulation-only algorithms), determined on-line from obstacle visual recognition results [19,22,29,31,33] or by manipulation tentative [13,14,16,23] (for real-world experiments). In order to be more realistic, other semantic information is used in more advanced approaches, like object kinematics and physics (mass, center of inertia, . . .), but successfully used only in simulated propositions [2,6,8,26,27], with mixed results in actual real-world implementations [29] (these characteristics are hard to determine with current robot sensing capabilities). Other types of obstacles than movable or unmovable, like humans or autonomously moving objects have never been considered in the NAMO literature: a standard hypothesis is that the robot is the only autonomous agent in the environment. We recapitulate this in the 'Movability' column of Table 1.

We must also say that rather few NAMO propositions have been applied in a real-world setting [8,13,19,22,29,31,33], and when they are, they always maintain a 3D representation of the world, though all NAMO algorithms execute their path finding subroutines in a 2D plane. 3D data is mainly used to allow for proper grasping of obstacles, but also for cross-plane rearrangement planning [33] (e.g. pick&place an object from ground to tabletop). Data is either acquired through external cameras and markers [8,22,29] to position priorly known polyhedral models of movable obstacles (eg. chairs, tables, ...), guaranteeing negligible uncertainty as to the environment's state, or by on-board sensors only [13,19,31,33]. A limited number of propositions actually are able to deal with no prior or partial geometric knowledge [13,14,19,23,31,33], uncertainty as to object positioning [8,13,17–19,26,27,29,31,33], object movability [13,17–19,29] or object kinematics/physics [18,29] (Recapitulated in Table 1, columns 'Prior', 'Uncertainty' and 'Real-World').

In the end, SAN and NAMO both depend on semantic knowledge in addition to spatial knowledge: the robot needs to differentiate objects, associate proper attributes with them, but also understand their relations to the whole environment. Systematic segmentation and identification of as many obstacles as possible thus appears to be a basic requirement for a Social NAMO.

Cost & Optimality. There is a wide variety of cost functions used in NAMO: distance, time, energy, number of moved obstacles, probability of success, that are sometimes combined or used alternatively: these are synthesized in Table 1, column 'Cost'. The choice of a cost that only takes displacement distance into account can be motivated by the hypothesis that the weight of the movable obstacles is negligible in regard to the physical capabilities of the robot. It is however evident that if manipulating an obstacle results in a significant change of speed and energy requirements compared to a sole navigation task, time and energy become way more appropriate choices.

NAMO Algorithms rarely seek completeness like [6,8,10,12,28]. None have achieved global optimality, and only Levihn [16,23] can claim a local optimality for a very simplified variant of the problem where a plan can only contain one movable obstacle (see Table 1, 'Comp.' and 'Opt.' columns). This situation actually makes sense, when one knows that a simplified variation of the NAMO problem, where the robot is considered as a square, all planar obstacles as rectangles of four sizes or "L-Shaped", parallel to the x- or y-axis, has been proved to be NP-Hard [1], and even PSPACE-hard if the final positions are predetermined. When obstacles are further reduced to square blocks limited to translations on a planar grid, the problem still remains NP-Complete [3].

In SAN, the presence of humans brings strong uncertainty that prevents proving global optimality and completeness of navigation strategies. It also results in the need to take social costs into account during navigation [20,24,30] to represent risk of disturbance to humans. In a Social NAMO, we must thus also take social costs into account, and extend them from the robot to the moved obstacles: other entities can now suffer the consequences and risks of a carelessly moved obstacle.

Manipulation. In [9], Stilman formalized three main classes of obstacle manipulation procedures: Grasping (constrained contact), Pushing (constrained motion), and Manipulation Primitives (relies on forward simulation of object dynamics, translational or rotational slip may occur). According to the results exposed in Table 1, Column 'Manipulations', grasping is the most popular class, likely because it is the most reliable. Pushing has also been considered because large objects cannot necessarily be grasped. Manipulation Primitives have also been experimented with, but real-world implementations require external cameras to work [8,29].

In order to reduce the manipulation search space, there are 3 common strategies. The first, applied by all but [2], is to consider that only one obstacle may be manipulated at once (no cascade effect on nearby movables). The second, also commonly used by all but [2,12,28] (which have never been applied in a real-world situation), is to consider a limited set of contact/grasping points, facilitating backward search for robot pose for manipulation. This semantically makes sense, in particular since some obstacles have specific contact points (eg. top of chair, regularly spaced points on table side, ...) [5,6,8,11,13,14,16–19,22,23,26,27,29,31,33]. Finally, the third strategy is to limit manipulation to translations in specific directions [8,12–14,16,17,23].

In a Social NAMO, the robot should bring a particular attention to human safety and comfort. Favoring the most reliable manipulation classes when possible, and reducing the complexity of the manipulation (thus, its chance to fail in a way that may put humans or their belongings at risk) would be of circumstance.

Planning Algorithms. While some solutions [2,26,27] propose tightly woven algorithms that do not clearly distinguish the different aspects of NAMO (iteration over movable obstacles, possible actions and path computations), we can usually tell apart a high-level decision planner and two path planning subroutines. These subroutines can loosely be identified as transit (robot only) and transfer (+obstacle) path planners.

The most proposition-specific planner is generally the high-level task planner. While some propositions are explicitly based on existing algorithms, like Dijkstra [2], DFS [6,8,11,28], BHPN [19], Markov Decision Processes + Monte-Carlo Tree Search [17,18,29], KPIECE+A* [26,27], others appear to have developed their approach from scratch [5,10,12–14,16,22,23,31,33], though [16,23] is based off [14], and [33] has been inspired by [14,23]. In order to reduce computation time, most high-level planners resort to ways of prioritizing the most promising obstacles but [2,10,12,19,22,26,27] do not. The most common way is to use a heuristic path planner that ignores movable obstacles to find 'blocking' obstacles [6,8,11,28,31,33]. Then, the last blocking object is selected by last intersection [6,8,11,28] or by least euclidean cost to go from obstacle to goal [33]. The propositions of Wu & Levihn [14,16,23] use a priority queue ordered by heuristic euclidean distance from obstacle to goal. Finally, the last approach is to use a graph that links obstacles to free space components so that obstacles are considered in the order they can be reached, as in Levihn & Scholz's NAMO-MDP [17,18,29] or Okada's Task Graph [5].

Table 1. Synthesis table with main differentiating criteria

Reference	Prior	Movability	Uncertainty	Comp.	Opt.	Cost	C-Space	Task P.	Transit P.	Transfer P.	Manipulations	Real-World
Chen [2]	Full	Given	None	-	-	D	Disc.	Dij. + GD	N/A	N/A	Prim.	No
Okada [5]	Full	Given	None	-	-	D‖E	Disc.	Custom	NG	NG	Grasp	No
Stilman [6]	Full	Given	None	RC	-	E+NMO	Disc.	DFS	A*	BFS	Prim.	No
Stilman [8]	Full	Given	Pos.	RC	-	E+NMO	Disc.	DFS	A*	BFS	Prim.	**Yes**
Nieuwenhuisen [10]	Full	Given	None	PC	-	D+PS	Cont.	Custom	RRT	RRT	Grasp	No
Stilman [11]	Full	Given	None	-	-	D+NMO	Disc.	DFS	A*	BFS	Grasp	No
Van den Berg [12]	Full	Given	None	PC	-	(D)	Disc.	Custom	N/A	N/A	Grasp	No
Kakiuchi [13]	**None**	Manip.	Pos. Mov	-	-	(D+NMO)	Cont.	Custom	RRT	N/A	Push	**Yes**
Wu [14]	**None**	Manip.	None	-	-	(D‖T‖E)	Disc.	Custom	A*	DFS	Push	No
Levihn [16,23]	**None**	Manip.	None	-	**LO**	(D‖T‖E)	Disc.	Custom	D*Lite	DFS	Grasp	No
Levihn [17]	Full	Given	Pos. Mov.	-	-	PS	Disc.	MDP + MCTS	N/A	N/A	Prim.	No
Levihn [18]	Full	Given	Pos. Mov. Kin.	-	-	T+E	Cont.	MDP + MCTS	PRM	RRT	Prim.	No
Levihn [19]	Partial	Recog.	Pos. Mov.	-	-	(D‖T‖E)	Cont.	BHPN	RRT	RRT	Grasp	**Yes**
Mueggler [22]	Full	Recog.	None	-	-	T	Disc.	Custom	A*	Dij.	Grasp	**Yes**
Castaman [23,26]	Full	Given	Pos.	-	-	T	Disc.	KPIECE + A*	N/A	N/A	Grasp‖Push	No
Moghaddam [28]	Full	Given	None	**CO**	-	E	Cont.	DFS	Dij. + VG	Dij. + VG	Grasp	No
Scholz [29]	Full	Recog.	Pos. Mov. Kin.	-	-	T+E	Cont.	MDP + MCTS	PRM	RRT	Prim.	**Yes**
Sun [31]	Partial	Recog.	Pos.	-	-	(D)	Cont.	Custom	RRT	RRT	Grasp‖Push	**Yes**
Meng [33]	Partial	Recog.	Pos.	-	-	D	**Cont. MP**	Custom	RRT	RRT	Grasp‖Push	**Yes**

Legend: () = Not given but likely; '+' = Combination of; '‖' = Alternative to; Manip. = Found through manipulation; Recog. = Found through visual recognition; Pos. = Manage uncertainty on position; Mov. = Same on movability; Kin. = Same on object kinematics; '-' = Depending on columns, either Not Optimal or Not Complete; RC = Resolution-Complete; PC = Probabilistically Complete; LO = Locally Optimal; D = Distance; E = Energy; T = Time; NMO = Number of Moved Obstacles; PS = Probability of Success; Disc. = Discrete; Cont. = Continuous; MP = Multi-Plane; Dij. = Dijkstra; GD = Generalized Distance; VG = Visibility Graph; NG = Not Given; N/A = Non Applicable; Prim. = Motion Primitives

As for transit path planners, used ones are traditional A* [6,8,11,14,22], D*Lite [16,23] over discrete environments, and RRT [10,13,19,31,33] or PRM [18,29] variants and Dijkstra over Visibility Graph [28] for continuous ones. On the other hand, obstacle placements are either decided through incremental application of motion primitives (forward search, eg. little translations/rotations) [2,6,8,10–14,16–19,23,29], or by growing sampling of possible placements in the obstacle's vicinity and subsequent path verification [5,22,26,27,31,33]. In some cases, when planning for successive obstacles, placement is constrained by the need to keep a taboo zone for the next manipulations [10–12,19,28,31,33]. In the end, in discrete environments, transfer path planners iterate over possible obstacle placements using Best-First Search [6,8,11] or Depth-First Search [14, 16,23], or in continuous ones, using an RRT variant [10,18,19,29,31,33] or again Dijkstra+VG [28].

Approaches mentioned for the three planning tasks are given in Table 1. We can note they are commonly found in SAN, thus incorporating social cost in NAMO planners should be possible. Although, many of them are offline planners: efficient online or anytime-oriented variants will be needed. In conclusion to this state of the art, we underline that none of the existing NAMO literature directly addresses social constraints, though a few references quickly mention the idea of taking object fragility into account [6,13].

3   Extension of NAMO Algorithms

3.1   Objectives of Socially-Aware NAMO

From our previous analysis, three general objectives of S-NAMO can be identified. The first is **Social Movability Evaluation**, or determining the movability of an object by human-acceptance for a robot to move it. The second is **Social Placement Choice**, or ensuring that the final environment reconfiguration is the least disturbing to humans compared to the initial one. Finally, the third is **Social Action Planning**, or making sure that all robot actions are in themselves as safe and comfortable for humans as possible.

In the light of the classification in SAN literature [20,24], we can elaborate three levels of problems of growing difficulty: *delayed human-object interaction* due to future human presence, *indirect interaction* due to actual human presence, and *direct human-robot interaction*. At the first level, like in usual NAMO, the robot can assume to be the only autonomous agent around (eg. cleaning robot servicing while humans are away), thus it only needs to be concerned about **Social Movability Evaluation** and **Social Placement Choice**. At the next levels, the robot must also integrate the dynamic and social aspects of human presence, and answer the additional objective of **Social Action Planning**, exhibiting behaviors such as kindly asking humans to let it pass. In the rest of the paper, we make a first S-NAMO proposition addressing **Social Movability Evaluation** and **Social Placement Choice**, in the context of *delayed human-object interaction*.

3.2   Extension of Wu and Levihn's Approach

We chose to build our proposition upon the solution proposed by Wu & Levihn [14,16,23] mainly for two reasons. First, it is designed for unknown environments, thus covers plan invalidation in the light of new knowledge, which is eventually essential for real-world applications. Second, as long as the problem is solvable by a single obstacle move in a single direction in the current robot knowledge, local optimality is guaranteed. It basically follows the general form of a NAMO algorithm presented in Sect. 2: iterate over known obstacles following a heuristic order, and evaluate potential plans that include obstacle movement as long as it can create a better plan. We introduce the S-NAMO Algorithm (see below), which extends the Wu & Levihn approach. The algorithm relies on two procedures: a main obstacle-level one, `make-and-execute-plan()`, that when needed calls a combined transfer/transit path planning sub-procedure `make-plan-for-obstacle()`. We first present these two procedures ignoring our S-NAMO extensions highlighted in red and blue in Algorithm 1, then detail the extensions.

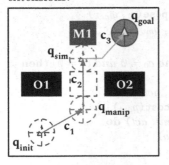

Fig. 1. The robot (grey disc) executes a three-step p_{opt} plan to move M1.

The main procedure, `make-and-execute-plan(`w, q_{init}, q_{goal}`)`, builds and executes the optimal navigation plan p_{opt} from world knowledge w (2D metric map with polygonal entities) and robot configurations $\{q_{init}, q_{goal}\}$. p_{opt} is either a path avoiding all obstacles or constructed from three path components (see Fig. 1): c_1, c_2, c_3, respectively paths from q_r to q_{manip}, from q_{manip} to q_{sim} where the robot stops moving obstacle o, and from q_{sim} to q_{goal}. It always first tries to find the best plan avoiding all obstacles, and only then, iterates over movable obstacles to find out whether moving one of them will yield a better plan. Robot knowledge is updated after each execution step, and if p_{opt} is no longer valid (future collision with other obstacles by robot or manipulated obstacle, failure in manipulation, or disrupting update of the manipulated obstacle geometry), re-planning is triggered. Since our contributions do not concern this procedure, we refer the reader to [23] to better understand the iteration through obstacles.

The sub-procedure, `make-plan-for-obstacle(`w, q_r, q_{goal}, o, p_{opt}`)`, is called during the iteration over obstacles, and returns the best plan p_{best} implying the manipulation of obstacle o. It iterates over actions act that can be done on o, assuming (line 4) there is only one robot configuration q_{manip} for every $\{o, act\}$ pair (middle of o's side). The plan components are computed sequentially, starting with c_1. If c_1 is found, successive unit actions act of constant length are simulated (*count* times) in a copy of w until impossible (collision with other obstacle). To avoid unnecessary computations of c_2 and c_3, the simulation is stopped as soon as an underestimated cost C_{est} of the currently evaluated plan gets higher than the one of p_{opt} (1.15). C_{est} is the sum of c_1's cost, a c_2 estimate (product of *count* by unit length), and a c_3 estimate (minimal euclidean distance between o and q_{goal}). Also, full evaluation is only done if a new local opening has been created around o (l.16, method described in [15]).

Algorithm 1: S-NAMO - Extension of the Wu&Levihn approach: Social Movability Evaluation in blue and Social Placement Choice in red

---

1 **Procedure** make-and-execute-plan(w, q_{init}, q_{goal})
2   ▷ when plan is invalidated, makes a plan avoiding all obstacles, then tries to improve it by iterating over obstacles and calling make-plan-for-obstacle(w, q_r, q_{goal}, o, p_{opt})

1 **Procedure** make-plan-for-obstacle(w, q_r, q_{goal}, o, p_{opt})
2    $p_{best} \leftarrow \emptyset$
3   **foreach** act **in** affordable-actions(o) **do**
4       $q_{manip}, c_1 \leftarrow$ q-for(o, act), A*(w, q_r, q_{manip})
5   **if** $c_1 \neq \emptyset$ **then**
6   **if** is-unknown(o) **then**
7             $q_{look} \leftarrow$ get-last-look-q(w, o, c_1)
8   **if** $q_{look} \neq \emptyset$ **then** $c_0, c_1 \leftarrow$ split-at-pose(c_1, q_{look})
9   **else** $c_0, c_1 \leftarrow$ compute-c_0-c_1(w, o, q_r, q_{manip})
10   **else** $c_0 \leftarrow \emptyset$
11   **if** is-movable(o) *or* (is-unknown(o) *and* $c_0 \neq \emptyset$ *and* $c_1 \neq \emptyset$) **then**
12             $w_{sim} \leftarrow$ copy(w)
13             $count, q_{sim} \leftarrow 1$, sim-one-step($w_{sim}$, act, o, q_r).
14   **while** $C_{est}(w_{sim}, c_1, count, act) \leq$ cost(p_{opt})
15   *and* is-step-success(q_r, q_{sim}, $count$, act) **do**
16   **if** check-new-opening(w, w_{sim}, o)
                  and not-in-taboo(w, o) **then**
17                   $c_2 \leftarrow$ line(q_{manip}, q_{sim})
18                   $c_3 \leftarrow$ A*(w, q_{sim}, q_{goal})
19   **if** $c_3 \neq \emptyset$ **then**
20                      $p \leftarrow$ plan(c_0, c_1, c_2, c_3, o, act)
21   **if** cost(p) < cost(p_{best}) **then** $p_{best} \leftarrow p$
22   **if** cost(p_{best}) < cost(p_{opt}) **then** $p_{opt} \leftarrow p_{best}$
23             $count, q_{sim} \leftarrow count + 1$, sim-one-step($w_{sim}$, act, o, q_{sim})

24   **return** p_{best}

1 **Procedure** compute-c_0-c_1(w, o, q_r, q_{manip})
2    $qL \leftarrow$ get-qL(w, o)
3    $paths$-qL-$q_{manip} \leftarrow$ multigoal-A*(w, q_{manip}, qL)
4    $paths$-q_r-$qL \leftarrow$ multigoal-A*(w, q_r, qL)
5   **return** shortest-c_0-c_1($paths$-q_r-qL, $paths$-qL-q_{manip})

Social Movability Evaluation. The initial approach of Wu & Levihn supposes that any obstacle is movable unless a manipulation tentative failed, in which case it is blacklisted. However, in S-NAMO this is not an acceptable behavior since it could lead to unauthorized objects manipulations. As a first approach, we propose a simple white-listing system: unregistered obstacles are considered unmovable. But a robot often relies on multiple sensors, and their respective Fields Of View (FOV) are not necessarily equal. An obstacle may have been detected geometrically, but not yet identified, leading to three possible states: unknown, movable, unmovable. As in the initial algorithm, we suppose a perfect conical 'geometry sensor' (eg. high resolution laser range finder), with perfect segmentation of obstacles (blue disk in Fig. 2a), but we add a perfect 'semantic sensor' that guarantees identification if the obstacle is in its FOV (eg. using a RGB-D Camera). The geometric FOV (G-FOV) is assumed to cover more space than the semantic one (S-FOV). White-listed obstacles are assumed to fit into the S-FOV, anything that doesn't is automatically classed as unmovable.

The `make-plan-for-obstacle()` procedure has been adapted to work under these hypotheses. When obstacle o is known as movable, the algorithm is unchanged. When o is unknown, we first check whether the usual computation of c_1 can provide observation certainty (lines 6–7); if not, we try to find another path that guarantees observation (line 9). To do that, in `compute-$c_0$-$c_1$()`, we determine the discrete robot configurations list qL that would allow observation (1.2): first, we get all non-colliding configurations within the area between the inflated obstacle polygons by minimal and maximal observation distances, and among them we only return these where o is included in the S-FOV. Then, we execute the multi-goal A* algorithm between q_{manip} and every configuration in qL (1.3). The same is done from the current robot configuration q_r to all elements of qL (1.4). Finally, we return the best pair of paths $\{c_0, c_1\}$ (1.5): see illustration Fig. 2b.

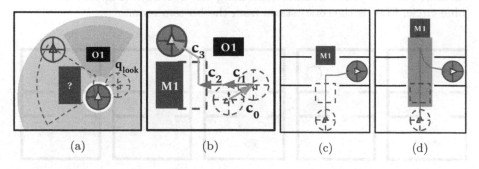

(a)   (b)   (c)   (d)

Fig. 2. In (a), G-FOV (blue) detected two obstacles, S-FOV (green) only identified unmovable obstacle O1. Robot is too close from other obstacle to observe it. Going through best intermediate observation configuration is necessary: final best path with c_0 is shown in (b). **(c)** represents two facing rooms separated by a corridor. In typical NAMO (c), robot will push M1 just enough to pass, blocking the other doorway. In our S-NAMO proposition, the taboo zone (red) prevents blocking, but may end up with a longer plan. (Color figure online)

Social Placement Choice. In current NAMO approaches, the robot does not care about placing obstacles in socially-critical spots (eg. around doors, often-used furniture, ...). As a first step, we answer this problem with a binary approach: either the zone is taboo for obstacle placement, or it is not.

We extend the definition of w by adding a social placement semantic map layer, where taboo zones are defined as a set of polygons P. We assume for now that P is provided by human users. Now, whenever the polygonal footprint of an obstacle intersects with any polygonal taboo zone in P, `not-in-taboo`(w, o) returns $False$, preventing full plan evaluation (see `make-plan-for-obstacle()` procedure, line 16). Figure 2(d) illustrates this process on a simple scenario. Next section presents experiments with more complex scenarios.

4   Experiments

We implemented the S-NAMO algorithm in a custom simulator based on ROS standards. This is a first step toward an implementation on a real robot (Pepper), simplifying object detection and identification, which could later be addressed with an existing package such as ED from TU-Eindhoven. For the sake of implementation ease, movable obstacles are assumed to be convex polygons. All computations are done on the 2D vectorial model, except for path planning, which is implemented as a grid-search A* Algorithm, as in [14][2].

Social Placement Choice. We tested the Social Placement Choice process in a scenario where a robot has to successively reach two goals represented as empty circles in Fig. 3. The environment consists of two rooms separated by a corridor, but two yellow boxes are blocking the doorways (Fig. 3a). The robot (blue circle, FOV is the cone) starts from the bottom room.

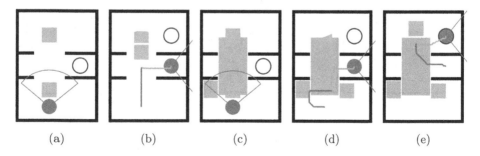

(a)   (b)   (c)   (d)   (e)

Fig. 3. Simulation of a two-goals scenario with NAMO (a,b) vs. S-NAMO (c,d,e)

In Fig. 3b we see that a standard NAMO approach like Wu & Levihn's results in blocking the other doorway: only the first goal is reached. In Fig. 3c we introduce the social semantic layer which consists in two taboo areas for objects

[2] All the code and its execution instructions are available on the following repository: https://gitlab.inria.fr/brenault/s-namo-sim.

(in red), respectively related to the doorways and a 'precious carpet'. Figure 3d shows how our algorithm deals with the first discovered object: the computed path moves the box on the right and outside taboo areas, leaving in particular the doorway area free. In Fig. 3e, the robot encountered the second box and pushed it outside the taboo area, leading to a path reaching the second goal. This S-NAMO scenario (and others) are available as videos[3].

Pushing Experiments with Pepper. In the view of a real-world implementation, we experimented with Pepper's base pushing abilities, using our existing robot architecture developed for the Robocup@Home 2018 [32]. In Fig. 4a and 4b, Pepper successfully pushes a garbage bin in a straight line with little deviation. We have also verified that with other light objects such as cardboard boxes, that when the object's side is properly centered relatively to the robot, pushes are more likely to succeed. However, we also learned that, as seen in Fig. 4c and 4d, heavier objects of interest such as chairs with wheel-casters will need to be accompanied with the arms in some way to avoid unpredictable drift, but even so, the manipulation could still fail (videos available at footnote 3). Thus, in our future work, we will also strive to address uncertainty as to manipulation success, like in [18].

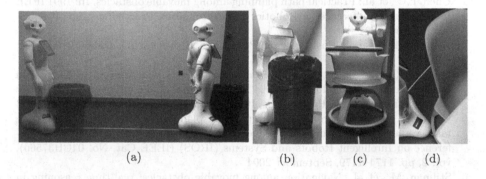

(a) (b) (c) (d)

Fig. 4. Pepper pushing a bin and a chair

---

[3] Link to videos: https://gitlab.inria.fr/brenault/s-namo-sim/wikis/Videos.

5   Conclusion

In this paper, we first analyzed existing NAMO approaches in order to adapt them to social constraints. This led us to extend the Wu&Levihn approach, by defining the S-NAMO algorithm which introduces Social Movability Evaluation and Social Placement Choice for object manipulations. We implemented these propositions in an open source ROS compatible simulator. Experiments showed how social semantic areas can prevent obstruction of places like circulation zones, and how the robot can identify obstacles to compute its plan. In future works, we plan to refine the semantic layer and address actual human presence with indirect or direct human-robot interaction, while integrating ways to manage uncertainty as to sensor data or success of manipulation. We will continue to experiment and validate these social NAMO abilities with robots such as Pepper and demonstrate their interest in the RoboCup@Home challenge.

References

1. Wilfong, G.: Motion planning in the presence of movable obstacles. Ann. Math. Artif. Intell. **3**(1), 131–150 (1991)
2. Chen, P.C., et al.: Practical path planning among movable obstacles. In: 1991 IEEE International Conference on Robotics and Automation Proceedings, pp. 444–449, vol. 1, April 1991
3. Demaine, E.D., et al.: PushPush and Push-1 are NP-hard in 2D. arXiv: cs/0007021, July 2000
4. Ota, J., Rearrangement of multiple movable objects - integration of global and local planning methodology. In: 2004 IEEE International Conference on Robotics and Automation, 2004, Proceedings, ICRA 2004, vol. 2, pp. 1962–1967, April 2004
5. Okada, K., et al.: Environment manipulation planner for humanoid robots using task graph that generates action sequence. In: 2004 IEEE/RSJ International Conference on Intelligent Robots and Systems (IROS) (IEEE Cat. No. 04CH37566), vol. 2, pp. 1174–1179, September 2004
6. Stilman, M., et al.: Navigation among movable obstacles: real-time reasoning in complex environments. Int. J. Humanoid Robot. **02**(04), 479–503 (2005)
7. Kim, D., et al.: Traversability classification using unsupervised on-line visual learning for outdoor robot navigation. In: 2006 IEEE International Conference on Robotics and Automation (ICRA), pp. 518–525, February 2006
8. Stilman, M., et al.: Planning and executing navigation among movable obstacles. Adv. Robot. **21**(14), 1617–1634 (2007)
9. Stilman, M.: Navigation among movable obstacles. PhD thesis, Carnegie Mellon University, Pittsburgh, PA, October 2007
10. Nieuwenhuisen, D., van der Stappen, A.F., Overmars, M.H.: An effective framework for path planning amidst movable obstacles. In: Akella, S., Amato, N.M., Huang, W.H., Mishra, B. (eds.) Algorithmic Foundation of Robotics VII. Springer Tracts in Advanced Robotics, vol. 47, pp. 87–102. Springer, Berlin (2008). https://doi.org/10.1007/978-3-540-68405-3_6
11. Stilman, M., et al.: Planning among movable obstacles with artificial constraints. Int. J. Robot. Res. **27**(11–12), 1295–1307 (2008)

12. van den Berg, J., Stilman, M., Kuffner, J., Lin, M., Manocha, D.: Path planning among movable obstacles: a probabilistically complete approach. In: Chirikjian, G.S., Choset, H., Morales, M., Murphey, T. (eds.) Algorithmic Foundation of Robotics VIII. Springer Tracts in Advanced Robotics, vol. 57, pp. 599–614. Springer, Berlin, Heidelberg (2009). https://doi.org/10.1007/978-3-642-00312-7_37
13. Kakiuchi, Y., et al.: Working with movable obstacles using on-line environment perception reconstruction using active sensing and color range sensor. In: 2010 IEEE/RSJ International Conference on Intelligent Robots and Systems, pp. 1696–1701, October 2010
14. Wu, H., et al.: Navigation Among Movable Obstacles in unknown environments. In: 2010 IEEE/RSJ International Conference on Intelligent Robots and Systems, pp. 1433–1438, October 2010
15. Levihn, M., et al.: Efficient opening detection. Technical Report, Georgia Institute of Technology (2011)
16. Levihn, M.: Navigation Among Movable Obstacles in unknown environments. Master's thesis, Georgia Institute of Technology, Atlanta, Georgia, May 2011
17. Levihn, M., Scholz, J., Stilman, M.: Hierarchical decision theoretic planning for navigation among movable obstacles. In: Frazzoli, E., Lozano-Perez, T., Roy, N., Rus, D. (eds.) Algorithmic Foundations of Robotics X. STAR, vol. 86, pp. 19–35. Springer, Heidelberg (2013). https://doi.org/10.1007/978-3-642-36279-8_2
18. Levihn, M., et al.: Planning with movable obstacles in continuous environments with uncertain dynamics. In 2013 IEEE International Conference on Robotics and Automation, pp. 3832–3838, May 2013
19. Levihn, M., et al.: Foresight and reconsideration in hierarchical planning and execution. In 2013 IEEE/RSJ International Conference on Intelligent Robots and Systems, pp. 224–231, November 2013
20. Kruse, T., et al.: Human-aware robot navigation: a survey. Robot. Auton. Syst. 61(12), 1726–1743 (2013)
21. Clingerman, C., et al.: Estimating manipulability of unknown obstacles for navigation in indoor environments. In: 2014 IEEE International Conference on Robotics and Automation (ICRA), pp. 2771–2778, May 2014
22. Mueggler, E., et al.: Aerial-guided navigation of a ground robot among movable obstacles. In: 2014 IEEE International Symposium on Safety, Security, and Rescue Robotics (2014), pp. 1–8, October 2014
23. Levihn, M., et al.: Locally optimal navigation among movable obstacles in unknown environments. In: 2014 IEEE-RAS International Conference on Humanoid Robots, pp. 86–91, November 2014
24. Rios-Martinez, J., et al.: From proxemics theory to socially-aware navigation: a survey. Int. J. Soc. Robot. 7(2), 137–153 (2015)
25. Clingerman, C., et al.: Dynamic and probabilistic estimation of manipulable obstacles for indoor navigation. In: 2015 IEEE/RSJ International Conference on Intelligent Robots and Systems (IROS), pp. 6121–6128, September 2015
26. Castaman, N., et al.: A sampling-based tree planner for navigation among movable obstacles. In: Proceedings of ISR 2016: 47st International Symposium on Robotics, pp. 1–8, June 2016
27. Castaman, N.: A sampling-based tree planner for robot navigation among movable obstacles. Master's thesis, University of Padova, Padova, Italy, July 2016
28. Moghaddam, S.K., et al.: Planning robot navigation among movable obstacles (NAMO) through a recursive approach. J. Intell. Robot. Syst. 83(3), 603–634 (2016)

29. Scholz, J., et al.: Navigation among movable obstacles with learned dynamic constraints. In: 2016 IEEE/RSJ International Conference on Intelligent Robots and Systems (IROS), pp. 3706–3713, October 2016
30. Charalampous, K., et al.: Recent trends in social aware robot navigation: a survey. Robot. Auton. Syst. **93**, 85–104 (2017)
31. Sun, H., et al.: Semantic mapping and semantics-boosted navigation with path creation on a mobile robot. In: 2017 IEEE International Conference on Cybernetics and Intelligent Systems (CIS) and IEEE Conference on Robotics, Automation and Mechatronics (RAM), pp. 207–212, November 2017
32. Jumel, F., et al.: Context aware robot architecture, application to the RoboCup@Home challenge. In: RoboCup symposium, pp. 1–12, Montreal, Canada, June 2018
33. Meng, Z., et al.: Active path clearing navigation through environment reconfiguration in presence of movable obstacles. In: 2018 IEEE/ASME International Conference on Advanced Intelligent Mechatronics (AIM), pp. 156–163, July 2018

Tell Your Robot What to Do: Evaluation of Natural Language Models for Robot Command Processing

Erick Romero Kramer[✉], Argentina Ortega Sáinz[✉], Alex Mitrevski[✉], and Paul G. Plöger[✉]

Hochschule Bonn-Rhein-Sieg, Sank[20], t Augustin, Germany
erick.romero@smail.inf.h-brs.de,
{argentina.ortega,aleksandar.mitrevski,paul.ploeger}@h-brs.de

Abstract. The use of natural language to indicate robot tasks is a convenient way to command robots. As a result, several models and approaches capable of understanding robot commands have been developed, which, however, complicates the choice of a suitable model for a given scenario. In this work, we present a comparative analysis and benchmarking of four natural language understanding models - Mbot, Rasa, LU4R, and ECG. We particularly evaluate the performance of the models to understand domestic service robot commands by recognizing the actions and any complementary information in them in three use cases: the RoboCup@Home General Purpose Service Robot (GPSR) category 1 contest, GPSR category 2, and hospital logistics in the context of the ROPOD project.

Keywords: Natural language understanding · Robot commands · Comparative analysis · Benchmarking

1 Introduction

In the context of service and particularly domestic robots, using natural language to give robot commands is a convenient way of interacting with a robot since it requires no specialized knowledge on the part of the human operator. A natural language command is composed of at least one action and a set of arguments that provide additional context to the indicated action. Different ways to replicate this form of communication in order to improve human-robot interaction (HRI) and use it in the context of domestic service robots have been explored in the literature.

Developing a system capable of understanding natural language commands is not trivial. One of the major challenges is dealing with the abstractions present in the way people speak, for instance ignoring grammar rules, changing the order

We gratefully acknowledge the support by the b-it International Center for Information Technology.

© Springer Nature Switzerland AG 2019
S. Chalup et al. (Eds.): RoboCup 2019, LNAI 11531, pp. 255–267, 2019.
https://doi.org/10.1007/978-3-030-35699-6_20

of words, and so forth. Because of the current rapid growth of the field of natural language understanding (NLU), an up-to-date comparative analysis of the state of the art models is missing. This lack of comparative analysis makes it difficult to determine which model would perform well when creating a system in which natural language commands should be used.

With this work, we provide a survey of the current state of the art of natural language models for robot command processing and analyze freely available options that can be used to develop such systems. In particular, we perform a comparative analysis of a selected set of available NLU frameworks - Mbot [20], Rasa [7], LU4R [4], and ECG [14] - and evaluate their effectiveness on three use cases: the RoboCup@Home General Purpose Service Robot (GPSR) category 1 contest [21], GPSR category 2, and hospital logistics in the context of the ROPOD project[1]. The models are evaluated using standard metrics, such as precision, recall, F-measure, and accuracy on predefined sets of natural language commands. The major objective of this work is to serve as a guideline for selecting a proper model to understand robot commands in a given context. A repository[2] has been set up containing the datasets and supplemental material used for the development of this paper.

2   State of the Art

Figure 1 presents an overview of different NLU approaches and their applications to robotics.

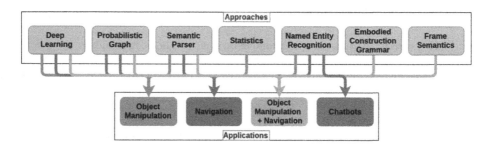

Fig. 1. Overview of different approaches that have been used for understanding natural language-based robot commands.

A recent survey in the field of NLP is presented by Wiriyathammabhum et al. [33], where the integration of computer vision techniques and NLP models for multimedia and robotics applications is introduced. Liu and Zhang [19]

---

[1] ROPOD is a Horizon 2020 project: http://cordis.europa.eu/project/rcn/206247_en.html.

[2] https://github.com/ErickKramer/NLU_Benchmarking.

explore various methodologies implemented for HRI using natural language. Otter et al. [26] review deep learning methods applied to NLP.

A *"functional benchmark"*, named Functional Benchmark on Speech Understanding (FBM3), was presented in [32]. The goal there was to measure and evaluate the performance of different architectures in the context of service robots operating in a home environment and in service robot competitions. The analysis done in this benchmark focuses more on comparing speech recognition rather than NLU models.

Several models that apply deep learning for understand robot commands have been used in the context of object manipulation [1,5,31,35], navigation [6,23,30], and both object manipulation and navigation [3,20]. A different approach is the application of probabilistic graphs to understand robot commands; such models have been used in the context of object manipulation [9,27], navigation [11], and both tasks combined [2,17,18,25].

In the field of semantic parsers, we can find the work done in [8,13,22,29]. A statistical model using a conditional random field for grounding natural language instructions is presented in [24]. A different approach is the implementation of named-entiry recognition (NER) to capture the entities inside the sentences, as shown in [7,10]. In [14], construction grammars are used to understand robot commands, while the work done by [4] and [15] relies on frame semantics to do so.

One limitation in the existing literature is the missing implementation of state of the art word embedding representations, such as BERT [12] or ELMo [28]. Additionally, there is no comparative analysis and benchmark of open source models capable of understanding robot commands. In particular, the surveys presented here do not perform a quantitative comparison of the existing NLU models. Similarly, most comparative studies only focus on models that use the same approach (e.g. deep learning), but do not compare models using different approaches, such as for instance grammar-based models and deep learning models, on the same benchmark.

3   Qualitative Comparative Analysis

Our analysis in this paper focuses on the following models:

– *Mbot* [20]: A model that follows a deep learning approach to understand robot commands. In particular, Mbot uses a recurrent neural network (RNN) with 500 long short-term memory (LSTM) cells to perform action detection and an RNN with two layers of 500 LSTM cells to perform slot filling. The action detection network identifies the corresponding action behind the commands, while the slot filling network assigns labels to all the words in the command following the IOB-format[3] and identifies slots such as *object, destination, source, sentence,* and *person.*

---

[3] B- Beginning word of the entity, I- Inside word of the entity, O- Out word.

- *Rasa* [7]: A Python library that contains two modules: Rasa Core, which is used as a dialogue manager, and Rasa NLU, which can perform NER and classify intentions. We used Rasa NLU as a second model, using a conditional random field (CRF) to perform NER, while an embedding classifier[4] is used to identify the actions in a command.
- *LU4R* [4]: A model that relies on the theory of frame semantics [16]. Its language understanding part contains four stages: (i) obtaining the morphological and syntactic information of the command, (ii) ranking the transcriptions obtained from a speech recognizer module, (iii) identifying the semantic frame that corresponds to the action in the command, and (iv) adding the proper labels as well as the corresponding category to the arguments in the command. The detection of the actions and arguments is performed using an support vector machine (SVM) with a Markovian formulation combined with the morphological and syntactic features found.
- *ECG* [14]: A model that uses the basic principles of construction grammars to construct a semantic formalism - the so-called denominated schemas - for expressing the meaning of commands. The language understanding part contains two main modules: (i) an *analyzer* that parses the sentences into a semantic specification schema using defined ontologies and grammars, and (ii) a *specializer* that extracts the information contained in the semantic specification using a set of predefined templates and generates an action specification schema.

These models were chosen based on the fact that they are freely available and, with the exception of LU4R, are open source; all models, with the exception of ECG, are also able to work offline and are capable of understanding robot commands.

Table 1 presents an overview of the different features each of the models have. Clarifying some of the terminology used in the table, "monologue" refers to sentences that contain more than one action. The "ready to use" feature expresses the fact that the authors have provided pre-trained models capable of dealing with a set of natural language commands. The linguistic knowledge required to train or adapt the models to a new domain is also expressed as a feature, such that a "high" level means that in order to use the full potential of the model, significant knowledge of linguistics is required, while a "moderate" level indicates that it is possible to implement the model without much linguistic knowledge. This feature is not applicable to LU4R since it cannot be adapted to new domains, due to the fact that it is not open source.

The features presented here indicate that Rasa NLU and Mbot are both quite attractive options. Both present customizable action and argument labels, which means that that the models can be used to identify most actions and entities. In addition, it is possible to change the interpretation format and use it to build a planner to execute actions. These models are also capable of ignoring unnecessary information in commands, such as intros and capturing entities composed of more than one word, similar to LU4R. For the case of Mbot, the model can

---

[4] Based on the StarSpace model [34].

be used out of the box to understand a large variety of actions, while for Rasa NLU, it is quite appealing that it can be used in any language. Regarding LU4R, it would be better if it was possible to retrain the model and adapt it to new domains, although the available model is already able to understand 18 semantic frames. Additionally, similar to Mbot, LU4R can deal with sentences containing multiple actions in them. The major drawback of ECG is the required linguistic knowledge to properly use the model; in addition, the model cannot understand entities composed of more than one word, such as "living room".

Table 1. Model comparison. ☑: a model has a given feature, ☒: it does not.

Features	Models			
	Mbot	Rasa NLU	LU4R	ECG
Customizable action labels	☑	☑	☒	☑
Customizable action arguments labels	☑	☑	☒	☑
Customizable output format	☑	☑	☒	☒
Supports sentences with intros	☑	☑	☑	☑
Supports multiple word entities	☑	☑	☑	☒
Supports monologues	☑	☒	☑	☒
Ready to use	☑	☒	☑	☒
Language	English	Any[a]	English, Italian	English
Programming language	Python	Python	Java	Java, Python
Used for robots	☑	☒	☑	☑
Linguistic knowledge required to adapt	Moderate	Moderate	NA	High

[a] As it was claimed in the documentation of the library http://rasa.com/docs/rasa/nlu/language-support/

4   Model Benchmarking

In this section, we set up a quantitative comparative analysis of the above models on three use cases. Our first and second use cases are the General Purpose Service Robot (GPSR) contest category 1 and category 2, which are part of the Robocup@Home competition. GPSR categories 1 and 2 concern tasks with low to moderate degrees of difficulty. The set of actions that were required for these use cases are *answer, find, follow, guide, take, tell, go, and meet.*

The third use case is the ROPOD project, where multiple logistics robots are deployed to a hospital for the purpose of transporting items, such as carts and beds, between different places in the hospital. The idea here is that the robotic platforms can be commanded around the hospital without the need of a GUI. For this use case, we defined the set of actions *attach, find, follow, guide, push, detach, and go.*

4.1   Datasets

We used three datasets for evaluating the selected NLU models - One for GPSR category 1, one for GPSR category 2, and one for ROPOD. The datasets for category 1 and 2 were created with the help of the GPSR command generator tool[5]. We started by generating a random set of 10,000 sentences for each category and preprocessed the sentences by (i) removing those that were not commands and (ii) converting them to lowercase letters. For each category, we chose a total number of 110 random sentences, ensuring that all actions involved are equally covered. We organized the sentences of each dataset in two inputs files, one containing single action sentences and one containing multiple action sentences. In those files, the sentences were organized in groups based on the action behind the command for the single action sentences and based on the number of actions for the multiple actions sentences. The dataset for ROPOD was built by manually creating a total number of 97 sentences. We included commands that we believe were suitable in the context of a hospital environment. The sentences in this dataset were split in a similar manner to the previous two datasets. For each single and multiple actions file, we manually developed an output file containing all the expected interpretations of the sentences following the interpretation format presented by Mbot [20]. We found this format to be quite useful as it displays the intention behind the sentences as well as the complementary arguments in a clear and concise way. All our experiments were performed on an Asus ROG GL552V with an Intel core i7 and 12GB of RAM.

Example sentences from the three datasets are shown in Table 2.

Table 2. Examples of sentences from the datasets in the three different use case. The colors here indicate either an intention or a slot.

Dataset	Input	Output
GPSR Cat 1 (Single)	Locate the pringles in the dining room	find object **pringles** destination **dining room**
	Give to tracy at the kitchen the soap from the towel rail	take person **tracy** destination **kitchen** object **soap** source **towel rail**
GPSR Cat 1 (Multiple)	Grasp the noodles from the towel rail and place it on the bookshelf	take object **noodles** source **towel rail** take object **it** destination **bookshelf**
	Navigate to the bathroom, locate someone, and tell the time	go destination **bathroom** find person **Someone** tell sentence **the time**

(continued)

5 https://github.com/kyordhel/GPSRCmdGen.

Table 2. *(continued)*

Dataset	Input	Output
GPSR Cat 2 (Single)	bring me the peach from the bookshelf	take person me object peach source bookshelf
	Guide morgan to the coffee table, you may find him at the shower	guide person morgan destination coffee table source shower
GPSR Cat 2 (Multiple)	Get the pear from the center table and put it on the fireplace	take object pear source center table take object it destination fireplace
	Go to the cabinet, look for the banana, and deliver it to taylor at the tv coach	go destination cabinet find object banana take object it person taylor destination tv coach
	Guide the nurse to the corridor	guide person nurse destination corridor
ROPOD (Single)	Undock from the station b	detach object station b
ROPOD (Multiple)	Follow the green robot and attach to the station f	follow object green robot attach object station f
	Go to the entrance, find the nurse and guide her to the room 10	go destination entrance find person nurse guide person her destination room 10

4.2 Evaluation Metrics

Similar to the benchmark presented in [32], we evaluated the performance of the models in terms of the following metrics:

- *Action Classification (AC)*: Measures the ability of the models to perform correct detection of the actions in the sentences. AC will be measured through the *precision* (Eq. 1), *recall*, (Eq. 2), and the *F1 score* or *F-measure* (Eq. 3) [10,32][6].

$$Precision = \frac{TP}{TP + FP} \qquad (1)$$

$$Recall = \frac{TP}{TP + FN} \qquad (2)$$

$$F1 = 2 \cdot \frac{Precision \cdot Recall}{Precision + Recall} \qquad (3)$$

- *Full Command Recognition (FCR)*: Measures the ability of the models to understands the commands completely, namely their ability to recognize the

---

[6] TP = True Positive, TN = True Negative, FP = False Positive, and FN = False Negative.

correct actions and complementary information. FCR will measured through the *accuracy* (Eq. 4) [20].

$$Accuracy = \frac{TP + TN}{TP + TN + FP + FN} \tag{4}$$

– *Runtime*: Measures the time required for the models to process the complete dataset. The values are going to be expressed in seconds.

4.3 Training and Adaptation

The three open source models - Mbot, Rasa, and ECG - required training and adaptation for our use cases. Both Mbot and Rasa were trained using labeled datasets[7] containing *200,000* commands for GPSR category 1 and 2, and *199,997* commands for ROPOD. Due to the nature of the ECG framework, it was not necessary to train it, but to add new vocabulary to the grammar file and the ontology. In order to do so, we took advantage of the ECG workbench[8] tool.

5 Results

The results obtained from the experiments with single action sentences are reported in Table 3 and plotted in Fig. 2a. The results shown in Table 4 and plotted in Fig. 2b corresponds to the experiments with multiple action sentences.

Table 3. Results of the experiments with single action sentences. The blue-colored values represent the best values obtained for each metric on each dataset.

Single action sentences														
Models	Metrics datasets													
	Action classification									Full command recognition				
	Precision			Recall			F1			Accuracy			Run-time		
	Cat1	Cat2	ROPOD	Cat1	Cat2	ROPOD	Cat1	Cat2	ROPOD	Cat1	Cat2	ROPOD	Cat1	Cat2	ROPOD
Mbot	1.0	0.97	0.92	1.0	1.0	1.0	1.0	0.98	0.96	1.0	0.75	0.77	3.85	3.36	4.23
LU4R	0.71	0.57	0.74	0.61	0.57	0.53	0.66	0.58	0.62	0.41	0.29	0.35	4.95	2.89	1.82
Rasa NLU	1.0	0.94	1.0	1.0	1.0	1.0	1.0	0.98	1.0	0.90	0.66	0.89	0.14	0.17	0.11
ECG	1.0	0.83	0.95	0.14	0.06	0.29	0.24	0.12	0.44	0.08	0.05	0.21	NaN	NaN	NaN

Based on these results, we can notice that both Mbot and Rasa NLU obtained better precision than LU4R and ECG across the three use cases. LU4R obtained the worst precision for all the datasets because it misclassified commands involving actions such as *tell, guide, and detach*. ECG had a decent performance in

---

[7] Generated using a modified version of a data generator script provided by the authors of Mbot in https://github.com/socrob/mbot_natural_language_processing.

[8] https://github.com/icsi-berkeley/ecg_workbench_release.

Table 4. Results of the experiments with multiple action sentences. The blue-colored values represents the best values obtained for each metric on each dataset.

Multiple action sentences															
Models	Metrics Datasets														
	Action classification									Full command recognition					
	Precision			Recall			F1			Accuracy			Run-time		
	Cat1	Cat2	ROPOD	Cat1	Cat2	ROPOD	Cat1	Cat2	ROPOD	Cat1	Cat2	ROPOD	Cat1	Cat2	ROPOD
Mbot	1.0	1.0	0.97	1.0	1.0	1.0	1.0	1.0	0.98	1.0	0.83	0.73	2.10	4.02	3.56
LU4R	1.0	0.83	0.89	0.67	0.48	0.57	0.80	0.60	0.68	0.17	0.07	0.15	1.62	1.34	0.91
Rasa NLU	1.0	1.0	1.0	1.0	1.0	1.0	1.0	1.0	1.0	0.58	0.80	0.81	0.06	0.14	0.09
ECG	1.0	1.0	0.96	0.25	0.23	0.40	0.40	0.36	0.56	0.04	0	0.15	NaN	NaN	NaN

terms of precision. It is also worth mentioning that Mbot practically guessed the actions behind the commands with words that are not in its dictionary.

In terms of recall, Mbot and Rasa obtained a full score for all the datasets, which means that they were able to provide an interpretation for all the commands. The low recall obtained by ECG shows that from all the commands, very few were actually classified. The results obtained by LU4R shows that it struggled to provide an interpretation for commands that contained actions not covered by the semantics frames on which it was already trained.

The F1 score gives us more insight into the actual ability of the models to classify the actions behind the given commands. We can see that for GPSR categories 1 and 2, both Mbot and Rasa NLU had an almost perfect score, which means that they were always able to both interpret the actions when receiving a command and correctly classify the interpreted actions. In the case of ROPOD, Rasa NLU outperformed Mbot, as Mbot misclassified some of the actions. This shows that the use of pretrained word embeddings by Mbot limits it to only understand words that are already present in its dictionary; since Rasa NLU created its own word embeddings during training, it was able to understand uncommon words such as *uncharge* or *undock*. ECG obtained the worst results on all the datasets, showing that it is likely not a good model to classify actions. The results obtained by LU4R were better than expected taking into account that it was not possible to retrain the model to our domains.

In terms of FCR, Mbot outperformed the other models for GPSR categories 1 and 2, while Rasa NLU obtained the best results for ROPOD. Rasa NLU had troubles differentiating between source and destination entities, which cause the model to perform suboptimally on the multiple sentence dataset for GPSR category 1. The results obtained for ECG show that the model failed to understand complete commands. The major reason for this is the inability of the model to understand two words tokens, which appear quite frequently in the datasets. LU4R failed mostly because it does not support some of the commands that were present in the datasets; in addition, the model struggled with complementary information involving people and locations.

The results in terms of runtime show that Rasa NLU was the fastest model across all the datasets. This could be due to the shallow structure of the CRF

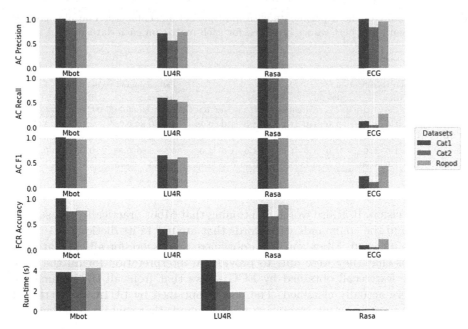

(a) Single-action commands

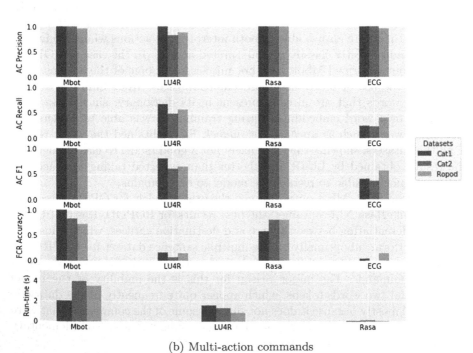

(b) Multi-action commands

Fig. 2. Results of the NLU models on our three use cases.

that performs NER and the embedding classifier that identifies the intentions. Both Mbot and LU4R were considerably slower than Rasa NLU, with LU4R having a shorter runtime than Mbot for GPSR category 2 and ROPOD, but only because LU4R could not understand some of the commands given in them, which means that no interpretation time was spent on those. We could not measure the runtime of ECG because of the delay in the communication process with the ECG analyzer; in other words, it was necessary to manually send the commands in the datasets one by one in order to verify that the generated interpretation coincided with the command sent.

6 Conclusion

This work presented a survey of the existing natural language understanding models for interpreting robot commands. A comparative analysis of a selected set of freely available models - Mbot, Rasa, LU4R, and ECG - was also performed. These models were benchmarked on three use cases: GPSR category 1, GPSR category 2, and ROPOD. Based on the obtained results, we can conclude that both Mbot and Rasa are suitable for robot command understanding; however, Mbot is slightly more suitable since Rasa has troubles differentiating certain location entities between *destination* and *source* categories.

To improve the results of the existing models and particularly Mbot and Rasa, state of the art word embedding representations could be used. Implementing an approach that takes into account the grounded information obtained from a semantic map to resolve ambiguous interpretations - similar to LU4R - could also be explored. For properly spliting multiple sentences into phrases, Google Syntaxnet[9] could be used, where each phrase would contain an action that needs to be executed. Finally, a pronoun resolution approach to properly identify implicit information in commands would be useful to develop.

References

1. Ahn, H., Choi, S., Kim, N., Cha, G., Oh, S.: Interactive Text2Pickup network for natural language based human-robot collaboration. CoRR abs/1805.10799 (2018). https://arxiv.org/abs/1805.10799
2. Arkin, J., et al.: Contextual awareness: Understanding monologic natural language instructions for autonomous robots. In: Robot and Human Interactive Communication (RO-MAN), 2017 26th IEEE International Symposium, pp. 502–509 (2017)
3. Arumugam, D., et al.: Grounding natural language instructions to semantic goal representations for abstraction and generalization. Auton. Robots **43**(2), 449–468 (2019). https://doi.org/10.1007/s10514-018-9792-8
4. Bastianelli, E., Croce, D., Vanzo, A., Basili, R., Nardi, D.: A discriminative approach to grounded spoken language understanding in interactive robotics. In: IJCAI, pp. 2747–2753 (2016)

---

9 https://opensource.google.com/projects/syntaxnet.

5. Bisk, Y., Shih, K.J., Choi, Y., Marcu, D.: Learning interpretable spatial operations in a rich 3D blocks world. CoRR abs/1712.03463 (2017). https://arxiv.org/abs/1712.03463
6. Blukis, V., Brukhim, N., Bennett, A., Knepper, R.A., Artzi, Y.: Following high-level navigation instructions on a simulated quadcopter with imitation learning. CoRR abs/1806.00047 (2018). https://arxiv.org/abs/1806.00047
7. Bocklisch, T., Faulker, J., Pawlowski, N., Nichol, A.: Rasa: open source language understanding and dialogue management. CoRR abs/1712.05181 (2017). https://arxiv.org/abs/1712.05181
8. Boldt, B., Gavran, I., Darulova, E., Majumdar, R.: Precise but natural specification for robot tasks. CoRR abs/1803.02238 (2018). https://arxiv.org/abs/1803.02238
9. Broad, A., Arkin, J., Ratliff, N., Howard, T., Argall, B.: Real-time natural language corrections for assistive robotic manipulators. Int. J. Robot. Res. **36**(5–7), 684–698 (2017)
10. Chesworth, D., Harmon, N., Tanner, L., Guerlain, S., Balazs, M.: Named-entity recognition and data visualization techniques to communicate mission command to autonomous systems. In: 2016 IEEE Systems and Information Engineering Design Symposium (SIEDS), pp. 233–238 (2016)
11. Chung, I., Propp, O., Walter, M.R., Howard, T.M.: On the performance of hierarchical distributed correspondence graphs for efficient symbol grounding of robot instructions. In: 2015 IEEE/RSJ International Conference on Intelligent Robots and Systems (IROS), pp. 5247–5252 (2015)
12. Devlin, J., Chang, M., Lee, K., Toutanova, K.: Bert: pre-training of deep bidirectional transformers for language understanding. CoRR abs/1810.04805 (2018). https://arxiv.org/abs/1810.04805
13. Dukes, K.: Semeval-2014 task 6: supervised semantic parsing of robotic spatial commands. In: Proceedings 8th International Workshop on Semantic Evaluation (SemEval 2014), pp. 45–53 (2014)
14. Eppe, M., Trott, S., Raghuram, V., Feldman, J.A., Janin, A.: Application-independent and integration-friendly natural language understanding. In: GCAI, pp. 340–352 (2016)
15. Evangelista, D., et al.: Grounding natural language instructions in industrial robotics (2017)
16. Fillmore, C.J.: Frames and the semantics of understanding. Quaderni di semantica **6**(2), 222–254 (1985)
17. Howard, T.M., Tellex, S., Roy, N.: A natural language planner interface for mobile manipulators. In: 2014 IEEE International Conference on Robotics and Automation (ICRA), pp. 6652–6659 (2014)
18. Kollar, T., et al.: Generalized grounding graphs: a probabilistic framework for understanding grounded commands. CoRR abs/1712.01097 (2017). https://arxiv.org/abs/1712.01097
19. Liu, R., Zhang, X.: A review of methodologies for natural-language-facilitated human-robot cooperation. CoRR abs/1701.08756 (2017). https://arxiv.org/abs/1701.08756
20. Martins, P.H., Custódio, L., Ventura, R.: A deep learning approach for understanding natural language commands for mobile service robots. CoRR abs/1807.03053 (2018). https://arxiv.org/abs/1807.03053
21. Matamoros, M., Rascon, C., Hart, J., Holz, D., Beek, L.: RoboCup@Home 2018: Rules and Regulations (2018). http://www.robocupathome.org/rules/2018_rulebook.pdf

22. Matuszek, C., Herbst, E., Zettlemoyer, L., Fox, D.: Learning to parse natural language commands to a robot control system. In: Experimental Robotics, pp. 403–415 (2013)
23. Mei, H., Bansal, M., Walter, M.R.: Listen, attend, and walk: neural mapping of navigational instructions to action sequences. In: AAAI, vol. 1, p. 2 (2016)
24. Misra, D.K., Sung, J., Lee, K., Saxena, A.: Tell me Dave: context-sensitive grounding of natural language to manipulation instructions. Int. J. Robot. Res. 35(1–3), 281–300 (2016)
25. Nyga, D., et al.: Grounding robot plans from natural language instructions with incomplete world knowledge. In: Conference on Robot Learning, pp. 714–723 (2018)
26. Otter, D.W., Medina, J.R., Kalita, J.K.: A survey of the usages of deep learning in natural language processing. CoRR abs/1807.10854 (2018). https://arxiv.org/abs/1807.10854
27. Paul, R., Arkin, J., Aksaray, D., Roy, N., Howard, T.M.: Efficient grounding of abstract spatial concepts for natural language interaction with robot platforms. Int. J. Robot. Res. 37(10), 1269–1299 (2018)
28. Peters, M.E., et al.: Deep contextualized word representations. CoRR abs/1802.05365 (2018). https://arxiv.org/abs/1802.05365
29. Sales, J.E., Freitas, A., Handschuh, S.: An open vocabulary semantic parser for end-user programming using natural language. In: 2018 IEEE 12th International Conference on Semantic Computing (ICSC), pp. 77–84 (2018)
30. Shah, P., Fiser, M., Faust, A., Kew, J.C., Hakkani-Tur, D.: FollowNet: Robot navigation by following natural language directions with deep reinforcement learning. CoRR abs/1805.06150 (2018). https://arxiv.org/abs/1805.06150
31. Sugiura, K., Kawai, H.: Grounded language understanding for manipulation instructions using GAN-based classification. In: 2017 IEEE Automatic Speech Recognition and Understanding Workshop (ASRU), pp. 519–524 (2017)
32. Vanzo, A., et al.: Benchmarking speech understanding in service robotics. In: 4th International Workshop Artificial Intelligence and Robotics (AIxIA), vol. 2054, pp. 34–40 (2017)
33. Wiriyathammabhum, P., Summers-Stay, D., Fermüller, C., Aloimonos, Y.: Computer vision and natural language processing: recent approaches in multimedia and robotics. ACM Comput. Surv. (CSUR) 49(4), 1–44 (2017)
34. Wu, L., Fisch, A., Chopra, S., Adams, K., Bordes, A., Weston, J.: StarSpace: Embed All The Things! CoRR abs/1709.03856 (2017). https://arxiv.org/abs/1709.03856
35. Zhong, J., Ogata, T., Cangelosi, A., Yang, C.: Understanding natural language sentences with word embedding and multi-modal interaction. In: Development and Learning and Epigenetic Robotics (ICDL-Epirob) (2017)

People Management Framework Using a 2D Camera for Human-Robot Social Interactions

Jacques Saraydaryan[1,2]([✉]), Raphael Leber[1], and Fabrice Jumel[1,2]

[1] CPE Lyon, Villeurbanne, France
jacques.saraydaryan@cpe.fr
[2] CITI Lab., Inria Chroma, Université de Lyon, Villeurbanne, France

Abstract. In order to perform tasks and offer socially acceptable human-robot interactions, domestic robots need the ability to collect various information about people. In this paper, we propose a framework that allows the extraction of high-level person features from a 2D camera in addition to tracking people over time. The proposed people management framework aggregates body and person features including an original pose estimation using only a 2D camera. At this time, people pose and posture, clothing colors, face recognition are combined with tracking and re-identification abilities. This framework has been successfully used by the LyonTech team in the RoboCup@Home 2018 competition with a Pepper robot from SoftBank Robotics where its utility for domestic robot applications was demonstrated.

1 Introduction

Interacting with humans in populated environments is a very challenging task for social robots. Many tasks, like people identification, intention recognition, navigation in crowed environments or situation description need to be performed by domestic robots.

The RoboCup@Home (part of the RoboCup international robotic competition) intends to evaluate current domestic robots through real life scenarios. The focus lies on human-robot-interaction, navigation and mapping in dynamic environments, computer vision, object manipulation and adaptive behaviors. A set of benchmark tasks is used to evaluate the robots' abilities and performance in realistic home environment settings. For example, during the "Party Host scenario" trials, robots provide general assistance to guests during a party (welcome, introduce a new guest to others, describe guests to the bartender, escort an exiting guest to a cab...).

Such interactions require abilities such as following an operator, finding a specific person in a crowd or comprehensibly describing a person. High level information about people (detected people, pose estimation, body description, clothing description...) has to be extracted from raw data provided by robot sensors.

© Springer Nature Switzerland AG 2019
S. Chalup et al. (Eds.): RoboCup 2019, LNAI 11531, pp. 268–280, 2019.
https://doi.org/10.1007/978-3-030-35699-6_21

As some characteristics (typically a person's positions) vary over time, the use of the tracking approach, more precisely, Multiple Object Tracking (MOT) [1], is needed. In recent works, the Deep Learning approach applied on large dataset has allowed the extraction of numerous human features (e.g. clothes color, gender, hat, hair color) [2,3]. All these approaches give important clues and tools to characterize and track people and could be based on simple sensors such as a 2D camera.

In the case of a domestic robot, we need a framework able to provide all these features with only onboard sensors. A modern approach would be to define all the characteristics needed and train a neural network. Unfortunately, at this time, the creation and labeling of such a large and complex dataset is not possible. The only practical approach is to aggregate different features extraction tools (mostly based on deeplearning) and merge them. For example, a RoboCup@Home team developed a general tracking tool for MOT called "wire" [4]. Another team defined a specific framework for "Person-Following" tasks [5] based on OpenPose tools [2] and color features extraction.

Relevant works have been made on MOT applied to people tracking [1], but few of them are from a human (or robot) eye's perspective (e.g. MOT16). Most MOT proposals consist of tracking scenes through a surveillance camera that is positioned much higher than the human eye. When people disappear and reappear, trackers need to re-identify people and associate them with a previous identity. This process, called Person Re-Identification (PReID) [6], uses different collected persons characteristics. In the context of domestic robots, the problem of re-identification is important, but in order to achieve various tasks, abilities to extract goal oriented people characteristics is essential. In this paper we propose a framework allowing the extraction of people's high-level information from a 2D camera and the tracking of people over time for future interactions. The proposed people management framework (available on github[1]) aggregates body and person features. At this time, people pose and posture, clothing colors, face recognition are combined with tracking and re-identification abilities. The paper is composed as follows: the Sect. 1 talked about the needs of people management abilities for domestic robots. The Sect. 2 presents an overview of our people features extraction and tracking framework. The people features extraction processes are detailed in Sect. 3. A proposed people tracking system is described in Sect. 4. The Sect. 5 presents results on pepper robot experiments. Finally, future works and improvement are discussed in Sect. 6.

2   Overview of the People Management Architecture

As presented in Sect. 1, managing social scenarios, with direct and indirect people interactions, involves to characterize, track people and understand their intentions.

---

[1] https://github.com/Robocup-Lyontech/People-Management-Framework.

To do so, we provide a framework collecting people information and extracting high-level semantic data. These semantic data, goal oriented, are crucial to achieve social robots scenarios.

The Fig. 1 presents the different framework blocks. First of all, the robot gets scene information through camera (2D picture). This image is processed in order to extract each person in the scene (OpenPose [2]). Semantic information are added concerning people posture, hand posture and estimated position (Pose Extraction). Then information such as face and clothes are used to identify a person (face detection, color detection and naming). Finally, all semantic information are gathered and sent to the robot decision process. Robot can identify people, understand intentions (e.g. hand call) and has an overview of the scene.

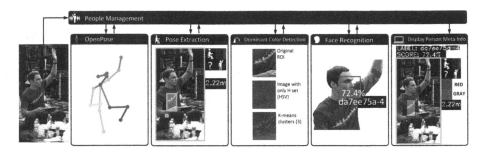

Fig. 1. People management architecture

Let a detected person noted $p \in P$, the following features are associated such as $p = (p^{face}, p^{shirt}, p^{trouser}, p^{posture}, p^{hand\_posture}, p^{pose})$ where:

- $p^{face} = (label, score)$ where $label$ and $score \in [0, 1]$ representing respectively the id of the detected face and the probability of matching with previously learned faces
- p^{shirt}, $p^{trouser}$ define the dominant colors of portion of the shirt and portion of the trouser. Each of theses items is a list of objects composed of a color name, the RGB value, the HSV value and the percentage of the portion of the targeted object (shirt or trouser). e.g. $p^{shirt} = \{p^{metaC_0}, p^{metaC_1}, ..., p^{metaC_m}\}$ where $p^{metaC_i} = (p^{rgb_i}, p^{hsv_i}, p^{name_i}, p^{score_i}), \forall i \in [0, m]$
- $p^{posture} \in \{standing, sitting, lying, undefined\}$ is the label of the detected posture
- $p^{hand\_posture}$ is an array of 2 objects (Left and Right arm), each object represents the posture of the arms $p^{hand\_posture} = (p^{hand_L}, p^{hand_R})$ such as $p^{hand_i} \in \{point\,left, point\,right, call, crossed, undefined\} | \forall i \in \{L, R\}$
- $p^{pose} = (x, y, \theta)$ is the estimated pose (position and orientation), expressed in a "top-view" map with the robot as the origin.

All those information are managed by the **People Management** block in charge of scheduling and launching people features detection blocks.

Indeed, the following workflow is executed: As soon as the **Openpose** block detects people, the **Pose Extraction** block is triggered. Information such as people pose (standing, sitting,...), people bounding box, shirt and trouser regions of interest (ROI) are then available. These ROI are used to extract main colors of shirt and trouser through the **Color Detection** block. The people bounding box becomes the input of the **Face Recognition** which identify people if they were already seen, register the current face otherwise. At the end, the **People Management** block gathers all these features to each detected people and publish information.

People and associated features are then collected by an additional block: the **People Tracker**, that creates and maintains a set of tracked persons over the time.

When information of observed person p at a given time t is collected, a score is computed for each p regarding to a list of already tracked people T_i. This score combines person attributes e.g. face, color and pose score. If the score is upper a threshold the current observed person p update the tracked person T_i, otherwise a new tracked person is created. A forget function removes tracked persons if they are not updated with new observations.

Sections below detail each processing block of the framework.

3   People Features Extraction

3.1   People Pose and Posture

For each detected person, OpenPose outputs a list of body parts, each given with a confidence and a point on the image. Those points are expressed in 2 dimensions but the third dimension is crucial to get people pose on a map, and gives more information for people posture. To compensate the lack of a depth measurement, we will explain how we lay on a main hypothesis and on a calibration dataset. The hypothesis is that the camera horizontal field of view is parallel to the ground. This hypothesis will be used in the computation of p^{pose} and $p^{posture}$. The calibration dataset will be used to estimate people distance with linear interpolation. Therefore the calibration enters in the computation of p^{pose}. The calibration dataset is made as follow: we recorded at every meter, an average size person, straight on his legs and facing the camera, in order to maximize the limbs components on the 2D camera plane.

People Pose. p^{pose} is computed in four steps. The first step is to estimate the depth of the persons ($p^{pose,x}$) in the image. To do so, we consider that at least one limb (e.g: one front leg, one arm, one flank,...) is seen with most of its components on the image plane (depth component small enough to be neglected) We find such limb $limb_{ref}$ in order to perform a distance evaluation. To find it, we normalized each limb size with its respective calibration limb size. Let call $limbs_{normalized}$ the list of normalized limbs. As we miss one dimension (image depth) we know that the biggest normalized limb is the one with the most components in the image plane, as it is in calibration data. Then we do $limb_{ref} = \max(limbs_{normalized})$ to select the biggest normalized limb as a reference to evaluate distance.

Once $limb_{ref}$ is found, it is compared to calibration data in order to find with the closest two calibrated distances. A linear interpolation is done between the two closest calibration data, in order to find $limb_{ref}$ distance ($d_{limb_{ref}}$), and therefore the measured body distance.

This distance is set in $p^{pose,x} = d_{limb_{ref}}$. Then we approximate $p^{pose,y}$ with Eq. 1

$$p^{pose,y} \sim p^{pose,x} * sin(\frac{H_{FOV} * (p^{neck,x} - (i_w/2))}{i_w}) \qquad (1)$$

with H_{FOV} the camera horizontal field of view, i_w the image width and $p^{neck,x}$ the horizontal coordinate of a person's neck on the image.

To complete pose on the map, Eq. 2 computes their orientation based on right and left confidence of people body parts (face and shoulder only). People front or back side are defined by shoulder sides and/or nose presence. Depending on front/back side, we compute α ($-\pi/2$ or $\pi/2$) and β (0 or π) in order to get an orientation angle $p^{pose,\theta} = \alpha * \psi + \beta$

$$\psi = \frac{\sum bodypart\_confidence_{right} - \sum bodypart\_confidence_{left}}{\sum bodypart\_confidence_{right} + \sum bodypart\_confidence_{left}} \qquad (2)$$

Posture

With a limited 2D information, multiple combinations could match with one of each posture. As well, a same combination could match for all the postures. To solve the first problem we use a scoring system on different combinations To fix the second problem we considered the hypothesis mentioned for pose detection. Here are the evaluation criteria for each position, starting with the body. "Standing" relies on xy thigh ratio and neck position on image height (i.e. hypothesis). "Sitting" checks height ratio of thigh and calf as well as knee angle. "Lying" test looks at legs xy ratio and also at head (each point) position on image height. About hands, "Pointing left/right" and arm "Crossed" compute forearms and clavicles as vectors. Hand "Call" checks wrist above shoulder or elbow above nose.

3.2 Color Detection

We optimized our previous color detection system [7] to give additional information to the **People Management** block. Although our color detection is still based on k mean-clustering on the H of the HSV image color, our system extracts dominant colors and associated readable names (E.g. Red, Dark Blue,...). To do so, main HSV color value is converted in RGB value given fixed S and V values (only the Hue value is considered). Then, the closest X11 color is used [8] to associate a name.

Information about saturation and value intensity is relevant to express darkness and extreme value such white and black. Based on the HSV color representations, thresholds on saturation and values are used to complete color name.

Future integration of deep learning color naming based approaches [9] will help to improved common issues concerning illumination and textures.

3.3   Face Recognition

The face recognition mechanism is based on the method provided by Adam Geitgey's based on the ResNet-34 of [10] library[2]. By adding automatic face learning if no matching exists, our method allows a dynamic people face learning and recognition. Using a set of face recognition options (HOG [11], Haar Cascades [12], bounding box from OpenPose), the learning face phase can be adapted according to the need. As a result, when the service is targeted with an image, the system return per detected face a percentage of matching of the more relevant learner face or unknown otherwise. If no known face is detected, the current detected face is learned automatically.

4   People Tracking

All persons with associated features need to be followed and tracked over time. Thus, a robot could keep a state of met people, called tracked people, that it could use for future tasks. The **People Tracker** block is a Multiple Object Tracker (MOT), that need, according to the literature [1], to cover 2 objectives: What is the number of objects? How to maintain object identities?

In the different targeted scenarios, the number of people is not previously known, tracked people is maintained during a time until to be removed by the system in accordance with the forgetting function. Identities of tracked people are fed by people observations that update the tracked people states. The tracked people update is triggered using a similarity function, resulting of the summation of multiple cues, between people observations and tracked people set. The greedy approach is used to associate observation with the most similar tracked person.

This state of met people is defined by a tracked person, noted $T_i \in T$ where T is the set of tracked persons. A tracked person T_i is composed of a set of person features like face, color and pose information updated with people, p, attributes when associated to T_i. Additional information such as a *weight* (how many time a detected person p is associated with the tracked person T_i), *lastUpdateTime* (referring to the last time a detected person p is associated with the tracked person T_i) are used to keep or forget a tracked person.

When the tracker receives detected people p, it computes a score of similarity between p and T_j based on attributes, e.g. $face$, $shirt\_color$, $trouser\_color$ and $pose$. The similarity score (called $general_{score}$) is defined as follows for the given attribute set:

---

[2] https://github.com/ageitgey/face_recognition.

$$general_{score}(p, T_j) = w_0.face_{score}(p, T_j) + w_1.color_{score}(p, T_j) + w_2.pose_{score}(p, T_j) \tag{3}$$

The different $general_{score}$ weights w_k can be adjusted according to the needs: if the pose information rate is high the importance of w_2 will increase. If the target scenario needs to identify people with specific color, the w_1 score weight should be higher. Furthermore, score weights could be computed using a Boosting based algorithm [1] (e.g. AdaBoost) given a training labeled dataset.

If the similarity score is over a threshold, the person p updates current tracked person T_i such as $T_i = \underset{T}{argmax}(general_{score}(p, T))$, otherwise a new tracked person is created and updated with p information. Other affections are possible using Hungarian method as used in [13]. For the rest of the article, only face, color and pose person attributes will be considered.

A tracked person T_i can be defined as follows:
$$T_i = (T_i^{pose}, T_i^F, T_i^C, T_i^{weight}, T_i^{last})$$
where:

- T_i^{pose} is the current tracked person pose,
- T_i^F contains information about the face of the tracked person,
$$T_i^F = \{T_i^{metaF_0}, T_i^{metaF_i}, ..., T_i^{metaF_o}\}/T_i^{metaF_j} = (T_i^{label_j}, T_i^{fweight_j}, T_i^{last_j})$$
$\forall j \in [0, o]$ where $T_i^{fweight_j}$ represents the number of observation matching the current face and $T_i^{last_j}$ the last update date.
- T_i^C contains clothes colors information, $T_i^C = \{T_i^{hsv_1}, T_i^{hsv_2}, ..., T_i^{hsv_p}\}$

4.1 Updating Tracked People

When a person p_i is associated to a tracked person T_i, the T_i attributes are updated. First of all, current tracked person weight and last update time are updated ($T_i^{weight}+ = 1$, $T_i^{last} = now$). This information is used to keep or remove a tracked person. T_i pose is adjusted to the observation pose values, $T_i^{pose} = p_i^{pose}$. The T_i color update process, given a queue size, adds the new main hsv color $p_i^{hsv_k}$ and removed the oldest hsv color if the queue size is reached (FIFO). Concerning face information, if the face label of the person is equal to one of T_i^F label, the weight and the last detected time of this one are updated. Otherwise, a new vector ($T_i^{label_{o+1}}, T_i^{fweight_{o+1}}, T_i^{last_{o+1}}$) is added to T_i^F such as $T_i^{label_{o+1}} = p_i^{face}$, $T_i^{fweight_{o+1}} = 1$ and $T_i^{last_{o+1}} = now$.

4.2 Forgetting Outdated Tracked People

In order to keep the system stable, outdated tracked people are removed. The forgetting function has to keep tracked persons for a given time from their respective updates. Moreover, tracked persons with a greater weight has to be kept longer. Considering these constraints, the following function based on classical forgetting curve is used as $forget$ function:

$$forget(T_i) = 1 + log\left(Th_t - \frac{Th_w}{min(Th_w, T_i^{weight})} * (now - T_i^{last})\right) \tag{4}$$

where Th_t define the maximum time that a tracked person would be kept if no update occurs, and Th_w is a weight threshold over which the tracked person would be kept during the maximum time. Moreover Th_w and Th_t can be customized for VIP tracked persons (for example operator in a people following task).

A tracked person updated regularly in the past will be kept by the tracker from its last update until the Th_t value (only if $T_i^{weight} \geq Th_w$).

Finally, given T_i, for a forget function value $forget(T_i) < 0$, the tracked person T_i is removed.

4.3 Face Similarity Score

The **Face detection** block associates to each person some face labels with confidence scores. When a person face is unknown, a new face is registered. So a same person can be associated to a set of faces (e.g. due to different camera/person settings). The face similarity score maintains for each tracked person T_i a set of face information T_i^F as defined in Sect. 4.

According to the detected person p with a given face label p^{face}. The face score (noted $face_{score}$) given by the current observation, is equal to the face weight $T_i^{fweight_k}$ of the person tracked, normalized with the sum of all people tracked face weight such as $T_i^{label_k} = p^{face}$.

This function gives values for an observed face, proportional to the past associated faces weights.

4.4 Color Similarity Score

When the face becomes unavailable, color information about clothes gives important clues to associate an observed person to a tracked person. Given an observed person p and a tracked person T_i, the used color score is the distance $d()$ between, for example, p^{shirt} and the average hsv color of T_i^C.

$d()$ function can be e.g. Hue distance value, Euclidean distance, one of the CIELAB $\Delta E*$ distances [14,15]. Other image distance/similarity can be computed like Color Histogram intersection [16].

4.5 Pose Similarity Score

Standard tracking system, such as Kalman filter or particle filter, are designed to track a single person according to move estimation and observed data. Knowing the pose of a tracked person, Kalman filter could be used to measure the similarity of the given measure p^{pose} and tracked person. To do so, the Kalman filter is applied on the current tracked person T_i with the observed person pose p^{pose} such as

$$(T_i^{pose}{}_t, \sum_t) = KF(T_i^{pose}{}_{t-1}, \sum_{t-1}, u_t, p_t^{pose})$$

where $\sum$ is the covariance error on the state and u the command applied on the system (in our case, $u = 0$ because no prior information about person's objectives is considered).

Then we define, the pose score as a distance between observation and the new state of the system. This pose score ($pose_{score}$) is also normalized in $[0,1]$ regarding to the distances of other tracked person pose.

The Kalman filter estimation is kept only on the T_i on which the observed people p is associated. For the other tracked persons the previous state is restored.

If the system guarantees a sufficient information rate (regarding to the human velocity max e.g. $5\,\mathrm{ms}^{-1}$), the Kalman filter can be applied. If the data rate is too low, the motion model of the Kalman filter becomes inefficient leading a great filter drift. We propose, in the case, to use only the last person tracked position and compute a function as an incertitude propagation model of the last position.

$$fn(T_i^{pose}, p^{pose}) = \begin{cases} 1 \text{ if } d(p^{pose}, T_i^{pose}) < d(T_i^{pose}, (T_i^{pose} \pm v_{max} \times \Delta T)) \\ 0 \text{ otherwise.} \end{cases} \tag{5}$$

where $d()$ is the distance function (in our case euclidean distance), v_{max} is the maximum human velocity considered and ΔT the time elapsed since the last person tracked update, $\Delta T = now - T_i^{last}$.

The pose score function to apply on low data rate is also normalized between $[0,1]$ regarding to other tracked person distances.

5   Experimental Evaluation

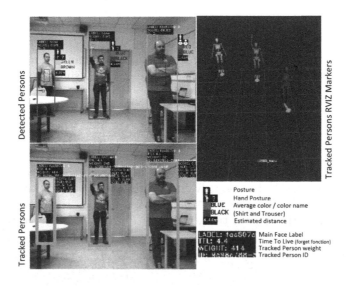

Fig. 2. Experimentation feedback

The Pepper robot from SoftBank Robotics is our evaluation platform collecting images of the scene. The camera of the pepper produces VGA (640 × 480) images at a rate fixed of 10 fps.

Several scenarios have been tested, the presented one (a video illustrating the results here[3]) is composed of a robot at a fixed position, (with head camera parallel to the ground) and 3 people appearing at different time. An example of robot feedback is displayed in Fig. 2.

In the first part of the scenario, a person (called person 1) is sitting in front of the robot (red shirt), after calling the robot (hand call), the person stands up and travels in the robot field of vision. Then, the person 1 sits again. In the second part of the scenario, a second person (called person 2) then appears (green shirt) and travels around the person 1. In a third scenario part, both person 1 and person 2 stand up and cross each other. Finally, a third person appears, walks and stands between person 1 and person 2. Then all people, walk in the robot direction and stand close to the robot.

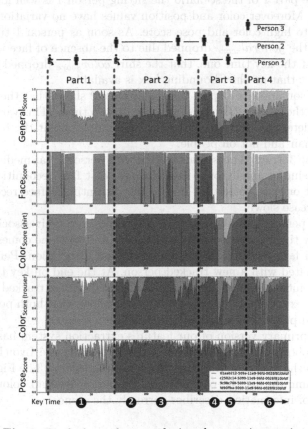

Fig. 3. Tracked people score during the experimentation

3 https://youtu.be/0qSulBGBarg.

During all the experiments different person features including shirt color, trouser color, person posture, hands posture are correctly identified. Some color names has some variation (especially between cyan and blue color names, same as red and pink). Few color name errors occurred. They are mainly due to a bad trouser ROI or due to the presence of the person's arm in the shirt ROI. Concerning person posture and arm posture, no errors has been identify during the experiments.

The Fig. 3 shows the different people tracked score according to the time.

On the top figure, the scenario situation is described. Indications such as how many people is there in the scene and what are the current people postures are available. Below all scores of generated tracked people are displayed during the time. Thus $general_{score}$[4], $face_{score}$, $color_{score}$ and $pose_{score}$ of tracked people are available. Tracked people are identified by a dedicated color and an universally unique identifier (UUID). Finally at the bottom of the picture, relevant scenario moments are indicated.

During the part 1 of the scenario the sitting person 1 is well identify by the face detector. Moreover color and position values have no variations during the time leading to high color and pose score. As soon as person 1 turns his back to the robot, the $general_{score}$ dropped due to the absence of face identification. One can see at the key time one, that the shirt $color_{score}$ dropped down, this is due to the fact that no shirt bounding box is available.

A new person appears at part 2, the key time 2 shows that the $color_{score}$ of the trouser of the person 2 dropped and rise up two times. This variation results of bad color detection. Indeed, the trouser bounding box at the both moments is apply on chair and not on people.

At key time 3, tracked person associated with person 2 has medium face score values, increasing gradually over time. In fact, first face recognition on person 2 is bad, next one are better but due to the discontinued face recognition, the $face_{score}$ increase slowly.

In part 3, person 1 and 2 cross each other and keep their associated tracked people. At key time 4, a person leaves the scene and when he comes back at key time 5, a bad face recognition prevents the good association. Person 1 for its part, is associated with a new tracked person. At the end on key time 6, a new person enters into the scene and is also associated with a tracked person until the end of the experiment. The present scenario shows that both people features extraction and people tracking has good results.

Finally, a primary version of our features extraction system has been tested during the RoboCup@Home 2018 competition, leading the LyonTech team to gain points to the Speech and Person Recognition scenario. The Fig. 4 displayed results obtaining during the competition. Despite a few bad color names processing most of information describes correctly the scene.

---

[4] Weights of the $general_{score}$ are chosen according the ground truth on several scenarios and results of a weight $w_0 = 0.5$ for the $face_{score}$, $w_1 = 0.15$ for the $color_{score}$ and $w_2 = 0.35$ for the $pose_{score}$.

Fig. 4. Result of speech and people recognition scenario during the RoboCup@Home 2018 challenge

6   Conclusion

To consider robot deployment in homes, people identification, intention recognition or situation description capabilities have to be developed with cheap and general purpose sensors such as a classical 2D camera.

Our main contribution is proposing a framework which equips robots with high-level information about individuals that in turn yields more productive social interactions. The framework is driven by domestic use cases (e.g. following people, locating people, checking if people sat, looking at people pointing, describing one person among others, coming to a person calling). It manages different blocks to extract people distinctive high-level features such as clothing colors, face recognition, position and posture.

Different real-life experimentation demonstrate the usability and relevance of the framework, especially during the RoboCup@Home 2018 competition.

Global performance could be enhanced with higher resolution images (better face recognition and better position evaluation) as well as more computation power (more FPS leading to better tracking).

Some block's improvements are still in development. Regarding to the tracker, weights of the scoring system could be optimized with reinforcement or adaptive learning. Concerning the pose extraction, The dependence between people position and people height can be reduced through other features (e.g. age, gender). To go further, the framework allows an easy addition of new blocks, even for new features, in order to answer new use-cases, or to have better performance on already covered use-cases. A coming block, is the implementation of the work of our colleagues [3] to get 45 more features (e.g. Causal/Formal upper/lower clothes, carrying plastic bag, gender) of people.

References

1. Luo, W., Zhao, X., Kim, T.-K.: Multiple object tracking: a review. CoRR, abs/1409.7618 (2014). Accessed 2017
2. Cao, Z., Hidalgo, G., Simon, T., Wei, S.-E., Sheikh, Y.: Openpose: realtime multi-person 2D pose estimation using part affinity fields. CoRR, abs/1812.08008 (2018)
3. Chen, Y., Duffner, S., Stoian, A., Dufour, J.-Y., Baskurt, A.: Pedestrian attribute recognition with part-based CNN and combined feature representations. In: VIS-APP 2018, Funchal, Portugal, January 2018
4. Elfring, J., Van Den Dries, S., Van De Molengraft, M.J.G., Steinbuch, M.: Semantic world modeling using probabilistic multiple hypothesis anchoring. Robot. Auton. Syst. **61**(2), 95–105 (2013)
5. Kim, M., et al.: An architecture for person-following using active target search. CoRR, abs/1809.08793 (2018)
6. Lavi, B., Serj, M.F., Ullah, I.: Survey on deep learning techniques for person re-identification task. CoRR, abs/1807.05284 (2018)
7. Jumel, F., et al.: Context aware robot architecture, application to the RoboCup@Home challenge. In: RoboCup symposium, Montreal, Canada, pp. 1–12, June 2018
8. Pettit, B.: (Microsoft Corporation) Steven Pemberton (CWI). Css color module level 3. W3c recommendation, W3C (2018). https://www.w3.org/TR/css-color-3
9. Yu, L., Cheng, Y., van de Weijer, J.: Weakly supervised domain-specific color naming based on attention. CoRR, abs/1805.04385 (2018)
10. He, K., Zhang, X., Ren, S., Sun, J.: Deep residual learning for image recognition. arXiv preprint arXiv:1512.03385 (2015)
11. Dalal, N., Triggs, B.: Histograms of oriented gradients for human detection. In: 2005 IEEE Computer Society Conference on Computer Vision and Pattern Recognition (CVPR 2005), vol. 1, pp. 886–893, June 2005
12. Viola, P., Jones, M.: Rapid object detection using a boosted cascade of simple features. In: Proceedings of the 2001 IEEE Computer Society Conference on Computer Vision and Pattern Recognition, CVPR 2001, vol. 1, p. I, December 2001
13. Bewley, A., Ge, Z., Ott, L., Ramos, F., Upcroft, B.: Simple online and realtime tracking. In: 2016 IEEE International Conference on Image Processing (ICIP), pp. 3464–3468 (2016)
14. McDonald, R., Smith, K.J.: Cie94-a new colour-difference formula*. J. Soc. Dyers Colour. **111**(12), 376–379 (1995)
15. Luo, M.R., Cui, G., Rigg, B.: The development of the CIE: colour-difference formula: CIEDE 2000. Color Res. Appl. **26**(5), 340–350 (2000)
16. Swain, M.J., Ballard, D.H.: Color indexing. Int. J. Comput. Vis. **7**, 11–32 (1991)

Gesture Recognition in RGB Videos Using Human Body Keypoints and Dynamic Time Warping

Pascal Schneider, Raphael Memmesheimer[✉], Ivanna Kramer,
and Dietrich Paulus

Active Vision Group, Institute for Computational Visualistics,
University of Koblenz-Landau, 56070 Koblenz, Germany
{pschneider,raphael,ivannamyckhal,paulus}@uni-koblenz.de
http://homer.uni-koblenz.de, http://agas.uni-koblenz.de

Abstract. Gesture recognition opens up new ways for humans to intuitively interact with machines. Especially for service robots, gestures can
be a valuable addition to the means of communication to, for example, draw the robot's attention to someone or something. Extracting a
gesture from video data and classifying it is a challenging task and a
variety of approaches have been proposed throughout the years. This
paper presents a method for gesture recognition in RGB videos using
OpenPose to extract the pose of a person and *Dynamic Time Warping*
(DTW) in conjunction with *One-Nearest-Neighbor* (1NN) for time-series
classification. The main features of this approach are the independence
of any specific hardware and high flexibility, because new gestures can
be added to the classifier by adding only a few examples of it. We utilize
the robustness of the Deep Learning-based OpenPose framework while
avoiding the data-intensive task of training a neural network ourselves.
We demonstrate the classification performance of our method using a
public dataset.

1 Introduction

Gesture recognition is an active field of research with applications such as automatic recognition of sign language, interaction of humans and robots or for new
ways of controlling video games. The main application we have in mind is an
accessible way to use gestures for interacting with service robots.

Deep learning-based approaches have set new records in classification tasks
in terms of their performance throughout the last few years. Consequently, they
have also been applied to the problem of gesture recognition, where they could
also provide good results. However, this usually comes at the cost of being very
data-intensive. As with many deep learning techniques, good performance can
usually only be reached with large amounts of labeled training samples. Our
goal is therefore to present an approach which allows adding new gestures to
the classifier with minimal effort. The training process we employ significantly

© Springer Nature Switzerland AG 2019
S. Chalup et al. (Eds.): RoboCup 2019, LNAI 11531, pp. 281–293, 2019.
https://doi.org/10.1007/978-3-030-35699-6_22

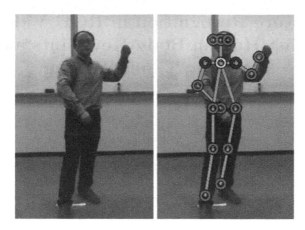

Fig. 1. Example for an extracted pose using OpenPose from the UTD-MHAD dataset [1].

reduces the overhead. Moreover, removing a gesture from the model does not involve any further cost, whereas for many other machine learning algorithms this would entail re-training the entire model [2].

Moreover, we want to avoid the need of any specific hardware. For example, the *Microsoft Kinect* is a popular platform for training models and collecting data for gesture recognition [3–6], since it provides not only an RGB video but also depth data. The task of gesture recognition can be simplified by placing special markers on the person's body [7] or special gloves for hand gestures [8]. Since the main application we have in mind is human-robot interaction for service robots, relying on installing hardware on humans or manipulating the environment beforehand are impractical.

We present a method that completely avoids proprietary platforms and the need of specific hardware and instead only relies on RGB video that can be recorded using any camera with reasonable video quality in attempt to make gesture recognition more accessible. The key idea is to combine the capability of the deep learning-based OpenPose framework for extracting poses from color images and DTW, a well-established method for time-series classification.

The paper is structured as follows: in Sect. 2 we give an overview of some recently proposed methods for gesture recognition as well as a selection of relevant papers for both OpenPose and Dynamic Time Warping. In Sect. 3 we describe our approach, which is summarized in Fig. 2. In Sect. 4 we present the results of our experiments. We conclude our findings in Sect. 5 and motivate possible future research in Sect. 6.

2   Related Work

Using Dynamic Time Warping for gesture recognition is an established approach [5, 9, 10]. For time-series classification (TSC) in general, DTW in combination with a *One-Nearest-Neighbor* (1NN) classifier has shown to provide very strong performance [11,12]. DTW has been prominently used in the field of speech recognition since the 1970's. A lot of research has been focused on reducing the computational complexity, e.g. by introducing global constraints such as the *Sakoe-Chiba-Band* [13], the *Itakura-Parallelogram* [14] or the *Ratanamahatana-Koegh-Band* [15]. Notable work in improving the performance of DTW has also been done by Salvador and Chan, who proposed an approximation of DTW with linear time and space complexity [16].

A detailed description of Dynamic Time Warping and the constraints is beyond the scope of this paper and hence omitted here. Introductions to the DTW algorithm and some extensions can be found in [17] and [18].

The growing popularity of deep learning has also influenced research in the field of gesture recognition. The method presented in this paper only uses deep learning for extracting the pose of people, not for the classification. Others have presented neural network architectures to address the problem of gesture recognition directly as a whole. Examples include the *Two Streams Recurrent Neural Network* proposed by Chai et al. [19] or the *Recurrent 3D Convolutional Neural Network* (R3DCNN) by Molchanov et al. [20].

The problem of recognizing gestures in a video or any other sequence of data can be split into two sub-problems: segmentation and recognition. A sequence of data might contain any number of gestures, therefore the individual gestures have to be segmented first. If both segmentation and recognition are performed, it is commonly referred to as *continuous* gesture recognition. Whereas if only recognition is done, this is called *isolated* gesture recognition. Our method only addresses the latter. An approach to extending a DTW-based gesture recognition to the continuous case is given in [9].

A general survey on different gesture recognition techniques can be found in [21], also including DTW as an approach.

There has also been research on performing gesture recognition on single RGB images using *Convolutional Pose Machines* and different supervised learning techniques [22]. The authors concluded that an extension towards using sequences rather than single images could presumably lead to significant improvements.

Our work is focused on how the human poses extracted by OpenPose can be processed and used as input signals for Dynamic Time Warping in such a way that these two components form a processing pipeline which ultimately yields a classification of human gestures using only RGB images. What sets this apart from proposed methods based on the *Microsoft Kinect* [3,5,23] is that we do not use depth data and extract the pose key points ourselves instead of relying on ones provided by the Kinect framework. This makes our approach independent of any special sensor hardware.

Rwigema et al. proposed an approach to optimize weights for gesture recognition when using weighted DTW [24]. They also used the *UTD-MHAD* dataset to verify the performance of their method and achieved an accuracy of 99.40%. The key difference compared to our method is their choice of data to perform the recognition on. While we restrict ourselves to only the RGB video, Rwigema et al. aimed at a multi-sensor setup using skeleton joint frames and data from a depth sensor and inertial sensor.

3   Approach

Figure 2 shows the basic processing pipeline of the proposed method approach. Its individual steps will be detailed in the following.

3.1   Recording RGB Videos

Avoiding the need for special hardware is one of the key aspects of the method we want to present. We therefore only use RGB videos. The image quality and resolution have to be sufficiently high to enable OpenPose to reliably extract the pose key points. Moreover, the video frame rate has to be high enough to provide adequate spatial resolution of the signals. Most customary web cams will nowadays meet this requirement which we hope will make this method very accessible.

3.2   Pose Estimation

To extract the pose, we use the OpenPose framework, which is based on Convolutional Pose Machines [25]. It features different pose models such as *MPI*, *COCO* and *BODY_25*. We chose the *COCO* model, because we consider its 18 key points to provide a good trade-off between a detailed representation of the human pose and complexity. OpenPose also supports extracting key points for the face, hands [26] and feet [27], but for our application aimed at full-body gestures these key points add hardly any useful information while greatly increasing the computational complexity.

3.3   Normalization

The pose key points from OpenPose are given in image coordinates. We normalize the key points first before passing them on to the DTW classifier to achieve scale invariance and translational invariance. This is necessary, because otherwise the key points' coordinates are dependent on the position of the person was standing relative to the camera. We ignore rotational invariance, since we consider this to be much less relevant, because humans can be expected to be in a mostly upright position under normal circumstances. However, adding rotational invariance might be necessary if tilt of the camera has to be corrected for.

The normalization is a simple coordinate transformation done in two steps:

1. **Translation:** All the key points are translated such that the neck key point becomes the origin of the coordinate system. This is achieved by subtracting the neck key points coordinates from all other key points.

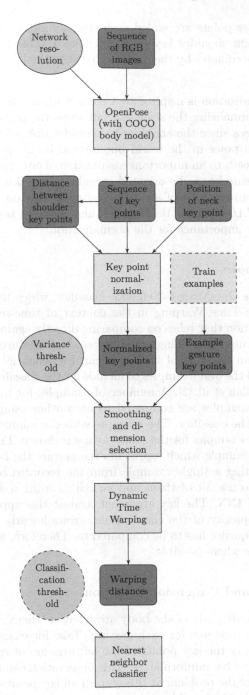

Fig. 2. Overview of the processing pipeline of our method. (Grey rectangles represent processing steps, blue rectangles represent data, ellipses represent parameters.) (Color figure online)

2. **Scaling:** The key points are scaled such that the distance between the left shoulder and right shoulder key point becomes 1. This is done by dividing all key points coordinates by the distance between the left and right shoulder key point.

The scale normalization is inspired by Celebi et al. [23]. It can be easily seen that this way of normalizing the scale can fail when the person is not oriented frontal to the camera since the shoulder-to-shoulder distance we consider here is not the actual distance in the world but instead its 2D projection onto the image plane. This leads to an important assumption of our approach: the person performing the gesture has to be oriented (roughly) frontal to the camera.

Figure 1 shows an example of an extracted pose skeleton for a video frame from the *UTD-MHAD* dataset [1]. The neck and shoulder key points are highlighted due to their importance for the normalization.

3.4   Train Examples

We employ a simple One-Nearest-Neighbor classifier, which has proven to work well with Dynamic Time Warping in the context of time-series classification [11,12]. A classification that relies on comparing directly against a set of labeled examples does not need a training stage per se. New gestures could be added simply by adding an example of it. Yet it can be beneficial to incorporate a training step to find the best examples to include for the classifier. Such a method is described by Gillian et al. [2]. A number of examples for the same gesture is recorded and the examples are compared to each other using the same DTW algorithm used by the classifier. The example with the minimum total warping distance to all other examples for the same gesture is chosen. This can be thought of as choosing the example which represents the gesture the best.

Instead of selecting a single example from the recorded ones for each gesture, you could also use all of them and switch to using a *k-nearest-neighbor* classifier instead of 1NN. The key argument against this approach is that the computational complexity of the classification grows linearly with the number of examples each sequence has to be compared to. Therefore, we try to limit the number of examples where possible.

3.5   Smoothing and Dimension Selection

For most gestures, only parts of the body are relevant. Hence, only a few of the key points might be relevant for each gesture. Take for example a *wave-with-left-hand* gesture: only the key points of the left arm are of relevance here and the others will usually be uninformative. This observation can be used to reduce the dimensionality of the problem at this step. If all key point sequences were to be used in the DTW, this would total up to 36 dimensions (18 key points with an x- and y-coordinate each). The neck key point coordinates will always be uninformative due to the normalization. To further reduce the number of signals to be processed by DTW, we perform a dimension selection. This step is greatly inspired by the work of ten Holt et al.

The criterion to select a dimension is the variance of its signal. Key points that do not move significantly during a gesture will cause the signals of the respective coordinates to be roughly constant with only little variance. All signals whose variance is below a threshold will be filtered out and are assumed to be uninformative. This filtering is done for the sequence to be classified as well as for the example sequences of each gestures. The set of dimensions for which DTW algorithm is then performed is the union of those dimensions for which the variance is above the threshold for either the sequence to be classified or the example sequence. If only those dimensions were considered where the variance is above the threshold for the sequence to be classified, some combinations of gestures could pose problems. Consider for example if there were a *wave-with-left-hand*, *wave-with-right-hand* and a *wave-with-both-hands* gesture. Classify a newly recorded *wave-with-left-hand* correctly is problematic if only its salient dimensions would be used in the DTW. Variance in the signal might also be due to noise. A noticeable source of noise was observed caused by the limited spatial resolution of the output from OpenPose. The quantization error caused sudden spikes in the signal. We therefore smooth the signal first before determining whether it should be included for the DTW. We use a median filter with radius $r = 3$ for the smoothing. The decision whether a dimension will be included for the DTW is done on the median filtered signal. However, the signal used for further processing is instead filtered using a Gaussian filter with $\sigma = 1$. This is done because the median filter is very effective at removing the noise spikes, but edges in the resulting signal are overly brought out. This worsened classification performance in our experiments, while the Gaussian filter is able to mitigate noise without these adverse effects.

In a last step before the DTW, the mean of the signal is subtracted from it, thus making it *zero-mean*. A common step for feature scaling is to also normalize the signal to have *unit-variance* by dividing the signal by its standard deviation. However, this had an adverse effect on classification performance in our experiments, possibly because differences in the amplitude of key point coordinate signals is relevant for classification. We therefore only transform the signals to zero-mean, but *not* to unit-variance.

3.6   Dynamic Time Warping

We employ the *FastDTW* method by Salvador and Chan [16] to perform DTW on each selected dimension separately. Their method is aimed at providing an approximation of DTW with less computational cost compared to the classical DTW algorithm. Finding the optimal warping path is not guaranteed with this method, but we consider this limitation to be outweighed by the superior computational performance. For the internal distance metric FastDTW uses we chose Euclidean distance. The result is the warping distances of the sequence to be classified to all gesture examples of the classifier.

Table 1. Selected actions from the *UTD-MHAD* [1] dataset to perform classification on

Identifier	Action description
a1	Right arm swipe to the left
a6	Cross arms in the chest
a7	Basketball shoot
a9	Right hand draw circle (clockwise)
a24	Sit to stand
a26	Forward lunge (left foot forward)

3.7 Classification

The classification is done using a simple *One-Nearest-Neighbor Classifier* (1NN). The metric used for determining the nearest neighbor is the warping distance. A new sequence is classified to a gesture class by calculating the warping distance to all training examples and choosing the class of the training sample for which the warping distance is minimal. An additional threshold can be used in order not to classify a gesture sequence to any class if it does not resemble any of the example gesture sequences. If the minimal warping distance is still very high, this sequence can be considered to contain none of the known gestures.

4 Experiments

4.1 Dataset

To evaluate the performance of our method we chose the multi-modal human action dataset of the University of Texas at Dallas (*UTD-MHAD* [1]). Each gesture is performed by eight subjects four times each. Since we want to operate on RGB data, we use the color videos they provide. These videos feature a resolution of 640×480 pixels at around 30 frames per second. Due to the limitations of the normalization method, we specifically selected gestures where the shoulder-to-shoulder key point distance remains roughly constant throughout the sequence. The selected gestures are given by Table 1.

4.2 Key Point Signals

Figure 3 shows the signals for every normalized coordinate of the extracted pose for a video sequence consisting of 44 images, i.e. it shows a separate signal for each x- and y-coordinate of each key point. Since the COCO body model has 18 key points, there are 36 individual signals. The video sequence shows a person performing the *right arm swipe to the left* gesture. Most signals are roughly constant throughout the sequence. However, four of the dimensions are highlighted in Fig. 3, since they can be considered salient and provide especially

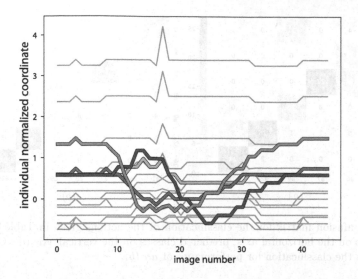

Fig. 3. Normalized key point coordinates for a sequence of 44 images from a person performing the *right arm swipe to the left* gesture in the *UTD-MHAD* dataset. The salient dimensions are highlighted.

good signal shapes for DTW to work with. Unsurprisingly, these dimensions belong to the x- and y-coordinate of the left hand and left arm key point.

The variations in the signals for key points of body parts which are not being moved during the *right arm swipe to the left* gesture (such as legs etc.) are mostly due to the noise caused by the limited resolution of the extracted pose. A conspicuous noise spike can be seen at frame 17. It is caused by the neck key point being located at a slightly higher position for one frame. Since the neck key point is the origin of our normalized coordinate system, it has a noticeable effect across multiple dimensions. A median filter with radius $r = 3$ will filter out most of these spikes, which is the reason why we introduce this filtering step.

4.3   Classification Performance

We selected six different gestures from the *UTD-MHAD* dataset. The selected gestures are given in Table 1. To select an example for each gesture, we only considered the gesture performances by subject one, i.e. from the four sequences for subject one for each of the gestures, one is selected as described in Sect. 3.4. The other three sequences are not considered for the classification. From the 168 sequences which were classified, 130 were classified correctly. This equates to approximately 77.4%. The confusion matrix is given by Fig. 4(a).

To further test the discriminative strength of the classification, we added another gesture to the classification: gesture *a8, right hand draw x*. The confusion matrix for this experiment is illustrated in Fig. 4(b). As can be seen, the classification performance deteriorated significantly. 125 of 196 sequences were

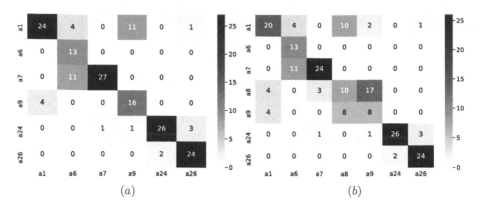

(a)   (b)

Fig. 4. Confusion matrix for the classification of the actions given in Table 1. Actual classes are on the horizontal axis, predicted classes on the vertical axis (a). Confusion matrix for the classification for performance of a8 (b).

Table 2. Percentage of correctly classified gestures for different variance thresholds t_{var}

t_{var}	Correctly classified	
	without a8	with a8
0.05	72.0%	63.3%
0.10	77.4%	63.8%
0.15	74.4%	67.9%
0.20	76.2%	66.8%

classified correctly (63.8%). Most notably, a9 was classified as a8 more often than it was classified correctly. This clearly shows the limitations of the method. Gestures that are too similar to each other can not be distinguished.

An important parameter for the processing is the variance threshold t_{var}. Choosing a very low threshold will result in many dimensions being selected for the DTW step, which makes computation slow. If the threshold is set too high on the other hand, possibly none of the signals will exceed it and the classification will fail because no data reaches it. Table 2 shows the classification performance for different values of t_{var}. Finding the appropriate value for t_{var} is not part of the method, so it has to be chosen a priori. We can not derive any general advice for how to choose t_{var} from this data, this question could be addressed in future research.

5   Conclusion

We presented a method for gesture recognition on RGB videos using OpenPose to extract pose key points and Dynamic Time Warping in conjunction with a

One-Nearest-Neighbor classifier to perform classification. We showed how this can be used to perform gesture recognition with only very little training data and without the need for special hardware. Our first tests using this method yielded promising results if the gestures where sufficiently different, but also revealed limitations in case of attempting to classify more similar gestures.

Recent methods for gesture recognition using multi-modal data are often able to outperform our results in terms of accuracy, even more so considering our focus on only few selected gestures. Examples include the method by Rwigema et al. [24] with an accuracy of 99.40% on the *UTD-MHAD* dataset, Celebi et al. [23] with an accuracy of 96.70% on their own dataset or Molchanov et al. [20] with up to 83.8% accuracy, also using their own custom dataset. Nonetheless, we find our results promising considering the substantially reduced amount of data available to our method by restricting ourselves to only RGB videos, which is often the most easily obtainable data in a real-world scenario.

6 Future Work

A variety of modifications to the original DTW algorithm have been presented through the years. Some have already been mentioned in Sect. 2. Others include for example methods for adding feature weighting [9], *Derivative Dynamic Time Warping (D-DTW)* [28] or *Multi-Dimensional* DTW [10]. The effect these modifications have on the performance of nearest neighbor classifiers based on warping distance is often times not obvious and also dependent on factors like noise in the signal [10]. Future research could try to work out general guidelines for when to use which variant of DTW. In addition to these fundamental algorithmic options, there are a number of other factors which can impact the classification performance parameters, such as the window size of DTW, the variance threshold or the choice of example gestures.

Only single-person gesture recognition has been regarded in this paper. Since OpenPose is also capable of detecting the poses of multiple people at once, upgrading to multi-person gesture recognition is a possible subject for future research. The *UTD-MHAD* dataset we used for our experiments was recorded in a very controlled environment, further tests should be conducted to find out how our results generalize to more realistic scenarios.

Another topic of research is how this method can be sped up, desirably up to the point where it reaches real-time capability.

References

1. Chen, C., Jafari, R., Kehtarnavaz, N.: UTD-MHAD: a multimodal dataset for human action recognition utilizing a depth camera and a wearable inertial sensor. In: 2015 IEEE International Conference on Image Processing (ICIP), pp. 168–172. IEEE (2015)
2. Gillian, N., Knapp, B., O'Modhrain, S.: Recognition of multivariate temporal musical gestures using n-dimensional dynamic time warping. In: NIME, pp. 337–342 (2011)

3. Rosa-Pujazón, A., Barbancho, I., Tardón, L.J., Barbancho, A.M.: Fast-gesture recognition and classification using Kinect: an application for a virtual reality drumkit. Multimed. Tools Appl. **75**(14), 8137–8164 (2016)
4. Jiang, F., Zhang, S., Wu, S., Gao, Y., Zhao, D.: Multi-layered gesture recognition with Kinect. J. Mach. Learn. Res. **16**(1), 227–254 (2015)
5. Ribó, A., Warchol, D., Oszust, W.: An approach to gesture recognition with skeletal data using dynamic time warping and nearest neighbour classifier. Int. J. Intell. Syst. Appl. **8**(6), 1–8 (2016)
6. Bautista, M.Á., et al.: Probability-based dynamic time warping for gesture recognition on RGB-D data. In: Jiang, X., Bellon, O.R.P., Goldgof, D., Oishi, T. (eds.) WDIA 2012. LNCS, vol. 7854, pp. 126–135. Springer, Heidelberg (2013). https://doi.org/10.1007/978-3-642-40303-3_14
7. Mitra, S., Acharya, T.: Gesture recognition: a survey. IEEE Trans. Syst. Man Cybern. Part C (Applications and Reviews) **37**(3), 311–324 (2007)
8. Kevin, N.Y.Y., Ranganath, S., Ghosh, D.: Trajectory modeling in gesturere cognition using CyberGloves® and magnetic trackers. In: 2004 IEEE Region 10 Conference TENCON 2004, pp. 571–574. IEEE, (2004)
9. Reyes, M., Dominguez, G., Escalera, S.: Feature weighting in dynamic time warping for gesture recognition in depth data. In: 2011 IEEE International Conference on Computer Vision Workshops (ICCV Workshops), pp. 1182–1188. IEEE (2011)
10. Ten Holt, G.A., Reinders, M.J., Hendriks, E.: Multi-dimensional dynamic time warping for gesture recognition. In: Thirteenth Annual Conference of the Advanced School for Computing and Imaging, vol. 300, p. 1 (2007)
11. Xi, X., Keogh, E., Shelton, C., Wei, L., Ratanamahatana, C.A.: Fast time series classification using numerosity reduction. In: Proceedings of the 23rd International Conference on Machine Learning, pp. 1033–1040. ACM (2006)
12. Bagnall, A., Lines, J., Bostrom, A., Large, J., Keogh, E.: The great time series classification bake off: a review and experimental evaluation of recent algorithmic advances. Data Min. Knowl. Discov. **31**(3), 606–660 (2017)
13. Sakoe, H., Chiba, S.: Dynamic programming algorithm optimization for spoken word recognition. IEEE Trans. Acoust. Speech Signal Process. **26**(1), 43–49 (1978)
14. Itakura, F.: Minimum prediction residual principle applied to speech recognition. IEEE Trans. Acoust. Speech Signal Process. **23**(1), 67–72 (1975)
15. Ratanamahatana, C.A., Keogh, E.: Making time-series classification more accurate using learned constraints. In: Proceedings of the 2004 SIAM International Conference on Data Mining, SIAM 2004, pp. 11–22 (2004)
16. Salvador, S., Chan, P.: Toward accurate dynamic time warping in linear time and space. Intell. Data Anal. **11**(5), 561–580 (2007)
17. Müller, M.: Information Retrieval for Music and Motion. Springer, Heidelberg (2007). https://doi.org/10.1007/978-3-540-74048-3
18. Senin, P.: Dynamic time warping algorithm review. Information and Computer Science Department University of Hawaii at Manoa Honolulu, USA, vol. 855, pp. 1–23 (2008)
19. Chai, X., Liu, Z., Yin, F., Liu, Z., Chen, X.: Two streams recurrent neural networks for large-scale continuous gesture recognition. In: 23rd International Conference on Pattern Recognition (ICPR), pp. 31–36. IEEE (2016)
20. Molchanov, P., Yang, X., Gupta, S., Kim, K., Tyree, S., Kautz, J.: Online detection and classification of dynamic hand gestures with recurrent 3D convolutional neural network. In: Proceedings of the IEEE Conference on Computer Vision and Pattern Recognition, pp. 4207–4215 (2016)

21. Liu, H., Wang, L.: Gesture recognition for human-robot collaboration: a review. Int. J. Industr. Ergon. **68**, 355–367 (2018)
22. Memmesheimer, R., Mykhalchyshyna, I., Paulus, D.: Gesture recognition on human pose features of single images. In: 2018 9th International Conference on Intelligent Systems (IS), pp. 1–7. IEEE (2018)
23. Celebi, S., Aydin, A.S., Temiz, T.T., Arici, T.: Gesture recognition using skeleton data with weighted dynamic time warping. In: VISAPP, no. 1, pp. 620–625 (2013)
24. Rwigema, J., Choi, H.-R., Kim, T.: A differential evolution approach to optimize weights of dynamic time warping for multi-sensor based gesture recognition. Sensors (Basel, Switzerland) **19**(5), 1007 (2019)
25. Wei, S.-E., Ramakrishna, V., Kanade, T., Sheikh, Y.: Convolutional pose machines. In: CVPR (2016)
26. Simon, T., Joo, H., Matthews, I., Sheikh, Y.: Hand keypoint detection in single images using multiview bootstrapping. In: CVPR (2017)
27. Cao, Z., Hidalgo, G., Simon, T., Wei, S.-E., Sheikh, Y.: OpenPose: realtime multi-person 2D pose estimation using Part Affinity Fields. arXiv preprint arXiv:1812.08008 (2018)
28. Keogh, E.J., Pazzani, M.J.: Derivative dynamic time warping. In: Proceedings of the 2001 SIAM International Conference on Data Mining, SIAM, pp. 1–11 (2001)

On the Use of Simulated Future Information for Evaluating Game Situations

Yudai Suzuki[✉] and Tomoharu Nakashima

Graduate School of Humanities and Sustainable System Sciences,
Osaka Prefecture University, Osaka, Japan
{yudai.suzuki,tomoharu.nakashima}@kis.osakafu-u.ac.jp

Abstract. A FOrward Simulation for Situation Evaluation (FOSSE) approach for evaluating game situations is proposed in this paper. FOSSE approach considers multiple future situations to quantitatively evaluate the current game situations. Since future situations are not available during an ongoing game in real time, they are generated by what is called forward simulation. Then the current game situation is evaluated using the future game situations as well as the current situation itself. First, we show the evaluation performance can be increased by using successive situations in time through preliminary experiments. Especially, the effectiveness of using future information rather than using past information is shown. Then, we present FOSSE approach where both the current and the future information of game situations are used to evaluate the current game situation. In the FOSSE approach, the future game situations are generated by forward simulation. Computational experiments are conducted to investigate the effectiveness of the proposed approach.

Keywords: Evaluating situation · Forward simulation · Recurrent Neural Network · Deep learning · Time series data · Soccer Simulation

1 Introduction

In sports, it is useful to perceive the superiority during a game. If the game situation can be evaluated quantitatively, the degree of dominance for teams can be accurately grasped. Furthermore, it is considered that the quantitative evaluation can be applied to strategy switching guidelines in a game and to the field of automatic live broadcasting of sports. However, quantitative evaluation is difficult in the dynamic game situation. For this problem, we employ machine learning method for quantitative evaluation.

As an experimental environment of this research, we use RoboCup Soccer Simulation 2D League [1]. For the metric of evaluating game situation, Pomas and Nakashima [2] proposed a metric called *SituationScore* which represents the degree of dominance in a soccer game. This paper also uses *SituationScore* with a minor modification to evaluate the game situation.

In general, only the current situation is considered when evaluating the game situation. However, since the game progresses dynamically, and accordingly the

© Springer Nature Switzerland AG 2019
S. Chalup et al. (Eds.): RoboCup 2019, LNAI 11531, pp. 294–308, 2019.
https://doi.org/10.1007/978-3-030-35699-6_23

situation drastically changes, especially in soccer, it is difficult to capture the degree of the dominance in the game with only a single situation information. In this paper, we investigate the use of multiple situations to capture the degree of the dominance in a game.

If future information is available during a game, it is possible to evaluate the game situation with higher accuracy than with only the current information as well as the past information. However, such future information is not available during an ongoing game. To solve this problem, we propose a FOrward Simulation for Situation Evaluation (FOSSE) approach for learning a machine learning model that generates future situations by simulation and then evaluates the current situation by using the generated future situations as well as the current one itself.

The proposed FOSSE approach consists of two parts. The first part is forward simulation for generating the estimated future game situations. The other one is situation evaluation for producing the value of *SituationScore* from the time series of game situations. We employ a Recurrent Neural Network (RNN) as the simulation model and a Deep Neural Network (DNN) as the evaluation model.

In the following sections, firstly, we show that the prediction accuracy of an evaluation model can be improved by using multiple-situation information comparing with a single-situation model. Secondly, the experiment using actual data shows that future information is more helpful than past information in an evaluation model. Finally, we indicate the effectiveness of the proposed method based on FOSSE approach through computational experiments.

It should be noted that the meaning of "evaluation" in this paper is to understand the field situation such as the degree of domination by a currently attacking team and the likeliness of scoring by that team. There are other research where the evaluation means the value of a state or an action in determining the next action by an individual player agent. Although the situation evaluation in this paper can also be used for such purpose in the future, this is not the focus of this paper. We focus on the evaluation of a field situation not from the view point of the soccer players who can only see the situation in their visual area, but from the view point of a coach or spectators who can watch the whole soccer field.

2   Quantitative Evaluation of Game Situations in RoboCup Soccer

We employ RoboCup Soccer Simulation 2D League [1] as the subject of study in this paper. Generally, as a measure to represent the degree of team dominance in a game, commonly used information would be the ball-possessing team and the ball location in the soccer field. However, such simple indices cannot accurately grasp the degree of team dominance. Therefore, another index that quantitatively expresses the game situation is required.

Pomas and Nakashima [2] proposed *SituationScore*, which represents the value of a game situation. In their work, a game situation is quantitatively evaluated by using time cycles until the next goal. This paper uses the same idea of *SituationScore* with a minor modification.

This section first introduces the RoboCup Soccer Simulation 2D League. Then, some modification to *SituationScore* is presented.

2.1   RoboCup Soccer Simulation 2D League

RoboCup [1] is a research project that focuses on the development of robotics and artificial intelligence. There are various leagues in this project. RoboCup Soccer Simulation 2D League is one of such leagues. It does not use real soccer robots but simulated soccer players. The players are represented by a two-dimensional circle as shown in Fig. 1. They play soccer in a two-dimensional virtual soccer field that is set up on a computer. The positions of the players and the ball are represented as a two-dimensional vector. Each player is programmed as an independent agent unlike a video soccer game where there is one central system that control all the objects such as all players. A game consists of 6,000 time cycles and one cycle is discretized in 0.1 s. When the game is over, a game log is generated in which all the game information such as the position coordinates of the player and the ball in each cycle are included.

2.2   Modification to *SituationScore*

Pomas and Nakashima [2] proposed a metric called *SituationScore*. This metric represents the value of a game situation. The value of *SituationScore* increases as the game situation is close to the time of goal scoring. In its original definition, the maximum value of *SituationScore* was 100 (when the left team scores), and the minimum value was −100 (when the right team scores). In the original definition of *SituationScore*, the superiority and inferiority of the teams are considered for all the time cycles. However, it is difficult to predict the value of *SituationScore* when it is close to zero, which is a boundary situation between the superiority and the inferiority of the teams. Due to this problem, some changes were made to *SituationScore* in this paper so that the lower limit is set to 0 assuming that *SituationScore* presents only the degree of dominance of either one team. Also, because it was also difficult to correctly predict the value of situations far from the goal, we only consider those situations where a goal is scored within 50 time cycles. As a result, in this paper, we slightly modify the definition of *SituationScore* as follows:

$$SituationScore(t) = 50 - n, \tag{1}$$

where n represents the number of remaining cycles from t until the next score. In this paper, the range of *SituationScore* is $0 \leq SituationScore \leq +50$, which means that we only consider the goals by the left team. The value of *SituationScore* for the right team can be separately defined by switching the sign of the value (i.e., positive to negative). Figure 2 shows an example game situation which is nine time cycles before the left team scores a goal along with its *SituationScore*.

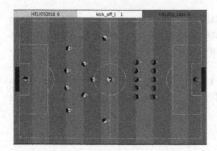

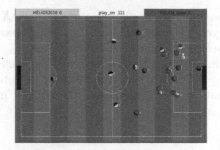

Fig. 1. Game screen of the RoboCup Soccer Simulation 2D League.

Fig. 2. Situation that is nine time cycles before the left team scores. The value of *SituationScore* is +41.

2.3 Dataset

The dataset in the computational experiments in this paper was generated by the following steps:

1. A game between HELIOS2018 [3] and agent2d [4] is performed for a specified number of times.
2. The log files of the games are analyzed by using Python scripts to detect at which cycles goals were scored.
3. The numerical information of the soccer field for 50 time cycles before each goal of the left team (i.e., HELIOS2018 [3]) are recorded as well as their corresponding *SituationScore* values. The recorded information is saved in a file for each of the time cycles. The numerical information includes the position of 22 players and the ball. The value of *SituationScore* is calculated as in (1). This *SituationScore* value is used as the ground truth for the situation evaluation.

A dataset containing the numerical field information for about 394,350 time cycles was constructed from 1,000 games. This dataset was then split into three parts as follows: training data ($5,490 \times 50$ time cycles), validation data (788×50 time cycles), and test data ($1,609 \times 50$ time cycles). In the rest of this paper, we use this dataset for all experiments.

3 Situation Evaluation with Multiple Situations

3.1 Evaluation Model

This section presents the investigation into the effect of using multiple situations on the accuracy of the trained model for situation evaluation. We employ a simple DNN as an evaluation model of game situations. This model produces the value of *SituationScore* at time cycle t. The overview of the DNN model is shown in Fig. 3. In this figure, X is the information of the game situation such as the position of the players and the ball. X_t is the information of the current (time cycle t) game state. X_{t-n_p} is the past state information (i.e., n_p time cycles before the current time cycle). X_{t+n_f} is the future state information (i.e., n_f time cycles after the current time cycle).

Numerical experiments are conducted in the next subsection in order to evaluate the performance of the trained model with various combination of input game situations.

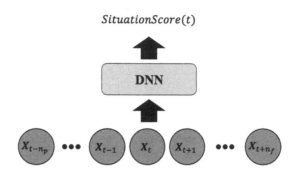

Fig. 3. The overview of deep neural network.

3.2   Experiment

Experimental Settings. The purpose of the experiments in this section is to examine the usefulness of using multiple field information with successive time cycles for evaluating the field situation (i.e., predicting the value of *SituationScore*). We compare the following four models with different combinations of game situations for the input of the DNN.

Model 1: Single situation (only the current game situation)
Model 2: Multiple situations (the current, past, and future game situations)
Model 3: Multiple situations (the current and past game situations)
Model 4: Multiple situations (the current and future game situations)

Each architecture is shown in Figs. 4, 5, 6 and 7. The number of hidden layers is fixed to 20 for all models, each hidden layer has 16 units, and the layers are fully-connected. For the training of the DNNs, we set the batch size to 64, and used Adam [5] optimizer with the initial learning rate $= 0.001, \beta_1 = 0.9, \beta_2 = 0.999$. Table 1 indicates the experimental settings. The dimensionality of input data in each situation is one of the following three types: two (the $x - y$ coordinates of the ball position), 24 (the $x - y$ coordinates of the ball position and the left team player's positions), and 46 (the $x - y$ coordinates of the ball position and the all player's positions). Past and future information of 5 time cycles are used for Models 2, 3, and 4.

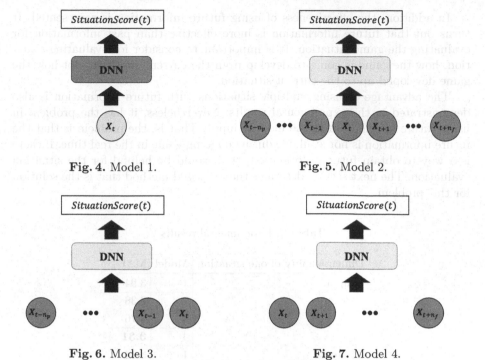

Fig. 4. Model 1.

Fig. 5. Model 2.

Fig. 6. Model 3.

Fig. 7. Model 4.

Table 1. Experimental settings.

Input data	Single situation (current)
	Multiple situations (current, past, and future)
	Multiple situations (current and past)
	Multiple situations (current and future)
Dimensionality for one situation	2 inputs (Ball pos)
	24 inputs (Ball pos, Left team's player pos)
	46 inputs (Ball pos, All player pos)
Output	SituationScore

We use Mean Absolute Error (MAE) as the quality measure of the trained model's accuracy.

Results. The experimental results are shown in Table 2. This table shows the effectiveness of using multiple situations compared with single situation. We can see that Model 1 with only a single situation (i.e., the current game situation) for input produced the largest value of MAE for all experimental settings. This is because the dominance trend in the dynamic game is captured by using multiple situations.

In addition, the effectiveness of using future information is represented. It turns out that future information is more effective than past information for evaluating the game situation. It is important to consider for evaluating situation, how the game is going to develop from the current situation, not how the game developed up to the current situation.

The advantage of using multiple situations with future information is also demonstrated in the experimental results. Nevertheless, it has the problem in using future information as the model's input. That is, the problem is that the future information is not available during ongoing game in the real time. If there is a way to obtain future information, that would be helpful for the situation evaluation. The next section describes the proposed method that is the solution for this problem.

Table 2. Experimental results.

Dimensionality of one situation	Model	MAE
2 inputs	1	3.94
	2	3.38
	3	3.76
	4	**3.31**
24 inputs	1	3.84
	2	3.36
	3	3.57
	4	**3.11**
46 inputs	1	3.51
	2	3.32
	3	3.45
	4	**3.07**

4   FOSSE Approach for Evaluating Field Situation

4.1   FOSSE Approach

In the last section, it was shown that using past and future multiple situations helps enhance the performance of the trained model for situation evaluation. Especially, using future situations produced the best accuracy among the considered four models. There is, however, a problem in real-time application that the future information is not available during an ongoing game. To solve this problem, we propose FOSSE (FOward Simulation for Situation Evaluation) approach. Figure 8 shows the overview of FOSSE approach. This approach consists of two parts: forward simulation part and situation evaluation part. The forward simulation part generates the estimation of the future information from the current and the past game situations. Using the generated future information as well as the past and the current field information, the situation evaluation part produces the value of *SituationScore* at time cycle t. The following subsections explain each part of FOSSE approach.

In this section, firstly, we explain forward simulation in detail. Secondly, we explain the method to evaluate situation by FOSSE approach. Finally, the computational experiments are conducted to show the effectiveness of the proposed methods.

4.2   Forward Simulation

The forward simulation part is shown Fig. 9. The forward simulation takes the past situations as input and generates the estimated field situation of the future.

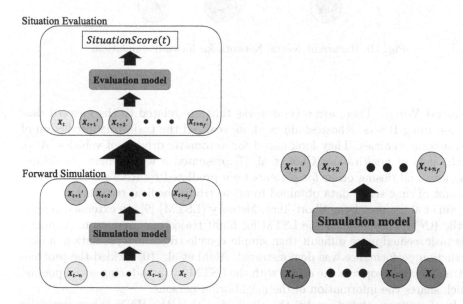

Fig. 8. FOSSE approach.   **Fig. 9.** Forward simulation.

Recurrent Neural Network. RNN is a type of neural networks that deals with time series data through its iterative use. It takes the output vector from the previous RNN block at time $t-1$ and the game situation at time cycle t as input. The output vector is used as the input of the next RNN block at time $t+1$. The future game situations are simulated through the above process. This process is called forward simulation for predicting the field situation of future time cycles (i.e., the future game situations). This process is shown in Fig. 10. This figure shows the process of generating the future game situation at time cycle $t+1$ with a time series of previous game situations from time cycle $t-n$ to time cycle t. Each piece of information in the time series $\{\boldsymbol{X}_{t-n}, \ldots, \boldsymbol{X}_t\}$ is processed by the same block. The block is generally represented as a hidden layer of the RNN. After the last piece of the time series is processed by the block, the estimated next situation is generated after a fully-connected layer (FC).

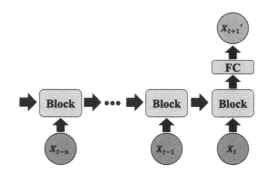

Fig. 10. Recurrent Neural Network for forward simulation.

Related Work. There are several works that are related to the forward simulation using RNNs. Khosroshahi et al. [6] realized the trajectory prediction of surrounding vehicles. They look ahead for automatic driving of vehicles. Also, in the field of health care, Choi et al. [7] presented a work where physicians' diagnosis and dosing order for patients were predicted by RNNs using the vast amount of time series data obtained from electronic medical records.

Shi et al. [8] uses Long Short-Term Memory (LSTM) [9], an extended version of the RNN. They applied the LSTM for flight trajectory prediction. Although this task seemed more difficult than simple vehicle trajectory prediction, a high prediction performance was demonstrated. Alahi et al. [10] tackled the problem of tracking the people in the crowd with the LSTM by introducing social pooling which shares the information of the neighboring persons.

In the above related works, they indicated that the RNN can successfully predict future situations from time series data. Furthermore, they also indicated that the effectiveness of the LSTM even in the difficult tasks. Based on these discussions, this paper also employs the LSTM as an architecture of RNN for the forward simulation part (i.e., we use the LSTM for the iterative block in Fig. 10).

Experiment. In the computational experiments of this subsection, we investigate the accuracy of the forward simulation using the LSTM. Specifically, we investigate the prediction accuracy of the future game situation that are generated by iteratively applying the trained LSTM. For training the LSTM model we set batch size to 512 and used Adam optimizer [5] with the initial learning rate = $0.001, \beta_1 = 0.9, \beta_2 = 0.999$. The LSTM generates a 512-dimensional output vector after taking a single-situation information and the output from the previous

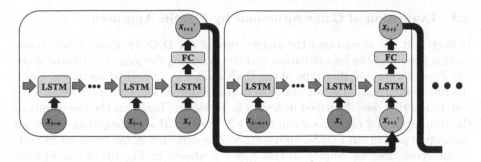

Fig. 11. The architecture of forward simulation by using LSTM.

LSTM block as the input for the next LSTM block. The output vector is used as a part of input for the next LSTM.

In the computational experiments, the number of generated future field situations by the forward simulation is specified to the number of the past situations in the input time series. Figure 11 shows this procedure. For example in the case of four past situations, first, the four past situations X_{t-4}, X_{t-3}, X_{t-2}, X_{t-1}, and the current situation X_t are given as the input to the model in order to generate the estimated next situation X'_{t+1}. A full-connection layer (FC) is used to generate the estimated next situation X_{t+1} after processing the last piece of the input time series. Then, X'_{t+2} is predicted with another five situations of X_{t-3}, X_{t-2}, X_{t-1}, X_t, X'_{t+1} (i.e., the predicted values in the last iteration). This procedure is repeated four times to finally generate the estimated future game situation X'_{t+4}. The error between the last predicted X'_{t+4} and the actual value is investigated. Evaluation of the each models is made based on MAE between the model's output and the ground truth of each of the corresponding objects' positions.

Table 3 indicates the results of the experiment. The results show that the prediction for three situations has less error than that for five situations. As a matter of course, the results indicate that prediction is more difficult as the number of situations increases, since the predicted values is repeatedly stacked as input instead of actual values.

Table 3. Experimental results of forward simulation using LSTM.

# of situations	Dimensionality of one field information	MAE
Three	2 inputs	1.27
	24 inputs	0.67
	46 inputs	0.62
Five	2 inputs	1.89
	24 inputs	1.12
	46 inputs	1.34

4.3   Evaluation of Game Situations by FOSSE Approach

In Sect. 3, it was shown that the architecture of the DNN that uses future information produced the best situation evaluation among the four investigated models. Thus, we employ that type of the DNN model as an evaluation model. Since the future information is not available during a game, we estimate it by forward simulation that was described in Sect. 4.2. Moreover, based on the the results of the computational experiments in Sect. 4.2, the LSTM is employed as a forward simulation part in our FOSSE architecture. The overview of the resultant FOSSE architecture that we employ in this paper is shown in Fig. 12. In our FOSSE architecture, a field situation is evaluated by using the predicted future information (i.e., $X'_{t+1}, \ldots, X'_{t+n_f}$) generated by forward simulation. The DNN model and the RNN model are separately constructed. In the forward simulation, the LSTM model predicts the field situation of the next time cycle as shown the bottom part of Fig. 12. Then, in the situation evaluation part, the $SituationScore$ of the current game situation is estimated using the current game situation as well as the estimated future game situations that are generated by the forward simulation.

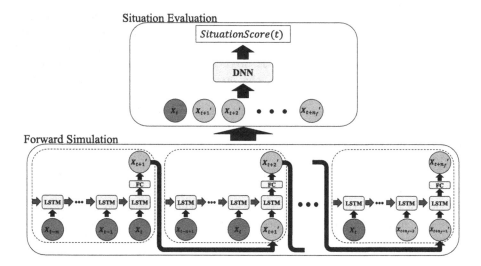

Fig. 12. The overview of our FOSSE architecture with DNN and LSTM.

4.4   Experiment

Experimental Settings. Table 4 indicates the settings of the models that are used in the computational experiment in this section. We compare the accuracy performance of four trained DNN models using single situation, multiple past situations, multiple future situations, and multiple predicted future situations (i.e., the proposed method).

Table 4. Experimental settings of evaluating situation.

Input	Single
	Past+current (Multiple-Past)
	Future+current (Multiple-Future)
	Predicted future+current (Multiple-Predict)
Dimensionality per situation	2 inputs (Ball pos.)
	24 inputs (Ball pos. and Left team's player pos.)
	46 inputs (Ball pos. and All player pos.)
# of input situations	1, 3, 5

Results. Table 5 shows the results of the experiments. It is shown that higher accuracy is demonstrated by the proposed method than using the field situation of a single situation. Besides, the performance of the proposed method is better than using multiple past situations when the field situations of three successive time cycles are used as input. As a result, it is shown that evaluation using predicted future situations by simulation model is more useful in the situation evaluation than using already-known past situations. Although using multiple future situations leads to a high accuracy of the trained model, this is only ideal because the future information is not available at the current time. Thus, using multiple future situations is not a real option for model building in real-time games. On the other hand, the proposed method can be used during ongoing games because the field situation of future time cycles is generated by forward simulation.

On the contrary, when the field situations of five successive time cycles are used, the proposed method outperforms using single situation. This, however, cannot show an effectiveness compared with the model using past situations. This is considered to be due to the fact that the error of the forward simulation model's output increases as the number of situations increases as described in Sect. 4.2. Although this paper employs a simple simulation model, it can be expected that the accuracy will be improved by elaborating more on the forward simulation model. The improvement of the forward simulation model is left for our future work.

The results of the computational experiments show the effectiveness of the proposed method that evaluates the situation combined with forward simulation. Accurate evaluation of game situations is important for the victory in many sports, not just in soccer. The other sports can be also benefitted by the FOSSE approach in evaluating the game situations.

Table 5. Experimental results (FOSSE model).

Dimensionality	Input	MAE (# of time cycles)		
		One	Three	Five
2 inputs	Single	3.94	-	-
	Multiple-Past	-	3.70	3.76
	Multiple-Future	-	3.33	3.31
	Multiple-Predict	-	3.63	3.77
24 inputs	Single	3.84	-	-
	Multiple-Past	-	3.62	3.57
	Multiple-Future	-	3.35	3.11
	Multiple-Predict	-	3.55	3.59
46 inputs	Single	3.51	-	-
	Multiple-Past	-	3.53	3.45
	Multiple-Future	-	3.28	3.07
	Multiple-Predict	-	3.44	4.09

5   Conclusion

In this paper, we proposed FOSSE approach for evaluating game situation of RoboCup Soccer Simulation 2D League. Three contributions in evalating a game situation were presented. The first contribution is to show the effectiveness of using the field situations of multiple time cycles rather than only a single situation. The second contribution is to show that future information is more valuable than past information. The third contribution, which is the main contribution, is to propose FOSSE approach where simulated future information was generated by forward simulation. The FOSSE approach consists of two parts: Forward simulation part and situation evaluation part.

In our FOSSE approach, a DNN with multiple future situations was used as the situation evaluation part, and the LSTM was used for the forward simulation part. From the computational experiments, the effectiveness of our model was shown. This achievement allows us to evaluate the game situation during the ongoing game in real time. It is expected that the FOSSE approach can be applied to other sports as well as soccer such as rugby and basket ball.

The idea of this approach is similar to human thinking processes. People often unconsciously perform forward simulation when evaluating the situation in real life. When humans guess *SituationScore* in a certain situation, it has possibility that they consider not only the current game situation but also expected future game situations. If it is proved that the proposed method is the same process as human thought process, it is considered effective to reproduce human thinking process by machine learning method.

6 Future Work

This paper conducted the computational experiments with only two teams. That is, only two teams were involved in the generation of training and test datasets. Considering the practical application where various teams are involved in a tournament, it is necessary to show that the proposed method works in general for any other teams. In the future, we will investigate the generalization of the proposed method. That is, it is necessary to examine the performance of the trained model to unknown teams that are not included in the generation process of the training dataset.

Furthermore, as already mentioned in the experiments of Sect. 4.4, it is necessary to consider improving the prediction accuracy of the forward simulation. For instance, different architectures of the forward simulation model and evaluation situation model can be used by increasing the number of hidden layers or by changing the number of situations for the input. Another idea is to adapt the FOSSE approach for accommodating field image data because it was indicated in [2] that using image data could lead to a better accuracy performance in evaluating game situations. In addition, we will consider machine learning method that computationally realizes human thinking processes. Incorporating human thought processes into machine learning method has the potential to contribute to the development of artificial intelligence.

Ultimately, we would like to implement it on the RoboCup soccer team and apply it as an indicator of tactical switching during the game. In addition to that, we would like to apply it for enhancing the game-watching experience, which is not related to the implementation of a team.

References

1. Kitano, H., Asada, M., Kuniyoshi, Y., Noda, I., Osawa, E., Matsubara, H.: RoboCup: a challenge problem for AI. AI Mag. **18**(1), 73–85 (1997)
2. Pomas, T., Nakashima, T.: Evaluation of situations in RoboCup 2D simulations using soccer field images. In: Holz, D., Genter, K., Saad, M., von Stryk, O. (eds.) RoboCup 2018. LNCS (LNAI), vol. 11374, pp. 275–286. Springer, Cham (2019). https://doi.org/10.1007/978-3-030-27544-0_23
3. Akiyama, H., Nakashima, T., Suzuki, Y., Ohori, A., Fukushima, T.: HELIOS2018: team description paper. In: RoboCup 2018, Montreal, p. 6 (2018)
4. Akiyama, H., Nakashima, T.: HELIOS base: an open source package for the RoboCup soccer 2D simulation. In: Behnke, S., Veloso, M., Visser, A., Xiong, R. (eds.) RoboCup 2013. LNCS (LNAI), vol. 8371, pp. 528–535. Springer, Heidelberg (2014). https://doi.org/10.1007/978-3-662-44468-9_46
5. Kingma, D.P., Ba, J.: Adam: a method for stochastic optimization. In: Proceedings of the International Conference on Learning Representations (2015)
6. Khosroshahi, A., Ohn-Bar, E., Trivedi, M.M.: Surround vehicles trajectory analysis with recurrent neural networks. In: Proceedings of the IEEE 19th Conference on Intelligent Transportation Systems (ITSC), pp. 2267–2271 (2016)
7. Choi, E., Bahadori, M.T., Schuetz, A., Stewart, W.F., Sun, J.: Doctor AI: predicting clinical events via recurrent neural networks. In: Proceedings of the Machine Learning for Healthcare 2016, pp. 301–318 (2016)

8. Shi, Z., Xu, M., Pan, Q., Yan, B., Zhang, H.: LSTM-based flight trajectory prediction. In: Proceedings of the 2018 International Joint Conference on Neural Networks (IJCNN), pp. 1–8 (2018)
9. Hochreiter, S., Schmidhuber, J.: Long short-term memory. J. Neural Comput. 9(8), 1735–1780 (1997)
10. Alahi, A., Goel, K., Ramanathan, V., Robicquet, A., Li, F.-F., Savarese, S.: Social LSTM : human trajectory prediction in crowded space. In: Proceedings of the IEEE Conference on Computer Vision and Pattern Recognition, pp. 961–971 (2016)

ROBO: Robust, Fully Neural Object Detection for Robot Soccer

Marton Szemenyei[1]($\boxtimes$) and Vladimir Estivill-Castro[2]

[1] Budapest University of Technology and Economics, Budapest, Hungary
szemenyei@iit.bme.hu
[2] Griffith University, Brisbane, QLD, Australia

Abstract. Deep Learning has become exceptionally popular in the last few years due to its success in computer vision [1–3] and other fields of AI [4–6]. However, deep neural networks are computationally expensive, which limits their application in low power embedded systems, such as mobile robots. In this paper, an efficient neural network architecture is proposed for the problem of detecting relevant objects in robot soccer environments. The ROBO model's increase in efficiency is achieved by exploiting the peculiarities of the environment. Compared to the state-of-the-art Tiny YOLO model, the proposed network provides approximately 35 times decrease in run time, while achieving superior average precision, although at the cost of slightly worse localization accuracy.

Keywords: Computer vision · Deep learning · Object detection

1 Introduction

Object detection is one of the fundamental tasks of computer vision, since accurately localizing and classifying relevant objects is a necessary component of scene understanding. Deep learning-based methods have achieved considerable success lately, and dominated this field in the last few years [2,3,7]. While these methods can provide state-of-the-art performance, their high computational requirements limit their use in low-power embedded systems.

In this paper, we present a fully neural object detection system for the Nao v6 robot, capable of detecting four object classes relevant to robot soccer (ball, line crossing, goalpost and robot) simultaneously. To achieve this, we propose the ROBO object detection architecture, which is based on the popular Tiny YOLOv3 model. ROBO exploits the idiosyncrasies of the robot soccer environment to provide a considerable (approximately 35 times) decrease in run time compared to the Tiny YOLOv3 method, while achieving superior accuracy.

The networks are pre-trained on a synthetic database, and subsequently fine-tuned and evaluated on a smaller real dataset. For the fine-tuning step, we propose a novel training method, called synthetic transfer learning, which allows us better convergence by only retraining the first few layers of the network.

© Springer Nature Switzerland AG 2019
S. Chalup et al. (Eds.): RoboCup 2019, LNAI 11531, pp. 309–322, 2019.
https://doi.org/10.1007/978-3-030-35699-6_24

During fine-tuning, the networks are pruned using L1 regularization for further improvement in speed.

We evaluate three slightly different versions of the ROBO architecture on our database demonstrating their superior speed and accuracy compared with the Tiny YOLOv3 model. We also demonstrate the effects of pruning and synthetic transfer learning. Our code for training, the databases used, and several pre-trained models are available online [8].

2 Previous Work

Deep neural networks have become a widely-used and powerful solution to numerous machine learning problems. The renewed interest in DNNs was largely sparked by the dramatic increase in the availability of high quality datasets and computational resources. The lack of these was one of the major barriers to training deep neural networks, in addition to some numerical problems [9]. Their applications are countless, ranging from natural language processing problems such as translation [4] or question-answering [5] to implementing Turing machines [6]. The use of deep learning is perhaps most prominent in the field of computer vision, where deep neural networks are used for standard classification [1] and object detection [2]. Lately, the applications expanded to several more complex areas, such as image captioning [10], translation and generation [11].

2.1 Object Detection

Deep learning detection methods can be divided into two categories: region-based methods, such as Faster-RCNN [2], and single-shot detectors, such as YOLO [3] or SSD [12]. Region-based methods first create object proposals using a region proposal network (RPN), followed by a classification step determining the type of object in the region. These methods usually have higher run time, and can be extended for instance segmentation [13].

One of the important additions of Faster-RCNN was the introduction of anchor boxes. Anchor boxes are basically template for the object bounding boxes, derived from the training dataset using clustering. During the region proposal step and the prediction of the final bounding box, the box parameters are estimated relatively to the anchor box. This solution helps the numeric convergence of these methods greatly, and was adopted by single-shot detectors as well [7].

Single-shot detectors skip the region proposal step, and predict the bounding box and class of the objects directly from the feature map. The YOLO [7] architecture for instance, makes k (the number of anchor boxes) object predictions for each cell in the downscaled feature map using a 1×1 convolutional layer. In order to avoid false detections, every prediction includes an *objectness* score signaling whether there is an actual object at that location. This means, that from every cell $k * (5 + N_{class})$ numbers are predicted. Every object must be predicted by the cell that contains its center, while the bounding box is predicted relative to the cell coordinates and the kth anchor box. To avoid multiple detections, non maximum-suppression is employed.

YOLO is a considerably faster, if less accurate object detection method, which tends to struggle with accurately predicting small objects. To resolve this, the v3 version of the architecture uses upscaling layers and makes predictions at multiple scales [14], similarly to the SSD method. YOLO also includes a smaller version, called Tiny YOLO [7,14], which uses a medium-sized convolutional base network, allowing it to run real-time on some embedded GPU platforms.

2.2   Computer Vision in Robot Soccer

The stated goal of RoboCup Soccer is to design a team of autonomous robots that are able to defeat the world champion soccer team using FIFA rules by the middle of the 21st century. Achieving human-level vision and scene understanding is an essential component of achieving this goal. In accordance with this insight, the RoboCup environment has steadily changed from featuring objects that are easy to recognize using low-level features, such as color, to ones that greatly resemble the actual objects used in human soccer.

The vision pipelines used by the competing teams have changed in tandem, going from human-engineered vision methods [15,16] to pipelines relying increasingly on machine learning. Several teams have used convolutional neural networks either for binary classification tasks [17,18] or to detect several relevant object categories [19,20]. Houliston and Chalup [21] used a technique called Visual Mesh to improve the performance of neural networks at multiple scales. These methods, however, use CNNs for classification only, therefore they still require a separate object proposal method, and the quality of the system may largely depend on the efficiency of the algorithm used to generate candidates for classification. A further disadvantage is that running the same neural network on potentially overlapping image regions is wasteful, since the same features are computed twice.

One of the most important advances of recent years is the work published by Hess et al. [22] in which they present a high-quality virtual RoboCup environment created in Unreal Engine. Using their work allows one to easily create large datasets of realistic images of a soccer field along with pixel-level semantic labeling. Since the performance of a trained neural network is highly dependent on the quality and quantity of the training data, and creating a large hand-labeled database is highly time-consuming, their work was profoundly valuable for our research. Notably, Dijk and Scheunemann [23] used a deep neural network to perform semantic segmentation on limited hardware. Their solution is capable of detecting balls and goalposts at multiple resolutions in real-time.

Last year, we proposed the first fully neural general scene understanding system [24]. This neural network was a semantic segmentation model that could detect the same four relevant categories, while running at 2–3 fps on the Nao v5 robot. By using optical flow to propagate labels between images the frame rate of the detection system could be increased to 12 fps. Also, the network was pruned [25] after fine-tuning to decrease the number of computations required.

However, the method of weight pruning did not use the advanced methods [26] to determine which weights should be pruned.

This solution had two major disadvantages: First, the decoder part of a semantic segmentation network effectively doubles the number of computations required, making this solution unnecessarily slow. Second, due to the pixel-wise classification loss, the network struggles to detect small objects, reducing the distance at which it can detect the ball.

3 The ROBO Architecture

The proposed ROBO model is heavily influenced by the popular Tiny YOLO [7] architecture. Tiny YOLO is a fully convolutional network with a stride of 32, meaning that if given a standard 416×416 input image, the output activation array has spatial dimensions of 13×13. The final layer of the model is a 1×1 convolutional layer predicting B bounding boxes at every location (grid cell). Each bounding box has $5 + N_c$ parameters, which are the center coordinates, width and height of the bounding box, the confidence score, and the N_c class scores.

Tiny YOLO also uses so-called anchor boxes, reference bounding boxes, acquired by running clustering on the boxes in the training set. The width and height of the bounding boxes are predicted relatively to one of the B anchor boxes. The center coordinates are predicted relatively to the grid cell. Predicting a certain object is the responsibility of the output with the most similar anchor box at the grid cell that contains the center of the object.

3.1 Improving the Model Efficiency

Despite its name, Tiny YOLO is a medium-sized network, with 20 layers (including pooling), some of which have 512 or even 1024 channels. This network was designed to perform well on complex datasets, like the Pascal VOC or COCO. To use such a large network for object detection in the robot soccer setting would be an overkill. Therefore, we propose the ROBO architecture, which is a 16 layer, fully convolutional network with the deepest convolutional layer having only 256 channels. This reduction in the number of channels is justified, since the robot soccer environment is considerably less complex and less varied than generic object recognition.

The ROBO architecture also replaces the max pooling layers in Tiny YOLO with strided convolution. This is due to the fact that max pooling discards spatial information, which reduces the performance of neural networks even for tasks where the spatial information is considerably less important, such as classification [27]. Arguably the effect of using max pooling is even worse for detection. To further allow the network to preserve some spatial information during downscaling, every strided convolutional layer increases the number of channels. Furthermore, this increases the complexity of the learnable features, since ROBO's network base has 15 subsequent convolutions, while Tiny YOLO only has 9 and 11 for its two outputs respectively.

To further increase the model's speed, the input image is downscaled aggressively. The first three layers of the network are all strided convolution, thus the spatial dimensions of the feature maps are reduced eightfold by the time the first conventional convolutional layer is applied. The total stride of the network (the ratio between the spatial size of input and output) is increased from 32 to 64, making the final part of the network four times faster. Notably, the aggressive downscaling and increased stride should in theory decrease the network's accuracy for smaller objects, the replacement of max pooling should counter that to some extent.

The ROBO architecture also exploits the fixed aspect ratio of the Nao robot's camera. All variants of YOLO are prepared for images of all size and shape, requiring a complex preprocessing step, where all images are padded and resized to 416 × 416. This is rather wasteful, however, since a fair share of the computation is wasted on padded parts of the image. On the other hand, the Nao robots have a 4:3 ratio camera, meaning that we can choose a fixed resolution of $k * 64 * (4 \times 3)$, where k is a positive integer to ensure that no pixel information or computation is wasted. In this paper, we chose $k = 2$, which results in an input resolution of 512 × 384.

3.2   Exploiting the Environment

Finally, the ROBO architecture also exploits prior knowledge about the relevant objects and their arrangement to make simplifications to the final layer of the model. The algorithm exploits the following properties of soccer fields:

- There are four classes (ball, line crossing, robot, goalpost)
- There is a limited number of all classes in the field
- Objects of the same class are not cluttered (robots are mild exceptions to this rule)
- Objects of the same class have similarly shaped bounding boxes (robots are mild exceptions to this rule, since they might fall over)

For the above reason, the ROBO model uses class-specific anchor boxes, meaning that from each cell on the final 8×6 grid, it makes exactly one prediction for each class. The anchor boxes are also computed separately per class by simply averaging the bounding box widths and heights (our method removes the need for clustering). Since the index of the anchor box now determines the class, the classification scores can be removed, meaning that our network has $N_{class} * 5 = 20$ outputs. This change simplifies both the loss function and the inference process somewhat, since the classification loss no longer has to be calculated, and non-maximum suppression is no longer necessary during training.

Since robots are mild exceptions to some of the rules above, we experimented with allocating 2 anchor boxes for the robot class, instead of just one. However, this did not yield noticeably different results, as even the single-box version was able to detect robot objects accurately. In the cluttered-robots scenario the model often predicts a single bounding box that encompasses both robots. In our opinion, correcting this minor issue is not worth the added complexity.

Finally, we changed the output logic of Tiny YOLO slightly: instead of upscaling the final feature layer of the network to produce an upscaled output, we simply produce the upscaled output from an earlier layer in the network. Also, instead of predicting all four classes at both outputs, the original output is responsible for predicting robots and goalposts, while the upscaled one predicts balls and crossings only. Our primary reason for doing this is that the ball and crossing classes are usually much smaller than the other two, so predicting them from a higher resolution feature map will increase the localization accuracy considerably.

For our experiments, we also made a slightly different version of ROBO, called ROBO-Bottleneck, or ROBO-BN for short. In this architecture, we doubled the number of channels in every convolutional layer. To account for the higher number of parameters and computational cost, we added 1×1 bottleneck convolutional layers to reduce the number of channels before 3×3 convolutions. The ROBO and ROBO-BN architectures are shown in Fig. 1.

4   Training

Our training procedure consists of two phases: First, the neural network is pre-trained on a large synthetic dataset, then the network is fine-tuned on a smaller dataset consisting of real images. The synthetic dataset was created using the Unreal Engine project published by Hess et al. [22]. First, we created 5000 test images, using 500 scene parameter (carpet color, lighting, color temperature, etc.) variations, and 10 different scene arrangements for each. Then, we created a test set with 1250 images using 250 scene parameter sets and 5 arrangements per set. Both the parameter sets and the arrangements were generated randomly. Annotations were generated for each image automatically using the object label map generated by the engine. Bounding boxes below a certain size threshold were discarded.

A smaller real dataset was also created, with training and test sets of approximately 550 and 160 images respectively. The images were collected from four locations, including the 2017 and 2018 RoboCup venues, an outdoors venue in Melbourne, and the field set up in the MIPAL lab in Brisbane. The train and validation sets were split randomly. Both datasets contain annotations for all four relevant object classes. The images are VGA resolution, and are converted to the YUV color space.

4.1   The Training Method

Aside from the network architecture, we made a few changes to the YOLO training method as well. The training is performed using the Adam optimizer with a learning rate of 10^{-3}. We use a cosine annealing-based learning rate

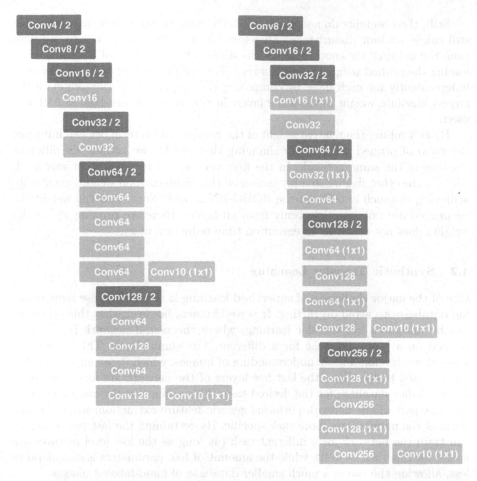

Fig. 1. The ROBO (left) and the ROBO-BN (right) architectures

schedule, with a minimal learning rate of $5 * 10^{-5}$. The training is ran for a total of 125 epochs. Moreover, we shuffle the training data before dividing them into minibatches of 64 images to further improve the stability of the optimization. We also use data augmentation to avoid overfitting: random horizontal flipping, and random variations of brightness, contrast, saturation and hue are applied to the images.

The most important change of our training method is the application of L1 regularization to the weights [28]. While L1 regularization is primarily a way to avoid overfitting, it has a desirable side effect: sparsifying the network's weight matrices. While most state-of-the-art methods of pruning devote considerable computational expense to find the least influential weights, using L1 regularization ensures that the majority of the weights are already effectively zero and can be pruned without affecting the network at all [28].

Still, these weights do not become exactly zero, therefore deleting them may still cause a minor disturbance. Therefore, after setting them to zero, we fine-tune the network for another 10 epochs using a learning rate of $5 * 10^{-5}$, while forcing the pruned weights to remain zero. The weights to be pruned are selected independently for each layer by comparing the magnitude of the weight to the largest absolute weight in the same layer. In this paper, a threshold of 0.01 was used.

By controlling the relative weight of the regularization term, we can influence the ratio of pruned weights. By changing this weight, we trained six different versions of the same network. In the first version, no regularization was used, while in the other five we steadily increased the regularization weight, eventually achieving as much as 97% on the ROBO-BN model. Note, that the weights to be pruned are not selected evenly from all layers, therefore pruning $x\%$ of the weights does not result in an execution time reduction of $x\%$.

4.2   Synthetic Transfer Learning

One of the major challenges of supervised learning is the need to use large training databases to avoid overfitting. It is well known, however, that this problems can be mitigated via transfer learning, where the neural network is first pre-trained on a large database for a different, but similar task. This allows the network to develop a basic understanding of images, which it can apply to other image-based tasks. Then, the last few layers of the network are fine-tuned on a much smaller database for the desired task. This scheme works mainly because the first part of the network performs generic feature extraction, while the last parts of the network are more task specific. By retraining the last part only, we can train the network for a different task (as long as the low level features are useful for this task as well), while the amount of free parameters is considerably less, allowing the use of a much smaller database of hand-labeled images.

Our training scheme is somewhat similar to transfer learning, in that we first pre-train the network on a large database, then we fine-tune it on a smaller one. The main difference in our case is that both databases are for the same object detection task, but come from different sources. As high quality and realistic the synthetic images may be, the distribution of their pixel values is fundamentally different from the real images. Also, the real images have complex, cluttered backgrounds, which can easily be confused with relevant foreground classes.

For the above reasons, we propose a different transfer learning scheme, in which the first few layer weights are retrained on the second database instead of the last few. We argue that this scheme is reasonable, since the first few layers of the network are responsible for extracting features from the image. We might also want to fine-tune middle-level layers to allow the network to learn more complex backgrounds. Note, that in most convolutional neural networks (including ROBO), the first few layers of the network contain much fewer parameters than the last few. This allows us to retrain more layers with similar amounts of data without overfitting, than is the standard transfer learning case.

5   Experimental Results

We evaluated the trained networks on both datasets, computing the Mean Average Precision (mAP) of the detections. We compared the Tiny YOLO v3 network with the proposed architectures, and also examined the effect of pruning. We used three model versions: ROBO, ROBO-BN and ROBO-HR, which is a cheaper, low-resolution (256×192) variant of ROBO. ROBO-HR is identical to ROBO, except the first strided convolutional layer is removed, ensuring that the outputs of the two models have the same scale. We determined the approximate number of operations required to run these models, and measured the average achievable FPS value of the entire vision pipeline on the Nao v5 robot using a single core.

5.1   Comparison of Detection Accuracy

We evaluated the models using several different Intersection over Union (IoU) thresholds. This threshold determines the minimum IoU value between the predicted and the ground truth bounding boxes required to consider a detection good. Lower threshold values mean that the evaluation is more lenient towards inaccurate localization. There is a slight problem with this method, however. In the case of tiny objects (such as the ball, and even more so the line crossing) even small errors in the localization can drastically decrease the IoU value. This will cause the evaluation method to be disproportionately punishing towards localization errors as opposed to classification or confidence errors.

To remedy this, we also compute the mAP values using a different error measure for localization, namely the Euclidean distance between the bounding box centers. It is worth mentioning, that this criterion ignores errors of the bounding box shape, although this is a relatively minor issue considering the rigidity of the detected objects. Table 1 shows the results on the synthetic and the real datasets respectively.

Table 1. mAP comparison on the synthetic and real databases

Database	Syn					Real				
IoU	0.75	0.5	0.25	0.1	0.05	0.75	0.5	0.25	0.1	0.05
Tiny YOLO	**29**	**65**	71	70	70	**21**	**65**	69	65	64
ROBO	16	51	72	80	82	16	55	76	80	**82**
ROBO-BN	24	59	**77**	**84**	**85**	20	62	**79**	81	82
ROBO-HR	15	48	69	77	78	16	52	73	79	80
Distance (px)	4	8	16	32	64	4	8	16	32	64
Tiny YOLO v3	**60**	70	70	70	70	**41**	**64**	69	65	64
ROBO	43	73	86	89	89	27	58	**80**	**84**	**85**
ROBO-BN	53	**79**	**88**	**90**	**90**	30	61	**80**	83	83
ROBO-HR	38	69	84	87	87	21	56	76	82	83

In all four cases the ROBO architectures respond to the change in the strictness of the localization criterion much more drastically, suggesting that they struggle more with accurate localization, while Tiny YOLO struggles with accurate detection and classification. This is underscored by the fact, that using a localization criterion that is loose enough, ROBO-based models invariably manage to outperform Tiny YOLO. We believe that this is largely due to the difference between the output generation methods employed. Importantly, ROBO outperforms Tiny YOLO more decisively on the real dataset. This is most likely due to the fact, that Tiny YOLO has several times more parameters, making it much easier to overfit on a small database.

Predictably, the somewhat more complex ROBO-BN outperforms the other two methods, although ROBO manages to achieve similar performance on the synthetic dataset with loose criteria. This suggests that higher parameter numbers help with accurate localization. Also, the two-channel version falls short of the other two by a few percentages, but still manages to clearly outperform Tiny YOLO. Figure 2 shows some example results of ROBO on the synthetic test dataset, and also some good and bad results on the real test dataset.

Fig. 2. Example results on the synthetic database (top row). Some good (middle) and bad (bottom) detection results on the real database both in- and outdoors.

The per-class AP results show that the network's performance does not depend strongly on the size of the objects. The model achieves the highest AP on the ball and goalpost classes (91 and 87 respectively), while it struggles more with the crossing and robot classes (83 and 77). Interestingly, the largest class appears to have the smallest average precision. As demonstrated in Fig. 2 the network is able to detect objects at a fair distance, although its localization is somewhat inaccurate with small objects. Recall, that qualitatively detection is more important than accurate localization, especially for small objects, since they are far.

5.2   Effects of Pruning

Figure 3 shows the effect of pruning on accuracy, as well as the number of operations required for each model version. Our results show that it is possible to prune approximately 90% of the ROBO model's parameters with only a negligible drop in accuracy, while reducing run time by 70%. Notably, the ROBO-HR version is slightly less affected by pruning, yielding a model with half the run time at the cost of a 1% drop in accuracy. Also, the share of parameters pruned from ROBO-BN is higher, since it as approximately twice the number of parameters. The drop in performance is also more steep in this case, making this model slightly inferior.

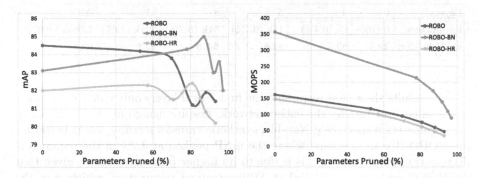

Fig. 3. Effect of pruning on the mAP (left) and the number of operations (right)

The single-core run time of ROBO on the Nao v6 robot is 438 ms, which translates to approximately 2.3 frames per second. With 88% pruning, however, the run time decreased to 179 ms, or 5.6 fps, while the 93% version produced 146 ms or 6.9 fps. It is worth noting, that this is considerably slower, than expected from floating point benchmarks of the robot's processor alone. This is largely because the large initial spatial size of the images makes efficient caching more difficult.

Moreover, using such a small network, the im2col operation that is part of the convolution takes up a considerable amount of the execution time in early layers. This motivated our ROBO-HR architecture, which performs 47% fewer operations, therefore the run time on the Nao robot decreases by a similar amount to 77 ms, which is 13 fps.

5.3 Effects of Synthetic Transfer Learning

We also ran experiments with synthetic transfer learning, as shown in Table 2. We ran several tests, where we changed the number of initial layers to retrain. By increasing this number, we allow the network to learn the real dataset better, resulting in faster convergence, but makes the network more likely to overfit. In these experiments, we fine-tuned the rest of the layers using a smaller learning rate (by a factor of ten) instead of freezing them completely.

Table 2. The results of synthetic transfer learning

	ROBO					
Layers	0	3	5	7	9	All
Parameters	0 (0%)	1.5k (0.3%)	8.5k (1.6%)	36k (6.5%)	110k (20%)	555k (100%)
mAP @ 32px	19.6	83.7	82.9	83.0	**84.6**	84.5
	ROBO-BN					
Layers	0	3	5	8	11	All
Parameters	0 (0%)	6k (0.4%)	11k (0.7%)	51k (3.2%)	221k (14%)	1,585k (100%)
mAP @ 32px	29.3	82.6	82.8	**84.3**	83.8	83.1

The results show that retraining the first 7 or 9 layers only can achieve superior results to retraining the entire network, despite using only 6.5 or 19.8% of the parameters respectively. Notably, synthetic transfer learning works better for the ROBO-BN architecture, where the mAP peaked at 3.2% of the parameters ($51k$) retrained. Arguably this is due to its higher parameter count, given that the ROBO architecture peaked at $110k$ retrained parameters, which is in the same order of magnitude.

6 Conclusion

In this paper, we presented a fully deep neural network-based object detection framework capable of detecting all relevant objects in robot soccer environments. We proposed a new architecture ROBO, and showed that it outperforms Tiny YOLO both in terms of speed and accuracy. We showed that these models can be trained using synthetic transfer learning to reduce the amount of data required. Our work also produced a small database of real images other teams can use freely. Our code, the pre-trained models, training and validation datasets are published online [8].

Yet, there are a few possibilities to improve our model. For instance, the network could be trained to detect the edges of the soccer field and ignore objects well outside. This way we could help the network learn by reducing the interference of complex backgrounds outside the field. Another important possibility is improving the regularization method, by using group L1 regularization [28]. This would allow us to prune entire convolutional filters instead of individual weights, which in turn would make the execution of the neural network considerably more efficient.

References

1. LeCun, Y., et al.: Gradient-based learning applied to document recognition. Proc. IEEE **86**(11), 2278–2324 (1998)
2. Ren, S., et al.: Faster R-CNN: towards real-time object detection with region proposal networks. IEEE Trans. Pattern Anal. Mach. Intell. **39**(6), 1137–1149 (2017)
3. Redmon, J., et al.: You only look once: unified, real-time object detection. In: 2016 IEEE Conference on Computer Vision and Pattern Recognition (CVPR). IEEE, June 2016. https://doi.org/10.1109/cvpr.2016.91
4. Sutskever, I., Vinyals, O., Le, Q.V.: Sequence to sequence learning with neural networks. In: 27th International Conference on Neural Information Processing Systems, pp. 1–9 (2014)
5. Yin, J., et al.: Neural generative question answering. In: Proceedings of the Twenty-Fifth International Joint Conference on Artificial Intelligence (IJCAI 2016), pp. 2972–2978 (2016)
6. Graves, A., Wayne, G., Danihelka, I.: Neural Turing machines. arXiv:1410.5401 (2014)
7. Redmon, J., Farhadi, A.: YOLO 9000: better, faster, stronger. In: 2017 IEEE Conference on Computer Vision and Pattern Recognition (CVPR). IEEE, July 2017. https://doi.org/10.1109/cvpr.2017.690
8. Szemenyei, M.: ROBO. https://github.com/szemenyeim/ROBO
9. Glorot, X., Bengio, Y.: Understanding the difficulty of training deep feedforward neural networks. In: Proceedings of the Thirteenth International Conference on Artificial Intelligence and Statistics, pp. 249–256 (2010)
10. Karpathy, A., Fei-Fei, L.: Deep visual-semantic alignments for generating image descriptions. IEEE Trans. Pattern Anal. Mach. Intell. **39**(4), 664–676 (2017)
11. Isola, P., et al.: Image-to-image translation with conditional adversarial nets. In: IEEE Conference on Computer Vision and Pattern Recognition (CVPR), pp. 5967–5976 (2017)
12. Liu, W., et al.: SSD: single shot multibox detector. In: Leibe, B., Matas, J., Sebe, N., Welling, M. (eds.) ECCV 2016. LNCS, vol. 9905, pp. 21–37. Springer, Cham (2016). https://doi.org/10.1007/978-3-319-46448-0_2
13. He, K., et al.: Mask R-CNN. In: 2017 IEEE International Conference on Computer Vision (ICCV). IEEE, October 2017. https://doi.org/10.1109/iccv.2017.322
14. Redmon, J., Farhadi, A.: YOLOv3: an incremental improvement. ArXiv, April 2018
15. Schwarz, I., Hofmann, M., Urbann, O., Tasse, S.: A robust and calibration-free vision system for humanoid soccer robots. In: Almeida, L., Ji, J., Steinbauer, G., Luke, S. (eds.) RoboCup 2015. LNCS (LNAI), vol. 9513, pp. 239–250. Springer, Cham (2015). https://doi.org/10.1007/978-3-319-29339-4_20
16. Metzler, S., Nieuwenhuisen, M., Behnke, S.: Learning visual obstacle detection using color histogram features. In: Röfer, T., Mayer, N.M., Savage, J., Saranlı, U. (eds.) RoboCup 2011. LNCS (LNAI), vol. 7416, pp. 149–161. Springer, Heidelberg (2012). https://doi.org/10.1007/978-3-642-32060-6_13

17. Javadi, M., et al.: Humanoid robot detection using deep learning: a speed-accuracy tradeoff. In: Akiyama, H., Obst, O., Sammut, C., Tonidandel, F. (eds.) RoboCup 2017. LNCS (LNAI), vol. 11175, pp. 338–349. Springer, Cham (2018). https://doi.org/10.1007/978-3-030-00308-1_28

18. Cruz, N., Lobos-Tsunekawa, K., Ruiz-del-Solar, J.: Using convolutional neural networks in robots with limited computational resources: detecting NAO robots while playing soccer. In: Akiyama, H., Obst, O., Sammut, C., Tonidandel, F. (eds.) RoboCup 2017. LNCS (LNAI), vol. 11175, pp. 19–30. Springer, Cham (2018). https://doi.org/10.1007/978-3-030-00308-1_2

19. O'Keeffe, S., Villing, R.: A benchmark data set and evaluation of deep learning architectures for ball detection in the RoboCup SPL. In: Akiyama, H., Obst, O., Sammut, C., Tonidandel, F. (eds.) RoboCup 2017. LNCS (LNAI), vol. 11175, pp. 398–409. Springer, Cham (2018). https://doi.org/10.1007/978-3-030-00308-1_33

20. Menashe, J., et al.: Fast and precise black and white ball detection for RoboCup soccer. In: Akiyama, H., Obst, O., Sammut, C., Tonidandel, F. (eds.) RoboCup 2017. LNCS (LNAI), vol. 11175, pp. 45–58. Springer, Cham (2018). https://doi.org/10.1007/978-3-030-00308-1_4

21. Houliston, T., Chalup, S.K.: Visual mesh: real-time object detection using constant sample density, 23 July 2018. arXiv:1807.08405v1 [cs.CV]

22. Hess, T., Mundt, M., Weis, T., Ramesh, V.: Large-scale stochastic scene generation and semantic annotation for deep convolutional neural network training in the RoboCup SPL. In: Akiyama, H., Obst, O., Sammut, C., Tonidandel, F. (eds.) RoboCup 2017. LNCS (LNAI), vol. 11175, pp. 33–44. Springer, Cham (2018). https://doi.org/10.1007/978-3-030-00308-1_3

23. van Dijk, S.G., Scheunemann, M.M.: Deep learning for semantic segmentation on minimal hardware, 15 July 2018. arXiv:1807.05597v1 [cs.LG]

24. Szemenyei, M., Estivill-Castro, V.: Real-time scene understanding using deep neural networks for RoboCup SPL. In: Holz, D., Genter, K., Saad, M., von Stryk, O. (eds.) RoboCup 2018. LNCS (LNAI), vol. 11374, pp. 96–108. Springer, Cham (2019). https://doi.org/10.1007/978-3-030-27544-0_8

25. Anwar, S., Hwang, K., Sung, W.: Structured pruning of deep convolutional neural networks. ACM J. Emerg. Technol. Comput. Syst. **13**(3), 1–11 (2017)

26. Molchanov, P., et al.: Pruning convolutional neural networks for resource efficient inference (2016). arXiv:1611.06440

27. Sabour, S., Frosst, N., Hinton, G.E.: Dynamic routing between capsules, 26 October 2017. arXiv:1710.09829v2 [cs.CV]

28. Scardapane, S., et al.: Group sparse regularization for deep neural networks. Neurocomputing **241**, 81–89 (2017). https://doi.org/10.1016/j.neucom.2017.02.029

A Real-Time Ball Detection Approach Using Convolutional Neural Networks

Meisam Teimouri[1]([✉]) [iD], Mohammad Hossein Delavaran[1] [iD], and Mahdi Rezaei[2] [iD]

[1] Mechatronic Research Laboratory, Qazvin Islamic Azad University, Qazvin, Iran
{m.teimouri,mh.delavaran}@qiau.ac.ir
[2] Auckland University of Technology, Auckland, New Zealand
mahdi.rezaei@aut.ac.nz

Abstract. Ball detection is one of the most important tasks in the context of soccer-playing robots. The ball is a small moving object which can be blurred and occluded in many situations. Several neural network based methods with different architectures are proposed to deal with the ball detection. However, they are either neglecting to consider the computationally low resources of humanoid robots or highly depend on manually-tuned heuristic methods to extract the ball candidates. In this paper, we propose a new ball detection method for low-cost humanoid robots that can detect most soccer balls with a high accuracy rate of up to 97.17%. The proposed method is divided into two steps. First, some coarse regions that may contain a full ball are extracted using an iterative method employing an efficient integral image based feature. Then they are fed to a light-weight convolutional neural network to finalize the bounding box of a ball. We have evaluated the proposed approach using a comprehensive dataset and the experimental results show the efficiency of our method.

Keywords: Ball detection · Convolutional neural networks · Humanoid robot · RoboCup

1 Introduction

Object detection is the task of classifying meaningful and semantic regions followed by precisely estimating the location of objects in an image [1]. It plays a crucial role in establishing the world model of a soccer-playing robot. One of the most important objects that every soccer-playing robot has to detect is the ball. It is a small moving object that in many situations is occluded by playing robots in the field. Also, ball detection is affected adversely by image blurring caused due to unstable walking of low-cost humanoid robots and slow shutter speed cameras mounted on them. The difficulty of ball detection increases, even more, when the standard size FIFA ball comes with a different pattern in every competition.

With the development of deep neural networks (DNNs), state-of-the-art methods have scored high accuracy in object detection [2, 3]. However, these methods are considered as real-time only by using dedicated graphic processing units (GPUs). In RoboCup 2018, most of the qualified teams in humanoid soccer leagues have used only a CPU for

© Springer Nature Switzerland AG 2019
S. Chalup et al. (Eds.): RoboCup 2019, LNAI 11531, pp. 323–336, 2019.
https://doi.org/10.1007/978-3-030-35699-6_25

all kind of tasks, including object detection, walking, world modeling, and behavior analysis. So implementing the DNN-based methods are not feasible on most soccer-playing humanoid robots. Recently several studies have been accomplished to adopt the DNNs for object detection, particularly ball detection on computationally low powered systems. These studies can be divided into two different approaches: single-stage detectors and candidate-based classifiers. Single-stage detectors process a full-sized image using a DNN to localize the position of the interested objects. These methods either lacked a real-time performance on a CPU or missed generalization performance on a real robot. On the other hand, candidate-based classifiers first extract ball candidates precisely and then each candidate is classified as a ball or background class separately. Although these approaches achieved some accurate results on low powered systems, they have highly relied on some manually-tuned heuristic methods to extract the candidates of a specific ball type.

In this paper, we propose a new ball detection method which achieves highly accurate results on a real robot, equipped only with a CPU in real-time performance. The method is described in two steps. In the first step, we find some coarse regions that may contain a ball. In the second step, these regions are fed into a convolutional neural network (CNN) to estimate the bounding box of the ball. The main contributions of this paper are: (i) proposing an iterative algorithm to find regions that probably contain a full ball using an efficient and novel feature extraction technique that is applicable for most soccer balls. (ii) introducing a light-weight CNN that localizes and classifies a ball within the candidate regions of interest. This network can inference the input in real-time on a computationally low powered system.

The rest of the paper is organized as follows: in Sect. 2 we review and investigate recently proposed ball detection methods. Our ball regions detector is presented in Sect. 3. Designing and training the proposed CNN are described in Sect. 4. In Sect. 5 we provide experimental results and then conclude in Sect. 6.

2   Related Works

As stated ball detection approaches in the context of humanoid soccer-playing robots are divided into two groups: single-stage detectors and multi-stage candidate-based classifiers.

Single-Stage Detectors. In [4] a CNN is presented that employs a full-sized $m \times n$ raw image to predict the center of the balls. It produces two m and n-dimensional vectors as output. These vectors are discrete distributions and indicate the probability that each row and column of the image hold the center coordinates of the ball. To let the network converge more quickly, they provided more solutions by using two normal distributions as the label. The major drawback of their network is the expensive inferencing that takes about one second to complete for each image. Moreover, there is no guarantee that the network produces two unimodal distributions. So the output must be post-processed to find the most promising row and column that show the center location of the ball. A fully convolutional neural network is proposed in [5] that can localize n objects simultaneously in an image. It uses an encoder-decoder design to produce n heat maps. Each heat map is a two dimensinal probability distribution that should be maximized at the interested location of an object belonged to a specific class. The proposed network has a real-time performance on a powerful GPU. Also, the network does not predict the boundary of objects. Another similar approach for ball detection is presented in [6]. The output of the network is a heat map that shows high values for ball pixels while contains near zero values for non-ball pixels. It achieved near real-time performance on a modern CPU without processing other tasks of the robot. In [7] a more efficient encoder-decoder architecture is proposed that maps an input image into a full-resolution pixelwise classification. To decrease the computation load they have used depthwise separable convolutions and removed skip connections. Although, this network achieved some good results in near real-time performance on a low-power processor, it trained and evaluated on a limited data set that contains only one ball type. A real-time CNN-based object detection approach for resource-constrained robotics is presented in [8]. Before feeding the input image to the network, it transforms the image using the object geometry to form a Visual Mesh. This mesh has a constant sample density for the object in different distances and it significantly reduces the computational complexity. To train the network a semi-synthetic data set is used. The data set is generated using 360 degree high dynamic range images and physics-based rendering. The proposed approach reported consistent and accurate precision and recall over all data set. However, the generalization performance of the method in a real robot is not evaluated.

Candidate-Based Classifiers. In [9] candidates are white blobs that satisfy expected color histogram, shape, and size of the target ball. For each candidate, a Histogram of Gradients feature is calculated and then classified by a cascade AdaBoost [10] method. The training time of this classifier was about 10 h that is an issue for on-site training during the competitions. Recently several neural network based classifiers are presented for classic ball detection in standard platform league [11–13]. In [11] ball candidates are examined using black pentagons of the ball. The topology and configurations of the proposed network are optimized using a genetic algorithm. A more general candidate generation is suggested by [12]. For each interested pixel, a Difference of Gaussian filter with a kernel size that is proportional to the expected ball radius at the location of the pixel is applied. Then highly responded blobs are fed to a cascade of two CNNs that the

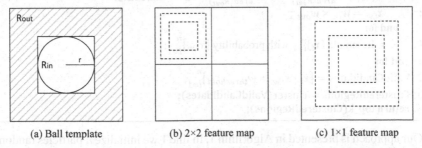

(a) Ball template   (b) 2×2 feature map   (c) 1×1 feature map

Fig. 1. (a) A template used to calculate importance weight of a particle in the ball proposed region detection algorithm. Inside region of the ball is approximated by the white box and outside region of the ball is illustrated by gray region. (b) and (c) show two feature maps and anchor boxes (dashed boxes).

first one reduces the number of proposals to five and the second one performs accurate classification. In [14] authors presented a simple and fast method to find the candidates. They divide the input image into a grid and then if the number of white pixels in each cell exceeds a threshold, it is considered as a ball candidate. They have investigated two CNNs for classification of the candidates. To accelerate the learning process they employed pre-trained networks and only retrained last layers for ball classification. Using a fixed grid for the whole image can lead to a candidate that either covers a portion of the ball or contains a small ball.

3 Ball Regions Proposal

The main goal of our region proposal algorithm is to find some bounding boxes, most likely containing a full ball in the image window. Thanks to the accurate localization of our network introduced in the next section, we have no concern in fitting a region to the boundary of the ball. Our method is partially influenced by a simple ball detection method introduced in [15]. In contrast, we have proposed an iterative method that quickly converges to some region of interests using an easy to implement and efficient to compute feature. This method requires to analyse the white and green mask of the image. In this work, we have used a learned lookup table to extract these two masks. However, to create a white mask we can use a thresholding method on the brightness channel. Also, the green mask could be generated by activating pixels fall into a predefined range on the hue channel [16].

Algorithm 1: Ball Regions Detection

1: $X = \text{Draw } \{x_i\}_{i=1}^n$ from white mask;
2: **for** $itt = 1 \; to \; m$ **do**
3:      **for** $i = 1 \; to \; n$ **do**
4:          R_{in} = region inside x_i;
5:          R_{out} = region outside of x_i;
6:          $w_{in} = \frac{n_{white}(R_{in})}{area(R_{in})}$;
7:          $w_{out} = \frac{n_{not\_white}(R_{out})}{area(R_{out})} \times 1(\frac{n_{green}(R_{out})}{area(R_{out})} > green_{threshold})$;
8:          $x_{i,w} = w_{in} \times w_{out}$;
9:      **end for**
10:     $X = \text{Resample } \{x_i\}_{i=1}^n$ with probability $\{x_{i,w}\}_{i=1}^n$;
11: **end for**
12: ValidCandidates $= \{x_i \mid x_{i,w} > w_{threshold}\}_{i=1}^n$;
13: ClusteredRegions = cluster(ValidCandidates);
14: **return** top_k(ClusteredRegions);

Our approach is presented in Algorithm 1. In line 1 we initialize n particles randomly at locations labeled as white. To accelerate converging and reduce the false regions, we have considered only white pixels located in a given distance (approximately eight meters). Each particle $x = [cx, cy, r, w]$ is a vector representing the parameters of a circle. The scalar r is the roughly estimated radius of a ball located at coordinates

(cx, cy) of the image. It can be derived using the camera matrix. An importance weight w is assigned to each particle that shows the likelihood of a ball. To estimate this weight we used a simple feature that can be computed efficiently. Considering a soccer ball on the playing field, we expect significant white pixels inside the ball (approximated by R_{in} in Fig. 1a). On the other hand, the region outside of the ball (approximated by R_{out} in Fig. 1a) should contains non-white pixels, especially green pixels. Following this feature analysis, we compute the weight of each particle in line 4 to 8. The function $n_c(R)$ calculates the number of pixels having color c inside the region R. This can be calculated efficiently considering a rectangular area around R using the integral image [17, 18]. Also, $1(expr)$ returns 1 if $expr$ interpreted as $true$ otherwise returns 0. The particles are converged through line 2 to 11. Each particle is replicated with a probability proportional to its weight in a resampling phase (line 10). In this phase, also every replicated particle is randomly translated and scaled to explore the neighborhood. Moreover, this random transformation makes finding candidates less sensitive to an accurate camera matrix. We repeat the weighting and resampling process until particles converge to some regions that may contain a ball. To reduce the number of particles we only keep the candidates with an importance weight exceeding a threshold (line 12). Then particles are clustered using an approach similar to non-maximum suppression. In contrast, we take an average of non-maximums to generate a cluster instead of suppressing them. This clustering method has a time complexity of $O(n^2)$. When the number of particles is large, a clustering algorithm with linear time complexity can be used in our method [19]. Since we have used a simple feature, it is likely that in some cases we miss the whole ball region; therefore, during the clustering phase, we increase the scale of the bounding box of each candidate, by a factor of two. To limit the maximum number of final regions we select k clusters that maximize the average importance weights (line 14).

4 Network Design and Training Phase

4.1 Design Phase

Here we propose a deep CNN architecture for ball detection, applicable in the region of interests, obtained in the previous step. To design the network we considered two main goals. Firstly, the network has to be fast in an embedded system with low computational resources. Secondly, it must be able to detect balls with different scales at a high precision rate. To achieve this network we inspired by the single shot multi-box detector (SSD) [2] and MobileNets [20] networks. SSD is an object detection network that uses some auxiliary multi-scales feature maps to detect objects at different sizes. Each feature map is tiled with some predefined anchor boxes in a convolutional way and produces a fixed set of boxes with per-class scores for each box. MobileNets is an efficient model for embedded systems which is established on separable convolutional blocks. A separable convolutional block is a depthwise convolution followed by a 1×1 convolution. A 3×3 separable convolution is 8 to 9 times faster than a normal convolution without significant reduction in its accuracy [20].

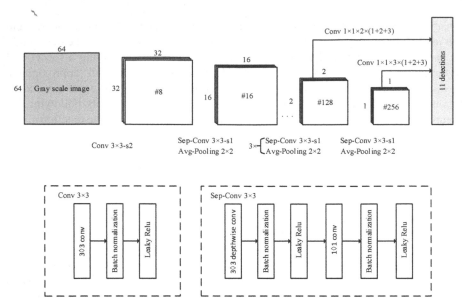

Fig. 2. The architecture of our deep convolutional network (BallNet) for ball detection (top). The microarchitecture of 3 × 3 normal and separable convolutions are shown in the bottom.

Our network is illustrated in Fig. 2. It merely consists of some low cost convolutional and average pooling layers. To compress information of the input image efficiently we downsampled the activation maps by a factor of two while doubling the number of channels. After all convolutions, we applied batch normalization (except for the convolutions applied to the feature maps). By normalizing the inputs of a layer, batch normalization acts as a regularizer and often eliminates the requirement of dropout [21]. In our case, this speeds up the training process while yielding consistent accuracy. To detect the balls, we have employed two last activation maps of the network as feature maps. At every $m \times n$ feature map with k associated anchor boxes to each cell, we produce $k \times m \times n$ detections. In this work, all anchor boxes are square shaped and located at the center of the feature map cells. Each detection can be considered as a vector of six scalars, in which each element is predicted by applying a 1×1 convolutional filter. To express the bounding box of a detection d_i we use a tuple $l_i = \left(l_i^{cx}, l_i^{cy}, l_i^{w} \right)$, where l_i^{cx} and l_i^{cy} are scale-invariant translations of the center coordinates and l_i^{w} is the log-space translation of the width relative to the corresponding anchor box a_i. Also, a tuple of two scalars $p_i = \left(p_i^{ball}, p_i^{bg} \right)$ is used to indicate the scores of the ball and background classes. The scalar c_i shows the confidence score of a detection. It reflects the confident level that the predicted bounding box fits the boundary of a ball. There are two anchor boxes related to each cell of the first 2×2 feature map with scales of 0.25 and 0.4 (Fig. 2b). The second feature map uses three anchor boxes with scales of 0.33, 0.5 and 0.75 (Fig. 2c). These scales and number of anchor boxes are determined so that the first feature map is more responsible for balls located at the corners, and the second one is more responsible for center located balls.

4.2 Training Phase

Training of the introduced network involves matching strategy of anchor boxes, optimization of a multi-task cost function, and preparing the dataset.

Assignment of Anchor Boxes. To match anchor boxes with an annotated label we follow SSD [2]. With each sample containing a ball, we first calculate the Jaccard overlap (also known as intersection over union) between the annotated box and each of the anchor boxes. Note that the location and size of the anchor boxes in the feature maps and the annotated box in the sample image are normalized. Then the anchor box with the best score in Jaccard overlap is selected as the best matching anchor box. As described in [2] we also match anchor boxes with Jaccard overlap above a value 0.5 to ease the learning procedure.

Loss Function. The loss function in our algorithm is based on both SSD [2] and YOLO [3]. We define the loss function as an ensemble of three terms named localization loss (L_{loc}), classification loss (L_{cls}), and confidence loss (L_{conf}):

$$L_{total} = \frac{1}{N}\left(\alpha L_{loc} + \beta L_{cls} + \gamma L_{conf}\right) \tag{1}$$

In which α, β and γ specify the contribution of the loss of each task and is determined by cross validation. N is the number of anchor boxes matched with the ground truth box. The localization loss counts only for the matched anchor boxes with the ground truth box:

$$L_{loc}(l, g) = \sum_{i \in pos}^{N} \sum_{m \in \{cx, cy, w\}} \left| l_i^m - \hat{g}_i^m \right| \tag{2}$$

$$\hat{g}_i^{cx} = \frac{\left(g^{cx} - a_i^{cx}\right)}{a_i^w} \qquad \hat{g}_i^{cy} = \frac{\left(g_i^{cy} - a_i^{cy}\right)}{a_i^w} \tag{3}$$

$$\hat{g}_i^w = \log\left(\frac{g_i^w}{a_i^w}\right) \tag{4}$$

where l_i is the predicted box related to the selected anchor box a_i and $\hat{g}_i$ is the ground truth box g encoded with respect to a_i. The classification loss is the sum of ball class losses for selected anchor boxes (i.e. positive boxes) and background class losses for anchor boxes which are not matched (i.e. negative boxes):

$$L_{cls}(p) = -\sum_{i \in pos}^{N} log\left(\hat{p}_i^{ball}\right) - \sum_{i \in neg}^{M} log\left(\hat{p}_i^{bg}\right) \tag{5}$$

where M is the number of negative boxes used. To balance between positive and negative examples we set M as twice of N at most. The negative boxes with high predicted scores for ball class are selected first. Also $\hat{p}_i^c$ is the softmax of a class $c \in \{ball, bg\}$:

$$\hat{p}_i^c = \frac{exp\left(c_i^c\right)}{\sum_c exp\left(p_i^c\right)} \tag{6}$$

We expect the confidence c_i of a positive box conveys the Intersection Over Union (IOU) between the decoded predicted box $d(l_i)$ and the ground truth g. So we defined the confidence loss as follows:

$$L_{conf}(c) = \sum_{i \in pos}^{N} \left| c_i - IOU_{d(l_i)}^{g} \right| \tag{7}$$

Optimization. To optimize the loss function we have used Adam optimizer with a piecewise constant schedule for learning rate. In our experiments, we begin with 1e-3 as starting learning rate. We perform a training phase for 5 k iterations followed by reducing the learning rate to 1e-4 and then continuing the training for 10 k iterations. We lowered the learning rate once more to 1e-5 for 3 k more iterations. We also tried other learning rate schedules like poly and exponential learning rate decay methods but we have found the piecewise constant schedule works better for our application.

We also set α, β and γ to 5, 0.6 and 1 respectively. In our experiments, we found the classification task is relatively easier than localization to learn. To avoid overfitting in the classification task we set β to 0.2 after 7 k iterations of training.

Data Set. One of the most important aspects of modern object detection systems is the data set. To prepare the data set we annotated 1 k images from various RoboCup competitions and our research lab, including 5 different types of balls and variety of negative candidates like robots, goal posts, penalty marker, humans, and other objects around the field. In the data set, all balls are located approximately at a distance up to 4 meters away from the camera. Then we generated 64 × 64 patches by applying the random crop, random scale, mirroring and random brightness around ball regions and other regions of the annotated images. To augment negative patches with more diverse regions we manually created some patches around goal posts, lines, and penalty markers. Our training set after augmentation contains 12 k images. Some positive and negative samples are shown in Fig. 3 rows 1–4.

4.3 Inference

At the inference stage, we assume that the category of a detection is the class with the maximum predicted score. Therefore it is possible that several detections report the ball class. Among these detections, we select a detection d_i maximizing the localization score $s_i = p_i^{ball} \times c_i$. As mentioned before the network only predicts a set of offsets to the assigned anchor box, hence to get final bounding box we decode the predicted bounding box l_i:

$$d^{cx}(l_i) = \left(l_i^{cx} * a_i^w\right) + a_i^{cx} d^{cy}(l_i) = \left(l_i^{cy} * a_i^w\right) + a_i^{cy} \tag{8}$$

$$d^w(l_i) = d^h(l_i) = exp\left(a_i^w\right) * a_i^w \tag{9}$$

Fig. 3. Row 1, 2: Positive samples in the training data set. Row 3 and 4: Negative samples in the training data set, Row 5: Positive samples of the validation data set. Row 6: Positive samples of generalization data set with a new ball pattern not used for training.

5 Experiments

In this section, we evaluate the performance of the ball regions detection algorithm. Then we show the effectiveness of the designed neural network under different conditions. Moreover, the overall performance of the proposed ball detection method is investigated in a real-world test. All experiments are performed in a kid-size humanoid robot [22] equipped with a Logitech c920 camera capturing 640 × 480 images at a rate of 30 frames per second and an Intel NUC with a Core i3 U6100 processor. The training is carried out on a Nvidia GTX 1080 GPU.

5.1 Region Proposal Analysis

We evaluated our *region proposal algorithm* on 400 images acquired from various conditions including moving, occluded, on the line, and near the goal post balls while the robot is either walking or standing. Then we initialized the algorithm with 500 particles and reduced it to 300 particles in the resampling step. After only two iterations particles are converged. We noticed that in 96% of images our algorithm finds at least one region that contains a full ball and in 4% of images, the clustered regions cover a portion of the ball. The step by step process of the algorithm is shown in Fig. 4. As shown in column three, our algorithm can detect regions with different ball patterns and sizes without any modification. Table 1 represents the run-time cost of the algorithm. The algorithm takes 1.46 ms in average that indicates it as a fast and real-time region proposal method.

Fig. 4. The process of generating the ball regions. Top row: initialized particles. Middle row: converged particles after two iterations. Bottom row: Final clustered regions.

Table 1. Run-time cost of ball region proposal algorithm in milliseconds.

Steps	Max	Average
Creating integral images	1.48	0.5
Converging particles	4.19	0.88
Clustering	1.22	0.08

5.2 Model Analysis

To evaluate our network (the BallNet) we prepared two datasets, the first set contains 2 k images of both positive and negative samples with the same ball patterns existed in training dataset (Fig. 3 row 5); The second set contains 1 k of only positive samples with a new ball pattern that are never used in training (Fig. 3 row 6). The second set tests the generalizability of our model. This is important because, in the humanoid soccer league, participating teams may face with new ball patterns in every RoboCup competition. Also, to investigate a speed-accuracy trade-off we trained a lighter network (BallNet-mini) in which all activation maps are halved compared to the BallNet.

Validation. Similar to other researchers we use the most common metrics of accuracy, recall rate, and precision rate to evaluate our classifiers. However, in the RoboCup soccer leagues, misclassification of the ball can lead to a score loss. Therefore we also analysed false positive rate. As can be seen in Table 2 the proposed BallNet model benefits from a high precision and recall rate while maintaining a low false positive rate, which means the trained model is able to accurately detect balls in most regions covering a ball. As mentioned earlier, the classification task is rather easier than the localization. Therefore the BallNet-mini model reported promising metrics, although all the metrics degraded slightly.

Table 2. Classification performance of the proposed networks

Model name	Accuracy	Precision rate	Recall rate	FP rate
BallNet	96.43	97.17	94.29	2.00
BallNet-mini	94.84	95.71	91.89	3.00

To evaluate the performance of the networks in the localization task we used average IOU and precision with IOU levels more than 0.5, 0.75 and 0.9. Note that only the samples labeled and classified as ball are used to calculate the metrics. Table 3 shows the high accuracy of BallNet model localization. As expected the BallNet model with more capacity outperforms the smaller model in localization task. Figure 5 shows the results with different IOU levels.

Table 3. Localization performance of the proposed networks

Model Name	Avg. IOU	P:0.5	P:0.75	P:0.9
BallNet	0.788	96.23	66.70	9.17
BallNet-mini	0.763	92.86	56.95	7.84

Generalization. Since there are no negative samples in the generalization set, we only used detection rate (number of samples detected as positive divided by the number of positive samples in the data set) to evaluate the classification performance of our models. As summarized in Table 4 the BallNet significantly outperforms the BallNet-mini at the generalization of both classification and localization tasks. Although the detection rate is significantly decreased in the BallNet, the result shows that there is a high possibility of increasing the model performance with fine-tuning during the competitions.

Time Complexity. We have evaluated the speed of the models at inferencing and training phases. As shown in Table 5, both models are very fast. Although we have halved the BallNet-mini, the inference time has not linearly decreased compared to the BallNet. The discrepancy may be more highlighted in a weaker computing device.

Table 5. Time and parameters complexity of the models.

Model Name	Inference (ms)	Train (minute)	Parameters	GFLOPS
BallNet	1.782	17.04	65,166	133,319
BallNet-mini	1.198	16.30	21,686	44,855

Fig. 5. The result of the ball detections with different IOU levels of P:0.9, P:0.75, and P:0.5 illustrated in the top, middle, and bottom row, respectively.

Table 4. The performance of the models on the generalization set.

Model Name	Detection rate	Avg. IOU	P:0.5	P:0.75	P:0.9
BallNet	70.9	0.768	94.30	69.2	10.11
BallNet-mini	53.53	0.69	90.0	40.75	3.20

5.3 Overall Performance

To evaluate the overall performance of the presented pipeline, we saved the input images, detected regions, and predictions of the BallNet once in every 10 frames from a 5-min real gameplay. The resulting measurements of the classification were as follows: 91.43% accuracy, 89.72% precision rate, 80.07% recall rate, and 3.30% of false ratio. Also, we measured a runtime cost of 5.13 ms in average for the entire detection pipeline while other tasks of the robot were running in parallel. As can be seen, due to different lighting conditions and more blurred images caused by robot movements, we experienced a weaker performance.

6 Conclusion

In this paper, we presented a fast and accurate ball detection pipeline for humanoid soccer playing robots. The first stage of the proposed method reliably extracts some regions that may contain a full ball and then the designed deep neural network (called the BallNet) predicts the exact location of the ball in each region, with a high recall and precision rate. We demonstrated that our region proposal algorithm can deal with different ball types without further modifications. The proposed pipeline also fulfilled the computational constraints of low-cost humanoid robots. The method is fast to train (about 17 min) and in average takes less than 5 ms to run on a standard Core i3 CPU. The pipeline can be applied for detecting other objects with known sizes like the goal posts and other robots. Our data sets and TensorFlow implementation of the network is publically available online[1] for other researchers and future works.

References

1. Zhao, Z., Zheng, P., Xu, S., Wu, X.: Object detection with deep learning: a review. IEEE Trans. Neural Networks Learn. Syst. 1–21 (2019)
2. Liu, W., et al.: SSD: single shot MultiBox detector. In: Leibe, B., Matas, J., Sebe, N., Welling, M. (eds.) ECCV 2016. LNCS, vol. 9905, pp. 21–37. Springer, Cham (2016). https://doi.org/10.1007/978-3-319-46448-0_2
3. Redmon, J., Divvala, S., Girshick, R., Farhadi, A.: You only look once: unified, real-time object detection. In: 2016 IEEE Conference on Computer Vision and Pattern Recognition (CVPR), pp. 779–788 (2016)
4. Speck, D., Barros, P., Weber, C., Wermter, S.: Ball localization for robocup soccer using convolutional neural networks. In: Behnke, S., Sheh, R., Sariel, S., Lee, D.D. (eds.) RoboCup 2016. LNCS (LNAI), vol. 9776, pp. 19–30. Springer, Cham (2017). https://doi.org/10.1007/978-3-319-68792-6_2
5. Schnekenburger, F., Scharffenberg, M., Wülker, M., Hochberg, U., Dorer, K.: Detection and localization of features on a soccer field with Feedforward Fully Convolutional Neural Networks (FCNN) for the Adult-Size Humanoid Robot Sweaty. In: Proceedings of the 12th Workshop on Humanoid Soccer Robots, 17th IEEE-RAS International Conference on Humanoid Robots, pp. 1–6. IEEE (2017)
6. Speck, D., Bestmann, M., Barros, P.: Towards real-time ball localization using CNNs. In: Holz, D., Genter, K., Saad, M., von Stryk, O. (eds.) RoboCup 2018. LNCS (LNAI), vol. 11374, pp. 337–348. Springer, Cham (2019). https://doi.org/10.1007/978-3-030-27544-0_28
7. van Dijk, S.G., Scheunemann, M.M.: Deep learning for semantic segmentation on minimal hardware. arXiv preprint arXiv:1807.05597 (2018)
8. Houliston, T., Chalup, S.K.: Visual mesh: real-time object detection using constant sample density. arXiv preprint arXiv:1807.08405 (2018)
9. Farazi, H., Allgeuer, P., Behnke, S.: A monocular vision system for playing soccer in low color information environments. arXiv preprint arXiv:1809.11078 (2018)
10. Rezaei, M., Klette, R.: Computer Vision for Driver Assistance: Simultaneous Traffic and Driver Monitoring. Springer, Cham (2017). https://doi.org/10.1007/978-3-319-50551-0
11. Felbinger, G.C., Göttsch, P., Loth, P., Peters, L., Wege, F.: Designing convolutional neural networks using a genetic approach for ball detection. In: Holz, D., Genter, K., Saad, M., von Stryk, O. (eds.) RoboCup 2018. LNCS (LNAI), vol. 11374, pp. 150–161. Springer, Cham (2019). https://doi.org/10.1007/978-3-030-27544-0_12
12. Leiva, F., Cruz, N., Bugueño, I., Ruiz-del-Solar, J.: Playing soccer without colors in the SPL: a convolutional neural network approach. arXiv preprint arXiv:1811.12493 (2018)

---

[1] https://github.com/mrl-hsl/cnnBallDetector.

13. Menashe, J., et al.: Fast and precise black and white ball detection for RoboCup soccer. In: Akiyama, H., Obst, O., Sammut, C., Tonidandel, F. (eds.) RoboCup 2017. LNCS (LNAI), vol. 11175, pp. 45–58. Springer, Cham (2018). https://doi.org/10.1007/978-3-030-00308-1_4

14. Gabel, A., Heuer, T., Schiering, I., Gerndt, R.: Jetson, where is the ball? Using neural networks for ball detection at RoboCup 2017. In: Holz, D., Genter, K., Saad, M., von Stryk, O. (eds.) RoboCup 2018. LNCS (LNAI), vol. 11374, pp. 181–192. Springer, Cham (2019). https://doi.org/10.1007/978-3-030-27544-0_15

15. Hayashibara, Y., et al.: CIT brains KidSize robot: RoboCup 2015 KidSize league winner. In: Almeida, L., Ji, J., Steinbauer, G., Luke, S. (eds.) RoboCup 2015. LNCS (LNAI), vol. 9513, pp. 153–164. Springer, Cham (2015). https://doi.org/10.1007/978-3-319-29339-4_13

16. Mühlenbrock, A., Laue, T.: Vision-based orientation detection of humanoid soccer robots. In: Akiyama, H., Obst, O., Sammut, C., Tonidandel, F. (eds.) RoboCup 2017. LNCS (LNAI), vol. 11175, pp. 204–215. Springer, Cham (2018). https://doi.org/10.1007/978-3-030-00308-1_17

17. Teimouri, M., et al.: MRL Team Description Paper for Humanoid KidSize League of RoboCup 2018. Mechatronics Research Lab, Department of Computer and Electrical Engineering, Qazvin Islamic Azad University, Qazvin, Iran (2018)

18. Rezaei, M.: Computer vision for road safety: a system for simultaneous monitoring of driver behaviour and road hazards (2016)

19. Laue, T., Röfer, T.: Pose extraction from sample sets in robot self-localization-a comparison and a novel approach. In: ECMR, pp. 283–288 (2009)

20. Howard, A.G., et al.: Mobilenets: efficient convolutional neural networks for mobile vision applications. arXiv preprint arXiv:1704.04861 (2017)

21. Normalization, B.: Accelerating deep network training by reducing internal covariate shift. CoRR.–2015.–Vol. abs/1502.03167. http://arxiv.org/abs/1502.03167 (2015)

22. Mahmudi, H., et al.: MRL Team Description Paper for Humanoid KidSize League of RoboCup 2019. Mechatronics Research Lab, Department of Computer and Electrical Engineering, Qazvin Islamic Azad University, Qazvin, Iran (2019)

Neural Semantic Parsing with Anonymization for Command Understanding in General-Purpose Service Robots

Nick Walker$^{(\boxtimes)}$ ⓘD, Yu-Tang Peng ⓘD, and Maya Cakmak ⓘD

Paul G. Allen School of Computer Science & Engineering, University of Washington,
Seattle, WA 98195, USA
{nswalker,pengy25,mcakmak}@cs.washington.edu

Abstract. Service robots are envisioned to undertake a wide range of
tasks at the request of users. Semantic parsing is one way to convert natural language commands given to these robots into executable representations. Methods for creating semantic parsers, however, rely either on
large amounts of data or on engineered lexical features and parsing rules,
which has limited their application in robotics. To address this challenge,
we propose an approach that leverages neural semantic parsing methods
in combination with contextual word embeddings to enable the training of
a semantic parser with little data and without domain specific parser engineering. Key to our approach is the use of an anonymized target representation which is more easily learned by the parser. In most cases, this simplified representation can trivially be transformed into an executable format,
and in others the parse can be completed through further interaction with
the user. We evaluate this approach in the context of the RoboCup@Home
General Purpose Service Robot task, where we have collected a corpus of
paraphrased versions of commands from the standardized command generator. Our results show that neural semantic parsers can predict the logical
form of unseen commands with 89% accuracy. We release our data and the
details of our models to encourage further development from the RoboCup
and service robotics communities.

Keywords: Natural language understanding · General-purpose service
robot · Semantic parsing

1 Introduction

General-purpose service robots (GPSRs) are envisioned as capable helpers that
will assist with everything from chores around the home to finding open conference rooms in the office. These robots are distinguished by their ability to
accomplish a wide variety of possible goals by recomposing basic capabilities
spanning navigation, manipulation, perception and interaction. One especially
desirable interface for these robots is natural language, because users are already
familiar with using language to ask for assistance.

ⓒ Springer Nature Switzerland AG 2019
S. Chalup et al. (Eds.): RoboCup 2019, LNAI 11531, pp. 337–350, 2019.
https://doi.org/10.1007/978-3-030-35699-6_26

Command understanding is commonly framed as executable semantic parsing [3,19], where the objective is to convert the user command into a logical representation that unambiguously captures the meaning of the command, decoupled from the surface characteristics of the language. For instance, both "Bring me a red apple from the kitchen" and "Could you get me a red apple from kitchen please" might be transformed into a λ-calculus representation like bring($\lambda\$1.$(apple($\$1$) $\wedge$ red($\$1$) $\wedge$ at($\$1$, "kitchen")). This representation can then be grounded immediately by finding satisfactory entities from the robot's ontology or later as a part of executing the resulting plan.

Traditionally, creating usable semantic parsers in a low-data domain has required an expert to craft lexical features or parsing rules. Recent neural semantic parsing approaches have lessened the need for domain specific engineering, but are not easily applied to robotics settings because of the dearth of available annotated data. This data-deficit is likely to persist because the contextual nature of commands makes it challenging to collect data without expensive extended interactions, and there is no deployed base of service robots with which interactions can be gathered en masse.

In this paper, we propose an approach to command understanding in a general-purpose service robot that can make use of recent advances in semantic parsing. Key to our approach is the use of a simplified target representation which trades immediate executablitity under certain circumstances for ease of learning. Further, we leverage pretrained contextual word embeddings to improve the model's generalizability. We evaluate this approach on a new corpus of command-semantics pairs created by crowd-sourcing paraphrases of the generated language used in the *General Purpose Service Robot* task from RoboCup@Home, demonstrating that learned parsers can predict the correct logical form of an unseen command with 89% accuracy.

2   Related Work

Several works have investigated neural methods for semantic parsing [14,16,20]. Our work is based on recent advances in translating language to logical forms using sequence-to-sequence encoder-decoder neural models [6]. Architectures that enforce the constraints of the target representation have been proposed, including recurrent neural network grammars [8], sequence-to-tree methods [6], course-to-fine methods [7], as well as other applications of constrained decoding tailored for semantic parsing [15]. Our work does not enforce decoding constraints, sacrificing potential performance gains for a higher degree of portability across target representations.

Anonymization, also referred to as delexicalization, is frequently used to overcome data sparsity in natural and spoken language systems. Our work is similar in spirit to the argument identification method used by Dong and Lapata [6], but instead of anonymizing entities into unique tokens, we abstract them by type into tokens representing their class. Perhaps closest to our approach is work on weakly-supervised parser learning aided by abstracted representations [12], which similarly proposes leveraging a small lexicon to simplify a visual reasoning domain. Copy mechanisms [13], which enable sequence-to-sequence models to copy portions of their input into their output, are also frequently used to combat data sparsity. Recent work has suggested that copying may dominate delexicalization for several semantic parsing tasks [4]. We do not consider a copy mechanism in this work, as avenues for integrating the robot's knowledge are less available when relying on a learned copying behavior.

The application of contextualized word embeddings to various language tasks is an active area and has seen several early applications to semantic parsing [9]. To our knowledge, this work is the first to evaluate whether contextual embeddings improve performance for semantic parsing in low-data domains.

Many researchers have investigated methods for giving commands to robots [19,24]. Our work is most closely aligned with research from Thomason et al. [25] on continually learning a command parsing and grounding system via dialogue. While we do not consider learning from dialogue interactions, we make the assumption that our understanding system will be used as part of a dialogue agent that can ask for confirmation or corrections. Further, where Thomason et al. initialized their parser by engineering a CCG lexicon against a set of user commands, we use neural methods that directly learn the correspondence between commands and logical forms.

While many teams have built systems motivated specifically by the RoboCup@Home GPSR task, they have largely adopted techniques that depend on knowledge of the command generation grammar [17]. Perhaps the most sophisticated system is that of Bastianelli et al., a frame-semantics based spoken language understanding system for service robots which can integrate and utilize visual information [1,2]. In contrast, our work considers solely the language aspect of command understanding, and takes advantage of the flexible nature of neural translation models to avoid prescribing a particular representation.

3   Approach

The thrust of our approach is to leverage the robot's knowledge base to simplify input utterances where possible, then parse them into an abstracted λ-calculus representation where argument slots are left as tokens representing the class of the argument. This simplifies the output space of the parser and enables us to use neural semantic parsing, which would otherwise be infeasible due to a lack of in-domain data. When important information is lost in this simplification, it can be retrieved easily by asking the user for clarification. An overview of this framing is shown in Fig. 1. We augment a standard encoder-decoder model with contextual embeddings to further ameliorate the challenge of data-scarcity.

3.1   Command Anonymizer

Though service robots operate in an open world and thus cannot assume complete knowledge of the environment, they are usually equipped with ontologies specifying basic knowledge about objects and locations. We leverage this

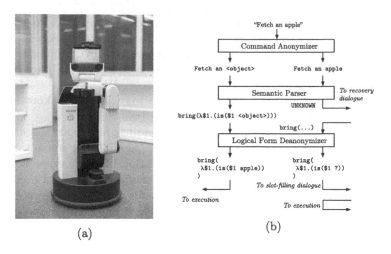

(a)

(b)

Fig. 1. (a) The Toyota Human Support Robot is used as a standard platform in the RoboCup@Home competition. (b) A high level overview of how the approach converts a natural language command to a logical form. The left path traces successful execution of each step. The right path shows how failures can be addressed by gathering additional information via dialogue interaction.

to anonymize commands where possible: Any token in the input command for which we have an name entry in the knowledgebase is replaced with a special token denoting its class. For instance, the command "Fetch an apple from the kitchen" would be anonymized to "Fetch an <object> from the <location>."

When anonymization is successful, it reduces the complexity of the semantic parsing task. For commands with arguments that fall within the robot's ontology, the model is no longer required to generalize parses across instantiations with slightly different entities. Further, anonymization guarantees that newly added entities can be used in the same commands that worked for previous entities. Because users will frequently refer to previously unknown objects or use unfamiliar language to refer to known objects however, the semantic parser must still be robust to partially- or even completely non-anonymized commands.

3.2 Semantic Parser

Following Dong and Lapata [6], our parser is a sequence-to-sequence (seq2seq) bidirectional LSTM encoder-decoder model with a bilinear attention mechanism which takes language input and translates it to a logical form. This architecture is shown in Fig. 2. Input tokens are represented with a concatenation of a contextualized word embedding and their 100D GloVe embedding [21]. For anonymized commands, the embedding provides a signal for which class of command is being asked for, as the interchangeability of verbs is captured. For partially anonymized commands, which the model receives when anonymization is unsuccessful, the embeddings may help if the unknown referent phrase embeds near arguments seen during training.

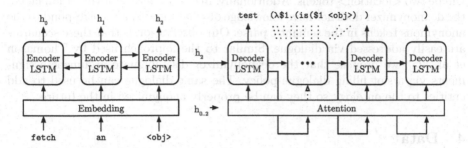

Fig. 2. The outline of the seq2seq architecture, shown encoding a command and decoding a logical form. Special start and end tokens are omitted for clarity. Arrows denote representations passing between modules.

We adopt λ-calculus for our logical representation, but counter to typical practice where output forms are fully specified, we use an intermediate, anonymized form. Similar to the anonymized form of a command, arguments to predicates are represented as abstract class tokens that encode the type of the argument but not its identity. For instance, the command "Navigate to the kitchen, look for the apple, and give it to Bill" has corresponding anonymized form

$$\text{bring}(\lambda\$1.(\text{is\_a}(\$1, <\text{object}>) \land \text{at}(\$1, <\text{room}>)), \lambda\$1.(\text{person}(\$1) \land \\ \text{name}(\$1, <\text{name}>))).$$

This representation retains the expressive power of λ-calculus, which can capture compositional aspects of common commands (e.g. "Bring me the [apple [from the counter [by the refrigerator]]]"), but discards the separate challenge of properly assigning arguments to leaf predicates. Our observation is that, by applying this abstraction, the space of output logical forms is significantly contracted for a set of representative robot commands, enabling us to train useful models even with relatively little data.

3.3 Logical Form Deanonymizer

The output of the semantic parser is an anonymized logical form. In order for the robot to execute the command however, this form must be deanonymized into a fully specified logical expression.

In cases where the anonymizer had replaced spans in the original input utterance, the deanonymizer has access to the correspondence between the class tokens and the original text that they replaced. In many cases, this allows the deanonymizer to automatically reconstruct the full logical form. In some cases, however, there may be multiple possible matchings between class tokens in the anonymized command and the anonymized logical form. For instance, for the command "Move the apple from the kitchen counter to the dining table", there will be two <location> tokens. Additionally, in cases where anonymization failed, the deanonymizer does not have knowledge of what input spans correspond to the anonymous tokens in the semantic parse. Our observation is that these scenarios are easily addressed via dialogue. Similar to the approach used by Thomason et al. [25], we propose that the deanonymizer disambiguate argument assignments via a slot filling dialogue policy. The same dialogue can be used to add entities to the ontology so they can be properly anonymized in the future.

4   Data

To our knowledge, there is no GPSR-style corpus of sufficient scale to evaluate our approach, so we constructed a set of anonymized command-semantics pairs based on the command generator[1] used in the *General Purpose Service Robot* task from the 2018 international RoboCup@Home domestic service robotics competition [18]. In the GPSR task, robots are read a generated command which they must carry out in a mock-apartment arena. These commands are intended to encompass all of the capabilities that are assessed in other tasks in the competition, including things like finding people and fetching objects. We supplemented the synthetic data from the generator with paraphrases gathered via crowdsourcing. In this section, we describe the details of the construction of these datasets.[2]

4.1   Generated

The generator is specified as a probabilistic context-free grammar with equal weighting on all production rules, split into three categories. Each category introduces both more complicated commands as well as more complicated desired goals. Example commands are provided for each category in Table 2 and summary information about the grammar is shown in Table 1.

The generator is distributed with an ontology describing objects, object categories, person names, gestures, question-answer pairs, common sayings, and household locations. Because commands have multiple highly-branching non-terminals representing entities from the ontology, the number of full expansions grows exponentially in the size of the ontology. However, we observe that the number of distinct anonymized commands is actually quite low, and the number of distinct logical forms is lower still.

---

[1] The generator is available at https://github.com/kyordhel/GPSRCmdGen. At the time of this work, the 2019 generator had not been finalized.

[2] The data and splits used for our experiments are available at https://doi.org/10.5281/zenodo.3244800.

Table 1. Summary of our annotations to the 2018 *General Purpose Service Robot* task command generator, broken down by category. "Annotations" refers to the number of logical templates that were annotated atop the grammar rules. "Logical forms" is the number of unique anonymized logical forms produced by expanding the annotations. Because categories overlap slightly, we count commands and logical forms as belonging to the first category that they appear in. Length is measured in tokens and includes all tokens that would be given or expected from a model. On average, 58% of logical form tokens are parentheses, quotation marks, or λ-calculus variable type markers.

Category	1	2	3	All
Anonymized commands	192	352	667	1211
Logical forms	17	39	45	101
Annotations	28	53	44	125
Complexity Measures				
Average command length	11.9	12.2	10.4	11.3
Average logical form length	28.4	27.0	22.6	25.1
Commands to forms ratio	11.3	9.0	14.8	12.0

We defined a logical domain consisting of 27 predicates (7 actions, 20 descriptive) and used them to create 125 annotations that provide logical forms for all 1211 distinct anonymized commands. These predicates cover concepts such as names, basic prepositions (e.g. `at`, `left_of`), and entity types (e.g. `person`, `object`).

There is no general correspondence between the structure of the generation grammar and the structure of the resulting logical representation; however expansions near the leaves frequently take forms that can be neatly tagged with a semantic template. Thus we annotate partial expansions from the generator with an accompanying semantic template which contains some of the same nonterminals, creating a shallow synchronous context free grammar that produces both commands and their logical representations when expanded.

For instance, a partial expansion that produces "bring" commands contains a nonterminal which produces synonymous verbs and another non-terminal which produces different objects. Its annotation incorporates the object non-terminal but discards the verb non-terminal as its expansions do not affect the semantics of the command:

$$\$vbbring\ me\ the\ \$object = bring(\lambda\$1.(is\_a(\$1, \$object)))$$

Continuing to expand both the command and this semantic template will result in a fully specified command-semantics pair. To produce pairs of anonymized commands and anonymized logical forms, we simply modify productions associated with ontology entities to produce our class tokens.

4.2   Paraphrases

Although the GPSR command generator is designed with naturalism in mind, it is nonetheless artificial. In order to understand how our approach will fair given more realistic input, we applied a similar methodology as that of Wang, Berant and Liang to crowdsource paraphrases of our generated dataset [26]. Crowd workers were provided fully-expanded generated commands and prompted to provide a paraphrased version—new text that captures all of the same information but uses different words or phrasing. We nudged workers to provide substantial paraphrases by presenting a warning UI if their input was below a threshold of Levenshtein (character) and Jaccard (word) distances from the original command. A similar warning was presented if the same metrics indicated that the paraphrase contained almost no overlap, as this almost always indicated that important information was discarded. To help filter out low-quality responses, we required crowd-workers to write their own commands based on their impression of what the robot could do. Spam responses to these questions consistently indicated spam responses to the paraphrasing task.

We used Amazon Mechanical Turk to collect 1836 paraphrases from 95 workers, ensuring there were at least 10 paraphrases per logical form. The mean Levenshtein and Jaccard distances between a paraphrase and its original command are 28.0 and 0.59 respectively. Sample paraphrases are shown in Table 2.

Table 2. Examples of fully-expanded commands, their anonymized forms, crowdsourced paraphrases, and corresponding logical forms from each category of the GPSR task.

Category	Example
1	tell me how many coke there are on the freezer
	tell me how many <object> there are on the <location>
	"how many cokes are left in the freezer"
	say(count(λ\$1.(is_a(\$1,<object>)) $\wedge$ at(\$1,<location>))))
2	tell me what's the largest object from the bar
	tell me what's the largest object from the <location>
	"Which is the largest object on top of the bar"
	say(λ\$1.(largest(\$1) $\wedge$ at(\$1,<location>)))
3	Could you give me the object on top of the glass from the coffee table
	Could you give me the object on top of the <object> from the <location>
	"can you bring be the thing from the coffee table thats on top of the glass"
	bring(λ\$1.(λ\$2.(is_a(\$2,<object>) $\wedge$ on_top_of(\$1,\$2))),<location>)

5   Experiments

We evaluate whether it is feasible to learn usable semantic parsers under our approach given the relatively small amount of data available. Our metric is exact-match accuracy; the percentage of logical forms that a model predicts exactly correctly on held-out test data.

Though we are primarily interested in how well models perform on the paraphrased data—as this best represents real language that a robot may encounter—we take advantage of the generated-paraphrased corpus' parallel nature to investigate a range of interesting configurations:

1. *Train generated, test generated* lets us see whether a learned model can approximate the performance of a grammar-based chart-parser, even without having access to the full grammar.
2. *Train generated, test paraphrased* exposes the extent to which the generator captures aspects of natural commands.
3. *Train paraphrased, test paraphrased* shows a model's capacity to generalize across real commands.
4. *Train generated and paraphrased, test paraphrased* can reveal whether there are any benefits to augmenting the paraphrased data with synthetic language.

To better approximate the conditions of a real service robot deployment, we do not use prior knowledge of entities in our experiments. Generated data consists purely of pairs of anonymized commands and anonymized logical forms. Paraphrased commands are not anonymized before being processed by the model.

We split both the generated data and the paraphrased data 70%/10%/20% into training, validation and test sets. Splits are such that no command appears in more than one set. As noted by Finegan et al., testing only generalization to unseen commands can reward models that learn to simply classify commands and produce memorized logical forms [10]. To evaluate whether models are able to produce correct, unseen logical forms, we use an additional logical split. This split forces the pools of logical forms in each part of the dataset to be disjoint. We ensure that the logical split roughly matches the proportions of the command split, and that the split is synchronized across generated and paraphrased data so that they can be combined without causing data leakage.

5.1   Training Regime

We use the Adam optimizer to minimize the cross entropy of the predicted output with the ground truth labels. Training is performed for 150 epochs with early stopping (patience $= 10$) based on accuracy evaluation on the validation set. We use an encoder dropout probability of 1. Test- and validation-time decoding is performed using beam search with a width of 5. Our experiments are built on top of AllenNLP [11] which uses the PyTorch deep learning framework.[3]

---

[3] The details of our implementation, including the full parameterization of our experiments, is available at https://doi.org/10.5281/zenodo.3246755.

We provide results using each of ELMo [22], OpenAI GPT1 [23], BERT$_{base}$, BERT$_{large}$ [5], with a comparison against a model that forgoes a contextual word embedding and simply uses GloVe. We leave the contextual word embedding frozen during training and instead allow tuning of the GloVe weights to avoid catastrophic forgetting.

5.2 Baseline Models

We compare our models against two simple baselines. GRAMMAR-ORACLE chart parses test samples using the generation grammar and looks up the corresponding annotation to return a logical form. Because it always has full access to the grammar, its predictions depend only on whether the test data are within the grammar. The K-nearest neighbors (KNN) model predicts the label of a test command by searching for its nearest neighbor amongst the training and validation data. We found empirically that using Jaccard distance and $K = 1$ worked well. This model is naturally incapable of predicting labels it has never seen before, so it always scores 0% when evaluated on a logical split.

6 Results

The results of our experiments are shown in Table 3. The columns of the table and our discussion are ordered to match the sequence of the descriptions given in Sect. 5.

1. When trained and evaluated on synthetic data, neural semantic parsing models easily fit to the surface characteristics of the data, achieving accuracy levels of 98.8% on unseen commands, despite not having access to the underlying grammar.
2. Models trained with the generated data achieve at most 27.6% accuracy on unseen paraphrased commands. All models are bested by the KNN baseline. As the generated training data doesn't contain any entities, it is unsurprising that test performance on the completely non-anonymized paraphrasing data is poor. The results indicate that around a quarter of the paraphrased commands can be resolved purely by looking for structural patterns learned from the generated language.
3. The best model trained on paraphrased data alone is able to achieve 78.5% accuracy on unseen commands, indicating that neural semantic parsers are reasonably capable of handling a realistic GPSR task. Comparing the best BERT-based model against the model with no contextual word embedding indicates that these large pretrained models can provide around an 8% performance improvement for this task.
4. Training with both the generated and paraphrased data leads to a consistent and large performance boost across all models, yielding the best performing model as evaluated on the paraphrasing test set. This result is possibly a reflection of headroom for improvement if more real data were available to the model.

Mirroring previously reported results on text-to-SQL tasks [10], the generalization achieved across unseen commands does not extend to unseen logical forms.

Table 3. Accuracy of models and ablations on different datasets. "C" indicates results from data split on commands while "λ" indicates results from data split on logical forms.

Train	Gen.				Para.		G. + P.	
Test	Gen.		Para.		Para.		Para.	
Split	C	λ	C	λ	C	λ	C	λ
GRAMMAR-ORACLE	100.0	100.0	1.1	0.9	1.1	0.9	1.1	0.9
KNN	63.0	0.0	**42.0**	0.0	42.8	0.0	49.8	0.0
SEQ2SEQ	95.9	0.0	13.0	0.0	64.4	0.0	79.6	0.0
+ GloVe	**98.8**	26.3	12.4	0.0	70.2	0.0	85.3	6.3
+ GloVe;ELMo	**98.8**	36.2	21.3	0.0	77.3	22.1	85.4	34.4
+ GloVe;OpenAI	97.9	24.6	27.6	1.8	78.2	26.3	89.0	**37.9**
+ GloVe;BERT$_{base}$	96.3	**56.9**	12.2	3.3	75.4	**31.3**	87.6	37.6
+ GloVe;BERT$_{large}$	97.9	54.7	27.1	**9.6**	**78.5**	30.4	**89.4**	37.6

6.1 Error Analysis

We manually inspected the predictions of the best paraphrase parsing model, seq2seq with GloVe and BERT$_{large}$, to better understand the model's generalization and common errors.

Table 4. Multiple inputs mapping to the same, incorrect logical form

x_1	"Bring an umbrella"
x_2	"Navigate to the hallway"
x_3	"Do this then that"
$y_1 = y_2 = y_3$ (go "<room>")	

Unexpected Defaults. As shown in Table 4, we observed that disparate commands can produce the same prediction. One explanation is that no probable solutions are found during decoding, so output tends to a default that is helpful for fitting the training data. Sampling additional commands that yield UNKNOWN might address this. Alternatively, a confidence threshold could be used to discard low scoring decodings.

Table 5. Predictions can change based on a single word

x_4	"Bring an umbrella to me"
y_4	(bring (λ \$1 e (is_a \$1 "<object>")))
x_5	"Bring an umbrella to Bob"
y_5	(go "<room>")
x_6	"Bring an umbrella to him"
y_6	(guide (λ \$1 e (person \$1) (name \$1 "<name>")) "<location>")

Overly Sensitive. As illustrated in Table 5, inputs that differ by a single word can be parsed to drastically different logical forms. Thus we suspect that the model put undue emphasis on the different arguments when predicting the first predicate.

7   Discussion

We have shown that the task of understanding commands in a general-purpose service robot domain can be successfully addressed using neural semantic parsing methods. Key to this success is the use of contextual word embeddings and a abstracted target representation which simplifies the learning task. Though anonymization may require a clarification dialogue for complex commands, such a dialogue would, in practice, occur regardless simply to confirm the command.

The dataset produced for this work is a strong common basis for command-taking in general-purpose service robots. Though the task and the generator are set in the home, the types of goals that arise from the commands apply to a wide variety domains. Thus, we expect that this data can be used to accelerate future efforts to bootstrap command understanding systems for service robots. We hope that the ease with which it is possible to train capable systems under this framework will motivate members of the RoboCup@Home and service robotics communities to expand their expectations of robot language understanding systems.

Acknowledgements. We thank Yuqian Jiang, Jesse Thomason, and the anonymous reviewers for their helpful feedback. This work was supported by HONDA award "Curious Minded Machines" and the National Science Foundation award IIS-1552427 "CAREER: End-User Programming of General-Purpose Robots."

References

1. Bastianelli, E., Castellucci, G., Croce, D., Iocchi, L., Basili, R., Nardi, D.: HuRIC: a human robot interaction corpus. In: Chair, N.C.C., et al. (eds.) Proceedings of the Ninth International Conference on Language Resources and Evaluation (LREC 2014). European Language Resources Association (ELRA), Reykjavik, May 2014

2. Bastianelli, E., Croce, D., Vanzo, A., Basili, R., Nardi, D.: A discriminative app-roach to grounded spoken language understanding in interactive robotics. In: Proceedings of the Twenty-Fifth International Joint Conference on Artificial Intelligence, IJCAI 2016, New York, NY, USA, 9–15 July 2016, pp. 2747–2753 (2016)

3. Chen, D.L., Mooney, R.J.: Learning to interpret natural language navigation instructions from observations, pp. 859–865, August 2011

4. Damonte, M., Goel, R., Chung, T.: Practical semantic parsing for spoken language understanding. In: Proceedings of the 2019 Conference of the North American Chapter of the Association for Computational Linguistics: Human Language Technologies, Volume 2 (Industry Papers), pp. 16–23. Association for Computational Linguistics, Minneapolis, June 2019

5. Devlin, J., Chang, M.W., Lee, K., Toutanova, K.: Bert: pre-training of deep bidirectional transformers for language understanding. arXiv preprint arXiv:1810.04805 (2018)

6. Dong, L., Lapata, M.: Language to logical form with neural attention. In: Proceedings of the 54th Annual Meeting of the Association for Computational Linguistics (Volume 1: Long Papers), pp. 33–43. Association for Computational Linguistics (2016). https://doi.org/10.18653/v1/P16-1004

7. Dong, L., Lapata, M.: Coarse-to-fine decoding for neural semantic parsing. In: Proceedings of the 56th Annual Meeting of the Association for Computational Linguistics (Volume 1: Long Papers), pp. 731–742. Association for Computational Linguistics, Melbourne, July 2018

8. Dyer, C., Kuncoro, A., Ballesteros, M., Smith, N.A.: Recurrent neural network grammars. In: Proceedings of the 2016 Conference of the North American Chapter of the Association for Computational Linguistics: Human Language Technologies, pp. 199–209. Association for Computational Linguistics, San Diego, June 2016. https://doi.org/10.18653/v1/N16-1024

9. Einolghozati, A., et al.: Improving semantic parsing for task oriented dialog. arXiv preprint arXiv:1902.06000 (2019)

10. Finegan-Dollak, C., et al.: Improving text-to-SQL evaluation methodology. In: Proceedings of the 56th Annual Meeting of the Association for Computational Linguistics (Volume 1: Long Papers), pp. 351–360. Association for Computational Linguistics (2018)

11. Gardner, M., et al.: AllenNLP: a deep semantic natural language processing platform (2017)

12. Goldman, O., Latcinnik, V., Nave, E., Globerson, A., Berant, J.: Weakly supervised semantic parsing with abstract examples. In: Proceedings of the 56th Annual Meeting of the Association for Computational Linguistics (Volume 1: Long Papers), pp. 1809–1819. Association for Computational Linguistics, Melbourne, July 2018

13. Gu, J., Lu, Z., Li, H., Li, V.O.: Incorporating copying mechanism in sequence-to-sequence learning. In: Proceedings of the 54th Annual Meeting of the Association for Computational Linguistics (Volume 1: Long Papers), pp. 1631–1640. Association for Computational Linguistics, Berlin, August 2016. https://doi.org/10.18653/v1/P16-1154

14. Kočiský, T., et al.: Semantic parsing with semi-supervised sequential autoencoders. In: Proceedings of the 2016 Conference on Empirical Methods in Natural Language Processing. Association for Computational Linguistics, Austin, November 2016

15. Krishnamurthy, J., Dasigi, P., Gardner, M.: Neural semantic parsing with type constraints for semi-structured tables. In: Proceedings of the 2017 Conference on Empirical Methods in Natural Language Processing, pp. 1516–1526. Association for Computational Linguistics, Copenhagen, September 2017. https://doi.org/10.18653/v1/D17-1160

16. Lewis, M., Lee, K., Zettlemoyer, L.: LSTM CCG parsing. In: Proceedings of the 15th Annual Conference of the North American Chapter of the Association for Computational Linguistics (2016)

17. Matamoros, M., Harbusch, K., Paulus, D.: From commands to goal-based dialogs: a roadmap to achieve natural language interaction in robocup@home. CoRR abs/1902.00754 (2019)

18. Matamoros, M., Rascon, C., Hart, J., Holz, D., van Beek, L.: Robocup@home 2018: rules and regulations (2018). http://www.robocupathome.org/rules/2018_rulebook.pdf

19. Matuszek, C., Herbst, E., Zettlemoyer, L., Fox, D.: Learning to parse natural language commands to a robot control system. In: Desai, J., Dudek, G., Khatib, O., Kumar, V. (eds.) Experimental Robotics, vol. 88, pp. 403–415. Springer, Heidelberg (2013). https://doi.org/10.1007/978-3-319-00065-7_28

20. Misra, D., Artzi, Y.: Neural shift-reduce CCG semantic parsing. In: Proceedings of the 2016 Conference on Empirical Methods in Natural Language Processing. pp. 1775–1786. Association for Computational Linguistics (2016)

21. Pennington, J., Socher, R., Manning, C.: Glove: Global vectors for word representation. In: Proceedings of the 2014 Conference on Empirical Methods in Natural Language Processing (EMNLP), pp. 1532–1543 (2014)

22. Peters, M.E., et al.: Deep contextualized word representations. In: Proceedings of NAACL (2018)

23. Radford, A., Narasimhan, K., Salimans, T., Sutskever, I.: Improving language understanding by generative pre-training (2018)

24. Tellex, S., et al.: Understanding natural language commands for robotic navigation and mobile manipulation. In: Proceedings of the National Conference on Artificial Intelligence (AAAI) (2011)

25. Thomason, J., et al.: Improving grounded natural language understanding through human-robot dialog. In: International Conference on Robotics and Automation (ICRA) (2019)

26. Wang, Y., Berant, J., Liang, P.: Building a semantic parser overnight. In: Proceedings of the 53rd Annual Meeting of the Association for Computational Linguistics and the 7th International Joint Conference on Natural Language Processing (Volume 1: Long Papers), pp. 1332–1342. Association for Computational Linguistics, Beijing, July 2015. https://doi.org/10.3115/v1/P15-1129

Efficient and Robust 3D Object Reconstruction Based on Monocular SLAM and CNN Semantic Segmentation

Thomas Weber[1](✉), Sergey Triputen[1](✉), Atmaraaj Gopal[1], Steffen Eißler[1], Christian Höfert[1], Kristiaan Schreve[2], and Matthias Rätsch[1]

[1] Reutlingen University, 72762 Reutlingen, Germany
{thomas.weber,sergey.triputen,matthias.raetsch}@reutlingen-university.de
[2] University of Stellenbosch, Stellenbosch, South Africa
kschreve@sun.ac.za
https://www.visir.org

Abstract. Various applications implement SLAM technology, especially in the field of robot navigation. We show the advantage of SLAM technology for independent 3D object reconstruction. To receive a point cloud of every object of interest void of its environment, we leverage deep learning. We utilize recent CNN deep learning research for accurate semantic segmentation of objects. In this work, we propose two fusion methods for CNN-based semantic segmentation and SLAM for the 3D reconstruction of objects of interest in order to obtain a more robustness and efficiency. As a major novelty, we introduce a CNN-based masking to focus SLAM only on feature points belonging to every single object. Noisy, complex or even non-rigid features in the background are filtered out, improving the estimation of the camera pose and the 3D point cloud of each object. Our experiments are constrained to the reconstruction of industrial objects. We present an analysis of the accuracy and performance of each method and compare the two methods describing their pros and cons.

Keywords: 3D reconstruction · SLAM · LSD-SLAM · Monocular camera · CNN · Semantic segmentation · Bin-picking · Collaborative robot · Depth estimation

1 Motivation

Our research is mainly motivated by tasks given by our industrial partners in facial recognition, industrial automation, and robot navigation.

T. Weber and S. Triputen—These authors contributed equally to this work.
This work is partially supported by a grant of the BMBF FHprofUnt program, no. 13FH049PX5.

S. Chalup et al. (Eds.): RoboCup 2019, LNAI 11531, pp. 351–363, 2019.
https://doi.org/10.1007/978-3-030-35699-6_27

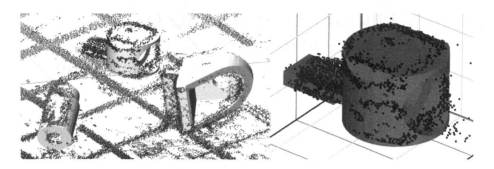

Fig. 1. (left) Point cloud produced from LSD-SLAM with the respective 3D model of the object aligned to its point cloud. (right) Point cloud of red labeled object of interest. (Color figure online)

While they have distinct specifications and requirements for their preferred task solutions, there is a common overlap of interest in 3D surface reconstruction, as seen in Fig. 1.

Therefore, our group has been looking for possible solutions or a combination of solutions to fulfill the 3D reconstruction challenge and to possibly improve it. In particular, we analyze our proposed solution and present the results concerning accuracy, performance and commercial feasibility.

In this paper, we propose two distinct methods for the 3D reconstruction of objects, characterized by semantic segmentation of the frames that are either input to an output from SLAM. To the best of our knowledge, this is the first work proposing a fusion with a focus of SLAM only to the points belonging to every single object of interest. The main contribution of this paper is a highly efficient and robust 3D object reconstruction. It is based on two different fusion methods of semantic segmentation via CNN and monocular visual SLAM. We focus the estimation of the 3D point cloud and camera trajectory obtained by SLAM to only the feature points belonging to every single object of interest. Therefore, robust and accurate 3D reconstruction, even in dynamic environments and in non-rigid world scenarios, can be obtained. Feature points not belonging to the object, within the background, or with low accuracy and noise are filtered out. We analyze the accuracy and performance of the fusion methods of CNN-based semantic segmentation with LSD-SLAM for 3D reconstruction.

We contribute (1) two fusion methods of CNN-based segmentation with SLAM for the 3D reconstruction; (2) an analysis of the accuracy and performance of the proposed methods; and as a significant novelty, (3) a pipeline to reconstruct the 3D point cloud of every single object of interest void of the background.

2   Problem Definition and Related Work

Our research targets to reconstruct the point cloud of a single object of interest with a monocular SLAM technology. There are various approaches available for 3D reconstruction. Considering the advantages that a relatively low-cost and smaller monocular camera could provide in an industrial environment, we choose to employ and improve the monocular SLAM technology in our experiments. The monocular camera is especially optimal for applications on embedded platforms, where CMOS image sensors are preferred. A further description of feasible depth sensing options is presented in [23], where the properties of different direct depth measurement sensors (i.e. stereo and RGB-D cameras, lasers, and optical scanning) and the depth estimation algorithm with SLAM are outlined.

There is a state-of-the-art visual odometry solution, the Semi-direct Visual Odometry (SVO) [7,8,19], which allows robust feature point tracking in dynamic environments and produces accurate point clouds. SVO is exceptionally stable and reliable when used with event-based cameras. These cameras are however significantly more expensive in comparison to monocular cameras and do not offer functionality to extract the point cloud of an object of interest. Nevertheless, the methods that we propose in this paper could be implemented with SVO to semantically label and reconstruct an object in the scene.

Since monocular SLAM produces semi-dense reconstruction [5,6,11,12,16,17], it is necessary that its accuracy is analyzed before approaching methods to improve the reconstruction quality. However, whenever monocular SLAM is employed there is the point cloud scaling and space alignment problem, which is a well-known problem among SLAM researchers and has been solved in various forms, i.e. through inertial measurement unit (IMU) sensor integration [9] and forward kinematics [23], to name a few.

The work in [18,22] propose solutions based on the combination of semantic segmentation with monocular SLAM, wherein they semantically label the point cloud from SLAM with bounding boxes [18] or pixel-wise [22]. Our goal is to reconstruct a point cloud for a single predetermined object instead of the whole scene. An example of an industrial bin-picking use-case for the point cloud would be to register it to the 3D model of the object, which scales the point cloud and then determines the gripping point on the object's surface. We propose a reconstruction solution with optimal accuracy based on CNN semantic segmentation [1,14,21] in combination with SLAM technology. Given that the CNN is trained to recognize a specific set of industrial objects, the real dimensions of the recognized object are known and could be used to scale the object's point cloud. Contrary to [18], we also measure and evaluate the accuracy of the reconstruction.

3   System Components Overview

In order to implement the proposed methods, we first outline our experimental constraints and the subsystems of choice. We present a list of objects of interest, the SLAM technology used, the CNN-based masking of the input data and framework of our proposed solution.

Fig. 2. The three industrial objects of interest and their 3D models: (f.l.t.r.) angle clamp bracket, universal-butt-fastener and automatic-butt-fastener.

3.1 Objects of Interest

We have determined the requirements for the objects of interest to improve our research result relevancy towards industrial applications. The chosen objects have to be present in industrial environments and their 3D CAD models have to be available to analyze the accuracy of reconstruction.

The objects we have selected, as shown in Fig. 2, are parts of the industrial building kit connectors from *item*®. The 3D CAD models of each of these objects are available for download in several formats from the online product catalog.

3.2 SLAM Technology Overview

Our proposed solutions could be incorporated into almost all available monocular SLAM systems. The SLAM technology that we have chosen to use for our experiments is the LSD-SLAM developed by the Computer Vision team from the Technical University of Munich [6], due to the prior experience and in-depth understanding of their open-source code. For most of the experiments done with LSD-SLAM, it is sufficient to consider the technology as a complete black box solution. However, our implementation requires that the processing pipeline of LSD-SLAM is understood. It is made up of several software nodes, namely the `slam_core` and the `slam_viewer`. These nodes have distinct functions.

`slam_core:` The task of the `slam_core` is to receive a stream of input frames and produce keyframes. Our research requires distinguishing the pre-processing and tracking components in `slam_core`. We prioritize a thorough understanding of the pre-processing stage and its functions. This section contains algorithms to determine feature points based on gradient vectors. These feature points would then be used by the tracking algorithm to estimate the camera pose. They are also the criteria to determine the subsequent keyframe. It is significant to note that the feature points are determined in the pre-processing section, based on the pixel gradients. Being aware of this assists in understanding the logic behind our proposed solution description. Additionally, the quality of the depth estimations in the keyframes is the basis for our accuracy analysis.

`slam_viewer:` The task of the `slam_viewer` is to receive all keyframes from the `slam_core`, compute the estimated depths based on the estimated camera pose and feature points, and represent these depths as a point cloud. Nonetheless, the node only provides the calculated final point cloud of the scene. This is insufficient for our research. We require further information to represent the estimated depths of a keyframe, and various mathematical and statistical tools for our keyframe-by-keyframe analysis. To comply with these requirements, we implement the slam_viewer node source code in a MATLAB environment, where a representation of the point cloud from each keyframe is visualized.

3.3 Semantic Segmentation Overview

The semantic segmentation of an image means assigning a class label pixel-wise. Multiple instances of the same objects in an image are assigned the same class labels. Thus they are not necessarily distinguishable or separated, so-called instanced. However mere segmentation of objects and "background noise" is sufficient for our task. The development of CNN architecture is not a part of our research. We opt for an Mask R-CNN with pre-trained weights for the MS COCO data-set [15] that we fine-tune in training based on our requirements. The semantic segmentation solution that we employ for our experiments is based on CNN because it boasts robust and accurate results [10]. Our requirements for a CNN based semantic segmentation solution are the ease of use, well documented with examples, compatible with well-known CNN frameworks (i.e. *Tensorflow, Caffe*) and lastly, also provides tools for data representation.

CNNs are commonly trained with more universal data, whereas for our (bin-picking) use-case, the data is constrained to objects and backgrounds of an industrial robot work-space. These constraints allow a more robust CNN semantic segmentation as it is trained with a larger volume of the work-space pictures and relatively few classes. There is also the advantage that industrial environments are controlled to yield stable conditions resulting in optimal segmentation.

We prepared large sets of semi-synthetic ground truth data for fine-tuning the CNN. For this, we combined real-world HDRI environment maps (360° photosphere pictures) as background with physically-based renderings of the industrial objects of interest, based on techniques like [24]. The image generation is done in the free and open source 3D creation suite *Blender* with its physically-based rendering engine *Cycles*. These renderings also contain ground truth pass with segmentation masks and class assignments. Images and ground truth passes are converted into the MS COCO data format to be used to fine-tune the CNN network in training.

This procedure provides us vast amounts of suitable training data without the need for tedious manual, labor-intensive image capturing, labeling and classification, which would be unfeasible for widespread industrial usage.

4   Proposed Solutions Overview

We attempt to solve the problems by implementing solutions based on the semantic segmentation methodology, which assigns a predefined class to each pixel of an image. The work [18] proposes a solution to this approach, wherein a form of object detection (or semantic segmentation) is used in combination with SLAM.

FLAIR feature encoding is used in this work to detect and build bounding boxes around the object(s) of interest. Furthermore, the problem their work seeks to solve is distinct to ours, as they employ SLAM to bolster the quality and accuracy of object recognition, whereas our goal is the inverse of it. We aim to measure and improve the accuracy of SLAM reconstruction of an object by object recognition. We expect that a CNN-based recognition would improve the accuracy of segmentation, because the latter exclusively labels each pixel of the objects of interest, while the bounding boxes from the former still include a part of the environment. We further hypothesize that a more accurate segmentation of the object(s) from the background results in a more precise reconstruction. The two methods we propose to employ CNN semantic segmentation supported monocular SLAM to reconstruct an object of interest in the scene. Although both yield a point cloud of an object isolated from its environment, there are differences in reconstruction accuracy and computing performance, we investigate.

4.1   Method I - CNN Semantic Segmentation Applied to Output Keyframes

Description: The idea of the first method is to apply semantic segmentation to the keyframes output by SLAM, as proposed in [18]. This method would result in a complete point cloud of the scene with the objects of interest labeled, allowing the object's point cloud to be extracted from its environment. The semantic segmentation system they employ is non-CNN in combination with monocular ORB-SLAM [16,17]. Accuracy and performance of their reconstruction are not measured nor analyzed. In contrast, we propose to use a CNN-based semantic segmentation [1,14,21] in combination with LSD-SLAM [6]. Their work proves the feasibility and advantages of labeling objects of interest in the SLAM reconstructed point cloud. Our aim is also to measure, analyze and improve the performance and accuracy of the 3D reconstruction. As there was no data on the accuracy of the reconstruction in their work, we re-implement this idea and measure the accuracy of the reconstruction and the computing performance of the system, with the constraints discussed in Sect. 3.1. We hypothesize that high recognition accuracy is achievable when a CNN is used for semantic segmentation. This CNN solution could be more processing power demanding, causing a drop in performance, depending on the optimization of the CNN architecture.

Implementation: We present a solution, where the semantic segmentation is applied to the keyframes output from the LSD-SLAM core, as shown in Fig. 3.

A keyframe is made up of the source camera frame, the estimated camera pose and the feature points determined. The camera frames from the tuple of keyframes are input to the semantic segmentation CNN block to recognize, segment and label the pixels in the frames. This block outputs frames, where the background pixels are labeled a monotone grey, while the pixels of interest are segmented and the masks are colored, as shown in Fig. 5(B). The labeled frames are used as a mask to recognize the feature points of interest, from which the feature points of the objects of interest could be determined and isolated. As the point cloud is constructed based on the feature points and the estimated camera pose, the point cloud of the object of interest could be recognized and isolated. Examples resulting from this solution are shown in Fig. 5(E, F, G).

4.2   Method II - CNN Semantic Segmentation Applied to Input Frames

Description: We propose another method of semantic segmentation integration with SLAM, where we recognize the objects in the stream of frames from the monocular camera, instead of the keyframes. As the keyframes themselves are determined based on the feature points on the stream of frames of the camera, we expect a difference in the accuracy and performance with this method. We expect to reduce a significant amount of background in the frame, which means LSD-SLAM would track, estimate the depth and produce a point cloud of only the object of interest. This could result in a better SLAM performance, as there are significantly fewer feature points in the frames. As a result of a focused area of interest on the frame and the background being filtered out, the tracking process in SLAM is speculated to be more efficient and accurate. This is due to minimal variance in the distance between the tracked feature points, given that the object of interest is generally much closer to the camera than the background is. As the camera moves, there will be a change in perspective. The displacement of the tracked feature points is proportional to the distance of the elements in the frame to the camera. Nevertheless, there would be a loss in performance as the semantic segmentation is executed on every camera frame. This could be limiting for embedded systems, but as deep learning frameworks have been optimized to be GPU-accelerated [13,20], this would still be a valid solution for use cases with GPU supported architectures.

Implementation: To solve this task, we extend the *Frames Source* section of LSD-SLAM, as shown in Fig. 4, by processing the frames before they are input to slam_core. While a tuple of RGB frames captured by the monocular camera is gray-scaled, the same tuple is input to the semantic segmentation CNN block to recognize, segment and label the pixels in the frames. Similar to the previous method, the background is labeled a monotone grey, and the objects of interest are respectively colored, as seen in Fig. 6(B). From the tuple of labeled frames, the label of the object of choice is determined (green in this example). We then build binary masks out of these frames by setting the determined pixels of interest generic white, and the rest generic black, as exemplified in Fig. 6(C). These masks are further blurred in gray-scale with a suitable blur factor to reduce the gradients at the edges of the pixel region of interest. This is a necessary step as the gradients are the criteria for determining feature points, and the shading done while building the mask would distort the gradients at the edges of the object. The tuple of masks with their blurred edges are used to filter the grey-scale frames tuple. The resulting frames present only the grey-scaled pixels of the object of choice, while the rest are colored black, as shown in Fig. 6(E). These frames with the background filtered out subsequently are input to slam_core.

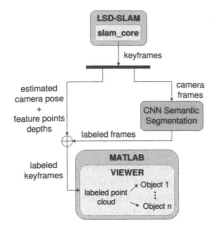

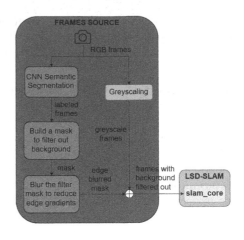

Fig. 3. Method I overview of the data flow and subsystems for the keyframes labeling solution.

Fig. 4. Method II overview of the data flow and subsystems for the all input frames labeling solution.

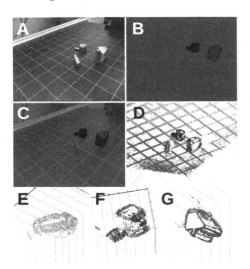

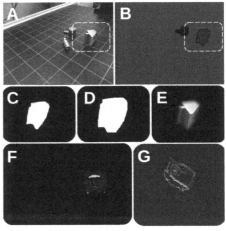

Fig. 5. The fusion of the CNN semantic segmentation with keyframes and the resulting isolated point clouds of each object in the frame. (a) The input camera frame from a selected keyframe. (b) The semantically labeled frame. (c) Input frame with labels overlay. (d) Semantically labeled point cloud of the selected keyframe. Point clouds of the (e) blue, (f) red and (g) green labeled objects of interest. (Color figure online)

Fig. 6. The fusion of the CNN semantic segmentation with the input frames. (a) An input camera frame. (b) The labeled frame. The yellow dashed line is the region of interest (ROI) with the selected object of interest. ROI of (c) the resulted mask from fusion (d) the blurred mask, and (e) the final filtered frame. (f) The LSD-SLAM debug frame with feature points highlighted green and (g) the reconstructed point cloud of the chosen object as shown in the slam_viewer. (Color figure online)

5   Accuracy Analysis

When it comes to 3D reconstruction, one of the primary metrics to determine the quality of reconstruction is the accuracy. A lot of the work in SLAM gives priority to and describes the accuracy of the estimated camera pose and path; however, we aim to analyze the accuracy of the reconstruction of a single object by a SLAM system. Hence, we describe here the methodology used for our result measurement and analysis. We define the accuracy of the reconstruction of an object as the normalized average error between the reconstructed point cloud and the 3D model of the object. The point cloud is first registered to the 3D model before the cloud-to-mesh distance is calculated. The registration is done to scale and transform the reconstructed point cloud to "fit" either the mesh or the dense point cloud from the 3D model. This is generally done via a minimization task that reduces the error between the two entities. There are many algorithms for the registration and cloud-to-mesh error calculation, and we choose to use the algorithms implemented in the open-source software for point cloud and 3D model processing, *CloudCompare* [4]. It provides several tools for manual editing and rendering of 3D point clouds and meshes, from which the most significant for our goal are tools for registration [2] and cloud-to-mesh distance computation [3].

To measure the accuracy of our reconstruction, we first import one instance of the point cloud, cf. Fig. 5(E, F, G), and one of the object's 3D model as a mesh, shown in Fig. 2. We then register the point cloud to the mesh, constraining the registration calculation with a parameter for the maximum error allowed. This results in the point cloud being optimally transformed and fitted to the mesh. From there on, we compute the cloud-to-mesh distance of every point in the point cloud. We obtain mean and standard deviation of the reconstruction error.

These steps are done for every keyframe with the parameters controlled, for both of the methods we propose.

6   Results

In this section, we present the results of our experiments. They are in the form of measurements and statistics of a set of metrics for the implementations of both proposed methods. The performance of both the proposed methods and accuracy of the 3D reconstruction are analyzed and compared to the original LSD-SLAM of the Technical University of Munich.

6.1   Performance Analysis Results

The processing time demanding block in the pipeline for each experiment is the tracking of feature points by slam_core and the semantic segmentation with CNN. Both methods increase processing time compared to the original LSD-SLAM, as there is the additional semantic segmentation of the frames. The empirical metrics defined before measuring the performance are listed in Table 1.

Table 1. Metrics for analyzing the performance obtained by averaging data from LSD-SLAM and CNN semantic segmentation.

Metric	Mean value
KF per frame factor	0.0765
Track time per KF [*ms*]	4311
CNN segmentation time per frame [*ms*]	128.14
Number of feature points per KF	87243

Table 2. Performance metrics for analysis of method II.

Metric	Method I	Method II
Mean feature point per KF factor	1	0.074
Mean KF per frame factor	0.0765	0.1832

The keyframe per frame factor is calculated by the ratio of the number of keyframes (KFs) to the number of input frames from the camera. We understand that the value from one experiment is non-reproducible, as it depends heavily on various variables, i.e., lighting, speed and trajectory of camera motion, and the camera frame rate, and so we obtain a mean value from several experiments. Similarly, the mean tracking time for every keyframe, mean time for CNN inference of a camera frame with a 640×480 *px* resolution and the mean number of feature points per keyframe.

Determining these parameters enables approximation of the time for tracking and segmentation in our methods. For method I, it is relevant to measure the factor between input and output keyframes, since we expect a large number of feature points. The run-time for method I is the sum of the processing time of the original LSD-SLAM to reconstruct the scene and keyframes CNN inference.

To evaluate the performance of method II, we calculate additional metrics as shown in Table 2. Specifically for method II, the performance is determined by the amount of background filtered before tracking. Therefore, we determine the ratio of feature points generated by this method to the mean number of feature points per keyframe, as given in Table 1. The parameter is dependent on the accuracy of the segmentation and the density of feature points in the keyframes. The run-time for method II also varies due to significantly fewer feature points being generated per keyframe. Given a tuple of camera frames with our system specifications, our results prove that method II is twice as fast as method I, based on the values of our performance metrics.

6.2   Accuracy Analysis Results

The analysis of the 3D reconstruction accuracy is carried out in the *CloudCompare* software, as described in Sect. 5. Our metrics for accuracy are the mean normalized error of the registered point cloud from the surface of the object's

Table 3. Mean normalized error of the registered point clouds from their respective 3D model surfaces.

Object	Method I	Method II
Red	0.1583	0.1501
Green	0.2151	0.2203
Blue	0.1688	0.1586

Table 4. Mean normalized standard deviation of the registered point clouds from their respective 3D model surfaces.

Object	Method I	Method II
Red	0.3071	0.1334
Green	0.6044	0.2462
Blue	0.2240	0.1189

mesh, and the mean normalized standard deviation of the errors. Table 3 shows that the mean error for both methods is similar. The mean standard deviation for every object from method II shown in Table 4 confers that the errors are less distributed and the points closer to the surface of the 3D mesh when reconstructed with method II. We infer therefore that method II reconstructs a more accurate point cloud of an object compared to method I. This agrees with our hypothesis of a more accurate 3D reconstruction, due to the reduced number of feature points when the background is filtered out.

7 Conclusion and Further Work

Both in this work proposed methods solve the initial task. We receive independent point clouds of all individual objects of interest.

In method I, we apply CNN-masking only on keyframes. The performance is slower compared to method II, albeit labeling only the keyframes. This is due to the larger number of feature points to be tracked in the keyframes, which increases process time in the LSD-SLAM block of the pipeline. Contrary to method II, we do not use a reduction of feature points for each frame. Method I is optimal for applications with minimal changes in the scene because no keyframe is generated while there is no major change. The semantic segmentation is done after the `slam_core`; thus the accuracy may be lowered due to further "background" feature points not belonging to the object. The method allows the extraction of several objects of interest from the scene's point cloud.

Method II is more resilient to motion in the background of the object and changes in the scene than method I. The camera pose is estimated by solving a minimization task between two point clouds. Point clouds are constructed based on the projection from the camera pose. This pose calculation is sensitive to feature points furthest away from its current position in the keyframes: A slight angular shift translates feature points the more the further away they are from the camera. The minimization task is expected to compute better camera pose estimate when the further feature points are filtered out. With refined, robust CNN-masking, most of the feature points should be concentrated on the object itself; "background noise" is filtered out. The `slam_core` produces keyframes at a higher rate compared to method I. Therefore method II is optimal for 3D reconstruction in dynamic environments and even non-rigid world scenarios.

Additionally, our work can be used as an alternative solution to the scaling problem in SLAM. The CNN semantic segmentation and pose estimation can be used to compute the scaling from the 3D model of the object. The accuracy of the 3D reconstruction is dependent on the accuracy of CNN semantic segmentation. Task- and object-specific CNN architectures could yield further improvements. Adapted CNN architectures may reduce run-time and require less demanding GPUs. As a result, the application could work in real time, even on lower-end hardware. Our further interest is investigating the feasibility, accuracy, and performance of the methods implemented on embedded low-cost systems.

As of now, the CNN semantic segmentation provides no additional information about the camera pose. However, an adapted CNN architecture could be trained to estimate information about the pose of the object. The object pose estimation could be an initial value input to the optimization task, which would facilitate faster solving and determination of the camera pose.

References

1. Badrinarayanan, V., Kendall, A., Cipolla, R.: SegNet: a deep convolutional encoder-decoder architecture for image segmentation. CoRR abs/1511.00561 (2015). http://arxiv.org/abs/1511.00561
2. Besl, P.J., McKay, N.D.: A method for registration of 3-D shapes. IEEE Trans. Pattern Anal. Mach. Intell. **14**(2), 239–256 (1992). https://doi.org/10.1109/34.121791
3. Cignoni, P., Rocchini, C., Scopigno, R.: Metro: measuring error on simplified surfaces, vol. 17, pp. 167–174, July 1998
4. Daniel, G.-M.: CloudCompare. http://www.cloudcompare.org/
5. Engel, J., Sturm, J., Cremers, D.: Semi-dense visual odometry for a monocular camera. In: 2013 IEEE International Conference on Computer Vision, pp. 1449–1456, December 2013. https://doi.org/10.1109/ICCV.2013.183
6. Engel, J., Schöps, T., Cremers, D.: LSD-SLAM: large-scale direct monocular SLAM. In: Fleet, D., Pajdla, T., Schiele, B., Tuytelaars, T. (eds.) ECCV 2014. LNCS, vol. 8690, pp. 834–849. Springer, Cham (2014). https://doi.org/10.1007/978-3-319-10605-2_54
7. Forster, C., Pizzoli, M., Scaramuzza, D.: SVO: fast semi-direct monocular visual odometry. In: 2014 IEEE International Conference on Robotics and Automation (ICRA), pp. 15–22, May 2014. https://doi.org/10.1109/ICRA.2014.6906584
8. Forster, C., Zhang, Z., Gassner, M., Werlberger, M., Scaramuzza, D.: SVO: semidirect visual odometry for monocular and multicamera systems. IEEE Trans. Rob. **33**(2), 249–265 (2017). https://doi.org/10.1109/TRO.2016.2623335
9. Engel, J., Sturm, J., Cremers, D.: Camera-based navigation of a low-cost quadrocopter. In: 2012 IEEE/RSJ International Conference on Intelligent Robots and Systems, pp. 2815–2821, October 2012. https://doi.org/10.1109/IROS.2012.6385458
10. Jafari, O.H., Groth, O., Kirillov, A., Yang, M.Y., Rother, C.: Analyzing modular CNN architectures for joint depth prediction and semantic segmentation. In: 2017 IEEE International Conference on Robotics and Automation (ICRA), pp. 4620–4627, May 2017. https://doi.org/10.1109/ICRA.2017.7989537
11. Klein, G., Murray, D.: Parallel tracking and mapping for small AR workspaces. In: 2007 6th IEEE and ACM International Symposium on Mixed and Augmented Reality, pp. 225–234, November 2007. https://doi.org/10.1109/ISMAR.2007.4538852

12. Klein, G., Murray, D.: Parallel tracking and mapping on a camera phone. In: 2009 8th IEEE International Symposium on Mixed and Augmented Reality, pp. 83–86, October 2009. https://doi.org/10.1109/ISMAR.2009.5336495
13. Li, C., Yang, Y., Feng, M., Chakradhar, S., Zhou, H.: Optimizing memory efficiency for deep convolutional neural networks on GPUs. In: International Conference for High Performance Computing, Networking, Storage and Analysis, SC 2016, pp. 633–644, November 2016. https://doi.org/10.1109/SC.2016.53
14. Lin, G., Milan, A., Shen, C., Reid, I.D.: RefineNet: multi-path refinement networks for high-resolution semantic segmentation. CoRR abs/1611.06612 (2016). http://arxiv.org/abs/1611.06612
15. Lin, T., et al.: Microsoft COCO: common objects in context. CoRR abs/1405.0312 (2014). http://arxiv.org/abs/1405.0312
16. Mur-Artal, R., Tardos, J.: ORB-SLAM: tracking and mapping recognizable features. In: Robotics: Science and Systems (RSS) Workshop on Multi View Geometry in Robotics (MVIGRO), July 2014
17. Mur-Artal, R., Tardós, J.D.: ORB-SLAM2: an Open-Source SLAM System for Monocular, Stereo and RGB-D Cameras. CoRR abs/1610.06475 (2016). http://arxiv.org/abs/1610.06475
18. Pillai, S., Leonard, J.J.: Monocular SLAM supported object recognition. CoRR abs/1506.01732 (2015). http://arxiv.org/abs/1506.01732
19. Pizzoli, M., Forster, C., Scaramuzza, D.: Remode: probabilistic, monocular dense reconstruction in real time. In: 2014 IEEE International Conference on Robotics and Automation (ICRA), pp. 2609–2616, May 2014. https://doi.org/10.1109/ICRA.2014.6907233
20. Strigl, D., Kofler, K., Podlipnig, S.: Performance and scalability of GPU-based convolutional neural networks. In: 2010 18th Euromicro Conference on Parallel, Distributed and Network-based Processing, pp. 317–324, February 2010. https://doi.org/10.1109/PDP.2010.43
21. Su, H., Maji, S., Kalogerakis, E., Learned-Miller, E.G.: Multi-view convolutional neural networks for 3D shape recognition. CoRR abs/1505.00880 (2015). http://arxiv.org/abs/1505.00880
22. Tateno, K., Tombari, F., Laina, I., Navab, N.: CNN-SLAM: real-time dense monocular SLAM with learned depth prediction. ArXiv e-prints April 2017
23. Triputen, S., Gopal, A., Weber, T., Hofert, C., Schreve, K., Rätsch, M.: Methodology to analyze the accuracy of 3D objects reconstructed with collaborative robot based monocular LSD-SLAM. CoRR abs/1803.02257 (2018). http://arxiv.org/abs/1803.02257
24. Zhang, Y., et al.: Physically-based rendering for indoor scene understanding using convolutional neural networks. CoRR abs/1612.07429 (2016). http://arxiv.org/abs/1612.07429

Development Track Papers

On Field Gesture-Based Robot-to-Robot Communication with NAO Soccer Players

Valerio Di Giambattista[1]([✉]), Mulham Fawakherji[1], Vincenzo Suriani[1],
Domenico D. Bloisi[2], and Daniele Nardi[1]

[1] Department of Computer, Control and Management Engineering,
Sapienza University of Rome, via Ariosto 25, 00184 Rome, Italy
`vincsur@gmail.com, nardi@diag.uniroma1.it`
[2] Department of Mathematics, Computer Science, and Economics,
University of Basilicata, viale dell'Ateneo Lucano, 10, 85100 Potenza, Italy
`domenico.bloisi@unibas.it`

Abstract. Gesture-based communication is commonly used by soccer players during matches to exchange information with teammates. Among the possible forms of gesture-based interaction, hand signals are the most used. In this paper, we present a deep learning method for recognizing robot-to-robot hand signals exchanged during a soccer game. A neural network for estimating human body, face, hands, and foot position has been adapted for the application in the robot soccer scenario. Quantitative experiments carried out on NAO V6 robots demonstrate the effectiveness of the proposed approach. Source code and data used in this work are made publicly available for the community.

Keywords: Communication protocols · Team coordination methods · Neural systems and deep learning

1 Introduction

Professional and amateur soccer players commonly use gesture-based communications during games. For example, players use arms to call plays on corner kicks signalling where the ball is heading to (one hand normally means the front post, two hands means the far post—see Fig. 1a and b). Also holding up an arm while shouting for the ball is a common way to get a teammate's attention (Fig. 1c).

In this paper, we describe a deep learning approach for robot-to-robot gesture-based communication to be used during RoboCup soccer matches as in human's soccer. Our goal is to meet the intentions of the RoboCup Standard Platform League (SPL) committee to achieve more and more realistic games. Using gesture recognition is a possible way to deal with (*i*) the recent introduction of free and corner kicks and (*ii*) the limitation of wireless communications (no more than 1 message per second allowed). SPL at RoboCup 2019 permits the use of the V6 version of the NAO humanoid robot manufactured by SoftBank

© Springer Nature Switzerland AG 2019
S. Chalup et al. (Eds.): RoboCup 2019, LNAI 11531, pp. 367–375, 2019.
https://doi.org/10.1007/978-3-030-35699-6_28

(a)   (b)   (c)

Fig. 1. Hand gesture during soccer games. Images from (a) http://thenews.org (b) https://www.dailymail.co.uk (c) https://www.gftskills.com/soccer-sign-language

Robotics that is equipped with a more powerful motherboard than previous versions. This increase in available computational power allows to use deep learning frameworks, such as TensorFlow, Keras or PyTorch, that were unavailable in the past years due to hardware limitations.

The main contributions of this work are:

– The description of a pipeline for estimating the position of body keypoints on the NAO robot.
– The definition of a gesture-based message protocol for robot-to-robot communication inspired to the one used in human's soccer.
– The release of the source code of the proposed approach together with the data used for evaluating it.

The remainder of the paper is structured as follows. Related work is discussed in Sect. 2. The proposed method is presented in Sect. 3. Experimental evaluation is shown in Sect. 4. Finally, conclusions are drawn in Sect. 5.

2   Related Work

Developing human-like robot behaviours is a key aspect for dealing with the RoboCup 2050's challenge, consisting in creating a team of fully autonomous humanoid robot soccer players able to win a soccer game complying with the rules of FIFA against the winner of the World Cup. The actual trend in the RoboCup competitions is to rely less on WiFi communication. In particular, SPL decided to test audio communications by promoting specific technical challenges. However, audio communications suffer a lot from interference and are not robust to noise. Thus, a pure audio approach seems not sufficient to cope with the 2050's challenge.

In 2014, SPL added a technical challenge, called Drop-in Player Competition, where robot originating from different teams and with different software had to play together. This serves as a testbed for cooperation without pre-coordination (see [6]). Pennisi et al. [12] presented an open source framework to extract the orientation of the NAO robots on the field in the same year. The extraction were carried out off the NAO board using external RGB-D sensors. More recently, extraction of NAO orientations in SPL field over short and medium distances has been carried out on the robot hardware both using a domain-specific approach [11] and a Convolutional Neural Network (CNN) [10].

Human-robot interaction using gesture recognition is an active research field. For example, [5,13]. In assistive scenarios, human-robot interaction can be performed with NAO robot platform using gesture communication [2]. In [8], a framework to track hand gestures has been proposed to interact with the same robot platform.

As a difference with existing work on human-robot interaction, we apply gesture based communication for exchanging messages between robots. Among the CNNs based approaches for human posture recognition, OpenPose [4] demonstrated to work well in a variety of scenarios. However, before the release of V6, NAO robots were too limited in computation power to perform CNN computation using general deep learning frameworks [1]. Inspired by human soccer, we propose in this paper a visual communication protocols based on robot posture. The use of postures to the robot-to-robot signal exchange problem is suitable for intention communication in mixed team competitions and in upcoming RoboCup scenarios such as corner kicks.

3   Methods

Figure 2 shows the three main steps of our pipeline. The raw RGB image coming from the NAO top camera is transformed into the HSV color space and it is processed to find the 2D locations of anatomical keypoints for each robot in the image. The pose of the robot is inferred from the list of detected keypoints.

To extract the keypoints we use the open-source library OpenPose[1] proposed by Cao et al. [3]. OpenPose exploits Part Affinity Fields (PAFs) for multi-robot pose estimation. PAFs are sets of 2D vector fields that encode the location and orientation of limbs over the image domain. Even if this approach is particularly cost effective, it can achieve high-quality results. First, a feedforward network

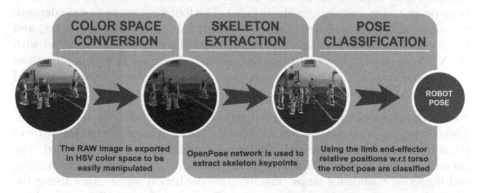

Fig. 2. Our pipeline for robot pose classification.

---

[1] https://github.com/CMU-Perceptual-Computing-Lab/openpose.

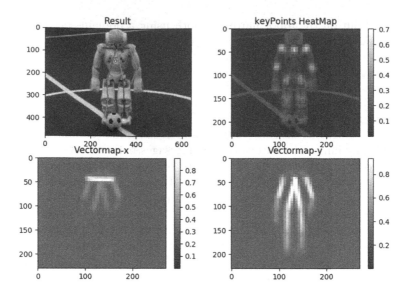

Fig. 3. Robot model.

predicts a set of 2D confidence maps S of body part locations and a set of 2D vector fields L of part affinities, which encode the degree of association between parts. In our pipeline, when the skeleton is extracted from the image, it is classified in one of the four possible poses of interest, namely one arm raised, two arms raised, one arm raised to the side, and no arms raised. Once the current pose has been classified, it is possible to associate a message to the pose for non-verbal coordination.

Robot Model. The skeleton structure used in OpenPose for multi-person 2D pose detection can be used also in the case of NAOs, being them humanoid robots. Figure 3 shows an example of the application of the OpenPose functions on an image containing a single NAO. The following keypoints are defined: *Shoulder, Elbow, Hip, Knee, Eye, Wrist* (left and right for all this parts) and the *Neck*. A dataset of images was created by collecting images acquired with the NAO top camera during outdoor tests simulating corner kick game situations and the position of the above listed keypoints were annotated in accordance of the standard COCO-dataset notation used by OpenPose.

Network Architecture. The original network was modified to increase the confidence range of robot recognition. In this way, the individual mechanical parts of the robot are recognized through the keypoints and then correctly labeled. The network iteratively predicts affinity fields that encode part-to-part association and detection confidence maps. The iterative prediction architecture treats the predictions over successive stages, $t \epsilon (1, ..., T)$, with an intermediate supervision at each stage. In our model the receptive field is preserved, while the computation is composed by three consecutive kernels and the output of each one of them is concatenated. This particular scheme allows to obtain accurate results and to deal with simultaneous detection and association.

We have used an auxiliary CNN model, build from the first 10 layers of VGG-19, to analyze the images taken by NAO robot's camera and extract a features map denoted as F. This features map F is processed by the first stage t_1, to generate a set of part affinity fields (PAFs) following $L_1 = \psi_1(F)$, where ψ_1 refers to the CNNs for inference at network's stage one. The output from this stage and their predictions concatenated with the initial F are used as input for the next stage (as features), to produce refined predictions. This process is repeated on every stage, with T_P iterations where T_P represent the total number of PAF stages. The process is repeated to detect the confidence maps, starting from the updated PAF prediction. In this way, the computation time is reduced and the prediction of confidence map, are done on top of the latest and most refined PAF predictions. At the end of each stage we applied a loss function, to iteratively guide the network's PAFs predictions of body-parts, in the first branch and confidence maps in the second branch.

Fine Tuning. To avoid a full training stage, we decided to carry out a fine-tuning on the models already available for people detection to obtain recognition even for NAO robots.

Implementation Details. OpenPose can run on different platforms and provides support for different hardware, such as OpenCL GPUs and CPU-only devices. The inference time of OpenPose outperforms all state-of-the-art methods with high-quality results, like Mask R-CNN [9] and Alpha-Pose [7] multi-person estimation libraries. To obtain better computational performance, instead of the original OpenPose implementation based on the Caffe framework, we have decided to use TF-Pose network[2], an implementation based on TensorFlow library.

The original network has been modified in order to obtain an optimal recognition, for this reason the parameters of threshold-part-confidence in the PAF module has been modified going to make a 10 % increase with regard to the upper-body detection and a 20% increase for the face detection. The network was trained with 640 × 480 input images, this to ensure that the input images were consistent with the dataset of the models already processed, and once the new model was obtained, true inference tests were performed with several image-sizes in input for optimal performance, as shown in the next section.

4   Experimental Results

To test the performance of the pose recognition task on challenging data, we created a dataset from a game scenario containing images captured outdoor with natural light conditions. This means that different areas of the scene may be subject to high contrast and changes in the brightness values. Figure 4 shows some image samples from the dataset, which is available from download

---

[2] https://github.com/ildoonet/tf-pose-estimation.

Fig. 4. Examples of images from the dataset used for the experimental evaluation.

Fig. 5. Examples with successful classification. (a) One arm raised. (b) Arm to the side. (c) Two arms raised. (d) None – no message.

at: http://www.dis.uniroma1.it/~labrococo/?q=node/459 as part of the **SPQR NAO image dataset**. The images were captured by using the top cameras of different players (i.e., NAO robots) in recreated game situations including corner and free kicks. Generated dataset contain 400 images, 100 images for each pose To the best of our knowledge, this is the first dataset for gesture recognition available in the RoboCup SPL specifically conceived for robot-to-robot gesture-based communication.

Quantitative Evaluation. Figure 5 shows four examples of correctly classified robot poses. The quantitative evaluation of the gesture recognition accuracy is given in the form of the confusion matrix shown in Fig. 6. The gesture denoted as *two_arms_raised* is recognized with an accuracy of 89%, while the other gestures are recognized with lower accuracy. In particular, the lowest accuracy of 68% is obtained for predicting the gesture denoted as *arm_to_the_side*. This is mainly

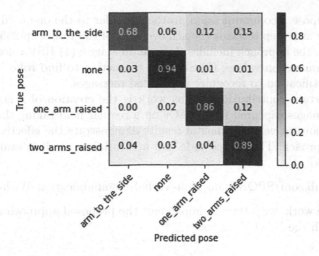

Fig. 6. Confusion matrix obtained using our robot gesture recognition approach

due to the overlap between body and arm of the NAO: 15% of the *one_arm_raised* pose is wrongly detected as *two_arms_raised* due to the similarity between the two poses.

Table 1. Runtime performance of our gesture recognition approach on NAO V6 robot.

Image size	CPU cores	CPU usage (avg.)	RAM usage	fps
232 × 217	4	67%	9%	2.1
320 × 240	4	85%	12%	1.2
432 × 368	4	96%	15%	0.88

Runtime Performance. NAO V6 robot is equipped with an Intel ATOM E3845 1.91 GHz quad core CPU 4GB RAM. To fully exploit the processing power provided by the CPU, the computational load has been spread over the four cores, obtaining the runtime performance shown in Table 1. Using an image size of 320 × 240 pixels it is possible to obtain a processing speed of about 1 frame per second (fps). It is worth noticing that, in our intention the gesture recognition module should be activated mainly in predefined game situations, such as corner kicks, thus a processing speed of 1 fps is feasible for possible use in RoboCup soccer matches.

5   Conclusion

We have presented a new approach for robot-to-robot gesture-based Communication based on a three-steps procedure to be used in the RoboCup SPL. Our aim is to propose a communication protocol similar to the one used in human's soccer games as a step towards the achievement of the Robocup 2050 challenge. In particular, the approach includes three main stages: (1) HSV color conversion to adjust illumination values; (2) Skeleton extraction to find robot's keypoints; (3) Pose classification to recognize predefined messages.

An important contribution of this work is the creation of a novel dataset, containing images captured from NAOs on a regular field taking three different gestures. Quantitative experimental results demonstrate the effectiveness of the proposed approach. The source code and a tutorial to use it is available at the following link:

https://github.com/SPQRTeam/Non-Verbal-Communication-With-NAO.

As future work, we intend to implement the proposed approach on the GPU provided with the NAO V6 robot.

References

1. Albani, D., Youssef, A., Suriani, V., Nardi, D., Bloisi, D.D.: A deep learning approach for object recognition with NAO soccer robots. In: Behnke, S., Sheh, R., Sariel, S., Lee, D.D. (eds.) RoboCup 2016. LNCS (LNAI), vol. 9776, pp. 392–403. Springer, Cham (2017). https://doi.org/10.1007/978-3-319-68792-6_33
2. Canal, G., Escalera, S., Angulo, C.: A real-time human-robot interaction system based on gestures for assistive scenarios. Comput. Vis. Image Underst. **149**, 65–77 (2016)
3. Cao, Z., Hidalgo, G., Simon, T., Wei, S.E., Sheikh, Y.: OpenPose: real-time multi-person 2D pose estimation using part affinity fields. arXiv preprint arXiv:1812.08008 (2018)
4. Cao, Z., Simon, T., Wei, S.E., Sheikh, Y.: Realtime multi-person 2D pose estimation using part affinity fields. In: CVPR, pp. 1302–1310 (2017)
5. Fujii, T., Lee, J.H., Okamoto, S.: Gesture recognition system for human-robot interaction and its application to robotic service task. In: Proceedings of the International Multi-Conference of Engineers and Computer Scientists (IMECS), vol. 1 (2014)
6. Genter, K., Laue, T., Stone, P.: The RoboCup 2014 SPL drop-in player competition: encouraging teamwork without pre-coordination. In: AAMAS (2015)
7. Fang, H.-S., Xie, S., Tai, Y.W., Lu, C.: RMPE: regional multi-person pose estimation. In: ICCV (2017)
8. Ju, Z., Ji, X., Li, J., Liu, H.: An integrative framework of human hand gesture segmentation for human-robot interaction. IEEE Syst. J. **11**(3), 1326–1336 (2017)
9. He, K., Gkioxari, G., Dollár, P., Girshick, R.: Mask R-CNN. In: ICCV (2017)
10. Leiva, F., Cruz, N., Bugueño, I., Ruiz-del-Solar, J.: Playing soccer without colors in the SPL: a convolutional neural network approach. CoRR abs/1811.12493 (2018)
11. Mühlenbrock, A., Laue, T.: Vision-based orientation detection of humanoid soccer robots. In: Akiyama, H., Obst, O., Sammut, C., Tonidandel, F. (eds.) RoboCup 2017. LNCS (LNAI), vol. 11175, pp. 204–215. Springer, Cham (2018). https://doi.org/10.1007/978-3-030-00308-1_17

12. Pennisi, A., Bloisi, D.D., Iocchi, L., Nardi, D.: Ground truth acquisition of humanoid soccer robot behaviour. In: Behnke, S., Veloso, M., Visser, A., Xiong, R. (eds.) RoboCup 2013. LNCS (LNAI), vol. 8371, pp. 560–567. Springer, Heidelberg (2014). https://doi.org/10.1007/978-3-662-44468-9_50
13. Sigalas, M., Baltzakis, H., Trahanias, P.: Gesture recognition based on arm tracking for human-robot interaction. In: 2010 IEEE/RSJ International Conference on Intelligent Robots and Systems, pp. 5424–5429. IEEE (2010)

An Open Source Vision Pipeline Approach for RoboCup Humanoid Soccer

Niklas Fiedler[(✉)], Hendrik Brandt, Jan Gutsche, Florian Vahl, Jonas Hagge, and Marc Bestmann

Hamburg Bit-Bots, Department of Informatics, University of Hamburg,
Vogt-Kölln-Straße 30, 22527 Hamburg, Germany
{5fiedler,8hbrandt,7gutsche,7vahl,5hagge,
bestmann}@informatik.uni-hamburg.de
http://robocup.informatik.uni-hamburg.de

Abstract. We are proposing an Open Source ROS vision pipeline for the RoboCup Soccer context. It is written in Python and offers sufficient precision while running with an adequate frame rate on the hardware of kid-sized humanoid robots to allow a fluent course of the game. Fully Convolutional Neural Networks (FCNNs) are used to detect balls while conventional methods are applied to detect robots, obstacles, goalposts, the field boundary, and field markings. The system is evaluated using an integrated evaluator and debug framework. Due to the usage of standardized ROS messages, it can be easily integrated into other teams' code bases.

Keywords: RoboCup · Open Source · Computer vision

1 Introduction

In RoboCup Humanoid Soccer, a reliable object recognition is the foundation of successful gameplay. To keep up with the rule changes and competing teams, continuous development and improvement of the detection approaches is necessary [2]. The vision pipeline we used previously was neither easily adaptable to these changes nor to our new middleware, the Robot Operating System (ROS) [15]. Additionally, it was hard for new team members to contribute.

Thus, we developed a completely new vision pipeline using Python. In the development, we focused on a general approach with high usability and adaptability. Furthermore, our team offers courses for students as part of their studies, in which they are able to work with our existing code base. Therefore, the code has to be optimized for collaboration within the team. It needs to be easily understandable, especially because the team members change regularly while the code base has to be actively maintained. In addition to that, it allows new participants to work productively with a short training period and thus providing a sense of achievement.

S. Chalup et al. (Eds.): RoboCup 2019, LNAI 11531, pp. 376–386, 2019.
https://doi.org/10.1007/978-3-030-35699-6_29

Fulfilling the requirements of our domain is made possible by versatile modules (see Sect. 3.1), which are designed to solve specific tasks (e.g. color or object detection), but are also applicable in more generalized use cases. Since we want to promote further development and encourage collaboration, we publish our code under an Open-Source license. Due to this and the usage of the ROS middleware as well as standardized messages [5], the vision pipeline can be integrated into code bases used by other teams.

2 Related Work

RoboCup Soccer encourages every participating team to continuously enhance their systems by adapting the laws of the game [2]. Thus, the number of teams using neural networks as a classifier for batches of ball candidates and even the amount of those employing Fully Convolutional Neural Networks (FCNNs) in their vision pipeline is increasing. This section is based on the team description papers submitted by all qualified teams for the RoboCup Humanoid Soccer League[1].

The most frequently used methods for object detection are single shot detectors (SSDs), based on existing models such as You Only Look Once (YOLO) [16]. In addition to the Hamburg Bit-Bots [4] (our team), the Bold Hearts [18] and Sweaty [7] are using fully convolutional neural networks (FCNNs) in their vision pipeline. With their FCNN [6], the Bold Hearts are detecting the ball and goalposts. Team Sweaty is additionally able to detect several field markings and robots with their approach [19]. In the Humanoid KidSize League, the processing hardware is restricted due to the size and weight limits. While the basic structure of a Convolutional Neural Network for classification is similar between teams (e.g. [1]), the candidate acquisition varies. The EagleBots.MX team uses a cascade classifier with Haar-like features [12]. Rhoban detects regions of interest by using information about the robot's state and "a kernel convolution on an Integral Image filter" [1]. The team Electric Sheep uses a color based candidate detection and relies solely on "number of pixels, ratio of the pixels in the candidate area and the size of the candidate area" [3] to classify them. In contrast to this, [11] proposes a method of candidate acquisition and classification for the Standard Platform League (SPL) based on high-contrast regions in grayscale images without the need of color.

The field boundary is usually detected by computing the convex hull around the largest accumulation of green pixels detected by a field color mask. The team MRL is working on a neural network based approach for field boundary detection [13]. For localization purposes, some teams detect field markings by color [4] while others are relying on the detection of landmarks, such as line crossings or the penalty marks [19].

---

[1] https://www.robocuphumanoid.org/hl-2019/teams/ last accessed: 2019-06-14.

3   Overview and Features

The vision pipeline is implemented as an adaption of the *pipe-and-filter* pattern [14]. Every module implements one or multiple filters. The data flow is defined in the main vision module. To accommodate the nonlinear data flow and to optimize the runtime performance, the output of filters is stored in the modules. This includes intermediate results of related tasks (e.g. when red robots are detected, general obstacle candidates are stored in the module, too). The stored measurements are invalidated as soon as a new image is received. Using launch scripts, the whole vision pipeline, as well as provided tools, can be started with a single command in a terminal. Additional parameters allow launching the vision pipeline with additional debug output, without the FCNN, or to be used in a simulation environment (rosbags or the Gazebo simulator).

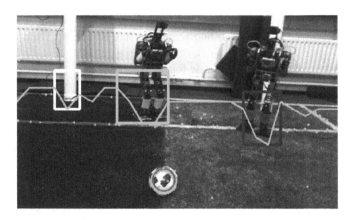

Fig. 1. Exemplary debug image. The detected field boundary is marked by a **red line**, field markings are represented as a set of **red dots**. Around detected obstacles, boxes are drawn (**red:** red robot, **blue:** blue robot, **white:** white obstacles i.e. goalposts). The best rated ball candidate and discarded candidates are indicated by a **green circle** or **red circles** respectively [4]. (Color figure online)

3.1   Modules

The following subsections present modules currently used in our vision pipeline by giving a general overview of their function (Fig. 2). Some modules contain multiple implementations of the same task as more efficient ones were developed and required evaluation. Modules which are no longer in use because they were replaced (e.g. a Hough-circle ball candidate detection and a classifier) are left out of this paper but kept in the repository.

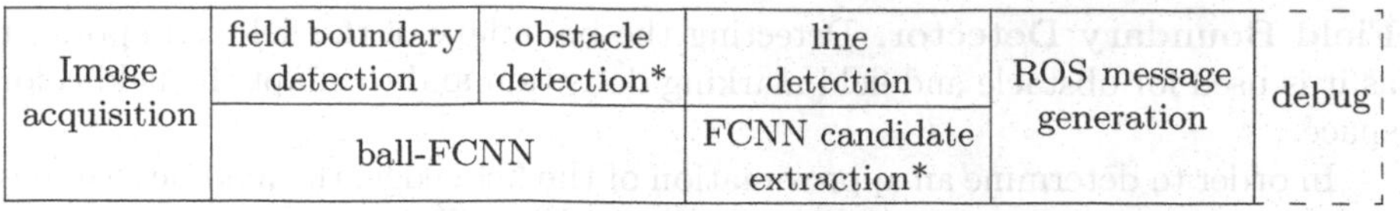

Image acquisition	field boundary detection	obstacle detection*	line detection	ROS message generation	debug
	ball-FCNN		FCNN candidate extraction*		

Fig. 2. Schematic representation of the vision pipeline. After the image acquisition, the pipeline is split into two threads. One handles conventional detection methods and the other handles the FCNN detecting the ball. Afterward, ROS messages and debug output are generated. The debug step is optional. Modules marked with an * implement the *Candidate Finder* class.

Color Detector. As many of the following modules rely on the color classification of pixels to generate their output, the color detector module matches their color to a given color space. These color spaces are configured for the colors of the field or objects like goalposts and team markers. Two types of color space definitions are implemented: Either it is defined by minimum and maximum values of all three HSV channels or by predefined lookup tables (provided as a Pickle file or YAML, a data-serialization language). The HSV color model is used for the representation of white and the robot marker colors, red and blue. The values of the HSV channels can be easily adjusted by a human before a competition to match the white of the lines and goal or the team colors of the enemy team respectively. This is necessary as teams may have different tones of red or blue as their marker color. On the other hand, the color of the field is provided as a YAML file to include more various and nuanced tones of green. These YAML files can be generated using a tool by selecting the field in a video stream (in the form of a live image or a ROS bag). Additional tools visualize included colors or increase the density of color spaces by interpolation between points in the RGB space.

The latest change of rules [17] also allowed natural lighting conditions. Therefore, pixels in the image mainly surrounded by pixels whose color is already in the color space are added.

However, only colors without any occurrences above the field boundary are chosen to ensure a stable adaptation to changes in shade and lighting. In Fig. 3, the images in the left column show an erroneous detection of the field boundary while the dynamic color space module has been deactivated. The color lookup table was deliberately chosen to be a bad representation of the green of this field which can be seen in the resulting color mask on the left. A few seconds after the activation of the dynamic color space using the dynamic reconfiguration feature, the field mask marks most of the field, which leads to an increased detection precision of the field boundary and therefore of obstacles. The dynamic color space feature is implemented in a separate ROS node and runs parallel to the main vision to increase runtime performance. It then publishes the updated color space for the vision.

Field Boundary Detector. Detecting the boundary of the field is important as it is used for obstacle and field marking detection and to adapt the field color space.

In order to determine an approximation of the field edge, the module searches for the topmost green pixels in columns of the image. To increase runtime performance not every pixel in every column is checked. Because of this, the resulting field boundary is not perfectly accurate which can be seen by the smaller dents in Fig. 1 in situations in which field markings are close to the edge of the field. These dents are too small to be classified as obstacles and therefore insignificant compared to the improvement of runtime performance.

Depending on the situation different algorithms are used to find the topmost green pixel. The first iterates over each column from top to bottom until green is found. As the robot will be looking down on the field most of the time, the field will be a large part of the image. Searching for it from the top is therefore very reliable and fast in most cases. However, this poses the problem that the robot might see green pixels in the background when looking up to search for objects which are further away (e.g. goalposts). Then these would be detected resulting in an erroneous measurement of the topmost point of the field.

To address this problem, a different algorithm iterates from the bottom of a column to the top until a non-green pixel is found. As the white lines inside of the field would then be falsely detected as the outer boundary, a kernel is applied onto the input image to take surrounding pixels into consideration.

Due to the use of a kernel, the second method is significantly slower and should only be used when necessary. It is therefore only chosen when the robots head is tilted upwards by a certain degree, which makes it likely that the background will occupy a large portion of the image.

After finding the field boundary, its convex hull is calculated. This is necessary because the actual border of the field might not be visible by the robot since obstacles can partially obstruct it. As a convex hull eliminates the dents in the detected field boundary that were caused by obstacles, it resembles a more accurate representation.

Line Detector. The Bit-Bots team uses field markings determined by the line detector to locate the robot in the field [4]. Unlike other teams (e.g. [8]), it does not output lines but points in the image which are located on a marking. This approach reduces the computation effort necessary to gather the information needed for the localization method. Pixels are randomly chosen in the image below the highest point of the field boundary. Afterward, the color of the pixel is matched to the color space representing the color of field markings via the *Color Detector.*

To improve the performance of this method, the point density is adapted accordingly to their height in the image. Additionally, the point density is increased in areas with line detections in the previous image.

Candidate Finder. As multiple modules (FCNN Handlers and Obstacle Detectors) detect or handle candidates which can be described in multiple ways (e.g. coordinates of corner points, one corner point and dimensions or center point and radius), a generalized representation is necessary. To approach this issue, the *Candidate* and *Candidate Finder* classes are used.

The *Candidate* class offers multiple representations of the same candidate as properties. Additionally, a function checking whether a point is part of the candidate is provided.

The *Candidate Finder* is an abstract class which is implemented by modules detecting candidates. It ensures a unified interface for retrieving candidates and thereby increases adaptability.

Obstacle Detector. Most obstacles obstruct the actual field boundary because they are inside the field and have a similar height as the robot. Therefore, the area between the convex hull of the field boundary and the detected field boundary itself is considered an obstacle, if its size is greater than a threshold. Possible objects in the field are robots of both teams, goalposts and other obstacles, like the referee. The classification of an obstacle is based on its mean color, as a goalpost will be predominantly white while robots are marked with their team color (blue or red).

FCNN Handler. The FCNN Handler module is used to preprocess images for a given FCNN-model and to extract candidates from its output. The preprocessing consists of a resize of the input image to fit the input size for the given model. As FCNNs return a pixel-precise activation (two-dimensional output of continuous values between 0 and 1), a candidate extraction is necessary. To optimize the runtime performance, the candidate extraction is implemented in C++ and accessed as a Python module.

For debug-purposes and to continue the processing of the FCNN-output in another ROS node, a generation of a ROS message containing the output in the form of a heatmap is included.

Currently, we are using an FCNN to locate the soccer ball in the image. It is based on the model proposed in [20] and trained on images and labels from the *Bit-Bots ImageTagger*[2] [9].

Debugging and Evaluation. To improve the results of the vision pipeline, it is essential to analyze and evaluate the results of algorithms and parameters in the pipeline. This is achieved by using ROS bags, the debug module, the *Evaluator* node and by analyzing messages between nodes.

To ease debugging, the *debug* module allows the user to create a debug image (the current input image with all detected features drawn into) via a simple interface, resulting in live insights into the vision pipeline (see Fig. 1).

---

[2] https://imagetagger.bit-bots.de last accessed: 2019-06-14.

Fig. 3. Demonstration of the dynamic color detector. A deliberately badly fitting color space was used on the top left image. The resulting color mask is shown in the bottom left. White pixels represent field-color detections. The dynamic color space adapted the original color space which resulted in the improved field-color detection depicted in the bottom right color mask which is based on the input image in the top right.

To measure the runtime of specific components, external profilers and internal time measurements are used. The neural networks are evaluated separately. To analyze the performance of the whole vision pipeline, we developed an external *Evaluator* node, which is presented in Sect. 4.

3.2   Configuration

Currently, the vision pipeline configuration consists of 80 parameters. Parameters are used to define variables which can have different optimal values depending on the environment (e.g. color definitions or stepsizes in scanline approaches). All parameters are defined in a single file in the YAML format. The ROS parameter server manages these parameters and parses the configuration file. Parameters are stored in the vision module to improve performance. Via its dynamic reconfiguration server, ROS allows the adaption of parameters in a graphical user interface while the module is running. A change of the value of a parameter triggers a callback in the vision pipeline which propagates the change to the modules. The dynamic configuration, which is applicable to all parameters, allows users to inspect the effect of the changed parameters with a minimal delay. The results are drawn into the debug image. Thereby, the user is able to adapt parameters intuitively based on runtime and detection performance.

4   Evaluation

To evaluate the vision pipeline, the *Evaluator* node from the *bitbots_vision_tools* package is used. The *Evaluator* reads a YAML file containing image names and corresponding object annotations from a whole image set. A corresponding export format and test data is provided in the *Bit-Bots ImageTagger* [9]. Afterward, the annotations are verified and preprocessed. Sequentially, it feeds the images into the vision pipeline (as ROS messages) and waits for the vision output.

On a Jetson TX2, the system processes 8.1 images per second without debug output generation. Our vision pipeline is not separated into several ROS nodes (except the dynamic color space node which is actively adapting the parameters of the pipeline) because of the delay in the message generation and passing process and because multiple modules require common information (e.g. the color module). ROS nodelets [22] cannot be used as they are currently not supported in rospy, the ROS interface for Python.

To determine the precision of a detection, the Jaccard-Index (Intersection over Union, see [21] is used. Two masks are generated for each annotation type. One mask is based on the label created or at least verified by a human and the other one on the output of the vision pipeline. A Jaccard-Index of 1 signifies a perfect detection, while 0 represents a completely wrong detection.

The results of our evaluation are presented in Table 1. The values are the mean of the Jaccard-Indices of all labels for each detection class. In this evaluation, a fully labeled and publicly available set[3] of 707 images was used.

Table 1. The mean Jaccard-Indices of the detections separated by detection class.

Class	Ball	Field boundary	Line	Goalpost	Robot red	Robot blue
Mean Jaccard-Index	0.677	0.925	0.021	0.183	0.149	0.380

The context of RoboCup Humanoid Soccer required compromising detection precision for runtime performance. For example, while the height of an obstacle is not relevant to avoid collisions, it has a significant impact on the used metric. The low rating for line detection is owed to our point based detection method compared to line based labels. In our case, we assume that the detected line points are sufficient for their purpose in the robot self-localization. The indices of the goalpost, robot and especially the obstacle detections are positively biased due to high numbers of negative samples included in the data set.

Despite the drawbacks of the metric, it allows a quantitative analysis of changes in parameters and algorithms. We propose this method of evaluation as it allows different vision pipelines to be automatically tested under the same

---

[3] https://imagetagger.bit-bots.de/images/imageset/261/ last accessed: 2019-06-14.

conditions. Therefore whole vision pipelines are comparable to each other within the same metric with one conveniently usable tool, given they are using ROS [15] and standardized messages [5].

5   Conclusion and Further Work

We presented a state of the art vision pipeline for the RoboCup Soccer context.

Through its implementation in Python, the system trades runtime performance for high adaptability and expandability while maintaining a usable frame rate and offering a state of the art neural network based ball-detection method. It is a starting point for new teams and teams transitioning to Python or ROS. Additionally, the modules can be integrated into existing vision systems. The *Evaluator* node offers a novel approach to analyze the complete vision pipeline while existing approaches solely evaluate isolated parts of the system. Thus, changes in a single module and their effect on other modules and overall performance can be evaluated.

In the future, we are planning to improve our FCNN to detect multiple object classes efficiently. In particular, the performance of our Neural Networks can be improved as we believe that our Jetson TX2 is not used to its full capacity. To achieve this and detect very distant objects reliably we are considering implementing the method proposed in [10].

Additionally, we are going to investigate the applicability of using more external information (e.g. the robot pose or a world model) in the vision pipeline for further optimizations.

We invite other teams to use (and adapt) the presented vision pipeline or modules in their own software stacks. The project is publicly available on GitHub via https://github.com/bit-bots/bitbots_vision.

Acknowledgments. Thanks to the RoboCup team Hamburg Bit-Bots, especially Timon Engelke and Daniel Speck, as well as Norman Hendrich. This research was partially funded by the German Research Foundation (DFG) and the National Science Foundation of China (NSFC) in project Crossmodal Learning, TRR-169. We are grateful to the NVIDIA corporation for supporting our research through the NVIDIA GPU Grant Program (https://developer.nvidia.com/academic_gpu_seeding). We used the donated NVIDIA Titan X (Pascal) to train our models.

References

1. Allali, J., Gondry, L., Hofer, L., Laborde-Zubieta, P., Ly, O., et al.: Rhoban football club - team description paper. Technical report, CNRS, LaBRI, University of Bordeaux and Bordeaux INP (2019)
2. Baltes, J., Missoura, M., Seifert, D., Sadeghnejad, S.: Robocup soccer humanoid league. Technical report (2013)
3. Barry, D., Curtis-Black, A., Keijsers, M., Munir, S., Young, M.: Electric sheep team description paper. Technical report, University of Canterbury, Christchurch, New Zealand (2019)

4. Bestmann, M., et al.: Hamburg bit-bots and wf wolves team description for RoboCup 2019 humanoid KidSize. Technical report, Universität Hamburg, Germany and Ostfalia University of Applied Sciences, Wolfenbüttel, Germany (2019)
5. Bestmann, M., Hendrich, N., Wasserfall, F.: ROS for humanoid soccer robots (2017)
6. van Dijk, S.G., Scheunemann, M.M.: Deep learning for semantic segmentation on minimal hardware. In: Holz, D., Genter, K., Saad, M., von Stryk, O. (eds.) RoboCup 2018. LNCS (LNAI), vol. 11374, pp. 349–361. Springer, Cham (2019). https://doi.org/10.1007/978-3-030-27544-0_29
7. Dorer, K., Hochberg, U., Ülker, M.W.: The sweaty 2019 RoboCup humanoid adult-size team description. Technical report, University of Applied Sciences Offenburg (2019)
8. Fan, W., et al.: Zjudancer team description paper. Technical report, State Key Laboratory of Industrial Control Technology, Zhejiang University, Hangzhou, China (2019)
9. Fiedler, N., Bestmann, M., Hendrich, N.: Image tagger: an open source online platform for collaborative image labeling. In: Holz, D., Genter, K., Saad, M., von Stryk, O. (eds.) RoboCup 2018. LNCS (LNAI), vol. 11374, pp. 162–169. Springer, Cham (2019). https://doi.org/10.1007/978-3-030-27544-0_13
10. Houliston, T., Chalup, S.K.: Visual mesh: real-time object detection using constant sample density. In: Holz, D., Genter, K., Saad, M., von Stryk, O. (eds.) RoboCup 2018. LNCS (LNAI), vol. 11374, pp. 45–56. Springer, Cham (2019). https://doi.org/10.1007/978-3-030-27544-0_4
11. Leiva, F., Cruz, N., Bugueño, I., Ruiz-del-Solar, J.: Playing soccer without colors in the SPL: a convolutional neural network approach. In: Holz, D., Genter, K., Saad, M., von Stryk, O. (eds.) RoboCup 2018. LNCS (LNAI), vol. 11374, pp. 122–134. Springer, Cham (2019). https://doi.org/10.1007/978-3-030-27544-0_10
12. Luna, J.P.V., Vázquez, S.G.R., Martinez, I.J.C.J., Ramírez, I.D.N.: Eaglebots.mx team description paper. Technical report, Highest Institute of Technology of Tepeaca (2019)
13. Mahmoudi, H., Fatehi, A., Gholami, A., et al.: MRL team description paper for humanoid KidSize league of RoboCup 2019. Technical report, Mechatronics Research Lab, Department of Computer and Electrical Engineering, Qazvin Islamic Azad University, Qazvin, Iran (2019)
14. Philipps, J., Rumpe, B.: Refinement of pipe-and-filter architectures. In: Wing, J.M., Woodcock, J., Davies, J. (eds.) FM 1999. LNCS, vol. 1708, pp. 96–115. Springer, Heidelberg (1999). https://doi.org/10.1007/3-540-48119-2_8
15. Quigley, M., Conley, K., Gerkey, B., Faust, J., Foote, T., Leibs, J., et al.: ROS: an open-source robot operating system. In: ICRA Workshop on Open Source Software, Kobe, Japan, vol. 3, p. 5 (2009)
16. Redmon, J., Divvala, S., Girshick, R., Farhadi, A.: You only look once: unified, real-time object detection. In: Proceedings of the IEEE Conference on Computer Vision and Pattern Recognition, pp. 779–788 (2016)
17. RoboCup Technical Committee: RoboCup soccer humanoid league laws of the game 2018/2019. Technical report (2019)
18. Scheunemann, M.M., van Dijk, S.G., Miko, R., Barry, D., Evans, G.M., et al.: Bold hearts team description for RoboCup 2019 (humanoid kid size league). Technical report, School of Computer Science, University of Hertfordshire (2019)

19. Schnekenburger, F., Scharffenberg, M., Wülker, M., Hochberg, U., Dorer, K.: Detection and localization of features on a soccer field with feedforward fully convolutional neural networks (FCNN) for the adult-size humanoid robot sweaty. In: Proceedings of the 12th Workshop on Humanoid Soccer Robots, IEEE-RAS International Conference on Humanoid Robots, Birmingham (2017)
20. Speck, D., Bestmann, M., Barros, P.: Towards real-time ball localization using CNNs. In: Holz, D., Genter, K., Saad, M., von Stryk, O. (eds.) RoboCup 2018. LNCS (LNAI), vol. 11374, pp. 337–348. Springer, Cham (2019). https://doi.org/10.1007/978-3-030-27544-0_28
21. Tan, P.N.: Introduction to Data Mining. Pearson Education India, Bengaluru (2006)
22. Tully Foote, R.B.R.: ROS Wiki: nodelet. https://wiki.ros.org/nodelet. Accessed 28 Mar 2019

A Simulation Platform Design and Kinematics Analysis of MRL-HSL Humanoid Robot

Amir Gholami[1]([✉]) [iD], Milad Moradi[2], and Majid Majidi[1] [iD]

[1] Department of Mechanical Engineering, Faculty of Industrial and Mechanical Engineering, Qazvin Branch, Islamic Azad University, Qazvin, Iran
amir.gholami@qiau.ac.ir
[2] Faculty of Electrical, Biomedical and Mechatronics Engineering, Qazvin Branch, Islamic Azad University, Qazvin, Iran

Abstract. This paper introduces MRL-HSL multibody simulation for the humanoid robot based on Matlab/Simulink and Simscape software, which can be used for designing control systems, enhancing the stability of the robot and etc. purpose. MRL-HSL real-time simulation is a virtual humanoid robot which is the safe way of educational and research purpose without damaging to the robot in the real environment and reducing the cost of implementation. The structure of the robot includes a rigid multibody of the robot, actuators, sensors and it can be developed simply for other types of robots. For the gaiting purpose and other movement control designing aims, the forward kinematics is solved by Denavit Hartenberg (D-H) method and the analytical solution is used for solving the inverse kinematics. The kinematics chain consists of the head, Legs and arms of the humanoid robot. The cad models of each part of the virtual humanoid robot designed by SolidWorks software.

Keywords: Humanoid robot · Simulation · Rigid multibody · Kinematics

1 Introduction

The MRL-HSL project was started in 2003 in the Mechatronics Research Laboratory in Islamic Azad University, Qazvin branch looking onward to enhance the knowledge of robotics and the MRL Humanoid Soccer League is aimed to develop a humanoid platform for research and education. MRL-HSL research center has the honor to hold the RoboCup from 2003 to 2018 [1].

The primary analysis before implementation in a real robot is needed to eliminate errors and reduce the costs. These analyses can lead to reducing damages and the process of time. The main purpose of this paper is a simulation for analysis forward and inverse kinematics of the MRL-HSL humanoid robot. This simulation includes several parts such as motors, sensors, controllers, physical modelling of the real robot architecture, robot body and joints which design in the Matlab/Simulink software. Humanoid robot platform simulation based on Matlab is a simple and reliable approach which is low cost and easy to operate. Also, according to the flexibility of Matlab, users can change

© Springer Nature Switzerland AG 2019
S. Chalup et al. (Eds.): RoboCup 2019, LNAI 11531, pp. 387–396, 2019.
https://doi.org/10.1007/978-3-030-35699-6_30

the environment parameters, degrees of freedom and study about the humanoid robot on various condition. It should be noted that it can be used for solving a variety of kinematics problems [2, 3]. Matlab has a growing number of tools for dynamics simulation, especially dynamic solver libraries. Ideally, the model and simulation should be a trustable representation of the real system, so the result between simulation and the real robot should be little or no difference. Some researchers proposes a humanoid robot framework with different simulator such as VERP [4] and OpenHRP [5]. In the matter of humanoid robots kinematics problems, Kofinas et al. present an analytical forward and inverse kinematics solution for NAO standard humanoid robot platform [6]. In the other hand, Williams solved the kinematics problem for Darwin-OP humanoid robot [7]. Import from cad model is one of the most important things for robot simulation. The overall popularity of Matlab in universities is another reason for this purpose. Also, it is making it even easier to develop controllers and estimators based on blocks of Simscape and Simulink. Simscape provides a multibody simulation and it is one of the needs of mechanical and control engineers. While it is possible to work easily with solids, joints, constraints and etc. in this simulator. A comparison of the simulator with other simulators is listed in Table 1.

Table 1. A comparison of the simulator with other simulators

Simulator	Physic engine	Import CAD	ROS interface	Open source
MRL-HSL	Simscape multibody physic engine	Yes	Yes	Yes
Gazebo	ODE, Bullet, Simbody, DART	No	Yes	Yes
Vrep	ODE, Bullet, Vortex Dynamics, Newton Dynamics	No	Yes	No
Webot	ODE	No	No	Yes

This paper presents a kinematic and dynamic simulator for MRL-HSL humanoid robot based on Matlab/Simulink, Simscape and SolidWorks, which can be expanded for many algorithms such as walking, kicking and other purposes. By this, physically more realistically motion simulation of the humanoid robot can potentially be achieved than with another common approach like Gazebo. This can be beneficial for the development of versatile humanoid robot motions and related controllers. The source code of the MRL-HSL humanoid robot simulation can find in [8] which is an open-source project. The simulation has been validated with a real humanoid robot.

This paper is organized as follows: Sect. 2, introduce the structure of MRL-HSL humanoid robot which including link parameters and diagram of the present simulation. Section 3 is about analysis of forward and inverse kinematics of the arm, leg and head. Section 4 discusses the results of solving the kinematics which is validated with real robot actions.

2 Structure of MRL-HSL Humanoid Robot

MRL-HSL real humanoid robot with 20 degrees of freedom (DOF) is equipped with Robotis Dynamixel MX series actuators which use two Dynamixel MX-28 in neck and head, six Dynamixel MX-106 for each leg and three Dynamixel MX-64 for each arm [9]. The overall structure of the robot has 83 cm in height and 6.6 kg weight (Fig. 1b) [10]. For the graphical purpose of simulation in a virtual environment, all of the components of the robot is designed by SolidWorks software with all details such as materials, inertias and weight of each part. Simulation of the humanoid robot is based on weight, inertia, canter of mass and graphical form of each component designed in the robot. For this reason, all of the part designed by SolidWorks has been moved to the Simulink software. The robot's overall shape in the Matlab needs assembling of each design components, so, for each part of the robot, a coordinate is defined and the robot assembly is based on these coordinates. Also, an end-effector coordinate is defined for kinematics purpose (Fig. 1a). Special thanks to [11], the robot simulation takes advantages of Dynamixel actuators in each joint, sub-controller (CM730) for using acceleration and gyroscope sensor, and force sensor which is located in the feet of the robots. The ID's number of each joint is like the Darwin-OP humanoid robot [12].

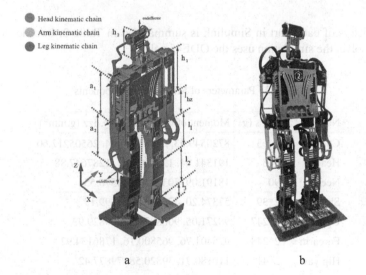

Fig. 1. MRL-HSL simulation humanoid robot and real humanoid robot

In Simulink model, the links coupled with one rotational degree of freedom and Simulink blocks have a definite physical meaning which is connected with other blocks by a signal line. MRL-HSL simulation humanoid robot has several chains consist of arms, legs, head and chest that they connected with each other and formed as an integral robot. Each chain defines as D-H parameters which express a transformation matrices. These transformation matrices that obtained from forward kinematics are in need because of solving inverse kinematics. The inverse kinematics gives joint angles, but since the

Dynamixel actuator is used in the robot, a Dynamixel convertor block applies which generates desire angles for the actuator. In sums with the actual angle from the encoder of the actuator, and the error goes to the actuator controller. The controller command to the actuator and all process will be visualized in Matlab (Fig. 2).

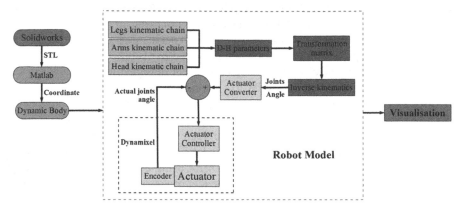

Fig. 2. Block diagram of the MRL-HSL simulation

Parameters of each part in Simulink is summarized in Table 2. In order to ensure accuracy solve, the simulation uses the ODE45 solver.

Table 2. Parameters of MRL-HSL components

Name	Mass (g)	Moment of inertia Ixx, Iyy, Izz (g.mm^2)
Chest	2463	8720549.93, 32362766.04, 26505212.60
Head	143	191341.94, 1210405.71, 1287647.88
Neck	90	18191.09, 30322.49, 32570.55
Shoulder	2*39	57374.20, 47657.93, 45699.19
Upper arm	2*247	98271.05, 906892.53, 919829.92
Forearm	2*248	925401.76, 965800.16, 1786134.92
Hip yaw	2*41	110180.71, 39820.58, 79877.42
Hip roll	2*358	416458.33, 552856.47, 235849.38
Thigh	2*263	154313.17, 5842352.97, 5810373.89
Tibia	2*129	127893.53, 1027984.81, 989075.93
Ankle	2*360	426375.54, 237912.72, 565177.63
Foot	2*267	1246236.11, 1307545.02, 617163.22
Total mass	6600	

3 Kinematics Analysis

A multi-body system consists of links which connected in a chain by revolute or prismatic joints and respectively create rotational or translational movement. With attaching coordinates to each joint, the circumstance for kinematics analysis is provided. Kinematics contains two portions, inverse and forward, which each of them is considered for a different purpose. Forward kinematics is a way for mapping from joint space to Cartesian space [13, 14]. The forward kinematics equation is written as:

$$x = f(\theta) \tag{1}$$

Where, the outputs of the Eq. (1) illustrate the position and orientation of the end effector respect to the reference frame that described by homogeneous transformation matrices. So transformation matrices describe cartesian space. Also, the inputs of the equation are joint angles. There are two different way of solving forward kinematics. In this paper, a modified D-H method is used for this purpose. On the other hand, inverse kinematics calculate joint angles with considering the position and orientation of end effector relative to the base frame. It means that the cartesian space mapping to joint space by Eq. (2).

$$\theta = f^{-1}(x) \tag{2}$$

Obtaining angles from Eq. (2) is not unique and multiple solutions exist. In the case of multiple solutions, there are two possible way, closed form and numerical solution. a closed-form solution is much faster than the numerical solution [15]. For this reason, the closed form solution is used in this article. In this paper forward and inverse kinematics problems are solved for arm, leg and head of the MRL-HSL humanoid robot. As shown in Fig. 1a there are five kinematics chains in humanoid robot and the reference frame of each chain located at the chest. With regard to the hardware design of the robot, human limits factor and rules of the RoboCup humanoid robot [16], all of the joint angles are limited in specific angles. These limitations are listed in the D-H table in each section.

3.1 Arm Kinematics

The MRL-HSL robot arm includes shoulder joint, upper arm, elbow joint, lower arm and end-effector. The arm has 3 DOF, two DOF located at the shoulder, the elbow has one DOF. The structure of the left arm is shown in Fig. 1a. The parameters of D-H are listed in Table 3. Which $traX$ means Translation of X-axis and $rotX$ means Rotation around X-axis and respectively Y and Z means Axis of them. According to D-H convention, the construction of the forward kinematics describes in Eq. (1).

$$T^{base}_{end} = \begin{bmatrix} c_2 s_6 - c_4 c_6 s_2 & c_2 c_6 - c_4 s_2 s_6 & -s_2 s_4 & p_x = a_2(c_2 s_6 - c_4 c_6 s_2) - a_1(c_4 s_2) \\ c_6 s_4 & -s_4 s_6 & -c_4 & p_y = s_4(a_1 + a_2 c_6) \\ -s_2 s_6 - c_2 c_4 c_6 & c_2 c_4 s_6 - c_6 s_2 & -c_2 s_4 & p_z = -a_2(c_2 s_6 + c_2 c_4 c_6) - a_1(c_2 c_4) \\ 0 & 0 & 0 & 1 \end{bmatrix} \tag{3}$$

Table 3. Three-DOF arm D-H parameters

i	α_{i-1} (deg)	a_{i-1} (mm)	θ_i (deg)	d_i (mm)	Variable range $(\theta_{min}, \theta_{max})$
1	$rotX(-90).rotZ(90)$				
2	0	0	θ_2	0	(−90, 180) [17]
3	90	0	θ_4	0	(0, 140) [18]
4	90	a_1	θ_6	0	(0, 145) [17]
5	$traX(a_2)$				

Where $s_i = \sin(\theta_i)$ and $c_i = \cos(\theta_i)$. To solve the inverse kinematics problem for obtaining the arm joints angles, kinematics problem decomposed into geometric and algebraic solution. Hence, because of the arm structure, to determine the elbow joint angle, the geometric method is used. Figure 3a demonstrate hand structure of the robot which is used for solving of hand inverse kinematics. On the other hand to calculate shoulder joint angles θ_2 and θ_4, the algebraic method is used. There are two solution for θ_2 and θ_6. It should be noted that this kinematics written for the left hand, the right hand kinematics is similar to the left one.

$$A = \frac{a_2^2 + a_1^2 - p_x^2 - p_y^2 - p_z^2}{2a_2a_1}$$
$$\theta_6 = 90 - \cos^{-1}(A) \; or \; -\cos^{-1}(A)$$
$$\theta_4 = \sin^{-1}\left(\frac{p_y}{a_1 + a_2 * c_6}\right) \quad (4)$$
$$B = -a_2s_6, \quad C = -a_1c_4 - a_2c_4c_6$$
$$\theta_2 = 2\tan^{-1}\left(\frac{C + \sqrt{B^2 + C^2 - p_x^2}}{B + p_x}\right) \; or \; 2\tan^{-1}\left(\frac{C + \sqrt{B^2 - C^2 - p_x^2}}{B + p_x}\right)$$

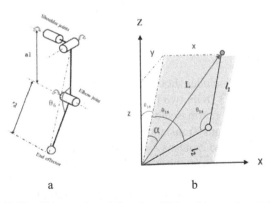

a   b

Fig. 3. (a) Hand kinematics of the robot (b) Leg kinematics of the robot

3.2 Leg Kinematics

Parameters of the leg serial chain in the D-H table listed as Table 4. The reference frame of this chain is located at the chest of the robot and the chain end effector is sitting at the bottom of the sole.

Table 4. Six-DOF leg D-H parameters

i	α_{i-1} (deg)	a_{i-1} (mm)	θ_i (deg)	d_i (mm)	Variable range $(\theta_{min}, \theta_{max})$
1	$traY(l_{hy}).traZ(l_{hz})$				
2	0	0	$90 + \theta_8$	0	(−45, 45)
3	90	0	$90 + \theta_{10}$	0	(0, 40) [19]
4	90	0	θ_{12}	0	(−45, 90)
5	0	$-l_1$	θ_{14}	0	(0, 120) [20]
6	0	$-l_2$	θ_{16}	0	(−90, 90)
7	− 90	0	θ_{18}	0	(−45, 45)
8	$rotZ(90).rotY(-90).traZ(-l_3)$				

Base on the D-H method with given θ_8 to θ_{18}, the very large matrix generated that the forward kinematics calculate it. Solving inverse kinematics for calculate the leg joints angles, kinematics problem decomposed into a geometric and algebraic solution. L is the distance between the ankle and the hip. As shown in Fig. 3b, with considering triangular Ll_1l_2 the angle of the knee is calculated. Also Fig. 3b shows the ankle roll and ankle pitch angles. By displacement, the transformation matrices with those elements that is calculated previously, hip yaw, roll and pitch angles will be attain in Eq. (5) [21].

$$L = x^2 + y^2 + z^2$$

$$\theta_{14} = \cos^{-1}\left(\frac{L - l_1^2 - l_2^2}{2l_1l_2}\right), \theta_{16} = atan2(y, z), \theta_{18} = \sin^{-1}\left(\frac{x}{\sqrt{L}}\right) - \sin^{-1}\left(\frac{l_1 \sin\theta_{14}}{\sqrt{L}}\right)$$

$$T = T_{base}^{end}.rotX(\theta_{18}).rotY(-\theta_{16} - \theta_{14}) = \begin{bmatrix} r_{11} & r_{12} & r_{13} & p_x \\ r_{21} & r_{22} & r_{23} & p_y \\ r_{31} & r_{32} & r_{33} & p_z \\ 0 & 0 & 0 & 1 \end{bmatrix}$$

$$\theta_8 = atan2(-r_{12}, r_{22}), \quad \theta_{10} = asin(r_{32}), \quad \theta_{12} = atan2(-r_{31}, r_{33})$$

$$(5)$$

3.3 Head Kinematics

According to the D-H table, parameters of the head serial chain are defined as Table 5. As mentioned earlier the reference frame of the head chain located at chest. As the robot

Table 5. Two-DOF head DH parameters

i	α_{i-1} (deg)	a_{i-1} (mm)	θ_i (deg)	d_i (mm)	Variable range $(\theta_{min}, \theta_{max})$
1	$traZ(h_1)$				
2	0	0	θ_{19}	0	(−90, 90)
3	− 90	0	θ_{20}	0	(−30, 90)
4	90	0	0	h_2	

needs to track the object, in the field of humanoid soccer robot the object is ball, the end effector coordinate is set at the camera.

Base on the D-H method with given θ_{19} and θ_{20}, the forward kinematics calculate the homogeneous transformation matrices which yield the following homogeneous matrices. Based on these parameter, according to the D-H rules, constructed the matrices, witch multiplied together, yield the following homogeneous.

$$
T^{base}_{end} = \begin{bmatrix} c_{19} + c_{20} & -(s_{19} + s_{20}) & 0 & p_x = 90(\cos(\theta_{19} + \theta_{20}) - \cos\theta_{19}) \\ s_{19} + s_{20} & c_{19} + c_{20} & 0 & p_y = 90(\sin(\theta_{19} + \theta_{20}) - \sin\theta_{19}) \\ 0 & 0 & 1 & p_z = h_2 + h_1 \\ 0 & 0 & 0 & 1 \end{bmatrix} \tag{6}
$$

The inverse kinematics of the head is solved base on algebraic solution as shown in Eq. (7). With given desired position in the space, the result of the inverse kinematics is joint angles of the head.

$$
\theta_{19} = atan2(p_y, p_x) \text{ or } atan2(-p_y, -p_z)
$$
$$
\theta_{20} = acos\left(\frac{p_z - h_1}{h_2}\right) \text{ or } - acos\left(\frac{p_z - h_1}{h_2}\right) \tag{7}
$$

4   Results and Conclusion

The MRL-HSL humanoid robot simulation in this paper was validated with a real robot. In order to validate the simulation, a kinematics algorithm is calculated. By giving different angles in joint space the position and orientation of the body are located at the same place in the space. In the other hand, the cartesian space was mapping to joint space by inverse kinematics as well as a real robot. The outputs of inverse kinematics have shown in Fig. 5 which is the output of the posture of the humanoid robot in Fig. 4. The red lines show the angle of each actuator which is read by the encoder in simulation and dot line show the outputs of the encoder of each joint of the actual robot. The results have shown that the behavior of the simulated robot is resembling the real robot. So this simulation can be used for controlling purposes and another aspect of the humanoid robots algorithm such as walking and kicking.

Fig. 4. The posture of the humanoid robot in simulated and real robot

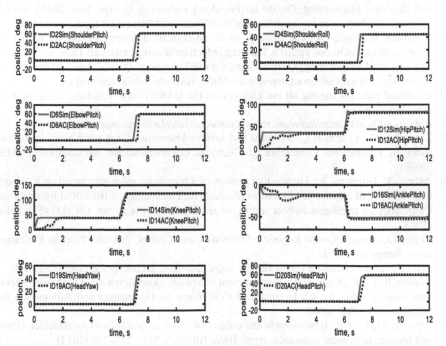

Fig. 5. Outputs of inverse kinematics simulated and real humanoid robot in different actuators (Color figure online)

References

1. Mahmoudi, H., Fatehi, A., Gholami, A., et al.: MRL team description paper for humanoid KidSize league of RoboCup 2019. Tech. rep., Mechatronics Research Lab, Dept. of Computer and Electrical Engineering, Qazvin Islamic Azad University, Qazvin, Iran (2019). https://submission.robocuphumanoid.org/uploads/MRL_HSL-tdp-5c05a863d9671.pdf
2. Li, Z.-W.: A simulation platform design of humanoid robot based on SimMechanics and VRML. Procedia Eng. **15**, 215–219 (2011)
3. Medrano-Cerda, G., et al.: Modelling and simulation of the locomotion of humanoid robots (2010)
4. Tong, G., Gu, J., Xie, W.: Virtual entity-based rapid prototype for design and simulation of humanoid robots. Int. J. Adv. Rob. Syst. **10**(7), 291 (2013)
5. Takubo, T., Inoue, K., Arai, T.: Pushing operation for humanoid robot using multipoint contact states. In: IEEE/RSJ International Conference on Intelligent Robots and Systems. IEEE (2005)
6. Kofinas, N., Orfanoudakis, E., Lagoudakis, M.G.: Complete analytical forward and inverse kinematics for the NAO humanoid robot. J. Intell. Rob. Syst. **77**(2), 251–264 (2015)
7. Williams, R.L.: DARwin-OP humanoid robot kinematics. In: International Design Engineering Technical Conferences and Computers and Information in Engineering Conference. American Society of Mechanical Engineers (2012)
8. Gholami, A. (2019). https://github.com/mrl-hsl/Simulator
9. Teimouri, M., Fatehi, A., Mahmoudi, H., et al.: MRL team description paper for humanoid TeenSize league of RoboCup 2018. Tech. rep., Mechatronics Research Lab, Dept. of Computer and Electrical Engineering, Qazvin Islamic Azad University, Qazvin, Iran (2018). https://www.robocuphumanoid.org/qualification/2018/TeenSize/MRL-HSL/tdp_corrected.pdf
10. Mahmudi, H., Fatehi, A., Gholami, A., et al.: MRL team description paper for humanoid TeenSize league of RoboCup 2019. Tech. rep., Mechatronics Research Lab, Dept. of Computer and Electrical Engineering, Qazvin Islamic Azad University, Qazvin, Iran (2019). https://submission.robocuphumanoid.org/uploads/MRL_HSL-tdp-5c05a7eb835c8.pdf
11. Unofficial page for sharing all our changes on the DARWIN-OP codebase. https://github.com/darwinop-ens
12. Robotis e-Manual. http://emanual.robotis.com/docs/en/platform/op/development/
13. Zannatha, J.I., Limon, R.C.: Forward and inverse kinematics for a small-sized humanoid robot. In: International Conference on Electrical, Communications, and Computers. IEEE (2009)
14. Asfour, T., Dillmann, R.: Human-like motion of a humanoid robot arm based on a closed-form solution of the inverse kinematics problem. In: Proceedings of IEEE/RSJ International Conference on Intelligent Robots and Systems (IROS 2003) (Cat. No. 03CH37453). IEEE (2003)
15. Craig, J.J.: Introduction to Robotics: Mechanics and Control, 3rd edn. Pearson Education India, Bengaluru (2009)
16. The rules of the humanoid league (2019). https://humanoid.robocup.org/materials/rules/
17. Gopura, R.A.R.C., Kiguchi, K.: Development of a 6DOF exoskeleton robot for human upper-limb motion assist. In: 4th International Conference on Information and Automation for Sustainability. IEEE (2008)
18. Rahman, M.H., et al.: Development and control of a robotic exoskeleton for shoulder, elbow and forearm movement assistance. Appl. Bion. Biomech. **9**(3), 275–292 (2012)
19. Zubrzycki, J., et al.: Structural analysis of the pelvic girdle before and after hip replacement procedure. Наука и техника **17**(2), 165–172 (2018)
20. Sanz-Merodio, D., et al.: Generation and control of adaptive gaits in lower-limb exoskeletons for motion assistance. Adv. Robot. **28**(5), 329–338 (2014)
21. Kajita, S., Hirukawa, H., Harada, K., Yokoi, K.: Introduction to Humanoid Robotics. STAR, vol. 101. Springer, Heidelberg (2014). https://doi.org/10.1007/978-3-642-54536-8

RoboCup@Home-Objects: Benchmarking Object Recognition for Home Robots

Nizar Massouh[✉], Lorenzo Brigato, and Luca Iocchi

Department of Computer Control and Management Engineering,
Sapienza University of Rome, Rome, Italy
{massouh,brigato,iocchi}@diag.uniroma1.it

Abstract. This paper presents a benchmark for object recognition inspired by RoboCup@Home competition and thus focusing on home robots. The benchmark includes a large-scale training set of 196K images labelled with classes derived from RoboCup@Home rulebooks, two medium-scale test sets (one taken with a Pepper robot) with different objects and different backgrounds with respect to the training set, a robot behavior for image acquisition, and several analysis of the results that are useful both for RoboCup@Home Technical Committee to define competition tests and for RoboCup@Home teams to implement effective object recognition components.

Keywords: Object recognition · Benchmarking · Service robots

1 Introduction

RoboCup@Home competition[1] aims at developing and benchmarking home service robots that can help people in everyday tasks. The competition is organized around a set of tasks in which several functionalities must be properly integrated [6,9]. Among these functionalities, *object recognition* is present in many tasks and it is thus very important for the competition as well as for actual deployment of home robots. Active object recognition was also benchmarked as a Technical Challenge in RoboCup@Home 2012. Homer@UniKoblenz achieved the highest score in this challenge by using SURF features and Hough transform clustering[2] applied to high resolution photos acquired by a digital camera. In this challenge, the robot had to move to the table where objects were located and thus active motion actions needed to be carefully designed to reach good view points for image acquisition.

In the last years, we have witnessed a significant effort in improving object recognition performance, specially boosted by the development of Convolutional Neural Networks (CNNs) and large-scale image databases (e.g., ImageNet [3]).

---

[1] https://athome.robocup.org.
[2] http://wiki.ros.org/obj_rec_surf.

© Springer Nature Switzerland AG 2019
S. Chalup et al. (Eds.): RoboCup 2019, LNAI 11531, pp. 397–407, 2019.
https://doi.org/10.1007/978-3-030-35699-6_31

Consequently, RoboCup@Home teams have shifted to machine learning techniques that promise very good results. However, such results are strongly influenced by the quality of training data and by computational resources available. Thus, many teams have to bring to the competition computational resources suitable to train CNNs and have to spend a lot of effort in acquiring images and train the networks during the setup days. While acquiring images about the specific objects chosen for the competition and training CNNs during the setup days is a suitable way of implementing the object recognition functionality of @Home robots, we believe that there are other processes that can help in implementing an effective object recognition functionality exploiting pre-trained CNNs and without requiring availability of competition objects, image acquisition and training during the setup days.

In this paper we present a benchmark for RoboCup@Home object recognition based on a large-scale training set acquired from the web and pre-trained models. More specifically, we provide: (1) a novel large-scale data set for RoboCup@Home (named **RoboCup@Home-Objects**) with over 196K images acquired from the web and automatically labelled with 8 main categories and 180 classes typically used in RoboCup@Home; (2) pre-trained CNNs on this data set that can be used by RoboCup@Home teams; (3) a test sets containing thousands of images acquired from the web with objects similar to the ones actually used in recent RoboCup@Home competitions; (4) a test set containing thousands of images taken from Pepper robot in a scenario similar to the ones encountered in the competitions; (5) a method based on active robot behaviors to improve quality of image acquisition and take advantages of pre-trained CNNs to improve actual performance of object recognition without any training on the specific competition objects; (6) a performance analysis that allows RoboCup@Home Technical Committee to better define competitions tasks involving object recognition. Although created for the RoboCup@Home community, we believe the benchmark, the models and the results will be interesting for all researchers aiming at integrating object recognition in home robots.

Data, models and results will be fully available in the web site https://sites. google.com/diag.uniroma1.it/robocupathome-objects[3].

2   Related Work

Ever since the exceptional results of Alexnet [7] in the ImageNet Large Scale Visual Recognition Challenge of 2012 (ILSVRC12) [3] the use of Deep Learning and CNNs for robot vision applications increased substantially. Deep Networks need large-scale annotated databases to be successfully trained or they will suffer from over-fitting. This made ImageNet the most used database for Deep network architectures. Another approach to avoid over-fitting and learn a new task is fine-tuning [1]. Fine-tuning is the method of re-training parts of a pre-trained network to fit a new task or new annotated data. Anyway fine-tuning still requires large-scale annotated data sets. As manually annotating large-scale

---

[3] Currently under development, will be completed before RoboCup@Home 2019.

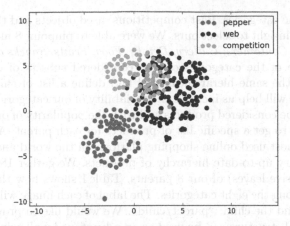

Fig. 1. The t-SNE visualization of the data-sets distributions' extracted features of the fully connected layer (FC7) with our Alexnet@Home180.

data sets requires too much human effort, automatic acquisition can produce suitable large-scale data sets with significantly lower effort. In particular, we can use the Web to collect many images related to a new task in an autonomous matter. In recent years successful attempts have been made to generate large scale databases from the web [2,4]. Work on automatic data collection for robot vision applications with deep networks was proposed for example in [8]. In the benchmark proposed in this paper, we have automatically downloaded images from the Web to build data sets for training and testing CNN-based object recognition for the RoboCup@Home competition.

3 Dataset Creation

In this section we will describe the process of creating 3 datasets: (1) a main dataset of 196K images acquired from the web that is used for training, (2) a benchmark dataset of about 5K images downloaded from the web as images similar to the ones published on RoboCup@Home github; (3) a benchmark dataset acquired from Pepper robot. It is important to notice that these datasets are acquired from different sources and thus come from different distributions, as shown in Fig. 1. Data acquired from different sources allows for a more realistic assessment of the performance that one can expect when using this technology. We thus believe that the experimental performance reported in this paper will provide a reliable estimation of expected performance of the tested networks in actual RoboCup@Home competition.

Below we will briefly describe the data sets acquired, while all the details are provided in the above mentioned web site.

RoboCup@Home-Objects Training Set. To successfully create a dataset that can be used for the RoboCup@Home competition we first need to define a structure for the categories. Past competitions' used objects and their categories can provide an insight to select ours. We were able to pinpoint 8 main categories: *Cleaning_stuff, Containers, Cutlery, Drinks, Food, Fruits, Snacks* and *Tableware*. Although some of the categories can be considered subsets of others we will place them at the same hierarchical level and define a list of children for each class. This step will help us increase the variability of our categories. Most of the categories can be considered products and with the popularity of online shopping we will be able to get a specific list of products for each parent. Amazon.com is currently the most used online shopping platform in the world and that allowed it to build a very up-to-date hierarchy of products. We gather 180 children (all mutually exclusive leaves) of our 8 parents. Table 1 shows how the children are distributed among the eight categories. The label of each image will be composed of the parent and the child: "parent/child". We would like to prove that having this hierarchical structure can be used as an advantage by allowing us to switch between a specific label to a more general category (parent category). This should prove useful when encountering never before seen objects.

Table 1. Distribution of the 180 classes of the RoboCup@Home-Objects dataset.

Parent name	Number of children
Cleaning_stuff	37
Containers	17
Cutlery	15
Drinks	17
Food	22
Fruits	23
Snacks	26
Tableware	23

The list of children is then used as a query list to search and download images on the web. With Google, Yahoo and Bing as our search engines we download images for each child's category name. These search engines are known to have a bias toward photos of objects with a clean background. After the data collection we use Perceptual Hashing on the images to identify and eliminate duplicates. After cleaning the database, we end up with a total of 196K images that we call RoboCup@Home-Objects.

RoboCup@Home github-seeded Web Benchmark. The RoboCup@Home github repository[4] contains the list and photos of objects actually used in several competitions. We have used these photos as seeds to create a benchmark from visually similar images collected from the web. We took advantage of the reverse

---

[4] https://github.com/RoboCupAtHome.

(a) Fruits (b) Food

(c) Containers (d) Cleaning stuff

Fig. 2. Examples of different categories from the RoboCup@Home github-seeded Web images.

image search provided by Google to produce this dataset. Google's reverse image search takes an image with an optional label and provides images that are visually and semantically similar. After collecting the competitions' images of objects we end up with 160 photos divided in 8 categories (our parent categories). We then proceed to use each of these photos as seeds providing their category as a label and we downloaded the first 50 returned images. After cleaning the duplicated images we end up with a total of 5,750 images labelled with the 8 parent categories defined above. As we can observe in Fig. 2 the downloaded images have the same visual features of the seeds used.

RoboCup@Home Pepper Objects Benchmark. RoboCup@Home Pepper Objects Benchmark has been acquired by using a Pepper robot, which is one of the standard platforms for RoboCup@Home. We selected a set of objects and placed each of them on a table (in different positions and different orientations with respect to a window to increase variability with respect to lighting conditions, including back-light situations).

Image acquisition was performed with an autonomous behavior of the robot reproducing operations during RoboCup@Home tasks. More specifically, the robot is *imprecisely* placed about 30 cm away from the table oriented towards it and executes the behavior illustrated in Fig. 3. For each run, 32 distinct images are thus automatically collected and organized in four groups: A (1 image), B (1 image), C (10 images), D (30 images), with $C \subset D$. Currently, we have acquired images of 14 objects (several runs in different locations), for a total of 2,624 images[5]. Some examples of acquired images are shown in Fig. 4.

---

[5] This data set will be further increased in the future, possibly as a community effort.

```
function TAKEIMAGES() → ⟨A, B, C, D⟩
    Stand posture
    Tilt head down
    Take image A
    Lean forward
    Take image B
    for i = 1, . . . , 10 do
        Random head motion
        Take image Cᵢ
        Copy image Cᵢ in Dᵢ
    end for
    Move left
    for i = 11, . . . , 20 do
        Random head motion
        Take image Dᵢ
    end for
    Move right
    for i = 21, . . . , 30 do
        Random head motion
        Take image Dᵢ
    end for
    return ⟨A, B, C, D⟩
end function
```

Fig. 3. Procedure to acquire images of an object for Pepper benchmark

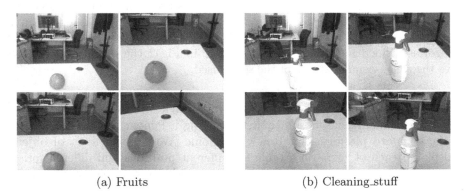

(a) Fruits   (b) Cleaning_stuff

Fig. 4. Pepper objects examples of different configurations: A - top left, B - top right, C - bottom left, D - bottom right.

4   Models Training

We proceeded to split our RoboCup@Home-Objects training set into 80% of images for training and 20% for validation. We fine-tuned an AlexNet [7] and a GoogleNet [10] pretrained on Imagenet's ILSVRC12 on our data, using the Caffe framework on NVIDIA Deep Learning GPU Training System (DIGITS).

We froze all the layers of the networks and learned the last fully connected layer for Alexnet and the last pool layer for Googlenet while boosting their learning multiplier by +1. We set our initial learning rate to 0.001 which we step down by 10% every 7.5 epochs. We trained both networks for 30 epochs with a stochastic gradient decent (SGD) solver.

We trained the same models on the training set using only the 8 parent categories. We ended up with 4 models: *Alexnet@home180* and *Googlenet@home180*, trained on all the children categories, *Alexnet@home8* and *Googlenet@home8*, trained on the parents categories only. For our models trained on the 180 children categories, we then execute a category mapper to map the result onto the 8 parents category. Table 2 shows the scored Top 1 accuracy percentage of the 4 models on the validation set and we can see that having less categories to learn made the task easier on the models.

Table 2. Validation accuracy percentage of our 4 models.

Model	Accuracy
Alexnet@home8	77.89%
Alexnet@home180	47.85%
Googlenet@home8	81.91%
Googlenet@home180	53.55%

5 Analysis of Results

In this section we present a brief summary of the results obtained using data and models described above. More details are provided in the web site.

Table 3. Top-1 and Top-5 parent majority accuracy of our 4 models trained with RoboCup@Home-Objects and tested on github objects (gh-o) and github-seeded dataset (gh-s).

Accuracy percentage	Top-1		Top-5 parent	
	gh-o (160)	gh-s (5.7K)	gh-o (160)	gh-s (5.7K)
Alexnet@Home180	70.44	65.86	**73.58**	70.84
Alexnet@Home8	67.29	66.74	67.29	66.74
Googlenet@Home180	64.78	67.33	70.44	**71.68**
Googlenet@Home8	**72.95**	**67.86**	72.95	67.86

5.1   Test Accuracy on Github-Seeded Web Benchmark

We are interested in the comparison of the results obtained in the two data sets collected from the web and of the models trained on the parents vs. the children.

As we can observe in Table 3, the results by all 4 models are very close to each other, with a little decrease of performance in the github-seeded benchmark (which contains 5.7 K images) in comparison with the 160 original github images. This means that our method for the creation of the github-seeded benchmark from web images is a successful data augmentation method that mimics the distribution of the source as we can see also in Fig. 1. We notice as well that Googlenet@Home8 slightly outperformed its child model and the other models. In the Top-5 parent section of Table 3 we used the top 5 predicted labels and returned the majority parent, i.e. if the top 5 predicted categories are: "tableware/bowl", "fruits/orange", "fruits/tangerine", "tableware/coffee_mug", "fruits/melon" the returned category is "fruits".

Finally, we observe an increase in accuracy when using the models trained on the 180 categories. Googlenet@Home180 was able to outperform our previous best by 4% for the github-seeded benchmark and for the github objects our new best is by Alexnet@Home180. This shows the advantages of mapping the result to the parent label (more general category) which adds flexibility in case of indecision.

5.2   Analysis on Pepper Benchmark

When using the Pepper dataset that, as already mentioned, has a very different distribution with respect to training, and without fine-tuning on the specific objects, there is a general decrease of performance in accuracy, but more importantly a very large variance of the results depending on the object.

By analyzing the performance of our models on this dataset without fine-tuning, we can assess the difficulty of recognizing each particular object. As discussed in the next section, this information can be very useful to competition organizers to choose proper objects for the competition as well as assigning a more suitable score to each kind of object. As an example, we show in Table 4 the result of the application of Googlenet@Home-180 on a set of objects of the Pepper benchmark averaged over all acquisition procedures. We can notice how different the result can change from one object to another. This wide range of results can be contributed to either the quality of the image taken or by how well the object represents its category. In the case of the Cookies our model kept predicting "Food" instead of "Snacks" which can be confusing since snacks can be considered a child category of Food. A detailed analysis has been done (available on the web site) on each object and a rank denoting the difficulty of recognizing every object without fine-tuning has been produced.

Active Image Acquisition. Finally, we have evaluated the active behavior of the Pepper robot in acquiring images from different view-points. To this end, we considered a subset of objects in the Pepper benchmark and two different

Table 4. Result of the Googlenet@Home-180 model on 7 different Pepper objects. The result is reported in Accuracy percentage over all acquisition procedures.

Category	Object	Accuracy
cleaning_stuff	cleaners	93.28%
tableware	cup	70.00%
fruits	orange	60.00%
drinks	water_bottle	43.33%
snacks	snack	36.67%
fruits	banana	9.68%
snacks	cookies	0.00%

Table 5. Accuracy on 5 selected objects varying robot acquisition behavior.

Model	A	B	C	D
Googlenet@Home-180	13.3%	43.3%	50.0%	50.0%
Mobilenet-Imagenet	26.7%	70.0%	73.3%	73.3%

models: Googlenet@Home-180 (as described above) and MobileNet model pre-trained on ImageNet [5]. These objects are: *banana, orange, cup, water_bottle*, and *plastic_bag*, whose labels are present within the 1,000 output categories of Imagenet trained models.

The results summarized in Table 5 show accuracy over 6 tests per each object and for each robot acquisition behavior A, B, C, D. For evaluating types with multiple images (i.e., C and D) a majority vote scheme was performed and the most voted class in all the images is compared with the true label. As shown, the behavior of leaning towards the object (B) gives significantly better results with respect to nominal behavior (A), while moving the head to view the objects from different view points (C, D) gives only a little additional advantage with respect to B. This observation should help researchers to properly balance acquisition time (C and D behavior are much longer) with recognition accuracy.

Finally, when we can assume that exactly one of these objects is in the image (as it is often the case during the competition), we can consider the highest confidence among only these 5 labels. In this way we obtained 100% accuracy in most cases.

6   Discussion and Conclusions

The results on the RoboCup@Home-Objects data can be useful for both @Home Technical Committee and teams.

From the perspective of the Technical Committee, an analysis of the difficulty in recognizing specific objects can drive choices about definition and scoring of the tests. We describe here three examples. (1) *Easy configuration*, choose a few objects (e.g., 5 to 10) that are within the RoboCup@Home-Objects/ImageNet labels and place exactly one of them in the environment: expected accuracy is almost 100% with a pre-trained model[6]. (2) *Medium configuration*, choose one object for each of the 8 parent categories of RoboCup@Home-Objects: expected accuracy is around 70% without fine tuning at the competition site, that can be enough in some cases, for example with a proper reasoning system or human-robot interactions to disambiguate or ask for confirmation. (3) *Difficult configuration*, choose objects with non-ImageNet labels among the ones that give worst accuracy results on our benchmark: expected accuracy is too low and on-site fine-tuning is necessary to perform well in the competition.

Another possibility for the Technical Committee is to define categories of objects granting more score for objects that are more difficult to recognize, possibly allowing the teams to choose. This would allow teams not willing to focus on object recognition to choose easy objects, use pre-trained models and focus their development on other functionalities (e.g., object manipulation or human-robot interaction), still having very good performance in object recognition. Evaluation of object recognition difficulty can be easily done by just use our pre-trained models on candidate objects selected for the competitions.

On-going and future work include extension of the data sets and involvement of the community (RoboCup@Home teams and other researchers) to improve the quality of the benchmark and of object recognition functionalities in home robots.

References

1. Chatfield, K., Simonyan, K., Vedaldi, A., Zisserman, A.: Return of the devil in the details: delving deep into convolutional nets. In: Proceedings BMVC (2014)
2. Cheng, D.S., Setti, F., Zeni, N., Ferrario, R., Cristani, M.: Semantically-driven automatic creation of training sets for object recognition. Comput. Vis. Image Underst. **131**, 56–71 (2015)
3. Deng, J., Dong, W., Socher, R., Li, L.J., Li, K., Fei-Fei, L.: Imagenet: a large-scale hierarchical image database. In: Proceedings CVPR, pp. 248–255 (2009)
4. Divvala, S.K., Farhadi, A., Guestrin, C.: Learning everything about anything: webly-supervised visual concept learning. In: Proceedings CVPR, pp. 3270–3277 (2014)
5. Howard, A.G., et al.: Mobilenets: efficient convolutional neural networks for mobile vision applications. CoRR abs/1704.04861 (2017). http://arxiv.org/abs/1704.04861
6. Iocchi, L., Holz, D., Ruiz-del-Solar, J., Sugiura, K., van der Zant, T.: RoboCup@Home: analysis and results of evolving competitions for domestic and service robots. Artif. Intell. **229**, 258–281 (2015)
7. Krizhevsky, A., Sutskever, I., Hinton, G.E.: Imagenet classification with deep convolutional neural networks. In: Proceedings NIPS (2012)

---

[6] This configuration was successfully tested at European RoboCup@Home Education Challenge 2019, where inexperienced high-school teams were able to use an almost perfect object recognition module.

8. Massouh, N., Babiloni, F., Tommasi, T., Young, J., Hawes, N., Caputo, B.: Learning deep visual object models from noisy web data: how to make it work. In: 2017 IEEE/RSJ International Conference on Intelligent Robots and Systems, IROS 2017, Vancouver, 24–28 September 2017, pp. 5564–5571 (2017). https://doi.org/10.1109/IROS.2017.8206444

9. Matamoros, M., Seib, V., Memmesheimer, R., Paulus, D.: RoboCup@Home; summarizing achievements in over eleven years of competition. CoRR abs/1902.00758 (2019). http://arxiv.org/abs/1902.00758

10. Szegedy, C., et al.: Going deeper with convolutions. CoRR abs/1409.4842 (2014)

Reusable Specification of State Machines for Rapid Robot Functionality Prototyping

Alex Mitrevski[(✉)] and Paul G. Plöger

Hochschule Bonn-Rhein-Sieg, Sankt Augustin, Germany
{aleksandar.mitrevski,paul.ploeger}@h-brs.de

Abstract. When developing robot functionalities, finite state machines are commonly used due to their straightforward semantics and simple implementation. State machines are also a natural implementation choice when designing robot experiments, as they generally lead to reproducible program execution. In practice, the implementation of state machines can lead to significant code repetition and may necessitate unnecessary code interaction when reparameterisation is required. In this paper, we present a small Python library that allows state machines to be specified, configured, and dynamically created using a minimal domain-specific language. We illustrate the use of the library in three different use cases - scenario definition in the context of the RoboCup@Home competition, experiment design in the context of the ROPOD project (ROPOD is an Innovation Action funded by the European Commission under grant no. 731848 within the Horizon 2020 framework program), as well as specification transfer between robots.

Keywords: State machines · Rapid prototyping · Experiment design

1 Introduction

The development of robot programs requires the integration of multiple functionalities that together allow a robot to perform useful tasks. Particularly for rapid prototyping, the development process often involves the use of finite state machines, which model the program execution by a set of states and transitions between them. State machines are attractive for robot program creation due to various properties, such as the fact that they can be used to make the program execution transparent and reproducible. This is particularly important for robot experiments, which need to be designed in a manner that allows different experimenters to obtain the same results under similar experimental conditions.

The development of state machines differs depending on the programming language, but most languages have dedicated libraries for defining and creating automata[1]. Due to the simplicity with which state machines can be created, it

---

[1] In Python, one such example is SMACH: https://github.com/ros/executive_smach.

© Springer Nature Switzerland AG 2019
S. Chalup et al. (Eds.): RoboCup 2019, LNAI 11531, pp. 408–417, 2019.
https://doi.org/10.1007/978-3-030-35699-6_32

is often the case that the specification of a state machine is interleaved together with the implementation[2]. Mixing up the specification and implementation of a state machine has various limitations however. First of all, keeping the specification together with the implementation leads to non-reusable specifications that are committed to a specific implementation. Furthermore, states can only be made reusable if they can be reconfigured, but this means that direct code changes are needed for reconfiguration, which is particularly problematic when reusing functionalities over different robots. Having the ability to load state machines dynamically is also more reasonable in certain cases, for instance when a robot operator needs to trigger an experiment remotely[3].

In this paper, we present a Python-oriented domain-specific language for specifying state machines as well as a small Python library that allows state machines to be dynamically created. We then illustrate the use of the library in three different use cases, namely (i) a pick-and-place experiment in the context of domestic robots, (ii) a docking and elevator entering experiment for a logistic robot, and (iii) reusing the pick-and-place state machine, but redefining a particular state for a specific robot. The limitations and possible extensions of the library are then discussed.

2   Related Work

In the context of full robot autonomy, state machine-driven development has various limitations, such as the lack of flexibility [12], but nevertheless, a state machine remains an invaluable tool for rapid functionality testing. For instance, the Amazon States Language [1] is a JSON-based state machine specification language that, in addition to including basic specification constructs, allows specifying conditional transitions, parallel state execution, as well as predefined error recovery behaviours. SCXML [13] is a similar XML-based language that also defines advanced constructs for complex state machine behaviours based on Harel statecharts [5]. The main aspect that distinguishes our library is that we consider the reusability of state machines and the redefinition of states. In contrast to language-based specifications, rcommander [11] can be used for creating state machines graphically; however, the library is SMACH-specific and it also does not address the reusability aspect. Bardaro and Matteucci [2] discuss the use of the Architecture Analysis and Design Language (AADL) for robot component modelling in the context of the Robot Operating System (ROS), though the use of the presented framework with other middlewares is also considered. Similarly, Li et al. [7] apply the RoboChart state machine framework [9] for modelling robot programs, such that, just as in [2], the specification can be used for code generation. Gogolla and Vallecillo [4] apply the Unified Modelling Language

---

[2] Various such examples can be found in the main repository of the b-it-bots@Work RoboCup team: https://github.com/b-it-bots/mas_industrial_robotics/tree/kinetic/mir_scenarios.

[3] This is for example necessary in the case of the ROPOD project, where robots need to be deployed to a hospital [8].

(UML) and the Object Constraint Language (OCL) for robot program description. The Lotos New Technology (LNT) language can also be used for specifying program behaviour and, additionally, fault diagnosis [6]. A Petri net [3] is an alternative formalism that is particularly suited for concurrent execution. All of these representations are formally rich, which can however make it difficult to apply them without dedicated training. In contrast, our state machine library is minimal and has the purpose of simplifying the process of rapid prototyping, but it should be noted that our intention is to supplement the more powerful frameworks, which remain essential in the context of architectural modelling and formal verification.

3   Use Cases

To motivate our state machine specification language and library, we will consider three different use cases: (i) definition and execution of a simple pick and place scenario in the context of the RoboCup@Home competition, (ii) experiment definition in the context of the ROPOD project, and (iii) state machine transfer between different robots.

In RoboCup@Home, a common task in different scenarios is picking and placing everyday objects. In practice, both picking and placing are error-prone activities due to the variation of objects in domestic environments, which is why it can be useful to investigate a robot's performance on both tasks experimentally, for instance on a common dining table. Such an experiment could involve going to the table and scanning all objects on it, picking one of the objects, and then placing it back at a different location. This would lead to the state machine shown in Fig. 1a.

In the ROPOD project, robots need to transport hospital items, such as carts and beds, between different parts of a hospital, possibly over multiple floors. Docking to a cart and navigating into an elevator with a cart attached are particularly interesting to consider since both actions can result in execution failures. An experiment that verifies the operation of both actions would be one in which a robot first has to dock to a cart and then enter an elevator, where the assumption is that the robot docks the cart right next to the elevator. This would be represented by the state machine shown in Fig. 1b.

The third use case we consider is that of reusing a state machine that is either robot-independent or specified for one particular robot on a different robot. As a concrete example, we will suppose that all states in the above pick-and-place state machine can be implemented in a robot-independent manner, except for the table scanning state, which needs to be reimplemented for different robots[4]. The objective in this case is to avoid redefining the complete state machine multiple times.

In the following section, we show how we specify, create, and execute state machines such as these.

---

[4] For instance, some robots may require taking the manipulator out of the camera's way before the table is scanned, while others may not.

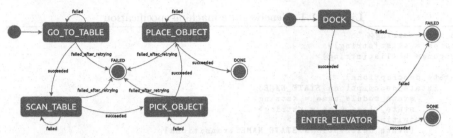

(a) A state machine for a simple pick and place experiment

(b) A state machine for a cart docking and elevator entering experiment

Fig. 1. State machines in the context of RoboCup@Home and ROPOD

4   State Machine Specification and Configuration

The general design of our Python library is illustrated in Fig. 2.

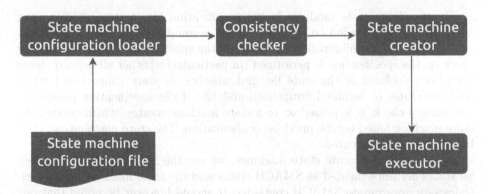

Fig. 2. Overview of the state machine specification library. A state machine is defined in a configuration file, such that state specifications include the names of the modules in which individual states are implemented. After a consistency check, the state machine is dynamically created from the specification and subsequently executed.

The state machine specification is at the core of the library, such that state machines are specified in a language embedded in TOML[5,6]. The language allows specifying the states in a state machine and the transitions between them, as well as passing arguments to the individual states and the state machine as a whole. In addition, our specification assumes that each state is implemented as a separate class; the names of the modules in which states are implemented and the names of the state classes are also specified in the configuration. A generic state machine specification template is shown below.

---

[5] https://github.com/toml-lang/toml.

[6] An earlier prototype, which we still actively use, was based on a YAML-based specification.

Listing 1.1. Generic state machine specification

```
sm_id = <string>
states = <list[string]>
outcomes = <list[string]>

[state_descriptions]
    [state_descriptions.STATE_NAME]
        state_module_name = <string>
        state_class_name = <string>
        initial_state = <bool>
        [state_descriptions.STATE_NAME.transitions]
            transition_1_name = <string>
            ...
            transition_n_name = <string>
        [state_descriptions.STATE_NAME.arguments]
            argument_1 = argument_1_value
            ...
            argument_n = argument_n_value
    ...

[arguments]
    argument_1 = argument_1_value
    ...
    argument_n = argument_n_value
```

By specifying state modules in the specification file, a state machine can be assembled and loaded on the fly[7]. This is accomplished in a three-step process, namely (i) a configuration loader reads the specification, (ii) a consistency check on the specification is performed (in particular, whether all defined states have been declared in the state list and whether all state transitions lead to declared states or terminal outcomes), and (iii) if the specification passes the consistency check, it is passed on to a state machine creator, which creates the state machine based on the provided configuration. The state machine can then be appropriately executed.

To create and execute state machines, we use the SMACH library, namely all states are implemented as SMACH states and the state machine creator initialises an appropriate SMACH container. It should however be noted that our library does not make any specific assumptions about the implementation of individual states or the actual state machine - other than the requirement that each state needs to be an individual class - which simplifies switching between state machine libraries without changing the state machine specification. In other words, switching between state machine libraries requires a change in the *implementation*, but not the *specification* of a state machine.

We can now illustrate how state machines can be described using our minimal description language in the context of the previously described use cases. The specification of the pick and place experiment[8] would be given as follows:

---

[7] In our Python library, this is achieved with the help of the *importlib* package.

[8] An implementation using the earlier YAML-based specification can be found at https://github.com/b-it-bots/mas_execution_manager; this is actively used for specifying RoboCup@Home scenarios in our domestic robotics repository: https://github.com/b-it-bots/mas_domestic_robotics.

Listing 1.2. State machine for a simple pick and place experiment

```
sm_id = "simple_pick_and_place"
states = ["GO_TO_TABLE", "SCAN_TABLE", "PICK_OBJECT", "PLACE_OBJECT"]
outcomes = ["DONE", "FAILED"]

[state_descriptions]
    [state_descriptions.GO_TO_TABLE]
        state_module_name = "mdr_navigation_behaviours.move_base"
        state_class_name = "MoveBase"
        initial_state = true
        [state_descriptions.GO_TO_TABLE.transitions]
            succeeded = "SCAN_TABLE"
            failed = "GO_TO_TABLE"
            failed_after_retrying = "FAILED"
        [state_descriptions.GO_TO_TABLE.arguments]
            destination_locations = ["TABLE"]
            number_of_retries = 3

    [state_descriptions.SCAN_TABLE]
        state_module_name = "mdr_perception_behaviours.perceive_planes"
        state_class_name = "PerceivePlanes"
        [state_descriptions.SCAN_TABLE.transitions]
            succeeded = "PICK_OBJECT"
            failed = "SCAN_TABLE"
            failed_after_retrying = "FAILED"
        [state_descriptions.SCAN_TABLE.arguments]
            plane_prefix = "table"
            number_of_retries = 3

    [state_descriptions.PICK_OBJECT]
        state_module_name = "mdr_manipulation_behaviours.
            pick_closest_from_surface"
        state_class_name = "PickClosestFromSurface"
        [state_descriptions.PICK_OBJECT.transitions]
            succeeded = "PLACE_OBJECT"
            failed = "PICK_OBJECT"
            failed_after_retrying = "FAILED"
            find_objects_before_picking = "SCAN_TABLE"
        [state_descriptions.PICK_OBJECT.arguments]
            picking_surface_prefix = "table"
            number_of_retries = 3

    [state_descriptions.PLACE_OBJECT]
        state_module_name = "mdr_manipulation_behaviours.place"
        state_class_name = "Place"
        [state_descriptions.PLACE_OBJECT.transitions]
            succeeded = "DONE"
            failed = "PLACE_OBJECT"
            failed_after_retrying = "FAILED"
        [state_descriptions.PLACE_OBJECT.arguments]
            placing_surface_prefix = "table"
            number_of_retries = 3
```

As can be seen in this specification, different arguments can be passed to the states depending on the needs; for example, the *GO_TO_TABLE* state takes a list of named locations to which the robot should go, while the *PICK_OBJECT* state receives the name of a surface from which the robot should grasp an object. This state machine also has some fault tolerance in its design, such that all states can be retried a predefined number of times before a global failure is reported.

The specification of the docking and elevator entering experiment in the ROPOD context is similarly shown below[9]:

Listing 1.3. State machine for a cart docking and elevator entering experiment

```
sm_id = "dock_and_enter_elevator"
states = ["DOCK", "ENTER_ELEVATOR"]
outcomes = ["DONE", "FAILED"]

[state_descriptions]
    [state_descriptions.DOCK]
        state_module_name = "ropod_experiment_executor.commands.dock"
        state_class_name = "Dock"
        initial_state = true
        [state_descriptions.DOCK.transitions]
            done = "ENTER_ELEVATOR"
            failed = "FAILED"
        [state_descriptions.DOCK.arguments]
            area_id = "Area1"
            area_name = "CartArea1"
            dock_action_topic = "/ropod_task_executor/DOCK"
            dock_progress_topic = "/task_progress/dock"
            timeout_s = 120.0

    [state_descriptions.ENTER_ELEVATOR]
        state_module_name = "ropod_experiment_executor.commands.
            enter_elevator"
        state_class_name = "EnterElevator"
        [state_descriptions.ENTER_ELEVATOR.transitions]
            done = "DONE"
            failed = "FAILED"
        [state_descriptions.ENTER_ELEVATOR.arguments]
            area_floor = 0
            elevator_id = 4
            elevator_door_id = 88
            wait_for_elevator_action_topic = "/ropod_task_executor/
                WAIT_FOR_ELEVATOR"
            enter_elevator_action_topic = "/ropod_task_executor/
                ENTER_ELEVATOR"
            elevator_progress_topic = "/task_progress/elevator"
            timeout_s = 120.0
```

The state machine describing this experiment is slightly simpler than the one for the pick-and-place case. What is worth noting is that the states require information from an OpenStreetMap environment description [10], which the robot is using for both navigation and docking. The complete workflow in ROPOD includes triggering such experiments through a web application[10]; because of this, dynamic state machine loading is particularly useful since an operator may want to run different experiments one after the other. In addition, the separation of the specification from the implementation makes it rather simple to visualise the state machine, as shown in Fig. 3.

Finally, to accomplish state machine transfer, we define hierarchical relations between state machines, such that the robot-independent state machine represents the parent and the robot-specific one the child[11]. When redefining a state,

---

[9] This specification, along with various other experiment definitions, can be found at https://github.com/ropod-project/ropod_experiment_executor.

[10] https://github.com/ropod-project/remote-monitoring.

[11] Multi-level hierarchies may also be beneficial, but our current implementation does not consider those.

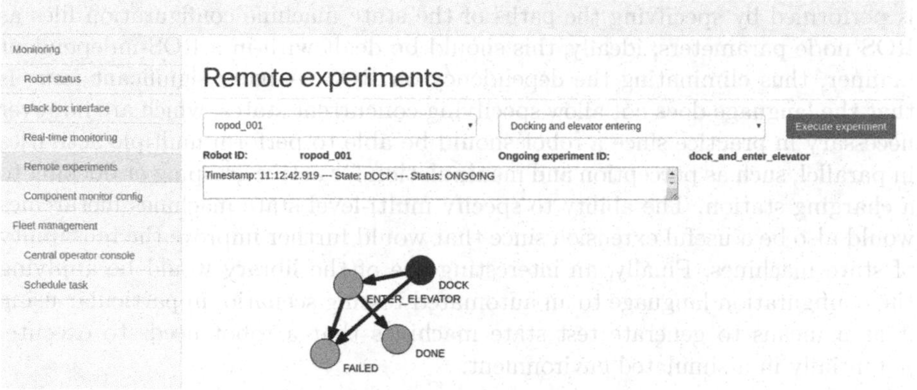

Fig. 3. Visualisation of the docking and elevator entering state machine. The green node denotes the currently active state, which is known due to the fact that the states continuously advertise their status. (Color figure online)

in principle we only need to modify the module and class names of the robot-specific state implementation; redefining the state transitions and arguments is possible as well, but not mandatory. In addition, the global state machine parameters, such as the name and list of states, can be modified as well. A redefinition of the *SCAN_TABLE* state for a specific robot can be done as shown below.

Listing 1.4. Robot-specific state redefinition in the pick-and-place state machine

```
sm_id = "robot_specific_simple_pick_and_place"

[state_descriptions]
    [state_descriptions.SCAN_TABLE]
        state_module_name = "my_robot_perception_behaviours.perceive_planes"
        state_class_name = "PerceivePlanes"
        [state_descriptions.SCAN_TABLE.arguments]
            arm_position = "folded"
```

In the above redefinition, we specify a new implementation for the *SCAN_TABLE* state and add an additional input argument that is specific to the new state.

It should be noted that we currently define hierarchical relations between state machines by specifying the paths to the parent and child state machines as ROS node parameters; this is thus the only ROS-dependent aspect of our library.

5   Discussion and Future Work

As described above, the state machine library presented in this paper is actively used and maintained in different contexts, but there are various potential improvements that can be made. First of all, as mentioned before, the definition of hierarchical relations between state machines is currently ROS-dependent and is performed by specifying the paths of the state machine configuration files as ROS node parameters; ideally, this should be dealt with in a ROS-independent manner, thus eliminating the dependency on ROS. A more significant issue is that the language does not allow specifying concurrent states, which are however necessary in practice since a robot should be able to perform multiple activities in parallel, such as perception and manipulation for active grasping or docking to a charging station. The ability to specify multi-level state machines hierarchies would also be a useful extension since that would further improve the reusability of state machines. Finally, an interesting use of the library would be applying the configuration language to an automated testing scenario, in particular using it as a means to generate test state machines that a robot needs to execute, potentially in a simulated environment.

Acknowledgements. We gratefully acknowledge the support by the b-it International Center for Information Technology. We would like to thank Argentina Ortega and Minh Nguyen for various suggestions about the library, the rest of the members of the b-it-bots@Home RoboCup team for its early adoption, as well as Dharmin Bakaraniya for actively contributing to the development.

References

1. Amazon.com: Amazon States Language. https://states-language.net/spec.html
2. Bardaro, G., Matteucci, M.: Using AADL to model and develop ROS-based robotic application. In: 2017 1st IEEE International Conference on Robotic Computing (IRC), pp. 204–207, April 2017
3. Costelha, H., Lima, P.: Modelling, analysis and execution of robotic tasks using petri nets. In: 2007 IEEE/RSJ International Conference on Intelligent Robots and Systems, pp. 1449–1454, October 2007
4. Gogolla, M., Vallecillo, A.: (An example for) formally modeling robot behavior with UML and OCL. In: Seidl, M., Zschaler, S. (eds.) STAF 2017. LNCS, vol. 10748, pp. 232–246. Springer, Cham (2018). https://doi.org/10.1007/978-3-319-74730-9_22
5. Harel, D.: Statecharts: a visual formalism for complex systems. Sci. Comput. Program. **8**(3), 231–274 (1987)
6. Hofer, B., Mateescu, R., Serwe, W., Wotawa, F.: Using LNT formal descriptions for model-based diagnosis. In: 29th International Workshop Principles of Diagnosis DX 2018 (2018)
7. Li, W., Miyazawa, A., Ribeiro, P., Cavalcanti, A., Woodcock, J., Timmis, J.: From formalised state machines to implementations of robotic controllers. CoRR abs/1702.01783 (2016)
8. Mitrevski, A., et al.: Deploying robots in everyday environments: towards dependable and practical robotic systems. In: 29th International Workshop Principles of Diagnosis DX 2018 (2018)
9. Miyazawa, A., Ribeiro, P., Li, W., Cavalcanti, A., Timmis, J., Woodcock, J.: RoboChart: modelling and verification of the functional behaviour of robotic applications. Softw. Syst. Model. **18**(5), 3097–3149 (2019)

10. Naik, L., Blumenthal, S., Huebel, N., Bruyninckx, H., Prassler, E.: Semantic mapping extension for OpenStreetMap applied to indoor robot navigation. In: IEEE International Conference on Robotics and Automation (ICRA), pp. 3839–3845 (2019)
11. Nguyen, H.: rcommander_core. http://wiki.ros.org/rcommander_core
12. Shpieva, E., Awaad, I.: Integrating task planning, execution and monitoring for a domestic service robot. Inf. Technol. **57**(2), 112–121 (2015)
13. World Wide Web Consortium (W3C): State Chart XML (SCXML): State Machine Notation for Control Abstraction. https://www.w3.org/TR/scxml/

Gliders2d: Source Code Base for RoboCup 2D Soccer Simulation League

Mikhail Prokopenko[1,2]([✉]) and Peter Wang[2]

[1] Complex Systems Research Group, Faculty of Engineering and IT,
The University of Sydney, Sydney, NSW 2006, Australia
mikhail.prokopenko@sydney.edu.au
[2] Data Mining, CSIRO Data61, PO Box 76, Epping, NSW 1710, Australia

Abstract. We describe Gliders2d, a base code release for Gliders, a
soccer simulation team which won the RoboCup Soccer 2D Simulation
League in 2016. We trace six evolutionary steps, each of which is encapsu-
lated in a sequential change of the released code, from v1.1 to v1.6, starting from agent2d-3.1.1 (set as the baseline v1.0). These changes improve
performance by adjusting the agents' stamina management, their pressing behaviour and the action-selection mechanism, as well as their positional choice in both attack and defense, and enabling riskier passes.
The resultant behaviour, which is sufficiently generic to be applicable
to physical robot teams, increases the players' mobility and achieves a
better control of the field. The last presented version, Gliders2d-v1.6,
approaches the strength of Gliders2013, and outperforms agent2d-3.1.1
by four goals per game on average. The sequential improvements demonstrate how the methodology of human-based evolutionary computation
can markedly boost the overall performance with even a small number
of controlled steps.

1 Introduction

The RoboCup Soccer 2D Simulation League contributes to the overall RoboCup
initiative, sharing its inspirational Millennium challenge: producing a team of
fully autonomous humanoid soccer players capable of winning a soccer game
against the 2050 FIFA World Cup holder, while complying with the official
FIFA rules [6]. Over the years, the 2D Simulation League made several important advances in autonomous decision making under constraints, flexible tactical
planning, collective behaviour and teamwork, communication and coordination,
as well as opponent modelling and adaptation [7,20,28–30,33,34,38,41]. These
advances are to a large extent underpinned by the standardisation of many low-
level behaviours, world model updates and debugging tools, captured by several
notable base code releases, offered by "CMUnited" team from Carnegie Mellon
University (USA) [35,37], "UvA Trilearn" team from University of Amsterdam
(The Netherlands) [15], "MarliK" team from University of Guilan (Iran) [40], and
"HELIOS" team from AIST Information Technology Research Institute (Japan)
[1]. As a result, almost 80% of the League's teams eventually switched their code

© Springer Nature Switzerland AG 2019
S. Chalup et al. (Eds.): RoboCup 2019, LNAI 11531, pp. 418–428, 2019.
https://doi.org/10.1007/978-3-030-35699-6_33

base to agent2d over the next few years [30]. The 2016 champion team, Gliders2016 [25,30], was also based on the well-developed code base of *agent2d-3.1.1* [1], and fragments of MarliK source code [40], all written in C++.

The winning approach developed by Gliders combined human innovation and artificial evolution, following the methodologies of *guided self-organisation* [19,21,22,26] and *human-based evolutionary computation* (HBEC). The latter comprises a set of evolutionary computation techniques that incorporate human innovation [8,16]. This fusion allowed us to optimise several components, including an action-dependent evaluation function proposed in Gliders2012 [27], a particle-swarm based self-localisation method and tactical interaction networks introduced in Gliders2013 [4,11,12,17,24], a new communication scheme and dynamic tactics with Voronoi diagrams utilised by Gliders2014 [23], bio-inspired flocking behaviour incorporated within Gliders2015 [32], and opponent modelling diversified in Gliders2016 [25]. The framework achieved a high level of tactical proficiency ensuring players' mobility and the overall control over the field.

We describe a base code release for Gliders, called *Gliders2d*, version v1, with 6 sequential changes which correspond to 6 evolutionary HBEC steps, from v1.1 to v1.6. Since Gliders2d release is based on agent2d, the version Gliders2d-v1.0 is identical to agent2d-3.1.1 (apart from the team name), but every next step includes a new release. It is important to point out that Gliders2d is an evolutionary branch separate from the (Gliders2012—Gliders2016) branch, and both branches evolved independently. The final version of the presented release, Gliders2d-v1.6, is neither a subset not superset of any of Gliders2012—Gliders2016 teams. However, as a point of reference, we note that Gliders2d-v1.6 has a strength approaching that of Gliders2013 [24], and future releases will improve the performance further.

Our objectives in making this first release are threefold: (a) it includes several important code components which explain and exemplify various approaches taken and integrated within the champion team Gliders2016; (b) it illustrates the HBEC methodology by showing some of the utilised primitives, while explicitly tracing the resultant performance (i.e., the fitness) for each sequential step from v1.1 to v1.6; (c) it demonstrates how one can make substantial advances, starting with the standard agent2d code, with only a small number of controlled steps. It may help new teams in making the first steps within the league, using the available base code.

2   Methodology and Results

The HBEC approach evolves performance across an artificial "generation", using an automated evaluation of the fitness landscape, while the team developers innovate and recombine various behaviours. The mutations are partially automated. On the one hand, the development effort translates human expertise into novel behaviours and tactics. On the other hand, the automated evaluation platform, utilised during the development of Gliders, and Gliders2d in particular, leverages the power of modern supercomputing in exploring the search-space.

Each solution, represented as the team source code, can be interpreted as a "genotype", encoding the entire team behaviour in a set of "design points". A design point, in the context of a data-farming experiment, describes a specific combination of input parameters [10], defining either a single parameter (e.g., pressing level), complex multi-agent tactics (e.g., a set of conditional statements shaping a positioning scheme for several players), or multi-agent communication protocols [14, 30, 41].

While some design points are easy to vary, others may be harder to mutate and/or recombine due to their internal structure. For example, a specific tactic (design point), created by a team developer, may be implemented via several conditional statements each of which comprises a condition and an action, involving multiple parameters and primitives (see next subsections for examples). These components can then be mutated and recombined as part of the genotype.

The solutions are evaluated against a specific opponent, over thousands of games played for each generation. In order to maintain coherence of the resultant code, which evolves against different opponents in parallel, auxiliary conditions switch the corresponding parts of design points on and off for specific opponents [30], in an analogy to epigenetic programming [39]. The fitness function is primarily based on the average goal difference, with the average points as a tie-breaker, followed by the preference for a lower standard error.

The main thread in the evolutionary branch described in this release aims to ensure a better control of the soccer field, by different means: (i) stamina management with higher dash power rates; (ii) more intense pressing of the ball possessing opponent; (iii) actions' evaluation aimed at delivering the ball to points stretching the opposition most; (iv) attacking players positioning to maximise their ball reachability potential; (v) defending players positioning to minimise the ball reachability potential of the opponents; (vi) risky passes. These improvements may in general be applied to robotic teams in physical RoboCup leagues.

In tracing the relative performance of Gliders2d from v1.1 to v1.6 we used three benchmark teams: agent2d-3.1.1 itself [1], Gliders2013 [24], and the current world champion team, HELIOS2018 [18]. For each sequential step, 1000 games were played against the benchmarks. Against agent2d, the goal difference achieved by Gliders2d-v1.6 improves from zero to 4.2. Against HELIOS2018, the goal difference improves from -12.73 to -4.34. Finally, against Gliders2013, the goal difference improves from -5.483 to -0.212, achieving near-parity. Tables 1, 2, and 3 summarise the performance dynamics, including the overall points for and against, goals scored and conceded, the goal difference, and the standard error of the mean.

2.1   Gliders2d v1.1: Stamina Management

The first step in improving upon agent2d performance, along the released evolutionary branch, is adding adjustments to the agents' stamina management (confined to a single source file `strategy.cpp`). Specifically, there are four additional assignments of the maximal dash power in certain situations, for example:

```
// G2d: run in opp penalty area
      else if ( wm.ball().pos().x > 36.0 && wm.self().pos().x > 36.0 && mate_min <
        opp_min - 4 )
              dash_power = ServerParam::i().maxDashPower();
```

This fragment of the source code demonstrates how these specific situations are described through conditions constraining the ball position, the agent position and its role, the offside line, and the minimal intercept cycles for the Gliders2d team (`mate_min`) and the opponent team (`opp_min`). Such constraints can be evolved by mutation or recombination of primitives (`argument (op) X`), where `X` is a constraint, the argument is a state of relevant variable, e.g. `wm.ball().pos().x`, and `(op)` is a relational operator, e.g., $<$, $>$, $==$, and so on. The action form may vary from a simple single assignment (the maximal dash power in this case), to a block of code.

Adding the stamina management conditions increased the goal difference against HELIOS2018 from -12.729 to -6.868, and against Gliders2013 from -5.483 to -2.684.

2.2   Gliders2d v1.2: Pressing

The second step along this evolutionary branch is adding adjustments to the agents' pressing behaviour (confined to a single source file `bhv_basic_move.cpp`). The `pressing` level, more precisely, level of *pressure*, is expressed as the number of cycles which separate the minimal intercept cycles by the agent (`self_min`) and the fastest opponent (`opp_min`). The intercept behaviour forcing the agent to press the opponent with the ball is triggered when `self_min < opp_min + pressing`. In agent2d the pressing level is not distinguished as a variable, being hard-coded as 3 cycles, and making it an evolvable variable is an example of a simple innovation. Specifically, there are several assignments of the pressing level, tailored to different opponent teams, agent roles and their positions on the field, as well as the ball location.

Again, adding the evolved conditions for pressing increased the goal difference against agent2d from near-zero to 1.288, against HELIOS2018 from -6.868 to -6.476 (this increase is within the standard error of the mean), and against Gliders2013 from -2.684 to -1.147.

2.3   Gliders2d v1.3: Evaluator

The third step modifies the action evaluator, following the approach introduced in Gliders2012 [27], which diversified the single evaluation metric of agent2d by considering multiple points as desirable states. The action-dependent evaluation mechanism is described in detail in [25,27], and the presented release includes its implementation (source files `sample_field_evaluator.cpp` and `action_chain_graph`).

In particular, a new variable, `opp_forward`, is introduced, counting the number of non-goalie opponents in a sector centred on the agent and extending to the points near the opponent's goal posts. The single evaluation metric of agent2d is invoked when there are no opponents in this sector, or when the ball is located within (or close to) the own half. Otherwise, the logic enters into a sequence of conditions (marked in the released code), identifying the "best" point out of several possible candidates offered by Voronoi diagrams. A Voronoi diagram is defined as the partitioning of a plane with n points into n convex polygons, so that each polygon contains exactly one point, while every point in the given polygon is closer to its central point than any other [13]. The best point is selected to be relatively close to the teammates' positions, and far from the opponents' positions. The distance between the identified best point and the future ball location, attainable by the action under consideration, is chosen as the evaluation result.

The action-dependent evaluation mechanism increased the goal difference against agent2d from 1.288 to 1.616, while not providing a notable improvements against the two other benchmarks, as it is applicable in attacking situations which are rare in these match-ups at this stage.

2.4 Gliders2d v1.4: Positioning

To make a better use of the new field evaluator, the positioning scheme of the players is adjusted by selecting the points according to suitably constructed Voronoi diagrams. For example, a Voronoi diagram may partition the field according to the positions of the opponent players; the candidate location points can be chosen among Voronoi vertices, as well as among the points located at intersections between Voronoi segments and specific lines, e.g., offside line, as illustrated in [23]. All the constrained conditions are evolvable.

The positioning based on Voronoi diagrams increased the goal difference against agent2d from 1.616 to 2.387, again maintaining the performance against the two other benchmarks.

2.5 Gliders2d v1.5: Formations

This step did not change any of the source code files—instead the formation files, specified in configurations such as `defense-formation.conf`, etc. were modified with fedit2. This approach, pioneered in the Simulation League by [2,3], is based on Constrained Delaunay Triangulation (CDT) [9]. For a set of points in a plane, a Delaunay triangulation achieves an outcome such that no point from the set is inside the circumcircle of any triangle. Essentially, CDT divides the soccer field into a set of triangles, based on the set of predefined ball locations, each of which is mapped to the positions of each player. Moreover, when the ball takes any position *within* a triangle, each player's position is dynamically adjusted during the runtime in a congruent way [2,3,30]. Overall, a formation defined via CDT is an ordered list of coordinates, and so, in terms of evolutionary computation, mutating and recombining such a list can be relatively easily automated and evaluated.

Figure 1 shows a CDT fragment; for example, the point 110, where the ball is located, defines the following intended positions for the players:

```
Ball -48.66 22.71
1 -50.72 6.07
2 -46.08 3.12
3 -47.6 10.53
4 -43.58 -3.75
5 -48.49 18.65
6 -44.3 13.29
7 -41.17 5.8
8 -40.32 17.03
9 -21.01 -17.44
10 -19.94 26.01
11 -22.62 5.8
```

The released changes in Gliders2d-1.5 formations are aimed at improving the defensive performance, placing the defenders and midfielders closer to the own goal. A notable performance gain was observed against all three benchmarks. The goal difference against agent2d increased from 2.387 to 3.210; against HELIOS2018: from −6.422 to −4.383; and against Gliders2013: from −1.039 to −0.344.

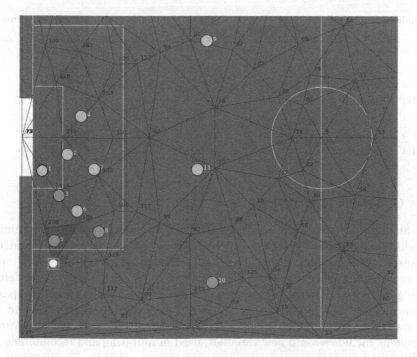

Fig. 1. Example of a Delaunay triangulation, used by `defense-formation.conf`, produced by fedit2. The triangle formed by points 106, 108 and 110 is highlighted. When the ball is located at 110, the players are supposed to be located in the shown positions.

Table 1. Performance evaluation for Gliders2d against agent2d, over ~1000 games carried out for each version of Gliders2d against the opponent. The goal difference improves from zero to 4.2, while the average game score improves from (2.29:2.29) to (5.21:1.01).

Gliders2d	Points for	Points against	Goals scored	Goals conceded	Goal diff.	Std. error
v0.0 (agent2d)	1.384	1.414	2.287	2.289	−0.002	0.040
v1.1 (stamina)	1.345	1.468	2.254	2.290	−0.036	0.049
v1.2 (pressing)	2.161	0.691	2.642	1.355	1.288	0.051
v1.3 (evaluator)	2.252	0.607	2.997	1.381	1.616	0.063
v1.4 (positioning)	2.515	0.367	3.849	1.461	2.387	0.086
v1.5 (formations)	2.785	0.154	3.995	0.785	3.210	0.181
v1.6 (risky passes)	2.840	0.116	5.214	1.014	4.200	0.172

Table 2. Performance evaluation for Gliders2d against HELIOS2018, over ~1000 games carried out for each version of Gliders2d against the opponent. The goal difference improves from −12.73 to −4.34, while the average game score improves from (0.12:12.85) to (0.26:4.60).

Gliders2d	Points for	Points against	Goals scored	Goals conceded	Goal diff.	Std. error
v0.0 (agent2d)	0.000	3.000	0.123	12.852	−12.729	0.514
v1.1 (stamina)	0.001	2.998	0.231	7.099	−6.868	0.276
v1.2 (pressing)	0.003	2.994	0.248	6.724	−6.476	0.140
v1.3 (evaluator)	0.004	2.992	0.269	6.821	−6.552	0.310
v1.4 (positioning)	0.002	2.996	0.298	6.720	−6.422	0.223
v1.5 (formations)	0.027	2.952	0.273	4.655	−4.383	0.197
v1.6 (risky passes)	0.024	2.961	0.260	4.600	−4.337	0.161

2.6 Gliders2d v1.6: Risky Passes

The final step of this release introduced `risk` level, expressed as the number of additional cycles "granted" to teammates receiving a pass, under a pressure from opponent players potentially intercepting the pass (`strict_check_pass_generator.cpp`). If `risk` level is set to zero, the default passing behaviour of agent2d is recovered. For positive values of `risk` the passes are considered as feasible even if an ideal opponent interceptor gets to the ball trajectory sooner than the intended recipient of the pass. The conditional statements include several new variables, used in mutating and recombining the conditions.

The addition of risky passes increased the goal difference against agent2d from 3.210 to 4.2; and against Gliders2013: from −0.344 to −0.212.

Table 3. Performance evaluation for Gliders2d against Gliders2013, over ~1000 games carried out for each version of Gliders2d against the opponent. The goal difference improves from −5.48 to −0.21, while the average game score improves from (0.57:6.05) to (0.78:0.99).

Gliders2d	Points for	Points against	Goals scored	Goals conceded	Goal diff.	Std. error
v0.0 (agent2d)	0.022	2.968	0.569	6.052	−5.483	0.213
v1.1 (stamina)	0.183	2.730	0.596	3.280	−2.684	0.071
v1.2 (pressing)	0.539	2.230	0.613	1.760	−1.147	0.063
v1.3 (evaluator)	0.657	2.109	0.770	1.800	−1.030	0.067
v1.4 (positioning)	0.603	2.160	0.700	1.739	−1.039	0.077
v1.5 (formations)	1.039	1.607	0.700	1.044	−0.344	0.026
v1.6 (risky passes)	1.111	1.527	0.776	0.988	−0.212	0.038

3   Conclusions

In this paper, we described the first version of *Gliders2d*: a base code release for Gliders (based on agent2d-3.1.1). We trace six sequential changes aligned with six evolutionary steps. These steps improve the overall control of the pitch by increasing the players' mobility through several means: less conservative usage of the available stamina balance (v1.1); more intense pressing of opponents (v1.2); selecting more diversified actions (v1.3); positioning forwards in open areas (v1.4); positioning defenders closer to own goal (v1.5); and considering riskier passes (v1.6).

As has been argued in the past, the simulation leagues enable replicable and robust investigation of complex robotic systems [5,31]. We believe that the purpose of the RoboCup Soccer Simulation Leagues (both 2D and 3D) should be to simulate agents based on a futuristic robotic architecture which is not yet achievable in hardware. Aiming at such a general and abstract robot architecture may help to identify a standard for what humanoid robots may look like in 2050, the year of the RoboCup Millennium challenge. This is the reason for focussing, in this release, on the features which can also be used by simulated 3D, as well as robotic, teams competing in RoboCup, aiming at some of the most general questions: when to conserve energy (stamina), when to run (pressing), where to kick the ball (actions), where to be on the field (positioning in attack and defense), and when to take risks (passes). While the provided specific answers may or may not be widely acceptable, general reasoning along these lines may bring us closer to a new RoboCup Humanoid Simulation League (HSL). In HSL, the Simulated Humanoid should be defined in a standard and generalisable way, approaching human soccer-playing behavior [36], while the behavioural and tactical improvements can be evolved and/or adapted to this standardised architecture.

The released code: http://www.prokopenko.net/gliders2d.html.

The last presented version, Gliders2d-v1.6, is comparable to Gliders2013, achieving the average score of (0.78:0.99) against this benchmark, and outperforms agent2d-3.1.1 with the average score (5.21:1.01).

In tracing this evolutionary branch, we illustrated the methodology of human-based evolutionary computation, showing that even a small number of controlled steps can dramatically improve the overall team performance.

Acknowledgments. We thank HELIOS team for their excellent code base of *agent2d*, as well as several members of Gliders team contributing during 2012–2016: David Budden, Oliver Cliff, Victor Jauregui and Oliver Obst. We are also grateful to participants of the discussion on the future of the RoboCup Simulation Leagues, in particular to Peter Stone, Patrick MacAlpine, Nuno Lau, Klaus Dorer, and Daniel Polani.

References

1. Akiyama, H., Nakashima, T.: HELIOS base: an open source package for the RoboCup soccer 2D simulation. In: Behnke, S., Veloso, M., Visser, A., Xiong, R. (eds.) RoboCup 2013. LNCS (LNAI), vol. 8371, pp. 528–535. Springer, Heidelberg (2014). https://doi.org/10.1007/978-3-662-44468-9_46

2. Akiyama, H., Noda, I.: Multi-agent positioning mechanism in the dynamic environment. In: Visser, U., Ribeiro, F., Ohashi, T., Dellaert, F. (eds.) RoboCup 2007. LNCS (LNAI), vol. 5001, pp. 377–384. Springer, Heidelberg (2008). https://doi.org/10.1007/978-3-540-68847-1_38

3. Akiyama, H., Shimora, H.: HELIOS 2010 team description. In: Ruiz-del-Solar, J., Chown, E., Plöger, P.G. (eds.) RoboCup 2010: Robot Soccer World Cup XIV. LNCS, vol. 6556. Springer, Heidelberg (2011)

4. Budden, D., Prokopenko, M.: Improved particle filtering for pseudo-uniform belief distributions in robot localisation. In: Behnke, S., Veloso, M., Visser, A., Xiong, R. (eds.) RoboCup 2013. LNCS (LNAI), vol. 8371, pp. 385–395. Springer, Heidelberg (2014). https://doi.org/10.1007/978-3-662-44468-9_34

5. Budden, D.M., Wang, P., Obst, O., Prokopenko, M.: RoboCup simulation leagues: enabling replicable and robust investigation of complex robotic systems. IEEE Robot. Autom. Mag. **22**(3), 140–146 (2015)

6. Burkhard, H.D., Duhaut, D., Fujita, M., Lima, P., Murphy, R., Rojas, R.: The road to RoboCup 2050. IEEE Robot. Autom. Mag. **9**(2), 31–38 (2002)

7. Butler, M., Prokopenko, M., Howard, T.: Flexible synchronisation within RoboCup environment: a comparative analysis. In: Stone, P., Balch, T., Kraetzschmar, G. (eds.) RoboCup 2000. LNCS (LNAI), vol. 2019, pp. 119–128. Springer, Heidelberg (2001). https://doi.org/10.1007/3-540-45324-5_10

8. Cheng, C.D., Kosorukoff, A.: Interactive one-max problem allows to compare the performance of interactive and human-based genetic algorithms. In: Deb, K. (ed.) GECCO 2004. LNCS, vol. 3102, pp. 983–993. Springer, Heidelberg (2004). https://doi.org/10.1007/978-3-540-24854-5_98

9. Chew, L.P.: Constrained Delaunay triangulations. Algorithmica **4**(1–4), 97–108 (1989)

10. Cioppa, T.M., Lucas, T.W.: Efficient nearly orthogonal and space-filling latin hypercubes. Technometrics **49**(1), 45–55 (2007)

11. Cliff, O.M., Lizier, J.T., Wang, X.R., Wang, P., Obst, O., Prokopenko, M.: Towards quantifying interaction networks in a football match. In: Behnke, S., Veloso, M., Visser, A., Xiong, R. (eds.) RoboCup 2013. LNCS (LNAI), vol. 8371, pp. 1–12. Springer, Heidelberg (2014). https://doi.org/10.1007/978-3-662-44468-9_1

12. Cliff, O.M., Lizier, J.T., Wang, X.R., Wang, P., Obst, O., Prokopenko, M.: Quantifying long-range interactions and coherent structure in multi-agent dynamics. Artif. Life **23**(1), 34–57 (2017)
13. Dylla, F., et al.: Approaching a formal soccer theory from the behavior specification in robotic soccer. In: Dabnicki, P., Baca, A. (eds.) Computers in Sport, pp. 161–186. Bioengineering, WIT Press, London (2008)
14. Gabel, T., Klöppner, P., Godehardt, E., Tharwat, A.: Communication in soccer simulation: on the use of wiretapping opponent teams. In: Holz, D., Genter, K., Saad, M., von Stryk, O. (eds.) RoboCup 2018. LNCS (LNAI), vol. 11374, pp. 3–15. Springer, Cham (2019). https://doi.org/10.1007/978-3-030-27544-0_1
15. Kok, J.R., Vlassis, N., Groen, F.: UvA Trilearn 2003 team description. In: Polani, D., Browning, B., Bonarini, A., Yoshida, K. (eds.) Proceedings CD RoboCup 2003. Springer, Padua (2003)
16. Kosorukoff, A.: Human based genetic algorithm. In: 2001 IEEE International Conference on Systems, Man, and Cybernetics, vol. 5, pp. 3464–3469. IEEE (2001)
17. Lizier, J.T., Prokopenko, M., Zomaya, A.Y.: Coherent information structure in complex computation. Theory Biosci. **131**, 193–203 (2012)
18. Nakashima, T., Akiyama, H., Suzuki, Y., Ohori, A., Fukushima, T.: HELIOS 2018: team description paper. In: RoboCup 2018 Symposium and Competitions: Team Description Papers, Montreal, Canada, July 2018 (2018)
19. Nehaniv, C., Polani, D., Olsson, L., Klyubin, A.: Evolutionary information-theoretic foundations of sensory ecology: channels of organism-specific meaningful information. In: Modeling Biology: Structures, Behaviour, Evolution, pp. 9–11 (2005)
20. Noda, I., Stone, P.: The RoboCup soccer server and CMUnited clients: implemented infrastructure for MAS research. Auton. Agents Multi-agent Syst. **7**(1–2), 101–120 (2003)
21. Prokopenko, M., Gerasimov, V., Tanev, I.: Evolving spatiotemporal coordination in a modular robotic system. In: Nolfi, S., et al. (eds.) SAB 2006. LNCS (LNAI), vol. 4095, pp. 558–569. Springer, Heidelberg (2006). https://doi.org/10.1007/11840541_46
22. Prokopenko, M., Gerasimov, V., Tanev, I.: Measuring spatiotemporal coordination in a modular robotic system. In: Rocha, L., Yaeger, L., Bedau, M., Floreano, D., Goldstone, R., Vespignani, A. (eds.) Artificial Life X: Proceedings of the 10th International Conference on the Simulation and Synthesis of Living Systems, Bloomington, IN, USA, pp. 185–191 (2006)
23. Prokopenko, M., Obst, O., Wang, P.: Gliders 2014: dynamic tactics with Voronoi diagrams. In: RoboCup 2014 Symposium and Competitions: Team Description Papers, Joao Pessoa, Brazil, July 2014 (2014)
24. Prokopenko, M., Obst, O., Wang, P., Budden, D., Cliff, O.M.: Gliders 2013: tactical analysis with information dynamics. In: RoboCup 2013 Symposium and Competitions: Team Description Papers, Eindhoven, The Netherlands, June 2013 (2013)
25. Prokopenko, M., Wang, P., Obst, O., Jaurgeui, V.: Gliders 2016: integrating multi-agent approaches to tactical diversity. In: RoboCup 2016 Symposium and Competitions: Team Description Papers, Leipzig, Germany, July 2016 (2016)
26. Prokopenko, M.: Guided Self-organization: Inception. Springer, Heidelberg (2013). https://doi.org/10.1007/978-3-642-53734-9
27. Prokopenko, M., Obst, O., Wang, P., Held, J.: Gliders 2012: tactics with action-dependent evaluation functions. In: RoboCup 2012 Symposium and Competitions: Team Description Papers, Mexico City, Mexico, June 2012 (2012)

28. Prokopenko, M., Wang, P.: Relating the entropy of joint beliefs to multi-agent coordination. In: Kaminka, G.A., Lima, P.U., Rojas, R. (eds.) RoboCup 2002. LNCS (LNAI), vol. 2752, pp. 367–374. Springer, Heidelberg (2003). https://doi.org/10.1007/978-3-540-45135-8_32

29. Prokopenko, M., Wang, P.: Evaluating team performance at the edge of chaos. In: Polani, D., Browning, B., Bonarini, A., Yoshida, K. (eds.) RoboCup 2003. LNCS (LNAI), vol. 3020, pp. 89–101. Springer, Heidelberg (2004). https://doi.org/10.1007/978-3-540-25940-4_8

30. Prokopenko, M., Wang, P.: Disruptive innovations in RoboCup 2D soccer simulation league: from Cyberoos'98 to Gliders2016. In: Behnke, S., Sheh, R., Sarıel, S., Lee, D.D. (eds.) RoboCup 2016. LNCS (LNAI), vol. 9776, pp. 529–541. Springer, Cham (2017). https://doi.org/10.1007/978-3-319-68792-6_44

31. Prokopenko, M., Wang, P., Marian, S., Bai, A., Li, X., Chen, X.: RoboCup 2D soccer simulation league: evaluation challenges. In: Akiyama, H., Obst, O., Sammut, C., Tonidandel, F. (eds.) RoboCup 2017. LNCS (LNAI), vol. 11175, pp. 325–337. Springer, Cham (2018). https://doi.org/10.1007/978-3-030-00308-1_27

32. Prokopenko, M., Wang, P., Obst, O.: Gliders 2015: opponent avoidance with bio-inspired flocking behaviour. In: RoboCup 2015 Symposium and Competitions: Team Description Papers, Hefei, China, July 2015 (2015)

33. Reis, L.P., Lau, N., Oliveira, E.C.: Situation based strategic positioning for coordinating a team of homogeneous agents. In: Hannebauer, M., Wendler, J., Pagello, E. (eds.) BRSDMAS 2000. LNCS (LNAI), vol. 2103, pp. 175–197. Springer, Heidelberg (2001). https://doi.org/10.1007/3-540-44568-4_11

34. Riley, P., Stone, P., Veloso, M.: Layered disclosure: revealing agents' internals. In: Castelfranchi, C., Lespérance, Y. (eds.) ATAL 2000. LNCS (LNAI), vol. 1986, pp. 61–72. Springer, Heidelberg (2001). https://doi.org/10.1007/3-540-44631-1_5

35. Stone, P., et al.: Overview of Robocup-2000. In: Stone, P., Balch, T., Kraetzschmar, G. (eds.) RoboCup 2000. LNCS (LNAI), vol. 2019, pp. 1–29. Springer, Heidelberg (2001). https://doi.org/10.1007/3-540-45324-5_1

36. Stone, P., Quinlan, M., Hester, T.: Can robots play soccer? In: Richards, T. (ed.) Soccer and Philosophy: Beautiful Thoughts on the Beautiful Game, Popular Culture and Philosophy, vol. 51, pp. 75–88. Open Court Publishing Company, Chicago (2010)

37. Stone, P., Riley, P., Veloso, M.: The CMUnited-99 champion simulator team. In: Veloso, M., Pagello, E., Kitano, H. (eds.) RoboCup 1999. LNCS (LNAI), vol. 1856, pp. 35–48. Springer, Heidelberg (2000). https://doi.org/10.1007/3-540-45327-X_2

38. Stone, P., Riley, P., Veloso, M.: Defining and using ideal teammate and opponent models. In: Proceedings of the 12th Annual Conference on Innovative Applications of Artificial Intelligence (2000)

39. Tanev, I., Yuta, K.: Epigenetic programming: genetic programming incorporating epigenetic learning through modification of histones. Inf. Sci. **178**(23), 4469–4481 (2008)

40. Tavafi, A., Nozari, N., Vatani, R., Yousefi, M.R., Rahmatinia, S., Pirdir, P.: MarliK 2012 soccer 2D simulation team description paper. In: RoboCup 2012 Symposium and Competitions: Team Description Papers, Mexico City, Mexico, June 2012 (2012)

41. Zuparic, M., Jauregui, V., Prokopenko, M., Yue, Y.: Quantifying the impact of communication on performance in multi-agent teams. Artif. Life Robot. **22**(3), 357–373 (2017)

ROS 2 for RoboCup

Marcus M. Scheunemann⁽⊠⁾ and Sander G. van Dijk

University of Hertfordshire, Hatfield, AL10 9AB, UK
marcus@mms.ai, sgvandijk@gmail.com
https://mms.ai
https://robocup.herts.ac.uk

Abstract. There has always been much motivation for sharing code and
solutions among teams in the RoboCup community. Yet the transfer of
code between teams was usually complicated due to a huge variety of
used frameworks and their differences in processing sensory information.
The RoboCup@Home league has tackled this by transitioning to ROS
as a common framework. In contrast, other leagues, such as those using
humanoid robots, are reluctant to use ROS, as in those leagues real-time
processing and low-computational complexity is crucial. However, ROS 2
now offers built-in support for real-time processing and promises to be
suitable for embedded systems and multi-robot systems. It also offers
the possibility to compose a set of nodes needed to run a robot into a
single process. This, as we will show, reduces communication overhead
and allows to have one single binary, which is pertinent to competitions
such as the 3D-Simulation League. Although ROS 2 has not yet been
announced to be production ready, we started the process to develop
ROS 2 packages for using it with humanoid robots (real and simulated).
This paper presents the developed modules, our contributions to ROS 2
core and RoboCup related packages, and most importantly it provides
benchmarks that indicate that ROS 2 is a promising candidate for a
common framework used among leagues.

Keywords: ROS 2 · Robot framework · Robot software · Embedded
system · Real-time system · Minimal hardware · Open source ·
Humanoid robots · Autonomous robots

1 Introduction

Having a common framework among teams (or even among leagues) has many
advantages. Most notably, rather than concentrating on increasing performance
or reliability of the framework, participants can focus on the implementation of
artificial intelligence. Solutions can be easily shared and distributed, with possibilities of benchmarking them against each other. The handover and knowledge
transfer within a team to a new generation can be done smoothly. If there is
a common framework not just within a league but between leagues, then this
may foster the collaboration between teams of different leagues. With an eye on

© Springer Nature Switzerland AG 2019
S. Chalup et al. (Eds.): RoboCup 2019, LNAI 11531, pp. 429–438, 2019.
https://doi.org/10.1007/978-3-030-35699-6_34

the goal of merging forces of different leagues and eventually merge leagues, a common framework is essential.

In a field such as a RoboCup league, where tasks and constraints are similar for each participating team, one might think that a common framework would naturally emerge. The RoboCup@Home Open Platform League is a good example that this indeed happens. Starting with two teams in 2010, in 2018 all teams announced within their team descriptions the use of the same software framework [9]. The used framework was the open-source Robot Operating System (ROS). In other leagues, such as the Humanoid League (HL) or the Standard Platform League (SPL), ROS didn't establish as a common framework despite some advances [1,2,5,14]. We argue that performance shortcomings on minimal hardware doesn't make it suitable for soccer playing humanoid robots [11]. In the SPL the self-developed framework from team B-Human was adopted by many teams instead. The performance strength is gained through a tight coupling between used software tools (e.g. simulator) and between modules [11]. However, this is also a shortcoming, as it restricts the community using the framework mostly to the football playing domain. NUClear is an example of a framework originating from RoboCup that is more loosely coupled, modular and applicable in different robot projects [7]. This framework solves the overhead of traditional message passing systems through specially optimised paths similar to those we will benchmark here. Additionally, it offers the ability of using more blackboard/whiteboard type data access patterns which are not directly available in the framework discussed in this paper.

The authors themselves developed several frameworks with teams in the Standard Platform League, Humanoid Kid-Size League and 3D Simulation League. Their current team, the Bold Hearts, used a self developed software framework, with almost all modules created from scratch [13]. Although shown to be capable of performing well, over the years the framework has become more and more complex. It is completely custom and some of the original developers have moved on, making it difficult to get new members started and to adapt it to new developments in the competitions. Code dependencies made it challenging to integrate well working modules from other teams or projects. For example, last year's change of the underlying vision pipeline towards a new semantic segmentation couldn't be easily achieved as third-party tools didn't integrate well together [3].

There are reasons why some leagues couldn't agree on a common framework yet. Naturally, without a central committee being in charge, there will always be some healthy argument or a fork of a different, perhaps slightly more efficient implementation.

The fact that ROS is a framework from 'outside' of RoboCup could provide a good common base, but has not been able to gain widespread adoption due to inherent limitations; ROS was never built with support for, e.g., multi-robot systems involving unreliable networks, for robots needing real-time processing capabilities or for robots with minimal hardware [4,8,11].

However, exactly these limitations sparked the development of a second, completely rewritten version of ROS. Although it is not yet deemed fully production ready, it has a wider support than a RoboCup team, a league or the whole community can offer: the support includes large entities from the industry, such as Intel and Amazon. With an eye on the future and the transferability of skills learned by our (student) members outside/beyond participation in RoboCup, we opted to use ROS 2 [13]. Some benchmarking suggests that ROS 2 is currently in a state that offers the possibility to use it for multi-robot teams, small platforms and real-time systems [6,8].

In this paper, we discuss why we think ROS 2 is a reasonable framework choice and also briefly present its advantages (Sect. 2). We further present the modules we have developed as a basis for participating in the RoboCup (Sect. 3). Additionally, we present two preliminary studies for benchmarking the system and showing the feasibility for using it in RoboCup (Sect. 4).

2   ROS 2 Architecture and Features

ROS 2 is based on the Data Distribution Service (DDS) standard for real-time systems [4,8]. DDS is a connectivity framework aiming to enable scalability and real-time data exchange using a Data-Centric Publish-Subscribe (DCPS) architecture [10].

DDS is specified by the Object Management Group (OMG), which is an open membership, not-for-profit computer industry standards consortium. It is developed for a wide variety of fields such as transportation systems, autonomous vehicles, and aerospace. ROS 2 sits on top of that, providing standard messages and tools to adapt DDS for robotic needs. A range of vendors providing implementations of DDS, such as eProsima's Fast RTPS and RTI Connext are fully supported [8,12]. Compared to ROS 1, ROS 2 has several beneficial features:

- Built-in support for real-time systems.
- Support for defining the 'Quality of Service' of topics. This allows one to make a range of trade-offs between strong reliability and 'best effort' policies, to deal with lossy communication. For instance, an efficient non-blocking 'best effort', 'UDP-like' service is acceptable for high frequency sensor data where missing individual messages is not detrimental. On the other hand, when each message is crucial, a reliable 'TCP-like' policy can be used.
- Nodes can be run in individual executables, or composed, using a variety of executors. In ROS 1, one has to maintain 'nodelet' versions of all nodes to make this possible. In ROS 2, this can be achieved natively, making it possible to remove much of the communication overhead between nodes by having them share memory. We provide a benchmark showing the appeal of this below.
- No need to run the ROS 1 `roscore` instance and maintain environment variables to make it and nodes reachable; with DDS, nodes discover each other through a network automatically.
- Communication between nodes can be strictly restricted by placing them in different 'domains'. This could be very useful in the RoboCup Simulation league for instance, where the programs of all robots in the same team run on the same machine but no communication between them should happen.

Together with the ability to compose all modules for one agent in a single executable, this makes ROS 2 a much better candidate to use as a platform in the simulation league than ROS 1.

3   ROS 2 and RoboCup Contributions

There are many modules that are not available yet, as ROS 2 is still relatively new. To be able to develop a full RoboCup team based on ROS 2, we have developed several modules, consisting of:

Hardware driver. Our robots are based on the Robotis CM-730 sub-controller. Robotis has released ROS 1 packages for their products, but at the moment there is no ROS 2 effort. We have created and published a ROS 2 driver for interacting with the CM-730, and controlling Robotis Dynamixel motors

Fig. 1. The upper image depicts a scene with a robot looking at a ball. The lower image is a screenshot of RViz2. It shows the camera image feed retrieved with our USB camera driver (left). Our CM-730 package publishes joint states, accelerometer and gyro information for building the robot model and compute its orientation with our IMU fusion package (both right).

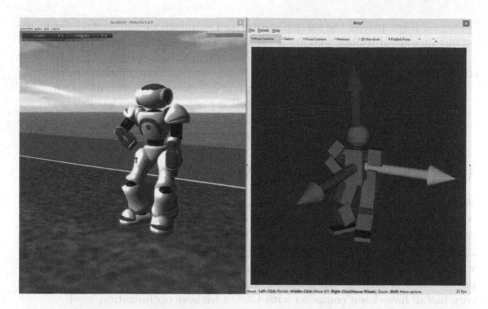

Fig. 2. Depicted is a scene from RCSSServer3D used in the 3D Simulation League (left, using RoboViz). Our package translates the servo information into standard ROS messages and publishes the topic /joint_state. Also, the simulated gyroscope and accelerometer information are published. Our IMU fusion package subscribes to the messages and computes the robot's orientation, exactly as for the real robot in Fig. 1. The interface package allows for using ROS 2 within the context of the 3D Simulation League.

attached to it[1]. Figure 1 (right) shows the result of the robot model built using the output of this driver. We also developed a USB camera driver[2], Fig. 1 (left) shows the output of the camera driver.

Ports of our modules. With all hardware interfaces in place, we now work on porting our existing modules over to the new platform. The IMU fusion filter[3] is one example. We complemented it with a package for visualizing the orientation of the robot in RViz2. Figures 1 and 2 (both right) show the visualization of the orientation.

Humanoid League. The RoboCup humanoid league uses a Game Controller application to manage a competition: it keeps track of and broadcasts the game state and events such as kick-off and penalties to the robots. We have created a package that forms a bridge between the communication protocol of the Game Controller and ROS 2 topics[4].

3D Simulation League. Taking advantage of the benefits described above, we have developed a ROS 2 interface for the RoboCup 3D Simulation

---

[1] https://gitlab.com/boldhearts/ros2_cm730

[2] https://gitlab.com/boldhearts/ros2_v4l2_camera

[3] https://gitlab.com/boldhearts/ros2_imu_tools

[4] https://gitlab.com/boldhearts/ros2_game_controller

Server [15][5]. It uses the same platform and standard message interfaces as for
our humanoid robots, making it easier for (new) members to experiment and
improve our modules, and deploy them to real robots directly.

ROS 2 core contributions. We have made several contributions to the core
ROS 2 project for issues discovered in our use cases, including fixes to make it
possible to compile ROS 2 for 32 bit ARM platforms[6], support modern Linux
64 bit library paths[7] and to set complex node parameters using command line
tools[8], along with smaller fixes for `geometry2`[9] and demo `image_tools`[10].

4   Benchmark Stand-Alone Versus Composed Nodes

We use the humanoid football robot BoldBot for the benchmarks. Its main board
is an Odroid-XU4. This device is based on a Samsung Exynos 5422 Cortex-A15
with 2 GHz and a Cortex-A7 Octa core CPU, which is the same as used in some
2015 model flagship smartphones [13]. The main board runs 32 bit Ubuntu 18.04
with a compiled version of ROS 2 Dashing Diademata, the first long-term support version of ROS 2. All packages used in these benchmarks and the ROS 2
core install have been compiled with GCC's highest optimization level.

In ROS 1, nodes are stand-alone executables. Communication between these
nodes is performed through a transport protocol, most often over TCP/IP. This
means that all communication between these nodes involves overhead from serial-
isation and memory copies. So called 'nodelets' were introduced to allow composing node-like building blocks into single executables to alleviate such overhead.
As these concepts are separate from normal nodes, a package developer has to
choose to support either nodes or nodelets, or maintain both.

In ROS 2, nodes were redesigned to make it possible to run them either stand-
alone or composed in a single process, either single or multi-threaded. ROS 2
Dashing Diademata even adds the ability to dynamically load and unload nodes
in a single process at runtime, as so called 'components'.

When nodes are composed in such a way, messages between them can be
shared directly, without any intermediate conversion overhead. ROS 2 explicitly supports this form of Intra-Process Communication (IPC), bypassing the
DDS layer and performing zero-copy communication where possible. To test
the impact of this, we perform several benchmarks of one of the most memory
intensive operations for robots: image processing.

4.1   Case 1: Simple Node Graph

A node is created that subscribes to the `/image_raw` topic provided by the
camera driver described earlier. This node applies a Sobel gradient operation to

---

[5] https://gitlab.com/boldhearts/ros2_rcss3d
[6] https://github.com/ros2/rcl/pull/365
[7] https://github.com/colcon/colcon-library-path/pull/10
[8] https://github.com/ros2/ros2cli/pull/199
[9] https://github.com/ros2/geometry2/pull/102
[10] https://github.com/ros2/demos/pull/288

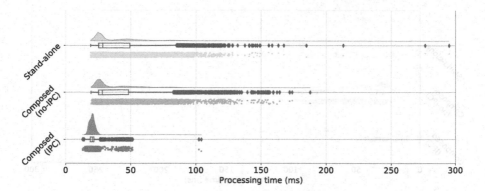

Fig. 3. Distributions of time measured from image capture by camera node until end of processing of a Sobel gradient operation on the full image done by processing node. Both nodes either run as stand-alone executables or run composed in a single executable, the latter with IPC disabled and enabled. Each plot shows the density (top), a boxplot (middle), and individual data points (bottom). 10.000 samples are measured in each case.

incur some actual processing cost to offset overhead costs against, and measures the time from initial image capture (provided in the Image header) until it finished processing the image.

Figure 3 shows the effects of composing nodes and intra-process communication. The end-to-end processing time for 10.000 images was compared when running the camera and processing nodes separately, or when composed in a single executable using a multi-threaded executor[11], the latter with IPC disabled and enabled. Composing the nodes seems to result in slightly more stable communication, with less extreme outliers than in the stand-alone case, but the difference is minimal.

However, a clear benefit can be seen when IPC is enabled, with the median processing time dropping by 33% compared to the stand-alone results, from 28.7 ms to 20.7 ms. The communication is also much more reliable, with a distinctly narrower distribution of processing times. The zero-copy transmission that is responsible for this improvement is achieved in ROS 2 by passing direct memory pointers to messages from publisher to subscriber, when using the C++ 'unique pointer' concept to signal that this is safe to do.

4.2   Case 2: Extended Node Graph

We extend the previous benchmark example to further understand the impact of communication overhead in a more realistic configuration with a larger set of nodes. To extend the image processing example, we further introduce nodes to publish and process IMU sensor and joint data, provided by our packages

---

[11] When using a single-threaded executor no processing actually happened, possibly due to the camera node claiming all execution time

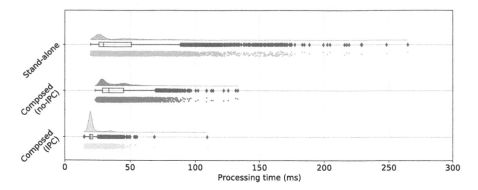

Fig. 4. Image processing times as in Fig. 3, but with the robot system extended with other necessary nodes and topics like /joint_states and /imu/data, for a total of 7 nodes running at a time. Each plot shows the density (top), a boxplot (middle), and individual data points (bottom). 10.000 samples are measured in each case.

described in Sect. 3. Our CM-730 package reads the servo information from the robot and publishes it as a standard topic /joint_state. It also publishes raw IMU readings of the accelerometer and the gyroscope. The IMU fusion package reads these raw messages and computes the robots' orientation and publishes the /imu/data topic. Altogether, 7 nodes are involved that communicate on 7 topics (including the image topic). For the benchmark using composition and IPC, only the /image_raw topic is IPC-enabled.

Figure 4 shows the results. The median computation time for the image processing for the stand-alone binary increases by 0.8 ms, only a slight increase when compared to the simple case from the previous section. However, the tail of the distribution has become longer, indicating further increase in communication variability.

This same effect is not seen in the composed, no-IPC results; the distribution is actually tighter, although the median processing time has increased from 28.4 ms to 33.6 ms. We do not know the reason for this change compared to the simple system. However, given the results when IPC *is* enabled, this mode is not recommended anyway.

This is because also in this extended case, enabling IPC gives significantly better results; hardly any effect of adding more nodes is visible in the image processing times, with the median time even 1 ms lower than in the simple case. These results show that a composed binary can prevent much of possible costs of creating a modular system without having to maintain any additional code, in contrast to ROS 1 for instance.

5   Conclusion and Future Work

We believe a common framework will ease the process of sharing and comparing solutions between teams and help them concentrate on their research interests.

This is valuable both within and between leagues. For instance, ultimately the simulation league aims more for strategic play, whereas the humanoid leagues focus heavily on developing robot hardware and lower level control. Given the goal of merging these leagues eventually, a common framework is an inevitable basis.

In this paper, we propose ROS 2 as a suitable choice for a framework for a RoboCup team with needs for real-time processing relying on minimal hardware. ROS 2 is supported by a large community, including big industrial partners, that the RoboCup community can benefit from. This makes it a potential candidate for a common framework. We presented our ROS 2 and RoboCup contributions, allowing to start with ROS 2 in the RoboCup. We supported the CM-730 sub-controller manufactured by Robotis, a very popular brand among RoboCup teams in the Humanoid League. Furthermore, we wrote an interface for using ROS 2 with the simulator of the 3D-Simulation League.

Our benchmarks indicate that ROS 2's capability to compose nodes can reduce the communicational overhead known from ROS 1. Our future work mostly includes porting over ROS 1 packages and our custom modules to the ROS 2 ecosystem.

References

1. Bestmann, M., et al.: Hamburg bit-bots and WF wolves team description for RoboCup 2019. Technical report (2019)
2. Bestmann, M., Hendrich, N., Wasserfall, F.: ROS for humanoid soccer robots. In: The 12th Workshop on Humanoid Soccer Robots at 17th IEEE-RAS International Conference on Humanoid Robots, p. 1 (2017)
3. van Dijk, S.G., Scheunemann, M.M.: Deep learning for semantic segmentation on minimal hardware. In: Holz, D., Genter, K., Saad, M., von Stryk, O. (eds.) RoboCup 2018. LNCS (LNAI), vol. 11374, pp. 349–361. Springer, Cham (2019). https://doi.org/10.1007/978-3-030-27544-0_29
4. Fernandez, E., Foote, T., Woodall, W., Thomas, D.: Next-generation ROS: building on DDS. In: ROSCon Chicago, September 2014. https://roscon.ros.org/2014/wp-content/uploads/2014/07/ROSCON-2014-Next-Generation-of-ROS-on-top-of-DDS.pdf
5. Forero, L.L., Yáñez, J.M., del Solar, J.R.: Integration of the ROS framework in soccer robotics: the NAO case. In: Behnke, S., Veloso, M., Visser, A., Xiong, R. (eds.) RoboCup 2013. LNCS, vol. 8371, pp. 664–671. Springer, Berlin Heidelberg (2014). https://doi.org/10.1007/978-3-662-44468-9_63
6. Gutiérrez, C.S.V., Juan, L.U.S., Ugarte, I.Z., Vilches, V.M.: Towards a distributed and real-time framework for robots: evaluation of ROS 2.0 communications for real-time robotic applications. https://arxiv.org/abs/1809.02595
7. Houliston, T., et al.: NUClear: a loosely coupled software architecture for humanoid robot systems. Front. Robot. AI **3**, 20 (2016). https://doi.org/10.3389/frobt.2016.00020
8. Maruyama, Y., Kato, S., Azumi, T.: Exploring the performance of ROS2.In: Proceedings of the 13th International Conference on Embedded Software.pp. 1–10. EMSOFT 2016, ACM, New York, NY, USA (2016). https://doi.org/10.1145/2968478.2968502

9. Matamoros, M., Seib, V., Memmesheimer, R., Paulus, D.: RoboCup@Home: summarizing achievements in over eleven years of competition. In: 2018 IEEE International Conference on Autonomous Robot Systems and Competitions (ICARSC). IEEE, April 2018. https://doi.org/10.1109/icarsc.2018.8374181
10. Object Management Group (OMG): Data Distribution Service (DDS), Version 1.4., April 2015. https://www.omg.org/spec/DDS/1.4. Accessed 20 Mar 2019
11. Röfer, T., Laue, T.: On B-human's code releases in the standard platform league – software architecture and impact. In: Behnke, S., Veloso, M., Visser, A., Xiong, R. (eds.) RoboCup 2013. LNCS (LNAI), vol. 8371, pp. 648–655. Springer, Heidelberg (2014). https://doi.org/10.1007/978-3-662-44468-9_61
12. ROS 2: ROS 2 Documentation, April 2019. https://index.ros.org/doc/ros2/. Accessed 18 April 2019
13. Scheunemann, M.M., van Dijk, S.G., Miko, R., Barry, D., Evans, G.M., Polani, D.: Bold Hearts Team Description for RoboCup 2019 (Humanoid Kid Size League). Technical report, School of Computer Science, University of Hertfordshire, College Lane, AL10 9AB, UK, December 2018. https://arxiv.org/abs/1904.10066
14. Schwarz, M., et al.: Humanoid TeenSize open platform NimbRo-OP. In: Behnke, S., Veloso, M., Visser, A., Xiong, R. (eds.) RoboCup 2013. LNCS (LNAI), vol. 8371, pp. 568–575. Springer, Heidelberg (2014). https://doi.org/10.1007/978-3-662-44468-9_51
15. Xu, Y., Vatankhah, H.: SimSpark: an open source robot simulator developed by the RoboCup community. In: Behnke, S., Veloso, M., Visser, A., Xiong, R. (eds.) RoboCup 2013. LNCS (LNAI), vol. 8371, pp. 632–639. Springer, Heidelberg (2014). https://doi.org/10.1007/978-3-662-44468-9_59

Game-Watching Should be More Entertaining: Real-Time Application of Field-Situation Prediction to a Soccer Monitor

Yudai Suzuki[1]($\boxtimes$), Takuya Fukushima[1], Léa Thibout[1],
Tomoharu Nakashima[1], and Hidehisa Akiyama[2]

[1] Osaka Prefecture University, Osaka, Japan
{yudai.suzuki,takuya.fukushima,tomoharu.nakashima}@kis.osakafu-u.ac.jp,
thiboutlea@eisti.eu
[2] Fukuoka University, Fukuoka, Japan
akym@fukuoka-u.ac.jp

Abstract. This paper describes an extension to a soccer monitor used in the RoboCup Soccer Simulation 2D League. The aim of the extension is to make the experience of watching games more entertaining. The audio effects and the visualization are focused on this purpose. The extended soccer monitor simulates the supporters' excitement in watching a game by estimating the time cycle until the next goal, which is called *SituationScore*. This paper describes how *SituationScore* is obtained using a machine learning model and also describes the resulting soccer monitor.
 – github: https://github.com/rinmunagi/spectator_app
 – YouTube demo: https://youtu.be/J_NgcwcFtQI

1 Introduction

Soccer is a sport as well as an entertainment. RoboCup soccer should have the same characteristics as the real soccer has. The current version of the official soccer monitor [1] shows only the status of the soccer field. This is a simple monitor just for watching games. *soccerwindow*2 [2] is an extended soccer monitor which is mainly for promoting a team development. For the team developers, *soccerwindow*2 is one of the most useful tools to analyze games and perceive about the thinking process of the players. Although the monitor is sufficient for the team developers to watch the games, If there were additional effects in accordance with the field status, such effects would make the spectator possible to enjoy the game more. For example, the audio narration would be helpful for the spectator to understand what is happening the ongoing game. For instance, Caspian monitor [3] has a function of on-line commentary that utters in the real time when passes and shoots are made. Another audio information is the sound from the virtual supporters inside the soccer monitor. The cheering and booing

© Springer Nature Switzerland AG 2019
S. Chalup et al. (Eds.): RoboCup 2019, LNAI 11531, pp. 439–447, 2019.
https://doi.org/10.1007/978-3-030-35699-6_35

could have non-verbal effect to enjoy watching the game. In this paper, we define "the supporters" as the virtual supporters inside the soccer monitor, and "the spectator" as the real-world people who watching the soccer monitor.

In this paper, we propose an application that extends *soccerwindow2* in the way the spectator does not miss the important scenes such as scoring. A prediction model is built by learning the field situation from a set of log files. Pomas and Nakashima [4] proposed a machine learning method to evaluate the game situation quantitatively from field images. We also use the same method in our application to express the excitement of the supporters. The prediction model takes the current field situation as an input and produces the number of expected time steps until the next goal, which is called a *SituationScore*. We have enhanced *soccerwindow2* so that it produces a sound effect and the visualization according to the *SituationScore*.

2   Soccer Simulation 2D League

Since the games in the Soccer Simulation 2D League happen on a virtual soccer field constructed within a computer, every piece of information regarding the games can be digitally stored. This stored information can be easily utilized for analysis purposes by team developers. Such logs contain, for example, the coordinates of the ball and all players' positions, the velocity of the ball and the players, and the players' body and neck angle for every cycle of a game. Therefore, it is not surprising that the log files play an important role when analyzing games and designing strategies.

Games can be visualized on computers even after the games are finished by using tools such as *soccerwindow2* [2] that displays the position of the ball and all players for every cycle of the game, with one computational cycle corresponding to one frame on it. A game consists of 6,000 cycles and one cycle is discretized in 0.1 second, which means a game consists of 6,000 frames. Figure 1 shows the example screen of the ongoing game on *soccerwindow2*. *soccerwindow2* is a component of HELIOS Base package [5]. This tool not only allows spectators to watch games, but also allows researchers to replay the same game, the same actions, in order to easily analyze them.

3   *SituationScore* Evaluation

In the RoboCup Soccer Simulation 2D League, there are various ways to define the degree of dominance in an ongoing game. Example metrics would be the number of those players who are on a specific part of the field, the target place and the partner teammate of passes, and the position and the player of the current ball holder. While such analysis can be easily conducted using numerical data from log files, it would be much more complicated to work only with field images that are provided by the soccer monitor. Therefore, another metric was defined in [4], which is called a *SituationScore*, that assesses the situation of a game without numerical data.

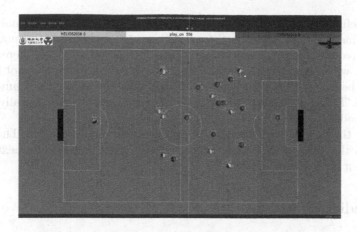

Fig. 1. Running a game on *soccerwindow*2.

In this paper, we also employ *SituationScore* of a frame f_r as the value of a field situation, which is defined by the following equation:

$$SituationScore(f_r) = \pm(100 - n),\qquad(1)$$

where n is the number of frames between f_r and the one corresponding to the next goal. It is assumed in this paper that the considered frames are at most 100 cycles away from the next goal. Therefore, in this formula, n should be lower than 100. The range of *SituationScore* is $-100 \leq SituationScore \leq 100$. The sign of *SituationScore* is determined by the team that will score the next goal. A positive value is assigned when the next goal is scored by the left team. On the other hand, a negative value is assigned when the next goal is scored by the right team. An example of soccer field images and its corresponding score is provided in Fig. 2.

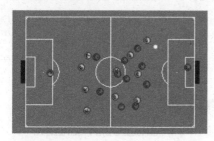 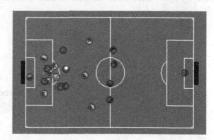

(a) 35 frames before the left team scores. The corresponding *SituationScore* is +65.

(b) 17 frames before the right team scores. The corresponding *SituationScore* is −83.

Fig. 2. The example of soccer field images and *SituationScore*.

The definition of the *SituationScore* in this paper brings us two main merits. The first merit is easy to assign *SituationScore* to newly produced images, as it does not require any complex computation. The second merit is inherent to our objective, which is to work only with images. *SituationScore* does not take into account the state of the field itself at all, but only the number of frames before next goal. Therefore, all situations or formations can be automatically covered by this model.

Using the defined *SituationScore*, a prediction model is built. That model estimates the value of *SituationScore* for any given frame. The next section talks about a prediction model.

4   Prediction Model

Nakashima et al. [4] showed high prediction accuracy of *SituationScore* by using a CNN model that handles image data. Therefore, we also employ a CNN for the prediction model of the *SituationScore*. This section first describes the CNN model in detail, and then describes the dataset used for training the model.

4.1   The CNN Model

The CNN model is trained with Python scripts and based on the images generated by *soccerwindow*2 during matches. We decided to use the TensorFlow library [6] for using the CNN model. A CNN architecture as well as its appropriate hyper-parameter values leading to satisfactory results have been determined by our preliminary experiments. Our architecture is illustrated in Fig. 3. The network structure is similar to the VGG architecture [7]. This structure has four convolutional blocks (blue boxes), four max-pooling layers (orange boxes), and a four-layered fully-connected block. ReLU (Rectified Linear Unit) is used as an activation function. Adam algorithm [8] is used as the optimizer. Our CNN was trained with an initial learning rate of 0.0001, then it was decreased by 5% every 1500 steps. The size of the mini batch was 16. It should be also noted that our

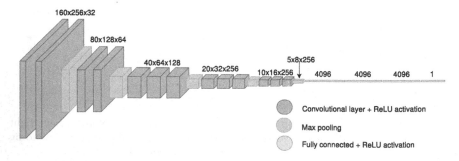

Fig. 3. Architecture of our CNN, composed of four convolutional blocks as in VGG, but with another fully-connected layer at the end of the network. (Color figure online)

CNN takes a 160×256 image as input and the dropout rate is 15% at the last layer of each convolutional block, as well as after each fully-connected layer.

4.2   Dataset for Training the Model

In order for our dataset to cover as many situations and formations as possible, games between several 16 different teams have been simulated.

Dataset-creation process is decomposed into the following five steps:

1. Games between each possible pair of teams are performed.
2. Log files of games without any goals are deleted.
3. For each game, every frame is saved using *soccerwindow2*.
4. Their corresponding log files are analyzed by using Python scripts to determine at which cycles goals have been scored.
5. The field situations of 0–100 frames before each of these goals are captured, and the value of *SituationScore* for these frames is computed. These frames are saved as an image data, and the name of the image file is specified so as to include their *SituationScore* value.

When using *soccerwindow2* in this procedure, some graphic options have been specified, mainly to enhance the frames' quality, to remove superfluous information, and to enlarge the players and the ball. These options include hiding score board, player numbers, view area, stamina and potential yellow card, as well as setting player size to 2.0, and ball size to 1.3. The size of the saved images has also been specified in these options, but because the minimum size from *soccerwindow2* is 280×167, captured frames have been then cropped to be of size 256×160. Soccer field images such as in Fig. 2 offers a good insight of frames contained in our dataset.

A dataset containing about 1.02 million soccer field images taken from 5,215 games was constructed. This dataset was then split into three parts: a training set containing ~720,000 images, a validation set containing ~156,000 images and a test set containing ~135,000 images. Images from a specific game are all included in only one of these sets. In other words, each of these sets contains images from different games. The CNN model trained by this dataset, and the performance to the test data was as high as $MeanAbsoluteError = 14.00$.

5   Application of the Prediction Model to Soccer Monitor

We developed a spectator application by extending *soccerwindow2* in order to pursue the entertaining aspect. This application expresses the supporters' excitement by sound effects and visualization.

First of all, this application calculates the *SituationScore* by using the trained CNN model described in Sect. 4.2. And then, the *SituationScore* is displayed on the window with color changing and sound effects like as supporters' cheering.

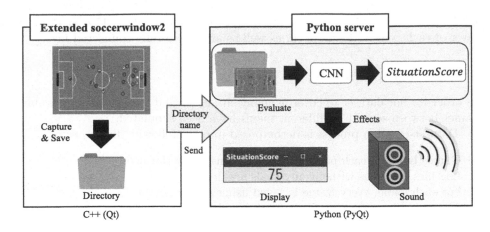

Fig. 4. The architecture of the spectator application.

The CNN model in the spectator application was trained from the dataset as described in Sect. 4.2. The *SituationScore* only have to be evaluated at the end of the match in the previous work [4]. This is because we could only take images after finishing the game. To use the trained model in real time, we need to capture images from the ongoing game in real time. This paper proposes to permit this score to be evaluated during a match, in real time. We store images from *soccerwindow*2 in real time and pass them into the already trained CNN model. Figure 4 shows the architecture of the spectator application. The application performs the following procedure:

The first procedure is to take the images from extended *soccerwindow*2 in real time using the Qt library. Then, *soccerwindow*2 sends the directory name of saving images to the Python server. And, the python server evaluates the saved images by using the trained CNN model. Finally, the application expresses the supporters' excitement by sound effects and color display according to the *SituationScore*. We use socket connection by TCP/IP protocol to connect between *soccerwindow*2 and the server, and the first one was coded in C++ and the second one in Python.

Once we begin a game between two teams, the images of the game in progress are stored every five frames in a local directory. Then, whenever an image is stored, *soccerwindow*2 sends the saved directory name as a signal to the Python server for evaluating the image. The trained CNN model calculates the *SituationScore* of the image in the directory when the Python server receives the signal. What is more, the Python server add sound effects and display the colored window according to the *SituationScore*. The image already used is sequentially moved to the other directory that store images of the past.

Figure 5a shows the window displays the *SituationScore* using PyQt library. This window's background is colored and changes the color according to the *SituationScore* as shown in Fig. 5b. If the situation is good for the yellow team,

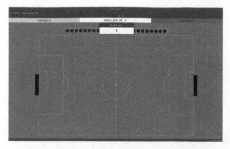 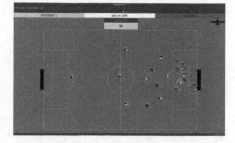

(a) The *SituationScore* displayed.   (b) The good situation for the yellow team.

Fig. 5. Example images displaying the *SituationScore*. (Color figure online)

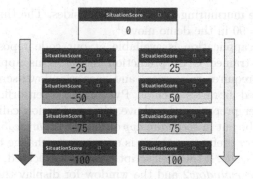

Fig. 6. The background color of the window gradually changes to red or yellow according to the *SituationScore*. (Color figure online)

the window gradually changes to yellow. And if the situation is good for the red team, the window gradually changes to red. It's shown in Fig. 6.

In addition, the application has the sound effects in order to make the game-watching experience more entertaining during a whole game. We employed the sounds library called Freesound [9]. The application implements real soccer game's supporters sound that is included in the Freesound library. The sound effects are changed according to the *SituationScore*. There are three kinds of sound effects: murmuring sounds (in stereo), cheering sound from the side of the dominating team (in monaural), and excited cheering sound from both sides of the teams (in stereo). Figure 7 shows the image of the sound effect. The choice of the sound out of the three is defined by using two thresholds $T1$ and $T2$ $(0 < T1 < T2 < 100)$ of *SituationScore*. When the *SituationScore* is higher than $T1$, which means it is a great opportunity for the yellow team (left team) to score, the sound volume from the left speaker is turned up. On the other hand, if the *SituationScore* is lower than $-T1$ which means the field situation is in favor for the red team (right team), the sound volume from the right speaker is turned up. Furthermore, if the *SituationScore* is greater than $T2$ or less than $-T2$, the sound is changed to more excited cheering. For the other cases, the

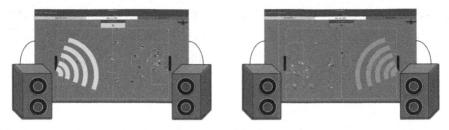

(a) The good situation for the yellow team. (b) The good situation for the red team.

Fig. 7. Sound effects of the supporters. (Color figure online)

sound is set to the murmuring noise from both sides. The thresholds are set as $T1 = 70$ and $T2 = 90$ in the demo movie[1].

The spectator application is available at our code repository[2]. This contains the already-trained CNN prediction model. This application works on Ubuntu OS, and requires rcssserver[3] and soccerwindow2-screenshot[4] as tools. The other required libraries include Python 2.7, Tensorflow 1.12.0, PyQt4 and opencv2. After preparing the above, the application called soccerwindow-screenshot should be put in *spectator_app* directory. If *librcsc* [5] is not installed in the system directory (default path), it is necessary to change the library path in the script called *execute*. If the shell script *execute* is executed, three windows are launched: two *soccerwindow*2 and the window for display the *SituationScore*. One of the launched *soccerwindow*2 is the main window for watching games and the other generates the images in order for the CNN to predict *SituationScore*. Next, the both soccerwindows should be connected to the rcssserver and run the team scripts to start a game. Lastly, a game is started with a 'KickOff' option.

The demonstration, the tutorial, and detailed information are described in the demo movie (See footnote 1).

6   Conclusions

In this paper, we described an extension to a soccer monitor that is used in the RoboCup Soccer Simulation 2D League. The extension is achieved by using *SituationScore* and a machine learning method. The extension involves visualization and sound effects by using the *SituationScore* that make the experience of watching games more entertaining.

---

[1] https://youtu.be/J_NgcwcFtQI.
[2] https://github.com/rinmunagi/spectator_app.
[3] https://github.com/rcsoccersim/rcssserver.
[4] https://github.com/rinmunagi/soccerwindow2-screenshot.

References

1. RoboCup Soccer Simulation Monitor. https://github.com/rcsoccersim/rcssmonitor. Accessed 8 June 2019
2. Akiyama, H.: RoboCup tools (2009). https://osdn.net/projects/rctools/releases/ 68532. Accessed 8 June 2019
3. Sedaghat, M.N., et al.: Caspian 2003 Presentation Description (2003). https:// archive.robocup.info/Soccer/Simulation/2D/TPs/RoboCup/2003/Caspian_SS2D_ RC2003_TP.pdf. Accessed 8 June 2019
4. Pomas, T., Nakashima, T.: Evaluation of situations in RoboCup 2D simulations using soccer field images. In: Holz, D., Genter, K., Saad, M., von Stryk, O. (eds.) RoboCup 2018. LNCS (LNAI), vol. 11374, pp. 275–286. Springer, Cham (2019). https://doi.org/10.1007/978-3-030-27544-0_23
5. Akiyama, H., Nakashima, T.: HELIOS Base: an open source package for the RoboCup soccer 2D simulation. In: Behnke, S., Veloso, M., Visser, A., Xiong, R. (eds.) RoboCup 2013. LNCS (LNAI), vol. 8371, pp. 528–535. Springer, Heidelberg (2014). https://doi.org/10.1007/978-3-662-44468-9_46
6. Abadi, M., et al.: TensorFlow: Large-scale machine learning on heterogeneous systems (2015). tensorflow.org
7. Karen, S., Zisserman, A.: Very deep convolutional networks for large-scale image recognition. arXiv preprint arXiv:1409.1556 (2015)
8. Kingma, D.P., Ba, J.: Adam: a method for stochastic optimization. In: International Conference on Learning Representations (2015)
9. Porter, A., et al.: Freesound (2005). https://freesound.org/. Accessed 8 June 2019

A JIT Compiler for Neural Network Inference

Felix Thielke[✉] and Arne Hasselbring

Fachbereich 3 – Mathematik und Informatik, Universität Bremen, Postfach 330 440,
28334 Bremen, Germany
{fthielke,arha}@uni-bremen.de

Abstract. This paper describes a C++ library that compiles neural network models at runtime into machine code that performs inference. This approach in general promises to achieve the best performance possible since it is able to integrate statically known properties of the network directly into the code. In our experiments on the NAO V6 platform, it outperforms existing implementations significantly on small networks, while being inferior on large networks. The library was already part of the B-Human code release 2018 [12], but has been extended since and is now available as a standalone version that can be integrated into any C++14 code base [18].

1   Introduction

Within the last years, convolutional neural networks (CNNs) have become a standard solution to image processing and computer vision problems such as object detection and image segmentation. The RoboCup competitions are no exception to this, with many teams using neural networks for the image processing part of their software. Due to the mostly independent operations within the layers of neural networks, massively parallel GPUs are well suited for their execution. However, they are often not available on mobile robots, due to size, weight or cost reasons. Even for robots that are equipped with a GPU, it might be advantageous to be able to run networks on the CPU, e. g. because frames from multiple cameras have to be processed simultaneously or only one large network is offloaded to the GPU while other smaller networks can be run on the CPU to maximize utilization of computational resources.

In order to achieve fast inference of neural networks on CPUs, we developed a C++ library that directly compiles neural network models to optimized machine code at runtime. It is targeted at x86/64 processors with the SSSE3/SSE4 instruction set extensions, especially the Atom and Silvermont microarchitectures present in the NAO and Pepper robots. This is different to most existing libraries that cannot take advantage of static knowledge about the network architecture and are rather optimized for GPUs than those CPUs. By this, we hope to enable the usage of more complex deep learning models on robots not only in RoboCup competitions.

© Springer Nature Switzerland AG 2019
S. Chalup et al. (Eds.): RoboCup 2019, LNAI 11531, pp. 448–456, 2019.
https://doi.org/10.1007/978-3-030-35699-6_36

The remainder of this paper is organized as follows: First, Sect. 2 discusses other available libraries for neural network inference. Afterwards, a description of our approach is given in Sect. 3. An evaluation of the performance of our library is presented in Sect. 4. Finally, the paper concludes in Sect. 5.

2 Related Work

There are several C++ libraries available for inferring neural networks. Of the popular deep learning frameworks, among others, TensorFlow [1] and Caffe [7] have C++ interfaces. Both also support training networks in the first place, but are rather heavyweight in their dependencies and mostly optimized for NVIDIA GPUs. TensorFlow includes the TensorFlow Lite library, which is targeted on embedded devices with an ARM processor, but is also able to run on x86 CPUs with SIMD using a NEON/SSE wrapper. Recently, the OpenCV project [2] also included support for inferring neural networks via their DNN module. It is able to read file formats of multiple deep learning frameworks and has support for different computation backends, including OpenCL. There are numerous smaller header-only libraries focused on ease of integration and versatility, including tiny-dnn [10] and frugally-deep [5]. Tiny-dnn also supports training of neural networks, but is not actively developed anymore. Frugally-deep is aimed to be compatible to Keras and claims to be faster than Keras itself with the Tensor-Flow backend on CPUs.

In the context of the RoboCup SPL, members of the Nao-Team HTWK created a fork of the Caffe library, in which they modified the layers for average pooling and the ReLU activation function to use SSE instructions [9]. Szemenyei and Estivill-Castro presented RoboDNN [16], based on the Darknet library, which is specialized on semantic segmentation networks for the NAO.

All of these libraries have in common that they are behaving like interpreters of neural networks, i.e. they include branches depending on the actual network structure read from a file that have to be taken on each execution pass. In order to speed up the inference of neural networks, TensorFlow comes with the XLA (Accelerated Linear Algebra) module that just-in-time compiles some layers of a network with optimizations for the target hardware. In addition, a program called tfcompile exists, which uses XLA to compile models ahead-of-time for inference. However, it does not support 32-bit x86 CPUs (thus not being compatible with NAO V5) and the JIT component seems to have a Python interface only.

The Nao Devils Dortmund however used MATLAB to train their neural networks and wrote a script to generate C++ code that performs the inference of the networks on the robot [6]. More recently they implemented the same approach in the Python language. This concept resembles our proposed library in principle, except that the compilation of networks takes place ahead-of-time, not at runtime. Apart from that, by generating C++ code, the optimality of their solution depends on the optimizations done by the C++ compiler, while our just-in-time compiler has complete control over the generated code and can thus theoretically produce the most efficient code without depending on external factors. Furthermore, it supports only a very limited selection of layers.

3   Approach

In order to achieve the best possible performance, the code for inferring a neural network can be optimized based on several static pieces of information about the model. Thus, we chose to implement our module in such a way that it reads pretrained models at runtime and translates them to machine code exposed as C++ functions by means of the AsmJit library [8].

While this approach allows for every possible optimization of the computations with respect to the target hardware, compiling the code just-in-time also provides flexibility and rapid deployment without an additional export step. However, it slightly increases the startup time of the software. In Sect. 4, the impact of this is measured for some typical models.

Considering that the main target hardware of our development, the NAO robot, contains an Intel Atom CPU, the code that our module generates is also targeted at this platform. This means that currently only x86 machine code can be emitted, making use of Streaming SIMD Extensions (SSE) up to version SSE4.2 for vectorized operations. Since the NAO's CPU does not have AVX support, we currently do not use it.

3.1   Front End

The front end and interface to the programmer of our library is represented by the Model class. Instances of this class contain a neural network architecture—i. e. a computational graph of layers—as well as the weights belonging to certain layers of that network. Currently, the Model class allows to load a network only from an HDF5 file as written by the Python library Keras [3]. For this purpose, our library depends on the HDF5 library [17] and includes a custom implementation of a JSON parser to obtain the model architecture. The Model class could potentially be extended to support other file formats.

In order to compile the inference code for such a model, it can be passed to an instance of the class CompiledNN. Once the code has been compiled, the method apply() of the CompiledNN instance can be used at any time to call the generated code that calculates the forward pass of the network. The input and output tensors of the network are owned by CompiledNN because it needs control over the actual memory layout.

In addition to this main functionality, the library also includes the class SimpleNN, which provides a straightforward, but slow implementation of neural network inference in C++. As this class was written to be as exact in its calculations as possible, it can be used to benchmark the compiler in terms of numeric precision.

3.2   Intermediate Processing

Internally, CompiledNN converts the nodes of the given network to a sequence of compilation units. Generally, each layer is mapped to one compilation unit, however sometimes layers are merged together or split into multiple compilation units if that is deemed beneficial for the compilation process or the performance of the generated code (cf. Sect. 3.5). Next, the inputs and outputs of all nodes are assigned to actual memory locations, taking into account that tensors with overlapping lifetimes must use different memory. At this stage, the individual layer compilers can indicate whether they want any of their outputs to use the memory of an input tensor that is not referenced afterwards. This way, many compilers can operate in-place, which results in better cache usage and less pointer register operations.

3.3   Common Principles

The performance of an x86 instruction depends on its latency and throughput on the given processor architecture. In this context, latency means the number of clock cycles the instruction takes until its result is available, which is relevant in dependency chains. The throughput on the other hand denotes the number of instructions of the same kind that can be executed per clock cycle, given that their operands are independent. Thus, the reciprocal throughput can be read as the number of clock cycles that an instruction takes if it follows a similar instruction and all its operands have already been computed [4].

On the microarchitectures that we target, the latency of all SIMD instructions is either larger than or equal to their reciprocal throughput. Thus, the code generated by our compiler generally follows a certain pattern to make sure that the limit for the performance of the generated code is the throughput of the instructions instead of the latency. In order to achieve this, our code subdivides the values to be computed into batches of up to $4 \cdot (n_{xmm} - k)$ elements, where n_{xmm} is the number of 128-bit XMM registers and k is an operation specific number of registers that are needed for intermediate results or weights (usually 2). Within each batch, first, all inputs are loaded into the registers. Then the operations, e.g. multiplications, are performed on all registers successively. Afterwards, the results are written to the destination addresses.

The core layers of CNNs are convolutional and fully connected layers. While the operation of a fully connected layer can be interpreted as a multiplication of a weight matrix with an input vector, the operation of a convolutional layer consists of a subdivision of the 3D input tensor along the width and height dimensions, followed by a series of multiplications of a kernel matrix with each of the resulting input vectors. Thus, the matrix-vector-product is the most important operation in our implementation. For this operation the compiler therefore generates specialized versions for several cases concerning the dimensions of the parameters. Besides, the calculation itself follows a scheme that uses the resources of the processor as well as possible. Using SIMD instructions, up to four floating point numbers can be used in a calculation at a time. The 4×4

matrix-vector-product as shown in Eq. 1 could then be implemented as shown in Eq. 2, where $\odot$ means element-wise multiplication.

The implementation in Eq. 2 would then need at least three registers: one register in which one column of the matrix is loaded at a time, one containing the input vector $\mathbf{x}$ and a third register that successively holds each of the four shuffled versions of the second register, containing only one of its elements at a time. The instructions needed are five load operations for the elements of the matrix and the input vector, four element-wise multiplications and four shuffle operations to broadcast the input vector.

However, the implementation that we use is shown in Eq. 3. Note that the elements of the matrix are parameters of the neural network known at compile time, so the memory layout of the matrix can be chosen arbitrarily without any impact on performance. This implementation allows to keep the elements of the input vector in the same register at all times, thus needing one less register. At the same time, it also needs only three shuffle operations as for the first element-wise multiplication, the input vector can be used directly. Saving the one register is crucial in this case as it increases the number of channels that can be computed per batch by 4.

$$
\begin{pmatrix} y_1 \\ y_2 \\ y_3 \\ y_4 \end{pmatrix} = \begin{pmatrix} a_{11} & a_{12} & a_{13} & a_{14} \\ a_{21} & a_{22} & a_{23} & a_{24} \\ a_{31} & a_{32} & a_{33} & a_{34} \\ a_{41} & a_{42} & a_{43} & a_{44} \end{pmatrix} \cdot \begin{pmatrix} x_1 \\ x_2 \\ x_3 \\ x_4 \end{pmatrix} \tag{1}
$$

$$
\begin{pmatrix} y_1 \\ y_2 \\ y_3 \\ y_4 \end{pmatrix} = \begin{pmatrix} a_{11} \\ a_{21} \\ a_{31} \\ a_{41} \end{pmatrix} \odot \begin{pmatrix} x_1 \\ x_1 \\ x_1 \\ x_1 \end{pmatrix} + \begin{pmatrix} a_{12} \\ a_{22} \\ a_{32} \\ a_{42} \end{pmatrix} \odot \begin{pmatrix} x_2 \\ x_2 \\ x_2 \\ x_2 \end{pmatrix} + \begin{pmatrix} a_{13} \\ a_{23} \\ a_{33} \\ a_{43} \end{pmatrix} \odot \begin{pmatrix} x_3 \\ x_3 \\ x_3 \\ x_3 \end{pmatrix} + \begin{pmatrix} a_{14} \\ a_{24} \\ a_{34} \\ a_{44} \end{pmatrix} \odot \begin{pmatrix} x_4 \\ x_4 \\ x_4 \\ x_4 \end{pmatrix} \tag{2}
$$

$$
\begin{pmatrix} y_1 \\ y_2 \\ y_3 \\ y_4 \end{pmatrix} = \begin{pmatrix} a_{11} \\ a_{22} \\ a_{33} \\ a_{44} \end{pmatrix} \odot \begin{pmatrix} x_1 \\ x_2 \\ x_3 \\ x_4 \end{pmatrix} + \begin{pmatrix} a_{12} \\ a_{23} \\ a_{34} \\ a_{41} \end{pmatrix} \odot \begin{pmatrix} x_2 \\ x_3 \\ x_4 \\ x_1 \end{pmatrix} + \begin{pmatrix} a_{13} \\ a_{24} \\ a_{31} \\ a_{42} \end{pmatrix} \odot \begin{pmatrix} x_3 \\ x_4 \\ x_1 \\ x_2 \end{pmatrix} + \begin{pmatrix} a_{14} \\ a_{21} \\ a_{32} \\ a_{43} \end{pmatrix} \odot \begin{pmatrix} x_4 \\ x_1 \\ x_2 \\ x_3 \end{pmatrix} \tag{3}
$$

3.4   Activation Functions

In neural networks, activation functions are operations that are applied on each input element independently, usually even independent of the position of the element in the input tensor. Therefore, they can not only be implemented in-place, meaning that the addresses of input and output in memory are the same, but also be appended to other operations, namely fully connected and convolutional layers. In that case, the activation function is applied before writing the result of the operation into memory. This avoids an additional loop with load and store operations.

However, some activation functions cannot be implemented that way. For example, *Softmax* needs two passes—one to calculate $x_i' = e^{x_i}$ for every input element x_i while at the same time calculating $\sum_i x_i'$ and a second pass to divide all resulting elements x_i' by this sum. In this case, the activation function is always compiled as a separate compilation unit.

Many usual activation functions utilized by neural networks, among them Softmax and the logistic function, need to calculate the exponential function. This poses a problem for our approach since there is no straightforward way of calculating $\exp(x)$ using SSE instructions. So instead, we chose to approximate these functions. For instance, the logistic function (sigmoid) can be expressed in terms of the tanh function (see Eq. 4) which in turn can be approximated by calculating a certain amount of steps of the continued fraction that converges to it (see Eq. 5). This reduces the operations needed to multiplications, additions and one division.

$$\text{sigmoid}(x) = \frac{\tanh\left(\frac{x}{2}\right) + 1}{2} \tag{4}$$

$$\tanh(x) = \cfrac{x}{1 + \cfrac{x^2}{3 + \cfrac{x^2}{5 + \dots}}} \approx \frac{(((36x^2 + 6930)x^2 + 270270)x^2 + 2027025)x}{(((x^2 + 630)x^2 + 51975)x^2 + 945945)x^2 + 2027025} \tag{5}$$

Alternatively, the exponential function can easily be approximated by exploiting the characteristics of the IEEE-754 floating point representation. Using the method described in [14], $\exp(x)$ can be calculated by one multiplication, one float-to-integer conversion and one integer addition, afterwards interpreting the result as a floating point number again. Approximating activation functions however impacts the precision of the calculations, which could lead to different outputs of the neural network.

3.5   Merging

Similarly to the aforementioned combination of activation functions into other compilation units, some layers can be eliminated entirely by merging them into adjacent ones. Specifically, batch normalization layers operate by multiplying a vector element-wise with the input tensor along the feature axis and afterwards adding an offset to it. If such a layer is immediately preceded or followed by a convolutional or fully connected layer, these calculations can be eliminated by removing the batch normalization step and adjusting the weights and biases of the other layer in such a way that they already include the factors and offsets of the normalization. Note that this changes the associativity of the calculations, which—because of the limited resolution of the representation of floating point numbers—might lead to a different result compared to the usual execution in two steps. If there is an activation function between the layers, the batch normalization is still fused into the other layer and applied after the activation, since it saves another loop and memory loads and stores.

4   Evaluation

To evaluate our library quantitatively, we benchmarked it on some models against other available inference libraries. These are frugally-deep [5], RoboDNN [16], TensorFlow Lite [1], and tiny-dnn [10]. The selected models include four networks relevant to the RoboCup SPL: The classifier that is used by Nao-Team HTWK [9], the ball classifier from B-Human [12], a detection network that predicts bounding boxes of robots on an entire camera image [11], and a network suitable to perform semantic segmentation into field/non-field on an 80 × 80 input. For comparison, MobileNetV2 [13] ($\alpha = 1$, without top) and VGG19 [15] have also been evaluated.

All libraries and the evaluation code have been compiled with optimizations enabled and the target architecture set to Silvermont. The runtimes are the average over multiple successive calls to the inference routine, after doing some unmeasured initial runs. Since RoboDNN and tiny-dnn do not support upsampling and depthwise separable convolution layers, the detection and segmentation networks and MobileNetV2 could not be tested. Table 1 shows the results.

Table 1. Inference times on the NAO V6's Intel Atom E3845 in milliseconds. C-HTWK denotes the classification network of Nao-Team HTWK, C-BH is the ball classifier from B-Human. The best runtime is marked bold. The last row lists the time in milliseconds our library needs to load and compile each network.

	C-HTWK	C-BH	Detector	Segmenter	MobileNetV2	VGG19
CompiledNN	**0.007**	**0.0447**	**1.995**	**7.859**	**145.1**	14993
frugally-deep	0.1724	0.5167	28.49	32.51	1036	11872
RoboDNN	0.0394	0.1383	–	–	–	20860
TensorFlow Lite	0.04276	0.3995	5.798	23.07	191.8	**10220**
tiny-dnn	0.1133	0.5297	–	–	–	100137
Compilation Time	6.5	9.5	26.6	18.1	335	13722

From an application perspective, our library allows the soccer SPL team B-Human to classify many more ball candidate patches per frame than any of the other solutions. This, in combination with a rather sensitive candidate generator, enables us to check for the ball in many locations of the image, decreasing the chance of missing it due to limited computational resources.

5   Conclusion and Future Work

In this paper, we presented a C++ library that compiles neural network models into machine code that performs inference. It is targeted at x86/64 processors, especially the Intel Atom and Silvermont microarchitectures that are used in the NAO and Pepper robots. The performance achieved on networks that are generally feasible to execute for each camera frame is significantly better than existing libraries, while being slower for particularly large models. The library is available on GitHub [18].

We are currently far from supporting all Keras layer types with all possible parameters, although the most commonly used ones are available. Some layers have limitations regarding the input dimensions. Optimizing the overall performance of the library is an ongoing effort without a foreseeable end.

References

1. Abadi, M., et al.: TensorFlow: Large-scale machine learning on heterogeneous systems (2015). https://www.tensorflow.org/
2. Bradski, G.: The OpenCV library. Dr. Dobb's Journal of Software Tools (2000)
3. Chollet, F., et al.: Keras (2015). https://keras.io
4. Fog, A.: Instruction tables: Lists of instruction latencies, throughputs and micro-operation breakdowns for Intel, AMD and VIA CPUs (2018). https://www.agner.org/optimize/instruction_tables.pdf
5. Hermann, T., et al.: frugally-deep: Header-only library for using Keras models in C++ (2019). https://github.com/Dobiasd/frugally-deep
6. Hofmann, M., Schwarz, I., Urbann, O., Larisch, A.: Nao Devils team report 2018 (2019). https://github.com/NaoDevils/CodeRelease/blob/master/TeamReport2018.pdf
7. Jia, Y., et al.: Caffe: convolutional architecture for fast feature embedding. arXiv preprint arXiv:1408.5093 (2014)
8. Kobalicek, P., et al.: AsmJit – Complete x86/x64 JIT and remote assembler for C++ (2019). https://github.com/asmjit/asmjit
9. Nao-Team HTWK: Team research report 2018 (2019). https://htwk-robots.de/documents/TRR_2018.pdf
10. nyanp, et al.: tiny-dnn: header only, dependency-free deep learning framework in C++14 (2018). https://github.com/tiny-dnn/tiny-dnn
11. Poppinga, B., Laue, T.: JET-Net: real-time object detection for mobile robots. In: Chalup, S., Niemueller, T., Suthakorn, J., Williams, M.-A. (eds.) RoboCup 2019: Robot World Cup XXIII. LNCS(LNAI), vol. 11531, pp. 227–240. Springer, Cham (2019)
12. Röfer, T., et al.: B-Human team report and code release 2018 (2018). http://www.b-human.de/downloads/publications/2018/coderelease2018.pdf
13. Sandler, M., Howard, A., Zhu, M., Zhmoginov, A., Chen, L.C.: MobileNetV2: inverted residuals and linear bottlenecks. arXiv preprint arXiv:1801.04381 (2018)
14. Schraudolph, N.N.: A fast, compact approximation of the exponential function. Neural Comput. 11(4), 853–862 (1999). http://nic.schraudolph.org/pubs/Schraudolph99.pdf
15. Simonyan, K., Zisserman, A.: Very deep convolutional networks for large-scale image recognition. In: International Conference on Learning Representations (2015)
16. Szemenyei, M., Estivill-Castro, V.: Real-time scene understanding using deep neural networks for RoboCup SPL. In: Holz, D., Genter, K., Saad, M., von Stryk, O. (eds.) RoboCup 2018. LNCS (LNAI), vol. 11374, pp. 96–108. Springer, Cham (2019). https://doi.org/10.1007/978-3-030-27544-0_8

17. The HDF Group: Hierarchical data format, version 5 (1997–2019). http://www.hdfgroup.org/HDF5/
18. Thielke, F., Hasselbring, A.: CompiledNN: A JIT compiler for neural network inference (2019). https://github.com/bhuman/CompiledNN

Human Support Robot as Research Platform of Domestic Mobile Manipulator

Takashi Yamamoto[1]([✉]), Yutaro Takagi[1], Akiyoshi Ochiai[2], Kunihiro Iwamoto[1],
Yuta Itozawa[1], Yoshiaki Asahara[1], Yasukata Yokochi[1], and Koichi Ikeda[1]

[1] Frontier Research Center, Toyota Motor Corporation, Toyota, Japan
tyamamoto@mail.toyota.co.jp
[2] Toyota Research Institute, Los Altos, CA, USA

Abstract. The Human Support Robot (HSR) has been used in Domestic Standard Platform League (DSPL) of RoboCup@Home since RoboCup Nagoya in 2017. Currently, the number of HSR users is expanding to 44 sites in 12 countries worldwide (as of 30th March, 2019). In this paper, we explain the design concept of HSR, and examples of recent activities of the developers community. We hope that it would contribute to RoboCup and researchers.

Keywords: Mobile manipulation · Domestic robots

1 Introduction

Domestic mobile manipulators are expected to perform physical work in living spaces worldwide in order to contribute to an aging population with declining birth rates with the expectation of improving quality of life (QoL). In order to achieve such robots, it requires tremendous research of algorithms in addition to the hardware which may coexist with people in their living space. We assume that the research will accelerate by using a common robot platform among researchers since that enables them to share their research results. Therefore we have developed a compact and safe research platform, Human Support Robot (HSR), which can be operated in an actual home environment and we have provided it to various research institutes to establish HSR Developers Community (Fig. 1) [7]. Regarding user experiences, HSR aims to support people having greater needs for daily life (Fig. 2).

2 Design of HSR

Here we explain the overview of HSR design, referring to [15,16]. Through several trial user tests with prototypes in [15], we concluded that the robot's motion appears to be complicated and unexpected because the arm starts moving after the wheels completely stop, resulting that it gives users uneasy feeling and impression of slow motion. Taking it into account, we started designing a

S. Chalup et al. (Eds.): RoboCup 2019, LNAI 11531, pp. 457–465, 2019.
https://doi.org/10.1007/978-3-030-35699-6_37

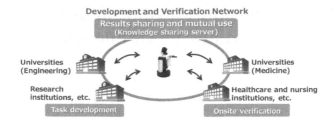

Fig. 1. HSR Developers Community [15].

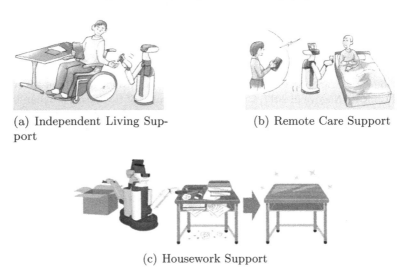

(a) Independent Living Support

(b) Remote Care Support

(c) Housework Support

Fig. 2. Utilization of HSR [15].

new simple mechanical structure based on coordinated movements of the wheels and the arm. Regarding the targets of the design, we set the maximum payload weight in arbitrary posture to 1.2 kg in order to grasp 43 classes of objects [9] from floor to desk (0–725 mm) in three directions (top, side, front) of the hand [16]. The target height is set to 1.35 m considering the reachability to furniture of shoulder height (1331 mm, referred from [14]), which could be normally accessed by general people standing. The maximum velocity is set to 0.8 km/h based on sensory evaluations using the previous prototype, considering real field tests to elderly people or people with disabilities, while giving them a sense of security. The width of the electric wheelchair is set to 700 mm or less and the width required for a wheelchair and a person facing the sideways to pass each other is set to 120 cm or more. Based on these conditions, the target width is set to less than 50 cm with a cylindrical telescoping body, taking into account the parallel running and passing with the wheelchair. In addition, we set targets with a step difference of 5 mm and a slope of 5° from the barrier free standard in Japan [3]. Moreover the height of the robot's standard posture is set to less than the eye

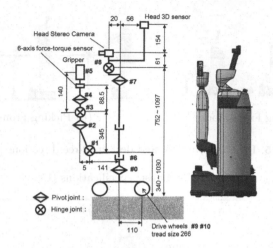

Fig. 3. Joint configuration of HSR [16].

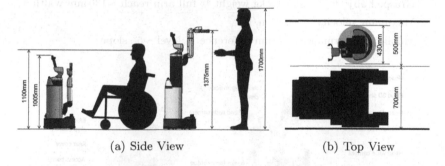

(a) Side View   (b) Top View

Fig. 4. Side and top view of HSR [16].

level of the wheelchair user (110 cm [8]), because we do not want to give the sense of intimidation to wheelchair users. Considering experiments under development in actual fields with people, we set the maximum kinetic energy 10 J or less.

Next, we describe actual results of the design. Figure 3 shows the joint configuration of HSR. Here, the shoulder extends twice the length of the head by the movement of joint #6.

As shown in Fig. 4, it is designed to meet the requirements of the size. In addition, it is designed to be able to handle from a floor to a desk by gripping postures in three directions as shown in Fig. 5. The basic specifications of HSR are shown in Table 1. With regard to the maximum kinetic energy, considering the worst case, we calculate the kinetic energy with the maximum speed of 0.36 m/s from the no-load rotation speed of the wheel motor, and the weight of 50 kg assuming to add 13 kg of additional devices. It is 3.24 J, which is lower than the target value 10 J. These results has clarified the features of HSR.

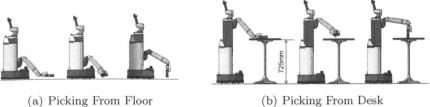

(a) Picking From Floor   (b) Picking From Desk

Fig. 5. Picking from floor and desk in three directions [16].

Table 1. HSR basic specifications [15].

Height	φ430 × 1,005 (~1,350) mm
Weight	37 kg
Arm length	600 mm
Shoulder height	340–1,030 mm
Grasped object	~1.2 kg weight @ full arm reach ~130 mm width
Maximum velocity	0.8 km/h
Mobility performance	~5 mm difference in level ~5° slope

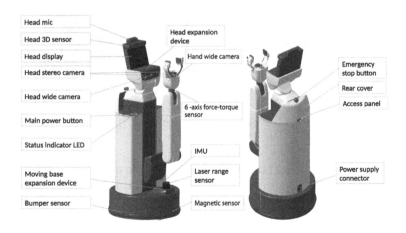

Fig. 6. Sensors and equipments of HSR [15].

Figure 6 shows the sensors installed in the HSR. Various sensors are installed for the ease of use as a research platform. Safety measures include reduction of pinch points by simplification of the arm, reduction of fall hazard through gravity compensation of the arm and self-lock mechanism of the hand, reduction of contact danger by driving thrust reduction and magnetic tape stop function to reduce the risk of fall from stairs and steps. It implements force control with a 6-axis force-torque sensor on the wrist, and compliance control using joint

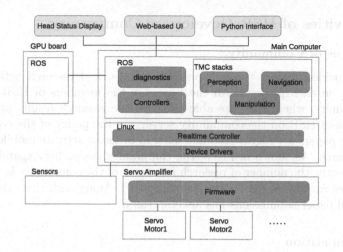

Fig. 7. Software architecture of HSR [15].

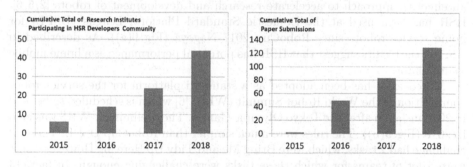

(a) Participants in Community   (b) Paper Submissions

Fig. 8. Statistics of HSR Developers Community.

modules based on series elastic actuators [11]. Regarding computational resources, CPU board (Intel©Core™ i7-4700EQ CPU 2.4 GHz) and GPU board (NVIDIA© Jetson™) are mounted inside HSR. When a large-scale calculation is required, it is possible to use an external server via wireless or wired LAN.

HSR's software architecture is built on ROS (Robot Operating System) [12]. The overview of the system architecture on ROS (Kinetic) is shown in Fig. 7.

The robot as a whole has 8 DoF for manipulation, comprised of the 3 DoF of the mobile base, 4 DoF of the arm, and 1 DoF of the torso lift. Thus, it is possible to generate flexible movement by moving the mobile base and the arm together. We developed a novel whole-body motion control method making better use of the configuration of this robot for coordination between transportation movement and the grasping operation [15].

3   Activities of HSR Developers Community

3.1   Status of Community

HSR is provided mainly through public offerings, and research activities are proceeding on each projects. All the users are the members of HSR Developers Community, where they are able to share the research results and receive information of HSR on the community server. As the policy of the community, submitting papers are highly recommended in order to activate mobile manipulation research. As shown in Fig. 8, the community is steadily expanding every year. Currently, the number of research institutes of the community is 44 sites in 12 countries worldwide (as of 30th March, 2019). Along with that, the number of accepted paper submissions has also increased.

3.2   Competition

In recent years, international robot competitions have attracted attention as an effective approach to accelerate research and development of robots [2,5,6]. HSR has been used at the Domestic Standard Platform League (DSPL) for home service robots since RoboCup 2017 Nagoya (Fig. 9(a)). As described in [15,16], the results suggest that HSR has potential performance as a home mobile manipulator.

Moreover, it has been adopted as a standard platform for the service robot competition of the World Robot Summit (WRS) [6] which is scheduled to be held in 2020 in Japan after the Tokyo Olympic Games. The preliminary WRS was held in 2018 (Fig. 9(b)). The rules were much simpler than RoboCup DSPL. The skill challenge had 2 tasks, which were Bring Me and Tidy Up Here [6]. However, there were a lot of teams for which these tasks were challenging enough. In fact, 14 teams joined the competitions and 6 teams did not get any points. It is clarified that one of the reasons was the short preparation time. Therefore we believe that WRS2020 should start the process of the public offering much earlier than WRS2018. Also it might be very hard for teams to do all the tasks perfectly at the competition place which they have never seen before the competition. Actually, it seemed not to be enough time to prepare all the settings for unknown test environment. Therefore it might be useful to use a simpler and smaller pre-announced competition space with furniture teams can get, which they can set on each sites. We think that it could be a standard regulation to share the same test conditions and compare each results clearly.

Currently, the WRS committee is preparing modified regulations for WRS2020, considering the results of WRS2018. The public offering is going to be held for WRS2020 and it is planned that the selected teams which have no HSR will receive it.

3.3   Research Activity

In the community, studies and field tests are being conducted in parallel. Figure 10 shows examples of these activities.

(a) RoboCup2017 Nagoya

(b) WRS2018 Tokyo

Fig. 9. International robot competitions using HSR.

(a) In-house Research of Autonomous Tidy-up Task [15]

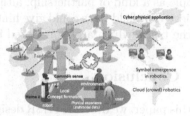

(b) CREST Project, Symbol Emergence in Robotics for Future Human-Machine Collaboration [1]

(c) Autonomous Tidying-up Robot System, CEATEC JAPAN 2018 [4]
©Preferred Networks, Inc.

(d) Test in Robotic Smart Home jointly with Fujita Health University [13]

Fig. 10. Research activities using HSR.

Regarding Fig. 10(a), we believe Tidy Up Here task is one of the most important tasks because it includes general solutions of autonomous technologies and it could be used to a lot of applications. Therefore we have been researching it since we started in-house development of HSR [10,15].

Next we introduce a example of government-funded projects (CREST) [1]. The project of Fig. 10(b) is using HSRs in each research institutes in order to establish the framework of "symbol emergence in robotics" [1]. The main target of the project is Tidy Up Here task. In the near future, the project is going to show the demonstration with their research results.

Figure 10(c) shows one of the best demonstrations of Tidy Up Here task. Throughout the event, HSRs were continuously tidying up the messy demonstration space [4] with the excellent deep learning technology. It has led to awards and increased interest in domestic mobile manipulators [4].

Figure 10(d) shows field tests for elderly people with a medical university. Here, we have experimented various applications of Bring Me task, with different user interfaces such as direct voice command through the microphone on HSR and tablet PCs or smart speakers set in each rooms for elder people. So far, it is too early to conclude it based on statistical methods. However we feel the existence of the robot might be able to give a enjoyable and positive life to elderly people as a kind of partnership, although the possible tasks are still limited. We believe that field tests could give hints of the research and evaluate the feasibility of the tasks, which are represented in Fig. 1.

4   Conclusion

In this paper, we described HSR design concepts and activities of HSR developers community. The design of HSR is still under active development and we will improve it by continually reflecting user and researcher requests. We are sure that the strong connection among researchers is very important to realize domestic mobile manipulators. Through these activities, we really hope to contribute to RoboCup and robotics researches.

References

1. CREST: Symbol Emergence in Robotics for Future Human-Machine Collaboration. https://www.jst.go.jp/kisoken/crest/en/project/1111083/15656632.html
2. DARPA Robotics Challenge. https://www.darpa.mil/program/darpa-robotics-challenge
3. MLIT Notification No. 1296. http://www.mlit.go.jp/notice/noticedata/pdf/20181219/20010803.pdf
4. Preferred Networks Inc.: Autonomous Tidying-up Robot System, CEATEC JAPAN 2018. https://hprojects.preferred.jp/tidying-up-robot/en/
5. RoboCup. https://www.robocup.org/
6. World Robot Summit. http://worldrobotsummit.org/en/
7. Toyota Shifts Home Helper Robot R&D into High Gear with New Developer Community and Upgraded Prototype, 16 July 2015. https://newsroom.toyota.co.jp/en/detail/8709541
8. Architectural Institute of Japan: Disability-friendly design guide. Design plan pamphlet 26 (1981)
9. Choi, Y.S., Deyle, T., Chen, T., Glass, J.D., Kemp, C.C.: A list of household objects for robotic retrieval prioritized by people with ALS. In: 2009 IEEE International Conference on Rehabilitation Robotics, pp. 510–517. IEEE (2009)

10. Hashimoto, K., Saito, F., Yamamoto, T., Ikeda, K.: A field study of the human support robot in the home environment. In: Proceedings of IEEE Workshop on Advanced Robotics and its Social Impacts, pp. 143–150, 7–9 November 2013
11. Pratt, G.A., Williamson, M.M.: Series elastic actuators. In: Intelligent Robots and Systems 1995, Human Robot Interaction and Cooperative Robots, Proceedings of 1995 IEEE/RSJ International Conference on Intelligent Robots and Systems, vol. 1, pp. 399–406. IEEE (1995)
12. Quigley, M., et al.: ROS: an open-source robot operating system. In: Proceedings of the International Conference on Advanced Robotics (ICAR), 22–26 June 2009
13. Tanabe, S., et al.: Designing a robotic smart home for everyone, especially the elderly and people with disabilities. Fujita Med. J. **5**, 31–35 (2019)
14. The National Institute of Advanced Industrial Science and Technology: AIST Human body dimension database 1991–92 (2005). https://unit.aist.go.jp/hiri/dhrg/ja/dhdb/91-92/data/list.html
15. Yamamoto, T., Terada, K., Ochiai, A., Saito, F., Asahara, Y., Murase, K.: Development of the research platform of a domestic mobile manipulator utilized for international competition and field test. In: Proceedings of 2018 IEEE/RSJ International Conference on Intelligent Robots and Systems (IROS), pp. 7675–7682. IEEE (2018)
16. Yamamoto, T., Terada, K., Ochiai, A., Saito, F., Asahara, Y., Murase, K.: Development of human support robot as the research platform of a domestic mobile manipulator. ROBOMECH J. **6**(1), 4 (2019)

Optimization of Robot Movements Using Genetic Algorithms and Simulation

Brandon Zahn, Jake Fountain, Trent Houliston, Alexander Biddulph,
Stephan Chalup, and Alexandre Mendes$^{(\boxtimes)}$

School of Electrical Engineering and Computing, Faculty of Engineering and Built
Environment, The University of Newcastle, Callaghan, NSW 2308, Australia
`Alexandre.Mendes@newcastle.edu.au`

Abstract. This work describes the optimization of two robot movements in the context of the Humanoid league competition at RoboCup. A multi-objective genetic algorithm (MOGA) was used in conjunction with the real-time physics simulator Gazebo. The motivation for this work was that the NUbots team, from the University of Newcastle, lacked a simulation platform for their soccer-playing robots. Gazebo was the preferred choice of simulator, offering built-in compatibility with the Robot Operating System (ROS). The NUbots robot software, however, uses a proprietary message-passing framework in place of ROS. This work thus describes the pathway to use Gazebo with non-ROS compliant applications. In addition, it describes how MOGA can be used to optimize complex movements in an efficient manner. The two robot movements optimized were a kick script and the walk engine. For the kick script, the resulting optimal configuration improved the kick distance by a factor of six, with 50% less torso sway. For the walk engine, the forward speed increased by 50%, with 38% less torso sway, compared to the manually-tuned walk engine.

Keywords: Simulation · Walk engine · Optimization · Multi-objective

1 Introduction

The use of optimization to fine-tune the movement of robots has been the focus of attention in recent years, particularly in the context of legged robots [3]. Those types of robots normally use controllers that allow them to maintain balance while performing complex tasks such as walking, turning and jumping. Some of those controllers might have several parameters, depending on the tasks that they perform, which need to be tuned. Just as an example, the walk controller used in this work has 46 parameters that can be individually tuned and finding the right trade-off between balance and speed is a difficult task. The work presented here is significant due to the combination of tools that it uses (the Gazebo simulator and a proprietary message-passing framework called NUClear) and the challenge that it posed. The lessons learned in terms of software engineering and how to effectively make the two systems communicate are

© Springer Nature Switzerland AG 2019
S. Chalup et al. (Eds.): RoboCup 2019, LNAI 11531, pp. 466–475, 2019.
https://doi.org/10.1007/978-3-030-35699-6_38

important contributions. From the perspective of optimization, the contribution is the demonstration of how NSGA-II [4] manages to obtain very good solutions in short periods of time and requiring few generations, which is an important aspect when the evaluation of individual solutions is a costly task.

Our work follows on the footsteps of other multi-objective optimization studies conducted on legged robots. Among those we cite [8], who used NSGA-II to optimize a walk controller for a quadruped robot. More recently, we have the work of Juang and Yeh (2017) [6], who also used NSGA-II in the optimization of a walk controller for a biped NAO robot. The results presented here indicate that the approach is suitable for the optimization of simpler movements (e.g. a kick script), as well as a considerably more complex walk engine.

2 Kick Script and Walk Engine Optimization

This work was developed with the NUgus robotic platform in mind [2]. The original *igus* platform was developed by the University of Bonn as an open platform in 2015 [1] and the NUbots team made a number of modifications to the original model, naming it NUgus afterwards. A simulation model of the NUgus was also derived from the original igus model, and used in our tests.

Two optimization problems are addressed. The first one is the tuning of the kick script used by the NUgus to kick the ball. The script consists of a sequence of six target positions for each of the 20 motors in the robot, i.e. they correspond to a sequence of poses. The first values in the sequence refer to the initial positions of each motor when the kick is triggered, and the last values refer to their final position after the kick is concluded. The four intermediate positions are strategic poses, e.g. the pose when the kick leg is brought backwards; the pose when the kick leg is at its maximum extension after ball contact, etc. The optimization goal is to find the positions of the motors in each of the four intermediate poses so that the ball's travelled distance is maximized, and maximum torso sway is minimized (to reduce the chances of the robot falling over while the kick is being executed). In order to provide information about how a solution for the problem is encoded, the values for motor positions are integers in the interval [0, 1024]. Therefore, there are 80 integer variables to be optimized, all of them within the interval above.

The second optimization problem refers to the walk engine, and the goal is to optimize 46 parameters used by the controller responsible for moving the robot forward. The goal in this case is to maximize forward speed, while minimizing maximum torso sway. The parameters are represented by real numbers in different ranges for each parameter. Again, to give an indication of the search space size for this problem, the largest interval among the controller's parameters is [0, 100].

3   Methodology

In this section we will explain four elements of this study: (1) the NUbots software system, (2) the Gazebo simulator, (3) the communication middleware and (4) the multi-objective genetic algorithm.

3.1   Nubots Software System - NUClear

In recent years, the NUbots developed a proprietary software architecture named NUClear [5]. It is a framework designed to aid in the development of real time modular systems and is built from a set of C++ template meta-programs that control the flow of information through the system. These meta-programs reduce the cost of routing messages between modules, resulting in faster communication times. Since NUClear utilises a co-messaging system, it allows for simple event callback functions through an expressive domain specific language (DSL). The DSL is highly extensible and provides several attachment points to develop new DSL keywords as required. NUClear has been successfully applied in several projects for robotics and virtual reality, and also in the NUgus Humanoid Platform [2]. A detailed description of NUClear is given in [5], which also provides a comparison with the Robot Operating System (ROS)[1] in terms of features and communication performance.

3.2   Gazebo Simulator

Gazebo is an open-source, physics-based robotics simulator. It is very popular with the simulation-league of RoboCup, being utilised by all teams to run their robots in simulations. Considerable support and information are available online to assist the integration of any ROS compliant robotic system with the Gazebo simulator. However, this is not the case for proprietary software, such as NUClear. Since Gazebo has strong connections with RoboCup, and resources such as 3D models and data for the igus platform are readily available, it would be a logical decision to choose Gazebo to integrate with the team's software architecture and NUClear. Integrating ROS into the NUbots' software architecture has been opposed due to the time required to re-factor the entire code, and also because NUClear is arguably more flexible than ROS, as described in [5].

Gazebo depends on several packages but the most significant for this work is the Ignition Transport library[2], which provides Gazebo with an intra- and inter-process co-messaging communication protocol for robot simulation (similar to NUClear). It is an open source communication library that allows sharing data between nodes that could be running within the same process in the same machine or in machines located on the same network.

---

[1] http://www.ros.org/.
[2] http://ignitionrobotics.org.

3.3   Communication Middleware

This section provides an overview of the communications configuration for this study. An online repository[3] has been created, where developers can download all necessary files and use them. The NUbots codebase repository[4] contains all the required source code for setting up a virtual machine (VM) that runs the NUbots software system under the NUClear framework. A diagram of the configuration for communications between Gazebo and the VM is shown in Fig. 1 and described below.

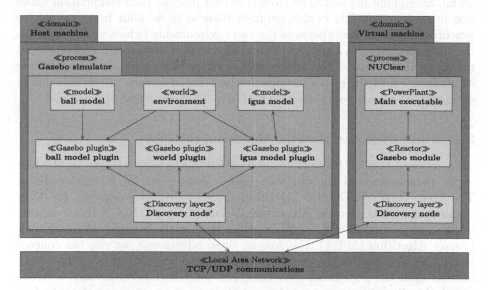

Fig. 1. The configuration for communications between the NUbots software system and Gazebo. On the left, we have the host machine, which runs the Gazebo simulator. On the right, we have a virtual machine that runs the NUbots software system. Two communication nodes (the Discovery nodes) were created using the Ignition Transport library – one for each module. Those nodes manage all the communication through the network and operate in a two-way, publish-subscribe fashion. In each communication cycle, the NUbots software in the virtual machine sends data to the Gazebo simulator about where to move each of the 20 motors, and the simulator sends back data about the position of each limb, as well as gyroscope and accelerometer data. The communication is in real time, via a common TCP/UDP communication layer.

The main contribution in terms of communication infrastructure was the creation of two communication modules. The first one sits within the Gazebo simulator in the host machine and is named *Discovery node'*. The goal of this module is to receive servo commands from the NUbots software that are then

---

[3] http://github.com/NUbots/Gazebo.

[4] http://github.com/NUbots/NUbots.

applied to the robot model in the simulation. In addition, it sends the position of each joint of the robot model, as well as gyro and accelerometer data back to the Nubots software, so it can be used in the walk engine. The second communication module sits within the NUbots software side (namely *Discovery node*). It manages the publishing of the data that its Gazebo counterpart subscribes to, and subscribes to the data published by the Gazebo's *Discovery node'*. The two modules communicate via a common TCP/UDP communication layer.

Integrating Gazebo with the NUClear framework required several iterations, until a configuration that was able to compile using the NUbots' toolchain was found. Several hurdles had to be crossed in that process, from compilation issues due to package conflicts (which required Gazebo to be built from source), to synchronization problems between the two environments (which was solved with the implementation of a custom clock function). For a thorough analysis of all the issues that occurred during the integration process and their corresponding solutions, we refer the reader to reference [10]. This reference will be valuable to developers who want to use Gazebo with non-ROS compliant applications.

3.4 Multi-Objective Genetic Algorithm (MOGA)

As mentioned before, this work focused on two optimization tasks: (a) the kick script parameters and (b) the walk engine parameters for forward walking. The Multi-Objective Genetic Algorithm (MOGA) implemented uses the Non-dominated Sorting Genetic Algorithm II (NSGA-II) [4]. NSGA-II has several advantages over other well-known MOEAs, such as the Strength Pareto Evolutionary Algorithm (SPEA) [11]. Among those advantages, we cite the concept of minimal distance between sets of solutions, which results in less fitness evaluations until the population converges, and most notably, maintains a strong population diversity throughout the evolutionary process. Now, we describe how MOGA was used in each of the optimization problems.

3.5 Optimizing the Kick Script

In order to optimize the kick script parameters using MOGA, firstly a suitable representation for a solution must be defined. The kick script is defined by a sequence of target positions for each motor (i.e. script frames). In out implementation, the first and last frames are fixed, and the MOGA can change the values for the intermediate frames, only. A valid solution contains 80 genes (20 motors and 4 intermediate poses), encoded as integers in the interval [0, 1024].

Objective Function. Two objective functions were chosen to evaluate the quality of the kick. Obj_1 was designed to measure the robot's stability. By using the IMU sensor in the torso, the accelerometer data is recorded during a kick and a maximum field plane sway $||\overrightarrow{fps_{max}}||$ value is calculated. The field plane sway $||\overrightarrow{fps}||$ is the 2D vector magnitude of the x and y components of the accelerometer sensor, calculated as:

$$\|\overrightarrow{fps}\| = \sqrt{\overrightarrow{x}^2_{accel} + \overrightarrow{y}^2_{accel}} \quad (\mathrm{ms}^{-2}) \tag{1}$$

$\|\overrightarrow{fps}\|$ is calculated each time a new sensor message arrives, which is 90 times per second, and Obj_1 is to minimize $\|\overrightarrow{fps_{max}}\|$.

Obj_2 is the maximization of the ball distance from the kick location. Since a minimization function is required by the MOGA framework, Obj_2 is defined as:

$$Obj_2 = min\left(\frac{1}{\text{ball distance}}\right) \quad (\mathrm{m}^{-1}) \tag{2}$$

3.6   Optimizing Walk Engine Parameters

This optimization involved the tuning of 46 parameters that describe how the walk engine generates waypoints for the joints during a walk cycle [9].

The representation of a solution consisted of 46 real values, and each of them was given minimum and maximum possible values, set at 50% of the original value in each direction. For example, if a parameter is originally set at 0.4, the minimum and maximum values then become 0.2 and 0.6, respectively. Notice that the original values correspond to the current hand-tuned walk engine, which already produces a relatively stable and fast walk. Thus, we expect the parameters of the optimized walk to be relatively close.

The two objective functions for walk evaluation were the minimization of the time required to walk a distance of 2.5 m, starting from a standing pose; and the minimization of the maximum 3D vector magnitude of the three components of the accelerometer, $\|\overrightarrow{accel_{max}}\|$, where:

$$\|\overrightarrow{accel}\| = \sqrt{\overrightarrow{x}^2_{accel} + \overrightarrow{y}^2_{accel} + \overrightarrow{z}^2_{accel}} \quad (\mathrm{ms}^{-2}) \tag{3}$$

4   Results

4.1   Results for the Kick Script Optimization

The MOGA framework ran for 300 generations with a population size of 40 individuals. Additional parameters are listed in Table 1 and the results are shown in Fig. 2. The parameters were determined after a series of exploratory tests and empirical observation of the evolution of the population of solutions.

In our tests, we opted for a high crossover probability, aiming at a fast evolution of the population, and a low mutation probability, since diversity would be handled by the minimum distance between solutions, which is part of NSGA-II. In Fig. 2, we highlight four solutions. Ind_O is the original, hand-tuned kick script (distance of 0.6 m; acceleration of 35.8 ms^{-2}) and becomes dominated already by generation 10. After 300 generations, several trade-off solutions were found, with a good concentration around the 3.3 m distance and instantaneous acceleration

Table 1. NSGA-II parameters used in the kick script and walk engine optimizations. For detailed information about those parameters, please refer to [4].

Test	popSize	gens	mutProb	crossProb	etaC	etaM
Kick script	40	300	0.025	0.8	15	40
Walk engine	40	50	0.025	0.8	13	20

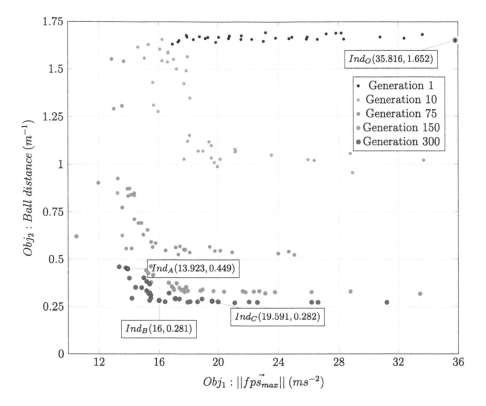

Fig. 2. Populations of solutions found during the evolutionary process for the optimization of the kick script on a simulated grass surface. Notice how the population converges to high quality solutions in 300 generations, with lower torso sway values and higher ball distances (in Obj_2 the values are inverted, so lower is better). Four individual solutions are highlighted for illustrative purposes.

of $15\,\text{ms}^{-2}$. In that group of solutions, we highlighted three, with Ind_B offering a good trade-off between the two objectives. That solution has a maximum torso acceleration of $16.0\,\text{ms}^{-2}$ and a resulting ball distance of 3.5 m. That represents an improvement of almost 6-fold for the distance travelled by the ball, while the maximum lateral acceleration was reduced to less than half of the original value.

Porting the Kick Script to the NUgus Robot: After completing the kick script optimization, we tested three candidate solutions on the robot itself, namely Ind_A, Ind_B and Ind_C. This test was fundamental to determine if the simulation settings were a correct representation of the real world. The so-called *reality gap* between simulation and real world is a major obstacle for the actual use of simulation results in real robotic platforms. For more information about this topic, we refer the reader to a recent survey [7]. Among the three solutions tested, the only one that resulted on the robot still standing at the end of the run was Ind_A. The other two led to the robot falling over at the end of the kick. The most probable reasons for that result might be the incorrect simulation of the friction between the studs on the robot's feet and the artificial grass surface; as well as the internal behaviour of the individual servos not being accurately simulated. This topic will require additional investigation in the future.

Figure 3 shows the time-lapse sequences for the kicks represented by Ind_A (top row) and Ind_B (bottom row), tested on the real robot. The top sequence shows the ball travelling a bit over 2 m from the middle of the field towards the goal (which is very similar to the simulated result), and the robot still standing on the last frame. The bottom sequence shows the ball travelling all the way to the goal (i.e. more than 3 m) but the robot falls over at the end.

Fig. 3. Time-lapse of two of the kick scripts highlighted in Fig. 2 – Ind_A (top) and Ind_B (bottom) – running on the real NUgus robot. In both cases, the distance travelled by the ball is very similar to the simulated results. However, only for solution Ind_A the robot still stands at the end, while Ind_B leads to the robot falling over – in the simulation, both scripts resulted in the robot standing at the end.

4.2 Results for Walk Engine

The framework was set up with the input parameters listed in Table 1 and was run for 50 generations. The low number of generations was chosen due to time constraints, as each evaluation of the walk required ≈ 1 min of simulation. The results are shown in Fig. 4. The evolutionary process was again successful. The time required for the robot to walk 2.5 m dropped from 32.5 s to 21.5 s (see solution Ind_A in Fig. 4, compared to the original, hand-tuned solution Ind_O), i.e. an increase of 50% in forward speed. The maximum torso acceleration was reduced from $70.7\,\mathrm{ms^{-2}}$ to $43.2\,\mathrm{ms^{-2}}$.

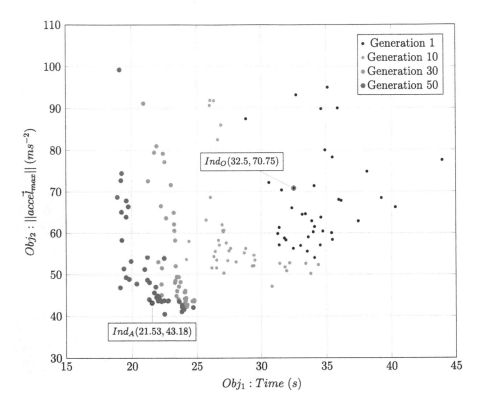

Fig. 4. Evolution of the populations during the walk engine parameters optimization. Notice how the population converges to high quality solutions in 50 generations, with lower times required to walk the 2.5 m distance, and smaller torso sway values. Two solutions are highlighted for illustrative purposes.

5 Conclusion

This work presented a multi-objective genetic algorithm approach for the optimization of two robot movements: kick and forward walk. Moreover, it also described how to setup a communication bus between the Gazebo simulator and a non-ROS compliant application. The results of the simulation were very good, with the optimized kick making the ball travel 6 times farther. For the walk simulation the results were also very good, with forward speed increasing by 50%. In both cases, the stability of the robot, represented by the maximum acceleration of the torso section, was also reduced, compared to the original, hand-tuned values. Future work will concentrate on bridging the reality gap between the results in simulation and the real robot. At this stage, kick scripts can be directly ported to the robotic platform, but the reality gap remains an issue for simulated kicks with a travelled distance greater than 2.5 m. The walk engine parameters will also require additional testing on the NUgus platform before porting is successfully achieved.

References

1. Allgeuer, P., Farazi, H., Schreiber, M., Behnke, S.: Child-sized 3d printed IGUS humanoid open platform. In: IEEE-RAS International Conference on Humanoid Robots (Humanoids), pp. 1–8 (2015)
2. Biddulph, A., Houliston, T., Mendes, A., Chalup, S.K.: Comparing computing platforms for deep learning on a humanoid robot. In: Cheng, L., Leung, A.C.S., Ozawa, S. (eds.) ICONIP 2018. LNCS, vol. 11307, pp. 120–131. Springer, Cham (2018). https://doi.org/10.1007/978-3-030-04239-4_11
3. Chalup, S., Murch, C., Quinlan, M.: Machine learning with AIBO robots in the four-legged league of robocup. IEEE Trans. Syst. Man Cybernet. Part C **37**(3), 297–310 (2007)
4. Deb, K., Pratap, A., Agarwal, S., Meyarivan, T.: A fast and elitist multiobjective genetic algorithm: NSGA-II. IEEE Trans. Evol. Comput. **6**(2), 182–197 (2002)
5. Houliston, T., et al.: Nuclear: a loosely coupled software architecture for humanoid robot systems. Front. Robot. AI **3**, 20 (2016)
6. Juang, C.F., Yeh, Y.T.: Multiobjective evolution of biped robot gaits using advanced continuous ant-colony optimized recurrent neural networks. IEEE Trans. Cybern. **48**(6), 1910–1922 (2017)
7. Mouret, J.B., Chatzilygeroudis, K.: 20 years of reality gap: a few thoughts about simulators in evolutionary robotics. In: Proceedings of the Genetic and Evolutionary Computation Conference Companion, pp. 1121–1124. GECCO 2017. ACM, New York (2017). https://doi.org/10.1145/3067695.3082052
8. Nygaard, T., Torresen, J., Glette, K.: Multi-objective evolution of fast and stable gaits on a physical quadruped robotic platform. In: IEEE Symposium Series on Computational Intelligence (SSCI), pp. 1–8 (2016)
9. Yi, S., Hong, D., Lee, D.: A hybrid walk controller for resource-constrained humanoid robots. In: 13th IEEE-RAS International Conference on Humanoid Robots, pp. 88–93 (2013)
10. Zahn, B.: Optimisation of a walk engine for a humanoid robot. Technical report, School of Electrical Engineering and Computing, The University of Newcastle, Australia (2018). http://github.com/NUbots/Gazebo
11. Zitzler, E., Laumanns, M., Thiele, L.: SPEA2: improving the strength pareto evolutionary algorithm. Technical report, Department of Electrical Engineering, Swiss Federal Institute of Technology, Zurich, Switzerland (2001). https://www.research-collection.ethz.ch/handle/20.500.11850/145755

Invited Champion Track Papers

Champion Team Paper: Dynamic Passing-Shooting Algorithm of the RoboCup Soccer SSL 2019 Champion

Zexi Chen, Haodong Zhang, Dashun Guo, Shenhan Jia, Xianze Fang,
Zheyuan Huang, Yunkai Wang, Peng Hu, Licheng Wen, Lingyun Chen,
Zhengxi Li, and Rong Xiong$^{(\boxtimes)}$

Zhejiang University, Zheda Road No. 38,
Hangzhou, Zhejiang, People's Republic of China
rxiong@zju.edu.cn
http://zjunlict.cn

Abstract. ZJUNlict became the Small Size League Champion of RoboCup 2019 with 6 victories and 1 tie for their 7 games. The overwhelming ability of ball-handling and passing allows ZJUNlict to greatly threaten its opponent and almost kept its goal clear without being threatened. This paper presents the core technology of its ball-handling and robot movement which consist of hardware optimization, dynamic passing and shooting strategy, and multi-agent cooperation and formation. We first describe the mechanical optimization on the placement of the capacitors, the redesign of the damping system of the dribbler and the electrical optimization on the replacement of the core chip. We then describe our passing point algorithm. The passing and shooting strategy can be separated into two different parts, where we search the passing point on SBIP-DPPS and evaluate the point based on the ball model. The statements and the conclusion should be supported by the performances and log of games on Small Size League RoboCup 2019.

Keywords: Damping · STMicrocontrollers · Off-the-ball running ·
Value-based criteria · CUDA searching

1 Introduction

ZJUNlict is a RoboCup Soccer Small Size League (SSL) team from Zhejiang University with a rich culture. We seek changes and upgrades every year from hardware to software, and try our best to fuse them together in order to form a better robot system. With a stable dribbler developed during 2017–2018, team ZJUNlict focused mostly on dynamic passing and shoot with the advantage of the stable dribbler in 2018–2019. In fact the algorithm helped us gain a ball possession rate[1] of 68.8% during 7 matches in RoboCup 2019.

---

[1] The possession rate is calculated by comparing the interception time of both sides. If the interception time of one team is shorter, the ball is considered to be possessed by this team.

© Springer Nature Switzerland AG 2019
S. Chalup et al. (Eds.): RoboCup 2019, LNAI 11531, pp. 479–490, 2019.
https://doi.org/10.1007/978-3-030-35699-6_39

To achieve the great possession rate, safe and accurate passing and shooting, our newly developed algorithm are developed into four parts:

1. The passing point module calculates the feasibility of all passing points, filters out feasible points, and uses the evaluation function to find the best passing point.
2. The running point module calculates the points where the offensive threat is high if our robots move there, to make our offense more aggressive.
3. The decision module decides when to pass and when to shoot based on the current situation to guarantee the success rate of the passing and shooting when the situation changes.
4. The skill module helps our robots perform passing and shooting accurately.

This paper focuses on how to achieve multi-robot cooperation. In Sects. 2 and 3, we discuss our main optimization on hardware. In Sects. 4 and 5, we discuss the passing strategy and the running point module respectively. In Sect. 6, we analyze the performance of our algorithms at RoboCup 2019 with the log files recorded during the matches.

2   Modification of Mechanical Structure of ZJUNlict

2.1   The Position of Two Capacitors

During a match of the Small Size League, robots could move as fast as 3.25 m/s. In this case, the stability of the robot became very important, and this year, we focused on the center of the gravity with a goal of lower it. In fact, there are already many teams got there hands busy with lowering the center of the gravity, e.g., team KIKS and team RoboDragons have their robot compacted to 135 mm, and team TIGERs have their capacitor moved sideways instead of regularly laying upon the solenoid [1].

Thanks to the open source of team TIGERs [1], in this year's mechanical structure design, we moved the capacitor from the circuit board to the chassis. On the one hand, this lowers the center of gravity of the robot and makes the mechanical structure of the robot more compact, On the other hand, to give the upper board a larger space for future upgrades. The capacitor is fixed on the chassis via the 3D printed capacitor holder as shown in Fig. 1, and in order to protect the capacitor from the impact that may be suffered on the field, we have added a metal protection board on the outside of the capacitor which made of 40Cr alloy steel with high strength.

2.2   The Structure of the Dribbling System

The handling of the dribbling part has always been a part we are proud of, and it is also the key to our strong ball control ability. In last year's champion paper, we have completely described our design concept, that is, using a one-degree-of-freedom mouth structure, placing appropriate sponge pads on the rear and the

Fig. 1. The new design of the capacitors

lower part to form a nonlinear spring damping system. When a ball with certain speed hits the dribbler, the spring damping system can absorb the rebound force of the ball, and the dribbler uses a silica gel with a large friction force so that the ball can not be easily detached from the mouth.

The state of the sponge behind the mouth is critical to the performance of the dribbling system. In RoboCup 2018, there was a situation in which the sponge fell off, which had a great impact on the play of our game. In last year's design, as shown in Fig. 2, we directly insert a sponge between the carbon plate at the mouth and the rear carbon plate. Under frequent and severe vibration, the sponge could easily to fall off [2]. In this case, we made some changes, a baffle is added between the dibbler and the rear carbon fiberboard, as shown in Fig. 3, and the sponge is glued to the baffle plate, which made it hard for the sponge to fall off, therefore greatly reduce the vibration.

Fig. 2. ZJUNlict 2018 mouth design   **Fig. 3.** ZJUNlict 2019 mouth design

3   Modification of Electronic Board

In the past circuit design, we always thought that the board should be designed into multiple independent boards according to the function module so that if there is a problem, the whole board can be replaced. But then we gradually realized that instead of giving us convenience, it is unexpectedly complicated, on the one hand, we had to carry more spare boards, and on the other hand, it was not conducive to our maintenance.

For the new design, we only kept one motherboard and one booster board, which reduced the number of boards, making the circuit structure more compact and more convenient for maintenance. We also fully adopted ST's STM32H743ZI master chip, which has a clock speed of up to 480 MHz and has a wealth of peripherals. The chip is responsible for signal processing, packet unpacking and packaging, and motor control.

Thanks to the open source of TIGERs again, we use Allergo's A3930 three-phase brushless motor control chip, simplifying the circuit design of the motor drive module on the motherboard. The biggest advancement in electronic this year was the completion of the stability test of the H743 version of the robot. In the case of all robots using the H743 chip, there was no robot failure caused by board damage during the game.

In addition, we replaced the motor encoder from the original 360 lines to the current 1000 lines. The reading mode has been changed from the original direct reading to the current differential mode reading.

4   Passing and Shooting Strategy Based on Ball Model

4.1   Real-Time Passing Power Calculation

Passing power plays a key role in the passing process. For example, robot A wants to pass the ball to robot B. If the passing power is too small, the opponent will have plenty of time to intercept the ball. If the passing power is too large, robot B may fail to receive the ball in limited time. Therefore, it's significant to calculate appropriate passing power.

Suppose we know the location of robot A that holds the ball, its passing target point, and the position and speed information of robot B that is ready to receive the ball. We can accurately calculate the appropriate passing power based on the ball model shown in Fig. 4. In the ideal ball model, after the ball is kicked out at a certain speed, the ball will first decelerate to 5/7 of the initial speed with a large sliding acceleration, and then decelerate to 0 with a small rolling acceleration. Based on this, we can use the passing time and the passing distance to calculate the passing power. Obviously, the passing distance is the distance between robot A and its passing target point. It's very easy to calculate the Euclidean distance between these two points. Passing time consists of two parts: robot B's arrival time and buffer time for adjustment after arrival. We calculate robot B's arrival time using last year's robot arrival time prediction algorithm. The buffer time is usually a constant (such as 0.3 s).

Since the acceleration in the first deceleration process is very large and the deceleration time is very short, we ignore the moving distance of the first deceleration process and simplify the calculation. Let d, t and a be the passing distance,

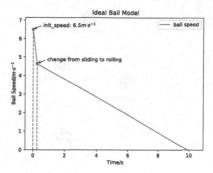

Fig. 4. Ideal ball model

time and rolling acceleration. Then, the velocity of the ball after the first deceleration and the passing power are given by the following:

$$v_1 = (d + \frac{1}{2}at^2)/t \tag{1}$$

$$v_0 = v_1/\frac{5}{7} \tag{2}$$

According to the capabilities of the robots, we can limit the threshold of passing power and apply it to the calculated result.

4.2 *SBIP*-Based Dynamic Passing Points Searching (DPPS) Algorithm

Passing is an important skill both offensively and defensively and the basic requirement for a successful passing process is that the ball can't be intercepted by opponents. Theoretically, we can get all feasible passing points based on the *SBIP (Search-Based Interception Prediction)* [2,3]. Assuming that one of our robots would pass the ball to another robot, it needs to ensure that the ball can't be intercepted by opposite robots, so we need the SBIP algorithm to calculate interception time of all robots on the field and return only the feasible passing points.

In order to improve the execution efficiency of the passing robot, we apply the searching process from the perspective of passing robot.

As is shown in Fig. 5, we traverse all the shooting power in all directions to apply the SBIP algorithm for all robots on the field. According to the interception time of both teammates and opponents under a specific passing power and direction, we can keep only the feasible passing directions and the corresponding passing power.

When considering that there is about 3 degree's error between the accurate orientation of the robot and the one obtained from the vision, we set the traversal interval of direction as $360/128°$. And the shooting power, which can be considered as the speed of ball when the ball just kicked out, is divided equally

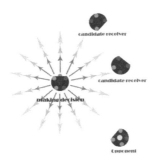

Fig. 5. Dynamic passing points searching process

into 64 samples between $1 \, \text{m/s}$ and $6.5 \, \text{m/s}$, which means the shooting accuracy is about $0.34 \, \text{m/s}$. Because all combinations of passing directions and passing power should be considered, we need to apply SBIP algorithm for 262144 times (we assume there are 16 robots in each team, 32 in the field), which is impossible to finish within about $13 \, \text{ms}$ by only serial computing. Fortunately, all of the 262144 SBIPs are decoupled, so we can accelerate this process by GPU-based parallel computing technique [5–7], and that's why the numbers mentioned above are 128, 64 and 32.

4.3 Value-Based Best Pass Strategy

After applying the DPPS algorithm, we can get all optional pass strategies. To evaluate them and choose the best pass strategy, we extract some important features $x_i (i = 1, 2, ..., n)$ and their weights $(i = 1, 2, ..., n)$, at last, we get the scores of each pass strategy by calculating the weighted average of features selected by Eq. 3 [8,9]

$$\sum_{i=1}^{n} \omega_i \cdot x_i \tag{3}$$

For example, we chose the following features to evaluate pass strategies in RoboCup2019 Small Size League:

- Interception time of teammates: close pass would reduce the risk of the ball being intercepted by opposite because of the ideal model.
- Shoot angle of the receiver's position: this would make the teammate ready to receive the ball easier to shoot.
- Distance between passing point and the goal: if the receiver decides to shoot, short distance results in high speed when the ball is in the opponent's penalty area, which can improve the success rate of shooting.
- Refraction angle of shooting: the receiver can shoot as soon as it gets the ball if the refraction angle is small. The offensive tactics would be executed smoother when this feature is added.

– The time interval between the first teammate's interception and the first opponent's interception: if this number is very small, the passing strategy would be very likely to fail. So only when the delta-time is bigger than a threshold, the safety is guaranteed.

After applying the DPPS algorithm, evaluating the passing points and choosing the best pass strategy, the results will be shown on the visualization software. In Fig. 6, the orange is the feasible passing points by chipping and the cyan is the feasible passing points by flat shot. The yellow line is the best chipping passing line, and the green line is the best flat shot passing line.

According to *a* in Fig. 6, there are few feasible passing points when teammates are surrounded by opponents. And when the passing line is blocked by an opponent, there are only chipping passing points. According to *b* in Fig. 6, the feasible passing points are intensive when there is no opponent marking any teammate.

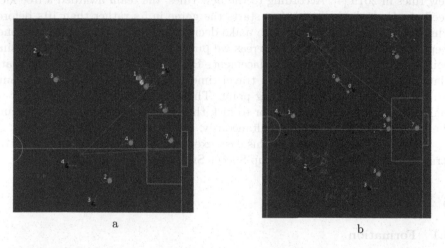

a   b

Fig. 6. Feasible pass points and best pass strategy (Color figure online)

4.4   Shooting Decision Making

In the game of RoboCup SSL, deciding when to shoot is one of the most important decisions to make. Casual shots may lead to loss of possession, while too strict conditions will result in no shots and low offensive efficiency. Therefore, it is necessary to figure out the right way to decide when to shoot. We developed a fusion algorithm that combines the advantages of shot angle and interception prediction.

In order to ensure that there is enough space when shooting, we calculate the valid angle of the ball to the goal based on the position of the opponent's robots. If the angle is too small, the ball is likely to be blocked by the opponent's robots. So, we must ensure that the shot angle is greater than a certain threshold.

However, there are certain shortcomings in the judgment based on the shot angle. For example, when our robot is far from the goal but the shot angle exceeds the threshold, our robot may decide to shoot. Because the distance from the goal is very far, the opponent's robots will have enough time to intercept the ball. Such a shot is meaningless. In order to solve this problem, the shot decision combined with interception prediction is proposed. Similar to the evaluation when passing the ball, We calculate whether it will be intercepted during the process of shooting the ball to the goal. If it is not intercepted, it means that this shot is very likely to have a higher success rate. We use this fusion algorithm to avoid useless shots as much as possible and ensure that our shots have a higher success rate.

4.5 Effective Free Kick Strategy

We generate an effective free kick strategy based on ball model catering to the new rules in 2019 [4]. According to the new rules, the team awarded a free kick needs to place the ball and then starts the game in 5 s rather than 10 s before, which means we have less time to make decisions. This year we follow our one-step pass-and-shoot strategy, whereas we put the computation for best passing point into the process of ball placement. Based on the ball model and path planning, we can obtain the ball travel time t_{p-ball} and the robot travel time $t_{p-robot}$ to reach the best passing point. Then we make a decision whether to make the robot reach the point or to kick the ball firstly so that the robot and the ball can reach the point simultaneously.

Results in Sect. 6 show that this easy-executed strategy is the most effective strategy during the 2019 RoboCup Soccer Small Size League Competition.

5 Off-the-Ball Running

5.1 Formation

As described in the past section, we can always get the best passing point in any situation, which means the more aggressiveness our robots show, the more aggressive the best passing point would be. There are two robots executing "pass-and-shot" task and the other robots supporting them [10]. We learned the strategy from the formation in traditional human soccer like "4-3-3 formation" and coordination via zones [11]. Since each team consists of at most 8 robots in division A in 2019 season [4], a similar way is dividing the front field into four zones and placing at most one robot in every part (Fig. 7). These zones will dynamically change according to the position of the ball (Fig. 8) to improve the rate of robot receiving the ball in it. Furthermore, we rasterize each zone with a fixed length (e.g. 0.1 m) and evaluate each vertex of the small grids with our value-based criteria (to be described next). Then in each zone, we can obtain the best running point x_R in a similar way described in Sect. 4.4.

There are two special cases. First, we can't guarantee that there are always 8 robots for us on the field for yellow card and mechanical failure, which means at this time we can't fill up each zone. Considering points in the zone III and IV have more aggressiveness than those in the zone I and II, at this time we prefer the best point in the zone III and IV. Secondly, the best passing point may be located in one of these zones. While trying to approach such a point, the robot may be possibly interrupted by the robot in this zone, so at this time, we will avoid choosing this zone.

Fig. 7. Four zones divided by front field

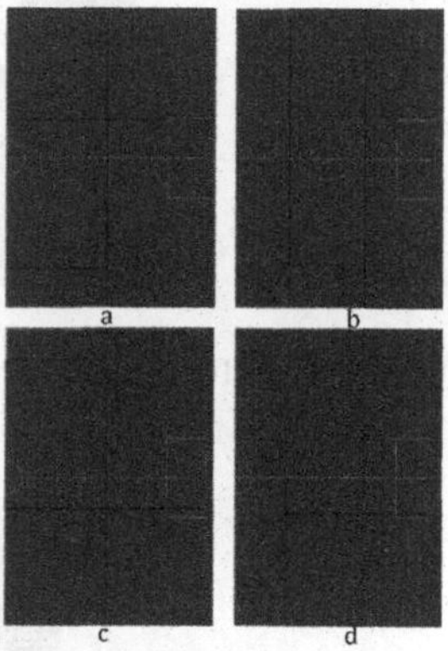

Fig. 8. Dynamically changed zoneaccording to the position of the ball

5.2 Value-Based Running Point Criteria

We adopt the similar approaches described in Sect. 4.3 to evaluate and choose the best running point. There are five evaluation criteria $x_i(i = 1, 2, ..., n)$ as follows. Figure 9 shows how they work in common cases in order and with their weights $\omega_i(i = 1, 2, ..., n)$ we can get the final result by Eq. 3 showed in f of Fig. 9 (red area means higher score while blue area means lower score).

- **Distance to the opponent's goal.** It is obvious that the closer robots are to the opponent's goal, the more likely robots are to score.
- **Distance to the ball.** We find that when robots are too close to the ball, it is difficult to pass or break through opponent's defense.
- **Angle to the opponent's goal.** It doesn't mean robot have the greater chance when facing the goal at 0°, instantly in some certain angle range.
- **Opponent's guard time.** Guard plays an important role in the SSL game that preventing opponents from scoring around the penalty area, and each team have at least one guard on the field. Connect the point to be evaluated to the sides of the opponent's goal, and hand defense area to P and Q (according to Fig. 10). Then we predict the total time opponent's guard(s) spend arriving P and Q. The point score is proportional to this time.

– **Avoid the opponent's defense.** When our robot is further away from the
ball than the opponent's robot, we can conclude that the opponent's robot
will approach the ball before ours, and therefore we should prevent our robots
being involved in this situation.

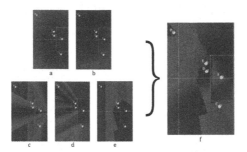

Fig. 9. How individual evaluation criterion affects the overall (Color figure online)

Fig. 10. Method to get location P and Q

5.3 Drag Skill

There is a common case that when our robot arrives at its destination and stops,
it is easy to be marked by the opponent's robot in the following time. We can
call this opponent's robot "defender". To solve this problem, we developed a new
"Drag" skill. First of all, the robot will judge if being marked, with the reversed
strategy in [3]. Assume that the coordinates of our robot, defender and the ball
are (x_{me}, y_{me}), $(x_{defender}, y_{defender})$ and (x_{ball}, y_{ball}). According to the coordinate information and Eq. (4) we can solve out the geometric relationship among
our robot, defender and the ball, while they are clockwise with $Judge > 0$ and
counterclockwise with $Judge < 0$. Then our robot will accelerate in the direction
that is perpendicular to its connection to the ball. At this time, the defender will
speed up together with our robot. Once the defender's speed is greater than a

certain value v_{min}, our robot will accelerate in the opposite direction. Thus there will be a huge speed difference between our robot and defender, which helps our robot distance defender and receive the ball safely.

The application of this skill allows our robots to move off the opponent's defense without losing its purpose, thus greatly improves our ball possession rate.

$$Judge = (x_{ball} - x_{me})(y_{defender} - y_{me}) - (x_{defender} - x_{me})(y_{ball} - y_{me}) \quad (4)$$

6   Result

Our newly developed algorithms give us a huge advantage in the game. We won the championship with a record of six wins and one draw. Table 1 shows the offensive statistics during each game extracted from the official log.

Table 1. Statistics for each ZJUNlict game in RoboCup 2019. The possession rate of Game UR1 is not included in the calculation due to the radio communication interference.

Game	Possession rate (%)	Goals by regular gameplay	Goals by free kick	Goals by penalty kick	Total goals
RR1	66.4	2	2	0	4
RR2	71.6	3	2	1	6
RR3	65.9	0	0	0	0
UR1	–	2	1	1	4
UR2	68.2	1	0	1	2
UF	69.2	1	1	0	2
GF	71.4	1	0	0	1
Total	–	10	6	3	19
Average	68.8	1.4	0.9	0.4	2.7

6.1   Passing and Shooting Strategy Performance

Our passing and shooting strategy has greatly improved our offensive efficiency resulting in 1.4 goals of regular gameplay per game. 52.6% of the goals were scored from the regular gameplay. Furthermore, Our algorithms helped us achieve a 68.8% possession rate per game.

6.2   Free-Kick Performance

According to the game statistics, we scored an average of 0.9 goals of free-kick per game in seven games, while 0.4 goals for other teams in nineteen games. And goals we scored by free kick occupied 32% of total goals (6 in 19), while 10% for other teams (8 in 78). These statistics show we have the ability to adapt to new rules faster than other teams, and we have various approaches to score.

7 Conclusion

In this paper, we have presented our main improvements on both hardware and software which played a key role in winning the championship. Our future work is to predict our opponent's actions on the field and adjust our strategy automatically. Improving our motion control to make our robots move faster, more stably and more accurately is also the main target next year.

References

1. Ommer, N., Ryll, A., Geiger, M.: TIGERs Mannheim extended team description for RoboCup 2019. In: RoboCup Wiki as Extended Team Description of TIGERs Mannheim Team, Leipzig, Germany (2019). Accessed 5 Apr 2019
2. Huang, Z., et al.: ZJUNlict: RoboCup SSL 2018 champion team paper. In: RoboCup 2018 Small Size League Champion. Robot Soccer World Cup. Springer, Heidelberg (2018)
3. Huang, Z., et al.: ZJUNlict extended team description paper for RoboCup 2019. In: RoboCup Wiki as Extended Team Description of ZJUNlict, Sydney, Australia (2019). Accessed 6 Mar 2019
4. Technical and Organizing Committee: Rules of the RoboCup Small Size League 2019. RoboCup Soccer SSL Official Web (2019). https://robocup-ssl.github.io/ssl-rules/sslrules.html. Accessed 26 June 2019
5. Sanders, J., Kandrot, E.: CUDA by Example: An Introduction to General-Purpose GPU Programming. Addison-Wesley Professional, Boston (2010). pp. 41–114
6. Harris, M.: Optimizing parallel reduction in CUDA. Nvidia Dev. Technol. **2**(4), 70 (2007)
7. Garland, M., et al.: Parallel computing experiences with CUDA. IEEE Micro **28**(4), 13–27 (2008)
8. Gyarmati, L., Anguera, X.: Automatic extraction of the passing strategies of soccer teams. arXiv preprint arXiv:1508.02171 (2015)
9. Marin, G., Guillermo, J., Arteche, M.M.: Robot soccer strategy based on hierarchical finite state machine to centralized architectures. IEEE Lat. Am. Trans. **14**(8), 3586–3596 (2016)
10. Phillips, M., Veloso, M.: Robust supporting role in coordinated two-robot soccer attack. In: Iocchi, L., Matsubara, H., Weitzenfeld, A., Zhou, C. (eds.) RoboCup 2008. LNCS (LNAI), vol. 5399, pp. 235–246. Springer, Heidelberg (2009). https://doi.org/10.1007/978-3-642-02921-9_21
11. Mendoza, J.P., et al.: Selectively reactive coordination for a team of robot soccer champions. In: Proceedings of AAAI 2016, the Thirtieth AAAI Conference on Artificial Intelligence, Phoenix, pp. 3354–3360 (2016)

Rhoban Football Club: RoboCup Humanoid KidSize 2019 Champion Team Paper

Loïc Gondry, Ludovic Hofer, Patxi Laborde-Zubieta[✉], Olivier Ly,
Lucie Mathé, Grégoire Passault, Antoine Pirrone, and Antun Skuric

Rhoban Football Club Team, LaBRI, University of Bordeaux, Bordeaux, France
team@rhoban.com, lucie.mathe@etu.u-bordeaux.fr,
{patxi.laborde-zubieta,gregoire.passault}@u-bordeaux.fr

Abstract. In 2019, Rhoban Football Club reached the first place of the KidSize soccer competition for the fourth time and performed the first in-game throw-in in the history of the Humanoid league. Building on our existing code-base, we improved some specific functionalities, introduced new behaviors and experimented with original methods for labeling videos. This paper presents and reviews our latest changes to both software and hardware, highlighting the lessons learned during RoboCup.

1 Introduction

This article presents some of the elements which led to the fourth consecutive victory of our team in the RoboCup KidSize Humanoid league. We also obtained the first place in the drop-in tournament for the third time in a row and the first place at the technical challenges competition for the first time. Our robots scored 30 goals, received 11 goals and performed the first in-game throw-in in the history of the Humanoid league.

This year we mainly pursued three objectives: moving toward more dynamic gameplay, improving our performance at the technical challenge competition and reducing the complexity of our code base which has grown each year since we first participated in 2011. While introducing several new functionalities, we still managed to reduce the total number of lines of code used for the competition from 196,000 to 163,000. All the code and configuration file we used during the competition are available[1] along with some documentation.

The structure of the paper is as follows: Sect. 2 introduces the tools used to model our robot, recent hardware changes are presented in Sect. 3, new motions and improvements are detailed in Sect. 4, our ongoing work regarding perception and data acquisition is described in Sect. 5 and finally the dynamical aspect of our strategy is presented in Sect. 6.

---

[1] https://www.github.com/Rhoban/workspace/releases/tag/public_2019.

© Springer Nature Switzerland AG 2019
S. Chalup et al. (Eds.): RoboCup 2019, LNAI 11531, pp. 491–503, 2019.
https://doi.org/10.1007/978-3-030-35699-6_40

2 Model

The 3D model of the robots used during Robocup 2019 can be accessed[2] in the online CAD software *OnShape*[3].

2.1 CAD to Standard Model (URDF/SDF)

Several CAD tools are commonly used to design robotics parts[4], mostly based on constraints geometry design. On the other hand, standard robot description format emerged, notably URDF and SDF[5], driven by the ROS community [8]. They are XML files describing the robot architecture, including transformation matrices, information about dynamics (mass, center of mass, inertia), collisions and visualisation geometry. In order to manufacture them, we used to design our robot with such CAD tools. But even if the model carried all the information needed for the standard robot description, the description was produced with separate tools. As a result, we could not ensure the consistency between the CAD and the description model. For that reason, we switched to *OnShape*, an emerging CAD software that includes an API allowing to request information about the 3D model. It allowed us to develop *onshape-to-robot*[6], a tool that seamlessly produces an URDF from a CAD model that can be used without any change for all our applications.

2.2 Using Model in Online Code

In order to compute frame transformations online using the robot, we developed a library on top of *RBDL* [3] to load the *URDF* and request it. *onshape-to-robot* allows you to attach manually frames in your model, directly in the CAD design-time, that appear in the final robot description and allow you to compute transformation matrices using the DOFs of your robot.

2.3 Physics Simulation

The robot description model that is produced this way can also be used for physics simulation, like *Bullet*[7]. However, simulating the collisions of the actual parts is computationally expensive, first because the exported parts are represented by unstructured triangular surfaces, but also because of all the small details (like screw holes) which are not relevant for our use case.

To tackle this issue, we introduced a semi-automatic system that allows to approximate those complex 3D shapes with pure geometry: union of cubes,

---

[2] https://cad.onshape.com/documents/f3bdef32bffd81536fce83d1/v/779c691df8f135b ba01eead1/e/a530b1889ee09acb5e1d7ff9.

[3] https://www.onshape.com/.

[4] Famous examples are *Dassault Solidworks*, *Autodesk Inventor* and *Catia*.

[5] http://sdformat.org/spec.

[6] https://github.com/rhoban/onshape-to-robot/.

[7] https://github.com/bulletphysics/bullet3.

spheres and cylinders (Fig. 1). This also allows to ignore some small parts that are not useful in the collision world. We are then able to simulate a physics model of our robot (Fig. 2). Even if the discrepancy between simulation and real world is high, motions like walking, kicking and standing up can be reproduced, allowing to do some motor test before porting it to the real robot.

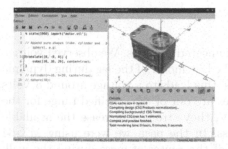

Fig. 1. Semi-automatic system to approximate 3D model with shape representation.

Fig. 2. Sigmaban approximated with 3D shapes in PyBullet physics simulator.

3   Hardware

We made only few changes on the hardware. We added some piano wire arcs to protect from falls, we switched to a four cells battery and we changed the shape of the feet and the hands. The last two improvements are described in Sect. 4.

3.1   Protections

One of the challenges in our league is that robots should be able to withstand falls. For example, our robots can fall up to 20 times during a game. It regularly resulted in the breaking of a motor of the neck. After several attempts, it was clear to us that a software safety on its own was not enough. Hence, to absorb a part of the impact we added 3 mm thick piano wire arcs at the front and at the back of the robot. By doing so, in 2018 and 2019 we had a significant decrease in the number of broken motors in the neck. But it is still not reliable enough as the many shoulder motors that we broke can tell.

To improve the protection of our robots, we would like to try other materials such as spring steel strips, which are less likely to bend perpendicularly to the impact, or dense foam. In order to assess rigorously the effectiveness of different solutions, the impacts when falling should be measured. For example, using motion capture or force platforms. Another way to protect the motors is to use clutches, but for the moment we did not find any solution fulfilling the requirements in term of weight and space used.

As mentioned during the second edition of the workshop "Humanoid Robot Falling: Fall Detection, Damage Prevention and Recovery Actions"[8], this problem is a research topic of growing importance. And the robots of the KidSize league happens to be an interesting benchmarking environment for this subject: solutions can be tested under realistic conditions during matches and it is much easier to safely experiment with smaller humanoid robots.

3.2 Battery

In our design, the 6 motors of a leg are connected in series. We observed voltage drop up to 4 volts between the first and the last motor of the leg during dynamic motions. When using three cells batteries, this leads to a voltage around 8 Volts in the ankle. While the four cells batteries are out of the specified range for the dynamixel motors since they deliver 16 V, they strongly increase the available torque and reduces the ohmic power loss. In the past, we were using MX-64 motors in the legs and a lower position of the center of mass during the walk motion, this led to frequent overheating when using four cells batteries. Now that we have MX-106 motors and a smoother walking engine, we can safely use four cells batteries without risking overheating. Increasing the voltage was one of the key elements to obtain a more powerful kick. When the ball was properly positioned, our robot managed to kick more than seven meters.

4 Motions

4.1 New Walk Engine

We designed a new walk engine, still based on single support, with the goal of reducing the complexity of the former one that included too many unused parameters, making it less maintainable. We now use cubic splines to represent the trajectories of the feet (see Fig. 3). They allow us to control both position and speed at specific knots. Trajectories are updated only at each support foot swap and described in the trunk frame.

We wanted the foot to reach its nominal speed before touching the ground and to decelerate after leaving the ground. This way, the foot in contact with the ground would have a constant speed which should lead to a steady and continuous speed of the trunk. However, the robot is performing much better when the foot touches and leaves the ground with vanishing speed. One hypothesis is that it is better to touch the ground with no speed for stability reasons. Moreover, the exact time when the foot touches the ground can vary from one step to one another.

The walk engine code can be found on our open source repository under `Motion/engines/` directory.

---

[8] https://iros2018wsfallingrobots.wordpress.com/.

Fig. 3. Trajectory of the feet during walk engine (physics simulation).

Fig. 4. Differents steps of the Throw-in.

4.2 Throw-In

This year, the throw-in rule has been introduced. While it is currently allowed for robots to perform it by kicking, we decided to move directly to human-like throw-in performed with the hands. The motion for the throw-in is created the same way as other kicks: we define splines associating time points with angular targets for the motors. The target between specified time points is obtained through linear interpolation.

We designed the throw-in motion using splines with several keypoints, see Fig. 4: initialization, bending the knees, unfolding the arms, leaning forward, holding the ball, straightening, lifting the arms and unfolding the knees, moving the arms behind the head, throwing the ball and back at initialization.

While simulation using *PyBullet* was not accurate, it allowed to design a coarse approximation of the motion before fine tuning the targets on the robot.

One of the main challenge to design the throw-in was to handle the fact that our arms have only three degrees of freedom. While the mechanical design is entirely sufficient for standing-up, it does not allow to control the distance between the hands when the elbow are bent. Therefore, amplitude of the motion on the elbow was limited in order to maintain grasp on the ball.

In order to lift the ball more easily, we designed new hands for the robot, see Fig. 5. The main idea was to create two metal plates in each side of the elbow motor and join them with spacer screws. On one side, the plate has a notch for the motor and, on the other side, there is large hole to surround the ball.

Fig. 5. Assembly of one hand of the robot in *OnShape*.

While designing the motion, we managed to have the ball bouncing and rolling up to 4.5 m. Since the field is only 6 m wide, we had to slow down the speed during the throw-in phase in order to have a more appropriate length for passes.

Next year, we plan to improve the throw-in so that the robot can adapt the direction by changing the orientation of the torso while the ball is in the air.

4.3   High Kick

One of the key aspect to lift the ball while kicking is the point in contact with the ball at impact. We refer to this part by the name of *kicker*. Previously, we used a *kicker* designed to give a rotational impulsion to ball so that it could roll on the grass. This year, in order to perform in the High Kick technical challenge, we designed new *kickers*.

To lift the ball, the contact point at impact has to be below the center of mass of the ball. Since we use high studs to stabilize on artificial grass and the ball has a radius of only 7.5 cm, the margin for the motion is relatively small. We decided to separate the new *kicker* in two different parts: the first one is thin and raises the ball which rolls over it, the second one hits the ball after it has left the ground making it easier to hit below the center of gravity.

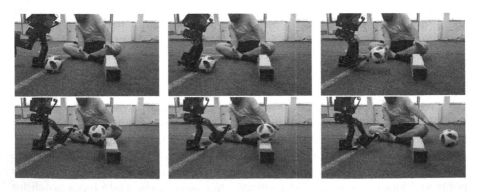

Fig. 6. Differents steps of the High kick.

This new kicker allowed us to outperform the other teams during the technical challenge, our robot scored over a bar of 20 cm, while the second best performance in our league was achieved by the CIT Brains who kicked the ball above 12 cm. Figure 6 shows the steps of this motion. An interesting fact about this high kick is that one of our robot did kick above another fallen robot during the quarter finals. Although not intentional, this kick is definitely a step toward the use of a third dimension in the RoboCup Humanoid league.

5   Perception and Localisation

This year, we aimed high regarding the modifications of our perception and localisation modules. Unfortunately, our system for labeling videos still lacked some robustness and the training procedure for our neural networks included a few bugs which impacted negatively its results during the competition. This sections presents our promising development of these modules along with preliminary conclusions based on their use during RoboCup 2019.

5.1   Labeling Videos

Most of the teams in the RoboCup Humanoid league now uses neural network to detect or classify features in their perception module. In order for the module to work on-site, it is generally required to manually label large datasets of images acquired on-site. The labeling of images requires a significant amount of human time and adding new features to detect for the robots increases the time spent labeling. We also previously used manual tagging, with the help of a collaborative on-line tool we developed for that purpose[9].

This year, we decided to take a paradigm shift, moving from labeling images to labeling videos. The main idea is quite simple, if we can retrieve the pose and orientation of the robots camera inside the field referential for each frame, then the position of field landmarks inside images can easily be obtained. Moreover, by synchronizing the video streams from multiple robots, it is possible to share annotations among them.

Accurate estimation of the orientation of the cameras is a difficult problem, in order to tackle it, we experimented two different methods: using ViveTrackers on the head of the robots and combining manual labeling with odometry. Both methods share similar issues regarding time synchronization between devices and its impact on orientation estimation. We used two complementary schemes to reduce the uncertainty on camera orientation.

---

[9] https://github.com/rhoban/tagger.

1. We used specific tool (`chrony`[10]) to synchronize all the information streams.
2. The impact of timing differences is mitigated using the following acquisition method for videos. Robots alternate between two different phases: walking to a randomly generated location and slowly scanning the environment while standing still. During extraction of labels, only the images obtained during the scanning phase are considered. This proved to be necessary because the head of the robot is shaking when the robot is walking, thus increasing the uncertainty on the orientation of the camera.

Access to the fields for data acquisition is a scarce ressource during the setup days. In order to optimize the usage of the time we were given, we created a specific training scenario in which the field is separated in as many zones as the number of robots used for acquisition.

– A zone is allocated to each robot.
– During 2 min, each robot alternates between moving to a random location inside its zone and scanning its environment.
– Zones are separated by a safety buffer of around 50 cm to reduce the risk of collision between robots.
– During the training, perception is disabled and robot relies solely on odometry to estimate its position.

Automatically Through Vive. *Vive* is an indoor tracking system developed by *HTC*. It is based on active laser emitters base stations called *Lighthouses* that sends laser sweeps on a known frequency. Infrared receivers are used and the time when they are hit by the sweeps of lighthouses is used to compute the position of the object they are attached to. There are two generation of the lighthouses. The first generation only works by pairs and covers a maximal tracking area of 5 m × 5 m. With the second version, the area can be increased up to 10 m × 10 m by using four lighthouses. Initially designed to track *Vive* controllers and helmets for virtual reality application, it is now also possible to buy simple trackers that you can attach to anything to track its position.

This makes ground truth possible with attaching a *Vive* tracker to the head of the robot, and capture some logs. The only thing that is required is then the transformation from the tracker frame to the camera frame, and the ability to project a known object 3D position onto image.

Vive trackers and lighthouses are easy to carry and deploy. Moreover, the calibration phase before being able to track objects is fast. This makes it a better choice than motion capture for on-site calibration, while being more affordable and with a wider working area. We used it during the *German Open 2019 Humanoid KidSize* competition to generate automatically labelled images.

A calibration phase is still needed to find the 3D transformation from the lighthouses to the field frame, and also to tag the balls position on the field every time we move them. To achieve that conveniently, we use a *Vive* controller which

---

[10] https://chrony.tuxfamily.org/.

is itself tracked and equipped with trigger button to mark some known position on the field and find the optimal 3D transformations, or show the balls position at the beginning of a log. We developed a custom tool to do that[11] on the top of OpenVR SDK[12].

Even if most of the data obtained this way was suitable for training our neural networks, the accuracy of such technology can be discussed [6]. In order to have a better control on the calibration and the data fusion algorithm used to compute the position using the IMU and light beam datas, the authors of LibSurvive[13] reverse engineered *Vive*. Having access to the low level data allowed better positioning results [2]. The support for the second lighthouse generation is currently being completed.

One of the drawbacks intrinsic to this method is that it cannot be used during real games.

Combining Labeling and Odometry. Finding a camera pose from 3D-2D correspondances is a well-known problem [5], by labeling the position of key-points of the field in an image, it is relatively easy to retrieve an accurate estimation of the pose of the camera which took the image. However, it is not realistic to apply this method for every image of a video for two majors reasons: this would require large amount of human-time to label a video and some frames do not even contain keypoints from the field.

Using odometry to extrapolate the pose of the camera before and after a labeled frame helps to strongly reduce the labeling burden. Experimentally, we noticed that labeling around 10 frames for a 2 min session containing more than 1500 usable frames hold satisfying results.

Currently, the major flaw of this method is that it requires the robots to stop walking and reduce the scanning speed in order to improve the pose estimation. Those conditions are rarely met during real games, making it difficult to extract data from real games, a crucial point to enhance opponent detection. In the future, we hope to take leverage on visual-inertial odometry methods [4] to enhance the accuracy of pose estimation in more dynamic situations. This would allow to easily label videos of entire games quickly, thus tackling the problem of building large datasets for neural network training.

5.2   Multi-class ROI and Classification

Last year, our perception system was mainly based on three specific pipelines, one for detecting the ball, a second one detecting the base of the goal posts and a third one to detect the corner of the arena field. The two first systems were roughly similar, but each system had its own neural network and some specificities to identify region of interests [7]. In order to make the perception system simpler while covering more type of features, we decided to use a single system to

---

[11] https://github.com/Rhoban/vive_provider.
[12] https://github.com/ValveSoftware/openvr.
[13] https://github.com/cnlohr/libsurvive.

identify the region of interests and classify the type of feature. While less accurate for centering the features in the region of interests, it allows to incorporate additional features such as line intersections or opponents more easily.

While this new system yielded promising results during the preparation of the RoboCup, we struggled to obtain decent results on-site and were forced to limit the perception to two different type of features: balls and base of goal posts. We initially thought that the main problem was the fact that the posts were thinner than the posts we used in our laboratory. However, after RoboCup, we ran a thorough code review and found 3 major bugs between the training process of the neural networks and the online prediction of the class. Once we solved them, we were able to include more classes while having an accuracy rate much higher than what we had during RoboCup. Due to these bugs, it is not possible to provide meaningful results for the code we used during RoboCup. However, the final results promise a strongly improved perception system for next year.

5.3 Localisation

We use a three-dimensional particle filter for localization which includes the position and the orientation of the robot on the field. It fuses information from both: the perception module and the odometry. Due to the major issues in perception at the beginning of the competition, we decided to strongly reduce the exploration for the first games. Increasing the confidence in the odometry allowed us to stay into the competition until we improved the perception part.

The position and the orientation of the robot used to be defined respectively as the average of the positions and the orientations of the particles. The major change we introduced this year was to fit a Gaussian mixture model on the set of particles by using the Expectation-Maximization [1] algorithm. It finds iteratively the partition in k disjoint subsets that maximizes the likelihood of the corresponding Gaussian mixture model. The choice of the k is done online as follows. Let $C_k = \{c_1, \ldots, c_k\}$ be the clustering into k disjoint subsets obtained by the Expectation-Maximization algorithm. Let $|c|$ and $\mathrm{Var_P}(c)$ denote respectively the number of particles and the variance of the particles positions. Finally, we define respectively the internal variances of position and orientation of C_k as

$$\mathrm{Var_P}(C_k) = \frac{\sum_{i=0}^{k} \mathrm{Var_P}(c_i) * |c_i|}{\sum_{i=0}^{k} |c_i|}.$$

Starting from $k = 1$, the number of clusters is increased until we reach $k = 5$ or $\mathrm{Var_P}(C_k) \geq 0.5\mathrm{Var_P}(C_{k+1})$. This ensures that adding a cluster is only done if it provides a major reduction of the variance. When several clusters are considered, only the most populated one is considered for high-level decisions.

The proposed method provides two main benefits with respect to the simple solution of taking the average of all particles. First, it allows to obtain meaningful orientation while the particle filter has not converged. This situations frequently occurs when a robot comes back from penalty from the side line. During games,

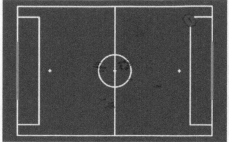 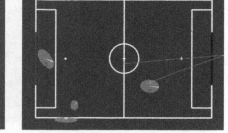

(a) Filtering of scattered particles: particles in blue, best cluster mean in red.

(b) Monitoring on field entry: Robot 1 enters the field from the side line.

Fig. 7. In-game examples of localization.

it allows to discard scattered particles which will be automatically attributed to a cluster containing the noise, see Fig. 7a. Second, representation of localization belief under the form of multiple clusters allows to store or broadcast the information at a much lower cost than sending the position of all the particles. Therefore, this method enables real-time monitoring under low bandwidth conditions, see Fig. 7b.

6 Strategy

In 2017, we introduced an off-line value iteration process to compute a kick policy that chooses a type of kick as well as the orientation aiming to optimize the time to score a goal with one robot on an empty field [7]. The reward function used for the optimization is simply the time needed for the robot to reach the next ball position, a penalty if the ball is kicked out of field and 0 if a goal is scored. This process produces a value function V that gives us an estimation of the time it takes to score a goal from a given position on the field.

This year, we also used an online value iteration that performs an optimization at depth one to include the current state of the game. It can roughly be described as follows. The discrete set of ball positions on the field is called S. An action is a type of kick together with a discrete orientation. We denote A the set of possible actions. Let $P_a(s, s')$ denotes the probability of reaching state s' from state s after performing action a kick with orientation a. The knowledge of the game is introduced with a reward function $r(s, s)$ described thereafter. The online policy is given by the formula

$$\arg \max_{a \in A} \sum_{s' \in S} P_a(s, s')(r(s, s') + V(s')).$$

To compute the reward r, we check if we are in a state where it is not allowed to score a goal. For example in the case of a throw-in, an indirect penalty kick or when we have the kick-off and the ball is still not in play (exited the center

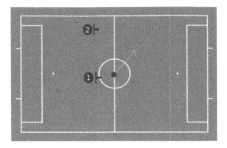

Fig. 8. An example situation using on-line Monte Carlo.

circle). In this case, a penalty score is given if a goal is scored. In that case, the robot will naturally kick the ball so that it does not score a goal, but placing it in the best situation possible to score a goal on the next kick. The reward $r(s, s')$ also includes the time for the closest robot to reach s' from which we subtract the time for the kicking robot to reach s'. Finally, we give penalties to kicks towards opponent robots if we have their location. As an example, in the situation of Fig. 8, the robot 1 is going for the ball, because he is the closest to it. He is not allowed to score a goal, because of the kick-off conditions. Hence, a short kick action getting the ball out of the center circle is preferred by the on-line iteration instead of a powerful kick that would certainly score. If the robot was alone on the field, the optimal orientation would be straight forward. However, the iteration produces this left oriented kick, because by the time we estimate the kick is done, the robot 2 will be properly positioned to handle the ball and score a goal faster than if robot 1 would have kicked straight.

References

1. Bilmes, J.A.: A gentle tutorial of the EM algorithm and its application to parameter estimation for Gaussian mixture and Hidden Markov models. International Computer Science Institute (1998). https://doi.org/10.1.1.119.4856
2. Borges, M., Symington, A., Coltin, B., Smith, T., Ventura, R.: HTC Vive: analysis and accuracy improvement. In: 2018 IEEE/RSJ International Conference on Intelligent Robots and Systems (IROS), pp. 2610–2615. IEEE (2018)
3. Felis, M.L.: RBDL: an efficient rigid-body dynamics library using recursive algorithms. Auton. Robots **41**(2), 495–511 (2017)
4. Gui, J., Gu, D., Wang, S., Hu, H.: A review of visual inertial odometry from filtering and optimisation perspectives. Adv. Robot. (2015). https://doi.org/10.1080/01691864.2015.1057616
5. Lepetit, V., Moreno-Noguer, F., Fua, P.: EPnP: an accurate O(n) solution to the PnP problem. Int. J. Comput. Vis. (2009). https://doi.org/10.1007/s11263-008-0152-6
6. Niehorster, D.C., Li, L., Lappe, M.: The accuracy and precision of position and orientation tracking in the HTC Vive virtual reality system for scientific research. i-Perception **8**(3) (2017). https://doi.org/10.1177/2041669517708205

7. Allali, J., et al.: Rhoban football club: RoboCup humanoid kid-size 2017 champion team paper. In: Akiyama, H., Obst, O., Sammut, C., Tonidandel, F. (eds.) RoboCup 2017. LNCS (LNAI), vol. 11175, pp. 423–434. Springer, Cham (2018). https://doi.org/10.1007/978-3-030-00308-1_35
8. Quigley, M., et al.: ROS: an open-source robot operating system. In: ICRA Workshop on Open Source Software, vol. 3, Kobe, Japan, p. 5 (2009)

Winning the RoboCup Logistics League with Fast Navigation, Precise Manipulation, and Robust Goal Reasoning

Till Hofmann[1]([⊠]), Nicolas Limpert[2], Victor Mataré[2], Alexander Ferrein[2], and Gerhard Lakemeyer[1]

[1] Knowledge-Based Systems Group, RWTH Aachen University, Aachen, Germany
{hofmann,gerhard}@kbsg.rwth-aachen.de
[2] MASCOR Institute, FH Aachen University of Applied Sciences, Aachen, Germany
{limpert,matare,ferrein}@fh-aachen.de

Abstract. The RoboCup Logistics League is a robotics competition in a Smart Factory scenario in which a team of robots has to assemble products for dynamically generated orders. In 2019, the Carologistics was able to win the competition with a redesigned manipulation system, improved navigation, and an incremental and distributed goal reasoning system. In this paper, we describe the major components of our approach that enabled us to win the competition, with a particular focus on this year's changes.

1 Introduction

The Carologistics RoboCup Team[1] is a cooperation of the Knowledge-Based Systems Group (RWTH Aachen University) and the MASCOR Institute (FH Aachen University of Applied Sciences), which was initiated in 2012. Doctoral, master's, and bachelor' students of both partners participate in the project and bring in their specific strengths to tackle the various aspects of the RoboCup Logistics League.

In the RoboCup Logistics League (RCLL), the goal is to maintain and optimize the material flow in a simplified Smart Factory scenario. Two competing teams of three robots each need to fulfill dynamically generated orders by assembling workpieces to products of varying complexities, ordered from C0 to C3. To assemble such products, the robots operate and transport workpieces between Modular Production System stations (MPSs). Each team has an exclusive set of seven machines of five different types, where each type of machine is capable to perform a different step of the production. The major challenges of the RCLL include navigation, perception and manipulation, as well as reasoning tasks such as planning, plan execution, and execution monitoring.

---

[1] https://carologistics.org/.

© Springer Nature Switzerland AG 2019
S. Chalup et al. (Eds.): RoboCup 2019, LNAI 11531, pp. 504–516, 2019.
https://doi.org/10.1007/978-3-030-35699-6_41

In the following, we describe our approach to the RCLL with a particular focus on the components that led to the success in 2019. To foster the development of the league, we have publicly released our software stack used in 2019[2]. We begin with the software architecture and major building blocks in Sect. 2 and summarize our development workflow in Sect. 3, which provided the means to effectively coordinate a team of ten developers in a competition environment. In Sect. 4, we describe our redesigned gripper system that allows precise grasping, and we summarize a multi-stage procedure using data from a laser range finder and an RGB/D camera to quickly and precisely align to a machine. We continue with improvements to path planning in Sect. 5, which enabled our robots to move across the playing field more quickly, a crucial aspect of a competitive production. In Sect. 6, we summarize our approach to high-level decision making using a goal reasoning approach with an incremental and distributed multi-agent strategy that is capable of an efficient production flow while reacting quickly to unexpected events, before we conclude in Sect. 7.

2   Architecture and Middleware

The software system of the Carologistics robots combines two different middlewares, Fawkes [13] and ROS [20]. This allows us to use software components from both systems. The overall system, however, is integrated using Fawkes. Adapter plugins connect the systems, for example to use ROS' 3D visualization capabilities.

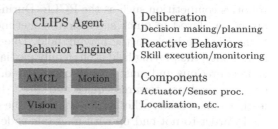

Fig. 1. Behavior layer separation [17]

In addition, using ROS within Fawkes allows to benefit from well-tested software solutions that solve lower level problems taking important roles in the RCLL such as navigation or several debugging functionalities including ROS-Bag to record the behavior and sensory of a robot and allow analyzation of the robots behavior. The overall software structure is inspired by the three-layer architecture paradigm [6]. As shown in Fig. 1, it consists of a deliberative layer for high-level reasoning, a reactive execution layer for breaking down high-level commands and monitoring their execution, and a feedback control layer for hardware access and functional components. The changes to the manipulation workflow, described in Sect. 4 give an insight on these aspects. The topmost layer is detailed in Sect. 6. The communication between single components – implemented as *plugins* – is realized by a hybrid blackboard and messaging approach [13].

---

[2] https://fawkesrobotics.org/p/rcll2019-release/.

2.1   Lua-Based Behavior Engine

In previous work we have developed the Lua-Based Behavior Engine (BE) [14]. It serves as the reactive layer to interface between the low- and high-level systems. The BE is based on hybrid state machines (HSM). They can be depicted as a directed graph with nodes representing states for action execution, and/or monitoring of actuation, perception, and internal state. Edges denote jump conditions implemented as Boolean functions. If a condition fires, the active state is changed to the target node of the edge. A table of variables holds information like the world model, for example storing numeric values for object positions. It remedies typical problems of state machines like fast growing number of states or variable data passing from one state to another. Behaviors, so-called *skills*, are implemented using the light-weight, extensible scripting language Lua.

3   Development Workflow

Over the years, it has become increasingly apparent that a healthy development workflow is an often underrated factor that can make or break a fast-paced robotics competition such as the RCLL. During an RCLL competition, matches are often played in quick succession, sometimes with only 1-h breaks before a team must be back on the playing field. Due to its relative expensiveness and complexity, the playing field is often only partially available for testing, so testing time is precious and must be well-coordinated. The short development windows create a tendency towards "quick-and-dirty" fixes, and the scarce testing often leads to uncertainty whether a feature can be considered stable or not.

In order to not end up with unusable code after a competition, these issues must be actively managed. During a typical, busy RCLL competition, there can easily be 50 or more feature branches in concurrent development. Here, it is most important to strictly separate branches that are supposed to become a stable feature (i.e. be merged back into the `master` branch) from location-specific tuning and dirty hacks. Although deployment to the robots is (aside from the merge conflicts) a straightforward task of simply merging all desired (stable or experimental) feature branches into a temporary (so-called `current`) branch, the job of feeding things back into the `master` remains important for a different reason: Since the `master` branch is the preferred starting point for all feature branches, it cannot fall too far back behind the on-going development. If some feature A is not in the `master`, any branch B that patches it has to be started from branch A, which should be avoided since it introduces an additional dependency. Even worse, if some feature C depends on two independent features A and B, at least one of A and B *must* be merged back into the master. Most importantly, branching any features off of the `current` branch is strictly forbidden, as `current`, and therefore anything branching from it, may contain things that turn out to be a bad idea.

To improve our assessment of code quality when merging back into the `master`, in 2019 we introduced continuous integration builds, a review process, as well as syntactic and semantic linter checks. To further improve reproducibility and reliability of our setup, we use Ansible [7] for configuration management. This allows us to quickly set up a robot from scratch and guarantees that all robots are set up with the same configuration. Additionally, we use Ansible to deploy the most recent changes to the robots by updating all repositories on the robot with a single Ansible playbook.

4   Improvements to Manipulation

In an ongoing effort to optimize picking and placing actions in terms of time and reliability, we modified both the gripper's hardware design and the design of the software components. Combining mechanical gripper adaptions for more robustness and reliability with a fast model-based perception to precisely estimate poses of either conveyor belts or the MPS's slides has had a major influence on the success of our system this year. Most of our hardware modifications have been described in our previous team description papers [8–10,19], so here we will focus on new developments only.

4.1   Gripper System

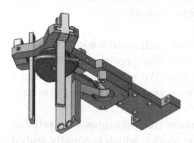

Fig. 2. New gripper with three self-centering fingers.

The Robotino base faces challenges on precise positioning in front of machines. The overall positioning tolerance of roughly ±2 mm on handling products at the MPS' conveyor belts requires precise motion. In 2018 we decided to extend the motion capabilities of the gripper [9] to overcome this issue. We added two axes for precise frontwards and sidewards gripper movement to get a higher placement tolerance of the Robotino base during product placing or picking actions. Previously, we could not align the Robotino with a sufficient precision, as it only allows motions with a certain speed threshold preventing position correction in the sub-centimeter range. The motor controllers have a limited minimal amount of rotations per minute which result in minimum translational velocities of $0.006 \frac{m}{s}$. In practice, the motion reported by the wheels lags behind the frequency of our software framework. In turn, the robot oscillates when the positioning tolerance is set too low. Our current setup sets a minimum translational tolerance of 0.02 m. Additionally, the position estimation reported by the global localization is inaccurate in front of a machine, due to the limited number of laser beams matching global map components and imprecise absolute machine positions. As a result we have to rely on the sensory gathering precise machine and conveyor belt positions (as denoted in the following section).

To overcome issues resulting from mechanical requirements of the gripper itself it has been redesigned in 2019 to grip the workpiece from above with three instead of two fingers, as shown in Fig. 2. The advantage is increased robustness and precision because the workpiece always centers between the three spring-loaded fingers, independently of any positioning error. Another advantage of the new design is that it retracts fully behind the robot's circular base shape, which significantly reduces the risk of damage and simplifies path planning.

4.2   Conveyor Belt Detection

Workpiece manipulation is one of the central challenges of the RCLL. In fact, production and delivery of a mere C0 already involves six pick or place operations. For a C2 with expensive rings, up to 18 manipulation operations are required. A manipulation failure is likely to result in a total loss of the handled product, so a single failure in handling an almost finished C2 will easily cause the loss of an entire game.

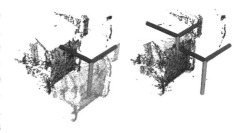

Fig. 3. Left: Model pointcloud (blue) roughly aligned to scene (black) based on initial guess. Right: After running ICP, the model is aligned to the scene precisely [8]. (Color figure online)

Consequentially, reliability is at the top of the priority list for manipulation in the RCLL. Since the conveyor belts are only a few millimeters wider than the workpieces, much of the reliability comes down to the precision of both the manipulator mechanics and the conveyor detection. We chose not to attempt detection of the workpieces themselves, but to concentrate on detecting the conveyor belts as reliably as possible.

The first step in that direction was to replace the notoriously unreliable RealSense F200 3D cameras with the newer SR300 model, which is equally suited for near-field operation with high resolution. It features a much more reliable USB 3.0 implementation and is supported by the redesigned librealsense2[3], which improves both OS support and stability. It is also better at dealing with the dark and reflective surfaces of most of the conveyor assembly, yielding less spotty pointclouds.

For maximum manipulation reliability, we need to determine the 6D pose (translation & rotation) of the conveyor belt. Our detection algorithm works purely on the 3D pointcloud data from the RealSense camera, disregarding any color information. For the RoboCup 2019, we built a multi-modal 3-stage pipeline that incorporates the two previous solutions as the first two stages, which each stage supplying an initial configuration for the next.

The first stage uses the LiDAR sensor mounted in the bottom base of the robot to roughly determine the pose of the MPS box in front of the robot. It uses a RANSAC approach [5] to fit a line parametrization that matches the width of

---

[3] https://github.com/IntelRealSense/librealsense.

the MPS table's flat side panel (error $\simeq$20 mm). The second stage uses the rough MPS pose to run a RANSAC-based plane fitting, this time where the conveyor belt can be expected in the point cloud data from the RealSense 3D camera. This stage reduces the translational error to $\sim$5 mm, supplying a suitable initial estimate for the next stage. The third stage is a highly precise ICP-based model fitting approach [4], as shown in Fig. 3. Its iterative nature makes it much more computationally expensive and sensitive to bad initial estimates, but it turns out to be the most reliable way to further reduce the pose jitter to something below 2 mm.

For the last stage, the quality of the model (i.e. the reference point cloud) that is fitted into the live data is of great importance. It should be sufficiently complex, i.e. it should contain points that describe multiple, non-parallel surfaces so as to be sufficiently defined in the translational component. Symmetries should also be minimal, and it should be sufficiently large in order to achieve high rotational precision.

With these conditions satisfied, and some tuning to compensate mechanical assembly tolerances, we were able to play entire games with no manipulation failures towards the end of the competition.

5 Path Planning

Throughout an entire game, navigation is one of the tasks that takes up most of the time. Changing to ROS Navigation [12] in 2017 has proven to be a flexible and reliable approach well-suited for the difficult navigation tasks in the RCLL. Path planning in such an environment requires a robust but fast navigation solution suitable to provide collision-free navigation with dynamic obstacles. From an agent's perspective it is desired to decrease the average time to reach navigational goals, which mainly depends on the average velocity, but also on path efficiency.

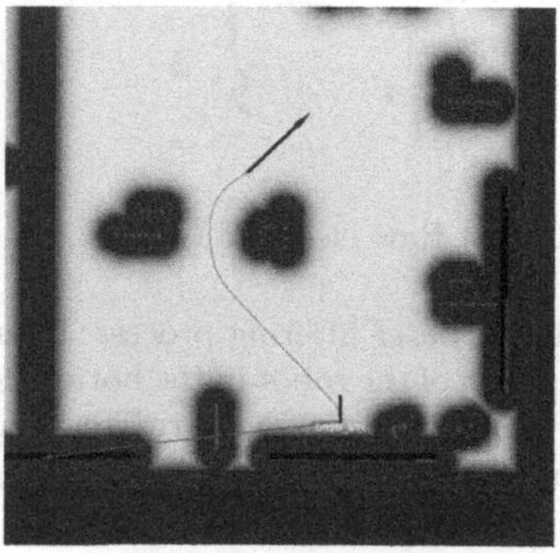

Fig. 4. Path planning in the RCLL. Obstacles are represented in occupancy grids which in turn are used for the path planning environment.

The classic separation between global and local path planning is of major use to quickly react to obstacles crossing the way in a small local frame. Figure 4 depicts an example of a robot navigating in the RCLL. The global path planner does not have to take kinematic constraints into account, as the Robotino base is omni-directional.

Since 2017, we have made use of a local planner based on a timed elastic band approach [22] as a controller running within our setup of ROS Navigation responsible for executing the planned path and optimizing a trajectory based on several properties of the robot base such as acceleration and velocity limits. The major advantage of this planner is its strafing capability. However, due to the kinematic freedom of the platform, we found that the complex workflow of the timed elastic band approach is not needed for us. As such, we implemented our own local planner based on the Vector Field Histogram approach [3], giving us considerably high loop rates of roughly 90 Hz (compared to an average maximum of 10 Hz of the previously used planner) resulting in much lower reaction times on dynamic obstacles, which allows to move closer to obstacles and use narrow passages that otherwise might lead to collisions as the robots do not react in appropriate time. However, we eventually realized that this approach requires a more elaborate solution to be a drop-in replacement for our local planner. The timed-elastic-band–based local planner has built-in features to smoothen translational and angular accelerations given the current obstacles around the robot, the current robot's velocities, the calculated trajectory and the difference between the robot and the absolute goal, which are lacking from the Vector Field Histogram planner. Thus, we decided to keep the previously used setup using the well-tested local planner and instead consider other aspects of navigation that will increase efficiency.

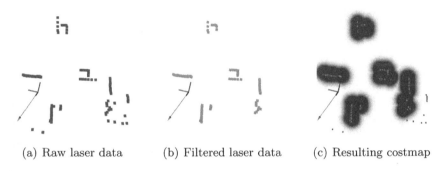

(a) Raw laser data   (b) Filtered laser data   (c) Resulting costmap

Fig. 5. Laser filtering process. Figure 5(a) shows the unfiltered laser readings and the position of the robot in the bottom left. Figure 5(b) depicts the filtered laser. Figure 5(c) is the resulting costmap representing filtered obstacles in an overlay to the filtered and unfiltered laser beams. Note the single laser beams in the bottom left and right corners that are not taken into account.

The planning environment in ROS Navigation is represented with occupancy grids [11]. The local planner's computation time is largely determined by the size of the occupancy grid. Therefore, shrinking its size reduces the planning time significantly. However, this approach impairs the local planner's foresight, which we remedy by implementing an additional controller for the local planner's maximum velocity based on plain laser data. To make the approach fast and reliable, we limit the maximum velocity when any laser beam reports obstacles within certain thresholds. We use three thresholds, which were empirically determined: A maximum velocity of $0.8 \frac{m}{s}$ if there are no obstacles, $0.6 \frac{m}{s}$ if there are obstacles within 0.6 m, and $0.3 \frac{m}{s}$ if there are obstacles within 0.3 m.

While this allows a maximum speed of $0.8 \frac{m}{s}$ in free environments, the system suffers from sensor noise gathered by raw laser data. In many cases, the laser reports false positives, showing obstacles at positions that are actually free, which results in occupied cells of the occupancy grid which are traversable. As a result, the path planner tries to avoid phantom obstacles. To overcome this issue, we filter the raw laser data by using an implementation of the fixed-radius near neighbour problem [2] in the PointCloud Library. Figure 5 shows an example scenario in which 247 beams are filtered down to 142 beams, while Fig. 5(c) shows the resulting costmap.

6   Goal Reasoning with the CLIPS Executive

We implemented an agent based on the the CLIPS Executive (CX) [16], which uses a goal reasoning model [1] similar to ACTORSIM [21]. We refer to [16] for an in-depth discussion of related work.

A goal describes objectives that the agent should pursue and can either *achieve* or *maintain* a condition or state. The program flow is determined by the *goal mode*, which describes the current progress of the goal. The mode transitions are determined by the goal lifecycle, as shown in Fig. 6. When a goal is created, it is first *formulated*, merely meaning that it may be relevant to consider. The goal reasoner may decide to *select* a goal, which is then *expanded* into one or multiple plans, either by using manually specified plans or automatic planners such as PDDL planners [15]. The reasoner then *commits* to one of those plans, which is *dispatched* after all required resources

Fig. 6. The goal lifecycle with all possible goal modes [16]

have been acquired, typically by executing a skill of the behavior engine. Eventually, the goal is *finished* and the outcome is *evaluated* to determine the goal's success.

The CX provides an explicit representation of the agent's world model, and its goals, plans, and actions. It separates the *domain model* with the available operators, predicates, and known facts from the *execution model*, which enhances the domain model by features that are only relevant for the execution of the plan, e.g., *exogenous actions* and *sensed predicates*.

Multi-robot Coordination. The CX also provides means for multi-robot coordination, in particular *world model synchronization*, *mutual exclusion*, and *resource allocation* [16]. To cooperate effectively, each agent must share (parts of) its world model with the other agents. The CX implements world model synchronization using a shared database [18,23]. Each robot uses a database instance for local (agent-specific) and global (shared) world model facts. The global world model database is synchronized as part of a replica set with the global instances of the other robots.

Based on the replicated database, the CX also implements a locking mechanism. To lock a mutex, an agent must request a *majority acknowledgment*, thereby avoiding two agents to hold the same mutex. To allow *mutual exclusion*, the CX specifies two actions *lock* and *unlock*, which may be used by the agent just as any other action. Additionally, each goal may be associated with one or multiple resources that are required in order to dispatch the goal. If one resource is currently unavailable, the goal is *rejected*. The agent holds the resource for the whole lifetime of the goal, once a goal is *retracted*, its acquired resources are released automatically. In contrast to that, other mutexes locked by *lock* and *unlock* actions are acquired and released explicitly by plan actions during the execution of the goal's plan. Resource locks are typically used if the resource is consumed or changed by the goal's plan and any other goal related to the resource may become invalid after the goal has finished, while lock actions are typically used to guarantee short-term mutual exclusion, e.g., to avoid two robots moving to the same location.

6.1   Goal Reasoning in the RCLL

Using goal reasoning in the CX, we implemented an incremental and distributed strategy for the RCLL. We split the production of an order into multiple goals, such that each step of the production of one order is a separate goal and each goal starts and ends at an MPS without a workpiece in the robot's gripper. With this approach, a robot can easily switch between tasks and orders, e.g., first mount a ring for a C2 and then switch to mounting a cap for a C0. All production goals are structured in a goal tree. The root of the tree is a PRODUCTION maintenance goal, with separate maintenance sub-trees for URGENT, FULFILL-ORDERS, PREPARE-RESOURCES, and NO-PROGRESS goals, with decreasing priorities of the order of the sub-trees. This way, the agent always selects an urgent goal if there is any, and otherwise tries to fulfill orders, e.g, by delivering a product. If this is not possible, it prepares resources not tied to a specific order, e.g., feeding raw material into the ring station. If there is no goal in any of the sub-trees, it selects a goal that does not progress the game, e.g., going to a waiting position.

Goal selection is solely based on the priority of the goal, i.e., we always select the formulated goal with the highest priority, which is currently defined manually for each goal class. Goals that continue the production of an already started product have higher priority than goals that start a new product, products of higher complexity have higher priority than products of lower complexity. Our goal selection implements an incremental strategy as our goal reasoner only decides which goal to pursue next rather than scheduling a set of goals ahead of time. We obtain a distributed multi-agent strategy that effectively fulfills order without an explicit decision which orders to pursue, thereby removing the need for a central agent.

Although the CX is capable of using a PDDL planner [15], we use a database of hand-crafted plans instead. This allows tighter control of the resulting plans and better execution monitoring and also avoids planning overhead during execution, but reduces the flexibility of the goal reasoner as we cannot easily dispatch the same goal in slightly different situations, e.g., start dispatch a goal with the robot holding a workpiece. Currently, PDDL is only used for the execution model to check whether all preconditions of an action are satisfied before executing an action, and also to specify the actions' effects.

To coordinate the three robots, we use a distributed approach using the locking mechanisms of the CX. More specifically, a production goal requires a workpiece and an MPS as resource if they are altered by the goal's plan. Additionally, all plans contain lock actions for locations and machines. The resource locks guarantee that we only dispatch one goal that depends on the current state of the workpiece (e.g., the number of rings mounted on the base) or the machine (e.g., whether a cap station has a buffered cap). The additional lock actions guarantee that no two robots try to move to the same location or operate the same MPS station at the same time, even if the station is not a required resource. This allows more efficient plan dispatching, as one robot may already start the execution of a plan, even if the plan contains an action at a station that is currently occupied.

Execution Monitoring. In most robotics scenarios and in the RCLL in particular, plan execution may fail for a number of reasons. For one, an action may simply fail due to imprecise sensors or actuators, e.g., picking a workpiece from an MPS may fail because the gripper is not properly aligned to the MPS. Also, another robot, either from the same or the opposite team, may interfere, e.g., by blocking a location or resetting an MPS. Additionally, a plan may fail due to the inherent uncertainties in the RCLL, e.g., an MPS being DOWN. Finally, we also need to deal with exogenous events and their effects on the agent's world model. We can distinguish three kinds of events: (1) an action may fail to execute, (2) a plan no longer has the intended effect, and (3) a goal is no longer useful. The CX already supports generic monitoring rules, e.g., retrying a failed action a number of times. In addition to that, we also implemented domain-specific monitoring rules, which deal with the specific aspects of the RCLL. Most of these domain-specific rules were created by observing undesired behaviors in test environments. Typical examples include resetting an MPS if it is in an unexpected state and removing unknown workpieces from the input or output of a machine. To implement and test our execution monitoring, we adapted the Gazebo-based simulation of the RCLL [24] to incorporate random failures. With this strategy, we were able to develop extended monitoring rules even for scenarios that we could not observe frequently in the real world.

7   Conclusion

In 2019, we continued the development of the CLIPS Executive (CX), a goal reasoning system which we use to pursue an incremental and distributed multi-agent strategy for the RCLL in a principled way. We redesigned our gripper system and replaced it with a three-finger manipulator that grasps workpieces from the top. We took a new approach to MPS alignment with a multi-stage strategy using RANSAC with a LiDAR sensor and ICP on an RGB/D image. We further improved our navigation, which allowed our robots to move more quickly across the playing field while avoiding collisions with static objects and robots of both our and the opposite team. All those changes provided the means to a more efficient production, which resulted in the team's success in the RoboCup Logistics League.

Acknowledgements. The team members in 2019 were David Bosen, Mario Claer, Sebastian Eltester, Christoph Gollok, Daniel Habering, Till Hofmann, Nicolas Limpert, Victor Mataré, Morian Sonnet and Tarik Viehmann.

Our special thanks go to T. Niemueller for his continued support and contributions both to the league and to our team.

We gratefully acknowledge the financial support of RWTH Aachen University and FH Aachen University of Applied Sciences.

T. Hofmann and V. Mataré were supported by the DFG grants *GL-747/23-1* and *FE-1077/4-1* (respectively) on Constraint-based Transformations of Abstract Task Plans into Executable Actions for Autonomous Robots (http://gepris.dfg.de/gepris/projekt/288705857).

N. Limpert was partly supported by the H2020 ROSIN project under grant agreement No 732287 (https://cordis.europa.eu/project/rcn/206395/factsheet/en) on ROS-Industrial quality assured software components.

We appreciate the financial and organizational support by the Cybernetics Lab IMA & IfU, RWTH Aachen University.

We are especially thankful to *Hans-Hermann-Voss-Stiftung* (https://www.hans-hermann-voss-stiftung.de/) for their financial support.

We thank our sponsors *ELTROPULS GmbH* (https://www.eltropuls.de/) and *Magazino GmbH* (https://www.magazino.eu/) for travel funding, as well as *AGVR GmbH* (http://www.agvr.eu/), *igus GmbH* (https://www.igus.de/) and *SICK AG* (https://www.sick.com/) for providing hardware and development support.

References

1. Aha, D.W.: Goal reasoning: foundations, emerging applications, and prospects. AI Mag. **39**(2), 3–24 (2018)
2. Bentley, J.L., Stanat, D.F., Williams Jr., E.H.: The complexity of finding fixed-radius near neighbors. Inf. Process. Lett. **6**(6), 209–212 (1977)
3. Borenstein, J., Koren, Y.: The vector field histogram-fast obstacle avoidance for mobile robots. IEEE Trans. Robot. Autom. **7**(3), 278–288 (1991)
4. Chen, Y., Medioni, G.: Object modelling by registration of multiple range images. Image Vis. Comput. **10**(3), 145–155 (1992)
5. Fischler, M.A., Bolles, R.C.: Random sample consensus: a paradigm for model fitting with applications to image analysis and automated cartography. Commun. ACM **24**(6), 381–395 (1981)
6. Gat, E.: Three-layer architectures. In: Kortenkamp, D., Bonasso, R.P., Murphy, R. (eds.) Artificial Intelligence and Mobile Robots, pp. 195–210. MIT Press, Cambridge (1998)

7. Hochstein, L., Moser, R.: Ansible: Up and Running. O'Reilly, Sebastopol (2014)
8. Hofmann, T., Limpert, N., Mataré, V., Ferrein, A., Lakemeyer, G.: The Carologistics RoboCup Logistics Team 2019. Technical report, RWTH Aachen University and FH Aachen University of Applied Sciences (2019). https://kbsg.rwth-aachen.de/~hofmann/papers/carologistics-2019-tdp.pdf
9. Hofmann, T., et al.: The Carologistics RoboCup Logistics Team 2018. Technical report, RWTH Aachen University and FH Aachen University of Applied Sciences (2018). https://kbsg.rwth-aachen.de/~hofmann/papers/carologistics-2018-tdp.pdf
10. Hofmann, T., et al.: Enhancing software and hardware reliability for a successful participation in the RoboCup Logistics League 2017. In: Akiyama, H., Obst, O., Sammut, C., Tonidandel, F. (eds.) RoboCup 2017. LNCS (LNAI), vol. 11175, pp. 486–497. Springer, Cham (2018). https://doi.org/10.1007/978-3-030-00308-1_40
11. Lu, D.V., Hershberger, D., Smart, W.D.: Layered costmaps for context-sensitive navigation. In: 2014 IEEE/RSJ International Conference on Intelligent Robots and Systems (IROS 2014), pp. 709–715. IEEE (2014)
12. Marder-Eppstein, E., Berger, E., Foote, T., Gerkey, B., Konolige, K.: The office marathon: robust navigation in an indoor office environment. In: International Conference on Robotics and Automation (2010)
13. Niemueller, T., Ferrein, A., Beck, D., Lakemeyer, G.: Design principles of the component-based robot software framework fawkes. In: International Conference on Simulation, Modeling, and Programming for Autonomous Robots (SIMPAR) (2010)
14. Niemüller, T., Ferrein, A., Lakemeyer, G.: A Lua-based behavior engine for controlling the humanoid robot Nao. In: Baltes, J., Lagoudakis, M.G., Naruse, T., Ghidary, S.S. (eds.) RoboCup 2009. LNCS (LNAI), vol. 5949, pp. 240–251. Springer, Heidelberg (2010). https://doi.org/10.1007/978-3-642-11876-0_21
15. Niemueller, T., Hofmann, T., Lakemeyer, G.: CLIPS-based execution for PDDL planners. In: ICAPS Workshop on Integrated Planning, Acting and Execution (IntEx) (2018)
16. Niemueller, T., Hofmann, T., Lakemeyer, G.: Goal reasoning in the CLIPS Executive for integrated planning and execution. In: Proceedings of the 29th International Conference on Planning and Scheduling (ICAPS) (2019)
17. Niemueller, T., Lakemeyer, G., Ferrein, A.: Incremental task-level reasoning in a competitive factory automation scenario. In: Proceedings of AAAI Spring Symposium 2013 - Designing Intelligent Robots: Reintegrating AI (2013)
18. Niemueller, T., Lakemeyer, G., Srinivasa, S.: A generic robot database and its application in fault analysis and performance evaluation. In: IEEE International Conference on Intelligent Robots and Systems (IROS) (2012)
19. Niemueller, T., et al.: Improvements for a robust production in the RoboCup Logistics League 2016. In: Behnke, S., Sheh, R., Sarıel, S., Lee, D.D. (eds.) RoboCup 2016. LNCS (LNAI), vol. 9776, pp. 589–600. Springer, Cham (2017). https://doi.org/10.1007/978-3-319-68792-6_49
20. Quigley, M., et al.: ROS: an open-source Robot Operating System. In: ICRA Workshop on Open Source Software (2009)
21. Roberts, M., Alford, R., Shivashankar, V., Leece, M., Gupta, S., Aha, D.W.: Actor-Sim: a toolkit for studying goal reasoning, planning, and acting. In: WS on Planning and Robotics (PlanRob) at International Conference on Automated Planning and Scheduling (ICAPS), London, UK (2016)

22. Rosmann, C., Feiten, W., Wosch, T., Hoffmann, F., Bertram, T.: Efficient trajectory optimization using a sparse model. In: European Conference on Mobile Robots (ECMR), pp. 138–143. IEEE (2013)
23. Zwilling, F.: A Document-oriented robot memory for knowledge sharing and hybrid reasoning on mobile robots. Master's thesis, RWTH Aachen University (2017)
24. Zwilling, F., Niemueller, T., Lakemeyer, G.: Simulation for the RoboCup logistics league with real-world environment agency and multi-level abstraction. In: RoboCup Symposium (2014)

Tech United Eindhoven Middle-Size League Winner 2019

W. Houtman[✉], C. M. Kengen, P. H. E. M. van Lith, R. H. J. ten Berge,
J. J. Kon, K. J. Meessen, M. A. Haverlag, Y. G. M. Douven,
F. B. F. Schoenmakers, D. J. H. Bruijnen, W. H. T. M. Aangenent,
J. J. Olthuis, M. Dolatabadi, S. T. Kempers, M. C. W. Schouten,
R. M. Beumer, W. J. P. Kuijpers, A. A. Kokkelmans, H. C. T. van de Loo,
and M. J. G. van de Molengraft

Eindhoven University of Technology,
De Rondom 70, P.O. Box 513, 5600 MB Eindhoven, The Netherlands
{techunited,w.houtman}@tue.nl
http://www.techunited.nl

Abstract. After the sequence of winning the RoboCup Middle-Size
League (MSL) in even years only (2012, 2014, 2016, 2018), Tech United
Eindhoven achieved its first RoboCup win during an odd year at
RoboCup 2019. This paper presents an evaluation of the tournament
and describes the most notable scientific improvements made in preparation of the tournament. These developments consist of our solution to
(unforeseen) localisation problems and the improvements in the control
architecture of our eight-wheeled robot. The progress in the shooting
lever is elaborated as well as the advancements in the arbitrary ball-
detection in order to improve our scoring during the Technical Challenge.
Additionally, research towards the application of artificial intelligence in
predicting the actions of opponents and recognizing the appearance of
the opponent robots will be presented.

Keywords: Robocup soccer · Middle-size league · Multi-agent ·
Localisation · Over-actuated control · Online calibration · Arbitrary
ball detection · Opponent prediction

1 Introduction

Tech United Eindhoven represents the Eindhoven University of Technology in
the RoboCup competitions. The team started participating in the Middle-Size
League (MSL) in 2006 and has been playing the final of the world championship
for 12 years now, while achieving the first place five times: 2012, 2014, 2016,
2018 and 2019. At the moment of writing, the MSL team consists of 6 PhD-, 8
MSc-, 4 BSc-, 6 former TU/e students, 3 TU/e staff members and two members
not related to TU/e. This paper describes the major scientific improvements
of our soccer robots over the past year and elaborates on some of the main

© Springer Nature Switzerland AG 2019
S. Chalup et al. (Eds.): RoboCup 2019, LNAI 11531, pp. 517–528, 2019.
https://doi.org/10.1007/978-3-030-35699-6_42

improvements or developments in preparation of the RoboCup 2019 tournament. First, in Sect. 2, an introduction of our fifth generation soccer robot is given. This is followed by some statistics of the latest tournament and our solution in robustifying the localisation-method in Sects. 3 and 4, respectively. Section 5 focuses on our efforts to make better use of our sixth generation soccer robot; the eight-wheeled platform. Section 6 continues with our progress in hardware and software to obtain a more reproducible shot. Section 7 describes two of our efforts to integrate methods from the domain of artificial intelligence into our robots. This paper is concluded in Sect. 8.

2   Robot Platform

Our robots, as shown in Fig. 1, have been named TURTLEs (acronym for Tech United RoboCup Team: Limited Edition). The development of the TURTLEs started in 2005. Through tournaments and numerous demonstrations, these platforms have evolved into the fifth generation TURTLE, a very robust platform. For an outline of our robot design the reader is referred to the schematic representation in [1]. A detailed list of hardware specifications, along with CAD files of the base, upper-body, ball handling and shooting mechanism, has been published on the ROP wiki[1]. The software controlling the robots is divided into four main processes: Vision, Worldmodel, Strategy and Motion. These processes communicate with each other through a real-time database (RTDB) designed by the CAMBADA team [2]. More detailed information on the software can be found in [3].

Fig. 1. Fifth generation TURTLE robots, with on the left-hand side the goalkeeper robot. (Photo: Bart van Overbeeke)

---

[1] http://www.roboticopenplatform.org/wiki/TURTLE.

3   RoboCup 2019 Statistics

Eight teams participated in the Middle Size League tournament of RoboCup 2019, of which team IRIS from Indonesia and Robot Club Toulon from France participated for the first time. The other teams were from Japan (Hibikino-Musashi), China (NuBot and Water), Portugal (CAMBADA) and the Netherlands (Falcons and Tech United Eindhoven). Six of these eight teams participated in the main soccer competition leading to a total of 34 matches, of which Tech United played 14 matches. Compared to the 2018 tournament, the average number of goals increased from 6.3 to 7.0 during these matches, while the number of opponent goals was approximately similar to last year with 0.9 goal per match on average this year versus 1.1 last year. Via 188 in-game passes and 146 passes during (re)starts of play, we were able to produce 121 shots on goal. Based on odometry-data, our robots drove more than a marathon, namely 46.9[km]. TURTLE 4 contributed most with 10.3[km], while the goalkeeper required a modest 0.7[km].

Noteworthy is our improvement in localisation. As the omnivision-system typically gives the most accurate estimate of the on-board sensors, the average fitting-error of the line detection of the omnivision pose is taken into consideration to validate the robot location. For a minimum of 50 and a maximum of 100 linepoints, the average fitting error is allowed to be 0.09[m]. This maximum number of linepoints is set to limit the computation-time. Last year, the average localisation percentage dropped due to the increased field size. The TURTLEs managed to localize almost 90% of the time [4]. Here TURTLE 4 outperformed the other robots by managing to localize 98% of the total time. This year, several improvements in the line detections were implemented, especially around the corners of the field. Together with the improved fusion of the gyroscope and accelerometer signals with the omnivision pose and odometry for the robot-pose estimate [5], this year, significant better results were achieved with an average localisation of 99.3% of the time. This year, the localization performance of all the robots varied between 98.0 and 99.9%. Even though the TURTLEs are similar in hardware and software, individual differences can be due to role, calibration accuracy or total playing time. Figure 2 confirms these numbers. In this figure, for last year and this year, both the correct (green) and missed locations (red) are indicated as function of the position of the field. For both years, the data from the latest Round Robin up to and including the final were taken into consideration. For the 2019 tournament, the data from the first match in the latest Round Robin were excluded, compensating for the overtime in the final match. The missed locations are estimated based on the pose estimate from a Kalman filter using gyro data and wheel-odometry. For visualisation purposes, the data of a single robot are visualized, in this case TURTLE 4. In both datasets, approximately 6.5[km] was covered. Due to the improvements, significant less misses are observed, confirming the percentages previously mentioned. Interestingly, a faster recovery behaviour is observed, as the sequences of consecutive missed positions are shorter in Fig. 2(b) compared to Fig. 2(a). This is due to less false positive and more true positive detected linepoints.

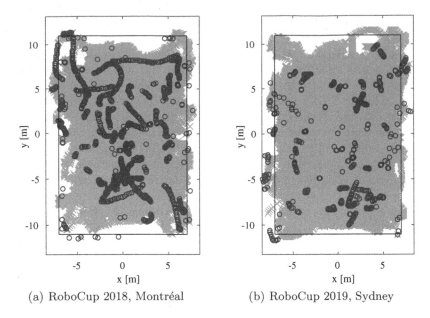

(a) RoboCup 2018, Montréal   (b) RoboCup 2019, Sydney

Fig. 2. Indication of correct (green) and missed locations (red) for TURTLE 4 as a function of the field positions over a subset of the matches played during last year's and this year's RoboCup. In both figures, a distance of approximately 6.5[km] was covered. The black lines indicate the outer field lines. (Color figure online)

4   Robustified Localisation

At the start of RoboCup 2019, major localization problems were observed, leading to unpredictable behaviour of our robots. This section elaborates the issues which were encountered, followed by the solution which was implemented during the tournament.

4.1   Challenge

Our main localisation algorithm functions by converting an omnivision camera image to a TURTLE pose in an optimization over this pose given a set of line points of the field. Due to the inherent symmetry of the lines of the soccer field, this algorithm needs an external input that indicates the heading of the TURTLE with respect to the center of the opponent's goal in order to uniquely determine the TURTLE's pose on the field. As the two possible orientations for a set of field points are 180[degrees] apart, a relative large error in the orientation-estimate is allowed. Empirical tests show that an error in the provided heading of up to approximately 30[degrees] will not hamper the optimization. To this extent, the integrated magnetometer of the Xsens MTi-3 was employed until this year to get such an estimate based on the magnetic field in the vicinity of the TURTLE. However, during RoboCup 2019, initial calibration of this sensor indicated that the magnetic field around the official field was heavily distorted, resulting in headings that were off by up to 70[degrees], thus rendering the magnetometer measurements useless. This resulted in extended periods in which localization was unavailable combined with false positive TURTLE poses, i.e. wrong positions on the field about which the algorithm was confident. Efforts to mitigate the dependence on the magnetic field by fusing the gyroscope and magnetometer were unfruitful, as the distorted field did not only have high variance, but was also heavily biased, varying with the position of the TURTLE.

4.2   Proposed Solution

The implemented solution for this problem consists of a stationary Kalman filter (i.e. a complementary filter) that fuses the gyroscope, which is unaffected by the distortion of the magnetic field, and the last confident omnivision orientation as an adaptation of [5]. In order to process the next sample(s) of the optimization algorithm of the omnivision-camera signal, the orientation-estimation of the Kalman filter replaces the heading input of the magnetometer measurements. This strategy has the disadvantage that a single confident outlier in the omnivision orientation could, through the heading estimate of the Kalman filter, cause the estimated omnivision orientation to return the flipped position on the field, i.e. the other orientation that also fits the line points. This also results in a false estimate of the TURTLE position, without having the explicit possibility to recover. By facing a robot to a specific goal when put on the field and by assuming that the robot is stationary when initialized, the filter can be initialized with a low covariance on both its heading and angular velocity estimate. Afterwards, the filter determines its heading by integrating the gyroscope and fusing the omnivision orientation. The gyroscope is the primary source of information, corresponding to a low covariance, while a high covariance is set on the omnivision orientation as its main purpose is to limit the drift of the heading induced by integrating the gyroscope. As this drift is bounded by 0.01[degree/s], the covariance matrices are set such that the resulting time constant of the filter is between 100 and 1000[s]. The covariance matrices were tuned within this band to accommodate for the rise time of the complementary filter, as the TURTLE will not be orientated towards its reference perfectly and thus the Kalman filter needs to converge to the sequence of found omnivision orientations after initialization. In combination with better line-detection around corner points, a better reduction of outliers and an improved tracking of the fieldline, the implemented solution ensured that our localization by omnivision was successful 99.3% of the time, which is significantly better compared to the 90% which was achieved last year.

5   Eight-Wheeled Platform

Last year, the mechanical design, presented in Fig. 3(a), and the first version of the low level control architecture of the eight-wheeled platform were presented [4]. The main advantages compared to the three-wheeled platform are the possibility to apply the torque delivered by the motors in the desired movement and the expectation to keep all wheels on the ground while accelerating. In this section, first the improvements in the low-level control will be discussed. As the eight-wheeled platform is non-holonomic while the current high-level software assumes the platform to be holonomic, some adaptations have to be made in order to be able to play soccer. Ideas on how to make this connection will be elaborated in Sect. 5.2.

5.1   Improved Low-Level Control Architecture

This platform consists of four sets each having two hub-drive wheels and thus five times over-constrained. As shown in Fig. 3(b), each pair of wheels can pivot around its suspension by actuating the corresponding wheels in opposite direction [4]. In order to actuate the platform, last year a kinematic control scheme was presented. The resulting performance was limited due to interaction between the wheels. As a result, the control-architecture as shown in Fig. 4 was designed.

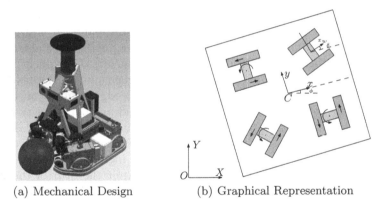

(a) Mechanical Design   (b) Graphical Representation

Fig. 3. The eight-wheeled platform with four suspended wheel combinations which are able to rotate around their center hinge.

For this controller, the aim is to manipulate the position x, y and orientation ϕ of the center C of the platform. First the left lower part of Fig. 4 is considered, which is marked with "Reference Generation of Pivots". In this part of the controller, the reference angle δ_{sp} of each wheel-unit $i = 1, 2, 3, 4$ is based on the desired platform velocity $v_{sp} = [\dot{x} \ \dot{y} \ \dot{\phi}]^T$ using the inverse kinematics G of the platform. At this stage, it is still assumed that the platform is holonomic. As this is not the case and in order to prevent step-responses, each pivot-setpoint is smoothed with a second order setpoint generator. Next, in the lower right part of Fig. 4, the "Pivot Controllers" are indicated. At these controllers, each reference angle of the pivots is controlled using a separate but identical position-to-force PD-controller C_δ. Here, the torque τ_w has an opposite direction for each wheel in a wheel-unit. By designing a feed-forward FF_δ for each pivot, the performance of these controllers is significantly increased. Using an estimate of the wheel-velocities v_w of each wheel and the rotation δ_i of each wheel unit, the platform-velocity v is determined using the forward kinematics J of the platform. This is required to control the motion of the platform, shown in the left-upper part of the figure. As the platform is non-holonomic, two velocity-to-torque PID-controllers are used to control three degrees of freedom. The first controller C_t controls the translation by projecting the velocity-errors $\dot{e}_x$ and $\dot{e}_y$ of both the x and y direction into the direction of the setpoint. This is considered as the controllable direction, as the wheels are kinematically oriented according to this reference. The orientation is controlled using a separate controller C_r. Finally, the wrench w_p is distributed among the eight-wheels. How to improve this distribution is an ongoing research.

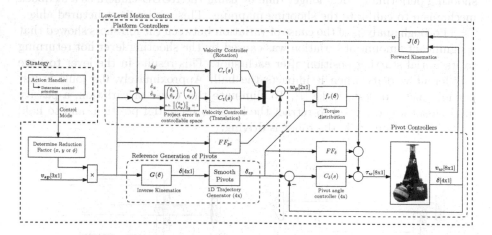

Fig. 4. Improved low-level control architecture of the eight-wheeled platform.

5.2 Integration into High-Level Software

The software used for the current three-wheeled platforms is designed assuming the platform to be holonomic. As a result, the motion software will attempt to control the position x, y, ϕ of the platform. For the eight-wheeled platform, this is however not possible due to the non-holonomic constraints set by the pivots. Therefore, in order to position at a specific location on the field, reducing small positioning errors requires the pivots to change orientation continuously. As a result, a large amount of energy is consumed in order to reduce these errors. However, in order to play soccer, it is not always necessary to control all three directions similarly. If, for example, the task of a robot is to intercept a pass, it is important that it positions itself on the line of the movement of the ball. In this situation, it is less important to position a bit more towards or a bit further away from the ball. Therefore, as shown in Fig. 4, depending on the action set by the high-level strategy, the relevant directions will be prioritized. This priority mode is then communicated to the motion controller, where it is used to lower the velocity references in the non-relevant directions.

6   Accurate Shooting

During matches it has been observed that the variation in the lob shots of the robots is too large, causing a lot of shots on goal to miss [6]. This section elaborates on improvements of the shooting performance of the robots, to make lob shots more reproducible. To this extent, two solutions are proposed. The first solution aims to gain improvements over short time, by adding a passive mechanism to the shooting mechanism. The second solution aims to improve the shooting performance over longer time by using the RGBD-camera as a feedback mechanism to calibrate the shooting mapping. This section is structured alike.

Thorough analysis of the cause of variation between the lob shots showed that a significant amount of variation was caused by the shooting lever not returning to its initial starting position after each shot. This results in the lever to have a different velocity when it impacts the ball. Approximately, 0.6 joule is lost per millimeter of lost stroke [7]. To eliminate this cause of variation, a passive mechanism was designed to retract the lever to its initial position, and to hold it at this position while the robot is driving.

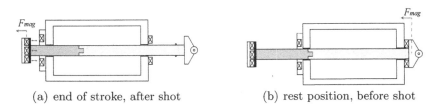

(a) end of stroke, after shot   (b) rest position, before shot

Fig. 5. Schematical representation of how two sets of magnets ensure a consistent initial position of the solenoid.

Figure 5(a) shows schematically how a set of repelling magnets push the lever backwards when it has moved fully forward after a shot. A second set of magnets at the front of the solenoid, shown in Fig. 5(b), pulls the lever into the initial starting position and hold it there. Experiments and theoretical analysis showed no observable decrease in shooting power using this mechanism. The force exerted by the solenoid over the stroke of the actuator is compared to the force exerted by the added permanent magnets. The work done by magnetic force generated by the permanent magnets is 0.11[J], which is 0.3% of the work generated by the solenoid, 32 [J] [7], over the first 60[mm] of the stroke where the solenoid is driving the ball. By implementing the permanent magnets, the reproducability of the shot increased as the standard deviation decreased from

0.32 to 0.08[m/s] and from 1.06 to 0.49[degrees] for the ball's starting velocity and angle respectively.

Over longer periods of time (weeks, months), small changes in the shooting system (lubrication, bearing performance) occur, which need to be compensated. To shoot at a specifc target, the inverse dynamics of the shooting mechanism is modeled in order to calculate the required robot inputs from a desired initial ball velocity v_0 and angle α_0. For this mapping a second order polynomial describing the robot shooting dynamics was chosen, since this was proven to be sufficient from previous research [8]. Using an Extended Kalman Filter (EKF), the polynomial coefficients can be recursively updated after each shot while taking the variation in the measured initial ball state into account. The state vector of the filter becomes $x = [a_0\ a_1\ a_2\ a_3\ a_4\ a_5]^T$, $u = [K\ L]^T$. $a_{[0,5]}$ are the polynomial coefficients, and K and L the shooting duty cycle and lever height settings respectively; the inputs of the shooting mechanism. Using the RGBD-camera mounted on the robot, the realised initial ball velocity v_0 and angle α_0 can be estimated in order to update the mapping.

Figure 6 shows the estimated initial ball velocity v_0 as function of the robot inputs. A corresponding mapping is created for the initial ball angle α_0. These maps need to be inverted in order to obtain the inverse dynamics in order to calculate the desired robot inputs for a specific shot.

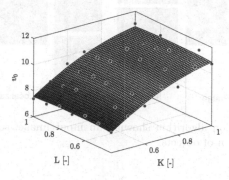

Fig. 6. Mapping between the robot initial ball state v_0, and the duty cycle setpoint K and lever height setpoint L. Fitted with a second order polynomial in both directions. Data obtained through the Kinect depth camera.

7 Artificial Intelligence

This section describes our efforts to arbitrary ball detection in Subsect. 7.1, and efforts towards learning opponent behavior in Subsect. 7.2. The latter is a continuation of our work on recognizing robots in camera images [9] and predicting robot behavior [10] as described in [3,4]. At the final paragraph of this section, current research on how to learn the response to these game situations is elaborated.

7.1 Arbitrary Ball Detection

Ball detection is currently based on the upper and lower bounds of the YUV values of the ball its color. This detection method works smoothly in most cases, however it comes with its limitations. For example, changes in the brightness make the calibration of the upper- and lower bounds less accurate. The algorithm is more likely to make false predictions if the color of the ball is similar to its environment, and the algorithm is only capable of detecting one-colored balls. To solve these inaccuracies and make the detection more robust, an approach using a machine learning algorithm is proposed. The new ball detection algorithm uses multiple convolutional layers to create feature mappings of the camera frame. These feature maps are then used to localize potential ball locations. Finally, the potential ball locations are classified through a neural network providing the probability-rate of a ball being present at the corresponding location. Figure 7 visually represents this algorithm.

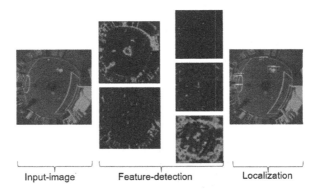

Input-image   Feature-detection   Localization

Fig. 7. Object detection algorithm showing an input image, some of the activation layers and the detection of objects.

A speed of 13 frames per second using only one CPU core with an accuracy of 80% on images with different balls with variable brightness and colors was achieved. In further research, our focus will be on implementation. The potential of a Jetson board will be explored. If necessary, other ways of integration will be analysed.

7.2 Opponent Behavior

The arbitrary ball recognition may be combined with previous work on recognizing robots [9] and forms the basis for a system to learn the behavior of competing teams and use this in the simulator of Tech United. The logfiles collected by the TURTLEs during a game are recorded with a frequency of about 10–30[Hz]. In that data Game Turnover Points (GTP) are identified. GTP's are points where a switch is made between attacking and defending. Such situations occur typically when the ball is lost or regained, or a shot at the goal is attempted. Using these GTP's all successful or failing episodes during a game are found. Episodes describe a game moment as a series of successive steps. The number of steps of an episode varies between just a few to sometimes several hundreds.

Having collected these episodes, two functions are performed. First a Game Situation Image (GSI) is created for each step of an episode, analogous to the work of Van't Klooster [10]. Then all episodes are classified according to its status as being one of the following: attack or defend, own half or opponent half, our ball or opponent ball and the starting situation, like kickoff, throw in, etc. For each step in an episode, the movements of the four field players of a team are calculated as single steps in the X and Y direction, forming a trail for each agent. The GSI and the agent trails are then fed into a neural network, which learns from this what each of the agent's role is during an episode. This way the network learns how a team responds to the various game situations.

Once the network has learned a team's behavior for every Game Situation, we use this network to pit two teams against each other, or to pit newly developed TURTLE behaviors against several opponents and use this to find weaknesses in our strategy. Currently, the project is in its early stages and the Game Situation Analysis is being developed and tested.

8 Conclusions

In this paper we have described the major scientific improvements of our soccer robots in preparation of the RoboCup 2019 tournament and the results we have achieved during the tournament. Not all of the developments have actively contributed to the result, but the methods developed will be integrated in preparation of future tournaments. By replacing the dependency of the magnetometer in the localization algorithm with an initialization procedure when putting the robots on the field, the localization-performance robustified. Our developments in the control of the eight-wheeled platform expand to the platform and strategy level, leading to its introduction during the Portugese Open 2019. The standard deviation in our shots was reduced by integrating magnets into the solenoid assembly, leading to an increased reproducibility. For arbitrary ball detection we have verified the feasibility of a neural network on the TURTLE's computational units. The research to modeling opponents continues, currently the classification process is revisited. Altogether we hope our progress contributes to an even higher level of dynamic and scientifically challenging robot soccer. The latter, of course, while maintaining the attractiveness of our competition for a general audience. In this way we hope to go with the top in Middle-size league for some more years and contribute to our goal in 2050 to beat the human World Champion in soccer!

References

1. Martinez, C.L., et al.: Tech United Eindhoven, Winner RoboCup 2014 MSL. In: Bianchi, R.A.C., Akin, H.L., Ramamoorthy, S., Sugiura, K. (eds.) RoboCup 2014. LNCS (LNAI), vol. 8992, pp. 60–69. Springer, Cham (2015). https://doi.org/10.1007/978-3-319-18615-3_5
2. Almeida, L., Santos, F., Facchinetti, T., Pedreiras, P., Silva, V., Lopes, L.S.: Coordinating distributed autonomous agents with a real-time database: the CAMBADA project. In: Aykanat, C., Dayar, T., Körpeoğlu, İ. (eds.) ISCIS 2004. LNCS, vol. 3280, pp. 876–886. Springer, Heidelberg (2004). https://doi.org/10.1007/978-3-540-30182-0_88
3. Schoenmakers, F., et al.: Tech United Eindhoven Team Description 2017 (2017). https://www.techunited.nl/media/images/Publications/TDP_2017.pdf
4. Douven, Y., et al.: Tech United Eindhoven middle size league winner 2018. In: Holz, D., Genter, K., Saad, M., von Stryk, O. (eds.) RoboCup 2018. LNCS (LNAI), vol. 11374, pp. 413–424. Springer, Cham (2019). https://doi.org/10.1007/978-3-030-27544-0_34
5. Kon, J., Houtman, W., Kuijpers, W., van de Molengraft, R.: Pose and velocity estimation for soccer robots. Student Undergraduate Research E-journal! 4 (2018). https://doi.org/10.25609/sure.v4.2840
6. Kengen, C.M., Douven, Y.G.M., Van De Molengraft, M.J.G.: Towards a more reproducible shot with the tech united soccer robots. Master's thesis, Eindhoven (2018). Reportnumber: CST 2018.097
7. Meessen, K.J., Paulides, J.J.H., Lomonova, E.A.: A football kicking high speed actuator for a mobile robotic application. In: IECON 2010–36th Annual Conference on IEEE Industrial Electronics Society, pp. 1659–1664. IEEE, November 2010. https://doi.org/10.1109/IECON.2010.5675433, http://alexandria.tue.nl/openaccess/Metis245159.pdf
8. Senden, J., Douven, Y., van de Molengraft, R.: A model-based approach to reach a 3D target with a soccer ball, kicked by a soccer robot. Master's thesis, Eindhoven University of Technology (2016). Reportnumber: CST 2016.078. https://www.techunited.nl/media/images/Publications/StudentReports/July2016/0716549-Jordy.pdf
9. Van Lith, P., van de Molengraft, M., Dubbelman, G., Plantinga, M.: A minimalistic approach to identify and localize robots in RoboCup MSL soccer competitions in real-time. Technical report. http://www.techunited.nl/uploads/Minimalist%20MSL%20Robot%20Location%205.0.pdf
10. Van 't Klooster, M., Nijmeijer, H., Dubbelman, G.: Deep learning for opponent action prediction in robot soccer middle size league. Master's thesis, Eindhoven University of Technology (2018). Reportnumber: DC 2018.050

Tech United Eindhoven @Home 2019 Champions Paper

M. F. B. van der Burgh, J. J. M. Lunenburg, R. P. W. Appeldoorn,
L. L. A. M. van Beek, J. Geijsberts, L. G. L. Janssen[✉], P. van Dooren,
H. W. A. M. van Rooy, A. Aggarwal, S. Aleksandrov, K. Dang,
A. T. Hofkamp, D. van Dinther, and M. J. G. van de Molengraft

Eindhoven University of Technology,
Den Dolech 2, P.O. Box 513, 5600 MB Eindhoven, The Netherlands
techunited@tue.nl
http://www.techunited.nl, https://github.com/tue-robotics

Abstract. This paper provides an overview of the main developments of
the Tech United Eindhoven RoboCup @Home team. Tech United uses an
advanced world modeling system called the Environment Descriptor. It
allows straightforward implementation of localization, navigation, exploration, object detection & recognition, object manipulation and robot-
robot cooperation skills based on the most recent state of the world.
Other important features include object and people detection via deep
learning methods, a GUI, speech recognition, natural language interpretation and a chat interface combined with a conversation engine. Recent
developments that aided with obtaining the victory during RoboCup
2019 include pointing detection, usage of HSR's display, a people detector and the addition of a custom keyboard in the chat interface.

1 Introduction

Tech United Eindhoven[1] (established 2005) is the RoboCup student team
of Eindhoven University of Technology[2] (TU/e), which joined the ambitious
@Home League in 2011. The RoboCup @Home competition aims to develop service robots that can perform everyday tasks in dynamic and cluttered 'home'
environments. Multiple world vice-champion titles have been obtained in the
Open Platform League (OPL) of the RoboCup @Home competition during previous years, and this year, whilst competing in the Domestic Standard Platform League (DSPL) for the first time, the world championship title was finally
claimed. In the DSPL, all teams compete with the same hardware; all teams compete with a Human Support Robot (HSR), and use the same external devices.
Therefore, all differences between the teams regard only the software used and
implemented by the teams.

---

[1] http://www.techunited.nl.
[2] http://www.tue.nl.

© Springer Nature Switzerland AG 2019
S. Chalup et al. (Eds.): RoboCup 2019, LNAI 11531, pp. 529–539, 2019.
https://doi.org/10.1007/978-3-030-35699-6_43

Tech United Eindhoven consists of (former) PhD and MSc. students and staff members from different departments within the TU/e. This year, these team members successfully migrated the software from our TU/e built robots, AMIGO and SERGIO, to HERO, our Toyota HSR. This software base is developed to be robot independent, which means that the years of development on AMIGO and SERGIO are currently being used by HERO. Thus, a large part of the developments discussed in this paper have been optimized for years, whilst the DSPL competition has only existed since 2017[3]. All the software discussed in this paper is available open-source at GitHub[4], as well as various tutorials to assist with implementation. The main developments that resulted in the large lead at RoboCup 2019, and eventually the championship, are our central world model, discussed in Sect. 2, the generalized people recognition, discussed in Sect. 4 and the head display, discussed in Sect. 5.3.

2   Environment Descriptor (ED)

The TU/e Environment Descriptor (ED) is a Robot Operating System (ROS) based 3D geometric, object-based world representation system for robots. ED is a database system that structures multi-modal sensor information and represents this such that it can be utilized for robot localisation, navigation, manipulation and interaction. Figure 1 shows a schematic overview of ED.

ED has been used on our robots in the OPL since 2012 and was also used this year in the DSPL. Previous developments have focused on making ED platform independent, as a result ED has been used on the PR2, Turtlebot, Dr. Robot systems (X80), as well as on multiple other @Home robots.

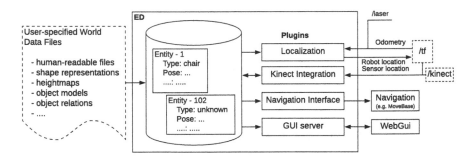

Fig. 1. Schematic overview of TU/e Environment Descriptor. Double sided arrows indicate that the information is shared both ways, one sided arrows indicate that the information is only shared in one direction.

ED is a single re-usable environment description that can be used for a multitude of desired functionalities such as object detection, navigation and human

---

[3] https://athome.robocup.org/robocuphome-spl.
[4] https://github.com/tue-robotics.

machine interaction. Improvements in ED reflect in the performances of the separate robot skills, as these skills are closely integrated in ED. This single world model allows for all data to be current and accurate without requiring updating and synchronization of multiple world models. Currently, different ED plug-ins exist that enable robots to localize themselves, update positions of known objects based on recent sensor data, segment and store newly encountered objects and visualize all this in RViz and through a web-based GUI, as illustrated in Fig. 9. ED allows for all the different subsystems that are required to perform challenges to work together robustly. These various subsystems are shown in Fig. 2, and are individually elaborated upon in this paper.

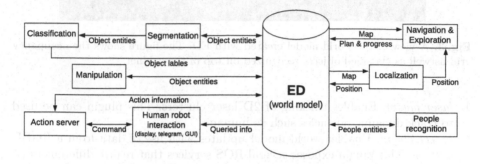

Fig. 2. A view of the data interaction with robot skills that ED is responsible for.

2.1 Localization, Navigation and Exploration

The *ed_localization*[5] plugin implements AMCL based on a 2D render of the central world model. With use of the *ed_navigation* plugin[6], an occupancy grid is derived from the world model and published. With the use of the *cb_base_navigation* package[7] the robots are able to deal with end goal constraints. The *ed_navigation* plugin allows to construct such a constraint w.r.t. a world model entity in ED. This enables the robot to navigate not only to areas or entities in the scene, but to waypoints as well. Figure 3 also shows the navigation to an area. Modified versions of the local and global ROS planners available within *move_base* are used.

2.2 Detection and Segmentation

ED enables integrating sensors through the use of the plugins present in the *ed_sensor_integration* package. Two different plugins exist:

---

[5] https://github.com/tue-robotics/ed_localization.
[6] https://github.com/tue-robotics/ed_navigation.
[7] https://github.com/tue-robotics/cb_base_navigation.

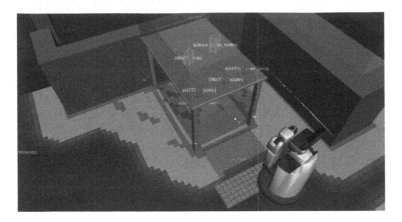

Fig. 3. A view of the world model created with ED. The figure shows the occupancy grid as well as classified objects recognized on top of the cabinet.

1. *laser_plugin*: Enables tracking of 2D laser clusters. This plugin can be used to track dynamic obstacles such as humans.
2. *kinect_plugin*: Enables world model updates with use of data from a RGBD camera. This plugin exposes several ROS services that realize different functionalities:
    (a) *Segment*: A service that segments sensor data that is not associated with other world model entities. Segmentation areas can be specified per entity in the scene. This allows to segment object 'on-top-of' or 'in' a cabinet. All points outside the segmented area are ignore for segmentation.
    (b) *FitModel*: A service that fits the specified model in the sensor data of a RGBD camera. This allows updating semi-static obstacles such as tables and chairs.

The *ed_sensor_integration* plugins enable updating and creating entities. However, new entities are classified as unknown entities. Classification is done in *ed_perception* plugin[8] package.

2.3 Object Grasping, Moving and Placing

The system architecture developed for object manipulation is focused on grasping. In the implementation, its input is a specific target entity in ED, selected by a Python executive and the output is the grasp motion joint trajectory. Figure 4 shows the grasping pipeline.

Movelt! is used to produce joint trajectories over time, given the current configuration, robot model, ED world model (for collision avoidance) and the final configuration.

---

[8] https://github.com/tue-robotics/ed_perception.

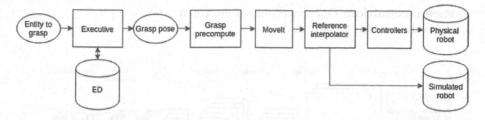

Fig. 4. Custom grasping pipeline base on ED, MoveIt and a separate grasp point determination and approach vector node.

The grasp pose determination uses the information about the position and shape of the object in ED to determine the best grasping pose. The grasping pose is a vector relative to the robot. An example of the determined grasping pose is shown in Fig. 5. Placing an object is approached in a similar manner to grasping, except for that when placing an object, ED is queried to find an empty placement pose.

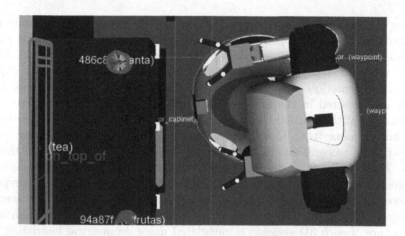

Fig. 5. Grasping pose determination result for a cylindric object with TU/e built robot AMIGO. It is unpreferred to grasp the object from behind.

3   Image Recognition

The *image_recognition* packages apply state of the art image classification techniques based on Convolution Neural Networks (CNN).

1. **Object recognition:** Tensorflow^{TM} with retrained top-layer of a Inception V3 neural network, as illustrated in Fig. 6.

2. **Face recognition:** OpenFace[9], based on Torch.
3. **Pose detection:** OpenPose[10].

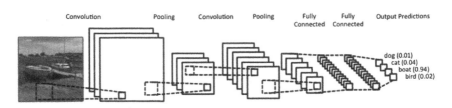

Fig. 6. Illustration of Convolution Neural Networks (CNN) used in our object recognition nodes with use of Tensorflow.

Our image recognition ROS packages are available on GitHub[11] and as Debian packages: *ros-kinetic-image-recognition*

4   People Recognition

As our robots need to operate and interact with people in a dynamic environment, our robots' people detection skills have been upgraded. This skill is upgraded to a generalized system capable of recognizing people in 3D. In the people recognition stack, an RGB-D camera is used as the sensor to capture the scene information. A recognition sequence is completed in four steps. First, people are detected in the scene using OpenPose and if their faces are recognized as one of the learned faces in the robots'database, they are labeled using their known name using OpenFace. The detections from OpenPose are associated with the recognitions from OpenFace by maximizing the IoUs of the face ROIs. Then, for each of the recognized people, additional properties such as age, gender and the shirt color are identified. Furthermore, the pose keypoints of these recognitions are coupled with the depth information of the scene to re-project the recognized people to 3D as skeletons. Finally, information about the posture of each 3D skeleton is calculated using geometrical heuristics. This allows for the addition of properties such as "pointing pose" and additional flags such as 'is_waving', 'is_sitting', etc.

4.1   Pointing Detection

This year's tournament challenges involved various non-verbal user interactions such as detecting to what object the user was pointing. In the previous section, our approach to people recognition is explained. This recognition includes information about the posture of each 3D skeleton. Once the people information is

---

[9] https://cmusatyalab.github.io/openface/.
[10] https://github.com/CMU-Perceptual-Computing-Lab/openpose.
[11] https://github.com/tue-robotics/image_recognition.

inserted into the world model, additional properties can be added to the persons that take also other entities in the world model into account, e.g. "is_ pointing_ at_ entity". This information is used by the toplevel state machines to implement challenges such as 'Hand Me That', the description of which can be found in the 2019 Rulebook[12]. However an additional check is inserted to ensure that the correct operator is found. This check is based on a spatial queries. By using such a query it is possible to filter out people based on their location. Finally, to determine at which entity the operator is pointing, ray-tracing is implemented. Figure 7 shows an example of the ray-tracing.

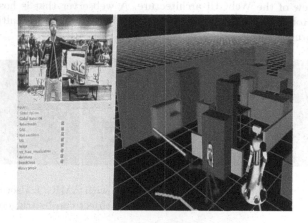

Fig. 7. Ray-tracing based on pose detection with AMIGO.

5   Human-Robot Interface

We provide multiple ways of interacting with the robot in an intuitive manner: WebGUI, Subsect. 5.1, and Telegram[TM] interface, Subsect. 5.2, which uses our *conversation_engine*, Subsect. 5.2.

5.1   Web GUI

In order to interact with the robot, apart from speech, we have designed a web-based Graphical User Interface (GUI). This interface uses HTML5[13] with the Robot API written in Javascript and we host it on the robot itself.

Figure 8 gives an overview of the connections between these components and Fig. 9 represents an instance of the various interactions that are possible with the Robot API.

---

[12] http://www.robocupathome.org/rules.
[13] https://github.com/tue-robotics/tue_mobile_ui.

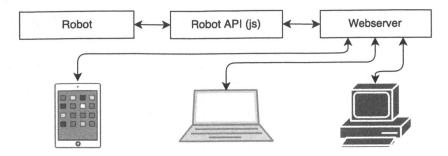

Fig. 8. Overview of the WebGUI architecture. A webserver that is hosting the GUI connects this Robot API to a graphical interface that is offered to multiple clients on different platforms.

Fig. 9. Illustration of the 3D scene of the WebGUI with AMIGO. User can long-press objects to open a menu from which actions on the object can be triggered

5.2   Telegram^{TM}

The Telegram interface[14] to our robots is a ROS wrapper around the *python-telegram-bot* library. The software exposes four topics, for images and text resp. from and to the robot. The interface allows only one master of the robot at a time. The interface itself does not contain any reasoning. This is all done by the *conversation_engine*, which is described in the following subsection.

Conversation Engine

The *conversation_ engine*[15] bridges the gap between text input and an action planner (called action_server). Text can be received from either Speech-to-Text or from a chat interface, like Telegram^{TM}. The text is parsed according to a (Feature) Context Free Grammar, resulting in an action description in the form of a nested mapping. In the action description, (sub)actions and their parameters are filled in. This may include references such as "it".

Based on the action description, the action_server tries to devise a sequence of actions and parameterize those with concrete object IDs. To fill in missing information, the conversation_engine engages with the user. When the user supplies more information, the additional input is parsed in the context of what info is

---

[14] https://github.com/tue-robotics/telegram_ros.

[15] https://github.com/tue-robotics/conversation_engine.

missing. Lastly, it keeps the user "informed" whilst actions are being performed by reporting on the current subtask.

Custom Keyboard, Telegram HMI

The user interface modality as explained above has been extended to reduce the room for operator error by only presenting the user with a limited number of buttons in the Telegram app. This has been realized through Telegrams *custom_ keyboards*[16] feature. This feature is especially useful if there are only a few options, such as when selecting from a predetermined selection of drinks, as has been shown in our finals during RoboCup 2019.

Since the competition, this feature has been employed to compose commands word-for-word. After the user has already entered, via text or previous buttons, for example "Bring me the ..." the user is presented with only those words that might follow that text according to the grammar, eg. "apple", "orange" etc. This process iterates until a full command has been composed. This feature is called *hmi_ telegram*[17].

5.3   Head Display

For most people, especially people who do not deal with robots in their day-to-day life, interaction with robots is not as easy as one would like it to be. It is often difficult to hear what the robot is saying and it is not always intuitive for people to know when to talk to the robot. To remedy this, the head display of HERO is used. On this display that is integrated in the Toyota HSRs' 'head', a lot of useful information can be displayed. Through the *hero_ display*[18] a few different functionalities are integrated. As per default, our Tech United @Home logo with a dynamic background is shown on the screen, as depicted in Fig. 10. When the robot is speaking the spoken text is displayed, when the robot is listening a spinner along with an image of a microphone is shown and it is possible to display images.

6   Re-usability of the System for Other Research Groups

Tech United takes great pride in creating and maintaining open-source software and hardware to accelerate innovation. Tech United initiated the Robotic Open Platform website[19], to share hardware designs. All our software is available on GitHub[20]. All packages include documentation and tutorials. Tech United and its scientific staff have the capacity to co-develop (15+ people), maintain and assist in resolving questions.

---

[16] https://github.com/tue-robotics/https://github.com/tue-robotics/telegram_ros/tree/rwc2019.
[17] https://github.com/tue-robotics/hmi_telegram.
[18] https://github.com/tue-robotics/hero-display.
[19] http://www.roboticopenplatform.org.
[20] https://github.com/tue-robotics.

Fig. 10. The default status of HERO's head display.

7 Community Outreach and Media

Tech united has organised 3 tournaments: Dutch Open 2012, RoboCup 2013 and the European Open 2016. Our team member Loy van Beek has been a member of the Technical Committee during the period: 2014–2017. We also carry out many promotional activities for children to promote technology and innovation. Tech United often visits primary and secondary schools, public events, trade fairs and has regular TV appearances. Each year, around 50 demos are given and 25k people are reached through live interaction. Tech United also has a very active website[21], and interacts on many social media like: Facebook[22], Instagram[23], YouTube[24], Twitter[25] and Flickr[26]. Our robotics videos are often shared on the IEEE video Friday website.

A HSR's Software and External Devices

A standard Toyota[TM] HSR robot is used. To differentiate our unit, it has been named HERO. This name also links it to our AMIGO and SERGIO domestic service robots.

HERO's Software Description. An overview of the software used by the Tech United Eindhoven @Home robots can be found in Table 1.

---

[21] http://www.techunited.nl.

[22] https://www.facebook.com/techunited.

[23] https://www.instagram.com/techunitedeindhoven.

[24] https://www.youtube.com/user/TechUnited.

[25] https://www.twitter.com/TechUnited.

[26] https://www.flickr.com/photos/techunited.

Table 1. Software overview

Operating system	Ubuntu 16.04 LTS Server
Middleware	ROS Kinetic [1]
Simulation	Gazebo
World model	Environment Descriptor (ED), custom https://github.com/tue-robotics/ed
Localization	Monte Carlo [2] using Environment Descriptor (ED), custom https://github.com/tue-robotics/ed_localization
SLAM	Gmapping
Navigation	CB Base navigation https://github.com/tue-robotics/cb_base_navigation Global: custom A* planner Local: modified ROS DWA [3]
Arm navigation	MoveIt!
Object recognition	image_recognition_tensorflow https://github.com/tue-robotics/image_recognition/tree/master/image_recognition_openface
People detection	Custom implementation using contour matching https://github.com/tue-robotics/ed_perception
Face detection & recognition	image_recognition_openface https://github.com/tue-robotics/image_recognition/tree/master/image_recognition_openface
Speech recognition	Windows Speech Recognition
Speech synthesis	Toyota^{TM} Text-to-Speech
Task executors	SMACH https://github.com/tue-robotics/tue_robocup

External Devices. *HERO relies on the following external hardware:*

- Official Standard Laptop
- USB power speaker
- Gigabit Ethernet Switch
- Wi-Fi adapter

References

1. Quigley, M., et al.: ROS: an open-source robot operating system. In: ICRA Workshop on Open Source Software (2009)
2. Fox, D.: Adapting the sample size in particle filters through KLD-sampling. Int. J. Robot. Res. **22**(12), 985–1003 (2003)
3. Fox, D., Burgard, W., Thrun, S.: The dynamic window approach to collision avoidance. IEEE Mag. Robot. Autom. **4**(1), 23–33 (1997)

UT Austin Villa: RoboCup 2019 3D Simulation League Competition and Technical Challenge Champions

Patrick MacAlpine[1]([✉]), Faraz Torabi[2], Brahma Pavse[2], and Peter Stone[2]

[1] Microsoft Research, Redmond, USA
patmac@microsoft.com
[2] The University of Texas at Austin, Austin, USA
{faraztrb,brahmasp}@utexas.edu, pstone@cs.utexas.edu

Abstract. The UT Austin Villa team, from the University of Texas at Austin, won the 2019 RoboCup 3D Simulation League, and in doing so finished with an overall record of 21 wins, 1 tie, and 1 loss. During the course of the competition the team scored 112 goals while conceding only 5. Additionally the team won the RoboCup 3D Simulation League technical challenge by accumulating the most points across two league challenges: fewest self-collisions challenge and free challenge. This paper describes the changes and improvements made to the team between 2018 and 2019 that allowed it to win both the main competition and technical challenge.

1 Introduction

UT Austin Villa won the 2019 RoboCup 3D Simulation League for the eighth time in the past nine years, having also won the competition in 2011 [1], 2012 [2], 2014 [3], 2015 [4], 2016 [5], 2017 [6], and 2018 [7] while finishing second in 2013. During the course of the competition the team scored 112 goals while conceding only 5 along the way to finishing with an overall record of 21 wins, 1 tie, and 1 loss. Many of the components of the 2019 UT Austin Villa agent were reused from the team's successful previous years' entries in the competition. This paper is not an attempt at a complete description of the 2019 UT Austin Villa agent, the base foundation of which is the team's 2011 championship agent fully described in a team technical report [8], but instead focuses on changes made in 2019 that helped the team repeat as champions.

In addition to winning the main RoboCup 3D Simulation League competition, UT Austin Villa also won the RoboCup 3D Simulation League technical challenge by winning each of the two league challenges: fewest self-collisions challenge and free challenge. This paper also serves to document these challenges and the approaches used by UT Austin Villa when competing in the challenges.

The remainder of the paper is organized as follows. In Sect. 2 a description of the 3D simulation domain is given highlighting differences from the previous year's competition. Section 3 details changes and improvements to the 2019 UT

© Springer Nature Switzerland AG 2019
S. Chalup et al. (Eds.): RoboCup 2019, LNAI 11531, pp. 540–552, 2019.
https://doi.org/10.1007/978-3-030-35699-6_44

Austin Villa team: reduction of self-collisions and use of a new pass mode, while Sect. 4 analyzes the contributions of these changes in addition to the overall performance of the team at the competition. Section 5 describes and analyzes the fewest self-collisions challenge, while also documenting the overall league technical challenge consisting of both the fewest self-collision challenge and a free/scientific challenge. Section 6 concludes.

2   Domain Description

The RoboCup 3D simulation environment is based on SimSpark [9,10], a generic physical multiagent system simulator. SimSpark uses the Open Dynamics Engine (ODE) library for its realistic simulation of rigid body dynamics with collision detection and friction. ODE also provides support for the modeling of advanced motorized hinge joints used in the humanoid agents.

Games consist of 11 versus 11 agents playing two 5 minute halves of soccer on a 30×20 m field. The robot agents in the simulation are modeled after the Aldebaran Nao robot, which has a height of about 57 cm, and a mass of 4.5 kg. Each robot has 22 degrees of freedom: six in each leg, four in each arm, and two in the neck. In order to monitor and control its hinge joints, an agent is equipped with joint perceptors and effectors. Joint perceptors provide the agent with noise-free angular measurements every simulation cycle (20 ms), while joint effectors allow the agent to specify the speed/direction in which to move a joint.

Visual information about the environment is given to an agent every third simulation cycle (60 ms) through noisy measurements of the distance and angle to objects within a restricted vision cone (120°). Agents are also outfitted with noisy accelerometer and gyroscope perceptors, as well as force resistance perceptors on the sole of each foot. Additionally, agents can communicate with each other every other simulation cycle (40 ms) by sending 20 byte messages.

In addition to the standard Nao robot model, four additional variations of the standard model, known as heterogeneous types, are available for use. These variations from the standard model include changes in leg and arm length, hip width, and also the addition of toes to the robot's foot. Teams must use at least three different robot types, no more than seven agents of any one robot type, and no more than nine agents of any two robot types.

One significant change for the 2019 RoboCup 3D Simulation League competition was penalizing self-collisions. While the simulator's physics model can detect and simulate self-collisions—when a robot's body part such as a leg or arm collides with another part of its own body—having the physics model try to process and handle the large number of self-collisions occurring during games often leads to instability in the simulator causing it to crash. To preserve stability of the simulator self-collisions are purposely ignored by the physics model. However, not modeling self-collisions can result in robots performing physically impossible motions such as one leg passing through the other when kicking the ball. In order to discourage teams from having robots with self-colliding behaviors, a new feature was added to the simulator this year to detect and penalize self-collisions when they happen. This feature signals a self-collision as having occurred if two body parts of a robot overlap by more than 0.04 m, and then all joints in any arm or leg of the robot involved in the self-collision are frozen and not allowed to move for one second. Freezing the joints in an arm or leg that has started to collide with another body part is an approximation of the physics model preventing body parts from moving through each other, and also detracts from the performance of the robot due to its limb being "numb" and immobile. After the second passes, the joints are unfrozen, and the robot is allowed to move its self-colliding body parts for two seconds without any self-collisions being reported. This two second period, during which previously collided body parts are no longer penalized and frozen for self-collisions, allows a robot time to reposition its body to no longer have a self-collision.

The other major change for the 2019 RoboCup 3D Simulation League competition from previous years was the addition of a new pass play mode to encourage more passing and teamwork. The pass play mode allows players some extra time on the ball to kick and pass it during which time the opponent is prevented from interfering with a kick attempt. A player may initiate the pass play mode as long as the following conditions are all met:

- The current play mode is PlayOn.
- The agent is within 0.5 m of the ball.
- No opponents are within a meter of the ball.
- The ball is stationary as measured by having a speed no greater than 0.05 m per second.
- At least three seconds have passed since the last time a player's team has been in pass mode.

Once pass mode for a team has started the following happens:

- Players from the opponent team are prevented from getting within a meter of the ball.
- The pass play mode ends as soon as a player touches the ball or four seconds have passed.
- After pass mode has ended the team who initiated the pass mode is unable to score for ten seconds—this prevents teams from trying to take a shot on goal out of pass mode.

3   Changes for 2019

While many components developed prior to 2019 contributed to the success of the UT Austin Villa team including dynamic role assignment [11], marking [12], and an optimization framework used to learn low level behaviors for walking and kicking via an overlapping layered learning approach [13], the following subsections focus only on those that are new for 2019: reduction of self-collisions and use of the new pass mode. A performance analysis of these components is provided in Sect. 4.1.

3.1   Reduction of Self-collisions

The UT Austin Villa team specifies motions for kicking, getting up, and goalie diving skills through a periodic state machine with multiple key frames, where each key frame is a parameterized static pose of fixed joint positions. Figure 1 shows an example series of poses for a kicking motion. The joint angles are optimized using the CMA-ES [14] algorithm and overlapping layered learning [13] methodologies.

Fig. 1. Example of a fixed series of poses that make up a kicking motion.

During learning the robot runs through an optimization task where it performs a skill (e.g. attempting to kick a ball or standing up after having fallen over). At the conclusion of the optimization task a *fitness* value is awarded for how well the robot performed on the optimization task (e.g. how far the robot kicked a ball or how quickly it was able to stand up). Prior to 2019 robots were not penalized for self-collisions, so many of the skills that were learned for the robots inadvertently contained self-collisions as there was no incentive during learning to avoid them. The skills that contained self-collisions no longer worked correctly with this year's introduction of penalizing self-collisions, however, so it was necessary to try to reduce the number of self-collisions as much as possible in order to fix the broken skills.

As a first step toward reducing self-collisions, it is necessary to determine which skills contain self-collisions. In order to identify the sources of self-collisions, UT Austin Villa played thousands of games against different opponents. During these games whenever an agent had a self-collision the skill the agent was performing at the time of the self-collision was recorded along with the agent's uniform number—the agent's uniform number can be used to identify the agent's robot model as robot models are assigned to an agent based on the agent's uniform number, and there is a different set of skills for each robot model due to the physical differences between robot models [3]. The total number of self-collisions for each executed skill for every agent uniform number (1–11) was then computed from the recorded data across all the games played. Table 1 shows an example of this data for the agent with uniform number 2.

From the data in the second column of Table 1 it is clear there are many self-collisions across different kicks, as well as a very large number of self-collisions

Table 1. The number of self-collisions recorded by the agent with uniform number 2 (a type 4 robot model with toes) for different skills across 6000 games both before and after reducing self-collisions.

Skill	Self-collisions	
	Before reduction	After reduction
SKILL_GETUP_BACK	152	89
SKILL_GETUP_FRONT	1363	0
SKILL_KICK_8M	14	0
SKILL_KICK_13M	67	0
SKILL_KICK_14M	313	0
SKILL_KICK_15M	964	0
SKILL_KICK_16M	485	0
SKILL_KICK_17M	126	0
SKILL_KICK_18M	649	0
SKILL_KICK_19M	812	0
SKILL_KICK_20M	737	1

when trying to get up after the robot has fallen on its front. To reduce the number of self-collisions occurring when executing these skills, the following strategies were employed:

Hand fix: When a self-collision occurs, the simulator reports which body parts of a robot collided with each other. For kicking skills the body parts that matter the most are those in the legs, so if a robot's arm is involved in a self-collision the arm's movement can probably be adjusted without affecting the kicking motion. Roughly half the kicking skills that had self-collisions involved the robots' arms in the self-collisions, so we were able to manually adjust the arms' joint angle positions to no longer self-collide while still exhibiting the same kicking motion through the ball.

Reoptimize current self-colliding behavior: In many cases it is not easy to hand adjust the motions of a skill to avoid a self-collision as doing so fundamentally changes the performance of the skill (e.g. adjusting the position of the legs of a robot for a kicking skill when the robot's legs self-collide). Instead of trying to fix things by hand, the current skill can be relearned with CMA-ES using the current self-colliding behavior as a starting point for learning, while also adding a large penalty value to the fitness of an agent if it has any self-collisions while performing the optimization task it is trying to learn.

Reoptimize starting from similar behavior: If the previous strategy does not work—possibly because the current behavior has too many self-collisions such that it is hard to find a behavior that does not have self-collisions when using the current self-colliding behavior as a starting point—one can instead attempt to learn using a similar related skill (e.g. similar distance kick) that has fewer collisions as a starting point for learning.

Reoptimize with a tighter threshold for self-collisions: Some skills have infrequent enough self-collisions that they do not always occur during a learning trial, but still experience a significant number of self-collisions during games. It can be especially hard to reduce the number of self-collisions for skills when self-collisions are not always detected during learning. As a way to decrease the chance of the robot assuming body positions that are right on the border of having a self-collisions, one can decrease the allowed amount of overlap between body parts in the simulator before a self-collision is considered to have occurred. By decreasing the amount of allowed overlap between body parts during learning it is less likely that a learned behavior will have self-collisions exceeding the actual allowed amount of overlap.

All of the strategies mentioned were used to to reduce self-collisions in 35 of UT Austin Villa's previously learned skills. This reduction of self-collisions dramatically lowered the average number of self-collisions exhibited by the team during a game from 10.507 down to 0.137, thus removing almost 99% of previous self-collisions. The large reduction in self-collisions can be seen in the third column of Table 1. The impact of reducing self-collisions on the team's performance is evaluated in Sect. 4.1, and the number of self-collisions UT Austin Villa had compared to other teams is detailed in the evaluation of the fewest self-collisions challenge in Sect. 5.2.

3.2   Pass Mode Strategy

To best take advantage of the new pass mode, players must carefully decide when to activate it. If players were to naively activate pass mode at every opportunity to do so they would have a difficult time scoring as a team must wait ten seconds after their pass mode ends before they are allowed to score. If a team never uses pass mode, however, they will miss out on opportunities to kick the ball without their opponent being able to interfere with the kick. Given these considerations, the following is the strategy UT Austin Villa employs for using pass mode:

- Only activate pass mode when an opponent is within 1.25 m of the ball. Activating pass mode before the opponent is close is unnecessary as the opponent is not yet a threat to interfere with a kick, and the later pass mode is activated the later it will time out leaving more time to kick the ball before pass mode eventually ends.
- Do not use pass mode when a player is close enough to take a shot on goal and score. Goals cannot be scored for ten seconds after pass mode ends, so it is better to attempt a shot and try to score than to pass the ball and then have to wait ten seconds to score.
- Do use pass mode if a player is not behind the ball even if the player is close enough to the opponent's goal to take a shot and score. The player will have to take some time to walk around the ball to get in position to take a shot,

and at that point it is likely the opponent will have gotten close enough to the ball to interfere with a potential shot.

The gain in team performance when using UT Austin Villa's pass mode strategy is evaluated in Sect. 4.1.

4   Main Competition Results and Analysis

In winning the 2019 RoboCup competition UT Austin Villa finished with an overall record of 21 wins, 1 tie, and 1 loss.[1] During the course of the competition the team scored 112 goals while conceding only 5. Despite the team's strong performance at the competition, the relatively few number of games played at the competition, coupled with the complex and stochastic environment of the RoboCup 3D simulator, make it difficult to determine UT Austin Villa being better than other teams by a statistically significant margin. At the end of the competition, however, all teams were required to release their binaries used during the competition. Results of UT Austin Villa playing 1000 games against each of the other six teams' released binaries from the competition are shown in Table 2.

Table 2. UT Austin Villa's released binary's performance when playing 1000 games against the released binaries of all other teams at RoboCup 2019. This includes place (the rank a team achieved at the 2019 competition), average goal difference (values in parentheses are the standard error), win-loss-tie record, and goals for/against.

Opponent	Place	Avg. goal diff	Record (W-L-T)	Goals (F/A)
magmaOffenburg	2	2.403 (0.048)	913-9-78	2496/93
WrightOcean	3	2.735 (0.042)	952-5-43	3006/271
HfutEngine	5	4.733 (0.054)	995-0-5	4751/18
BahiaRT	4	6.360 (0.054)	1000-0-0	6361/1
FCPortugal	6	7.309 (0.052)	1000-0-0	7489/180
ITAndroids	7	9.670 (0.063)	1000-0-0	9721/51

UT Austin Villa finished with at least an average goal difference greater than 2.4 goals against every opponent. Additionally, UT Austin Villa's win percentage was greater than 91% against each team, and out of the 6000 games that were played in Table 2 the team only lost 14. These results show that UT Austin Villa winning the 2019 competition was far from a chance occurrence. The following subsection analyzes the contributions of reducing self-collisions and use of a new pass mode (both described in Sect. 3) to the team's dominant performance.

---

[1] Full tournament results can be found at http://www.cs.utexas.edu/~AustinVilla/?p=competitions/RoboCup19#3D.

4.1   Analysis of Components

To analyze the contribution of new components for 2019—reduction of self-collisions and use of the new pass mode (Sect. 3)—to the UT Austin Villa team's performance, we played 1000 games between a version of the 2019 UT Austin Villa team with each of these components turned off—and no other changes—against each of the RoboCup 2019 teams' released binaries. Results comparing the performance of the UT Austin Villa team with and without using these components are shown in Table 3.

Table 3. Different versions of the UTAustinVilla team when playing 1000 games against the released binaries of all teams at RoboCup 2019. Values shown are average goal difference with values in parentheses being the difference in performance from the team's released binary.

Opponent	No pass mode	Self-collisions	No pass mode + Self-collisions
UTAustinVilla	−0.677 (−0.677)	−1.986 (−1.986)	−2.075 (−2.075)
magmaOffenburg	1.843 (−0.560)	1.814 (−0.589)	1.312 (−1.091)
WrightOcean	2.104 (−0.631)	1.487 (−1.248)	0.765 (−1.970)
HfutEngine	4.391 (−0.342)	3.509 (−1.224)	3.333 (−1.400)
BahiaRT	6.255 (−0.105)	5.409 (−0.951)	4.863 (−1.497)
FCPortugal	6.966 (−0.343)	4.869 (−2.440)	4.653 (−2.656)
ITAndroids	9.379 (−0.291)	6.461 (−3.209)	6.128 (−3.542)

Results show that without using pass mode or reducing self-collisions the team's performance drops significantly. Furthermore, if UT Austin Villa had not used either pass mode or reduced self-collisions, the team would have only beaten WrightOcean by an average of 0.765 goals which correlates to 60.8% of games being wins, 23.9% ties, and 15.3% losses.

4.2   Additional Tournament Competition Analysis

To further analyze the tournament competition, Table 4 shows the average goal difference for each team at RoboCup 2019 when playing 1000 games against all other teams at RoboCup 2019.

It is interesting to note that the ordering of teams in terms of winning (positive goal difference) and losing (negative goal difference) is transitive—every opponent that a team wins against also loses to every opponent that defeats that same team. Relative goal difference does not have this same property, however, as a team that does better against one opponent relative to another team does not always do better against a second opponent relative to that same team. UT Austin Villa is dominant in terms of relative goal difference, however, as UT Austin Villa has a higher goal difference against each opponent than all other teams against the same opponent.

Table 4. Average goal difference for each team at RoboCup 2019 (rows) when playing 1000 games against the released binaries of all other teams at RoboCup 2019 (columns). Teams are ordered from most to least dominant in terms of winning (positive goal difference) and losing (negative goal difference).

	UTA	mag	Wri	Hfu	Bah	FCP	ITA
UTAustinVilla	—	2.403	2.735	4.733	6.360	7.309	9.670
magmaOffenburg	−2.403	—	0.021	1.376	2.783	3.286	3.464
WrightOcean	−2.735	−0.021	—	1.160	2.503	4.599	5.105
HfutEngine	−4.733	−1.376	−1.160	—	0.315	0.981	1.525
BahiaRT	−6.360	−2.783	−2.503	−0.315	—	0.633	0.386
FCPortugal	−7.309	−3.286	−4.599	−0.981	−0.633	—	0.084
ITAndroids	−9.670	−3.464	−5.105	−1.525	−0.386	−0.084	—

5   Technical Challenges

During the competition there was an overall technical challenge consisting of two different league challenges: free and fewest self-collision challenges. For each league challenge a team participated in, points were awarded toward the overall technical challenge based on the following equation:

$$\text{points}(rank) = 25 - 20 * (rank - 1)/(numberOfParticipants - 1)$$

Table 5. Overall ranking and points totals for each team participating in the RoboCup 2019 3D Simulation League technical challenge as well as ranks and points awarded for each of the individual league challenges that make up the technical challenge.

Team	Overall		Free		Fewest Self-collisions	
	Rank	Points	Rank	Points	Rank	Points
UTAustinVilla	**1**	**45**	**2**	**20**	**1**	**25**
FCPortugal	2	36.7	1	25	5	11.7
magmaOffenburg	2	36.7	3	15	2	21.7
ITAndroids	4	28.3	4	10	3	18.3
WrightOcean	5	15	—	—	4	15
BahiaRT	6	13.3	5	5	6	8.3
HfutEngine	7	5	—	—	7	5

Table 5 shows the ranking and cumulative team point totals for the technical challenge as well as for each individual league challenge. UT Austin Villa won the fewest self-collisions challenge and finished second in the free challenge resulting in a first place finish in the overall technical challenge. The following subsections detail UT Austin Villa's participation in each league challenge.

5.1 Free Challenge

During the free challenge, teams give a five minute presentation on a research topic related to their team. Each team in the league then ranks the presentations with the best receiving a score of 1, second best a score of 2, etc. Additionally several respected research members of the RoboCup community outside the league rank the presentations, with their scores being counted double. The winner of the free challenge is the team that receives the lowest score. Table 6 shows the results of the free challenge in which UT Austin Villa was awarded second place.

Table 6. Results of the free challenge.

Team	Score
FCPortugal	28
UTAustinVilla	**38**
magmaOffenburg	40
ITAndroids	51
BahiaRT	68

UT Austin Villa's free challenge submission[2] presented research on learning skills by observing a single demonstration of a skill by another agent [15]. In particular, we showed that an agent could use a PID controller as an inverse dynamics model to mimic and improve upon its opponent's soccer skills by combining the use of a single demonstration and the environment-provided sparse reward. Moreover, this single demonstration consists of only joint angles per time-step, i.e., the learner is only exposed to how the opponent's joint configuration is transitioning each time-step, it has no knowledge of the torque applied to achieve the transition. Using the yearly released binary files, we artificially created the opponent demonstration by triggering desired behaviors by, for example, placing the ball in specific locations to induce a long distance kick. In order to retrieve the joint angles per time-step for specific tasks, we modified the simulator to output the joint angles of the agent when performing the task.

The other teams participating in the free challenge also presented interesting work:[3] FCPortugal presented work on how to learn fast human-like running and sprinting behaviors [16,17], magmaOffenburg talked about learning a walk behavior utilizing toes from scratch, ITAndroids discussed Bottom-Up Meta-Policy Search (BUMPS) for learning robot skills, and BahiaRT presented a set of tools for learning set plays from demonstration [18].

---

[2] Free challenge entry description available at http://www.cs.utexas.edu/~Austin Villa/sim/3dsimulation/AustinVilla3DSimulationFiles/2019/files/UTAustinVilla FreeChallenge2019.pdf.

[3] All participating teams' free challenge entry descriptions available at http://archive. robocup.info/Soccer/Simulation/3D/FCPs/RoboCup/2019/.

5.2   Fewest Self-collisions Challenge

Results of the fewest self-collisions challenge are shown in the second column of Table 7. UT Austin Villa won the challenge by only having one recorded self-collision during the entire competition. The average number of self-collisions when each team plays 1000 games against each of the other teams' released binaries is show in the third column of Table 7. UT Austin Villa also had the fewest number of self-collisions when playing 1000 games against each of the other teams' released binaries suggesting that UT Austin Villa winning the fewest self-collisions challenge was statistically probable.

Table 7. Average number of self-collisions per game for each team as recorded for the fewest self-collisions challenge and as measured when playing 1000 games against each of the other teams' released binaries

Team	Avg. self-collisions per game	
	Challenge	Many games
UTAustinVilla	**0.1**	**0.137**
magmaOffenburg	0.2	0.315
ITAndroids	2.0	2.936
WrightOcean	3.2	4.360
FCPortugal	3.5	2.732
BahiaRT	5.7	7.392
HfutEngine	8.5	8.069

6   Conclusion

UT Austin Villa won the 2019 RoboCup 3D Simulation League main competition as well as the overall league technical challenge.[4] Data taken using released binaries from the competition show that UT Austin Villa winning the competition was statistically significant. The 2019 UT Austin Villa team also improved from 2018 as it was able to beat the team's 2018 champion binary by an average of 0.7 ($\pm$0.044) goals across 1000 games.[5]

In an effort to both make it easier for new teams to join the RoboCup 3D Simulation League, and also provide a resource that can be beneficial to existing

---

[4] More information about the UT Austin Villa team, as well as video from the competition, can be found at the team's website: http://www.cs.utexas.edu/~AustinVilla/sim/3dsimulation/#2019.

[5] So as to be compatible with the 2018 version of the team's binary the simulator was modified to not report when pass play mode was active to the 2018 team (the play mode was reported as still being PlayOn during pass mode to the 2018 team's agents), and self-collisions were not penalized.

teams, the UT Austin Villa team has released their base code [19].[6] This code release provides a fully functioning agent and good starting point for new teams to the RoboCup 3D Simulation League (it was used by two other teams at the 2019 competition: WrightOcean and HfutEngine). Additionally the code release offers a foundational platform for conducting research in multiple areas including robotics, multiagent systems, and machine learning.

Acknowledgments. This work has taken place in the Learning Agents Research Group (LARG) at UT Austin. LARG research is supported in part by NSF (IIS-1637736, IIS-1651089, IIS-1724157), ONR (N00014-18-2243), FLI (RFP2-000), ARL, DARPA, Intel, Raytheon, and Lockheed Martin. Peter Stone serves on the Board of Directors of Cogitai, Inc. The terms of this arrangement have been reviewed and approved by the University of Texas at Austin in accordance with its policy on objectivity in research. Patrick MacAlpine is an employee of Microsoft and supported by Microsoft Research.

References

1. MacAlpine, P., et al.: UT Austin Villa 2011: a champion agent in the RoboCup 3D soccer simulation competition. In: Proceedings of 11th International Conference on Autonomous Agents and Multiagent Systems (AAMAS 2012) (2012)
2. MacAlpine, P., Collins, N., Lopez-Mobilia, A., Stone, P.: UT Austin Villa: RoboCup 2012 3D simulation league champion. In: Chen, X., Stone, P., Sucar, L.E., van der Zant, T. (eds.) RoboCup 2012. LNCS (LNAI), vol. 7500, pp. 77–88. Springer, Heidelberg (2013). https://doi.org/10.1007/978-3-642-39250-4_8
3. MacAlpine, P., Depinet, M., Liang, J., Stone, P.: UT Austin Villa: RoboCup 2014 3D simulation league competition and technical challenge champions. In: Bianchi, R.A.C., Akin, H.L., Ramamoorthy, S., Sugiura, K. (eds.) RoboCup 2014. LNCS (LNAI), vol. 8992, pp. 33–46. Springer, Cham (2015). https://doi.org/10.1007/978-3-319-18615-3_3
4. MacAlpine, P., Hanna, J., Liang, J., Stone, P.: UT Austin Villa: RoboCup 2015 3D simulation league competition and technical challenges champions. In: Almeida, L., Ji, J., Steinbauer, G., Luke, S. (eds.) RoboCup 2015. LNCS (LNAI), vol. 9513, pp. 118–131. Springer, Cham (2015). https://doi.org/10.1007/978-3-319-29339-4_10
5. MacAlpine, P., Stone, P.: UT Austin Villa: RoboCup 2016 3D simulation league competition and technical challenges champions. In: Behnke, S., Sheh, R., Sarıel, S., Lee, D.D. (eds.) RoboCup 2016. LNCS (LNAI), vol. 9776, pp. 515–528. Springer, Cham (2017). https://doi.org/10.1007/978-3-319-68792-6_43
6. MacAlpine, P., Stone, P.: UT Austin Villa: RoboCup 2017 3D simulation league competition and technical challenges champions. In: Akiyama, H., Obst, O., Sammut, C., Tonidandel, F. (eds.) RoboCup 2017. LNCS (LNAI), vol. 11175, pp. 473–485. Springer, Cham (2018). https://doi.org/10.1007/978-3-030-00308-1_39
7. MacAlpine, P., Torabi, F., Pavse, B., Sigmon, J., Stone, P.: UT Austin Villa: RoboCup 2018 3D simulation league champions. In: Holz, D., Genter, K., Saad, M., von Stryk, O. (eds.) RoboCup 2018. LNCS (LNAI), vol. 11374, pp. 462–475. Springer, Cham (2019). https://doi.org/10.1007/978-3-030-27544-0_38

---

[6] Code release at https://github.com/LARG/utaustinvilla3d.

8. MacAlpine, P., et al.: UT Austin Villa 2011 3D simulation team report. Technical report AI11-10, The University of Texas at Austin, Department of Computer Science, AI Laboratory (2011)

9. Obst, O., Rollmann, M.: Spark – a generic simulator for physical multi-agent simulations. In: Lindemann, G., Denzinger, J., Timm, I.J., Unland, R. (eds.) MATES 2004. LNCS (LNAI), vol. 3187, pp. 243–257. Springer, Heidelberg (2004). https://doi.org/10.1007/978-3-540-30082-3_18

10. Xu, Y., Vatankhah, H.: SimSpark: an open source robot simulator developed by the RoboCup community. In: Behnke, S., Veloso, M., Visser, A., Xiong, R. (eds.) RoboCup 2013. LNCS (LNAI), vol. 8371, pp. 632–639. Springer, Heidelberg (2014). https://doi.org/10.1007/978-3-662-44468-9_59

11. MacAlpine, P., Price, E., Stone, P.: SCRAM: scalable collision-avoiding role assignment with minimal-makespan for formational positioning. In: Proceedings of the Twenty-Ninth AAAI Conference on Artificial Intelligence (AAAI-15) (2015)

12. MacAlpine, P., Stone, P.: Prioritized role assignment for marking. In: Behnke, S., Sheh, R., Sariel, S., Lee, D.D. (eds.) RoboCup 2016. LNCS (LNAI), vol. 9776, pp. 306–318. Springer, Cham (2017). https://doi.org/10.1007/978-3-319-68792-6_25

13. MacAlpine, P., Stone, P.: Overlapping layered learning. Artif. Intell. **254**, 21–43 (2018)

14. Hansen, N.: The CMA Evolution Strategy: A Tutorial (2009). http://www.lri.fr/~hansen/cmatutorial.pdf

15. Pavse, B.S., Torabi, F., Hanna, J., Warnell, G., Stone, P.: RIDM: reinforced inverse dynamics modeling for learning from a single observed demonstration. In: Imitation, Intent, and Interaction (I3) Workshop at ICML 2019 (2019)

16. Abreu, M., Lau, N., Sousa, A., Reis, L.P.: Learning low level skills from scratch for humanoid robot soccer using deep reinforcement learning. In: 2019 IEEE International Conference on Autonomous Robot Systems and Competitions (ICARSC), pp. 1–8. IEEE (2019)

17. Abreu, M., Reis, L.P., Lau, N.: Learning to run faster in a humanoid robot soccer environment through reinforcement learning. In: Chalup, S., et al. (eds.) RoboCup 2019: Robot World Cup XXIII. LNAI, pp. 3–15. Springer (2019)

18. Simões, M., Nogueira, T.: Towards setplays learning in a multiagent robotic soccer team. In: 2018 Latin American Robotic Symposium, 2018 Brazilian Symposium on Robotics (SBR) and 2018 Workshop on Robotics in Education (WRE), pp. 277–282. IEEE (2018)

19. MacAlpine, P., Stone, P.: UT Austin Villa RoboCup 3D simulation base code release. In: Behnke, S., Sheh, R., Sariel, S., Lee, D.D. (eds.) RoboCup 2016. LNCS (LNAI), vol. 9776, pp. 135–143. Springer, Cham (2017). https://doi.org/10.1007/978-3-319-68792-6_11

MRL Champion Team Paper in Humanoid TeenSize League of RoboCup 2019

Hamed Mahmudi(✉)🆔, Amir Gholami🆔, Mohammad Hossein Delavaran🆔,
Soheil Khatibi, Saeid Bazargan, Milad Moradi, Bita Alaee, Arash Rahmani,

Kazem Firouzmandi Bandpey, Peyman Fallahzadeh, and Meisam Teimouri(✉)🆔

Mechatronics Research Lab, Department of Computer and Electrical Engineering,
Qazvin Islamic Azad University, Qazvin, Iran
{mahmudihamed,m.teimouri}@qiau.ac.ir
http://hsl.mrl.ir, http://hsl.mrl.ir

Abstract. RoboCup uses soccer competitions as a research area to promote robotics and artificial intelligence. The ultimate goal of the RoboCup is to develop a team of humanoid robots that can win against the human world champion soccer team in 2050. This paper presents the approach of the MRL TeenSize humanoid team to improve its hardware and software which leads to achieving first place in soccer competition and Drop-In games, second place in the technical challenge and third-best humanoid award.

Keywords: Champion team paper · RoboCup · Humanoid league · Bipedal locomotion

1 Introduction

The MRL project was started in 2003 in the Mechatronics Research Laboratory at Islamic Azad University, Qazvin branch looking onward to enhance the knowledge of robotics. The MRL humanoid soccer team is aimed to develop a humanoid platform for research and education. Our humanoid soccer-playing team has participated in the RoboCup Humanoid KidSize since 2011 [1–3]. As RoboCup uses soccer as a research area to develop a team of humanoid robots, we decided to participate in the TeenSize category from 2018 in order to move toward the goal of RoboCup and face new challenges. MRL earned first place in the TeenSize main league competition as well as Drop-In games and won second place in TeenSize Technical challenges and third-best humanoid award in the RoboCup 2019, Sydney, Australia.

The rest of this paper can be summarized in the following. In Sect. 2 an overview of the system is described. The electronic parts are discussed in Sect. 3. In Sect. 4 recent development of our software including methods of developing for visual perception and robot behavior are clarified. We will continue with solutions developed to overcome the technical challenges and advances made to increase the efficiency of robot kicking in Sect. 5. Finally, the paper is concluded in Sect. 6.

S. Chalup et al. (Eds.): RoboCup 2019, LNAI 11531, pp. 553–564, 2019.
https://doi.org/10.1007/978-3-030-35699-6_45

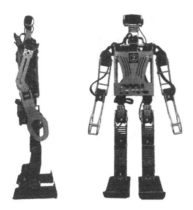 

Fig. 1. Left: Amir humanoid TeenSize robot. Right: MRL-HSL team at RoboCup 2019 competition Sydney, Australia.

2 Overview of the System

Amir is our new humanoid robot with 20 degrees of freedom (Fig. 1). Our robots have a well-known 20 degree of freedom structure with a height of 83 cm and a weight of 6.6 kg. All joints are equipped with Robotis Dynamixel MX series actuators. We have used six Dynamixel MX-106 for each leg, three Dynamixel MX-64 for each arm and two Dynamixel MX-28 in neck and head. The robot is powered by a 3-Cell, 5000mAH LiPo battery. The main processing unit is an Intel NUC 7th generation and power management is done by our self-constructed controller board which will be described below.

Visual perception is done by a Logitech C920 normal webcam with a 78° field of view. All mechanical parts of the robot are made of aluminum alloy 6061. We manufactured robot components by utilizing CNC Milling in order to increase accuracy.

Our software architecture is based on the UPennalizers RoboCup released code [4]. The Vision, world model, and behavior modules are completely rewritten and the walk engine is enhanced to address disturbances more efficiently.

3 Electronic

3.1 Control Manager

Last year, we designed our control manager board (Fig. 2 left) that was responsible for power supply, actuator communication and attitude estimation of the robot. In MRL-CM1, we divided the actuators lane into three separate lanes to reduce the load. So the transmission speed between the mainboard and actuators located in different chains increased. However, we need to read sensors data with a higher rate to get smoother motion controllers. Reading actuators and sensors data through the same BUS makes the rate of reading constrained by the speed of actuators reading that is considerably lower than sensors reading. Moreover adding extra measuring instruments to the system makes it even slower. To cope with this problem, a new control manager board (Fig. 2 right) is designed that consists of two separated boards (actuators and sensors board).

Fig. 2. Left: MRL-CM1. Right: New control manager board (MRL-CM2).

Each board is individually connected to the mainboard and transfers the data using the standard Dynamixel packets. The block diagram of the new system is demonstrated in Fig. 3.

Sensor Board. The processing unit of the actuators board is an ARM STM32F405VE microcontroller. The firmware is developed under standard HAL drivers [5]. This board is equipped with 2 inertial sensors (gyroscope and accelerometer). Also, it has a lane for communicating with strain gauges. Since its task is just to read data sensors and it has no communication with actuators, we can read data faster. An OLED display is attached for monitoring and debugging. In addition, it should be mentioned that another aim of this board is estimating roll, pitch, and yaw employing a complementary filter [6].

Actuator Board. The tasks of power management and actuators data streaming are accomplished by this board. The processing unit of the actuator board is the same as the sensor board. This board is designed to communicate with both TTL and RS-485 protocols simultaneously, but because of our available R series actuators of Dynamixel and efficiency of RS-485 over long distances between legs actuators, we used RS-485

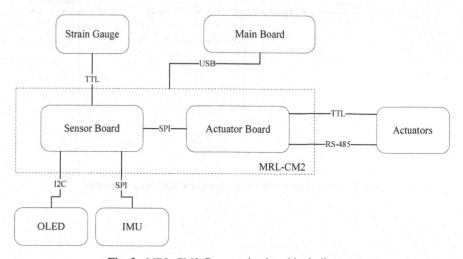

Fig. 3. MRL-CM2 Communications block diagram

protocol as our serial communication. Similar to MRL-CM1, to reduce the heavy load of data transfer, we have divided the communication lane into five independent lanes, each one has its own FIFO queue.

As well, the actuator board is able to supply the required power for the entire robot. We used a DC-DC boost converter in MRL-CM1 which provided 18V-5A at a frequency of 350 kHz, but there were some problems. It was used only to supply mainboard voltage and we got the actuator voltage directly from the battery and we had no way to change and control it. So, in this version of the board, we used a DC-DC buck converter to supply the voltage and current needed for the mainboard and actuators, as explained below.

DC-DC Buck Converter. The battery is the main input power supplier of the robot and its voltage drops over time. By implementing this system, we can keep motors voltage constant and apply desired voltage to the motor in different situations, such as higher voltage than usual when the robot is kicking or when the robot is standing up. Moreover, the process of motion calibration of the robot becomes simpler.

Buck converters are switched-mode step-down DC-DC converters; the output voltage of buck converters is a function of the PWM duty cycle which controls the MOSFETs status. The output signal is an average of the PWM square wave [7].

The architecture of the closed-loop DC-DC buck converter is depicted in Fig. 4. It is consisting of a power stage and a controller. The converter power stage consists of a second-order LC low-pass filter and it is prone to become unstable. In this design, we have to satisfy two important characteristics: the capability of rejecting disturbances and stability in all operating conditions. So a PID controller is implemented to enhance system stability and adjust the output voltage [8].

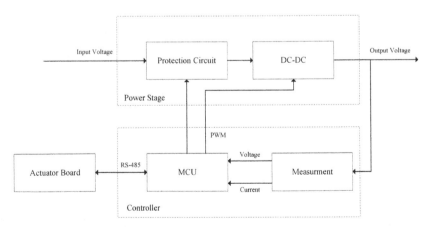

Fig. 4. Block diagram of the designed DC-DC buck converter.

4 Software

4.1 Visual Perception

Vision is the most important source of perception in a humanoid soccer playing robot. In this section, we briefly summaries the pipeline of our vision system and investigate the details of our segmentation module in the following subsection.

Like most of the participating teams, we use a monocular vision system. The captured image at first is fed to a segmentation module to perform semantic segmentation. Based on this segmented image the boundary of the field is determined. Then all object detection algorithms are applied only on the pixels located in the field boundary. The field lines and their intersections are detected using the Hough Transform [2]. For ball detection, first, some coarse regions of interest that may contain a ball are extracted using the segmentation map and camera matrix. Then each region is fed to a deep convolutional neural network to predict whether the region contains a ball or not and estimate the exact location of the ball in that region. The details of our ball detection approach are described in [9].

Semantic Segmentation. In RoboCup 2019 an important step toward outdoor conditions was taken by advancing to natural light in drop-in matches. Most humanoid teams used pixel-level image segmentation as the first step of vision pipeline, but due to the continuous changes of illumination in natural light, methods such as thresholding and lookup tables often yield unreliable and ineffective results. To overcome this challenge, we have used semantic segmentation [10] as the first step of our vision pipeline. This segmentation module uses a deep fully convolutional neural network which we will briefly describe in the following subsections.

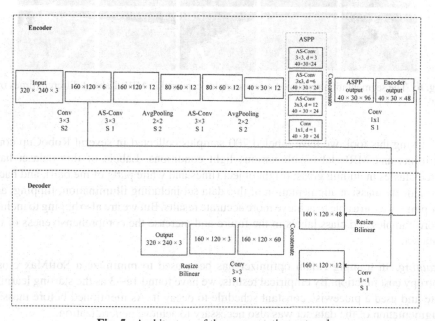

Fig. 5. Architecture of the segmentation network.

Model Architecture. Since most humanoid robots carry only a CPU as the processing units, semantic segmentation as a dense prediction task could be computationally expensive. By considering the limitations of our robots we have designed a segmentation model made an efficient trade off between accuracy and computational cost.

The designed model is highly inspired by DeepLab v3+ [10]. Following DeepLab our model has two parts: an encoder for downsampling and a decoder for upsampling. With the same scheme as DeepLab v3+, the encoder has a small base network followed by an Atrous Spatial Pyramid Pooling (ASPP) [10] module. In the decoder, low-level features have been pulled from the base network of the encoder and then concatenated with the upsampled output of the encoder. Finally, to produce the un-normalized class probabilities, a convolutional layer is applied. The output must be upsampled once more to match the input resolution. For the sake of reducing the computational cost of inference in most layers of the network, Atrous Separable Convolutions [10] (AS-Conv) has been used instead of the traditional convolutions. The details of the network and each layer is demonstrated in Fig. 5.

Data Set. Training of the described segmentation module requires samples with pixel-level labels and manual labeling of this data set is a challenge. Therefore, we have created a tool to ease up the labeling and save annotation time.

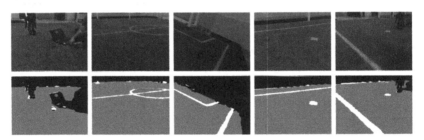

Fig. 6. The segmentation results on a few samples captured in MRL Labs at different times of a day.

Using this tool, we have labeled 700 samples collected in several RoboCup competitions and MRL labs with various light conditions. Labels of this dataset have three classes including grass, bright object (lines and white parts of the ball), and background. By massive augmentation of this data set including illumination, flipping, and cropping we were able to achieve more accurate results. But we are also hoping to include more samples and class labels in the future and increase the comprehensiveness of the data set.

Training. In training Adam optimizer has been used to minimize a SoftMax cross-entropy cost function. By empirical results, we have found $1e-3$ as the starting learning rate and used a piecewise constant schedule to decay it. As mentioned before massive augmentation of the data set was also necessary to achieve generalization.

Training of the network takes about 30 min on an Nvidia GTX 1070 TI GPU. Also, the entire training code was implemented using TensorFlow and will be available on the MRL-HSL GitHub page[1].

In RoboCup 2019 we used the trained model for all matches, and we achieved accurate results. Also, the trained model has been tested and used at various times of the day with different light conditions in our lab. As it is shown in Fig. 6 the segmentation results are accurate with fine edges.

The entire segmentation module can be processed as fast as 22 frames per second on an Intel Core i3 7th gen CPU alongside with other operations needed for a real game of play.

It is obvious that the work is not finished. During RoboCup 2019 we experienced some disturbances caused by the effect of direct sunlight on the grass. However, using multi-task learning other vision tasks of the robot can share the base network with the segmentation module. Furthermore, a0dding more classes to segmentation and making a benchmarking data set for the base of compression can be a good path toward the future of this work.

4.2 Behavior

Role Assignment. Our role set consists of four roles named Goalkeeper, Attacker, Defender, and Supporter which have their own responsibility description. The Goalkeeper is a static role which does not change while the others do according to the game situation. Hence the Goalkeeper stands in the middle of its goal and when the ball enters the goal area and no other teammates are close to it, the Goalkeeper comes to clear it. We assign a role to other robots in the field considering two factors. First, the chance of approaching the ball that is a combination of ball model probability and cost of reaching it facing the opponents goal. Second, distance to the own goal. The Attacker role is assigned to the robot which has the biggest chance to approach the ball. Then the robot that is not an Attacker and is closer to its own goal than others will be Defender. It should block the way that ball can be kicked toward our goal and be ready to chase the ball when needed. Finally, the last one will be Supporter. Supporter is a quite important role which can drastically improve the performance of each team by supporting both attacking and defending through apt positioning. It is quite dependent on accurate localization and error can cause serious problems like collision that impairs the team performance rather than improving it. In recent years we have been able to practice this role due to significant improvement in our localization accuracy. When our Attacker detects the ball the Supporter starts following it with a certain shift with respect to it in order to become Attacker in the case that the current Attacker loses the ball. This shift can vary according to different positions of the ball and the Attacker [11]. When the Attacker does not detect the ball (which means that none of the robots detect it), the Supporter plays like a Defender. It covers the other side that the Defender does not cover so that the goal area becomes safe. On the other hand, the Attacker can search for the ball not being concerned about conceding a goal.

---

[1] https://github.com/mrl-hsl.

Active Vision. Due to the limited field of view, our robot is not able to see every important observation in a specific head position. To avoid this problem, some teams have used cameras with a wider field of view and some others have used cameras with higher fps so that the robot can move its head fast and observe all important things around. But we have started to develop an active vision algorithm in which the robot goes through some predefined actions. The goal is to improve the models of self-localization and the ball. The uncertainty of a belief given by Shannon entropy can be a good benchmark to determine whether an action improves the models [12].

Calculating the entropy after doing an action consists of updating the models for all of the visible observations. The visibility of observations is determined with a polygon formed by projecting four corners of the image on the field. But we experienced serious problems while implementing this algorithm. Firstly, issues like losing the ball can occur because of projection and localization errors. Secondly, We do not have any feedback from the environment after taking action. For instance, If the robot can not detect a landmark due to the occlusion, there is no way to find it out. To solve these problems we are investigating a deep reinforcement learning network that takes a sequence of raw images as input and selects the best action to move the head through the right position and fix the error.

5 Motion Control

5.1 Push Recovery by Stepping

In the previous year, the hip-knee-ankle strategy for push recovery was applied using the PID controller for each joint [13]. Also, for more stability, the arm controller was added to the hip-knee-ankle strategy. This made the robot to resist more against pushes coming from the front, rear and sides of the robot [14].

For RoboCup 2019 our push recovery approach is extended by adding a simple stepping method. This method is activated against strong forces coming from the front, rear, and sides of the robot. To recover the stability by stepping method, an Inertial Measurement Unit (IMU) is required to get angle feedback of the upper body. When the humanoid robot is impacted by external forces, the ground projection of the CoM position starts to leave the support polygon, so there is a possibility for the robot to fall down. If the ground projection of the CoM position exceeds a predefined threshold, the robot increases the velocity of stepping in the direction of pushes and walks forward, backward or sides more quickly (Fig. 7). When CoM returns to the desired state, the velocity of stepping comes back to the normal condition.

Fig. 7. Push recovery by stepping meth

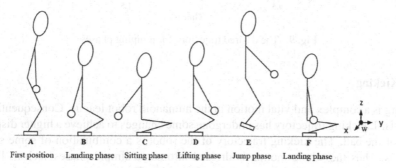

A	B	C	D	E	F
First position	Landing phase	Sitting phase	Lifting phase	Jump phase	Landing phase

Fig. 8. Jump phases

5.2 High Jump

In this section, a motion planning method for the humanoid robot is proposed which can perform the vertical jump. A stable vertical jump is accomplished by maintaining the ground projection of the Center of Mass (CoM) in the support polygon. To satisfy the stability we have used arms. Therefore, the robot pulls back its arms while it is sitting down and subsequently pulls forward while it is jumping in the vertical direction. On the other hand, movement of the arms helps to make the robot do a higher jump [15].

The states of the robot in the jumping phases are shown in Fig. 8. The first phase of jumping (i.e. phase A) starts while the robot standing in an upright position. The robot moves downward by bending its knees and ankles (phase B). When it reaches to sitting position (phase C), stay in this position for 0.3 s. Take-off from the ground needs a fast response to reach the desired trajectory with overshoot. So the robot extends its lower body in a moment (phase D) and as a result, the robot takes off the ground (phase E). Landing without losing stability is remarkably important, hence the robot must be kept stable in this situation and the controller will help the robot to do this job correctly (phase F).

The designed trajectory is approximated from phase A to D using two linear equations and from phase D to F by the Fourier series as shown in Fig. 9. During the lifting phase, controlling the CoM position is the main problem and in order to solve this, a PD controller is designed to control the CoM position. The gains of the PD controller is tuned with Ziegler–Nichols method.

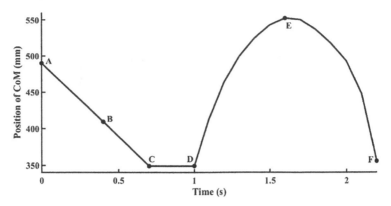

Fig. 9. The desired trajectory for jumping phases

5.3 Kicking

Kicking is a complex and vital motion in the humanoid robot league. Consequently, the MRL-HSL kicking trajectory has undergone some changes to achieve a higher displacement of the ball. The kicking trajectory of the robot is a combination of some simple motions. Thus the whole motion is divided into some simple phases such as lifting, kicking, landing and stabilizing the CoM of the robot. Furthermore, the upper body has the opposite movement compared to the swing foot which causes to provide more power to the ball (Fig. 10). The trajectory of kicking is designed by using [16].

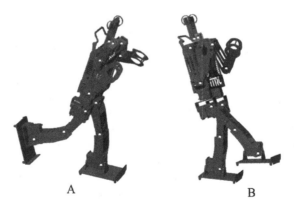

Fig. 10. Movement of body during kicking

6   Conclusion

In this paper, we have presented the specifications of the hardware and software of the MRL TeenSize humanoid robot system developed under the RoboCup 2019 rules.

The mentioned improvements including new control manager board, buck convertor, semantic segmentation, deep convolutional ball detector network, high jump motion and stepping push recovery strategy lead us to take four awards in Robocup 2019 competitions. In soccer competition we got first place by winning all matches. In drop-in games with 11 points we won the first place award and in the technical challenge by taking 14 points from two push recovery and high jump challenges second place is achieved. Overall we honored as the third-best humanoid team.

Also, We use our self-designed and self-constructed robots and we are working on this platform with some interested researchers and students optimizing vision, motion control, world modeling, behavior, and embedded control board.

References

1. Teimouri, M., et al.: MRL Team Description Paper for Humanoid KidSize League of RoboCup 2017. Mechatronics Research Lab, Department of Computer and Electrical Engineering, Qazvin Islamic Azad University, Qazvin, Iran (2017)
2. Teimouri, M., et al.: MRL Team Description Paper for Humanoid KidSize League of RoboCup 2018. Mechatronics Research Lab, Department of Computer and Electrical Engineering, Qazvin Islamic Azad University, Qazvin, Iran (2018)
3. Mahmoudi, H., et al.: MRL Team Description Paper for Humanoid KidSize League of RoboCup 2019. Mechatronics Research Lab, Department of Computer and Electrical Engineering, Qazvin Islamic Azad University, Qazvin, Iran (2019)
4. https://github.com/UPenn-RoboCup/UPennalizers
5. ST Microelectronics: RM0090 Reference manual STM32F405xx. STM32F407xx, STM32F415xx and STM32F417xx advanced ARM-based
6. Allgeuer, P., Behnke, S.: Robust sensor fusion for robot attitude estimation. In: 2014 IEEE-RAS International Conference on Humanoid Robots, pp. 218–224. IEEE (2014)
7. Kazimierczuk, M.K.: Pulse-Width Modulated DC-DC Power Converters. Wiley, Hoboken (2015)
8. Guo, L.: Implementation of digital PID controllers for DC-DC converters using digital signal processors. In: 2007 IEEE International Conference on Electro/Information Technology, pp. 306–311. IEEE (2007)
9. Teimouri, M., Delavaran, M.H., Rezaei, M.: A real-time ball detection approach using convolutional neural networks. In: Proceedings of 23rd RoboCup International Symposium. Sydney, Australia (2019)
10. Chen, L.-C., Zhu, Y., Papandreou, G., Schroff, F., Adam, H.: Encoder-decoder with atrous separable convolution for semantic image segmentation. In: Proceedings of the European Conference on Computer Vision (ECCV), pp. 801–818 (2018)
11. Petersen, K., Stoll, G., von Stryk, O.: A supporter behavior for soccer playing humanoid robots. In: Ruiz-del-Solar, J., Chown, E., Plöger, P.G. (eds.) RoboCup 2010. LNCS (LNAI), vol. 6556, pp. 386–396. Springer, Heidelberg (2011). https://doi.org/10.1007/978-3-642-20217-9_33
12. Seekircher, A., Laue, T., Röfer, T.: Entropy-based active vision for a humanoid soccer robot. In: Ruiz-del-Solar, J., Chown, E., Plöger, P.G. (eds.) RoboCup 2010. LNCS (LNAI), vol. 6556, pp. 1–12. Springer, Heidelberg (2011). https://doi.org/10.1007/978-3-642-20217-9_1
13. Teimouri, M., et al.: MRL Team Description Paper for Humanoid TeenSize League of RoboCup 2018. Mechatronics Research Lab, Department of Computer and Electrical Engineering, Qazvin Islamic Azad University, Qazvin, Iran (2018)

14. Mahmudi, H., et al.: MRL Team Description Paper for Humanoid TeenSize League of RoboCup 2019. Mechatronics Research Lab, Department of Computer and Electrical Engineering, Qazvin Islamic Azad University, Qazvin, Iran (2019)
15. Sakka, S., Yokoi, K.: Humanoid vertical jumping based on force feedback and inertial forces optimization. In: Proceedings of the 2005 IEEE International Conference on Robotics and Automation, pp. 3752–3757. IEEE (2005)
16. Gholami, A., Moradi, M., Majidi, M.: A simulation platform design and kinematics analysis of MRL-HSL humanoid robot. In: Proceedings of 23rd RoboCup International Symposium, Sydney, Australia (2019)

Adaptive Learning Methods for Autonomous Mobile Manipulation in RoboCup@Home

Raphael Memmesheimer[(✉)], Viktor Seib, Tobias Evers, Daniel Müller, and Dietrich Paulus

Active Vision Group, Institute for Computational Visualistics,
University of Koblenz-Landau, 56070 Koblenz, Germany
{raphael,vseib,tevers,muellerd,paulus}@uni-koblenz.de
http://homer.uni-koblenz.de, http://agas.uni-koblenz.de

Abstract. Team homer@UniKoblenz has become an integral part of the RoboCup@Home community. As such we would like to share our experience gained during the competitions with new teams. In this paper we describe our approaches with a special focus on our demonstration of this year's finals. This includes semantic exploration, adaptive programming by demonstration and touch enforcing manipulation. We believe that these demonstrations have a potential to influence the design of future RoboCup@Home tasks. We also present our current research efforts in benchmarking imitation learning tasks, gesture recognition and a low cost autonomous robot platform. Our software can be found on GitHub at https://github.com/homer-robotics.

1 Introduction

This year, team homer@UniKoblenz became RoboCup@Home world champion for the fourth time. This makes our team the most successful team in the Open Platform League of the RoboCup@Home!

Team homer@UniKoblenz started in 2008 by borrowing rescue robot "Robbie" from our prior existing RoboCup Rescue team for their own participation in a so far unknown at home environment. The next year homer@UniKoblenz participated for the first time with their own robot "Lisa". Thanks to the endeavors of the team leaders and the commitment of all team members over time we managed to be among the top 5 teams frequently. As our team that arises from new students every year, going beyond the 5th place was not easy. We had to develop strategies to teach and mentor new students and allow them to start being productive after a short introductory period. Most importantly, we had to come up with a software architecture and organization structure, which enable programming on different abstraction levels and, despite their complexity, are easy to comprehend and to learn for new team members. In this paper we first present our strategies and solutions to overcome common challenges. We provide several software package used by our team during the competition and give an

S. Chalup et al. (Eds.): RoboCup 2019, LNAI 11531, pp. 565–577, 2019.
https://doi.org/10.1007/978-3-030-35699-6_46

insight on how we collect data for object recognition. We hope all of these will serve as guidelines for new teams. Finally, we discuss our demonstration in the finals of 2019 and describe the results of the competition.

2   Team homer@UniKoblenz

The key to success in a competition is a good team. Here we describe our selection process for new team members and give an overview over our robotics hardware.

2.1   Members

In our case only one academic employee is working with Lisa. That employee is the team leader and conducts research for his PhD thesis on Lisa. Since the major part of the team is formed by students and there is only a limited amount of persons, which can be effectively supervised, these students have to be selected carefully. Thus, students have to write a formal application and will be invited to an interview. The application process is necessary in order to identify especially those students, which are most motivated and willing to put extensive work into the project. A student does not have to be exceptionally talented in any field to be accepted. The main requirement is to show motivation and willingness to learn. Two weeks before the start of the course all selected students participate in a daily training to learn the basics of version control, operating the robots and using ROS. The goal is to enable the students to work on their own with the robots. This is achieved by using a modular software architecture with different abstraction levels. Please consult [1,2] for details on the organization of our software. During the course focus is put on preparations for the competition. In two weekly meetings the team analyzes the requirements of the different tests and develops strategies to solve them. Over the years we reduced the amount of formal requirements engineering and software specifications to a minimum in favor of agile and permanent development. We integrate Jenkins as a build server for continuous, multi-architecture integration and deployment. Further, at all times students are encouraged to test their code using the robots at place with real sensor data or recorded ones, e.g. from ROS bagfiles. On a regular basis we organize simulated RoboCup events at which each RoboCup task is tested and scored according to the current rules. This allows to honestly assess the progress made during the course.

2.2   Robots

We use a custom built robot called Lisa and a PAL Robotics TIAGo [3] depicted in Fig. 1. Each robot is equipped with a workstation notebook with an 8 core processor and 16 GB RAM. We use Ubuntu Linux 16.04 and ROS Kinetic. Each robot is equipped with a laser range finder and wheel encoders for navigation and mapping. Further, both robots have a movable sensor head with an RGB-D camera and a directional microphone. Lisa features a 6-DOF robotic arm

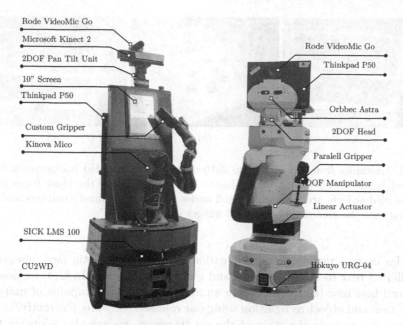

Rode VideoMic Go

Microsoft Kinect 2

2DOF Pan Tilt Unit

10" Screen

Thinkpad P50

Custom Gripper

Kinova Mico

SICK LMS 100

CU2WD

Rode VideoMic Go

Thinkpad P50

Orbbec Astra

2DOF Head

Paralell Gripper

7DOF Manipulator

Linear Actuator

Hokuyo URG-04

Fig. 1. The robots Lisa (left) and TIAGo (right). We use Lisa first and foremost for human robot interaction related tasks. The 10 in. screen supports guided interactions. TIAGo is used mainly as a mobile manipulation platform. The work range is far higher and the arm controllers are more reliable.

(Kinova Mico) for mobile manipulation. The end effector is a custom setup and consists of 4 Festo Finray-fingers. An Odroid C2 mini computer inside the casing of Lisa handles the robot face and speech synthesis. In contrast to Lisa, TIAGo is able to move its torso up and down and has a wider working range. This allows TIAGo to use his 7-DOF arm to reach the floor, as well as high shelves.

3   Contributing Software and Dataset

We omit a detailed description of the current approaches used by our team as these can be found in recent team description papers. Instead, in this section we focus on our contributions in the form of released software and dataset. We hope, this will help new teams to catch up with the evolved RoboCup@Home community and allow them to participate and reach a similar performance level more easily.

3.1   Software

We started releasing our packages for ROS in our old repository[1]. Now we decided to make our contributions more accessible through our GitHub profile[2]. This

---

[1] Previous homer repositories: http://wiki.ros.org/agas-ros-pkg.
[2] Current homer GitHub profile: https://github.com/homer-robotics.

(a) (b) (c)

Fig. 2. Examples from the RoboCup 2019 dataset. We recorded backgrounds like in
(a) and labeled images containing objects like e.g objects of the class *fruits* in (b).
The labeled objects are then augmented under a variety of transformations and then
mapped onto the recorded background images (c).

includes custom mapping and navigation packages, a robotic face, integration
to different text to speech systems and gesture recognition. In [2, 4] we describe
in detail how new teams can create an autonomous robot capable of mapping,
navigation and object recognition using our released software. Currently, as deep
learning has become the state of the art in vision, we are also adopting these
methods. Meanwhile, our point cloud recognition software with recent enhance-
ments is described in [5] and can also be found on GitHub[3]. As development
continues, we plan to release more packages and instructions on how they can
be used.

3.2   RoboCup@Home 2019 Dataset

During the RoboCup 2019 competition we created a dataset that gives an insight
in what data we gather for the competition attendance. In total, we recorded
189 images containing objects of different classes and 12 background images. The
pixel-wisely labeled images in conjunction with the labeled object images were
used to project the extracted objects to a variety of backgrounds. The backgrounds represent manipulation locations from inside the arena. In total 60572
labels were generated on 33539 augmented images. Figure 2 shows examples of
backgrounds, object images and augmented images. The dataset is available
online[4].

4   Final Demonstration

During the final demonstration we showed three approaches that could potentially influence the way how RoboCup tasks will be designed in the future. The
first two approaches are addressing the challenge of how robots can perform

---

[3] Point cloud recognition: https://github.com/vseib/PointCloudDonkey.
[4] RoboCup@Home 2019 dataset: https://agas.uni-koblenz.de/datasets/robocup_2019_
sydney/.

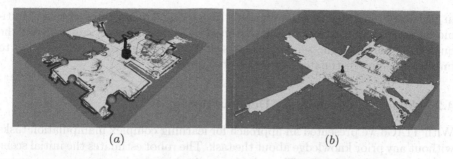

(a) (b)

Fig. 3. LISA exploring the apartment during the RoboCup@Home finals. (a) shows a map created shortly after entering the apartment. Tables and chairs are added to the semantic representation. (b) shows the explored map at the end of the final demonstration. Once finished with the apartment the robot started to explore the outside area.

complex tasks without much prior knowledge. We demonstrated an approach for autonomous semantic exploration on our robot Lisa and an approach for adaptive learning of complex manipulation tasks. In addition, we proposed an approach for touch enforcing manipulation. A video showing the final demonstration during the RoboCup@Home 2019 is available on YouTube[5].

4.1   Autonomous Semantic Exploration

Currently, at RoboCup@Home semantic information about the arena and the objects are provided during the setup days. After publication the majority of teams records maps, defines locations and trains objects. All this data is translated to a semantic knowledge representation which can be understood by the robot. Maps are commonly stored as occupancy grid maps with additional layers for rooms and points of interest. Object recognition tends to be trained using recent object detectors [6,7]. This strategy works fine in an competition environment as long as the state of the arena remains unchanged or undergoes only minor modifications. In the finals, we demonstrated a more general idea addressing the question "How can we make robots behave more autonomously in previously unknown environments?". There is a variety of pre-trained models nowadays which contains a wide variety of classes found in daily life. The COCO [8] dataset contains classes like *Chairs, Dining Table, Refrigerators, Couch*. The wide variety of training examples allows for creation of a generalized object detector which yields good results in completely different scenarios. We make use of the strength of those object detectors and combined them with a traditional method for exploration based on occupancy grid-maps. An example, as shown during the finals is shown in Fig. 3. Based on the autonomously created semantic representation, robots could execute manipulation tasks in the future

---

in previously unknown environments without any human intervention. Multimodal sensor data extraction that is fused on different levels can increase the quality and level of the semantic representation. For our approach we plan to improve the pose estimates of the detected objects.

4.2   Adaptive Learning by Demonstration

With TIAGo we presented an approach for learning complex manipulation tasks without any prior knowledge about the task. The robot estimates the initial scene state by detecting objects. The robot's arm is then put into gravity compensation mode, which allows for seamless human guidance. A human demonstrated relevant arm trajectories for a given task. During the demonstration trajectories are recorded relatively to the estimated objects and a static local reference.

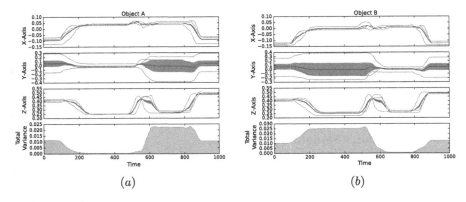

(a)   (b)

Fig. 4. Average relative position and variance of Object A and Object B. Gray lines in X-, Y- and Z-Axis represent single demonstrations. Blue lines represent average positions and blue areas variances. The total variances are shown in gray in the bottom graphics. (Color figure online)

(a)   (b)

Fig. 5. TIAGo learning by demonstration how to pour a drink (a) and cleaning a toilet using a touch enforcing approach and a sponge end-effector (b).

The reference allows demonstrations with just one or no object at all as reference. With multiple demonstrations, it can be predicted if a specific object is involved in the task. More precisely, the variance in relative position of an object to the end effector over time can be calculated. A low variance indicates high importance of the object within the task at that moment and vice versa. Examples of variances are shown in Fig. 4, where an object A has been placed in an object B. The total variance of object A is low between 200–500 (Fig. 4(a)), where it has been grasped and thus is involved in the task during that time period. On the other hand the total variance of object B is low between 600–800 Fig. 4(b). The end effector moved over object B and let go in that time period. Knowing the average position of the robot's end effector relative to the appropriate objects and estimating its importance allows to calculate a position for every time step and finally build a trajectory for any scene. Our approach is based on the ideas of Reiner et al. [9]. Yet, we use deviations of the trajectories to align the multiple trajectories. Aligning them is necessary in order to compute precise variances, since demonstrations by humans are never executed in the exact same speed. The Levenberg-Marquardt algorithm is used, which shall grand a more stable handling of singularities [10]. Figure 5(a) shows the approach as presented during the finals. Future work on this approach will include integration of joint efforts. Currently only joint angles are taken into account during the recording and reproduction. This has side effects like that if an object is grasped by closing the gripper it will be grasped with the same end effector joint states as in the demonstration. This means objects are held only loosely or smaller objects will not be stably grasped. Therefor, we suggest to also take the motor effort into account during the demonstration and reproduction.

4.3 Touch Enforcing Manipulation

In the final demonstration we also built on top of our previously presented effort based manipulation approach [11]. We propose to enforce contact during a manipulation action by continuously observing the joint efforts. Our previous approach was used in an open loop control, where a movement is interrupted once a certain effort has been reached. This is suitable for grasping where you want to determine when the effector touches the surface supporting the object. Our novel approach proposes to hold a certain effort in closed loop control. This was demonstrated during the finals as a case sample of cleaning a toilet (Fig. 5(b)). This approach can be used for a variety of tasks like cleaning tables or windows and slightly moving objects.

5   Results

This year's tasks were categorized in two scenarios: Housekeeper and Party Host. Both scenarios contained five tasks each and teams could choose to perform three of those per scenario. For detailed descriptions of the tasks we refer to the RoboCup@Home rulebook [12]. Results from the OPL are shown in Fig. 6.

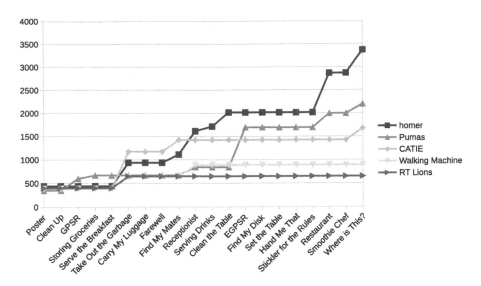

Fig. 6. Scores after Stage 1 and Stage 2 for the top five ranked teams. Stage 1 ended with *Serving Drinks*. Note: Tasks not attended by teams are still listed with no increase in points.

In Stage 1 of the Housekeeper scenario, we participated first in *Take Out The Garbage* (Fig. 7a) where we gathered 500 points. The robot grasped two garbage bags with our previously introduced closed loop touch enforcing approach. The bins were detected by finding circular patterns in the laser scan. For the *Storing Groceries* task we trained a semantic segmentation approach [6] with augmented images. Semantic annotations contained grasping trajectories. Due to a robot damage during transportation, the calibration was off and we scored 0 points. We further participated in the *Serving Breakfast* task. In *Find My Mates* we scored 175 points and additional 500 in the *Receptionist* task. We used convolutional pose machines [13] and projected them using the RGB-D camera in order to calculate distances of the persons in relation to locations of the map. This way we could estimate free seat locations and introduce the new guest to the others. In *Serving Drinks* we scored 100 points (Fig. 7b).

Table 1. The finals results

Team	Stage 1	Stage 2	Final
homer	1715	3365	100
Pumas	845	2195	78.05
CATIE	1425	1675	–

(a)   (b)

Fig. 7. TIAGo grasping a trash bag during the *Take Out The Garbage* task using an effort based grasping approach to ensure that the bag was grasped successfully (*a*) and Lisa handing over a drink to a guest during the *Serving Drinks* task.

(a)   (b)

Fig. 8. LISA learning an unknown restaurant and then serving customers in the *Restaurant* task (*a*) and TIAGo gently placing a in the *Clean the Table* task (*b*) during a test run.

Stage 2 consisted of *Clean the Table, Enhanced General Purpose Service Robot (EGPSR), Hand Me That, Restaurant, Stickler for the Rules Where Is This?*. No team attended the tasks *Find My Disk, Smoothie Chef* or *Set The Table*. In *Clean the Table* (Fig. 8b) we achieved 300 points. Points were given only if the whole task was completed. We used the effort based gripping approach and successfully verified our grasping approaches. When having failed to grasp the object, we asked for a handover by describing the object we had intended to take. Our approach for *Hand me That* was based on finding the operator by estimating human poses [13]. As multiple persons could be in the environment, the robot asked the operator to take a distinguishable pose. We gathered 0 points, however we demonstrated robust human robot interaction. For *Restaurant* (Fig. 8a) we used again a gesture recognition based on estimated human poses [13]. Maps were created on-line and as tables and chair's in unknown environments are hard to see obstacles we fused the laser range finder and RGB-D camera in an obstacle layer of the mapping. We managed to serve two customers and deliver three orders with a forth order on the way. In total we gathered 850 points. For the *Where Is This?* task we decided to use naive operators. We managed to guide two randomly chosen children from the audience to the object they were looking for, another 500 points for us. Table 1 shows the final results of the first three teams.

6   Current Research

We now briefly highlight our current research and ongoing developments related to RoboCup@Home.

Simitate: A Hybrid Imitation Learning Benchmark. Imitation learning approaches for manipulation tasks lack comparability and reproducibility. Therefore we developed a benchmark [14] which integrates a dataset containing RGB-D camera data as it is available on most robots. The RGB-D camera is calibrated against a motion capturing system. The calibration furthermore allows the reconstruction in a virtual environment which allows quantitative evaluation in a simulated environment. For that we propose two metrics that assess the quality on a trajectory and a effect level.

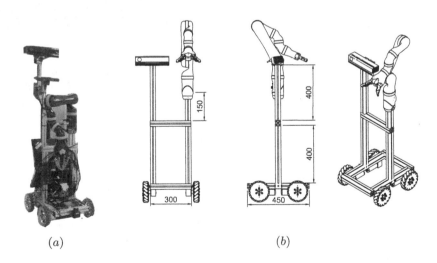

(a)   (b)

Fig. 9. Assembled *Scratchy* (a) and exemplary dimensions in (b).

A Lightweight Modular Autonomous Robot for Robotic Competitions. We proposed a novel modular robotic platform [15] for competition attendance and research. The aim was to create a minimal platform, which is easy to built, reconfigurable, offers basic autonomy and is low in cost to rebuilt. Thus researchers can concentrate on their respective topics and adapt sensors and appearance depending on their needs. *Scratchy* allows also low cost participation in robot competitions as the weight is low and the robot can be compressed up to a hand luggage size.

Gesture Recognition. Gesture recognition in RoboCup@Home becomes more and more mandatory. First we propose a gesture recognition approach on single RGB-D images. We extract human pose features and train them using a set of classifiers [16]. We then extended the approach to image sequences [17] using Dynamic Time Warping [18] and a one nearest neighbour classifier. This allows gesture classification with just one reference example.

Updating Algorithms. In the past we successfully used classic approaches for 3D point cloud processing [5] and affordance estimation [19]. We believe that transferring these ideas to the powerful domain of deep neural networks will further enhance the performance of these algorithms. Currently, we investigate methods that allow for a lightweight network structure while still retaining the performance of the classic approaches.

7   Conclusion

With our success this year we demonstrated a robust robotic architecture that is adaptable to various kinds of robots and setups. This architecture was constantly developed and improved over the years - and we will continue into the same direction. This paper gave a brief insight into the internal organisation of our teams and presented our robots. We further published some important software components on our GitHub profile. We hope that all of these will be helpful to new team who join the RoboCup@Home league. Our final demonstration of this year focused on the topic of autonomy in unknown environments. We want to motivate the league to follow this track and encourage autonomous robots that operate in previously unseen environments and execute loosely specified tasks. This will increase the flexibility of the robots and allow more research related activities in RoboCup@Home. Our methods on imitation learning, programming by demonstration, autonomous mobile exploration can be seen as potential directions. We believe that recent research results like on benchmarking imitation learning approaches, gesture recognition and a minimal autonomous research platform can support current and new teams.

Acknowledgement. We want to thank the participating students that supported in the preparation, namely Ida Germann, Mark Mints, Patrik Schmidt, Isabelle Kuhlmann, Robin Bartsch, Lukas Buchhold, Christian Korbach, Thomas Weiland, Niko Schmidt, Ivanna Kramer. Further we want to thank our sponsors (Univeristy of Koblenz-Landau, Student parliament of the University of Koblenz-Landau Campus Koblenz, PAL Robotics, Einst e.V., CV e.V., Neoalto and KEVAG Telekom GmbH).

References

1. Seib, V., Manthe, S., Memmesheimer, R., Polster, F., Paulus, D.: Team homer@UniKoblenz — approaches and contributions to the RoboCup@Home competition. In: Almeida, L., Ji, J., Steinbauer, G., Luke, S. (eds.) RoboCup 2015. LNCS (LNAI), vol. 9513, pp. 83–94. Springer, Cham (2015). https://doi.org/10.1007/978-3-319-29339-4_7

2. Memmesheimer, R., Seib, V., Paulus, D.: homer@UniKoblenz: winning team of the RoboCup@Home open platform league 2017. In: Akiyama, H., Obst, O., Sammut, C., Tonidandel, F. (eds.) RoboCup 2017. LNCS (LNAI), vol. 11175, pp. 509–520. Springer, Cham (2018). https://doi.org/10.1007/978-3-030-00308-1_42

3. Pages, J., Marchionni, L., Ferro, F.: Tiago: the modular robot that adapts to different research needs. In: International Workshop on Robot Modularity, IROS (2016)

4. Seib, V., Memmesheimer, R., Paulus, D.: A ROS-based system for an autonomous service robot. In: Koubaa, A. (ed.) Robot Operating System (ROS). SCI, vol. 625, pp. 215–252. Springer, Cham (2016). https://doi.org/10.1007/978-3-319-26054-9_9

5. Seib, V., Theisen, N., Paulus, D.: Boosting 3D shape classification with global verification and redundancy-free codebooks. In: Tremeau, A., Farinella, G.M., Braz, J. (eds.) Proceedings of the 14th International Joint Conference on Computer Vision, Imaging and Computer Graphics Theory and Applications, vol. 5, pp. 257–264. SciTePress (2019)

6. He, K., Gkioxari, G., Dollár, P., Girshick, R.: Mask R-CNN. In: Proceedings of the IEEE International Conference on Computer Vision, pp. 2961–2969 (2017)

7. Redmon, J., Divvala, S., Girshick, R., Farhadi, A.: You only look once: unified, real-time object detection. In: Proceedings of the IEEE Conference on Computer Vision and Pattern Recognition, pp. 779–788 (2016)

8. Lin, T.-Y., et al.: Microsoft COCO: common objects in context. In: Fleet, D., Pajdla, T., Schiele, B., Tuytelaars, T. (eds.) ECCV 2014. LNCS, vol. 8693, pp. 740–755. Springer, Cham (2014). https://doi.org/10.1007/978-3-319-10602-1_48

9. Reiner, B., Ertel, W., Posenauer, H., Schneider, M.: LAT: a simple learning from demonstration method. In: 2014 IEEE/RSJ International Conference on Intelligent Robots and Systems, pp. 4436–4441. IEEE (2014)

10. Buss, S.R., Kim, J.-S.: Selectively damped least squares for inverse kinematics. J. Graph. Tools **10**(3), 37–49 (2005)

11. Memmesheimer, R., Mykhalchyshyna, I., Seib, V., Evers, T., Paulus, D.: homer@UniKoblenz: winning team of the RoboCup@Home open platform league 2018. In: Holz, D., Genter, K., Saad, M., von Stryk, O. (eds.) RoboCup 2018. LNCS (LNAI), vol. 11374, pp. 512–523. Springer, Cham (2019). https://doi.org/10.1007/978-3-030-27544-0_42

12. Matamoros, M., et al.: Robocup@home 2019: Rules and regulations (draft) (2019). http://www.robocupathome.org/rules/2019_rulebook.pdf

13. Cao, Z., Simon, T., Wei, S.-E., Sheikh, Y.: Realtime multi-person 2D pose estimation using part affinity fields. In: Proceedings of the IEEE Conference on Computer Vision and Pattern Recognition, pp. 7291–7299 (2017)

14. Memmesheimer, R., Mykhalchyshyna, I., Seib, V., Paulus, D.: Simitate: a hybrid imitation learning benchmark. arXiv preprint arXiv:1905.06002 (2019)

15. Memmesheimer, R., et al.: Scratchy: a lightweight modular autonomous robot for robotic competitions. In: 2019 IEEE International Conference on Autonomous Robot Systems and Competitions (ICARSC), pp. 1–6. IEEE (2019)

16. Memmesheimer, R., Mykhalchyshyna, I., Paulus, D.: Gesture recognition on human pose features of single images. In: 2018 International Conference on Intelligent Systems (IS), pp. 813–819. IEEE (2018)

17. Schneider, P., Memmesheimer, R., Kramer, I., Paulus, D.: Gesture recognition in RGB videos using human body keypoints and dynamic time warping. arXiv preprint arXiv:1906.12171 (2019)

18. Salvador, S., Chan, P.: Toward accurate dynamic time warping in linear time and space. Intell. Data Anal. **11**(5), 561–580 (2007)

19. Seib, V., Knauf, M., Paulus, D.: Affordance Origami: unfolding agent models for hierarchical affordance prediction. In: Braz, J., et al. (eds.) VISIGRAPP 2016. CCIS, vol. 693, pp. 555–574. Springer, Cham (2017). https://doi.org/10.1007/978-3-319-64870-5_27

An Approach for Distributed Constraint Optimization Problems in Rescue Simulation

Yuki Miyamoto[1], Taishun Kusaka[1], Yuki Okado[1], Kazunori Iwata[2(✉)], and Nobuhiro Ito[1]

[1] Department of Information Science,
Aichi Institute of Technology, Toyota, Japan
`ait-rescue2019@maslab.aitech.ac.jp`
[2] Department of Business Administration, Aichi University,
Nagoya, Japan
`kazunori@vega.aichi-u.ac.jp`

Abstract. The "task assignment problem" of RoboCupRescue Simulation (RRS) can be regarded as a Distributed Constraint Optimization Problem (DCOP). However, it is difficult to apply the DCOP algorithm to the problem on the current simulator. In this paper, we propose an extension on RRS-ADF for the difficulty. We introduce a new communication system that agents can use to communicate repeatedly within each step of this extension. Furthermore, we also describe an example that applies a DCOP algorithm and then discuss its effectiveness. The results confirmed that our extension is effective.

1 Introduction

A typical problem in RoboCupRescue Simulation (RRS) is the task assignment problem. The task assignment problem consists of determining an approach to assign n agents to m tasks according to their purpose. This problem can be modeled as a Distributed Constraint Optimization Problem (DCOP) [4]. RMAS-Bench [2] was proposed as an attempt to solve the task assignment problem of RRS using a DCOP and its algorithm. RMASBench is a benchmark system for the task assignment problem that introduces pseudo-agents and pseudo-communication between them on the RRS system. Research on RMASBench [3] has demonstrated that the DCOP algorithm works effectively for the task assignment problem on RRS.

Therefore, in this research, we propose an extension of RRS-ADF to use the DCOP algorithm in the task assignment problem on RRS. However, since RMASBench introduced pseudo-communication, it is difficult to use the DCOP algorithm on the current simulator. Therefore, the extension proposed in this research provides a similar pseudo-communication system on the present system. Additionally, we confirm that it operates effectively by applying the max-sum algorithm [6] which is a typical approximate solution method for the DCOP.

In Sect. 2, we first describe the DCOP, max-sum algorithm, and RMASBench as background information. In Sect. 3, we describe the pseudo-communication

S. Chalup et al. (Eds.): RoboCup 2019, LNAI 11531, pp. 578–590, 2019.
https://doi.org/10.1007/978-3-030-35699-6_47

system that we introduce and the extension of RRS-ADF that uses this system. In Sect. 4, we apply the DCOP to the task assignment problem of ambulance teams and implement the max-sum algorithm for the problem on the extension. In Sect. 5, we present the experiment used to confirm that our extension and the max-sum algorithm implementation work effectively. As a result of the experiment, we confirm that they work sufficiently well.

2   Background

2.1   DCOP: Distributed Constraint Optimization Problem

The DCOP is the problem of determining a combination of variable values that maximize utility when they have a constraint between a variable that corresponds to a distributed agent and other variables. The definition of the DCOP is as follows [1]:

$\mathbf{A} = \{a_1, \ldots, a_n\}$
    is a set of agents, where a_i is an agent.
$\mathbf{X} = \{x_1, \ldots, x_m\}$
    is a set of variables. However, $m \geq n$, where m is the number of variables and n is the number of agents.
$\mathbf{D} = \{D_1, \ldots, D_m\}$
    is a set of ranges for each variable $x_i \in X$, where D_i represents the range of corresponding variable x_i.
$\mathbf{F} = \{f_1, \ldots, f_k\}$
    is a set of functions (called utility functions) that express constraints between variables. The utility function is represented by the following expression: $f_i \colon \times_{x_j \in \mathbf{x}^i} D_j \to \mathbb{R}$, where $\mathbf{x}^i$ is the set of variables whose constraint relation is represented by f_i. The utility function maps a combination of arbitrary values included in the value range for each variable of $\mathbf{x}^i$ to a real number. The value obtained by the utility function is called the "utility."
$\alpha \colon \mathbf{X} \to \mathbf{A}$
    is a mapping function that expresses a relationship between an agent and a variable. Each agent corresponds to a distinct variable.

Objective function $\mathbf{F}_g(\mathbf{X})$ for optimization is defined as

$$\mathbf{F}_g(\mathbf{X}) = \sum_{f_i \in \mathbf{F}} f_i\left(\mathbf{x}^i\right) \tag{1}$$

by the utility functions. Then, the optimized assignment σ^* which maximizes $\mathbf{F}_g(\mathbf{X})$, is expressed as

$$\sigma^* = \arg\max_{\sigma \in \mathcal{D}} \mathbf{F}_g(\sigma) \tag{2}$$

In this case, $\mathcal{D}$ is a direct product set of all ranges in $\mathbf{D}$, which means a set of possible assignments. Note that Eq. (2) is used only when a combination that maximizes the objective function is the optimized assignment.

2.2 Max-Sum Algorithm

The max-sum algorithm is one of the major approximate solution methods for the DCOP. It optimizes the overall utility by propagating the utility to each constraint. The target of this algorithm is a problem that can be modeled as the factor graph. The factor graph is an undirected graph that consists of variable nodes that represent variables, factor nodes that represent utility functions between variable nodes, and edges that represent mutual relationships between variable nodes and factor nodes. An example of the factor graph is shown in Fig. 1.

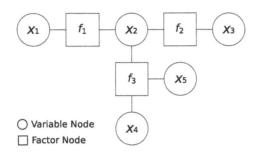

Fig. 1. Example of the factor graph

In Fig. 1, the factor node has a constraint, which is a utility function, on neighboring variable nodes. Additionally, a corresponding agent calculates a utility for each variable value according to its own range and the constraints of the neighboring factor nodes in the variable node. First, initial utilities are calculated in variable nodes by corresponding agents according to the condition. Then the utilities gradually propagate to other variable nodes through neighboring factor nodes. The propagation (calculation) continues until the updating of utilities is stopped or when the designated iteration number is reached.

The following is an evaluation function [3], and is used when variable node x of the equation sends the utility on a value of the variable node to the factor node f:

$$\mu_{x \to f}(\mathbf{x}) = \sum_{g \in \mathcal{N}(x) \setminus \{f\}} \mu_{g \to x}(\mathbf{x}) \tag{3}$$

where $\mathbf{x}$ is the value calculated by an appropriate agent and included in the range of the variable node x; $\mathcal{N}(x)$ is a set of factor nodes that neighbor variable node x; and $\mu_{g \to x}$ is the utility calculated on factor node g and sent to variable node x. Equation (3) calculates the sum of the utilities received from neighboring factor nodes except for the factor node that is the destination. The calculated value is in the range of variable node x.

The following is an evaluation function [3], and is used when factor node f sends the utility on a value to variable node x:

$$\mu_{f \to x}(\mathbf{x}) = \max_{\mathbf{Y}} \left(f(\mathbf{x}, \mathbf{Y}) + \sum_{y \in Y} \mu_{y \to f}(\mathbf{y}) \right) \qquad (4)$$

where Y is the set of variable nodes that neighbor factor node f except for x, $\mathbf{Y}$ is the set of values that are calculated by appropriate agents on Y, $\mu_{y \to f}$ is the utility from variable node y to factor node f, and $\mathbf{y}$ is the value of variable node y that is included in $\mathbf{Y}$. Equation (4) calculates the maximum value of the sum of a value of a utility function for $\mathbf{x}$ and $\mathbf{Y}$, and a sum of $\mu_{y \to f}$ for $y \in Y$ on $\mathbf{Y}$.

When the propagation is complete, the optimal assignment is calculated by

$$\sigma^* = \arg \max_{x \in \mathbf{X}} \sum_{f \in \mathcal{N}(x)} \mu_{f \to x}(\mathbf{x}) \qquad (5)$$

Equation (5) calculates an assignment that maximizes the sum of values of utility functions for each factor node.

2.3   Previous Research: RMASBench

RMASBench was proposed in 2013 to conduct DCOP research of RRS. It is a benchmark system for the task assignment method for multi-agent systems, and an evaluation system for DCOP algorithms.

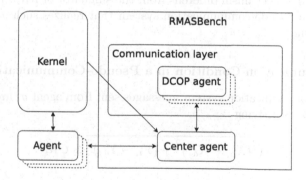

Fig. 2. System structure of RMASBench

The system structure of RMASBench is illustrated in Fig. 2. The center agent can obtain current states from each agent and current situations of the disaster simulation from the kernel. Additionally, the system introduces a pseudo-communication layer (communication layer) and pseudo-agents (DCOP agent) that correspond to agents on the pseudo-communication layer, so that the pseudo-agents can communicate without restrictions imposed by the RRS system. Then, the center agent performs task assignments by making the pseudo-agents send and receive many messages repeatedly in the layer. The result of the task assignments on the pseudo-agents is communicated to the agents from the center agent directly.

This approach achieves the application/implementation of DCOP algorithms to the task assignment problem of RRS. However, this approach cannot solve the task assignment problem based on the local communication of the DCOP, although it can solve the problem based on global communication.

3   RRS-ADF Extension

3.1   Necessity of Multiple Communications Within a Step with the Pseudo-Communication System

The max-sum algorithm requires sending and receiving many messages repeatedly to propagate utilities among agents. By contrast, agents of RRS can send/receive messages only once per simulation timestep, which means 1 min in real time because agents of RRS are assumed to communicate by voice. Therefore, multiple steps are required to execute the algorithm.

The Distributed Stochastic Algorithm (DSA) is one of the major approximate solution methods for DCOP similar to the max-sum algorithm. The experiments of Zhang et al. [7] demonstrated that the DSA requires approximately 60 iterations to converge to a solution. By contrast, RRS performs from 200 steps to 300 steps. This fact means that it is difficult for RRS to use the DSA effectively because the algorithm requires many steps.

To solve this problem, RMASBench enables multiple communications within each step, with a mechanism different from the simulator of RRS. In this paper, we introduce a pseudo-communication system that realizes such a communication mechanism.

3.2   Communication Condition in a Pseudo-Communication System

In a pseudo-communication system, messages sent from agent a_i are received by other agents a_j, satisfying

$$\sqrt{\left(X_{a_i} - X_{a_j}\right)^2 + \left(Y_{a_i} - Y_{a_j}\right)^2} \leqq CR, \tag{6}$$

X_{a_i} : X coordinate at which a_i is located

Y_{a_i} : Y coordinate at which a_i is located

CR : Communication radius centering on an agent

3.3   Design of the Pseudo-Communication System

It is difficult to extend the communication system of the current simulation kernel, to introduce a pseudo-communication system. Therefore, our pseudo-communication system uses a new pseudo-communication server that manages communication among agents, and a new pseudo-communication client for current agents. In the max-sum algorithm, an agent needs to synchronize with the other agents when the agent sends/receives each message. Agents that intend to communicate with the other agents need to send/receive each message repeatedly until all agents lose the intention to continue communication.

The pseudo-communication server receives the following information from clients to confirm whether the communication condition is satisfied:

- X and Y coordinate where the agent is located; and
- an intention to continue communication.

When all agents lose the intention to continue communication, the server regards the simulation step as complete and initializes the states of the agents on the server.

3.4 Implementation of a Task Assignment Module for the DCOP with Our Pseudo-Communication System

We implemented a task assignment module (*DCOP Target Detector*) using the pseudo-communication system. This module was implemented by inheriting the task assignment module (*Target Detector*) of RRS-ADF. *DCOP Target Detector* internally manages a pseudo-communication client and assigns a task to its agent based on the communications of a DCOP algorithm. Figure 3 shows the program structure and data flow in the RRS simulator with our extension.

In this approach, the pseudo-communication server is implemented as an independent program with the kernel. Additionally, the server receives information required for communication from agents. However, when we used this system for competitions, we assumed that it was appropriate to implement it as an extension to the communication component of the kernel from the viewpoint of fairness.

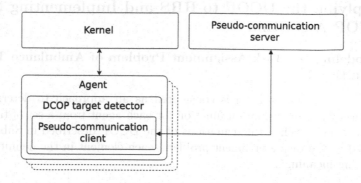

Fig. 3. Part of the program structure and the data flow

In the *DCOP Target Detector*, the following procedure is executed:

1. Initialize state (according to the user definition).

2. Receive all messages simultaneously.
3. Execute task assignment based on the DCOP algorithm (according to the user definition).
4. Send all messages simultaneously.
5. Return to step 2, if necessary.

In step 3, the module returns the task that is assigned to the agent, and whether a repeat of the procedure is required. In step 5, the module repeats in the case in which a repeat is required in step 3 or until the number of repeats reaches the defined limit. To execute this procedure, *DCOP Target Detector* provides the new methods shown in Table 1. The user then has to define the method shown in Table 2.

Table 1. Methods provided by *DCOP Target Detector*

Definition	Explanation
void send(CommunicationMessage)	Add a message to a blanket sending list
List<CommunicationMessage> receive()	Receive blanket received messages

Table 2. User-defined methods in *DCOP Target Detector*

Definition	Explanation
void initialize()	Initialize the state at the beginning of the procedure
Pair<EntityID, Boolean> improveAssignment()	Execute task assignment

4   Applying the DCOP to RRS and Implementing the DCOP Algorithm

4.1   Modeling the Task Assignment Problem of Ambulance Teams as a DCOP

The task assignment problem is considered as an approach to determine an optimal task with an evaluation function for each agent from a set of tasks recognized by agents. When the definitions of the DCOP described in Subsect. 2.1 are applied to the task assignment problem, each element in the definitions has the following meaning:

$\mathbf{A} = \{a_1, \ldots, a_n\}$
   denotes the set of all ambulance agents existing in a simulation.
$\mathbf{X} = \{x_1, \ldots, x_n\}$
   denotes the set of variables x_i that represent the task selected by agent $a_i \in \mathbf{A}$. A task that is eventually the value of $x_i \in \mathbf{X}$ means a task that a_i will take.

$\mathbf{D} = \{D_1, \ldots, D_n\}$

denotes the set of a task set D_i that agent $a_i \in \mathbf{A}$ can select. $D_i \in \mathbf{D}$ for an ambulance team is composed of the following two elements:

- multiple rescue tasks for multiple civilians that a_i recognizes; and
- a single situation search task that a_i performs to recognize a simulation situation.

The situation search tasks are gathered into only one task because of RRS-ADF handles that assigning civilian rescue tasks and situation search tasks to agents as different problems.

$\mathbf{F} = \{f_1, \ldots, f_k\}$

denotes the set of utility functions f_j that corresponds to the combination of value $\mathbf{x}_i$ of variable $x_i \in \mathbf{X}$. In the evaluation of civilian rescue tasks, the final civilian survival number is the most important. Therefore, it is necessary to minimize the cost of the tasks after assigning the number of agents required to keep a civilian alive in each task. For the reasons stated above, objective function $\mathbf{F}_g(\mathbf{X})$ for civilian rescue tasks can be defined as

$$\mathbf{F}_g(\mathbf{X}) = \sum_{x_i \in \mathbf{X}} C\left(\alpha\left(x_i\right), \mathbf{x}_i\right) + \sum_{d \in \bigcup_{i=1}^{n} D_i} P\left(d, |\{\mathbf{x}_i | \mathbf{x}_i = d \wedge x_i \in \mathbf{X}\}|\right) \quad (7)$$

using the equations

$$C(a, d) = \begin{cases} \frac{\sqrt{(X_a - X_d)^2 + (Y_a - Y_d)^2}}{\tau} & \text{(if } d \text{ is a civilian rescue task)} \\ 0 & \text{(if } d \text{ is a situation search task),} \end{cases} \quad (8)$$

which is a function that calculates the length of time required by agent a to start to execute task d;

$$P(d, n) = \begin{cases} \rho\left\{1 - \left(\frac{min(REQ(d),n)}{REQ(d)}\right)^2\right\} & \text{(if } d \text{ is a civilian rescue task)} \\ 0 & \text{(if } d \text{ is a situation search task),} \end{cases} \quad (9)$$

which is a function that determines the penalties arising from an insufficient number of agents when n agents are assigned to task d; and

$$REQ(d) = \frac{BD_d \times DT_d}{HP_d} + 1 \quad (10)$$

which is a function that estimates the number of agents required to rescue the civilian in task d by considering the civilian's current state, where

$\mathbf{x}$: value of variable x

BD_d: the buried depth of the civilian in task d

DT_d: physical strength that the civilian in task d loses per step

HP_d: physical strength of the remaining civilians in task d

τ: constant representing an estimated value of the movable distance per step $(0 < \tau)$

ρ: constant representing a penalty $(0 \leq \rho)$

$\alpha\colon \mathbf{X} \to \mathbf{A}$

denotes the function that finds agent $a_i \in \mathbf{A}$ that manages variable $x_i \in \mathbf{X}$. Because the RRS agent cannot perform more than one task simultaneously, the variable managed by agent $a_i \in \mathbf{A}$ is always limited to one variable. Therefore, this function is always bijective.

We then minimize the value obtained from Eq. (7). To obtain the same result as objective function $\mathbf{F}_g(\mathbf{X})$, fitting utility function $f_j \in \mathbf{F}$ for the max-sum algorithm is defined in Subsect. 4.2.

4.2   Applying the Max-Sum Algorithm

In this subsection, we describe the method of forming a factor graph and its utility functions to execute the max-sum algorithm.

Method for Forming a Factor Graph

As described in Subsect. 2.2, the factor graph consists of variable nodes that represent variables, factor nodes that represent utility functions between variable nodes, and edges that connect a variable node to a factor node. The factor graph has a feature such that a utility function affects multiple variables represented as factor nodes. Such a utility function is needed for each task, such as function $P(d, n)$ shown in Eq. (9). However, tasks cannot manage factor nodes. The factor nodes are managed by the closest agent to the task's location instead of the task to solve such a situation. The nearest agent is determined by each agent that received information from the other agents. When an agent for a factor node and an agent for a variable node can communicate with each other according to the restriction of the communication range, an edge is created between the factor node and variable node. As an example of constructing a factor graph, Fig. 5 shows the factor graph constructed by an agent and a task that has the relationship shown in Fig. 4. The agent for variable node x_3 is the closest to the location of the task, and factor node f_1 for the task is managed by the same agent as x_3.

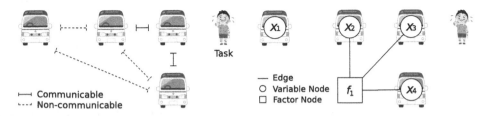

Fig. 4. Example of the communication availability between agents and the task state

Fig. 5. Factor graph constructed from the state of Fig. 4

Definition of the Utility Function

The max-sum algorithm uses utility functions related to agents and factor nodes. Additionally, the utility function related to a single agent is used as the variable node. Thus, objective function $\mathbf{F}_g(\mathbf{X})$ shown in Eq. (7) is divided according to a relationship among the agents and used as a utility function. The following equations, respectively, show utility function $f_{MSV}(x_i)$, which is used for variable node x_i to calculate the cost required for the agent to work the task, and utility function $f_{MSF}(d_j)$, which calculates penalties from the task and a set of neighboring variable nodes used on the factor node related to task d_j:

$$f_{MSV}(x_i) = C\left(\alpha(x_i), \mathbf{x}_i\right) \tag{11}$$

$$f_{MSF}(d_j) = P\left(d_j, |\{\mathbf{x}|\mathbf{x} = d_j \wedge x \in \mathcal{N}(d_j)\}|\right) \tag{12}$$

Additionally, the method [5] proposed as the cardinality-based potentials is applied to the calculation on the factor node because utility function $f_{MSF}(d_j)$ of the factor node calculates the utility based on the number of assigned agents.

5   Experiment and Consideration

5.1   Experimental Method

In this section, we confirm the effectiveness of our proposed approach. We, therefore, check whether our task assignment method with the max-sum algorithm works properly.

In this experiment, our implemented max-sum algorithm is compared with the Closest[1] and Greedy[2] methods with respect to the task assignment of RRS. These three methods were evaluated in the simulation result, that is, the "score", of RRS through some simulations. In this experiment, the VC3 and the Eindhoven3 scenarios of RoboCup 2018 were used, except entities that were not related to the ambulance team and rescue of civilians were removed from those scenarios. Furthermore, four types of communication range (distance) were applied to each scenario because the results of the simulations were strongly influenced by communication ranges.

Each scenario had the following features:

VC3

Platoon agents were densely located while the locations of refuges and civilians were dispersed (Table 3).

Table 3. Simulation settings of VC3

Initial score	Refuges	Ambulance teams	Civilians
293.0	5	32	292

---
[1] Task assignment with a greedy method on the distance between an agent and a task.
[2] Task assignment with a greedy method on the time required for an agent to complete a task.

Eindhoven3

The locations of platoon agents were more dispersed than for VC3. The locations of refuges and civilians were also dispersed (Table 4).

Table 4. Simulation settings of Eindhoven3

Initial score	Refuges	Ambulance teams	Civilians
401.0	4	15	400

5.2   Experimental Results

Tables 5 and 6 show the experimental results for each communication range in VC3 and Eindhoven3, respectively. The communication range "1/4" indicates that communicable range for an agent was 1/4 for the entire map. The communication range "4/4" indicates that agents could communicate globally with each other in the map. The results are averages and standard deviations, which are the numbers in parentheses, of scores for 30 simulations for each algorithm and communication range. Additionally, the results of "Max-Sum" indicate the case in which agents sent and received messages 100 times in each step for task assignment using the max-sum algorithm.

Table 5. Experimental results on VC3

Agent	Communication range			
	1/4	2/4	3/4	4/4
Closest	329.18 (±1.89)	328.45 (±1.75)	328.22 (±1.73)	328.15 (±1.69)
Greedy	328.62 (±1.68)	326.43 (±1.07)	325.73 (±1.00)	325.50 (±0.88)
Max-Sum	330.11 (±1.17)	329.88 (±2.27)	330.01 (±1.79)	330.25 (±1.60)

Table 6. Experimental results on Eindhoven3

Agent	Communication range			
	1/4	2/4	3/4	4/4
Closest	329.18 (±1.89)	328.45 (±1.75)	328.22 (±1.73)	328.15 (±1.69)
Greedy	328.62 (±1.68)	326.43 (±1.07)	325.73 (±1.00)	325.50 (±0.88)
Max-Sum	330.11 (±1.17)	329.88 (±2.27)	330.01 (±1.79)	330.25 (±1.60)

For VC3, the score of Closest was the highest, although Max-Sum was a high score. For Eindhoven3, the results demonstrate that Max-Sum was the highest score.

5.3   Considerations for Experiments

The experimental results show the following from the features of the algorithms.

Closest determines task assignments only from a distance between an agent and the rescue task of a civilian; that, the scenarios in the experiment were only suitable for the Closest, although the results demonstrated a high score.

Greedy determines the task assignment with priorities calculated based on the time for solving the task. However, agents work sequentially according to the priorities only. As a result, agents sometimes cannot work decentrally. This method did not have the worst score if the scenarios included concurrent multiple tasks.

By contrast, Max-Sum could decentrally assign appropriate tasks according to the situation with utility functions for all tasks. Additionally, we confirmed that Max-Sum worked effectively from the results, even if the communication range was restricted. Therefore, we confirmed that the max-sum algorithm is an effective approach for the solution of the task assignment problem of RRS.

The above discussion has demonstrated that the three methods worked properly on RRS. Furthermore, we showed that our proposed extension of RRS-ADF is valid and effective for RRS.

6   Conclusions

In this paper, we proposed an extension of RRS-ADF to apply the DCOP algorithm to the task assignment problem of RRS. We described the necessity of multiple communications within each step for the DCOP as a reason for introducing the extension. As a result, we designed a pseudo-communication system to realize this communication and implemented *DCOP Target Detector* for that system.

Finally, we confirmed that this extension is sufficient for applying the DCOP algorithm to RRS through designing and implementing the max-sum algorithm on RRS. We also confirmed that our max-sum algorithm implementation worked effectively using some simulations. Additionally, because the max-sum algorithm provided high scores, even in the simulation in which the situation recognition/communication range was restricted, we concluded that the algorithm is effective for the task assignment problem of RRS.

However, this extension is difficult to use in agent competitions because it is an extension to the RRS simulator. When we adopt this extension in our RRS, we need to discuss the specification and configuration in detail according to our purpose. We hope that our extension or idea is useful for the RRS community through some discussions.

References

1. Fioretto, F., Pontelli, E., Yeoh, W.: Distributed constraint optimization problems and applications: a survey. J. Aritf. Intell. Res. **61**, 623–698 (2018)
2. Kleiner, A., Farinelli, A., Ramchurn, S., Shi, B., Maffioletti, F., Reffato, R.: RMAS-Bench: benchmarking dynamic multi-agent coordination in urban search and rescue. In: Proceedings of the 2013 International Conference on Autonomous Agents and Multi-agent Systems, AAMAS 2013, pp. 1195–1196. International Foundation for Autonomous Agents and Multiagent Systems, Richland (2013). http://dl.acm.org/citation.cfm?id=2484920.2485139
3. Pujol-Gonzalez, M., Cerquides, J., Farinelli, A., Meseguer, P., Rodríguez-Aguilar, J.A.: Binary max-sum for multi-team task allocation in RoboCup Rescue. In: Optimisation in Multi-Agent Systems and Distributed Constraint Reasoning (OptMAS-DCR), Paris, France (2014)
4. Ramchurn, S.D., Farinelli, A., Macarthur, K.S., Jennings, N.R.: Decentralized coordination in RoboCup Rescue. Comput. J. **53**, 1447–1461 (2010)
5. Tarlow, D., Givoni, I.E., Zemel, R.S.: HOP-MAP: efficient message passing with high order potentials. In: AISTATS (2010)
6. Weiss, Y., Freeman, W.T.: On the optimality of solutions of the max-product belief-propagation algorithm in arbitrary graphs. IEEE Trans. Inf. Theory **47**, 736–744 (2001)
7. Zhang, W., Wang, G., Wittenburg, L.: Distributed stochastic search for constraint satisfaction and optimization: parallelism, phase transitions and performance. In: Proceedings AAAI 2002 Workshop on Probabilistic Approaches in Search, January 2002

b-it-bots: Our Approach for Autonomous Robotics in Industrial Environments

Abhishek Padalkar, Mohammad Wasil, Shweta Mahajan, Ramesh Kumar,
Dharmin Bakaraniya, Raghuvir Shirodkar, Heruka Andradi,
Deepan Padmanabhan, Carlo Wiesse, Ahmed Abdelrahman, Sushant Chavan,
Naresh Gurulingan, Deebul Nair, Santosh Thoduka[⊠], Iman Awaad,
Sven Schneider, Paul G. Plöger, and Gerhard K. Kraetzschmar

Department of Computer Science, Hochschule Bonn-Rhein-Sieg,
Grantham-Allee 20, 53757 Sankt Augustin, Germany
{abhishek.padalkar,mwasil.wasil,shweta.mahajan,kumar.kumar,
dharmin.bakaraniya,raghuvir.shirodkar,heruka.andradi,deepan.padmanabhan,
carlo.wiesse,ahmed.abdelrahman,sushant.chavan,
naresh.gurulingan}@smail.inf.h-brs.de,
{deebul.nair,santosh.thoduka,iman.awaad,sven.schneider,
paul.ploeger,gerhard.kraetzschmar}@h-brs.de
http://www.b-it-bots.de

Abstract. This paper presents the approach of our team, b-it-bots, in the RoboCup@Work competition which resulted in us winning the World Championship in Sydney in 2019. We describe our current hardware, including modifications made to the KUKA youBot, the underlying software framework and components developed for navigation, manipulation, perception and task planning for scenarios in industrial environments. Our combined 2D and 3D approach for object recognition has improved robustness and performance compared to previous years, and our task planning framework has moved us away from large state machines for high-level control. Future work includes closing the perception-manipulation loop for more robust grasping. Our open-source repository is available at https://github.com/b-it-bots/mas_industrial_robotics.

1 Introduction

The RoboCup@Work league was established in 2012 as a demonstration league, and became a regular league in 2016. It is aimed at robots working autonomously in industrial environments in collaboration with humans. A typical task involves transporting objects from one location to another, using skills such as autonomous navigation, object perception, manipulation and task planning.

A. Padalkar, M. Wasil, S. Mahajan, R. Kumar, D. Bakaraniya, R. Shirodkar, H. Andradi, D. Padmanabhan, C. Wiesse—Current team member.

© Springer Nature Switzerland AG 2019
S. Chalup et al. (Eds.): RoboCup 2019, LNAI 11531, pp. 591–602, 2019.
https://doi.org/10.1007/978-3-030-35699-6_48

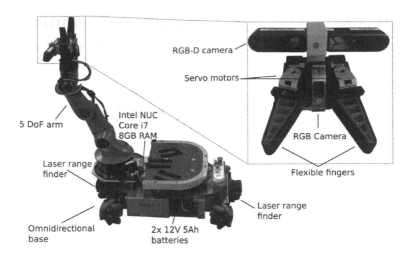

Fig. 1. b-it-bots robot configuration based on the KUKA youBot

Our team, b-it-bots, has participated in RoboCup@Work since its inception, and has regularly performed well at both the World Championships and RoboCup German Open. This year, our team achieved the first place after a closely fought competition with teams from Germany, Singapore, Iran and the Netherlands.

The team consists of Master of Science in Autonomous Systems students from Hochschule Bonn-Rhein-Sieg, who are advised by PhD students and professors. Although RoboCup activities are not part of the academic curriculum, the students participate voluntarily and results from class projects, research and development projects and Master's theses have been deployed on the robot over several years. Collaboration between team members is achieved by regular team meetings every Friday, development and issue tracking on Github and development sprints before competitions. Our main research interests include mobile manipulation in industrial settings, navigation in unconstrained environments, robot perception, task planning and failure detection and error recovery.

In this paper, we describe our approach for the RoboCup@Work competition including our robot platform in Sect. 2, software framework in Sect. 3, navigation in Sect. 4, our approach for different perception tasks in Sect. 5, manipulation and control in Sect. 6 and task planning in Sect. 7.

2   Robot Platform

As most other teams in the league, we use the KUKA youBot as the applied platform for RoboCup@Work (see Fig. 1). It is equipped with a 5-DoF manipulator, a two finger gripper and an omni-directional platform. The standard internal computer of the youBot has been replaced with an Intel NUC with a

Core i7 processor and 8 GB of RAM. Two Hokuyo URG-04LX[1] laser range finders are mounted vertically flipped in the front and the back of the platform.
For perception-related tasks, the manipulator is fitted with an ASUS Xtion Pro
Live[2] RGB-D camera on the gripper palm. Additionally, an RGB camera is fitted
between the fingers of the gripper for close-range perception of objects.

Another custom modification has been made for the youBot gripper (based
on the design of [6]) which enhances the opening range and enables grasping of a
wider range of objects. The gripper (see Fig. 1) is actuated with two Dynamixel
AX-12A servo motors which provide a position interface and force-feedback information. A final modification was performed on the back platform of the youBot.
It has been replaced with a new light-weight aluminium version, the position of
which can be manually adjusted forward and backward. All technical drawings
to the previously described modifications, as well as various 3D printed sensor
mounts have been made public[3].

3 Robot Software Framework

We use the Robot Operating System (ROS) [15] as the middleware to pass data
and events between components. We primarily use topics since they support
non-blocking communication and the possibility of monitoring the communication between two or more nodes at any time. We have standardized our nodes
with the addition of *event in* and *event out* topics. Our components listen to the
event in topic and expect simple command messages for starting, stopping or
triggering (run once) the component. The components provide feedback of their
status on the *event out* topic when they finish. This allows us to coordinate and
control the components with either simpler state machines or task planning; in
either case, the control flow and data flow between the components remains separated, following a similar approach as proposed in GenoM3 [13]. The software
is organized in an hierarchical manner (see Fig. 2) with the low level components
implemented as ROS nodes. Higher level actions are developed as SMACH [10]
state machines wrapped around ROS action servers, and include actions such
as *move base to location*, *perceive location*, *pick object*, and *place object*. For
task planning, the Mercury task planner [11] is used within the framework of
ROSPlan, with actions in the task plan corresponding to the actions mentioned
earlier.

4 Navigation

For navigation, we use *move_base* from the ROS navigation stack, along with
accompanying components such as the occupancy grid map, global and local

---

[1] https://www.hokuyo-aut.jp/search/single.php?serial=166.
[2] https://www.asus.com/us/3D-Sensor/Xtion_PRO_LIVE.
[3] https://github.com/mas-group/technical_drawings.

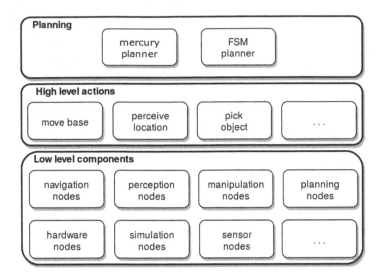

Fig. 2. Software architecture organization

path planner (Dynamic-Window-Approach) and Adaptive Monte Carlo Localization (AMCL). The parameters for *move_base*, such as inflation radius and maximum linear velocity, were configured by running experiments in simulation in various environments. Based on the experiments, we fixed 3 sets of parameters for low, medium and high speed navigation; currently the speed settings are chosen manually based on the complexity of the environment. We use the force-field recovery behaviour developed by smARTLab@Work [6], which moves the robot away from obstacles when it gets stuck.

A direct base controller has been implemented, which allows the robot to move in a local frame relative to its current position without requiring a map or global localization. This is used, for example, for local motions while picking objects from a workstation.

Yellow and black barrier tapes on the floor indicate areas in the environment to be avoided. Using the RGB-D camera, we detect the barrier tape in 2D using a colour filter and convert the pixels to 3D using the point cloud. The point cloud is republished as a laser scan which forms an additional sensor source for the costmap, hence treating the barrier tapes as static obstacles.

5   Perception

Several components have been developed for processing the image and point cloud data from the arm-mounted RGB-D camera. In the current configuration, the RGB-D camera faces downwards when the arm is fully stretched upwards; this allows the robot to perceive the entire area of the workstation.

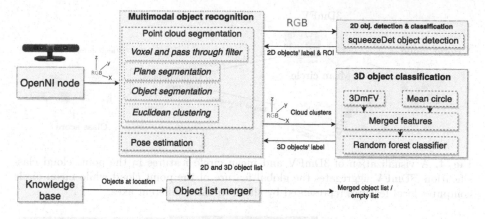

Fig. 3. Object perception pipeline

5.1 Object Recognition

Perception of objects relevant for industrial environments is particularly challenging because they are typically textureless and made of reflective materials such as metal. For the object detection and recognition task, we use the RGB-D camera with both 3D and 2D methods as outlined in Fig. 3.

3D Perception. For 3D segmentation and classification, we capture a single point cloud, downsample it using a voxel grid filter, and crop it using passthrough filters in order to reduce the computational complexity. To perform plane segmentation, we use a sample consensus method to segment a single horizontal plane. The convex hull of the segmented plane is computed and represented as a planar polygon. The prism of points above the polygon are segmented and clustered to individual object point clouds.

We extract the features of each cluster using 3D modified Fisher vector (3DmFV) [4] and mean circle features [19]. The 3DmFV features represent a global description of the point cloud using a generative model which is formulated using Gaussian mixture model (GMM). The mean circle features include the radius of circles fit on slices of the point cloud along all three axes, dimensions of the bounding box, mean colour, etc. The combined 3DmFV and mean circle features are used to learn a random forest classifier as illustrated in Fig. 4. The training data for 3D perception consists of approximately 300 segmented point clouds per object.

2D Perception. In previous years, we used graph-based segmentation [9] to segment objects from the background. However, since the requirement to pick from arbitrary surfaces has been included in the rulebook for RoboCup@Work [2], an approach for object segmentation which does not rely on a uniform background is required. We use SqueezeDet [20], a convolutional neural network for object

3DmFV

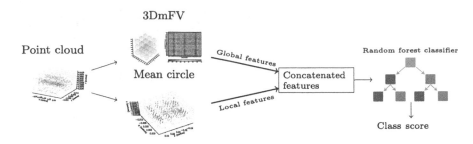

Fig. 4. A visualization of 3DmFV and mean circle features in the point cloud classification. 3DmFV aggregates the global feature of the point cloud while mean circle computes local features represented by slices on three different axes.

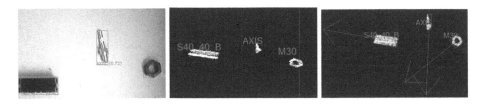

Fig. 5. Recognized objects using 2D (left) and 3D (middle) methods. The right image illustrates the estimated pose of each object.

detection in which the region proposal and classification are integrated into one stage. It uses the `ConvDet` layer to output coordinates for bounding boxes and the class probabilities for each bounding box.

Given the 2D bounding box, we find the corresponding 3D point for each pixel in the box and fit a 3D bounding box to determine the position and orientation of the object. Sample outputs are shown in Fig. 5. The training data for 2D classification consists of approximately 700 annotated images per object.

Inference from both models together runs at approximately 2 FPS. This is achieved by running inference on the two models (squeezeDet and random forest) in parallel. The two object lists are received by the *object list merger* node, which intelligently combines the lists into a unified one. The *object list merger* uses information such as class probabilities from both classifiers, prior knowledge regarding the accuracies for certain objects by each classifier, and inventory at the current location being perceived (which is retrieved from the *knowledge base* used by the task planner as described in Sect. 7).

For the precision placement test, the robot is required to insert objects into cavities. Given an input image of the workstation, canny edge detection is applied to extract the edges around the cavities and the workspace. The resulting edges are dilated and combined into contours, which are filtered based on their area. The cropped cavity images are classified using a MobileNetV2 [17] network. The pose of each cavity is estimated in a similar manner as the 2D objects - by fitting oriented 3D bounding boxes to the corresponding 3D points of the 2D contour.

5.2   Object Tracking

In the rotating table test, the robot is required to pick up a specified list of objects which are placed on top of a rotating table along with several other objects. The table spins at an arbitrary speed within a known range; this is set at the start of the run and remains fixed throughout. The robot needs to track the objects, classify them, and estimate their motion model in order to anticipate their arrival in front of the robot. Once an object has been identified for a grasp, the gripper-mounted RGB camera is used to estimate the precise grasp time.

For tracking, the robot's arm is moved to a predefined configuration such that more than half of the table is within the field of view of its RGB-D camera. At a rate of 10 Hz, 150 point clouds are captured and processed once capturing is complete. For each point cloud, object clusters are extracted in a similar manner as described in Sect. 5.1. In our current approach, we track objects by using the detections from every frame and establish temporal correspondences based on the distance between the centroids of all pairs of objects. This naive approach is possible since there are no occlusions and the objects all rotate at a constant speed. A list of tracked objects is maintained, where each tracked object consists of a list of centroid positions and timestamps.

Given the tracked positions of the objects, a least squares solution for the center of rotation is obtained using SVD, and the angular velocity is estimated as the median of angular velocities for each tracked object. The velocity and center of rotation are used to estimate the time and position at which a given object will arrive in front of the robot. Once an object has been classified and selected for grasping, the arm is positioned such that the gripper is directly above the expected grasp location. In order to determine the exact grasp time, background change detection is performed on the images of the gripper-mounted RGB camera during a small window around the estimated arrival time.

Future improvements aim at incorporating the size and orientation information of the objects for calculation of the exact grasp time using background change detection to allow more flexibility in the placement of objects.

6   Manipulation and Control

We use MoveIt! [1] as our base framework for basic manipulation tasks, but in order to grasp objects reliably, several additional components have been developed and integrated on the robot. We developed our own interpolation-based planner for MoveIt! as it produces more deterministic trajectories for the arm movement. This is used for motions of the arm to pre-defined positions.

For grasping, the grasp pose of the object is the input to the *pre-grasp planner*, which computes a pre-grasp arm configuration based on the type of grasp, a distance offset and constraints imposed by the robot's manipulator and end effector. Finally the trajectories to reach the pre-grasp and grasp pose are concatenated and executed in sequence. Once the end effector reaches the grasp pose, the gripper of the robot is closed. A grasp monitor checks whether the object is grasped successfully utilizing the force and position feedback of the two Dynamixel motors.

6.1   Cartesian Motion

Given that the manipulator has only 5 degrees of freedom, an exact inverse kinematic solution which satisfies both position and orientation of a particular pose is not always possible. Hence, we deploy a Cartesian motion control framework which can provide an approximate kinematic solution for a particular pose by removing constraints on the orientation. The Cartesian motion control provides joint velocities for target task-space or Cartesian velocities; it relies on an approximate inverse kinematic velocity solution near singularities and joint limits of the arm. The method we use to obtain such inverse kinematic solutions for task space velocities is called Weighted Damped Least Square (WDLS) [8]. Our implementation uses the *WDLS inverse kinematic velocity solver* provided by the OROCOS KDL library. The use of such approximate solutions allows us to manipulate objects in scenarios where positional accuracy is not the primary objective, such as when inserting an object in a box. This method allows us to ignore constraints on specific degrees of freedom (angular degrees of freedom in this case) and the object can be placed in the box by reaching the area above it in any orientation. The Cartesian motion controller also allows the robot to execute motions subject to task-space constraints on the trajectory, such as curve-tracing. The Cartesian controller is an instantaneous incremental motion controller, hence online changes in the target position can be handled easily by the velocity controller.

6.2   Learning from Demonstration

Complex manipulation skills can be transferred to the robot by the learning from demonstration (LfD) framework developed using Dynamic Movement Primitives and Cartesian control. Dynamic movement primitives use nonlinear dynamic equations to learn the shape of the motion [18]. Skills are demonstrated to the robot by a teacher using an arUco marker board; the robot records the motion by tracking the board with a camera and the motion is then learned using the LfD framework [14][4]. This framework was implemented and used to teach the robot motion profiles which are hard to engineer. We plan to use this for teaching motion profiles such as those for picking from or placing on shelves.

7   Task Planning

Finite state machines (FSMs) are sometimes used for high-level control in robotic applications, and in particular in competition settings where the objects involved, locations and the tasks are well-specified and the action set is relatively small. Such FSMs of whole scenarios may, over time, become complex

---

[4] https://youtu.be/jEtlm96KAbA.

and difficult to understand and maintain. In our architecture, small, easily-understandable, debuggable and maintainable FSMs (in the form of SMACH scripts) are used for executing actions such as *perceive location, pick object* and *move base to location.* The high-level control is handled through the use of a task planner which produces a sequence of fully ordered actions to achieve a goal. Listing 1.1 shows a sample plan for transporting a *bearing* from *WS03* to *WS10.*

Listing 1.1. Sample plan	**Listing 1.2.** PDDL definition for *pick*

```
(move_base youbot-brsu start ws03)
(perceive youbot-brsu ws03)
(pick youbot-brsu ws03 bearing-00)
(stage youbot-brsu platform_left bearing-00)
(move_base youbot-brsu ws03 ws10)
(unstage youbot-brsu platform_middle
        bearing-00)
(place youbot-brsu ws10 bearing-00)
```

```
(:action pick
  :parameters (?r - robot ?l - location ?o -
          object)
  :precondition (and    (on ?o ?l)
                        (at ?r ?l)
                        (perceived ?l)
                        ( gripper_is_free ?r)
                        (not (holding ?r ?o))
                        (not (heavy ?o))
                )
  :effect (and    (holding ?r ?o)
                  (not (on ?o ?l))
                  (not ( gripper_is_free ?r))
                  (increase (total-cost) 2)
          )
)
```

We have, for the past couple of years, been using the Mercury task planner [11], a winner at the 2014 International Planning Competition (IPC). Our planning domain contains seven basic operators: *move base to location, perceive location, pick object, stage object to robot platform, unstage object from robot platform, place object,* and *insert object.* As an example, the PDDL representation of the *pick* operator is shown in Listing 1.2. The limited number of operators also serves to help with tractability, which remains a problem, as is often the case with task planners, in particular given the limits on time in the arena to complete the various tests. In addition to the operators, the domain also includes literals representing locations, the robot, objects and the robot platform (representing the spaces on the robot which are used to transport up to three objects at a time). Eleven predicates such as *on, occupied, gripper is free* and *perceived* are also included. Further details on the modelling of the domain and the planner's integration into the system can be found in [7] and [12].

As the task to be carried out is received from the referee box, it is parsed and the facts that make up the initial state and the goal statement are added to the knowledge base (KB) within the ROSPlan framework. Due to the time necessary to generate an optimal plan, the *problem generator* chooses three goals to be achieved and outputs the PDDL problem file which is then sent to the planner along with the PDDL domain file containing the operators, their preconditions and effects. The first plan that it may produce is far from optimal. As the planner continues, the quality of the generated plan improves (see [11]). Here, a time limit of 10 s is set. The latest generated plan at that time is then sent to the *plan executor* which schedules each action and dispatches it for execution by triggering the SMACH scripts which are tailored specifically to perform the actions given runtime constraints such as location type and object type. The *plan executor* monitors the action execution and, upon completion, updates the KB

Table 1. Quantitative comparison of task planners for the @Work problem

Planner	Time limit (s)	Plan length	Plan cost	Plan redundancies
Mercury 2014	10	65	570	5
	15	65	570	5
FDSS(2) 2018	10	79	588	0
	15	65	486	0
LAMA 2011	10	57	420	0
	15	56	400	0

to reflect the changes to the world that the action has resulted in (the action's effects), thus ensuring that the current state is available in case any replanning is needed. In the case of a failure during the execution of an action, and depending on the action, the *plan executor* either retries the action or triggers a re-plan.

Parallel execution of base and arm motion has helped to reduce execution time as the robot is able to partially execute part of the following action along with the current one. For example, as the robot is arriving at a workstation (the current action) it may move the arm in preparation for a perceiving action (the following action). This is handled entirely within the state machines which have knowledge of the next action in the plan.

Ideally, the planner should take into consideration the different points awarded for different items/locations in the RoboCup@Work scenarios, the time constraints of the tests and the tendency for certain actions to succeed more often than others. The planning system would then be able to provide a plan that prioritises actions which are highly likely to succeed and high-reward goals. The problem would then be a resource-constrained planning problem with expectation maximisation in a Markov decision process (MDP). MDPs are known to be hard to solve and are, therefore, usually solved offline and assume that all possible situations are in the model. This kind of a solution is not readily available off-the-shelf (and to our knowledge remains an open research topic) and yields a more complex modelling process than what is currently being used in our system.

Looking ahead, and following the results of a comparative study [3] of planners submitted to the 2018 IPC that was carried out to investigate whether to continue with our current planner or switch to another, the LAMA planner [16] will be integrated and tested, mainly due to its ability to produce near-optimal plans in limited time (see Table 1).

8   Current Research Activities

Currently, robustness in perception and grasping of objects is an area for improvement. Our current approach involves perceiving the objects once and performing an open-loop grasp with only minimal grasp verification after the grasp is complete. We would like to improve this by closing the perception-manipulation loop, incorporating continuous perception before and during the grasp, and continuous grasp monitoring after grasping. We plan to use neural compute sticks such as Intel Movidius[5] or Google Coral[6] to reduce the inference time for object recognition. Additionally, smart machine vision cameras such as JeVois[7] are being considered for use at the end-effector. For manipulation, we aim to achieve coordinated motion between the base and the arm by modeling the entire robot as an 8 DOF manipulator (3 DOF base + 5 DOF arm).

9 Conclusion

In this paper, we presented our approach for the RoboCup@Work competition including modifications applied to the standard youBot hardware configuration as well as the functional core components of our current software architecture. Our combined 2D and 3D approach to object recognition has resulted in improved performance compared to previous years, while keeping up with the increased complexity of the tasks over the years. The task planning framework allows us to easily attempt new types of tasks, without having to deal with large state machines. We applied the component-oriented development approach defined in BRICS [5] for creating our software, allowing us to compose several heterogeneous components into a complete system and even reuse components on different robots. Our current work is focussed on improving the robustness of grasping, by incorporating continuous perception during manipulation and additional sensors for grasp monitoring. Additionally, we eventually aim to move our software to a different platform since the youBot is no longer in production.

Acknowledgement. We value the advice and guidance over the years by Professor Gerhard Kraetzschmar, who sadly passed away this year. He was one of the founders of RoboCup@Work and actively involved in the team activities of b-it-bots. We gratefully acknowledge the continued support of the team by the b-it Bonn-Aachen International Center for Information Technology, Bonn-Rhein-Sieg University of Applied Sciences and AStA H-BRS.

References

1. MoveIt! motion planning. http://moveit.ros.org. Accessed 07 October 2019
2. RoboCup@Work Rulebook 2019. https://atwork.robocup.org/wp-content/uploads/2019/02/Rulebook_2019.pdf. Accessed 05 September 2019
3. Abdelrahman, A., Chavan, S., Tran, N.: Evaluation of New Planners. Unpublished manuscript. Hochschule Bonn-Rhein-Sieg (2019)
4. Ben-Shabat, Y., Lindenbaum, M., Fischer, A.: 3DmFV: three-dimensional point cloud classification in real-time using convolutional neural networks. IEEE Robot. Autom. Lett. **3**(4), 3145–3152 (2018)

---

[5] https://software.intel.com/en-us/neural-compute-stick.
[6] https://coral.withgoogle.com/products/accelerator/.
[7] http://www.jevois.org/.

5. Bischoff, R., et al.: BRICS - best practice in robotics. In: Proceedings of the IFR International Symposium on Robotics (ISR 2010), Munich, Germany, June 2010
6. Broecker, B., Claes, D., Fossel, J., Tuyls, K.: Winning the RoboCup@Work 2014 competition: the smARTLab approach. In: Bianchi, R.A.C., Akin, H.L., Ramamoorthy, S., Sugiura, K. (eds.) RoboCup 2014. LNCS (LNAI), vol. 8992, pp. 142–154. Springer, Cham (2015). https://doi.org/10.1007/978-3-319-18615-3_12
7. Carrion, O.L.: Task planning, execution and monitoring for mobile manipulators in industrial domains. Master's thesis, Bonn-Rhein-Sieg University of Applied Sciences, Grantham Allee 20, 53757 St. Augustin, Germany, April 2016. https://github.com/oscar-lima/isr_planning/blob/kinetic/oscar_lima_master_thesis.pdf
8. Chiaverini, S., Siciliano, B., Egeland, O.: Review of the damped least-squares inverse kinematics with experiments on an industrial robot manipulator. IEEE Trans. Control Syst. Technol. **2**(2), 123–134 (1994)
9. Felzenszwalb, P.F., Huttenlocher, D.P.: Efficient graph-based image segmentation. Int. J. Comput. Vision **59**(2), 167–181 (2004)
10. Tim Field. SMACH documentation, July 2011. http://www.ros.org/wiki/smach/Documentation
11. Katz, M., Hoffmann, J.: Mercury planner: pushing the limits of partial delete relaxation. In: IPC 2014 Planner Abstracts, pp. 43–47 (2014)
12. Lima, O., Ventura, R., Awaad, I.: Integrating classical planning and real robots in industrial and service robotics domains. In: Proceedings of the 6th Workshop on Planning and Robotics (PlanRob) at ICAPS (2018)
13. Mallet, A., Pasteur, C., Herrb, M., Lemaignan, S., Ingrand, F.: GenoM3: building middleware-independent robotic components. In: 2010 IEEE International Conference on Robotics and Automation, pp. 4627–4632. IEEE (2010)
14. Mitrevski, A., Padalkar, A., Nguyen, M., Plöger, P.G.: "Lucy, take the noodle box!": domestic object manipulation using movement primitives and whole body motion. In: Chalup, S., Niemueller, T., Suthakorn, J., Williams, M.-A. (eds.) RoboCup 2019. LNCS (LNAI), vol. 11531, pp. 189–200. Springer, Cham (2019)
15. Quigley, M., et al.: ROS: an open-source Robot Operating System. In: ICRA Workshop on Open Source Software (2009)
16. Richter, S., Westphal, M., Helmert, M.: LAMA 2008 and 2011. In: International Planning Competition, pp. 117–124 (2011)
17. Sandler, M., Howard, A., Zhu, M., Zhmoginov, A., Chen, L.-C.: MobileNetV2: inverted residuals and linear bottlenecks. In: Proceedings of the IEEE Conference on Computer Vision and Pattern Recognition, pp. 4510–4520 (2018)
18. Schaal, S.: Dynamic movement primitives - a framework for motor control in humans and humanoid robotics. In: Kimura, H., Tsuchiya, K., Ishiguro, A., Witte, H. (eds.) Adaptive Motion of Animals and Machines, pp. 261–280. Springer, Tokyo (2006). https://doi.org/10.1007/4-431-31381-8_23
19. Thoduka, S., Pazekha, S., Moriarty, A., Kraetzschmar, G.K.: RGB-D-based features for recognition of textureless objects. In: Behnke, S., Sheh, R., Sarıel, S., Lee, D.D. (eds.) RoboCup 2016. LNCS (LNAI), vol. 9776, pp. 294–305. Springer, Cham (2017). https://doi.org/10.1007/978-3-319-68792-6_24
20. Wu, B., Iandola, F., Jin, P.H., Keutzer, K.: SqueezeDet: unified, small, low power fully convolutional neural networks for real-time object detection for autonomous driving. In: Proceedings of the IEEE Conference on Computer Vision and Pattern Recognition Workshops, pp. 129–137 (2017)

UTS Unleashed! RoboCup@Home SSPL Champions 2019

Sammy Pfeiffer[✉], Daniel Ebrahimian, Sarita Herse, Tran Nhut Le,
Suwen Leong, Bethany Lu, Katie Powell, Syed Ali Raza, Tian Sang,
Ishan Sawant, Meg Tonkin, Christine Vinaviles, The Duc Vu, Qijun Yang,
Richard Billingsley, Jesse Clark, Benjamin Johnston, Srinivas Madhisetty,
Neil McLaren, Pavlos Peppas, Jonathan Vitale, and Mary-Anne Williams

University of Technology Sydney, 15 Broadway, Ultimo, NSW 2007, Australia
{Sammy.Pfeiffer,Sarita.Herse,TranNhut.M.Le,Su.W.Leong,Bethany.Lu,
Katie.A.Binns,Tian.Sang-1,Ishan.Sawant,Margaret.Tonkin,
Christine.Vinaviles,TheDuc.Vu,Qijun.Yang}@student.uts.edu.au,
{Richard.Billingsley,Jesse.Clark,Daniel.Ebrahimian,Benjamin.Johnston,
Srinivas.Madhisetty,Neil.McLaren,Pavlos.Peppas,Syed.Raza,
Jonathan.Vitale,Mary-Anne.Williams}@uts.edu.au

Abstract. This paper summarizes the approaches employed by Team *UTS Unleashed!* to take First Place in the 2019 RoboCup@Home Social Standard Platform League. First, our system architecture is introduced. Next, our approach to basic skills needed for a strong performance in the competition. We describe several implementations for tests participation. Finally our software development methodology is discussed.

Keywords: RoboCup@Home · RoboCup · Social Standard Platform League · Social robotics · UTS Unleashed!

1 Introduction

UTS Unleashed! is the only Australian team to participate in 2017, 2018 and 2019 RoboCup@Home Social Standard Platform League. It was awarded the Human-Robot Interface Award in 2017, and able to achieve second place in the competition in both 2017 and 2018. In 2019 the team demonstrated significant problem solving and software development capability for developing sophisticated behaviours for Softbank Pepper robots to win the competition. To prepare for the 2019 RoboCup competition the team focused on system robustness by running all its code locally on the robot, while making fault-tolerant use of external computing resources when available and necessary.

M.-A. Williams—Team Leader.
Authors are listed in alphabetical order after the student development lead, Sammy Pfeiffer: students are followed by researchers.

S. Chalup et al. (Eds.): RoboCup 2019, LNAI 11531, pp. 603–615, 2019.
https://doi.org/10.1007/978-3-030-35699-6_49

2   System Architecture

Our system architecture was designed to tackle the specific challenges of the
Pepper [1] robotic platform, the type of goals to be achieved in the different
RoboCup@Home tests and the available network infrastructure constraints and
performance at the RoboCup competition. It also takes into consideration the
profile of our team composition which includes a mix of multi-disciplinary skills
(Human-Robot Interaction, User Experience, Psychology, Machine Learning,
Software Engineering, Design, Business and Law). Our diverse team members
ranged from Undergraduate through Masters and PhD students and possessed
a wide range of technical skills.

A diagram of our system architecture is illustrated in Fig. 1. All software
modules were implemented with on-board deployment in mind and can be run
externally as well. To run directly on the robot itself, dependencies and software
needed to be compiled and configured for that purpose. This was accomplished

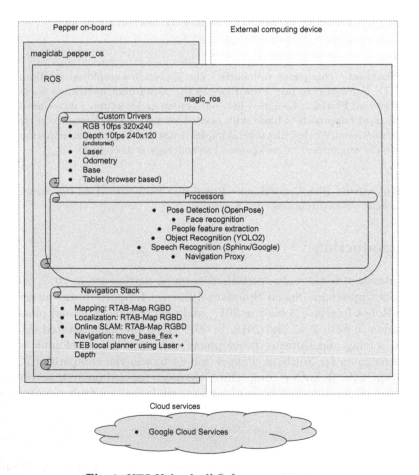

Fig. 1. UTS Unleashed! Software architecture.

by the base OS, `magiclab_pepper_os`. Services that benefit from running on an external computer or having a cabled internet connection are also run in the external computer and used automatically when the network is available using our sophisticated `magic_ros` framework.

2.1   Base Operating System

A common challenge faced by all teams in the SSPL (Social Standard Platform League) is the need to build a large number of updated and new dependencies in order to enable usage of state-of-the-art algorithms and tools as found in the ROS middleware [2]. The challenge comes from the Pepper platform using a 32 bits Gentoo Operating System (OS)[1] with no root access, making developers unable to use standard software deployment strategies (e.g. `sudo apt-get install` as in a typical Ubuntu distribution). Building every package by hand was found to be extremely time consuming so a better solution was developed.

`pepper_os` [3] was designed and implemented, a 32bits Docker image based on a dump of the disk image of the Pepper robot[2] with Gentoo Prefix [4] and ROS_overlay [5] already built with a big set of commonly used ROS packages (e.g. `navigation`, `perception`, `rosbridge`, `naoqi_driver`...). Additionally, some extra useful (and hard to compile on a 32 bits OS) libraries like Tensorflow [7] can be found. A user must only extract the latest release onto the home folder of their robot and the robot will boot with a `roscore` ready to be used.

Furthermore `magiclab_pepper_os` [6] contains the full image used in our robots for the competition, including other hard to build libraries like PyTorch [8], RTAB-Map [9], OpenNI2 [10], dlib [11] and spatio_temporal_voxel_layer [12].

2.2   The `magic_ros` Framework

During the previous years of the competition, the team identified difficulties for some team members to learn and use ROS quickly and effectively. Also, similarly to other robotics competitions, teams have to optimize to make the best use of wireless networking during the competition but not completely depend on it. Hence, the library `magic_ros` [13] was born, implementing the following features:

- ROS complexity is hidden: Auto initialization of uninitialized nodes; no need to use ROS message format as you can pass native Python datatypes around; autoconversion of images to cv2/numpy format.
- Helper informative messages, setting parameters such as `ROS_MASTER_URI`, `ROS_IP`, `init_node`,....

---

[1] The OS image is dated as built in November 2016 with binaries and shared libraries dated from 2014.

[2] To be able to build in exactly the same conditions than the real robot, as the provided Virtual Machine by the manufacturer does not match the real system precisely.

- Message Providers with subscription, query-able acquisition models and a buffer. This also enables easy logging and recording of data. They are network efficient, as `magic_ros` automatically detects if messages are to be delivered on-board or through the network, using information compression when necessary.
- Processors are nodes that enable remote calls, with the ability to have multiple nodes in the network doing the same task, different selection strategies are used to choose which processor to run first. Calls are guaranteed to go through the network if it is possible. As an example a full OpenPose [14] call (containing RGB + Depth images and returning a dictionary with all the available 3D skeleton data and Regions Of Interest (ROI) of faces found and additional data) takes just 0.6–0.8 s (±0.1 s standard deviation) added to the processing time. Messages are compressed as much as possible usually fitting into a single TCP packet. All clients do not need to do any work to take advantage of nodes running in more powerful external computers when they are available, this is transparent to the user.
- Automatic diagnostics publication, making it easy to monitor and debug.

Custom Drivers. Some drivers were re-written using `magic_ros` to have more control of the on-board processing pipeline. It was also an opportunity to double check and confirm if the drivers were correct. It is worth mentioning we found that the default laser driver provided by `naoqi_driver` provides inaccurate data. We implemented a better approximation on a virtual single laser which improved our navigation stack. A query-based interface was created for the camera images, which ran at 10 Hz at low resolutions (320 × 240 px RGB, 240 × 120 px Depth) to minimize computing costs while still providing enough useful data. We also benchmarked the robot's odometry and discovered it was surprisingly good.

3   Skills

Some robot skills are of utmost importance to ensure a high performance in RoboCup@Home SSPL. The approach UTS Unleashed! took to prioritize foundational robot skills is outlined in this section.

3.1   Navigation

Autonomous navigation is necessary in all RoboCup tests, therefore, considerable effort was devoted to this topic.

Mapping. RTAB-Map (Real-Time Appearance-Based Mapping) [9] is used for mapping with RGB and Depth images. The robot odometry is consumed at a rate of 10 Hz. RTAB-Map is able to provide 3D localisation but to minimise computational cost is constrained to 2D. A set of rosbags were recorded on the robot following trajectories that the robot is expected to pursue during

Fig. 2. RoboCup@Home SSPL arena gridmap used for global path planning and visualization on the top left corner. The rest of the image is an example of the 3D pointcloud and default gridmap provided by RTAB-Map with some real-time RGB+Depth data shown in the lab.

the different tests while taking care to face the robot towards fixed landmarks. Examples of landmarks are walls, doors and other fixed furniture like kitchen sinks. We also positioned the head of the robot to look at a 45° angle towards the floor to maximize the amount of close-range, visible features that can be recognized for localisation later. Some rosbags were used for the mapping process, while others were used for map verification.

Once the rosbag-recording stage is completed, we run the mapping process on a powerful external computer. A 2D projection of the map is created with the RTAB-Map library, then manually cleaned and obstacles are inflated for use in global path planning and visualisation purposes as shown in Fig. 2.

Localisation. Localisation was also achieved using RTAB-Map, but running on-board at 10 fps. We discovered that relying on laser data alone proved to be insufficient.

Navigation Stack. It is based on `move_base_flex` [18], hence generating a navigation state machine.

On receiving a navigation goal, a global path is queried to the standard ROS navigation stack, *global_planner/GlobalPlanner*. When a valid plan is found, it is executed by the local planner. We use Time-Elastic Bands (TEB) local planner [19] running on-board. To do real-time obstacle avoidance we use Pepper's laser (6 Hz publishing frequency) and its depth camera (at 10 Hz) as sensing sources. To be able to compute this information on-board we make use of spatio_temporal_voxel_layer [12] to feed pointcloud data to the plugin *costmap_converter::CostmapToPolygonsDBSMCCH* which converts this information into something processable in real-time.

We stop the navigation stack software while the robot is not moving to save CPU cycles by adapting the Linux approach of sending a signal of *SIGSTOP* to the RTAB-Map localisation process and the navigation state machine and sending *SIGCONT* when a new navigation goal is received until it is finished.

The specific configuration of our navigation stack and the TEB local planner will be available at our code release.

3.2   Speech Recognition

Speech recognition was performed by running multiple speech recognition engines in a concurrent fashion. On-board the robot, CMU PocketSphinx [15] provided a fallback recognition strategy when external cloud-based recognition was not available. When network conditions allowed cloud-based speech recognition, Google Cloud Speech to Text [16] was used. To improve performance over unreliable WiFi connections, audio data is streamed over the network using the compressed Opus [17] audio codec and decompressed on an external computing device before being forwarded to the cloud-based recognition service. As many cloud-based speech recognition services do not support controlled grammars, the recognized text is post-processed using a grammar. A dictionary is used to convert English transcriptions into phonemes, and then an approximate match is performed to find a high-probability parse.

3.3   Perception

Object Recognition. Our object recognition module is built on YOLO [20] version 3. Named `dark_magic` because it is built on `darknet_ros` [21], a subset of YOLO for ROS, is able to produce rapid object detection with extrapolated 3D locations. On a machine with a GPU this is close to real-time; on Pepper's CPU, it detects objects within approximately 3.3 s.

Altogether, approximately 200–250 images are needed for each object to be trained. The number of images per object in the training data should be kept approximately equal, in order to prevent detection bias affecting the results. With the data sets prepared, we separated them into training and testing batches.

From an RGB image, the module will output the name of the detected object, the detection confidence, and a bounding box. With depth image added, 3D location in robot and world space of each object can also be extracted.

We improved the efficiency of the network by fine-tuning certain configurations such as mini-batch and network resolution. At times, this meant finding a compromise where the resolution of the images were small enough for fast detection, but still provided enough information for accuracy, due to computational limitation on CPU. A higher resolution was kept in the full (GPU) model.

People Perception. We made extensive use of OpenPose [14] to detect people in an unconstrained environment like RoboCup@Home. As with other libraries, we created a `magic_ros` server and a client called `magic_pose`. The server automatically detects if the machine on which it is running has GPU access (external machine) or not (Pepper) and initializes the appropriate model (either GPU or CPU based). The client is the same for both, the GPU and CPU servers.

We also used OpenPose to estimate people's poses, one of which was if the person was sitting. This was achieved by measuring the height of the person and setting a threshold below which the person was estimated to be sitting.

Finally, we also used OpenPose to crop faces and further extract facial features, especially for non-frontal and far away faces which are harder to detect with our face detector.

When it was possible to make simpler assumptions on the location of the person (e.g. expecting a person within 1.5 m and in front of the robot) we could rely on a different library to detect faces. We used the Python module `face_recognition` [24] that makes use of dlib [11]. As we did for OpenPose, we wrapped these APIs in client/server processors of our architecture. This library was also used to extract face encodings for face identity recognition tasks.

3.4   Human Robot Interaction

We developed our own web-based tablet interface with UTS-branded aesthetics including simple animations to express what the robot is doing. It became a useful debugging tool for programmers in addition to aiding the robot users in understanding what is happening and how to interact. We provided a simple API to increase adoption. A separate paper about this is to be published.

4   Test Implementation Highlights

We consider designing and implementing in a well-thought manner. Every test is important and here we show what we consider as key elements of our results in this edition of RoboCup@Home. We chose these tests by common decision in our team by taking into account our strengths, weaknesses, and opportunity for success. Most tests were implemented as State Machines. This section details some of these tests, while the full test descriptions can be found in the official RoboCup@Home rules website.

4.1   Stage I

Clean Up. We used the `dark_magic` module for object recognition. Once the model arrived at an acceptable accuracy, we focused on HRI elements, particularly expressing the locations of the found objects to the operator in a clear and effective way, via both speech and tablet display and then ensuring the operator places the object on it's predefined location by detecting the object again.

Find My Mates. We detected all the people in the room from a fixed set of safe viewpoints, which were selected to prevent blind spots. For each person detected we estimated an accurate position in the map, and achieved higher accuracy by correcting distortions of the depth camera images. People estimated within 20 cm from a previously estimated person in the map were joined together as a single person. Face recognition was used to further reinforce this strategy. People detected outside the considered room were disregarded (e.g. audience).

After collecting the positions of all the people in the room, we estimated their pose (either standing or sitting), which was affirmed by checking if the person was located near a seating landmark. We also cropped the face of the person and a portion of the torso.

To predict facial features we trained several SVM (Support Vector Machines) models to classify facial features by using the Large-scale CelebFaces Attributes (CelebA) dataset [22]. We first cropped the faces of the dataset and then extracted face encodings using the Python module `face_recognition` and its function `face_encodings`. We thought that the face encodings generated by the face_recognition module would most likely include information about features characterizing the physical appearance of the person's face to distinguish them. Our approach achieved 95% prediction accuracy when testing our models for facial features: facial hair, dark colored hair, gray hair, eyeglasses and gender.

To predict the color of the t-shirt we collect only the pixels in the torso with higher depth, to avoid occlusions. We then increased the luminance and saturation of the collected pixels and used a median filter with window size 3 to reduce the noise and unnecessary fine details. After this pre-processing we transformed the image patch from RGB space to CIELAB space. In the CIELAB space the distances reflect those in a perceptual space more closely, which is ideal when the task is to report colors to a human. The pixels of the patch were clustered together down to 3 colors through a k-means algorithm. Finally we employed a color dictionary with a limited set of colors we used to estimate distances of each pixel to a color in the dictionary. Each color belonged to a color group (e.g. blue, red, etc.). To compute perceptual distances between colors in our color dictionary we used the CIEDE2000 color difference distance [23]. This returned better results than employing a simple Euclidean distance or colors represented in HSV space. The likelihood of each detected color was calculated by the number of pixels bucketed in a specific color group over the number of total pixels of the patch. Finally, we estimated the color of the t-shirt using thresholds for the estimated likelihoods: a single color if a color reached 70% likelihood, multiple colors with over 50% likelihood, if any, or no color was returned otherwise.

In addition, we used Google Cloud Vision to detect text from the torso. If we detected any text from the torso we reported the collected characters back.

Our strategy revealed success in reporting the correct location and a unique description for one of the mates the robot was asked to find.

Receptionist. Finding an empty seat was the hardest task in this test and the most crucial to score points. Our approach to finding an empty (sofa) seat was based on a simple heuristic that any surface with height within a range (say 40 cm to 60 cm) from the ground would be a seat. To differentiate seats from tables we also detect a seat back, by looking for a vertical surface just behind the horizontal surface. To return a location of an empty seat in the sitting area, the robot turned its head from left to right and calculated area for each empty seat found. Finally, the location was returned with the largest seat area as an empty seat.

Take Out the Garbage. Given the placement of the trash cans is known beforehand the main challenge for this test was carrying rubbish bags over a few minutes. The bags may come loose and fall or the robot's arms may overheat. We asked an operator using speech and a descriptive tablet interface to have a bag placed between the hip of the robot and under the arm, then we continuously send commands to keep the arm in position. We repeat this approach with the second bag and finally navigate to the drop-off point.

4.2   Stage II

Find My Disk. The robot provided specific instructions to the blind person about how to position the disk in front of its camera, and then compared text visible on the disk with the operator's desired disk. While disk positions were tracked using the robot's depth sensors, a naive strategy for disk tracking was not appropriate because of the depth sensor's limitations. In particular, the depth sensor is unable to measure the distance of objects that are held too close to the camera or highly glossy objects at angles that reflect the sensor's infrared laser light directly back into the sensor. In such cases, the result may contain depth ranges with no valid value and it is non-trivial to distinguish between objects that are either too close or objects that are at an appropriate distance but are simply glossy. Close-proximity objects can be handled by making the robot provide instructions to step backwards but glossy objects are a challenge to the sensor itself. Using in-lab experimentation, a set of simple heuristics was developed based on a binned histogram of depth ranges. These heuristics were simple if-then rules that mapped depth data into spoken commands to the operator.

The operator's desired disk was recognized verbally using Google Cloud Speech to Text. The currently held disk was recognized by using depth camera data to determine an appropriate crop of RGB camera data. The cropped RGB image was then sent to Google Vision for optical character recognition (OCR). The two transcriptions (speech and OCR) were then compared using a Levenshtein distance, The OCR transcription is modified by deletions at its start or end to make it zero cost.

Hand Me That. The main problem was detecting pointing. We tried several methods in order to assess the direction that the person was pointing in. In the end we used data directly from our `magic_pose` module providing 3D joint poses. To see most of the human body in the frame, we used raw data from the deep learning module to assess the likelihood of pixel clusters representing elbows and wrists, which ended up improving accuracy. In the test, while detecting the person, our robot would get closer and look only at their hip area to find the arm joints.

Restaurant. We scanned for waving people while turning around via `magic_poses`. The robot waves with both arms as an example of how we would like clients to wave. Naive users tend to wave with both arms imitating the robot increasing the chances of a wave detection. If we find a client we navigate towards it by using our navigation stack.

If we don't find a waving person after a full turn of the robot looking for them, we repeat the strategy but taking HD images and scanning sections of them. This approach, while much slower, enabled us to find people waving up to 9 m away (but without depth information given the range and noise of the depth camera). If someone waving far away is found, we navigate closer in the detection direction, and detect again.

The map location of the robot is saved for delivering the order as the customer is within reach, as it's known the robot can safely navigate to this point.

Due to the limited manipulation ability of Pepper's arms, all of the manipulation aspects of the test were managed by using HRI. The robot holds its arms outstretched in front, and the operator is instructed to place an off-the-shelf tray on the robot's arms, with the ordered items following.

Between orders, the robot interacts with the barman to remove the tray from its arms to allow the robot to return its arms to a neutral position. This step is required to manage the heat produced by the arm motors which tend to overheat very quickly especially when carrying weight. On top of this, while navigating with the tray the depth camera loses a major section of its field of view, therefore making navigation less safe. Speed limits are thus lowered.

Where Is This? For this challenge, we developed a social navigation overlay on top of the global and local planner otherwise used for robot navigation. A dense map of socially meaningful way-points, socially meaningful connections between way-points and objects of interest was assigned to the arena. A human expert then assigned socially meaningful descriptions to the way-points and connections. When asked the location of an object or place, the robot first finds a shortest path through the social navigation overlay. A plain-English explanation is generated by concatenating the expert descriptions. The robot then uses the global and local planner to physically navigate through the arena along a path that approximates the social navigation overlay.

5   Software Development Methodology

We believe our success this year was aided thanks to our approach to the software development process. Some key elements of our approach are shown here.

5.1   Standard Software Development Practices

We made use of the available standard software development tools and practices such as Git, GitLab, automated testing, continuous integration and continuous deployment, coding standards and code reviews.

During different moments of the project the strictness to adhere to these practices needed to be re-evaluated in order to allow for smooth development across all team members.

We chose Python as our main programming language for its ease of learning and usage, and also the availability of useful libraries. We chose the ROS middleware for similar reasons.

5.2   Operational Readiness Tests

Three months out from the competition we conducted Operational Readiness Tests (ORT) every two weeks. Closer to the date of RoboCup we moved to weekly ORTs. Other teams have advised that they ran similar events weekly all year long. At RoboCup 2019 we simulated the conditions of the RoboCup@Home SSPL competition as closely as possible in our ORTs. For this exercise we used a house-like scenario inside of our laboratory similar to a real RoboCup@Home arena. This testing space was reconfigured from time to time both to practice for the competition setup days and to find new, unexpected challenges.

We believe this exercise helped in advancing the development of necessary robot skills and tests. It also allowed the team to brainstorm effectively and generally strengthen the team spirit.

5.3   Mentoring and Pair Programming

Initially each person was allocated a Stage 1 task to work on and at least one partner to work with. This was so that each member would be supported by each other, and to allow more discussions and creative solutions.

When the pairs were finished with their task, they could either choose to work with another pair who did not have as much progress, or begin working on a stage 2 task either in the same pair or with other people. This gave team members the chance to develop new skills, and to collaborate with people who they may not have interacted with much previously.

6   Summary and Outlook

In this paper we described the approach used to win the first place in RoboCup@Home SSPL 2019. The key elements and motivations of our architecture was discussed with special attention to some key skills that were implemented in our tests. Additionally, our software project implementation model was detailed, which includes regular readiness check, mentoring and pair programming, which we found extremely beneficial to ensure steady progress during development.

Our code release at https://utsunleashed.webnode.com/software contains our stack of software used for the competition.

Acknowledgements. We want to thank Cecilio Angulo and Bence Magyar for their help on polishing this paper and the Australian Research Council, WiseTech Global, NSW Chief Scientist and Engineer, Commonwealth Bank of Australia and University of Technology Sydney for the support and crucial funding for the team to compete.

References

1. Pandey, A.K., Gelin, R.: A mass-produced sociable humanoid robot: pepper: the first machine of its kind. IEEE Robot. Autom. Mag. **25**(3), 40–48 (2018)
2. Quigley, M., et al.: ROS: an open-source robot operating system. In: ICRA Workshop on Open Source Software 2009 May 12, vol. 3, no. 3.2, p. 5 (2009)
3. https://github.com/awesomebytes/pepper_os
4. https://wiki.gentoo.org/wiki/Project:Prefix
5. https://github.com/ros/ros-overlay
6. https://gitlab.com/uts-unleashed/magiclab_pepper_os
7. Abadi, M., et al.: Tensorflow: a system for large-scale machine learning. In: 12th USENIX Symposium on Operating Systems Design and Implementation (OSDI 16), pp. 265–283 (2016)
8. Paszke, A., Gross, S., Chintala, S., Chanan, G.: Pytorch: tensors and dynamic neural networks in python with strong gpu acceleration, p. 6. Tensors and dynamic neural networks in Python with strong GPU acceleration, PyTorch (2017)
9. Labbé, M., Michaud, F.: RTAB-Map as an open-source lidar and visual simultaneous localization and mapping library for large-scale and long-term online operation. J. Field Robot. **36**(2), 416–446 (2019)
10. https://github.com/OpenNI/OpenNI2
11. King, D.E.: Dlib-ml: a machine learning toolkit. J. Mach. Learn. Res. **10**(Jul), 1755–1758 (2009)
12. https://github.com/SteveMacenski/spatio_temporal_voxel_layer
13. magic_ros library https://gitlab.com/uts-unleashed/magic_ros
14. Cao, Z., Hidalgo, G., Simon, T., Wei, S.E., Sheikh, Y.: OpenPose: realtime multi-person 2D pose estimation using Part Affinity Fields. arXiv preprint arXiv:1812.08008
15. Huggins-Daines, D., Kumar, M., Chan, A., Black, A.W., Ravishankar, M., Rudnicky, A.I.: PocketSphinx: a free, real-time continuous speech recognition system for hand-held devices. In: 2006 IEEE International Conference on Acoustics Speech and Signal Processing Proceedings, 14 May 2006, vol. 1, p. I. IEEE (2006). https://github.com/cmusphinx/pocketsphinx

16. Google Cloud Speech to Text. https://cloud.google.com/speech-to-text/
17. Valin, J.M., Maxwell, G., Terriberry, T.B., Vos, K.: High-quality, low-delay music coding in the opus codec. arXiv preprint arXiv:1602.04845, 5 February 2016
18. Pütz, S., Simón, J.S., Hertzberg, J.: Move base flex. In: 2018 IEEE/RSJ International Conference on Intelligent Robots and Systems (IROS), pp. 3416–3421, 1 October 2018
19. Rösmann, C., Feiten, W., Wösch, T., Hoffmann, F., Bertram, T.: Efficient trajectory optimization using a sparse model. In: Proceedings of IEEE European Conference on Mobile Robots, Spain, Barcelona, pp. 138–143 (2013)
20. Redmon, J., Farhadi, A.: YOLOv3: an incremental improvement. arXiv (2018)
21. https://github.com/leggedrobotics/darknet_ros
22. Liu, Z., Luo, P., Wang, X., Tang, X.: Proceedings of International Conference on Computer Vision (ICCV), December 2015
23. https://en.wikipedia.org/wiki/Color_difference#CIEDE2000
24. https://github.com/ageitgey/face_recognition

Fractals2019: Combinatorial Optimisation with Dynamic Constraint Annealing

Mikhail Prokopenko[1,2(✉)] and Peter Wang[2]

[1] Complex Systems Research Group, Faculty of Engineering,
The University of Sydney, Camperdown, NSW 2006, Australia
`mikhail.prokopenko@sydney.edu.au`
[2] Data Mining, CSIRO Data61, PO Box 76, Epping, NSW 1710, Australia

Abstract. Fractals2019 started as a new experimental entry in the RoboCup Soccer 2D Simulation League, based on Gliders2d code base, and advanced to become a RoboCup-2019 champion. We employ combinatorial optimisation methods, within the framework of Guided Self-Organisation, with the search guided by local constraints. We present examples of several tactical tasks based on the Gliders2d code (version v2), including the search for an optimal assignment of heterogeneous player types, as well as blocking behaviours, offside trap, and attacking formations. We propose a new method, *Dynamic Constraint Annealing*, for solving dynamic constraint satisfaction problems, and apply it to optimise thermodynamic potential of collective behaviours, under dynamically induced constraints.

1 Introduction

The RoboCup Soccer 2D Simulation League provides a rich dynamic environment, facilitated by the RoboCup Soccer Simulator (RCSS), aimed to test advances in decentralised collective behaviours of autonomous agents. The challenges include concurrent adversarial actions, computational nondeterminism, noise and latency in asynchronous perception and actuation, and limited processing time [3,5,7,29,37,38,42,43,46]. The League progress has been supported by several important base code releases, covering both low-level skills and standardised world models of simulated agents [1,22,45,47]. The release in 2010 of the base code of HELIOS team, *agent2d-3.0.0*, later upgraded to agent2d-3.1.1, was particularly influential. By 2016, about 80% of the teams adopted agent2d as their base code, including the champion team, Gliders2016 [33,38], which also used fragments of MarliK source code [47], and by 2019 this fraction exceeded 90%.

Gliders2016 was developed using Human-based Evolutionary Computation (HBEC) [23,33]. In 2018, we released the code base *Gliders2d* [40], version v1, comprising six HBEC steps. In this paper we present the second version of *Gliders2d* (v2), with six additional steps:

© Springer Nature Switzerland AG 2019
S. Chalup et al. (Eds.): RoboCup 2019, LNAI 11531, pp. 616–630, 2019.
https://doi.org/10.1007/978-3-030-35699-6_50

– Gliders2d-v2.1: blocking behaviour (disrupting the opponents in possession of the ball; based on simplified MarliK source code [47]; bhv_basic_move.cpp);
– Gliders2d-v2.2: offside trap behaviour (bhv_basic_move.cpp);
– Gliders2d-v2.3: assignment of heterogeneous player types (sample_coach.cpp);
– Gliders2d-v2.4: back action (allowing players to select actions which evaluate worse than the current action; action_chain_graph.cpp);
– Gliders2d-v2.5: tackle action (higher risk in defense); bhv_basic_move.cpp);
– Gliders2d-v2.6: wing attacking formation (strategy.cpp).

Some of these steps are relatively simple, while some involve substantial code changes. Nevertheless, the performance improvements are tangible, and we will detail these in Sect. 2. Gliders2d uses librcsc 4.1.0 [1]. It is different from the competition branch (Gliders2012—Gliders2016), being a separate evolutionary branch, created over 2018–2019 to experiment with Fractals2019. We will exemplify how Guided Self-Organisation (GSO) allows us to optimise the performance, using the transition between v2.2 to v2.3 which improved an assignment of heterogeneous player types.

Fractals2019 is a new team which is partially based on Gliders2d [39], while retaining some elements of our previous champion team Gliders2016 [33,38]. To a large extent, Fractals2019 is an experimental entry, motivated by a new set of aims. Specifically, we redefined the fitness landscape used by optimisation in terms of dynamic constraints, rather than in terms of the performance metrics alone. Our overall approach uses *guided self-organisation* of tactical behaviour, shown here for the transition between v2.2 to v2.3, now extended by a thermodynamic characterisation of collective action, Sect. 3, with results described in Sect. 4.

2   Gliders2d: Version v2

Each HBEC solution can be seen as a "genotype", encoding the entire team behaviour in a set of "design points" [10,40], which may vary from a single parameter (e.g., blocking depth), to an ordering of heterogeneous types with respect to some criterion (e.g., a list of integers representing players' roles), to complex multi-agent communication schemes [17,38,50].

Each solution is typically evaluated against a specific opponent, over thousands of games, with the fitness function being the average goal difference, while the average points and standard error provide tie-breakers [40]. In other words, a design point (possibly conditioned on the name of a specific opponent) is accepted only if it outperforms every single opponent in the pool of available opponents. This strict acceptance criterion may be adjusted by assigning different weights to the available opponents, set in proportion to their respective strengths which are "statically" determined in advance. These weights can be based on the competition ranking of the previous year, or can be specified more precisely, using the points achieved in a multi-game round-robin tournament involving these opponents [41]. In this evolutionary/optimisation approach, the overall fitness is determined as a weighted average computed across the opponents in the pool. As a consequence, a design point may be accepted even it underperformed against a relatively weaker opponent (if it performed strongly against other, stronger, opponents). Rarely, a design point may even be accepted if it underperformed against the strongest opponent, provided that the other performances outweighed this loss on average.

The weighted fitness function, accommodating relative strengths of the opponents, achieves several aims. Firstly, it better accounts for the absence of transitivity in teams' relative strengths [41]. Secondly, it reduces the development and computation time required to ensure that any given design point outperforms all available opponents. Thirdly, it produces a simple and more general-purpose code, with fewer conditional branches. It is interesting to point out the similarity of the weighted fitness function with the concept of "Nash averaging" recently introduced by Balduzzi et al. [6], who distinguished between two basic scenarios: agent-vs-agent and agent-vs-task. Nash averaging was utilised in a "dynamic" setting, where at each round the strength of the evolving team (the "agent") itself contributed to the relative strengths of the opponents. Most recently this was carried out by DeepMind in the AlphaStar League, while evolving an agent excelling in the real-time strategy game StarCraft II. The final AlphaStar agent comprised the elements of the Nash distribution of the league, capturing the most effective mixture of strategies discovered by the evolution guided by Nash average [14]. In RoboCup Simulation League scenarios, this would mean that the weights of the opponents in a pool are re-evaluated in a round-robin tournament which includes the evolving solution (design point) itself, providing a better quality of the solutions—but at a prohibitive computational cost (at this stage).

A balanced pool of opponents (an "ecosystem") in which Gliders2d were evolved from v2.1 to v2.6, using a weighted fitness function, included four benchmark teams: Gliders2013 [32], the 2018 world champion team, HELIOS2018 [27], the 2018 third-ranked team, MT2018 [49], and the 2018 sixth-ranked team, YuShan2018 [9]. For each sequential step and for the baseline Gliders2d-v1.6 (the latest step in version v1), 2000 games were played against these four benchmarks.

Against Gliders2013, the goal difference achieved by Gliders2d-v2.6 improves from -0.2 to zero. Against YuShan2018, the goal difference improves from -0.8 to zero, achieving parity as well. Against MT2018, the goal difference improves from -2.1 to -1.0. Finally, against HELIOS2018, the goal difference improves from -4.4 to -2.4. The latter case will be detailed specifically, for the transition between v2.2 and v2.3, when the goal difference improved from -4.2 to -3.0, i.e., by more than a single goal, merely due to a better assignment of heterogeneous players. Table 1 summarises the performance dynamics, including the overall goal difference and the standard error of the mean, for each of the match-ups. Adoption of the weighted fitness function ensures the progression at several steps: for example, from v1.6 to v2.1.

The released code, including the six sequential steps comprising version v2, is located at:

http://www.prokopenko.net/gliders2d.html.

Table 1. Performance evaluation of Gliders2d against benchmarks, over ~2000 games for each version of Gliders2d against the opponent. The match-up marked by $\star$ involved ~16000 games (Sect. 4).

Version	Gliders2013		YuShan2018		MT2018		HELIOS2018	
	Goal diff.	Std. error	Goal diff.	Std. error	Goal diff.	Std. error	Goal diff.	Std. error
v1.6	-0.242073	0.029355	-0.827273	0.032821	-2.05796	0.040560	-4.43894	0.046226
v2.1	-0.124561	0.028637	-0.499497	0.030966	-1.74109	0.038903	-4.48316	0.046027
v2.2	-0.128321	0.028243	-0.461384	0.031010	-1.52841	0.038033	-4.17144	0.045290
v2.3	-0.103206	0.029718	-0.422634	0.031381	-1.33676	0.036293	$-2.95471^{\star}$	0.013678
v2.4	-0.129081	0.029207	-0.190190	0.029751	-1.27683	0.034613	-2.72030	0.036411
v2.5	-0.138122	0.030924	-0.128192	0.029237	-1.12130	0.033411	-2.52632	0.034567
v2.6	-0.030105	0.028551	-0.016525	0.033414	-1.01404	0.035441	-2.39538	0.036255

The differences can be easily identified by consecutively comparing the files indicated for each step across versions v2(n) and v2(n+1), for $n \geq 0$ (with v2.0 being v1.6). For example, differentiating the file bhv_basic_move.cpp between v1.6 and v2.1 will show the changes implementing the blocking behaviour (with the acknowledged fragments of Marlik source code [47]), while checking the differences in the same file between v2.1 and v2.2 will highlight the offside trap behaviour of Gliders2d. The offside trap is produced by collective motion of the defenders synchronised by their perception of relevant situational variables. The changes in the last three steps are self-explanatory, and also involve several variables describing situational patterns, forming design points evolved by HBEC or GSO. The step from v2.2 to v2.3 deserves a more detailed analysis, being quite illustrative of the difference between HBEC and GSO approaches, and showing how self-organisation can be guided by thermodynamic properties of collective behaviour.

3   Fractals2019: Thermodynamically Driven Collective Behaviours

Guided Self-Organisation constrains self-organisation within a dynamical system to paths leading towards specific attractors or outcomes. It integrates two techniques: (i) self-organising exploration of the search space, and (ii) traditional design following a "blueprint" [34,35]. GSO has been studied in several robotic scenarios, combining (i) universal objective functions, and (ii) task-dependent constraints on the system dynamics, often using generic information-theoretic or thermodynamic methods [4,15,18,20,26,28,30,31,35,36]. An example of combinatorial optimisation carried out in a noisy potential field using information-theoretic tools is described by Kim et al. [19] in a study which complemented hill-climbing using information entropy. The class of simulated annealing algorithms is also characterised by a thermodynamic analogy [25].

3.1   Problem Formulation

In statistical-mechanical terms, each candidate solution (a design point) can be interpreted as a configuration of the suitably defined statistical system, so that the fitness of the solution can be considered as the energy of the system in that particular configuration. Hence, one may in general represent an optimisation problem as a search for an equilibrium state of a system which optimises the appropriate thermodynamic potential (e.g., minimises the free energy).

In developing Fractals2019 we combine (i) the standard (weighted) fitness function defined by the goal difference, which is inevitably measured only imprecisely, and (ii) local constraints which indirectly represent collective behaviour. The constraints are defined with respect to the elements of the design point under consideration, restricting the search-space. In HBEC approach, these constraints are specified before the search begins, by human designers. Importantly, under our GSO approach, these constraints are not given in advance, but are induced during the first phase of combinatorial optimisation which is driven by maximising the goal difference alone. Given the landscape of the fitness function, partially discovered during the first phase, the method identifies the regions around local maxima, and induces partial constraints that represent these local fitness sub-spaces. At the second phase of optimisation, we use the thermodynamic analogy and guide the search from the attained local optimum towards the constrained sub-space, shaped by the discovered constraints.

For example, a design point can be specified as an assignment of heterogeneous player types to player roles, represented as an ordered list of integers, e.g., the assignment of *agent2d-3.1.1* sets $X = \{11, 2, 3, 10, 9, 6, 4, 5, 7, 8\}$, with function $\rho : \mathbb{N} \to \mathbb{N}$ defining the rank in this list, e.g., $\rho(11) = 1$. This list is used by the coach agent in assigning the strongest heterogeneous player type (defined according to some criterion, for instance, the fastest player type) to the first player from this list, i.e., player 11 (centreforward). The second best type is assigned to the second player on the list, i.e., to player 2 (left central defender), and so on, so that the weakest, slowest, type is assigned to player 8 (right midfielder). The goalkeeper, player 1, is assigned a type separately. A constraint can be specified as a preference over the ranks, e.g., $\rho(6) < \rho(10)$ would mean that player 6 should have preference in the assignment over player 10. In general, ranking constraints have the form: $\rho(i) < \rho(j)$ for players i and j.

Finding the assignment which maximises the fitness function f_X over all possible 10! candidate solutions $X \in \mathcal{X}$ in the search-space is the specific optimisation problem solved at the transition between v2.2 and v2.3. Even on a high-performance computing cluster with 100 two-minute games running in parallel, checking all 3,628,800 permutations over 1000 games each (to account for the score fluctuations due to the simulation noise), would require over 138 years of continuous computation. A hill-climbing optimisation method would cut this time considerably but is likely to find only inferior local optima. We advocate instead a GSO approach which combines elements of hill-climbing optimisation and dynamic constraint satisfaction problems, with insights from simulated annealing, informed by the thermodynamic analogy.

One may think of our assignment problem as a variant of the Traveling Salesman Problem (TSP), where each player needs to be assigned only one role, and the objective is to maximise the fitness (rather than minimise the cost). The "distances" between the players (the nodes along a directed path) are not known, so we cannot simply aggregate the path segments into the total path length d. Instead, the approximate overall path distance is provided by the noisy fitness function (the average goal difference resulting from the assignment), and so the values f_X and f_Y of two neighbouring solutions X and Y can produce the difference $\delta = f_X - f_Y$.

3.2   Phase 1: Hill-Climbing and Dynamically Induced Constraints

During the first phase, we use a hill-climbing algorithm [44] based on a variant of insertion sort [21]. Hill climbing is a greedy local search algorithm which always moves in the direction of increasing fitness f by comparing with values of local neighbours, terminating when it reaches a solution without neighbours with a higher fitness. Defining a suitable neighbour function makes a significant impact on the success of this algorithm. In TSP problems one often defines a simple k-node flip neighbour function where a sequence of k nodes of one solution is flipped to produce a candidate. For example, a 2-flip neighbour function applied to $X = \{11, 2, 3, 10, 9, 6, 4, 5, 7, 8\}$ at rank 4 produces a candidate $Y = \{11, 2, 3, 9, 10, 6, 4, 5, 7, 8\}$, with the ranks of players 10 and 9 reversed, not unlike a bubble sort algorithm that would compare f_X and f_Y before deciding if the flip should be accepted. Insertion sort is a more efficient sorting algorithm that produces a sorted list by finding a location for a given element within the current list. Starting with the initial assignment, the insertion sort algorithm picks one element from the data (e.g., in the ranked order), and finds the optimal location for this element within the list by comparing the fitness values corresponding to different locations. Having inserted this element, the algorithm iterates to the next element, until all elements are properly inserted. At every location test, only a better candidate is accepted, following the hill climbing approach.

The challenge is that the fitness function f_Y must be computed for every location choice, that is, thousands of games need to be played for the assignment Y against the benchmark. This is needed in order to reduce the effects of fluctuations—an aspect particularly relevant when assigning heterogeneous types which are stochastically generated before each game. Nevertheless, the fitness remains noisy even for a large number of games, making hill climbing problematic.

To address this challenge and reduce the overall number of tests, we make two extensions. Firstly, we use a heuristic: an assumption of "iteration" convexity, that is, we assume that the fitness landscape is convex along the insertion path of each element. Secondly, in addition to identifying the best location for an element, the algorithm checks the neighbourhood of the identified location, and induces local constraints over the ranks, whenever possible. This approach is broadly in line with dynamic constraint satisfaction problem (DCSP) solvers in which the constraints are dynamically evolved while the CSP is being solved [48]. It differs from constraint recording techniques, in which newly learned constraints represent inconsistencies in the problem formulation, rather than the fitness landscape as such.

Let us consider the iteration of inserting 11, traced in Table 2. Initially the rank of the player is 1, i.e., $\rho(11) = 1$, and the corresponding fitness is $f = -4.17144$. Several locations are then iteratively tested, until a local maximum $f^* = -3.89289$ is found at rank $\rho(11) = 4$. The assumption of convexity along an iteration allows us to stop after the first maximum is identified during the iteration, that is, after checking the rank $\rho(11) = 5$ with the inferior fitness. At this stage we induce ranking constraints for 11: specifically, $\rho(10) < \rho(11)$ is induced by comparing tests 2 and 3, and $\rho(11) < \rho(9)$ is induced by comparing tests 3 and 4. Basically, the assignment differences between the tests are converted into constraints, to match the corresponding differences in fitness (if these differences are sufficiently large). For example, the difference between the tests 2 and 3 is the 2-flip at rank 3, picking 11 and 10, and since $f_2 < f_3$, it is induced that $\rho(10) < \rho(11)$. This preference impacts the collective behaviour of the team, resulting in the overall fitness (the thermodynamic potential), and so the fitness is used to induce the ranking.

Inducing such local constraints may appear redundant, as the maximum identified in this example reflects them already. However, not every iteration will improve on the current maximum, but may still identify local constraints that partially represent the structure of the search-space (see Sect. 4 for more examples, summarised in Table 3). All these constraints will be used in the second phase, guiding a more refined search.

Our use of DCSP is motivated by the noisy fitness function. The fluctuations in the fitness function appear due to a dynamic and distributed RoboCup environment where the outcomes change from game to game—and so estimating the fitness across multiple games forms a changing problem environment. In general, problems tend to have structure, and the local constraints induced during the first phase partially discover this structure.

Table 2. Hill climbing with insertion sort. A local maximum, $\rho(11) = 4$, is marked $*$. Two constraints are induced: $\rho(10) < \rho(11)$ and $\rho(11) < \rho(9)$. Each test $i > 0$ involved ~1000 games, test 0: ~2000 games.

Test i	Assignment	Goal difference f_i	Standard error	Induced constraint
Inserting 11				
0	11 2 3 10 9 6 4 5 7 8	−4.17144	0.045290	
1	2 11 3 10 9 6 4 5 7 8	−4.04819	0.065453	
2	2 3 11 10 9 6 4 5 7 8	−4.04100	0.061556	
3	2 3 10 11 9 6 4 5 7 8	−3.89289*	0.061798	$\rho(10) < \rho(11)$
4	2 3 10 9 11 6 4 5 7 8	−4.06928	0.060939	$\rho(11) < \rho(9)$

3.3   Phase 2: Constraint Satisfaction via Annealing

After carrying out iterations for all elements of the design point, and obtaining a local maximum X, as well as a set of local constraints, we begin the second phase guided by a thermodynamic characterisation of the fitness landscape. In a seminal work, Černý [8] argued that the analogy with thermodynamics offers a new insight into optimisation problems such as TSP: the length d_X of a given trip, defined as a sequence/permutation of the nodes (in our terms, a given assignment of the player types), can be seen as the energy E_X of the system in that particular configuration X. Crucially, "simulating the transition to the equilibrium and decreasing the temperature, one can find smaller and smaller values of the mean energy of the system (= length of the trip)" [8]. This argument provided strong motivation for simulated annealing algorithms [16,25], where the probability of a candidate solution X generated during an exploration of the search-space, while minimising the path length, is given by the Boltzmann-Gibbs distribution, for some temperature T and normalisation constant Z:

$$P(X) = Ze^{-E_X/T}. \tag{1}$$

Given a current minimum d_Y, the chances of accepting a worse candidate X with $d_X > d_Y$, are not zero, but depend on the (energy) difference $\delta = d_X - d_Y$. More precisely, a worse candidate is accepted with probability $e^{-\delta/T}$. When the annealing temperature becomes sufficiently low, the acceptance probability for non-optimising solutions reduces as well.

We use simulated annealing in guiding the exploration of the search-space. Once a locally optimal solution X is obtained, we generate candidate solutions Y in some proximity of the local optimum, but keeping closer to, and preferably within, the region of the search-space restricted by the discovered local constraints ("closer" in terms of a simple neighbourhood function, e.g., insertion sort again). The probability of accepting a worse candidate Y, with $d_X > d_Y$ is given by $e^{-\delta/T}$, for $\delta = d_X - d_Y$, with acceptable Y replacing X as the current best candidate. Thus, this algorithm shares Černý's insight quoted earlier, in exploring the search-space thermodynamically, i.e., along the landscape of a thermodynamic potential, guided by local constraints towards an optimum (equilibrium) state. In the beginning of the search, when the temperature T is higher, acceptable solutions can be found deeper within the constrained subspace, but when the search cools down, candidate solutions may sit very close to the currently identified optimum. Section 4 demonstrates the second search phase for our main example, see Table 4.

We refer to our second phase as *constraint satisfaction via annealing*. It differs from the "constraint annealing" technique [24] which interprets constraints as objective functions and applies standard simulated annealing to the redefined problem. The main overall difference, of course, lies in our use of dynamically induced constraints, and so we refer to the entire optimisation method introduced in this paper as *Dynamic Constraint Annealing*.

In general, the objective function and, thus the dynamic local constraints, may be chosen to represent different aspects of the problem structure:

624   M. Prokopenko and P. Wang

maximisation of spatiotemporal coordination [30,31], maximisation of information flows [11,12], maximisation of thermodynamic efficiency which contrasts the gain in the uncertainty reduction with the required work [13], etc.

4   Results

In this section we develop our leading example, detailing the two optimisation phases. Let us continue with the hill-climbing phase: having inserted element 11, we iterate insertion sort algorithm for other elements, while applying the convexity heuristic and avoiding testing the assignments which have been checked earlier, as shown in Table 3.

The dynamically induced local constraints construct a partial ordering underlying an optimal assignment, shown in Fig. 1. It is evident that the local maximum attained by test 34 does not satisfy all these local constraints, highlighting the need for a second, constraint satisfaction, phase. The algorithm continues with the best solution $X_{34} = \{2, 3, 5, 4, 8, 10, 11, 9, 6, 7\}$, re-evaluated after 16000 games in order to ensure a higher precision, attaining $f_{34} = -3.14496$, and then generates the candidates closer to and within the constrained sub-space, as shown in Table 4, for a specified number of tests, e.g., 10 additional tests. The maximum attained at the end of this phase is given by $X_{44} = \{5, 4, 2, 3, 7, 6, 8, 10, 11, 9\}$ with $f_{44} = -2.95471$, reducing the goal deficit by further 0.2. This solution fully satisfies the local constraints.

Not surprisingly, this assignment which was optimised against the world champion of 2018, is assortative: it prefers to place the fastest players in defence (defenders 5, 4, 3, 2, with the wing defenders 5 and 4 assigned the best types), followed by midfielders (7, 6, 8), and leaving the weakest types for forwards (10, 11, 9). To re-iterate, this is carried out at the transition step from Gliders2d-v2.2 to v2.3, which is still a relatively weak team overall. In general, such an optimisation should be repeated after each tactical improvement, adjusting the collective behaviour of heterogeneous players to the latest tactics. In fact, every time when the optimal assignment changes in response to newest tactics, it signifies an important step in the development of collective behaviour. Our winning entry, Fractals2019, maintained a more balanced assignment than Gliders2d-v2.6, disassortatively mixing the roles across types to fit a more attacking style—the final optimisation was carried out in the last days before the championship. The Dynamic Constraint Annealing method described in this study takes about three days of computation on a high-performance cluster with 100 parallel games in the RCSS synchronisation mode (about 2 min per game), with the first and second phase taking roughly 12 h (∼35000 games) and 54 h (∼160000 games) respectively. And so such a re-optimisation becomes feasible.

Optimisation of other design points can also be carried out with Dynamic Constraint Annealing, given a suitably chosen discretisation of situational variables, so that relevant local constraints can be induced during the iterative hill-climbing phase.

Table 3. Hill climbing with insertion sort: continuing after first four tests which inserted 11 at rank 4 (Table 2). The current maxima are marked with ∗. Tests 3 and 4 are shown repeatedly, to clarify the comparisons which induced constraints. When the difference between fitness values is smaller than the standard error, a possible constraint, shown within [], is not induced. Each test is carried out over ∼1000 games.

Test i	Assignment X_i	Goal difference f_i	Standard error	Induced constraint
3	2 3 10 11 9 6 4 5 7 8	−3.89289*	0.061798	$\rho(10) < \rho(11)$
Inserting 2				
5	3 2 10 11 9 6 4 5 7 8	−3.96985	0.064817	$\rho(2) < \rho(3)$
Inserting 3				
6	2 10 3 11 9 6 4 5 7 8	−4.24600	0.066165	$\rho(3) < \rho(10)$
Inserting 10				
7	10 2 3 11 9 6 4 5 7 8	−4.23547	0.063354	$[\rho(2) < \rho(10)]$
Inserting 9				
8	9 2 3 10 11 6 4 5 7 8	−4.14766	0.064273	
9	2 9 3 10 11 6 4 5 7 8	−4.23695	0.065580	
10	2 3 9 10 11 6 4 5 7 8	−4.08133	0.063088	
4	2 3 10 9 11 6 4 5 7 8	−4.06928	0.060939	
3	2 3 10 11 9 6 4 5 7 8	−3.89289*	0.061798	$\rho(11) < \rho(9)$
11	2 3 10 11 6 9 4 5 7 8	−3.93493	0.063252	$[\rho(6) < \rho(9)]$
Inserting 6				
12	6 2 3 10 11 9 4 5 7 8	−4.03722	0.065353	
13	2 6 3 10 11 9 4 5 7 8	−4.14874	0.061345	
14	2 3 6 10 11 9 4 5 7 8	−3.98894	0.065420	$\rho(3) < \rho(6)$
15	2 3 10 6 11 9 4 5 7 8	−4.07251	0.062459	$\rho(6) < \rho(10)$
Inserting 4				
16	4 2 3 10 11 9 6 5 7 8	−3.79618*	0.060502	
17	2 4 3 10 11 9 6 5 7 8	−3.72417*	0.059761	
18	2 3 4 10 11 9 6 5 7 8	−3.69539*	0.058036	$[\rho(3) < \rho(4)]$
19	2 3 10 4 11 9 6 5 7 8	−3.80542	0.060862	$\rho(4) < \rho(10)$
Inserting 5				
20	5 2 3 4 10 11 9 6 7 8	−3.22312*	0.055354	
21	2 5 3 4 10 11 9 6 7 8	−3.19860*	0.052708	
22	2 3 5 4 10 11 9 6 7 8	−3.15800*	0.056941	$[\rho(3) < \rho(5)]$
23	2 3 4 5 10 11 9 6 7 8	−3.28815	0.055315	$\rho(5) < \rho(4)$
Inserting 7				
24	7 2 3 5 4 10 11 9 6 8	−3.44869	0.059632	
25	2 7 3 5 4 10 11 9 6 8	−3.41141	0.059249	
26	2 3 7 5 4 10 11 9 6 8	−3.35772	0.059014	
27	2 3 5 7 4 10 11 9 6 8	−3.31795	0.057105	
28	2 3 5 4 7 10 11 9 6 8	−3.18036	0.057603	$\rho(4) < \rho(7)$
29	2 3 5 4 10 7 11 9 6 8	−3.34604	0.057504	$\rho(7) < \rho(10)$
Inserting 8				
30	8 2 3 5 4 10 11 9 6 7	−3.39980	0.058509	
31	2 8 3 5 4 10 11 9 6 7	−3.41106	0.058709	
32	2 3 8 5 4 10 11 9 6 7	−3.31891	0.056437	
33	2 3 5 8 4 10 11 9 6 7	−3.30924	0.055972	
34	2 3 5 4 8 10 11 9 6 7	−3.12261*	0.057369	$\rho(4) < \rho(8)$
35	2 3 5 4 10 8 11 9 6 7	−3.19157	0.056433	$\rho(8) < \rho(10)$

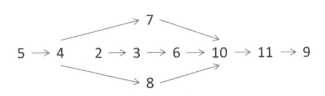

Fig. 1. A partial ordering underlying an optimal assignment implied by induced local constraints. Ranking preference $\rho(i) < \rho(j)$ is depicted as $i \to j$.

Table 4. Constraint satisfaction via annealing: continuing after the first phase (Table 3) for 10 additional tests. The current maxima are marked with *, worse but accepted solutions – by a, and worse but rejected solutions – by r. Each test is carried out over ~16000 games.

Test i	Assignment X_i	Goal difference f_i	Standard error	Annealing temp. T	Acceptance prob. P
34	2 3 5 4 8 10 11 9 6 7	-3.14496^*	0.014086		
36	2 5 3 4 8 10 11 9 6 7	-3.12690^*	0.013852	0.10	1
37	2 5 3 4 8 7 10 11 9 6	-3.11121^*	0.013912	0.09	1
38	2 5 3 4 7 8 10 11 9 6	-3.05126^*	0.013869	0.08	1
39	2 5 3 4 7 8 6 10 11 9	-3.05799^a	0.013767	0.07	0.90833
40	2 5 3 4 7 6 8 10 11 9	-3.04399^*	0.013761	0.06	1
41	5 2 3 4 7 6 8 10 11 9	-3.11263^r	0.014044	0.05	0.31854
42	2 5 4 3 7 6 8 10 11 9	-3.00621^*	0.013789	0.04	1
43	5 2 4 3 7 6 8 10 11 9	-2.98825^*	0.013473	0.03	1
44	5 4 2 3 7 6 8 10 11 9	-2.95471^*	0.013678	0.02	1
45	5 4 2 3 6 7 8 10 11 9	-2.96470^r	0.013397	0.01	0.36825

5   Conclusions

Team Fractals2019 is based on recently released Gliders2d code base [40]. The second version of Gliders2d is described and traced in this study against a pool of benchmark opponents, using a fitness function weighted by relative strengths of the benchmarks. We followed the methodology of Guided Self-Organisation in optimising for strong team performance, within a noisy fitness landscape affected by fluctuations inherent in the nondeterministic RoboCup simulation environment. This is achieved by employing a thermodynamic analogy in characterising the global objective function, as well as local constraints which are dynamically discovered during the combinatorial optimisation. We proposed a new method, *Dynamic Constraint Annealing*, which improves on greedy search such as hill-climbing techniques, by (i) dynamically inducing local constraints, and (ii) guiding the constraint satisfaction phase by a simulated annealing carried out along a trajectory approaching or within the constrained sub-space. We illustrated this method for a specific problem, an optimal assignment of heterogeneous player types to player roles, interpreted as a variant of the Traveling Salesman Problem (TSP), demonstrating a tangible increase of fitness over a series of tests. This technique may be generally applicable to combinatorial optimisation and constraint satisfaction problems in changing distributed environments.

Fractals2019 allowed us to verify the applicability of the GSO approach to combinatorial optimisation problems within a challenging environment of RoboCup simulation. RoboCup-2019 competition included 15 teams from 7 countries: Australia, Brazil, China, Germany, Iran, Japan, and Portugal. Fractals2019 played 22 games during several rounds, winning 16 times, with the total score of 59:10, or 2.68:0.45 on average. The final game against team HELIOS2019 (Japan) went into the extra time, and ended with Fractals2019 winning 1:0. Post-tournament we carried out a 16000-game experiment between the two finalists, using their released binaries [2,39], with the champion team, Fractals2019, out-performing the runner-up by 0.22 goals (the average score 0:79:0.57) with 0.009 of standard error.

Acknowledgments. We thank HELIOS team for their excellent code base of *agent2d*, as well as several members of Gliders team contributing during 2012–2016: David Budden, Oliver Cliff, Victor Jauregui and Oliver Obst.

References

1. Akiyama, H., Nakashima, T.: HELIOS base: an open source package for the RoboCup soccer 2D simulation. In: Behnke, S., Veloso, M., Visser, A., Xiong, R. (eds.) RoboCup 2013. LNCS (LNAI), vol. 8371, pp. 528–535. Springer, Heidelberg (2014). https://doi.org/10.1007/978-3-662-44468-9_46
2. Akiyama, H., Nakashima, T., Fukushima, T., Suzuki, Y., Ohori, A.: Helios 2019: team description paper. In: RoboCup 2019 Symposium and Competitions, Sydney, Australia (2019)
3. Akiyama, H., Noda, I.: Multi-agent positioning mechanism in the dynamic environment. In: Visser, U., Ribeiro, F., Ohashi, T., Dellaert, F. (eds.) RoboCup 2007. LNCS (LNAI), vol. 5001, pp. 377–384. Springer, Heidelberg (2008). https://doi.org/10.1007/978-3-540-68847-1_38
4. Ay, N., Bertschinger, N., Der, R., Guttler, F., Olbrich, E.: Predictive information and explorative behavior of autonomous robots. Eur. Phys. J. B **63**, 329–339(11) (2008)
5. Bai, A., Wu, F., Chen, X.: Online planning for large Markov decision processes with hierarchical decomposition. ACM Trans. Intell. Syst. Technol. **6**(4), 45:1–45:28 (2015)
6. Balduzzi, D., Tuyls, K., Perolat, J., Graepel, T.: Re-evaluating evaluation. In: Proceedings of the 32nd International Conference on Neural Information Processing Systems, USA, pp. 3272–3283 (2018)
7. Budden, D.M., Wang, P., Obst, O., Prokopenko, M.: RoboCup simulation leagues: enabling replicable and robust investigation of complex robotic systems. IEEE Trans. Robot. Autom. **22**(3), 140–146 (2015)
8. Černý, V.: Thermodynamical approach to the traveling salesman problem: an efficient simulation algorithm. J. Optimiz. Theory App. **45**(1), 41–51 (1985)

9. Cheng, Z., et al.: YuShan2018 team description paper for RoboCup2018. In: RoboCup 2018 Symposium and Competitions, Montreal, Canada (2018)
10. Cioppa, T.M., Lucas, T.W.: Efficient nearly orthogonal and space-filling Latin hypercubes. Technometrics **49**(1), 45–55 (2007)
11. Cliff, O.M., Lizier, J.T., Wang, X.R., Wang, P., Obst, O., Prokopenko, M.: Towards quantifying interaction networks in a football match. In: Behnke, S., Veloso, M., Visser, A., Xiong, R. (eds.) RoboCup 2013. LNCS (LNAI), vol. 8371, pp. 1–12. Springer, Heidelberg (2014). https://doi.org/10.1007/978-3-662-44468-9_1
12. Cliff, O., Lizier, J., Wang, X.R., Wang, P., Obst, O., Prokopenko, M.: Quantifying long-range interactions and coherent structure in multi-agent dynamics. Artif. Life **23**(1), 34–57 (2017)
13. Crosato, E., Spinney, R.E., Nigmatullin, R., Lizier, J.T., Prokopenko, M.: Thermodynamics and computation during collective motion near criticality. Phys. Rev. E **97**, 012120 (2018)
14. DeepMind: AlphaStar: Mastering the Real-Time Strategy Game StarCraft II (2019). https://deepmind.com/blog/article/alphastar-mastering-real-time-strategy-game-starcraft-ii
15. Der, R., Martius, G.: The Playful Machine – Theoretical Foundation and Practical Realization of Self-Organizing Robots. Springer, Heidelberg (2012). https://doi.org/10.1007/978-3-642-20253-7
16. Eglese, R.W.: Simulated annealing: a tool for operational research. Eur. J. Oper. Res. **46**(3), 271–281 (1990)
17. Gabel, T., Klöppner, P., Godehardt, E., Tharwat, A.: Communication in soccer simulation: on the use of wiretapping opponent teams. In: Holz, D., Genter, K., Saad, M., von Stryk, O. (eds.) RoboCup 2018. LNCS (LNAI), vol. 11374, pp. 3–15. Springer, Cham (2019). https://doi.org/10.1007/978-3-030-27544-0_1
18. Hamann, H., et al.: Hybrid societies: challenges and perspectives in the design of collective behavior in self-organizing systems. Front. Robot. AI **3**, 14 (2016)
19. Kim, P., Nakamura, S., Kurabayashi, D.: Hill-climbing for a noisy potential field using information entropy. Paladyn **2**(2), 94–99 (2011)
20. Klyubin, A., Polani, D., Nehaniv, C.: Representations of space and time in the maximization of information flow in the perception-action loop. Neural Comput. **19**(9), 2387–2432 (2007)
21. Knuth, D.E.: The Art of Computer Programming, vol. 3. Addison-Wesley, Boston (1997)
22. Kok, J.R., Vlassis, N., Groen, F.: UvA Trilearn 2003 team description. In: Polani, D., Browning, B., Bonarini, A., Yoshida, K. (eds.) Proceedings of the CD RoboCup 2003. Springer, Heidelberg (2003)
23. Kosorukoff, A.: Human based genetic algorithm. In: 2001 IEEE International Conference on Systems, Man, and Cybernetics, vol. 5, pp. 3464–3469. IEEE (2001)
24. Kropaczek, D.J., Walden, R.: Constraint annealing method for solution of multiconstrained nuclear fuel cycle optimization problems. Nucl. Sci. Eng. **193**(5), 506–522 (2019)
25. Laarhoven, P.J.M., Aarts, E.H.L. (eds.): Simulated Annealing: Theory and Applications. Kluwer Academic Publishers, Norwell (1987)
26. Martius, G., Herrmann, J.M., Der, R.: Guided self-organisation for autonomous robot development. In: Almeida e Costa, F., Rocha, L.M., Costa, E., Harvey, I., Coutinho, A. (eds.) ECAL 2007. LNCS (LNAI), vol. 4648, pp. 766–775. Springer, Heidelberg (2007). https://doi.org/10.1007/978-3-540-74913-4_77

27. Nakashima, T., Akiyama, H., Suzuki, Y., Ohori, A., Fukushima, T.: HELIOS2018: team description paper. In: RoboCup 2018 Symposium and Competitions, Montreal, Canada (2018)

28. Nehaniv, C., Polani, D., Olsson, L., Klyubin, A.: Evolutionary information-theoretic foundations of sensory ecology: channels of organism-specific meaningful information. In: Modeling Biology: Structures, Behaviour, Evolution, pp. 9–11 (2005)

29. Noda, I., Stone, P.: The RoboCup soccer server and cmunited clients: implemented infrastructure for MAS research. Auton. Agents Multi-Agent Syst. **7**(1–2), 101–120 (2003)

30. Prokopenko, M., Gerasimov, V., Tanev, I.: Evolving spatiotemporal coordination in a modular robotic system. In: Nolfi, S., et al. (eds.) SAB 2006. LNCS (LNAI), vol. 4095, pp. 558–569. Springer, Heidelberg (2006). https://doi.org/10.1007/11840541_46

31. Prokopenko, M., Gerasimov, V., Tanev, I.: Measuring spatiotemporal coordination in a modular robotic system. In: Rocha, L., Yaeger, L., Bedau, M., Floreano, D., Goldstone, R., Vespignani, A. (eds.) Artificial Life X: Proceedings of The 10th International Conference on the Simulation and Synthesis of Living Systems, Bloomington IN, USA, pp. 185–191 (2006)

32. Prokopenko, M., Obst, O., Wang, P., Budden, D., Cliff, O.M.: Gliders 2013: tactical analysis with information dynamics. In: RoboCup 2013 Symposium and Competitions, Eindhoven, The Netherlands (2013)

33. Prokopenko, M., Wang, P., Obst, O., Jaurgeui, V.: Gliders 2016: integrating multi-agent approaches to tactical diversity. In: RoboCup 2016 Symposium and Competitions, Leipzig, Germany (2016)

34. Prokopenko, M.: Guided self-organization. HFSP J. **3**(5), 287–289 (2009)

35. Prokopenko, M. (ed.): Guided Self-Organization: Inception. ECC, vol. 9. Springer, Heidelberg (2014). https://doi.org/10.1007/978-3-642-53734-9

36. Prokopenko, M., Einav, I.: Information thermodynamics of near-equilibrium computation. Phys. Rev. E **91**, 062143 (2015)

37. Prokopenko, M., Wang, P.: Evaluating team performance at the edge of chaos. In: Polani, D., Browning, B., Bonarini, A., Yoshida, K. (eds.) RoboCup 2003. LNCS (LNAI), vol. 3020, pp. 89–101. Springer, Heidelberg (2004). https://doi.org/10.1007/978-3-540-25940-4_8

38. Prokopenko, M., Wang, P.: Disruptive innovations in RoboCup 2D soccer simulation league: from Cyberoos'98 to Gliders2016. In: Behnke, S., Sheh, R., Sariel, S., Lee, D.D. (eds.) RoboCup 2016. LNCS (LNAI), vol. 9776, pp. 529–541. Springer, Cham (2017). https://doi.org/10.1007/978-3-319-68792-6_44

39. Prokopenko, M., Wang, P.: Fractals 2019: guiding self-organisation of intelligent agents. In: RoboCup 2019 Symposium and Competitions, Sydney, Australia (2019)

40. Prokopenko, M., Wang, P.: Gliders2d: source code base for RoboCup 2D soccer simulation league. In: Chalup, S., Niemueller, T., Suthakorn, J., Williams, M.-A. (eds.) RoboCup 2019. LNCS (LNAI), vol. 11531, pp. 418–428. Springer, Cham (2019). arxiv.org/abs/1812.10202

41. Prokopenko, M., Wang, P., Marian, S., Bai, A., Li, X., Chen, X.: RoboCup 2D soccer simulation league: evaluation challenges. In: Akiyama, H., Obst, O., Sammut, C., Tonidandel, F. (eds.) RoboCup 2017. LNCS (LNAI), vol. 11175, pp. 325–337. Springer, Cham (2018). https://doi.org/10.1007/978-3-030-00308-1_27

42. Reis, L.P., Lau, N., Oliveira, E.C.: Situation based strategic positioning for coordinating a team of homogeneous agents. BRSDMAS 2000. LNCS (LNAI), vol. 2103, pp. 175–197. Springer, Heidelberg (2001). https://doi.org/10.1007/3-540-44568-4_11

43. Riedmiller, M., Gabel, T., Trost, F., Schwegmann, T.: Brainstormers 2D - team description 2008. In: RoboCup 2008 (2008)

44. Russell, S.J., Norvig, P.: Artificial Intelligence: A Modern Approach. Prentice Hall, New Jersey (2003)

45. Stone, P., Riley, P., Veloso, M.: The CMUnited-99 champion simulator team. In: Veloso, M., Pagello, E., Kitano, H. (eds.) RoboCup 1999. LNCS (LNAI), vol. 1856, pp. 35–48. Springer, Heidelberg (2000). https://doi.org/10.1007/3-540-45327-X_2

46. Stone, P., Veloso, M.: Task decomposition, dynamic role assignment, and low-bandwidth communication for real-time strategic teamwork. Artif. Intell. **110**(2), 241–273 (1999)

47. Tavafi, A., Nozari, N., Vatani, R., Yousefi, M.R., Rahmatinia, S., Pirdir, P.: MarliK 2012 soccer 2D simulation team description paper. In: RoboCup 2012 Symposium and Competitions, Mexico City, Mexico (2012)

48. Verfaillie, G., Schiex, T.: Solution reuse in dynamic constraint satisfaction problems. In: Proceedings of the Twelfth National Conference on Artificial Intelligence, AAAI 1994, vol. 1, pp. 307–312. American Association for Artificial Intelligence, Menlo Park (1994)

49. Yang, Z., et al.: MT2018: team description paper. In: RoboCup 2018 Symposium and Competitions, Montreal, Canada (2018)

50. Zuparic, M., Jauregui, V., Prokopenko, M., Yue, Y.: Quantifying the impact of communication on performance in multi-agent teams. Artif. Life Robot. **22**(3), 357–373 (2017)

RoboCup 2019 AdultSize Winner NimbRo: Deep Learning Perception, In-Walk Kick, Push Recovery, and Team Play Capabilities

Diego Rodriguez[✉], Hafez Farazi, Grzegorz Ficht, Dmytro Pavlichenko,
André Brandenburger, Mojtaba Hosseini, Oleg Kosenko, Michael Schreiber,
Marcel Missura, and Sven Behnke

Autonomous Intelligent Systems, Computer Science,
University of Bonn, Bonn, Germany
rodriguez@ais.uni-bonn.de
http://ais.uni-bonn.de

Abstract. Individual and team capabilities are challenged every year
by rule changes and the increasing performance of the soccer teams at
RoboCup Humanoid League. For RoboCup 2019 in the AdultSize class,
the number of players (2 vs. 2 games) and the field dimensions were
increased, which demanded for team coordination and robust visual perception and localization modules. In this paper, we present the latest
developments that lead team NimbRo to win the soccer tournament,
drop-in games, technical challenges and the Best Humanoid Award of
the RoboCup Humanoid League 2019 in Sydney. These developments
include a deep learning vision system, in-walk kicks, step-based push-
recovery, and team play strategies.

1 Introduction

The Humanoid League contributes to the goal of beating the human soccer world
champion by 2050 by gradually making the game rules more FIFA alike. Additionally, individual and team skills are also encouraged by a set of technical challenges. This year, for the AdultSize class, the teams were allowed to be composed by
two team players. Correspondingly, the field dimensions were updated to 14×9 m.
These modifications pose several challenges in terms of perception (further away
balls and goalposts to be detected), locomotion (longer distances demanding for
a faster gait), localization (robust line detection and state estimation), and team
play (coordination between players). This paper presents our recent developments
to address these modifications and shows their performance in the competition.
These developments include in-walk kicks, a step-based push recovery approach,
a vision system based on deep learning and team play strategies.

S. Chalup et al. (Eds.): RoboCup 2019, LNAI 11531, pp. 631–645, 2019.
https://doi.org/10.1007/978-3-030-35699-6_51

632   D. Rodriguez et al.

Fig. 1. Humanoid AdultSize team NimbRo at RoboCup 2019 in Sydney.

Our robots won all AdultSize 2019 competitions, namely the soccer tournament, the drop-in games and the technical challenges. Additionally, the NimbRo team was given with Best Humanoid award of the Humanoid League. In RoboCup 2019, we used our fully open-source 3D printed humanoid platform NimbRo-OP2(X) [1,2], shown in Fig. 1 with our human team members. We released a video of the 2019 competition highlights[1].

2   Robot Platforms

During the competition three different robots have been used — NimbRo-OP2 (Fig. 1 first from right), NimbRo-OP2X (Fig. 1 first from left) and Copedo (Fig. 1 second from left). These platforms lead team NimbRo to win all possible competitions last year in the AdultiSize League of RoboCup 2018 [3]. Despite the visible differences in the kinematic structure and outer appearance, there is a fundamental level of similarity between the platforms. The joints of all robots are actuated with Robotis Dynamixel actuators. These are controlled through a Robotis CM740 microcontroller board, which also incorporates an IMU with a 3-axis gyroscope and accelerometer. For visual perception, a Logitech C905 USB camera in combination with a wide-angle lens was used.

NimbRo-OP2(X). NimbRo-OP2 [1] and NimbRo-OP2X [2] are our self-developed humanoid robots, where both the hardware[2] and software[3] components are completely open-source. Although the platforms share a similar design and name, there is a number of differences between them. With the same height of 1.34 m, the robots place on the lower end of the AdultSize class requirements. Their 3D printed plastic structure mainly contributes to the low weights

---

[1] RoboCup 2019 NimbRo highlights video: https://youtu.be/ITe-seb4PsA.
[2] NimbRo-OP2X hardware: https://github.com/NimbRo/nimbro-op2.
[3] NimbRo-OP2X software: https://github.com/AIS-Bonn/humanoid_op_ros.

of 17.5 kg (OP2) and 19 kg (OP2X). Both robots share a similar joint layout with 18 Degrees of Freedom (DoF), with 5 DoF in a parallel kinematics arrangement per leg, 3 DoF per arm, and 2 DoF actuating the head. A Shuttle X1 Gaming computer with an Nvidia GTX 1060 and an Intel Core i7-7700HQ CPU was mounted inside the hollow trunk of the NimbRo-OP2. For the NimbRo-OP2X we increased the available space in the trunk to fit a standard Mini-ITX motherboard, with a i7-8700T CPU and a GTX 1050 Ti GPU. Other significant differences With the NimbRo-OP2X, a new type of Dynamixel X actuator—the XH540—was used. Equipped with thicker gears and a fully metal casing, the servomotors are more durable and reliable, compared to the MX-106 from the NimbRo-OP2. Both robots use external gearing to produce the required torque in the leg roll and yaw joints. Initially, they were custom-milled out of brass for the OP2. Due to weight and procurement factors, the OP2X utilizes 3D-printed double-helical gears, which are fast to manufacture.

Copedo. Copedo was built using milled carbon composite and aluminum parts. These provide the necessary rigidity, while keeping the total weight down. Initially, Copedo was built (in 2012) as a TeenSize robot. With the introduction of one vs. one games in the AdultSize class in 2017, we have rebuilt him to have a weight of 10.1 kg and a height of 131 cm [4]. Dynamixel EX-106+ were chosen to power the 5 DoF legs. The legs are additionally equipped with tension springs, which allow for energy storage during locomotion. The 1 DoF arms and 2 DoF neck use RX-64 servos, due to lower torque and speed requirements for their joints. A small, light-weight and efficient Intel NUC NUC7I7BNH (i7-7567U CPU) computer was fitted into Copedo to complete the build.

3   Deep Learning Visual Perception

Our visual perception pipeline improved significantly since RoboCup 2018. Thanks to our new unified perception convolutional neural network (NimbRoNet2), we now can reliably perceive the environment in extremely low and very bright lighting condition. The visual perception system can recognize soccer-related objects, including a soccer ball, field boundaries, robots, line segments, and goalposts through the usage of texture, shape, brightness, and color information.

Our deep-learning-based visual perception system is robust against brightness, viewing angles, and lens distortions. To achieve this, we designed a unified deep convolutional neural network to perform object detection and pixel-wise classification with one forward pass. After post-processing, we managed to outperform our previous non-deep learning approach to soccer vision [5] as well as our previous deep-learning-based model [2]. Our perception system is also able to track [6] and identify our robots [7].

The system has two output heads; one for object detection, and the other for pixel-wise segmentation. The detection head gives the location of the ball, robots, and goalposts. The segmentation head is for line and field detection. Our model uses an encoder-decoder architecture similar to pixel-wise segmentation models like SegNet [8], and U-Net [9]. Due to computational limitations and the necessity of real-time perception, we have made several adaptations, e.g., using a shorter decoder than the encoder. Thus, the number of parameters has been reduced for the cost of losing fine-grained spatial information which can be alleviated using sub-pixel post-processing. To minimize annotation efforts, we utilized transfer-learning. A pre-trained ResNet-18 is chosen as the encoder. Since ResNet was originally designed for recognition tasks, we removed the Global Average Pooling (GAP) and the fully connected layers in the model. Transpose-convolutional layers are used for up-sampling the representations. To use location-dependent features, we used newly proposed location-dependent convolutional layer [10]. In order to limit the number of parameters used, a shared learnable bias between both output heads is implemented. The proposed visual perception architecture is illustrated in Fig. 2.

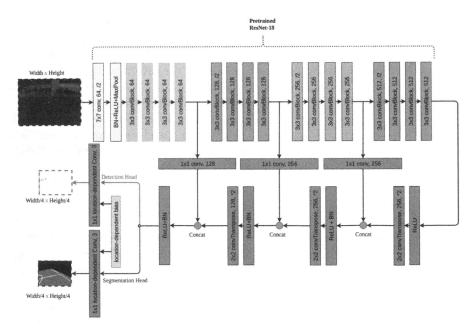

Fig. 2. NimbRoNet2 architecture. Similar to ResNet, each convBlock consists of two convolutional layers followed by batch-norm and ReLU activations. For simplicity, residual connections in ResNet are not depicted. Note that instead of a convolutional layer we used a location-dependent convolution in the last layer.

Different losses were used for different network heads. For detection head, similar to SweatyNet [11], the mean squared error is employed. The target is constructed by Gaussian blobs around the ball center and bottom-middle points of the goalposts and robots. In contrast to last year model, NimbRoNet2 uses a bigger radius for robots with the intuition that annotating a canonical center point is more difficult, thus a bigger radius would less penalize the network for not outputting the exact human labels. In the classification head, we used pixel-wise Negative Log Likelihood. We also added Total Variation loss to the output of all result channels except the line segmentation channel. Total Variation loss encouraged blob response thus helped to have less false positives, especially in field detection.

One other difficulty of this year of RoboCup was very thin goalposts which were hard to detect. However, with many training samples, the network finally managed to learn it very robustly. After sufficient training, goal posts were detected even when they were hard to recognize by a human. This might be explained by inferring their presence from other features of the pitch like field boundary and lines. One detected hard-to-recognize goal post is shown in the last row of Fig. 3.

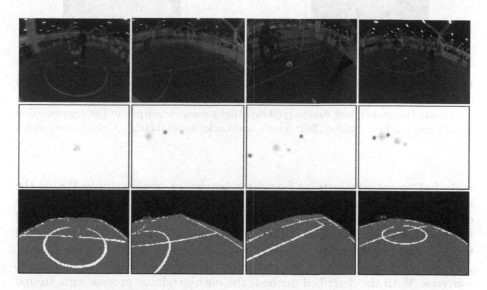

Fig. 3. Object detection results. Upper row: captured images by our robots. Middle row: the output of the network with balls (cyan), goal posts (magenta), and robots (yellow). Bottom row: the output of the segmentation branch with lines (white), field (gray), and background (black). (Color figure online)

Despite using Adam optimizer, which has an adaptable per-parameter learning rate, finding a suitable learning rate is still a challenging prerequisite for training. To determine an optimal learning rate, we followed the approach presented by Smith et. al. [12]. Each batch contained only some samples for one of the output heads. We used progressive image resizing that uses small pictures at the beginning of training, and step by step increase the dimensions as training progresses, a method inspired by Brock et. al. [13] and by Yosinski et al. [14]. In early iterations, the inaccurate randomly initialized model will

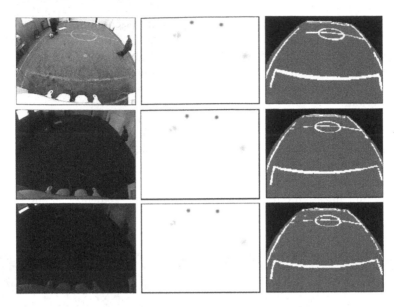

Fig. 4. Object detection under various lighting conditions. Left column: captured images by our robots. Middle column: output of the network indicating balls (cyan), goal posts (magenta), and robots (yellow). Right column: output of the segmentation branch showing lines (white), field (gray), and background (black). (Color figure online)

make fast progress by learning from large batches of small pictures. Within the initial fifty epochs, we used downsampled training images, whereas the weights on the encoder part are frozen. Throughout the following fifty epochs, all parts of the models are jointly trained. In the last fifty epochs, full-sized pictures are used to learn fine-grained details. A lower learning rate is employed for the encoder part, with the intuition that the pre-trained model needs less training time to converge. With the described method, the entire training process with around 9k samples takes less than three hours on a single Titan X GPU with 12 GB of memory. Examples from the test set are pictured in Fig. 3. To annotate more data as quickly as possible, we designed an annotation tool which automatically annotates the input based on the previously trained model. The user then only had to correct those samples which were wrongly classified. This semi-automatic annotation tool was crucial for us to gather as many samples as possible from the RoboCup 2019 environment.

The output of the network is of lower resolution and has less spatial information than the input image. To account for this effect in the detection part, we calculate sub-pixel level coordinates based on the center of mass of a detected contour. There was no need to account for lower resolution output in the field and line segmentation.

After detecting soccer-related objects, we filter them and project each object location into egocentric world coordinates. Using NimbRoNet2, we can detect objects which are up to 10 m away. The complete perception pipeline, including a forward-pass of the network, takes approximately 36 ms on the robot hardware. Using a unified network helped both detection and segmentation. The network learned to exclude the balls which were outside of the field, hence reducing false detection rate. Outside field object removal was previously done only after post-processing. In addition, the robot was able to play soccer in pitch black, and the perception was robust in different lighting conditions, including direct sunlight and without ambient light (Fig. 4). Unfortunately, this year, all AdultSize games were played with artificial light, thus we could not test our new development for lighting conditions during the competition.

Table 1. Results of the detection branch of our visual perception network.

Type	F1	Accuracy	Recall	Precision	FDR
Ball (NimbRoNet2)	**0.998**	**0.996**	0.996	**1.0**	**0.0**
Ball (NimbRoNet)	0.997	0.994	**1.0**	0.994	0.005
Ball (SweatyNet-1 [11])	0.985	0.973	0.988	0.983	0.016
Goal (NimbRoNet2)	**0.981**	**0.971**	0.973	**0.988**	**0.011**
Goal (NimbRoNet)	0.977	0.967	**0.988**	0.966	0.033
Goal (SweatyNet-1 [11])	0.963	0.946	0.966	0.960	0.039
Robot (NimbRoNet2)	**0.979**	**0.973**	**0.963**	**0.995**	**0.004**
Robot (NimbRoNet)	0.974	0.971	0.957	0.992	0.007
Robot (SweatyNet-1 [11])	0.940	0.932	0.957	0.924	0.075
Total (NimbRoNet2)	**0.986**	**0.986**	0.977	**0.994**	**0.005**
Total (NimbRoNet)	0.983	0.977	**0.982**	0.984	0.015
Total (SweatyNet-1 [11])	0.963	0.950	0.970	0.956	0.043

Table 2. Results of the semantic segmentation of our visual perception network.

Type	Accuracy	IOU
Field	0.986	0.975
Lines	0.881	0.784
Background	0.993	0.981
Total	0.953	0.913

Our visual perception pipeline is compared on different soccer-related objects against SweatyNet [11] and our previous model NimbRoNet [2] (Table 1). We also evaluated our segmentation head (Table 2). We have outperformed SweatyNet and NimbRoNet, whose results were one of the best-reported in terms of detecting soccer objects. This achievement was also accompanied by being approximately two times faster than SweatyNet in training phase. The reduced training time can be attributed to the progressive image resizing and transfer learning techniques.

4   Robust Omnidirectional Gait with In-Walk Kick

Team NimbRo has developed a motion and a gait control framework capable of absorbing pushes from any direction at any time during the gait cycle. This year, for the first time, our NimbRo-OP2(X) adult-sized platforms incorporated step-based push recovery capabilities and in-walk kicks.

Compliant Actuation. Motions performed by the robot are sensitive to the tracking capabilities of the control system. We developed a feed-forward control scheme which modifies the joint trajectories based on the commanded position and inverse dynamics [15]. The model incorporates factors such as battery voltage, joint frictions, and body inertias.

Open-Loop Walking. The walking gait is based on an open-loop central pattern generator calculated from a gait phase angle proportional to the desired gait frequency. To formulate this open-loop gait, we use three different spaces: joint space, Cartesian space and abstract space [16]. The open-loop gait is further extended by the integration of an explicit double support phase, modification of the leg extension profiles, and velocity and acceleration-based leaning strategies [17]. These extensions resulted in passive damping of oscillations and smooth transition between swing and support phases.

Feedback Mechanisms. Several basic feedback mechanisms, namely arm angle, hip angle, continuous foot angle, support foot angle, CoM shifting, and virtual slope, have been built around the open-loop gait core to stabilize the walking [17]. These PID-like feedback mechanisms derive from the state estimation and add corrective action components to the central pattern generated waveforms.

Capture Steps Gait. We use the Capture Step Framework [18, 19] to make our robots recover balance. The Capture Step Framework is a composition of central pattern-generated open-loop step motions and a linear inverted pendulum model-based balance controller. In each iteration of the motion control loop, timing and location of the next footstep are computed using the linearized equations of the inverted pendulum model such that the Center of Mass (CoM) would return to a stable limit cycle while also following a commanded walking velocity. Our robots showed stable walking throughout the competition, including balance-restoring capture steps after collisions in games and excelled in the technical challenge.

4.1   In-Walk Kick

Our in-walk kick approach integrates the kick directly into the gait to avoid unnecessary stops (Fig. 5), which were required in our previous kicking motions. Thus, a significantly boosting of the overall pace of the game on the larger field has been achieved.

Fig. 5. In-walk kick performed during a soccer match.

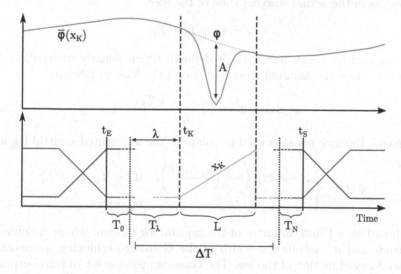

Fig. 6. A schematic visualization of the kick phase x_K and the sagittal leg angle $\bar{\varphi}$. The upper part shows the augmented leg angle $\bar{\varphi}$ in sagittal direction during a kick, where the vertical dashed lines symbolize the start and the end of the kicking motion. The lower part displays the timing parameters used to calculate x_K, where the red line resembles the support coefficient of the kicking leg and the blue line of the supporting leg respectively. The timing parameter λ can be used to move the motion of length L inside the legal execution window of size ΔT.

A general schematic of the approach can be seen in Fig. 6. In our approach, an allowed time window ΔT is defined for the kick. Generally, a kick can be performed between the end t_E of the previous support transition phase and the start t_S of the next transition phase respectively. Nevertheless, for $T_0, T_N > 0$, it is advantageous to prohibit kicks in boundary intervals $[t_s, t_s + T_0]$ and $[t_E - T_N, t_E]$ to prevent unwanted foot contact with the ground during the kick execution. In this manner, we define

$$\Delta T = t_E - t_S - T_0 - T_N \tag{1}$$

as the length of the interval where we can safely perform a kick. In addition, given a motion duration $L < \Delta T$, it is possible to perform the kick inside an arbitrary location of the allowed interval. This enables us to define a timing parameter $0 \leq \lambda \leq 1$ resulting in a delay interval

$$T_\lambda = \lambda \left(\Delta T - L \right), \tag{2}$$

controlling the starting time of motion execution inside the allowed time window. This is particularly important for the soccer behaviors, since it allows for exact control of the location of the foot at the start and apex of the kick. Altogether, this results in the actual starting time of the kick

$$t_K = t_S + T_0 + T_\lambda. \tag{3}$$

Consequently, a kick phase x_K is defined, which linearly interpolates from -1 to 1 between the nominal start and end of the kicking motion:

$$x_K \left(t \right) = 2 \frac{t - (t_S + T_0 + T_\lambda)}{L} - 1. \tag{4}$$

In the end, the kick phase is used to compute the augmented sagittal leg angle:

$$\bar{\varphi}\left(t \right) = \begin{cases} \varphi - A \exp\left(-\frac{1}{2} \left(\frac{x_K(t)}{\sigma} \right)^2 \right), & \text{if } t \in [t_K, t_K + L] \\ \varphi, & \text{otherwise} \end{cases} \tag{5}$$

by subtracting a Gaussian curve of the sagittal leg motion, where A defines the amplitude and σ controls the width of the Gaussian, achieving a smooth but distinct forward motion of the leg. The Gaussian term is set to zero beyond the interval boundaries $[t_K, t_K + L]$. Thus, σ has to be small enough such that the activation of the Gaussian can be neglected at the borders, ensuring that the transition to the kick is smooth.

5   Soccer Behaviors

We refer to soccer behaviors to the decision process required to play football. These decisions include, for example, to search for the ball if this is not detected, to go for the ball if we are far from it, or to activate the kick if all the conditions for kicking are granted. The decision process is modeled as a hierarchical Finite State Machine (FSM) with two main layers [20]. The state of the upper layer is established by the state of the game defined in part by the game controller and the role of the player (goalie, striker or defender). The states of the lower FSM represent individual skills of the players such as: move, stop, kick, dribble, dive, among others. Collision avoidance, i.e., avoidance of other robots—either from the opponent team or our team—is part of the lower state machine.

Team Play Strategies. In general, the function of the team play is to safely assign the game roles to each of the players. In this manner, for example, having two strikers simultaneously is not desired in order to avoid collisions between robots of the same team when they are going for the ball. The task assignment is implemented as a server/client architecture where the striker is the server and it is the only one allowed to accept task renegotiation requests. The other players, i.e., defenders and goalies, are allowed to make requests if they find themselves in a better position than the striker, e.g., being closer to the ball. During drop-in games, no task renegotiation was allowed, mainly due to the lack of game roles of other teams. Thus, our players were assigned to fixed roles from the beginning of the match. However, team capabilities were still exhibited during drop-in games, e.g., by our goalkeepers clearing out balls and returning to their corresponding goal. For a deeper discussion about the team play strategies, please refer to [20].

6 Technical Challenges

Technical challenges is a separate competition, where robots have to perform isolated independent tasks during a limited time period. Since the time period for executing all tasks is limited to only 25 min, robustness and reliability have the highest importance when designing a solution for each challenge. At RoboCup 2019 there were four technical challenges: push recovery, high jump, high kick and goal kick from moving ball.

Fig. 7. Technical Challenge: Push Recovery. Several capture steps allow the robot to regain balance after a very strong push of a 5 kg pendulum.

6.1 Push Recovery

In this *Push Recovery* challenge, a robot has to withstand three pushes in a row while walking on spot. The pushes are performed by releasing a previously retracted pendulum which then hits the robot at the height of the CoM. The pushes are performed randomly from the front and from the back. The weight of the pendulum is 5 kg and the robots are ranked by the distance of pendulum retraction for the series of three successful attempts. The Capture Step Framework allowed our robot to withstand very strong pushes, making a series of capture steps to regain balance (Fig. 7), and to finish first in this challenge.

6.2 High Jump

The goal of the *High Jump* is to remain airborne during a vertical jump as long as possible and upon landing remain in a stable sitting or standing posture. For this challenge, motions were pre-designed using key-frames and a simple geometry-based mass distribution principle [21]. By lowering and rapidly lifting the CoM, the accumulated linear momentum at full CoM height propels the robot into the air. After the leap is performed, there is a possibility to decrease the CoM height, which results in folding the legs. This would increase the time in the air by postponing the contact with the ground plane even with a weaker jump upwards. However, we observed that this rapid leg movement caused the robot to often lose balance upon landing. Due to the bent knees, the force upon impact was also damaging to the gears in the knee actuators. In our experience, we have found that landing on extended legs increased the durability of the actuators and made the landing more reliable. This was largely due to the integrated tension springs in the legs. They provide passive compliance during landing and also contributed greatly to the strength of the jump. Our robot remained airborne for 0.262 s and came in second with a difference of 13 ms to the first.

6.3 High Kick

In the *High Kick* challenge, the robot has to score a goal over an obstacle which is positioned on the goal line. The ball is initially positioned at the penalty mark. The goal is only valid if the ball surpassed the obstacle without touching it. The height of the obstacle can be adjusted and the teams are ranked by the height of the successfully over-kicked obstacle. Since it is allowed to touch the ball multiple times, we first move the ball close to the goal line by executing a pre-designed kicking motion. Having the ball close to the obstacle, we execute a pre-designed high kick motion. During this motion the tip of the foot makes first contact with the ball as close to the ground plane as possible. From that point, the foot moves forward and upwards. In order to improve the efficiency of this motion, we use a modified foot with a "scoop" shape. It ensures a prolonged contact with the ball during the high kick motion and—hence—transfer of more energy to the ball, which allows to kick over higher obstacles. Our team came in second in this challenge, successfully kicking over an obstacle of 26 cm height.

6.4   Goal Kick from Moving Ball

The goal of this challenge is to score a goal by kicking a moving ball. The robot is placed at the penalty mark. The ball is positioned at the corner of the field and is passed to the robot either by a human or by another robot. The teams are ranked by the number of successful goals out of three consecutive attempts. In order to know when the robot has to kick, we predicted the time-of-travel of the ball to get in front of the robot foot by estimating its velocity and acceleration from a series of consecutive ball detections, separated in time by a time interval $\epsilon = 0.1\,\text{s}$. Our robot performing this challenge is shown in Fig. 8. Our team took the first place in this challenge, successfully scoring the goal from the moving ball three out of three times.

Fig. 8. Technical Challenge: Goal Kick from Moving Ball.

7   Game Performance

During the AdultSize 2 vs. 2 Soccer competition of RoboCup 2019, our robots scored 48 goals while receiving none. The robots have shown outstanding performance during the whole tournament including winning the final game 8:0. While 2 vs. 2 competition games have shown individual and team capabilities, drop-in games demonstrated individual skills of each single robot. In the Drop-in tournament, our robots scored 31:7 goals in 6 drop-in games—resulting in winning 57 points with a margin of 33 points to the second best team. Compared to the soccer tournament, we received goals during drop-in games mainly due to the lack of a second field player (our partner teams normally placed goalkeepers), and due to the lack of diving motions when our robots were goalkeepers. The capabilities of our robots were once more demonstrated by winning the AdultSize Technical Challenges. Consequently, NimbRo received the 2019 Best Humanoid Award of the Humanoid League.

8   Conclusions

In this paper, we presented the approaches that lead us to win all possible competitions in the AdultSize class for the RoboCup 2019 Humanoids League in Sydney: soccer tournament, drop-in games and technical challenges. Special emphasis was put on the deep learning based computer vision system that lead our robots to be robust against different lighting conditions and to detect reliably balls up to 10 m. Part of our success in the games was explained by the novel in-walk kick, making our games very dynamic and hard to counteract by the opponents. We also presented a step-based push recovery approach that was demonstrated during the competition with impressive performance. Finally, the decision making process and team play strategies were presented, which are responsible for integrating and making use of all individual components.

Acknowledgements. This work was partially funded by grant BE 2556/13 of German Research Foundation.

References

1. Ficht, G., Allgeuer, P., Farazi, H., Behnke, S.: NimbRo-OP2: grown-up 3D printed open humanoid platform for research. In: 17th IEEE-RAS International Conference on Humanoid Robots (Humanoids) (2017)
2. Ficht, G., et al.: NimbRo-OP2X: adult-sized open-source 3D printed humanoid robot. In: 18th IEEE-RAS International Conference on Humanoid Robots (Humanoids) (2018)
3. Farazi, H., et al.: NimbRo robots winning RoboCup 2018 humanoid adultsize soccer competitions. In: Holz, D., Genter, K., Saad, M., von Stryk, O. (eds.) RoboCup 2018. LNCS (LNAI), vol. 11374, pp. 436–449. Springer, Cham (2019). https://doi.org/10.1007/978-3-030-27544-0_36
4. Ficht, G., et al.: Grown-up NimbRo robots winning RoboCup 2017 humanoid adultsize soccer competitions. In: Akiyama, H., Obst, O., Sammut, C., Tonidandel, F. (eds.) RoboCup 2017. LNCS (LNAI), vol. 11175, pp. 448–460. Springer, Cham (2018). https://doi.org/10.1007/978-3-030-00308-1_37
5. Farazi, H., Allgeuer, P., Behnke, S.: A monocular vision system for playing soccer in low color information environments. In: 10th Workshop on Humanoid Soccer Robots, IEEE-RAS International Conference on Humanoid Robots (2015)
6. Farazi, H., Behnke, S.: Real-time visual tracking and identification for a team of homogeneous humanoid robots. In: Behnke, S., Sheh, R., Sarıel, S., Lee, D.D. (eds.) RoboCup 2016. LNCS (LNAI), vol. 9776, pp. 230–242. Springer, Cham (2017). https://doi.org/10.1007/978-3-319-68792-6_19
7. Farazi, H., Behnke, S.: Online visual robot tracking and identification using deep LSTM networks. In: IEEE/RSJ International Conference on Intelligent Robots and Systems (IROS) (2017)
8. Badrinarayanan, V., Kendall, A., Cipolla, R.: SegNet: a deep convolutional encoder-decoder architecture for image segmentation. IEEE Trans. Pattern Anal. Mach. Intell. **39**(12), 2481–2495 (2015)
9. Ronneberger, O., Fischer, P., Brox, T.: U-Net: convolutional networks for biomedical image segmentation. In: Navab, N., Hornegger, J., Wells, W.M., Frangi, A.F. (eds.) MICCAI 2015. LNCS, vol. 9351, pp. 234–241. Springer, Cham (2015). https://doi.org/10.1007/978-3-319-24574-4_28

10. Azizi, N., Farazi, H., Behnke, S.: Location dependency in video prediction. In: Kůrková, V., Manolopoulos, Y., Hammer, B., Iliadis, L., Maglogiannis, I. (eds.) ICANN 2018. LNCS, vol. 11141, pp. 630–638. Springer, Cham (2018). https://doi.org/10.1007/978-3-030-01424-7_62
11. Schnekenburger, F., Scharffenberg, M., Wülker, M., Hochberg, U., Dorer, K.: Detection and localization of features on a soccer field with feedforward fully convolutional neural networks (FCNN) for the Adult-size humanoid robot Sweaty. In: Proceedings of the 12th Workshop on Humanoid Soccer Robots, IEEE-RAS International Conference on Humanoid Robots(Humanoids) (2017)
12. Smith, L.N.: Cyclical learning rates for training neural networks. In: IEEE Winter Conference on Applications of Computer Vision (WACV), pp. 464–472 (2017)
13. Brock, A., Lim, T., Ritchie, J.M., Weston, N.: Freezeout: accelerate training by progressively freezing layers. arXiv:1706.04983 (2017)
14. Yosinski, J., Clune, J., Bengio, Y., Lipson, H.: How transferable are features in deep neural networks? In: Advances in Neural Information Processing Systems (NIPS), pp. 3320–3328 (2014)
15. Schwarz, M., Behnke, S.: Compliant robot behavior using servo actuator models identified by iterative learning control. In: Behnke, S., Veloso, M., Visser, A., Xiong, R. (eds.) RoboCup 2013. LNCS (LNAI), vol. 8371, pp. 207–218. Springer, Heidelberg (2014). https://doi.org/10.1007/978-3-662-44468-9_19
16. Behnke, S.: Online trajectory generation for omnidirectional biped walking. In: Proceedings of 2006 IEEE International Conference on Robotics and Automation (ICRA) (2006)
17. Allgeuer, P., Behnke, S.: Omnidirectional bipedal walking with direct fused angle feedback mechanisms. In: 16th IEEE-RAS International Conference on Humanoid Robots (Humanoids) (2016)
18. Missura, M.: Analytic and learned footstep control for robust bipedal walking. Ph.D. dissertation, Universitäts-und Landesbibliothek Bonn (2016)
19. Missura, M., Behnke, S.: Walking with capture steps. In: IEEE-RAS International Conference on Humanoid Robots, p. 526 (2014)
20. Rodriguez, D., et al.: Advanced soccer skills and team play of RoboCup 2017 TeenSize winner NimbRo. In: Akiyama, H., Obst, O., Sammut, C., Tonidandel, F. (eds.) RoboCup 2017. LNCS (LNAI), vol. 11175, pp. 435–447. Springer, Cham (2018). https://doi.org/10.1007/978-3-030-00308-1_36
21. Ficht, G., Behnke, S.: Online balanced motion generation for humanoid robots. In: IEEE-RAS 18th International Conference on Humanoid Robots (Humanoids) (2018)

B-Human 2019 – Complex Team Play Under Natural Lighting Conditions

Thomas Röfer[1,2(✉)], Tim Laue[2], Gerrit Felsch[2], Arne Hasselbring[2], Tim Haß[2], Jan Oppermann[2], Philip Reichenberg[2], and Nicole Schrader[2]

[1] Deutsches Forschungszentrum für Künstliche Intelligenz, Cyber-Physical Systems, Enrique-Schmidt-Str. 5, 28359 Bremen, Germany
thomas.roefer@dfki.de
[2] Universität Bremen, Fachbereich 3 – Mathematik und Informatik, Postfach 330 440, 28334 Bremen, Germany
{tlaue,s_uhei4h,arha,hasst,jan_opp,s_ksfo6n,nicole2}@uni-bremen.de

Abstract. In the RoboCup Standard Platform League 2019, the team B-Human won the main competition and, together with Berlin United - Nao-Team Humboldt, the Mixed Team Competition. For being successful in such a competitive environment, many sophisticated solutions for a variety of robotics tasks need to be found and integrated in a reliable and efficient manner. In this paper, we focus on three aspects that we consider as crucial for this year's success and that have not been published before: a system of neural networks for ball classification and position estimation, a new framework for behavior specification along with its application to passes and set plays, and a set of approaches for maintaining the reliability of our robot team throughout a game.

1 Introduction

B-Human is a joint RoboCup team of the University of Bremen and the German Research Center for Artificial Intelligence (DFKI) that continuously participates in the Standard Platform League since 2009. We participated in ten RoboCup German Open competitions, the RoboCup European Open 2016, and eleven RoboCups and only lost six official games. As a result, we won all German Open competitions except for one as well as the European Open competition, and the RoboCups 2009, 2010, 2011, 2013, 2016 and 2017. This year, we won both the main competition and, together with the team Berlin United – Nao Team Humboldt as team *B&B*, the Mixed Team Competition. We also reached second place in the technical challenges, i.e. the open research challenge and the directional whistle challenge. In this paper, we present three major aspects that we consider to have significantly contributed to this year's success: the ball detection, a new behavior structure, and the overall system reliability.

For some years, starting with the *Outdoor Competition* at RoboCup 2016, the Standard Platform Leagues aims for natural lighting conditions on the playing fields. This means possible changes of the ambient brightness during a game

© Springer Nature Switzerland AG 2019
S. Chalup et al. (Eds.): RoboCup 2019, LNAI 11531, pp. 646–657, 2019.
https://doi.org/10.1007/978-3-030-35699-6_52

Fig. 1. Playing under natural lighting conditions during a practice match in Bremen (left) and at one of the *outdoor fields* at RoboCup 2019 (right)

as well as the possibility of bright spots and dark shadows, caused by structures in the environment or by the robots themselves, as depicted in Fig. 1. As an increasing number of games under such conditions has been foreseeable (at RoboCup 2019, B-Human actually played most games close to huge windows, e.g. on the field shown in the right part of Fig. 1), we decided to increase our development efforts towards more flexible vision approaches and to test more under such difficult conditions. One currently very popular and successful approach for object detection in such environments is the application of *Convolutional Neural Networks* (CNN). At the RoboCup Symposium 2019, we presented our CNN-based robot detection [1], which has been used throughout the whole competition. In this paper's Sect. 2, our new CNN-based approach for ball classification is presented. Both approaches make use of our new library for fast neural network inference on NAO robots. Its implementation has been released as open-source [7] and was also presented at the RoboCup Symposium [8].

In 2018 and 2019, multiple Standard Platform League rule changes directly affected the implementation of the robots' behavior by introducing new set plays such as corner kicks and kick-ins. Their proper handling – when being in defense as well as when being in offense – together with reasonable transitions to the normal game behavior significantly increases the complexity of the overall behavior. As the previously used C-based Agent Behavior Specification Language (CABSL) [6] together with libraries turned out to be too inflexible to be used as the only means of specifying behaviors, a new behavior framework has been developed. It is presented in Sect. 3, along with some of the innovations we implemented this year.

One important aspect of robot football, which is perhaps underrated as it is not a clearly defined field of research, is the overall team reliability. Whenever a single robot breaks or becomes removed for a rule violation, the opponent team immediately gains a numerical advantage for some time. In Sect. 4, we describe multiple measures that we took to decrease the likelihood of such situations. Furthermore, we present and discuss the corresponding game statistics recorded at RoboCup 2019.

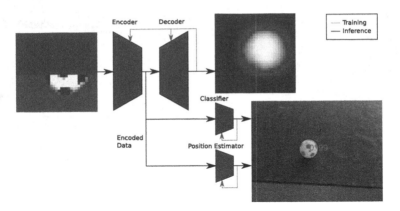

Fig. 2. System of neural networks for ball classification and position estimation. The encoder is a CNN, the classifier and the position estimator are DNNs. The architectures of the networks that are executed on the robot are shown in Table 1.

2   Ball Detection

Detecting a ball under natural lighting conditions means detecting it in very different conditions, be it in bright light, in completely shadow, or only partly covered by it. CNNs are currently a very popular approach for such problems. We have been using them for ball classification on extracted 32×32 patches since 2018 [4]. Instead of collecting more data and tuning hyperparameters, we aim to improve this approach by integrating additional knowledge.

2.1   Encoding Relevant Knowledge

This year, we used CNNs to estimate the exact *position* of the ball in a given patch. For this task, the labels of the existing dataset were extended by the position of the ball in the patch and the ball radius. If it is assumed a ball is always round, it is possible to create ball segmentation images from those labels. An example of such a segmentation image pair is shown in Fig. 3. A segmented image contains much more knowledge than a simple classification label. Some of this knowledge is relevant for ball classification and determining the ball position. If an encoder-decoder architecture is successfully trained to predict this segmentation from the original ball patches, this knowledge is also contained somewhere in the encoded features. Ideally, the features would comprise whether a ball is present in the image, which specific pixels carry the information that a ball is present, that a ball is round and connected even if a part is obscured, and the position and size of the ball.

   Features containing this information could both be used for ball classification and position estimation. In the example shown in Fig. 3, this knowledge was incorporated by the autoencoder. Despite the input showing only one half of a ball, the segmented image shows a whole circle, where the ball would be.

Table 1. Architectures of the three neural networks for ball detection

(a) Encoder

Layer Type	Output Size
Input	32x32x1
Convolutional	32x32x8
Batch Normalization	32x32x8
ReLU Activation	32x32x8
Max Pooling	16x16x8
Convolutional	16x16x16
Batch Normalization	16x16x16
ReLU Activation	16x16x16
Max Pooling	8x8x16
Convolutional	8x8x16
Batch Normalization	8x8x16
ReLU Activation	8x8x16
Max Pooling	4x4x16
Convolutional	4x4x32
Batch Normalization	4x4x32
ReLU Activation	4x4x32
Max Pooling	2x2x32

(b) Ball Classifier

Layer Type	Output Size
Input	2x2x32
Flatten	128
Dense + Batch Norm + ReLU	32
Dense + Batch Norm + ReLU	64
Dense + Batch Norm + ReLU	16
Dense + Batch Norm + Sigmoid	1

(c) Position Estimator

Layer Type	Output Size
Input	2x2x32
Flatten	128
Dense + Batch Norm + ReLU	32
Dense + Batch Norm + ReLU	64
Dense + Batch Norm + ReLU	3

This hints on the ability to detect partly obscured balls, which is very important under natural lighting conditions.

Figure 2 shows the resulting system for ball classification and position estimation. After feature extraction by the encoder, ball classification and position estimation are done by two separate deep neural networks (DNN). The position is only estimated if the image was classified as containing a ball.

2.2 Results

For evaluation purposes, the performance of the new network was compared to the performance of the one we used during the German Open 2019. This was done by running both ball detectors on data recorded during a test game in front of a large window front and during the RoboCup 2019 final in Sydney.

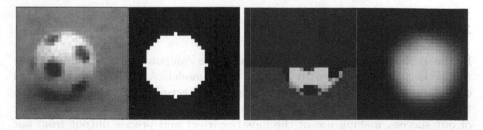

Fig. 3. Training ball segmentation. The left image shows a training example, the right image shows an exemplary inference result.

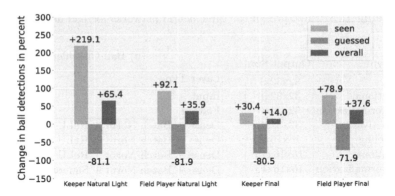

Fig. 4. Change in occurrence of different confidence levels by using the new network instead of the old one that was used at the RoboCup German Open 2019. The changes are in percent based on the detections of the old network.

For both games, the detections of the keeper and a field player from the first half were used. The evaluation was completely automated by considering ball detections as invalid that are not consistent with the team's belief of the actual ball position, which is a feature of the modeling we use in games. This method does not identify all false positives, but it makes it possible to compare both detectors on a relatively large dataset without manual labeling. We use two different confidence levels of detected balls, *seen* and *guessed*, that differ in the threshold that the classifier output must surpass.

As can be seen in Fig. 4, the new network detects overall more balls than the old one. Specifically, the number of actual sightings has risen, while there was a decrease in the number of times patches were classified as guessed. This effect could also be achieved by lowering the thresholds for the guessed and seen labels. Such an adjustment would also result in reduced precision. Figure 5 shows that this is not the case. For a reliable ball detection it is also important to be able to evaluate every frame provided by the NAOs cameras. Using our library for fast neural network inference [7], computation of the shared features requires 192 μs per evaluated patch on the NAO V6 and inference of the classifier 3.1 μs per patch. This is fast enough to allow processing of the 60 frames per second the NAO provides. Additional estimation of the ball position takes 2.5 μs per frame and is therefore almost insignificant compared to encoding multiple patches.

3   Behavior

In the B-Human software, the *behavior* is the component that decides about the actions to be taken with a given world model. Actions are then passed on to the motion system, which generates the actual joint angles and sends them to the controllers. The behavior of B-Human has always been a key part of our success, making use of the mostly correct and precise output from our state estimation and the extensive features and stability of our motion system.

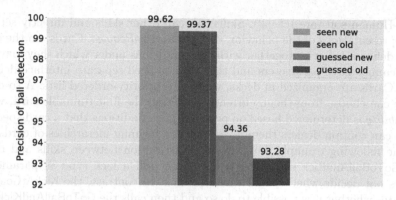

Fig. 5. Precision at different confidence levels of the new and the old network

However, handling uncertainty is still crucial in order to achieve stable decisions. We also often integrate ideas of other teams that we observe to be successful and try to optimize them.

3.1   Defining a Framework

Decomposition and hierarchy are necessary to specify behaviors for complex tasks such as playing soccer. From 2013 to 2017, B-Human used a single hierarchy of CABSL options to specify the behavior. This approach had some short-comings: Adding or removing high level behaviors required modification of other options. This also meant that an option would often be in a different place than the conditions under which it would become active, which is not easy to maintain. Furthermore, some behaviors are simply not suitable to be modeled with finite state machines, need large calculations, or keep additional state. Some functionality was therefore outsourced to so-called *libraries*, which also spread closely related code across different places.

In 2018, we already started to move away from a single hierarchy of CABSL options (cf. [4, p. 34]). The main problem with the *behavior options* in 2018 was that they could not be passed any parameters, making them useless for behaviors such as walking to a point or doing a specific kick. On the other hand, this anonymity was a desired property to achieve exchangeability of behavior components. We realized that it might not be a good idea to try to fit all behavior levels in the same formalization, but instead split the behavior into two layers: one that would decide *what* the robot should do, where options could easily be added or removed, and another one that would realize *how* the robot fulfills this request.

We call our new framework the *Skills and Cards* system. Skills are separated into an interface declaration and an implementation, where the interface defines the signature of a skill. This allows us to develop multiple methods for the same task, just as representations can be provided by different modules in the B-Human software (cf. [3]). Skills can call other skills and directly set output representations of the behavior, e.g. the *MotionRequest*. Cards, on the other hand, define a behavior together with the conditions under which they may run. They cannot have parameters and thus do not need separate interface declarations. Cards are organized in decks, which are priority-ordered lists. A so-called *dealer* can choose from them, currently selecting the first runnable card, where *runnability* is determined based on pre- and postconditions that a card specifies. Cards can contain dealers themselves, thereby forming hierarchies of cards.

The following example illustrates the distinction between skills and cards: The GoToBallAndKick skill takes a kick pose and a kick type as parameters. It does not decide whether and where to kick. In contrast, the KickAtGoalCard evaluates whether it is possible to do so and then calls the GoToBallAndKick skill with the appropriate parameters. Of course, the GoToBallAndKick skill is also called from other cards, such as passing to a teammate.

3.2   Passing into Space

For this year, we abandoned the idea of taking passes using specialized motions. Instead of kicking the ball directly at a teammate, we found that it would be much better to pass into space, acknowledging the inaccuracy of our kicks over long ranges. Furthermore, when passing upfield, the ball should end up between the receiving teammate and the opponent's goal because this reduces the time the receiver needs to walk around the ball after reaching it. Therefore, robots positioning for receiving a pass walk to the flanks of the opponent's half, oriented such that the ball can still be seen, but with a tendency towards the center of the field. This way, the passing robot can aim at an area next to its teammate, including a safety margin to minimize the probability that the ball actually ends up behind the receiver.

A particular instance of this kind of passing is the kick-off. While we are not the first team to implement a passing kick-off (the concrete variant with two robots entering the opponent's half is inspired by the team rUNSWift), we seem to be the only team that repeatably executes it with success. The kick-off occurred 10 times during the competition, and while a direct goal after two ball contacts could be scored only once, in all cases our robot had the second ball contact after the kick-off far inside the opponent's half. In some cases, only the opponent's goalkeeper could prevent an immediate goal, which is acceptable and still a strong opening. This also means that we are ready for potential rule changes which require two different robots touch the ball before a goal can be scored.

3.3   Taking Advantage of Set Plays

One of this year's changes in the SPL rule book [2] was the expansion of set plays with the introduction of kick-ins and corner kicks. If not handled properly, these situations could either allow the opponent to easily score a goal or deny a crucial goal in a game. On the highest level, our system distinguishes between

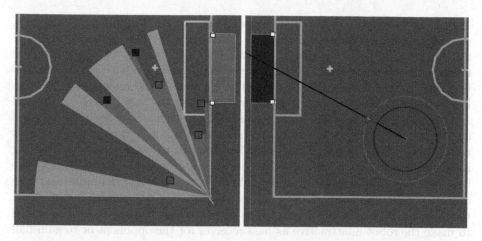

Fig. 6. Offensive and defensive free kicks. The left drawing shows the candidate kick direction intervals (green) and blocked sectors (red) during an offensive corner kick. The right drawing shows a defensive wall building scene. (Color figure online)

own (or *offensive*) and opponent (or *defensive*) free kicks. Both of them have their own deck, although they share most cards with the normal play deck.

The first card in the own free kick deck is a direct shot at the goal, which is the same that is used during normal play and executed as soon as possible. If this is not the case (e.g. due to obstacles blocking the goal or being too far from the goal), different variants exist for the different types of set plays, i.e. goal free kick, corner kick, kick-in and pushing free kick, that try to move the ball closer to the goal and ideally close to a teammate. For example, a striker executing the CornerKickToOwnRobotCard calculates all angular intervals around the ball that point inside the field of play and are not blocked by obstacles (regardless of their team affiliation), as shown in Fig. 6. Up to two of them are chosen, e.g. they must have a minimum width, and broadcast to its teammates. Simultaneously, up to two supporting robots can execute the WaitForCornerBallCard. They listen to the potential kick directions that the striker sends and position themselves such that the expected ball position after the pass is between them and the goal, according to the passing paradigm described above. As soon as the selected kick direction is stable or 15 s have passed, the kick is executed. Stability is determined by checking whether the candidate direction intervals calculated each frame intersect by a certain amount in successive frames for some time.

The behavior during an opponent's free kick, on the other hand, is always aimed at preventing a goal and does so in different ways depending on the possibilities available. All ball-playing cards are removed from this deck, however, there are three special cards in addition to the usual supporting behavior during normal play. Most importantly, one robot tries to form a wall between the own goal and the ball (cf. Fig. 6). The position is chosen just outside the clear area around the ball in an angle such that the own goal is covered as wide as possible. Keeping a robot close to the ball has the additional purpose to regain ball possession quickly when the free kick is not executed properly. A special case is when the ball is in one of the own corners, such as in an opponent's corner kick. In this case, the robot does not stand between the ball and its own goal but walks to a position close to the sideline. The goal is then still covered by the defenders and the goalkeeper. If a free kick takes place directly in front of the own goal such that a wall between the ball and the own goal is no longer possible, an attempt is made to delay or prevent the opponent from taking the free kick. This is done by walking in front of the opponent which is nearest to the ball. This forces the opponent to walk around the blocking robot (which continuously adjusts its position) or even makes it lose track of the ball. As third option, if there are five robots or more in the defending team, one of them considers marking an opponent. Candidates are opponents that are closer to the own goal than the ball and probably not taking the free kick. The goal is to make the robot unattractive as pass receiver for the opponent or to gain ball possession if a pass is done nevertheless.

Finally, it is important to keep track of the ball during free kicks. At least during goal free kicks and corner kicks, the ball is replaced in a different location than it went out, which may be outside the field of view of all robots. The robots, however, know the type of free kick from the referee computer message. Therefore, they can specifically search the positions where the ball should have been put. Although we make a guess about the side (i.e. left or right) based on the observed ball trajectory, both possibilities are investigated with two robots, if available. For kick-ins, the ball is searched for at the position where it went out, if that has been observed.

4   Reliability

In human soccer, it is considered a huge disadvantage to play with fewer players than the opponent, usually due to a penalty. Unless the level of play is very different between the two opposing teams, this assumption is also valid for robot soccer. Therefore, we try to keep our robots on the field as long as possible, i.e. to avoid receiving penalties as much as possible. In the 2019 SPL Champions Cup competition, we generally succeeded in that goal—with one exception.

4.1   Obeying the Rules

Throughout the competition, our robots received no penalties for *leaving the field*, *illegal defender*, *illegal positioning*, and *illegal motion in set*. The absence of the first three of these penalties is a result to our reliable self-localization [5], the last one originates from our robust whistle detection [3, p. 86] that was improved this year. In fact, the only penalties the robots received were four pushing calls throughout the competition, a result of our good obstacle detection [1] and careful behavior near opponent players. No team received less. The only problem that we had this year was that the operating system on the NAOs sometimes terminated our software as a response to terminal output, which resulted in 15 penalties for *inactive players*. It took us the first two games in the Champions Cup and one in the Mixed Team Competition to identify and solve this problem.

4.2   Avoiding Hardware Damage

Another reason for a low count in penalties is the avoidance of hardware damage. In general, the new version 6 of the NAO helped a lot with this, because it appears to be a lot more robust than its predecessors. In addition, our robots execute protective measures when they fall, i.e. they kneel down when falling backwards, turn the head straight and pitch it away from the fall direction, and lower the joint stiffness before impact. They determine over which edge of the support polygon they might fall and use an Unscented Kalman Filter to preview whether they actually will. This allows them to start the safety measures very early. An indicator that our fall protection works better than others is the cover of the loudspeakers in the head of the NAO V6. It is a little bit loose and it pops off quite easily when a robot falls, as could be observed during many games. However, our robots never lost this part, most likely due to the lower force with which the heads hit the ground.

4.3   Getting Up

In previous years, our robots had problems with getting up on the artificial grass the field is made of. After a robot fell, it tried different getup motions in a row, from fast and risky to slow and safe, until it could actually get up. This resulted in many failed attempts and sometimes also in *fallen robot* penalties. In addition, the get up motions had to be manually tuned for the carpet at each competition, sometimes even for individual robots.

The main problem with robustly getting up is that NAO's joints sometimes do not follow the commands they were given or at least not as fast as they should. This changes the overall trajectory that the body follows during the get up motion, which often results in the robot falling over again. In particular, this can happen when the NAO has to get its legs together from a wide crouch, which requires a lot of force. The key idea in our current approach is to observe whether each joint of the robot actually follows the commands it was given. If it lags too much behind, the error is distributed over other joints according to predefined weights. Although this cannot produce the same overall trajectory as the original motion, it takes away the load from the lagging joint, which can then catch up more easily to its target angles. As a result, we now only have a single get up motion for each fall direction of the robot, i.e. front and back, with no adjustments needed. All of our robots, even the old ones, get up in their first attempt in more than 96% of the cases if there are no obstacles in the vicinity that could prevent this.

Table 2. Average number of penalties per game (PPG) and average number of robots in play (RIP, also for 1st and 2nd half) for the three SPL competitions at RoboCup 2019

(b) Challenge Shield

Team	PPG	RIP	1st	2nd
Camellia Dragons	10.5	4.44	4.66	4.22
SABANA Herons	10.5	4.44	4.50	4.37
NTU RoboPAL	9.9	4.36	4.51	4.21
Starkit	10.6	4.22	4.28	4.16
MiPal	16.2	4.07	4.04	4.10
Naova ETS	14.8	3.96	4.01	3.90
UPennalizers	20.3	2.85	3.16	2.57
RoboEireann	23.3	2.80	2.89	2.72
Average	14.5	3.89	4.01	3.78

(a) Champions Cup

Team	PPG	RIP	1st	2nd
B-Human	2.7	4.81	4.65	4.98
Nao Devils Dortmund	4.0	4.78	4.76	4.79
TJArk	4.7	4.77	4.81	4.74
Berlin United	4.8	4.77	4.71	4.82
Nao-Team HTWK	5.1	4.67	4.81	4.50
HULKs	3.3	4.65	4.79	4.51
NomadZ	9.6	4.57	4.67	4.46
rUNSWift	9.9	4.50	4.58	4.42
Bembelbots	10.5	4.42	4.35	4.49
SPQR Team	8.9	4.38	4.38	4.39
Dutch Nao Team	12.4	4.20	4.18	4.21
UT Austin Villa	15.3	3.90	4.16	3.60
Average	7.6	4.53	4.57	4.49

(c) Mixed Team Competition

Team	PPG	RIP	1st	2nd
B&B	7.0	5.69	5.63	5.75
Team Team	8.0	5.56	5.70	5.42
Devil SMASH	8.0	5.52	5.56	5.48
SwiftArk	9.3	5.49	5.47	5.51
SPQR-Starkit	16.8	4.60	4.41	4.82
Average	9.8	5.37	5.35	5.39

4.4   Results

Table 2 shows the average penalties per game and the average number of robots that were on the field during actual play. It shows that B-Human was the team with the least penalties and with the most robots on the field. Also in the Mixed Team Competition, where teams play with six instead of five robots, B&B, our joint team with Berlin United, also was the best one in this regard. As can be seen, there is a general tendency to have fewer robots on the field in the second half, in particular in the Challenge Shield. This is mainly due to the incremental nature of the penalty time, i.e. according to the rule book, each penalized robot has to stay 10 s longer off the field than the previous one. However, some teams also start taking robots off the field to save them for the next game, when the current game has basically already been decided in their favor. This is, e.g., the case for the team HULKs, which had fewer robots on the field in the second half, although they have the second-lowest penalty count per game.

5   Conclusion and Future Work

In this paper, we described three – out of many – aspects that contributed to our success in the RoboCup 2019 competitions. While the overall reliability of our robots is already quite close to the aim of having always the full number of robots on the field, without any penalties or fallen robots, the vision system as well as the team behavior, although they already provided very good results, can still be considered as work in progress.

Due to the much higher computing power of the NAO v6 robots, we are now able to run multiple deep neural networks for ball detection as well as for robot detection in parallel. However, these components are still embedded in our old, partially lighting-dependent vision system that still requires a few manual calibration steps before each game. Thus, currently ongoing research deals with the replacement of these parts, for instance by applying neural-network-based semantic segmentation.

This year's competitions showed that our new ability of playing passes after set plays as well as during the normal course of the game is definitely an advantage. However, so far, we only developed few variants for the respective situations, which is why our robots did not find a proper solution in some situations. As our new behavior framework allows an easy integration of new variants for passes, we are looking forward to an even more sophisticated team play at RoboCup 2020.

References

1. Poppinga, B., Laue, T.: JET-Net: real-time object detection for mobile robots. In: Chalup, S., et al. (eds.) RoboCup 2019: Robot World Cup XXIII. LNAI, pp. 227–240. Springer (2019)
2. RoboCup Technical Committee: RoboCup Standard Platform League (NAO) rule book (2019). https://spl.robocup.org/wp-content/uploads/downloads/Rules2019.pdf
3. Röfer, T., et al.: B-Human team report and code release 2017 (2017). http://www.b-human.de/downloads/publications/2017/coderelease2017.pdf
4. Röfer, T., et al.: B-Human team report and code release 2018 (2018). http://www.b-human.de/downloads/publications/2018/CodeRelease2018.pdf
5. Röfer, T., Laue, T., Richter-Klug, J.: B-Human 2016 – robust approaches for perception and state estimation under more natural conditions. In: Behnke, S., Sheh, R., Sariel, S., Lee, D.D. (eds.) RoboCup 2016. LNCS (LNAI), vol. 9776, pp. 503–514. Springer, Cham (2017). https://doi.org/10.1007/978-3-319-68792-6_42
6. Röfer, T.: CABSL – C-based agent behavior specification language. In: Akiyama, H., Obst, O., Sammut, C., Tonidandel, F. (eds.) RoboCup 2017. LNCS (LNAI), vol. 11175, pp. 135–142. Springer, Cham (2018). https://doi.org/10.1007/978-3-030-00308-1_11
7. Thielke, F., Hasselbring, A.: CompiledNN: a JIT compiler for neural network inference (2019). https://github.com/bhuman/CompiledNN
8. Thielke, F., Hasselbring, A.: A JIT compiler for neural network inference. In: Chalup, S., et al. (eds.) RoboCup 2019: Robot World Cup XXIII. LNAI, pp. 448–456. Springer (2019)

Author Index

Printed in the United States
By Bookmasters